Tribal People and Globalization

Christian Heritage Rediscovered

The Series, as the name suggests, is meant to focus on Christian Faith & Living vis-à-vis topics like Literature & Poetry, Indigenous Philosophizing, Ethical response towards Agriculture, Health & Healing, Science & Technology, Eco-feminist Theology, Sociological approach towards Human Rights, Law & Politics, Arts, History of Ideas, Ancient Civilizations, Cultural Contiguity, Religious Cosmologies & Mysticism, Footsteps of famous Theologians, World Peace & Harmony, Global Capitalism, Network Marketing, Cybertheology, Population & Demographics, Epigraphic Studies, Contextualized Education, and many others. We welcome a Mss. on any topic/s mentioned, whether they are original works, scholarly monographs, collections of conference papers, revised dissertations, or translations of historical documents. Through the Series we, the Publishers, are striving to put forward published works that may help Institutions, Academic Bodies, Researchers, Scholars and the World at large in furthering their respective knowledge and understanding on the concerned subject. We welcome your comments on our efforts and further suggestions on how we can foster the upcoming thought provoking theologically grounded books.

Christian Heritage Rediscovered - 70

Tribal People and Globalization

A Theological Perspective

S. Hayong

CWI
Christian World Imprints(TM)

First Published in 2018 by

Christian World Imprints™
Christian Publishing & Books from India
H-12 Bali Nagar, **New Delhi-110015**
info@christianworldimprints.com
www.ChristianWorldImprints.com
Phone: +91 11 25465925

ISBN: 978-93-5148-299-4 (HB) ISBN: 978-93-5148-300-7 (PB)

Cataloging in Publication Data--DK
Courtesy: D.K. Agencies (P) Ltd. <docinfo@dkagencies.com>

Hayong, S., author.
Tribal people and globalization : a theological perspective / Dr. S. Hayong.
pages cm. -- (Christian heritage rediscovered ; 70)
"This book is the outcome of my D.th thesis submitted to the Senate of Serampore"--Acknowledgement.
Study conducted in United Khāsi-Jaintia Hills of Meghalaya, India.
Includes bibliographical references.
ISBN 9789351482994 (HB)
ISBN 9789351483007 (PB)

1. Khasi (Indic people)--India--United Khāsi-Jaintia Hills--Economic conditions. 2. Globalization--Social aspects--India--United Khāsi-Jaintia Hills. 3. Theology, Doctrinal--India--United Khāsi-Jaintia Hills. I. Title. II. Series: Christian heritage rediscovered ; 70.

LCC DS432.K5H39 2018 | DDC 305.89593 23

Printed in India.

That the book in its original form is the thesis submitted to the Senate of Serampore College, towards the D.Th degree and is published with written permission. The candidate is responsible for the title, contents and opinions expressed in it.

Contents

Foreword

Globalization has come to be a principal characteristic feature of the new millennium and it has become an inescapable reality in today's society. No community and society can remain isolated from the forces of globalization. The general characteristic of globalization process is the liberalization of the movements of goods, services, investment and finance across national borders, and the expansion of global information flows and the acceleration of the speech of information exchanges. It involves a process by which economies of different countries are oriented to a global market and are controlled by multinational and global financial institutions. It is not merely an economic process; it is also a cultural process. With the help of media, it creates a mono-culture – a culture of rich and powerful. This book, *Tribal People and Globalization: A Theological Perspective,* makes a critical examination of globalization process from the perspective of tribal people locating in their experience.

While affirming the importance of development, the author argued the uncritical acceptance of market capitalism and pointed out that it will liberate the poor and tribal people from the yoke of misery and hunger. It operates with a basic ideology, i.e., maximum profit, maximum capital accumulation, and maximum exploitation of labour supported by global military hegemony. This ideology of ever-increasing growth and the thirst for maximization of profit and absolute domination of the earth's resources is a threat for future humanity. He further highlighted that in this development process, while rich nations have tremendous economic advantages, the developing countries are becoming poorer and more and more dependent. He argued that this will not only affect political rights but also widen gap between the rich and poor countries as the powerful countries to control and manipulate natural resources of other poorer countries, global trade, and world market for their own benefits and interests.

Nature has been bestowed with an abundance of resources for the support and maintenance of life-systems on planet earth. However, humankind, considering themselves to be the lone beneficiaries of the goodness of nature, thought it their right and privilege to exploit them for their own needs and welfare. This has led to a wasteful and extravagant use of the resources of nature. Since, the natural resources are something to be made use of and hence to yield maximum profit, preferably as quick as possible, the survival problem of tribal people is at threat. Being driven away from their home base, tribal people lost their means of resource generation and left to fend for themselves in situations where they are untrained to cope with.

In the globalized free market, the only people who count are those who have goods to sell and those who have the money to buy. This in turn drives many to the margins of the economic life. The small entrepreneurs and tribal communities who depend on land and forest resources have very little chance of survival in this system. The weak, the poor tribal people and the inexperienced ones are pushed to the outer rims of the society. In short, globalization works for the benefits of the rich while the poor and tribal people become commodities since they are used as cheap labours. It has created a situation of marginalization, exclusion and social disintegration.

One of the vehicles that accelerate globalization is commercial tourism industry which need to be taken note in tribal context. Tourism is ever hungry for land, water, electricity, and a variety of infrastructure. In most cases, these are generously provided by governments for the construction and maintenance of hotels, resorts, golf courses, amusement and theme parks, state of the art airports and highways. Most of these developments in NE are continuously on the rise to cater the growing numbers of tourists. Even though local communities themselves are obviously in need of these resources that are consumed by tourism operations, this sector continues to be given a priority on these over the local people. This is in the face of what is obvious to anyone that their poverty is in sharp contrast to the affluence enjoyed by a few, namely the tourism interests and the tourists themselves. Sensitive travelers would have observed this aspect of tourism in the countries, regions, and tourism areas especially in North East India they have visited.

To meet the demand of the tourist, the hosts have to sacrifice many things including their culture and bodies. The social costs through abused, including trafficking, of women and children. Due to the informal and underground character of this 'businesses, and its lack of transparency, it is difficult to arrive at exact figures of those exploited. However, estimates of women and children victimized in sex tourism and slavery, both worldwide and regionally, are placed at consistently high levels. This is not surprising with the situation of entrenched poverty of communities and victims making it a strong push factor driving sex tourism. In an activity subject to the laws of supply and demand, a service or commodity that is desired is generally be met by those with a profit motive, intermediaries such as pimps and other middlemen in the case of sex tourism. The treatment of women as a service or commodity is in stark contrast to the countercultural attitudes and teachings of Jesus. With usually little education, hardly any skills, and negligible employment opportunities, these disadvantaged women, and children, take recourse to using the only asset they have – their bodies. Children are even more helpless. Trafficked women and children have little control over their situation brought about by the ruthless 'merchants' and their agents peddling sex tourism motivated mainly by the lure of money. Tourists who take advantage of such human beings, and those who enable this to happen, are exploiters of the poor in an unequal relationship of power and money.

In most of the tourist destination, one will observe that local people are employed mostly as manual labour jobs like watchman, waiter, cleaner in hotels and massage parlors! Generate income for whom? Income goes mostly for hotels, tour agencies and government machinery. In the process of tourism development, local people are forcefully evicted from their ancestral places without adequate compensation. Along with denial of fishing, hunting and cultivation rights, their cultural assets are also increasingly marketed as tourism products by privatizing their land and natural resources. In the process of being re-packaged for visitor's consumption, tribal people's historical and religious sites, rituals, festivals, arts and crafts are often unrecognized, distorted and commercialized. This creates poverty, indecent living style, identity and spiritual crises.

The land, the river and forest have been the home and life sustaining source of tribal people for centuries. But today they are being misused and raped to meet the growing demand of consumerism. Forest and fishing resources are depleted for quick profits. Mining companies rape resources with little regard to the environmental and social costs. The sustaining power of the earth for nurturing life is being destroyed. The whole planet is at threat. But today one cannot deny the fact that land and resources have become the greatest single cause of strife and warfare between nations and people of different communities within a nation. Resources are hoarded by a few and denied to others. Possession of resources, instead of being used as an opportunity for mutual sharing, as of an unmerited gift of God, has become a matter of conquest and seizure, a tool of oppression, greed and power. This trend is becoming more and more alarming particularly in India.

I congratulate Rev. Dr. Shanbha Hayong for this scholarly and comprehensive theological analysis on the impact of globalization on the tribal communities in India. I hope the issues and theological perspectives articulated in the book will be taken seriously by the policy makers of our governments, NGOs and churches for a future world.

Wati Longchar

Acknowledgement

This book is the outcome of my D.th thesis submitted to the Senate of Serampore. Hence, here I would like to acknowledge my deep appreciation and gratitude to the following persons and Institution for their contribution towards the successful completion of the research work.

First of all, I would like to express my sincere gratitude to my supervisor, Rev. Dr. K. G. Pothen, Professor in Theology, Mar Thoma Theological Seminary, Kottayam, for his immeasurable help with valuable suggestions and scholarly advice which enable me to complete my research work. I also would like to express my sincere gratitude to Rev. Dr. Wati Longchar for helping me to write the Forward of the book.

I owe my deep sense of indebtedness to the Librarians and staff at the Otto Hopfenmueller Library of Sacred Heart Theological College, Shillong; ICSSR Library, Shillong; NEC Library, Shillong; Rev. T B Phillips Memorial Library of John Roberts Theological Seminary, Shillong; State Central Library, Shillong; Deputy Commissioner's Record Room, Shillong; Jeebon Roy Memorial Library, Shillong; Mr. L. G. Shullai's- Shillong Collection Centre, Shillong; Directorate of Archives, Gauhati, Assam; Department of Historical and Antiquarian Studies, Gauhati; West Bengal Archive, Kolkata; National Library, Kolkata; Asiatic Society Library, Kolkata; The Goethals Indian Library & Research Society, Kolkata; United Theological College Library, Bangalore; Princeton Theological Seminary Library, Princeton; Princeton University Library, Princeton; Santhom Library of St. Thomas Apostolic Seminary, Vadavathoor; Mar Thoma Theological Seminary, Kottayam; Orthodox Theological Seminary Library, Kottayam; and Mahatma Gandhi University Library, Kottayam for their valuable help and co-operation during my research work.

I also express my deep gratitude to Rev. Dr. I. Kharkongor; Rev. Dr. M. J. Hynniewta, Principal John Roberts Theological Seminary, Governing Board John Roberts Theological Seminary for their constant help and encouragement in different capacities throughout the entire course of study.

I would also like to express my sincere gratitude to all those friends, whom I have interviewed for sparing their time and energy despite of their busy scheduled, that could enriched and make the research work success.

I am deeply grateful to my wife Ayesha D. Warjri, my daughter Wandi K. Warjri, my father and mother in law, my parents, brothers and sisters for bearing with me during the whole course of my research work.

Above all, I would like to express my thanks and gratitude to the Almighty God for providing me with good health and knowledge during the entire research work.

Abstract

The purpose of this book is to investigate the challenges posed by globalization to the daily life experiences of the Khasi people, especially their economic life and make a theological response for the same. The process of globalization has adversely affected the entire life situation of the tribals in general and their economic life in particular. It has broken the delicate balance of the entire eco-system such as land and natural resources. Such a situation demands theological response that will help the Khasi people as well as other tribal groups in their daily struggles for survival.

Chapter I deals with the traditional social, political, cultural and religious life of the Khasi people. It is found that all these aspects in one way or the other, contributed to the economic life of the people. It also attempts to study the Khasi economy prior to the coming of the British colonial rule, during the British period and the post independence era. The research found that before the coming of the British rule in these hills, though the people has to import some items from the neighboring plain people of Assam and East Bengal (now Bangladesh) like rice and other household items, their overall life situation in general and economic life in particular was generally self sufficient. The arrival of the British colonial rule had adverse affect on the tribal life, including their economy. Trade activities, especially items with important economic value like coal, lime stone and oranges, which were under complete control of the Khasi people, were captured by the British colonial master. This severely affected the economic life of the Khasis. Furthermore, to extend the horizon of their empire the colonial rulers also brought with them, people from outside the region to assist them in different capacities like offices, trade activities and so on. This caused large influx of people from outside the region to these hills. In due course people from outside the tribal communities took complete control over the entire trade activities thereby denying the local indigenous population of different employment opportunities. These problems faced by the tribal people became worst in the post independent era, where the entire trade activities both wholesale and retail are being captured by the immigrants especially the Marwaris. In other words, when the British colonial rule left these hills, the economy of the local Khasi people was in a deplorable state. At the time when the tribal economy was insecure and weak, the arrival of the present phase of globalization worsened the situation for the tribal people.

Chapter II examines different phases of globalization, namely, the colonialist globalization, the post war globalization and the present day globalization. The first phase reveals that with the vision to exploit the rich natural resources of the colonies, the colonial rulers not only went to plunder the raw materials of the colonies to support the demand of industrial sectors of Europe, but also converted the colonies into a dumping ground for the manufactured goods produced by different factories in Europe. That is the colonial masters turned the colonies into captive market to serve their interest in their attempt to exploit the economic resources of the colonies. The second phase shows the emergence of two super powers (USA and USSR), making all efforts, to capture and dominate different countries of the world. The collapse of USSR opened up the way for the capitalist countries under the leadership of USA, to take control of the economy of the entire world. The third phase or the present day globalization demonstrates the emergence of the agencies of globalization or the so called neo-colonial forces at the expense of national states. The research found that the present day globalization not only divides the world countries between the rich and the poor, developed and underdeveloped, or the First and the Third World countries but even within the countries, it divided the people between the rich and the poor. In turn, the rich countries or the G7 countries, coupled with the agencies of the present day globalization make all efforts to exploit the economic resources of the world especially that of the Third World countries. Thus, the present day globalization is nothing, but the replication of the colonialist globalization.

The Third chapter discusses how India joins the process of globalization and integrates its economy with the global economy. The research found that it was the economic crisis of the 1990s that compelled India to restructure its economy, by implementing the New Economic Policy of 1991 based on Liberation, Privatisation and Globalization or the LPG model. It is believed that by joining the process of economic globalization, India has nothing to lose but many things to gain in the process. However, though the country achieved rapid economic progress within short period, the ground realities tells a different story. Though the country achieved promising economic growth in the recent past, majority of the population do not benefit from the process. In other words, the process of economic globalization benefitted only a small section of population, whereas the majority poor and marginalized, especially Dalits and the tribals are further relegated to the margin of economic development with little hope for a better future.

Chapter IV studies the challenges of globalization to tribal economy particularly the Khasi context. In the context of the Khasi people, the challenges of globalization were experienced both in the first phase or the colonialist globalization, and the present day globalization. With its mission to exploit and plunder the economic resources of the colonies, the advent of British rule had severely affected the growth and development of the Khasi economy. When the colonial masters left the Khasi and Jaintia Hills, the economy of the people was in a bad shape. Moreover, in the post-independence era, the development activities implemented by the government of India in the tribal areas, using the "top-down" model could not help raise the living conditions and the economic life of the Khasi people. To state differently, tribal people were made objects not the subject of development. Hence, even after six decades of independence, the living conditions of the tribals have not improved and some are even worse than earlier. At the time, when the Khasi economy was insecure and weak, the coming of the present phase of globalization makes the situation no better for the local people. With the mission to achieve unlimited and quick profit, the agencies of globalization make all effort to exploit and plunder the natural resources of the local people. The research found that besides damaging the surrounding environment, the present phase of globalization divided the tribal people between the rich and the poor thereby pushing the major chunk of the population to the margin of economic life. Such a situation calls for a serious and authentic response from the theological point of view. It is believed that appropriate response from the perspective of the Khasi people, will not only able to correct the drawbacks of globalization, but it will also help provide meaningful and practical suggestions for the good and betterment of the local indigenous population.

Chapter V deals with a theological response from the indigenous Khasi tribal perspective. In the process to achieve unlimited profit within short span of time, globalization not only brought damage to the surrounding environment, but also make the lives of majority poor more impoverished than before. Hence, revisiting the eco-spirituality of the tribals that emphasize on respect for the value and importance of nature, and the rediscovery of the tribal religio-ethical norms like the concept of *Tipbriew Tipblei*[1] and *Kamai ia ka Hok*[2] are proposed to correct some of the drawbacks of globalization. The research also found that one has to move beyond sustainable development towards realizing the inherent value and worth of the natural environment thereby bringing justice to the health of the earth as well as humans. Besides in the present day context where the survival of humans as well as non-human creatures is under threat, we have to move beyond

---

[1] The concept of *Tipbriew Tipblei* literally means to know God and to know human beings. It can also be translated as to have right relationship with God and other fellow humans. A person who has right relationship with God and other human beings will not like to see that other fellow beings are exploited and discriminated. But a person who is *Tipbriew Tipblei* would like to see that the rights of the poor and marginalised are protected and respected.

[2] The concept of *Kamai ia ka Hok* means to earn righteously. It is against the ideology of exploiting the earth resources by the rich sections at the expense of the poor and marginalised.

the biblical concept of stewardship which will be still tainted by the element of anthropocentrism and move towards kinship of the earth. Kinship with the earth is based on the interdependence of human and nature. It is seen that, the concept of stewardship depicts more concern for the benefit and welfare of human community rather than the welfare of other creations. At the same time, it can go hand in hand with the oppressive structures without challenging them. Thus it will not be able to save the earth from ecological crisis. If humans and other creatures are to live in a healthy atmosphere the health of the earth need to be taken seriously, and this could only be achieved through kinship with the earth.

Abbreviations

ACISCA	Association of Christian Institutes for Social Concern in Asia.
ASEAN	Association of South East Asian Nations.
BIMSTEC	Bangladesh, India, Myanmar, Sri Lanka, Thailand Economic Cooperation.
BOT	Build Operate Transfer.
BPL	Below Poverty Line.
BTESSC	Board of Theological Education of the Senate of Serampore.
Cf	Compare.
CHC	Community Health Centre.
CMEA	Council for Mutual Economic Assistance.
CSWO	Civil Society Women Organisation.
DBCIC	Don Bosco Centre for Indigenous Cultures.
Ed.	Edition.
Etc	*et cetera.*
Et al	and others.
EU	European Union.
FDI	Foreign Direct Investment.
FKJGP	Federation of Khasi Jaintia Garo People.
GATT	General Agreement on Trade and Tariff.
GDP	Gross Domestic Products.
G7	Group 7.
HNYF	Hynniewtrep National Youth Front.
Ibid	Same source.
ICSSR	Indian Council of Social Science and Research.
i.e	That is to say.
IMF	International Monetery Fund.
ISPCK	Indian Society for Promoting Christian Knowledge.
ITI	Industrial Training Institute.
JHADC	Jaintia Hills Autonomous District Council.
JYF	Jaintia Youth Federation.

KSU	Khasi Student Union.
LEP	Look East Policy.
LPG	Liberalization, Privatisation and Globalization.
MAA	Meghalaya Adventure Association.
MGNREGS	Mahatma Gandhi National Rural Employment Guarantee Scheme.
MNCs	Multinational Companies.
MOU	Memorandum of Understanding.
MPA	Meghalaya Progressive Alliance.
MPHRC	Meghalaya People Human Right Commission.
MT	Metric Ton.
MUA	Meghalaya United Alliance.
NAM	Non Alliance Movement.
NCCI	National Council of Churches in India.
NCCR	National Council of Churches Review.
NEC	North Eastern Council.
NEHU	North Eastern Hill University.
NEI	North East India.
NEP	New Economic Policy.
NER	North Eastern Region.
NGO	Non Government Organization.
NHRM	National Rural Health Mission.
NOC	No Objection Certificate
PCUSA	Presbyterian Church of Unites States of America.
PHC	Primary Health Centre.
PIL	Public Interest Litigation.
SAARC	South Asia Association Regional Conference.
SAL	Structural Adjustment Loan.
SAP	Structural Adjustment Programme.
SATHRI	South Asia Theological Research Institute.
SEZs	Special Economic Zones.
SSA	Sarve Siksha Abhiyan.
TNCs	Transnational Companies.
UPA	United Progressive Alliance.
USA	United States of America.
USSR	Union Soviet Socialist Republic.
Vol.	Volume.
WB	World Bank.
WCC	World Council of Churches.
WTO	World Trade Organization.

Glossary

Bakhraw	The original clan.
Blei	God.
Byrsieh	Taint or stigma.
Durbar Hima	State Assembly.
Durbar Kur	Clan Assembly.
Durbar Raid	*Raid* Assembly, below the State Assembly.
Durbar Shnong	Village Assembly.
Elaka	A small administrative unit that comprise few villages.
Hats	Markets at the border.
Hukum	Law giver.
Hynniew Skum	Seven Families.
Hynniew Trep	Seven huts.
Iawbei Tynrai	First ancestress.
Jaid Syiem	Syiem clan.
Jutang	Covenant.
Ki Khun Ki Hajar	Citizen of the state.
Ki Ksuid ki khrei	he evil spirit.
Kni Rangbah	Eldest maternal uncle.
Kpoh	The smaller unit within the clan.
Kur	Clan.
Lyngdoh	Priest.
Mawkynthei	Table stones in front of menhirs.
Mawshynrang	Menhirs.
Meikha	Paternal grandmother.
Mei Ramew	Mother Earth.
Myntri	Elected member of the state.
Niam	Religion.
Nongtymmen	Inherited Property.
Raid	A small administrative unit that comprise few villages, similar with *Elaka*.

Ri Kynti	Private land.
Rangbah Shnong	Village Headman.
Ri Raid	Community Land.
Riti	Unwritten constitution.
Ryngkew	Dry land.
Ryngkew u Basa	Village Patron God.
Saidnia	First maternal uncle.
Sang	Taboo.
Sohbam	Fruits given to labourers to take home after the labour.
Syiem	Chief.
Thawlang	First ancestor.

Introduction

The process of globalization has adversely affected the tribal life, in general, and tribal economy, in particular. It has broken the delicate balance of the tribal economic resources, such as, land and natural resources. Such a situation calls for a theological formulation, which will help the tribal people, in general, and Khasis, in particular, to respond to these challenges of globalization, which influence their day-to-day life.

For centuries, prior to the British rule, Khasis, like most tribals groups in the North East India (NEI), lived in isolation from their neighbors[1] except for the main two reasons: (1) they had trade contact with their neighbors.[2] (ii) Conquest of the vast tract of land both in the Surma valley or East Bengal in the south, and the plain of Assam in the North by the Khasi rulers in the Pre-British era.[3] Hence, though the majority of the people in these hills were isolated from the outside world, many of them had substantial contacts with their neighbors. This study intends to examine how such contact contributed to the economic life of the tribal people of Khasi-Jaintia Hills.

---

[1] According to Nataranjan, the rugged physical feature of the land has contributed to the isolation of the people. See, Nalini Nataranjan, *The Missionary among the Khasis* (New Delhi: Sterling Publishers Private Limited, 1977), 9.

[2] Nalini argued that were trade relationship between the Khasi people and the people of Assam in the north, through barter system. See Nataranjan, *The Missionary*, 134-135. Snaitang suggests that the people of Ri War area in the south had trade relationship with the plain people of Sylhet in East Bengal now Bangladesh. See O. L. Snaitang, *Christianity and Social Change in Northeast India* (Shillong: Vendrame Institute, 1993), 37.

[3] In the Pre-British period some of the Khasi rulers, ruled over a large area of plain land, both in Assam in the north and the plain of Sylhet in the south. For instance, the Syiem of Sutnga, established his kingdom up to the plain of Sylhet, and made Jaintiapur (now in Bangladesh) his winter resort. So also, the territory of the *Syiem* of Khyrim covered many areas, in the plain of Assam. See Helen Giri, *The Khasis Under the British Rule, 1824-1947* (New Delhi: Regency Publications, 1998), 32-33.

Notably, like most tribal societies, traditional Khasi economy was self-sufficient.[4] Primarily, their economy was based on agriculture[5] and trade.[6] However, with the passage of time, their economic life, in particular, and their whole life situation, in general, underwent significant changes. Like many tribal groups, in due course, the increase of population brought tremendous pressure on land and forest. Land and forest products, that formed one of the sources of income to tribal people became insufficient to support and meet the demand and needs of the people. Nevertheless, the serious problem that the tribal communities face is the challenge posed by globalization. In the context of the tribal people of NEI in general, and Khasi people in particular, the challenges of globalization has been strongly experienced both in the first phase or the colonist globalization and the third or modern phase of globalization.

The advent of the British rule[7] had mixed bearing on the tribal life, including economy. On one hand, the tribals had their first experience/contact with the outside world and the process of modernization that has positively contributed to the welfare and development of the tribal society. On the other hand, the process of modernization/colonialist's globalization seems to diminish several traditional and cultural values. Many of the virtues present in the tribal culture like, respect and love for the nature, etc., began to be overlooked and ignored for the sake of temporary monetary benefits. As the tribal way of life cannot be separated from nature, to undermine nature, means to be detached from their way of life. This brought serious challenges to the whole life situation of the tribal people especially their economic life.

Moreover, the coming of the British rule or the first phase of globalization had adverse effect on the tribal economy. Some among several effects of colonialist globalization are: first, the capturing the entire trade of important trade items like orange, coal and lime stone.[8] Second, the dismantling of the iron smelting industries of the Khasis,[9] and third, when the British government declared Shillong

[4] Nataranjan, *The Missionary*, 178. See also, J.B. Bhattacharjee "The Eastern Himalayan Trade of Assam in the Collonial Period," in *Studies in the Economic History of North East India,* edited by J.B. Bhattacharjee (New Delhi: Har-Anand Publications, 1994), 188.

[5] In agriculture, they practiced both shifting cultivation or *jhumming* and also permanent cultivation like wet cultivation. See Sousmen Sen, *Social and State Formation in Khasi-Jaintia Hills* (Delhi: B. R. Publishing Corporation, 1985), 35-37.

[6] Sen, *Social and State Formation in Khasi-Jaintia Hills,* 35.

[7] The British occupation in Khasi Jaintia Hills started in 1826. See Giri, *The Khasis under the British Rule, 1824-1947,* 63. By 1835, the Britishers took complete control over the whole land. See Snaitang, *Christianity and Social Change in Norteast India,* 44-45.

[8] Cf. Giri, *The Khasis under the British Rule, 1824-1947,* 42.

[9] A. C. Mohapatra, "Locational Pattern of Markets in Pre and Early British Period in North East India (Khasi, Jaintia and Garo Hills)," in *Studies in the Economic History of North East India,* edited by J. B. Bhattacharjee (New Delhi: Har-Anand Publications, 1994), 166.

as the Provincial capital in 1874, the British rulers brought people from other places like East Bengal for different required services.[10] This has not only caused an influxes of the people from outside the region to these hills, but in due course of time, the people from outside the region also took control of the whole trade and commerce,[11] which denied significant job/employment opportunities to the local tribal population. Hence, the first phase of globalization creates enormous challenges to the economic life of the Khasi people.

Alongside the British colonial rule, Christianity marked its arrival during this period in these hills.[12] Its services through education, health ministry, and social work have positively contributed to the welfare of the tribal people. Nevertheless, its theology which emphasized on salvation of human soul led to the valuation of humans above everything including the created world. Such type of Christian theology detached from the real life situation of the tribal community is other worldly, anthropocentric and detached from the soil. In this context, to accept Christian faith means to abandon all traditional cultural practices, which the missionaries termed as evil, superstitious, derogatory and devoid of any merit.[13] This has caused severe blow to the economic life of the tribal, in particular, and their whole life situation, in general.

In the post-independence era, the economic policy of the Government of India, implemented in the tribal society using the idea of "catch up" policy[14] through the implementation of Five Years Plan of development, does not fit well in the tribal context. It has made the people the object not the subject of development. This idea of top-down model[15] without proper analytical study of tribal context,

---

[10] David R, Syiemlieh, "Influence and contribution of Bengali Settler in Khasi Hills," *The Shillong Times*, 21st April 2009, 4.

[11] The population of Shillong which was only 4000 in 1881, had increased to 26,536 in 1931.According to the Census 2001, the recorded population of Shillong rose to 2, 67,662, i.e., only the permanent residence (whereas the real population of Shillong today due to heavy influx of the people outside the region, is approximately more than 4 lakhs). See Census of India 1931, Volume III, p 32. Census of India, 2001.

[12] The Welsh Calvinistic Methodist Foreign Mission came to establish their mission work in 1841, and fifty years later, the Roman Catholic Mission began their mission work in 1890. See Snaitang, *Christianity*, 68-82.

[13] For the missionaries, all traditional customs like festivals, dances, songs, etc., has no value at all, therefore regarded as evil. At the same time, Christians were forbid to take part in any traditional cultural functions. Any one that stepped against such restriction has to face disciplinary action like excommunication from the church. See A. Wati Longchar, "The need for doing Tribal Theology," in *Tribal Theology: A Reader*, edited by Shimreingam Shimray (Jorhat: Tribal Study Centre, 2003), 7.

[14] Longchar, "The Need for doing Tribal Theology," 3.

[15] The word "top down model" in this context, means everything is decided from Delhi, for the development of the tribal people and implemented in the tribal areas, without allowing the tribal people to participate in the development process. Therefore, the tribals besides having no knowledge on those particular projects have not much role to play in the whole process.

where majority are poor and marginalized fail to lift-up the economic life of the tribal people. The result is that the tribals who were economically self-sufficient prior to the coming of the British rule have to depend on the Central Government for their overall development and economic survival.[16]

The most serious problem emerging in the tribal context, in general, and tribal economy in particular is the challenge of the modern phase of globalization.[17] With India adopting the policies of Globalization, Liberalization and Privatization and the implementation of the New Economic Policy (NEP), the problems face by the tribals became worse. Some among several challenges posed by the process of globalization include: first, reduction of expenditure in social sector, cutting down in employment, government subsidies, etc., as imposed by the agencies of globalization on the Indian government.[18] Second, ruthless exploitation of mineral resources like coal, lime stone and other mineral resources to meet the demand of the contemporary globalized era unmindful of its consequence to humans and natural environment as well.[19] Third, the free entry of big companies and TNCs/MNCs to the tribal areas likes Khasi and Jaintia Hills.[20] Consequently, with the entry of giant companies, the tribals are not only being alienated from their land and natural resources, but tribals found themselves unskilled in several employment opportunities too.[21]

The advent of globalization, though, brought positive result with a promise of better future, is only one sided. In other words, it is only the rich, the powerful and the privilege class, which are benefitted. The majority poor and the marginalized suffer major setbacks in multiple areas of their life. Hence, the gap between the rich and the poor keep on widening

Such a situation entails authentic and concrete response both from the biblical theological point of view and the tribal perspective, in order, to help the tribal people to realize the gravity of the problem they are facing. In our attempt to develop an indigenous theology in the era of globalization today, one of the

---

[16] Thanzauva, *Theology of Community: Tribal Theology in the Making*, 51-53.

[17] The present day globalization or the modern phase of globalization has its roots in the colonial period or the colonialist globalization. It is important to note that, the modern phase of globalization is but the replication of the colonialist globalization.

[18] Matthews George Chunakara, "Globalization and its Impact on Human Rights," in *Globalization and its Impact on Human Rights,* edited by Matthews George Chunakara (Thiruvalla: Christava Sahitya Samithy, 2000), 96.

[19] Corky Chakraborty, "Economic Policy and North East-Looking beyond Neo-Classical Praxis," in *Globalization and North East India,* edited by Bimal J. Deb, Keya Sengupta and B. Datta Ray (New Delhi: Concept Publishing Company, 2008), 181.

[20] "MPHRC Cries Hoarse over Lafarge's Project," *The Shillong Times,* 26 October 2007. See also Toki Blah, "The MAA and its PIL-the untold story," *The Shillong Times,* 17 August 2008, 4.

[21] See "Hato ka khlaw Narpuh kan sah tang ha ki Khana Pateng?" *Mawphor,* 10 May 2002. See also "Cave may remain in history only," *The Shillong Times,* 31 October 2002.

essential task[22] is to rediscover and reinterpret these insights from the traditional cultural heritage that are liberative and life affirming which could help us to respond to the contemporary problems of the society today. It is hoped that this will enable us to formulate a theology, which is meaningful, liberative, inclusive and accommodative. In other words, it means a theology, which emphasizes the holistic well being of the community or a healthy community. This does not mean to say 'no' to development but development should be community based. Hence, economic activities must be planned in such a way that it is protecting, rather than alienating from the habitat.

Importance of the Study

First, though many writers from the region often referred to the challenges of globalization to the life and culture of the tribal people in their writings, there has not been any significant attempt to study the impact of globalization on the tribal economy, especially, in the Khasi context. Therefore, an in-depth study on the subject will not only highlight the seriousness of the issue but also provides some theoretical and practical suggestions relevant for tribal people, in general, and Khasi people in particular.

Second, though the challenge of globalization to the tribal economy is very serious, majority of Khasi people are not aware of it. In the process of globalization, the most affected and marginalized communities among many are those who belong to the poorer sections of the society like, the Dalit and the tribal people though they may not be aware of it. Hence, this research work will definitely be able to make the tribal people in general, and Khasi people, in particular, aware and sensitive to the challenges of globalization in their day to day life.

Method of Research

Analyzing the challenges of globalization on the economic life of the tribal people involves more than one approach. Hence, integrated tools will be employed in this research work. In the first place, as the area of study, involves the colonial era, the researcher will employ Postcolonial tools, to critically analyze the Khasi context during the colonial era, both from the colonial point of view and the colonies point of view. It will also involve, criticism of the economic theories, which support globalization, and the criticism will be based on the ecological critique of economic. Towards the end, the researcher will try to integrate, the insights from the Khasi traditional heritage, both in the past and the present, with the insights drawn from Process thought. This will help formulate an indigenous people theology relevant to the tribal context. The study will involve both

[22] Apart from those, mention above this research work will try to incorporate the theological and biblical insights from the Early Church and the Process thought related on the subject of research.

library and empirical research. For the library sources, books, Reports, and other materials related with the Khasi people written both during and after the British rule will served as important sources. For empirical research, personal interviews and Focus Group Discussion especially in Shella areas[23] and Lumshnong areas[24] the two areas mostly affected by the operation of the Big and MNCs/TNCs will be conducted to supplement and support the research study.

Hypothesis

The proposed research is an attempt for theological response on the challenges posed by globalization on the economic life of the tribal people, particularly, the Khasi tribe of Meghalaya. Tribal societies underwent a series of changes through their interaction with the process of modernization, Christianization and globalization. Through these contacts, some positive result emerged, but there are some areas that have negatively affected the tribal way of life. Hence, the context impels for theological response. Therefore, formulating an indigenous theology relevance to the contemporary tribal context involves rediscovering the traditional cultural values that are liberating and life affirming. In addition, integrating the insights from tribal heritage, with the insights drawn from the Process thought could help develop an indigenous theology that is inclusive, accommodative, empowering and life affirming.

Limitation of the Study

Keeping in mind the vastness of the entire area of tribal society in the North East India, this research work will concentrate only within the Khasi Hills Jaintia Hills areas of Meghalaya. There are two main reasons for this i.e., first, to make the scope of study manageable, and second, an attempt is made to concentrate particularly on the Khasi tribe of Meghalaya, delving with the burning issue that confront and affect the contemporary Khasi society in their daily life.

Previous Research

There have been a number of studies conducted by different scholars from the NEI on Tribal Theology[25] but so far, there is no scholarly work concerning the

[23] Shella area here is referred to those areas surrounding Shella Village.

[24] Lumshnong areas include several villages around Lumshnong village.

[25] Several books published by the Tribal Study Centre Viz. *An Exploration of Tribal Theology (1997)* and *In Search of Identity and Tribal Theology: A Tribute to Dr. Renthy Keitzer, (2000)*, edited by A. Wati longchar, *The Tribal Worldview and Ecology (1998)* edited by A. Wati Longchar and Yangkahao Vashum, *Doing Theology with Tribal Resources, (*1999), edited by A. Wati Longchar and Larry W. Davies, etc. These books are good works, which attempt to develop tribal theology, by using indigenous resources based on the context of Nagaland and served as good resource materials for Tribal studies. However, they do not deal with the subject on globalization. There are books written by K. Thanzauva Viz. *Towards a Tribal Theology: The Mizo Perspective (1989) and Theology of Community: Tribal Theology in the Making (1997*), which are also good attempt to develop Tribal

challenges of globalization on the tribal economy in the Khasi context in particular and the NEI, in general. The book *Transforming Theology: A Theological Basis for Social Transformation* by K. Thanzauva contains a small section on globalization, in general, but it does not deal directly with the impact of globalization on tribal economy. The book *Tribal Theology: A Reader* edited by Shimreingam Shimray includes one useful article "Globalization and Indigenous People: Challenge for doing Theology in Asia" by A. Wati Longchar. However, this article deals generally with the impact of globalization on the indigenous people of the Third World not specifically on the North East tribal. Another book *Globalization and North East India* edited by Bimal J. Deb, Keya Sengupta and B. Datta Ray contains 29 small articles based on different areas and context of North East India. Most of the articles in this book were written in the context of the New Economic Policy (NEP) but these articles besides not being detailed research, are also inadequate methodologically. Another book, *Globalization and Women's Substinence Labour: A Third World Theological Perspective* by W. S. Annie published by BTESSC/SATHRI(2009), which is the outcome of her thesis[26] is a good and well researched work. However, the book deals only with the subsistence labour of women based mainly on the mainland India and it does not include North East India as part of the researched work. Another research work, *Towards a Theology of Community in a Tribal Perspective: A Theological Response to Cultural Globalization with special Reference to the Zo People in North East India* by L. Liankhanlal Simte under the Senate of Serampore and is still in the process. This research work deals specifically on the Cultural Globalization as a threat that may lead to the extinction of the Zo culture of Manipur. This research work apart from excluding the economic challenges of globalization on the life of the tribal people, it has also made no reference on the Khasi people. Moreover, this research study is based on the context of the Zo people in Manipur, a context that is different from the Khasi context. Hence, so far there is no scholarly research work with regard to the challenges of globalization on the economic life of the tribal people of the North East India in general and the Khasi people, in particular.

Definitions

Khasi

The Khasi people as one of the tribal group in North East India (NEI), is a group of homogenous community comprising of the seven sub-tribes such as the Khynriams, Pnars, Bhois, Wars, Marams, Lyngngams and the never heard

Theology, by using tribal resources, from the context of Mizoram. However, these books, though they are scholarly written they do not contain writings on globalization.

[26] The Thesis entitled, *A Theological Evaluation of Labour in an Age of Globalization: A Third World Perspective with Special Reference to Women in India* under the Senate of Serampore.

Diko,[27] living in Khasi Jaintia Hills of Meghalaya State.[28] However, today people also referred to them as Khasi Jaintia people, or Khasi-Pnar[29] based on their geographical settlement. However, it is important to note that, they are meant for the same group of people coming from the same origin. The Khasi people also called themselves as *Ki Hynniew Trep* meaning the Seven Huts based on their traditional myths and legends.[30] However, all the four nomenclature viz., Khasi, Khasi-Jaintia, Khasi-Pnar and Hynniew Trep is referred, to the same group of people. In this research study the author, prefer to use the term Khasi.

Khasi States

The term Khasi states is referred to the 25 states of Khasi-Jaintia Hills which function independently from each other as autonomous political unit. Each of these states comprise several villages. In the Khasi local language, they are called *hima* and were ruled by the Chiefs known as *Syiem.* Each state had a similar form of government, which was basically democratic, to look after the welfare and well-being of the citizens. However, after joining with the Indian union their role is not as strong as before.

The Structure

The first chapter deals with the general back ground of the Khasi people. It seeks to demonstrate how the social, religious and cultural life of the people contributed to their economic life. It also examines the economy of the Khasis in the pre-colonial, British and post Independence period. There are several changes with regards to the economy of the people in the different periods mentioned above. The Khasi people which were economically self sufficient prior to the coming of British colonial rule have to depend on the central funding of the central government for their economic survival in the post Independence or postcolonial period.

---

[27] The Dikos were a group of people living in the border of Garo Hills. Gurdon opines that the Dikos or Hanas are Garos who observe the Khasi custom of erecting memorial stones. It may be due to their physical appearance resembling the Garos. The Census of India, 1891 shows that out of the total population of 1,78,630 members of the Khasis, the Diko's population is only 673 people. However, this group of Khasis is never heard off nowadays. See P. R. T. Gurdon, *The Khasis,* Reprinted. (Delhi: Low Price Publications, 2010), 62. See also Census of India 1891, 156.

[28] It is important to note that apart from those living in Khasi Jaintia hills, a large number of Khasi people are living Noth Cachar and Cachar areas of Assam and Bangladesh. But these are not included in the area of this research. Cf. H. Bareh, *The History and Culture of the Khasi People,* 3rd ed. (Guwahati: Spectrum Publications, 1997), 9-10.

[29] The word Khasi is generally understood today by some people as those living in Khasi Hills area and the word Pnar is generally referred by some author for all the Khasis living in Jaintia Hills area. Hence, the word Khasi-Pnar.

[30] See Kynpham Sing Nongkynrih, *Around the Hearth: Khasi Legends* (New Delhi: Penguin Books, 2007), 1-5.

Chapter II discusses the general overview of the process of globalization. It is an attempt to portray different phases of globalization-colonialist globalization, post war globalization and the present day globalization. It points out how the world view, agencies and culture of globalization contribute to the growth and expansion of globalization to different parts of the globe.

Chapter III examines how India joining in the process of globalization. After decades of restriction and protection, India opened up its economy to the global economy. It demonstrates that the grim financial crisis which compelled India to join the process of globalization through the implementation of the New Economic Policy based on liberalization, globalization and privatisation. However, it reveals that joining the process of economic globalization brings more harm than good to different sections of population especially the vulnerable sections of population like the Dalits and the tribals.

Chapter IV deals with the challenges of globalization to tribal economy particularly the Khasi economy. It tries to point out that both the colonialist and the present day globalization brought severe challenges to the economic life of the people. At a time when the Khasi economy is weak and insecure the advent of globalization in the form of neo-colonial forces makes the situation worse for the tribals. Globalization not only damages the delicate balance of the eco-system, but also further pushed the majority of the marginalised tribal people to the margins of economic survival.

Chapter V discusses the indigenous Khasi tribal theological responses to the process of globalization that has challenged the economic survival of the Khasis. It reveals that there are plenty of traditional cultural elements which are liberative, lives affirming and inclusive that could serve as alternatives to the process of globalization. Coupled with the biblical, theological resources and the sources from the Process Theology, an indigenous Khasi tribal response could provide a better alternative to the tribal people in their daily struggles for economic survival against the challenges of the present phase of globalization.

Chapter 1

The Khasi Setting

This section attempts to investigate the general background of the Khasi people of Meghalaya. It will mostly deal with the traditional social, political, and cultural life of the people. At the same time it will analyse the economy of the Khasi people in the pre-colonial era, during the British colonial rule and the post independence period.

Geographical Description

The Khasi and Jaintia Hills comprise of the central and the eastern parts of Meghalaya state in North East India, lying between Brahmaputra valley in the north and the Surma valley or the plain of Bengal now Bangladesh in the south. It is situated between 24*58' and 26*7' N and 90*45' and 92*51' E.[1] The entire region is composed of hilly country with the highest point, the Shillong peak in the central region, rises to 6,450 feet above the sea level.[2] It may be noted that prior to the coming of the British rule, several Khasi states possessed certain areas of land either in the Brahmaputra valley in the north or the Surma valley in the south. The plain land, served as immense sources of income from the revenue collected by the Khasi chiefs from the inhabitants of the plain.[3] However with the establishment of the British colonial rule all these plain areas were annexed to the British territory.[4] Hence, there have been several changes with regard to the area

[1] Henry Frowde, *Imperial Gazetteer of India, Karachi to Kottayam,* Vol. XV, New Edition (Oxford: Clarendon Press, 1908), 254.

[2] B. C. Allen, *Gazetteer of the Khasi & Jaintia Hills, Garo Hills, Lushai Hills,* 2nd edtion (Delhi: Giant Publications, 1980), 4.

[3] Bareh, *The History and Culture of the Khasi People,* 262.

[4] For instance, Mills reports that the Raja of Jaintia had large possession of land both in the plain of Sylhet and Assam which were annexed to the British rule. See A. J. M. Mills, *Report of*

of the land. The Census of Assam reported that the area of the region was 6,157 sq. miles.[5] Later, it was reduced to 6,027 sq. miles.[6] However, with the merger of Block I and Block II to Mikir Hills now Karbi Anglong of Assam in 1960, the area of Khasi and Jaintia hills was again reduced to 5,541 sq. miles.[7]

Geographical Division of the Land

The entire region is divided into three zones.[8] The first division is the northern zone called the *Ri Bhoi.* Starting from the central belt, this area consists of "a compact plateau with associated flat lands and open valley, its northern extremity gradually sloping towards the Brahmaputra valley."[9] The area is covered with dense forests and bamboo groves.[10] Earlier, this belt was found to be unhealthy and sparsely populated.[11] There are also no records available that reveal any agricultural products produced in the area. Nevertheless, in the last few decades, it was found that *Ri Bhoi* is the most fertile area in Khasi and Jaintia Hills. The main agricultural products in the area are ginger, betel leaf, broom, betel nut, pine apple, paddy, tomato, banana, etc. It may be noted that among all the products, the first three items are the major sources of income to the people of the area.

The next zone is the central portion or the *Ri Lum.* This part comprises of irregular plateau stretching from Jowai region in the east up to Garo hills border in the west. The entire area marks the total absence of thick forests. Nevertheless, the abundant presence of pine trees and short grasses adds beauty to the land.[12]

---

the Khasi and Jaintia Hills, 1853 (Shillong: North Eastern Hill University, 1985), 2. Cf. William Robinson, *A Descriptive Account of Assam* (Calcutta: Ostel and Lepage, 1841), 407. Pamberton reports that the Raja of Nartung had large portions of plain land in the direction of Goalpara, but later taken away from him and annexed to the British territory. The name "Nartung" though it is a Khasi name, is quite confusing as no states known to bear that name. However, it indicates that many Khasi states possesses considerable portion of lands both in the plain of Assam and Sylhet. See B. R. Pamberton, *The Eastern Frontier of India*- Reprinted. 1st Printed as *Eastern frontier of the British Territories, 1835,* (New Delhi: Mittal Publications, 2000), 239.

[5] See *The Census of Assam 1881,* (Calcutta: Office of the Superintendent Printing, India, 1883), 163. See also W.W. Hunter, *A Statistical Account of Assam,* vol. 2, Reprinted (Guwahati: Spectrum Publications, 1998), 203.

[6] Henry Frowde, *Imperial Gazetteer of India: Karachi to Kottayam,* 254.

[7] Bareh, *The History and Culture of the Khasi People,* 7. Cf. B. B. Vaghaiwalla, *Census of India, 1951,* (Bombay: Municipal Printing Press, 1954), 4.

[8] Pamberton, *The Eastern Frontier of India,* 241-246. See also Mills, *Report of the Khasi and Jaintia Hills,* 2-4.

[9] Bareh, *The History and Culture of the Khasi People,* 7.

[10] O. L. Snaitang, *Christianity and Social Change in Northeast India* (Shillong: Vendrame Institute, 1993), 11.

[11] Snaitang, *Christianity and Social Change in Northeast India,* 11.

[12] Pamberton suggests that the abundance of short rich grass in the area will be good for cattle rearing. See Pamberton, *The Eastern frontier of India,* 250.

The main agricultural products in this region include potatoes, paddy, vegetables of different varieties,[13] and various kinds of fruits[14] and so on. Besides, the area possesses rich mineral resources like coal,[15] uranium,[16] etc. The iron industry of the Khasis in the earlier times was mainly located in this belt. Hence, the availability of natural resources and different agricultural products could enhance the economic life[17] of the people.

The third division is the *Ri War* area runs along the border of Bengal region, now Bangladesh, extending from Ratachera in Jaintia Hills in the east, up to the Garo hills border in the west. Besides the abundant presence of limestone, the area is also rich in agricultural plantation. The main agricultural products are oranges, banana, jack-fruit, pineapple, betel nuts, betel leaves, broom, bay leaves, black pepper, etc.[18] At present, except betel nut other agricultural items do not yield much source of income to the people of the region.

Land

Like all tribal[19] groups, land occupies the most important place in the life of the Khasis. For them, land is the source of livelihood. The entire source of living derives from land. The perception that "land is life"[20] indicates their recognition of the value and importance of land to human survival. Iscot Marbaniang observes that "the main basis of the economic condition of the people has since time immemorial been the land."[21] This implies that for the tribal people, land and its resources is the only economic source worth mentioning. Accordingly, the ancestral parents of the Khasis make all effort to see that all members of the

---

[13] This area produces different types of vegetables like tomato, cabbage, carrot, beet roots, reddish, chilly, squash, etc.

[14] The area is good for various kinds of fruits like the plum, pear, Khasi cherry or *sohiong,* many types of wild fruits and so on.

[15] This belt is also very rich in coalmines like in Bapung area of Jaintia Hills, Cherapunjee, Shahlang and Borsara area of West Khasi Hills, etc.

[16] Uranium of large quantity is found in Domiasiat area of West Khasi Hills District. The uranium deposit is yet to be mined as there is strong opposition from the Non Governmental Organizations (NGOs) like the Khasi Student Union (KSU), Federation of Khasi Jaintia Garo Peoples (FKJGP) and others on the basis that it will damage the environment and displacing many of the local people in the area.

[17] The economic life here can be referred to the relationship between people and economy. Economy can be defined as the source of livelihood that support the people in their struggle for survival.

[18] Cf. Pamberton, *The Eastern Frontier of India,* 242.

[19] In this research work, the word tribal and indigenous people are used interchangeably.

[20] Nirmal Minz, "Tribal Perspective on Ecology," in *The Tribal Worldview and Ecology,* edited by A. Wati Longchar and Yangkahao Vashum (Jorhat: Tribal Study Centre, 1998), 4.

[21] Iscot Marbaniang, *Assam in a Nutshell* (Shillong: Chapala Book Stall, 1970), 97.

community could have at least a small piece of land. This is clearly reflected in their land tenure system which has been followed in different parts of the land.

Land Tenure System

According to the Land Reforms Commission for Khasi Hills 1979[22] the whole land in these hills can be classified into two categories, namely, i) *Ri Kynti* or the private land and ii) *Ri Raid* or the community land.

Ri Kynti Land

Ri Kynti land means private land that belongs exclusively to particular family or clan. *Ri Kynti* lands consist of two types, i) ancestral and ii) Self-acquired. The former is referred to the land inherited from the ancestors/ancestress while the latter means land acquired by the person concerned. However, self-acquired land can also become ancestral land when it passes from generation to generation.[23] The entire management and control of the *Ri Kynti* land lies in the hands of the *dorbar Kur* or the clan assembly. It is the *dorbar Kur* who has the absolute proprietary and transferable right over these lands. The states or the *Raid* have no authority over these lands except to settle the dispute that may occur at any period of time.[24] David Roy maintains that the origin of the *Ri Kynti* land can be referred to the time when the *Bakhraw* or the leading families came and occupied the land which naturally became their absolute possession.[25] The *Bakhraw* here is understood as the founding clan who first came and occupied the new land. As they are the first settlers, naturally they have absolute control and authority over the land they have occupied. Bareh maintains that as the first settlers, they became the 'proprietor' and earned a 'permanent ownership' of that particular land. He further states that such a clan "became a legitimate ruling clan and extended protection to future comers in its fold."[26] It may be noted that, it was the custom of the Khasis, when the existing cultivated land became insufficient to meet the needs of the growing population; some groups migrated to new places in search of new land for cultivation and established their villages accordingly.[27] In this

[22] This Land Reforms Commission is done only for the Khasi Hills area. However, the land tenure system in other parts of the land is more or less the same with different variations here and there could be found such as the term used and others.

[23] Cf. *Report of the Land Reforms Commission for Khasi Hills,* 1974, 20.

[24] See *Report of the Land Reforms Commission on Khasi Hills,* 1974, 20. Cf. R. T. Rymbai, "The pattern of Landholding of the Khasi Pnars," in *Tribal Institution of Meghalaya,* edited by S. K. Chattopadhyay (Guwahati: Spectrum Publications, 1985), 189.

[25] See David Roy, "Land Tenure in the States" in *Notes on Khasi Law,* by Sir Keith Cantlie's, 2 nd ed. (Shillong: Chapala Publishing House, 2008-2009), 121.

[26] Bareh, *The History and Culture of the Khasi People,* 39.

[27] Cf. Helen Giri, *The Khasis under the British Rule, 1824-1947* (New Delhi: Regency Publications, 1998), 12.

way, people began to scatter in different parts of Khasi and Jaintia Hills. Hence, the first settlers or the founding clan could occupy certain areas of land in certain places as they deem it necessary. These lands occupied by the founding clans in due course became the *Ri Kynti* land of those particular clans. The proprietary and the heritable rights to these lands belong exclusively to the descendants of the clan. The rest of the remaining land normally kept aside for the need of the increasing population and the late comers, hence converted to the *Ri Raid* land or community land.[28]

Ri Raid Land

Ri Raid land is the land that was set apart for the need of the community as a whole. Hence, it belongs to the community. The community may be a village or group of villages and so on.[29] The whole management or control of such lands rest with the community. Any member of the community has the right to occupy or use any part or plot of the community land without payment of revenue or tax. But a person cannot occupy more than what actually he/she needs. At the same time, right of occupancy does not include heritable or transferable rights. The occupation is normally temporary and cultivation is mostly seasonal in nature.[30] Nevertheless, such lands if remain unused for a minimum period of three years will return back to the *Raid.* There are certain circumstances where the *Ri Raid* land or community land can become *Ri Kynti* land.[31] First, if the occupant of the *Ri Raid* land has made permanent development on the said land, such as wet paddy fields, terrace cultivation, fish ponds, etc. The said land can be considered as *Ri Kynti* land. Second, certain parts of *Ri Raid* land can be transferred as *Ri Kynti* land to a particular "person or a family or clan for certain yeoman's service rendered to the *Elaka*"[32] or *Raid* as a mark of respect or recognition for the invaluable service sacrificed for the community. But even in such cases the community can reclaim back any of the lands if the owner ceased to utilise it for a period of three years.

The above discussion on land tenure system indicates the fact that the ancestral parents of the Khasis realises the importance of land to the well being of the people in the community. Hence, they made a system of land classification which could benefit all inhabitants. As land is closely linked to the economic life of the tribals, every member in the community should be abled to enjoy the

[28] Chowdhury, *Ki Khun Khasi Khara (The Khasi People),* 220-221.

[29] R. T. Rymbai, *The Pattern of Landholding of the Khasi-Pnar*, 189.

[30] See *Report of the Land Reforms Commission for Khasi Hills, 1974,* 18.

[31] See *Report of the Land Reforms Commission for Khasi Hills, 1974,* 17. Cf. Government of Meghalaya, Art & Culture Department, *Meghalaya District Gazetteers Khasi Hills District,* 1991, 63.

[32] *Elaka* consists of number of villages under the supervision of one head named *Doloi.*

benefit of it. T. Nongbri argues that the main intention regarding this system of land classification is "to ensure availability of land to all sections of population"[33]

Khasi Polity

The traditional political organization of the Khasis is essentially democratic in nature. While Nataranjan compares it with the 'Swiss Cantons,'[34] Dutta opines that they are near parallel with the 'Polis' of the ancient Greece.[35] A. B. Lish on the other hand, suggest that Khasi polity is 'Republican.'[36] All these suggestions point to the fact that Khasi polity is basically democratic. The unique characteristic of Khasi polity is the hierarchy of the *Dorbars* that connect the clan council at the lowest level to the *Dorbar Hima* or state assembly at the highest level.[37] Thus, the Khasi political system is basically a four tier system of administration. There are some writers who suggest that Khasi polity is a three tier system of government[38] and there are those who seem to suggest only two tier system of administration.[39] But here we will try to follow a four tier system of administration. This political structure can be broadly classified as i) the Clan *Dorbar*, ii) the Village *Dorbar*, iii) the *Dorbar Raid* and iv) the State Assembly or the *Dorbar Hima*.[40]

The Clan Dorbar

The clan is one of the most important units of the Khasi society. In a matrilineal[41] society like the Khasis, the clan consists of different families that originates from the same *Iawbei Tynrai* or the first ancestress of the clan. It is this common origin

---

[33] T. Nongbri, "The Khasi Land Tenure System: Need for Conceptual Refinement," in *Land Relation in North East India,* edited by B. B. Dutta and M. N. Karna (New Delhi: People Publishing House, 1987), 73.

[34] See Nalini Nataranjan, *The Missionary among the Khasis* (Guwahati: United Publishers, 1977), 37.

[35] See Promatha Nath Dutta, *Impact of the West on the Khasis and Jaintia* (New Delhi: Cosmo Publications, 1982), 15.

[36] A. B. Lish, "A Brief Account of the Khasees," *Calcutta Christian Observer* VII/70 (March, 1838): 133.

[37] See Homiwell Lyngdoh, *Ki Syiem Khasi bad Synteng* (Shillong: Desmond P. Reade Diengdoh, 3 rd ed. 2003), xv.

[38] Those who suggest a three tier system, ignores the role of the Clan Council. They opine that Khasi polity started with the Village Council at the lowest level up to the State council at the highest level. Cf. Dutta, *Impact of the West on the Khasis and Jaintias,* 15. See also, David R. Syiemlieh, "Traditional Institutions of Governance in the Hills of North East India: The Khasi Experience," *Man and Society: A Journal of North East Studies* III (Spring, 2006), 124.

[39] See J. N. Choudhury, *Ki Khun Khasi Khara,* 171.

[40] Cf. Snaitang, *Christianity and Social Change in Northeast India,* 14. Cf. Nataranjan, *The Missionary among the Khasis,* 37.

[41] The matrilineal society here means that the descent line and property pass on from the mother to the daughter.

that binds together all members of the clan into one single unit. All members are closely attached to their *Kurs* or clan. The clan is again sub-divided into different *Kpohs.* It is important to note that if the clan serves as a binding unit of all the members, this bond is stronger and well establish within the particular *Kpoh* the smaller unit.[42] Notably, the tribals used to identify themselves by the place to which one belongs.[43] But for the Khasis besides land, it is also the clan that provide them identity and personhood. Whenever two Khasis meet for the first time, after knowing the place one belongs, the next question will be to which clan he or she belongs. By knowing the clan or *Kurs,* they will understand that a person is from Ri Bhoi or War Khasi and so on.

Each and every clan have their respective *dorbar* known as *Dorbar Kur* or clan assembly. It is a custom of the Khasis that every family has to send at least one person as member or representative to the clan *dorbar.*[44] The eldest male member or *U Kni Rangbah* of the clan is usually elected as the Chairman or the executive head of the clan. He is also called *U Saidnia,* that is his role is to mediates or speak on behalf of the clan[45] In other words, being the eldest person he must be a mature person and has the personality and ability to maintain the overall development of the entire clan. In most cases he is to perform the role of the *Lyngdoh* or priest for the entire clan. Hence, he has "both secular and sacerdotal power."[46] At the same time, as the executive head he is expected to convene the *Dorbar Kur,* listen to the problems of different members or families, and bring them to the clan *dorbar* for any solution needed and so on.[47] Snaitang argues that the main duty of the clan *dorbar,*

> Were to look after the clan property (Ri Kur) and to settle dispute among clan members, including trying cases of theft, adultery, trespass, damage to

---

[42] Though the clan binds together all the members into one unit, kinship obligation is stronger within the particular *Kpoh.* This is clearly seen either in time of joy or sorrow, looking after or extending assistance to the members who are poor and needy and so on. This does not mean that the clan has no role to play, but the stronger the bond within the *Kpoh* the better will be for the welfare of the whole clan.

[43] See J. N. Chowdhury, *Ki Khun Khasi Khara (The Khasi People)* (Shillong: Published by the Author, 1996), 6.

[44] Snaitang opines that only male member are allowed to attend the *Dorbar Kur,* but today any member including female members of the clan attend different meetings of the *Kur* or clan. Cf. Snaitang, *Christianity and Social Change in Northeast India,* 17.

[45] Cecile A. Mawlong, "Megalith and Social Formation in Khasi-Jaintia Hills," in *Society and Economy in North-East India,* edited by Mignonette Momin and Cecile A. Mawlong (New Delhi: Regency Publications, 2004), 42.

[46] *Ibid,* 42.

[47] In the last few decades, all the clan councils have been better organized with different office bearers elected from time to time among the matured members of the clan to look after the entire welfare of the clan.

property, etc. It is also responsible for looking after the clan's general welfare, including the provision of assistance to landless members.[48]

According to the Khasi traditional custom and usage, it is the duty and responsibility of the clan to look after the general welfare of the clan members. In other words, moral behaviour of all the members, their wrong doings, the dispute or conflict that may arise among clan members must be settled within the clan council.[49] Moreover, it is the responsibility of the clan to look after the economic life and well being of its members especially the poor and the landless. It is generally the belief that the clan council is able to help the economic problems of clan members and provide advice or direction for different circumstances and so on. Hence, if the living condition of any person or even a family is so poor, that has attracted the attention of others, the Khasis use to say *um/kim don kur don jaid?* This means that the person or the family concerned has no relatives or clan members to help them in such a situation?[50] In other words, it is a shame for the whole clan if it does not provide help or rescue its member in such a situation. It is because of this practice that a beggar is unknown or never seen in a Khasi society. Since "clan loyalty among the Khasis is very strong" argues Kynpham Singh "it is considered a dishonour to a clan to have a member begging because of poverty."[51] The Khasis believe that it is the responsibility of the clan to look after the economic well being of its member especially the poor and the needy.

The Village Dorbar

Another important feature of Khasi political institution is the village *dorbar* or the *dorbar Shnong*. As stated earlier, during the migratory period one or more than one clan came to settle in a new land and became the original settler or the founding clan. Later some new clans joined them; therefore together they formed a village.[52] The head of the founding clan was naturally preferred to be the village headman or the *Rangbah Shnong*. B. Pakem maintains that such a leader must have been a very powerful person and "could not be a democratic leader." He further argues that the head of the village was assisted by the village

---

[48] See Snaitang, *Christianity and Social Change in Northeast India*, 18.

[49] However, this does not mean that the family or the parents has no role to play here, but it means that it is also the responsibility of other members or relatives concerning the moral behavior of the person. It is the belief of the Khasis that anything wrong committed by the member, it affects not only the person concern or the family but it also affects the whole clan.

[50] This saying also applies to a person who is committing any wrong doing in public, for the Khasis belief that such an action affects the integrity of the whole clan.

[51] Kynpham Singh, "Khasi and Jaintia Religion," in *Khasi Heritage*, edited by Hipshon Roy Kharshiing (Shillong: Seng Khasi, 1979), 103.

[52] Mawlong, "Megalith and Social Formation in Khasi-Jaintia Hills," 42. Cf. Gurdon, *The Khasis*, 2010), 64.

dorbar or the *Dorbar Shnong.*[53] In the earlier time it was only the *Rangbah Shnong* and the *Dorbar Shnong* who looked after the general welfare and the overall development of the village. In the later period, besides these two institutions the Village Committee also instituted to assist the *Rangbah Shnong,* for the smooth functioning of the village development. It may be noted that even today, in many villages the post of *Rangbah Shnong* is kept aside for the original clan.[54] However, all male members above the age of 18 years are able to take part in the election of the *Rangbah Shnong.*[55] However, though the *Rangbah Shnong* is the head of the village, the final authority with regard to any affairs of the village rests with the *Dorbar Shnong.* It is the *Dorbar Shnong* as the highest body that has to approve all important decision for the total welfare of the village. Snaitang argues that apart from the judicial function,[56] the Village *Dorbar* is responsible to "maintain law and order, administer public ponds, bridle paths, bridges and forests, and look after the village security."[57] Though the role of the Village *Dorbar* in the economic life of the people is insignificant, it is its responsibility to take care and maintain the village land and the village forests. With regard to the former the Village *Dorbar* is responsible in allotting certain plot of land to any members who are in need for constructing a dwelling house. While in the latter, it is the Village *Dorbar* which normally used to distribute the forest land for those required for *Jhum* cultivation However, right of occupancy in the village land, either for the purpose of house building or cultivation belongs exclusively to the member of the village not to the outsider.[58]

The Raid Dorbar

Above the villages there is a *Raid.* The *Raid* is formed by a conglomeration of several villages in one particular area. Hence, the *Raid Dorbar* as a council has to look after a bigger area which comprises several villages under its jurisdiction. The members of the *Raid Dorbar* includes all the Village Headmen within the *Raid* with an addition of some more representatives if need arise.[59] The head of the *Raid Dorbar* is preferably the senior most male person usually elected among the

[53] B. Pakem, "State Formation in Pre-Colonial Jaintia," in *Tribal Polities and State Systems in Pre-Colonial Eastern and North Eastern India,* edited by Surajit Sinha (Calcutta: K. P. Bagchi & Company, 1987), 243.

[54] But there are villages like Sohkha in War Jaintia where the post of *Rangbah Shnong* and all committee members are open to all clans in the village not only to the original clans.

[55] Pakem, "State Formation in Pre-Colonial Jaintia," 245.

[56] The important judicial function of the Village *Dorbar* is to settle criminal cases that have taken place within its jurisdiction, like murder, theft, robbery, assault, adultery, rape cases, etc. before sending them to the police for proper investigation.

[57] Snaitang, *Christianity and Social Change in Northeast India,* 17.

[58] J. N. Choudhury, *The Khasi Canvas* (Calcutta: Srimati Jaya Choudhury, 1978), 163.

[59] Snaitang, *Christianity and Social Change in Northeast India,* 16-17.

Village Headmen. The main activities of the Raid *Dorbar* comprise management and care for the *Raid* land and forests, allotment of land for the landless members, dwelling house and cultivation and so on.[60] In other words, it indicates that the important function of the *Raid Dorbar* is basically to look after the economic life of its members. As stated earlier, the intention of the ancestors/ancestress in keeping the *Ri Raid* land is for the benefit of all members in the community. *Ri Raid* land is not meant for sale but is land to be shared. Hence, it is the responsibility of the *Raid Dorbar* to see that all members of the *Raid* could obtain certain areas of land for cultivation or residential building without any discrimination.

The Dorbar Hima

The *Dorbar Hima* is the supreme political body in the Khasi society.[61] It is the highest decision making body in the administrative set up that regulates the affairs of the state. Besides the *Syiem* and the *Myntri* or the *Bakhraw*, its members comprise representatives from the *Raid* and the Village council.[62] Hence, there is a close connection between the *Hima* as the supreme administrative body and the people in different *Raids* and villages. The Chief presides over the *Dorbar* and all important meeting of the state. According to the customary belief, though the Chief is the head of administration, he cannot make any important decision with regard to the affairs of the *Hima* without consulting and attaining the approval of the *Dorbar*.[63] In other words, an authority concerning the welfare and development of the entire states lies not with the chief as the head, but with the democratic right and liberties of the people. It is the *Dorbar Hima* which is the sole authority in the administrative set up of state. Nataranjan argues that the *Dorbar Hima* performs its duty strictly under the guidance of *Ka Riti*-an unwritten constitution that emphasised on the usages and practices of the people.[64] Snaitang on the other hand maintains that according to the traditional custom, the *Dorbar* does "not legislate new laws but was, rather, responsible for the proper implementation of traditional laws, customs manners and usages."[65] The main functions of the *Dorbar Hima* include maintaining law and order, protecting the rights of the people, settles different cases that could not solve by the lower courts, supervising the affairs of the common market, rivers, forests and state religious ceremonies,

[60] Snaitang, *Christianity and Social Change in Northeast India,* 17. Cf. Rymbai, "The Pattern of Landholding of the Khasi Pnar," 189.

[61] Kyn pham Singh, "Syiems and Durbars in Khasi Polity," in *Tribal Institutions of Meghalaya,* edited by S. K. Chattopadhyay (Guwahati: Spectrum Publications, 1985), 20.

[62] Snaitang, *Christianity and Social Change in Northeast India*, 16. Cf. J. N. Choudhury, *Ki Khun Khasi Khara*, 174.

[63] Dutta, *Impact of the West on the Khasis and Jaintias,* 22.

[64] Nataranjan, *The Missionary among the Khasis,* 38.

[65] Snaitang, *Christianity and Social Change in Northeast India,* 16.

etc.[66] This indicates that the *Dorbar* has different roles to play for the economic well being of the people or *Ki Khun Ki Hajar*.[67]

The Role of the Chief

The Chief or *Syiem* is the executive head of the state. Edward Gait who has written about the early history of the Khasis, argues that there is no record which suggest that the Khasis were ruled by one Chief.[68] It is believed that in the early period, the Khasis were ruled by the *Basans* and *Lyngdohs* normally elected from among the founding clan.[69] However, with the increase of population new socio-economic problems evolved;[70] such as opening of markets, execution of marriage laws, codification of land tenure matters, execution of judgement on criminals, settlement of the wealth and properties of those people whose clan has become extinct and so on.[71] It was said that no members of the founding clan or *Jaid Bakhraw* would like to take the role of Syiemship, for it is the bounded duty of the *Syiem* to execute unpleasant judgement like imprisonment, capital punishment, to collect the property of those whose clan has become extinct for the fear of *Ka Byrsieh* that is defilement or taint that could befall on their descendants.[72] Both the *Basans* and the *Lyngdohs* were not in a position to deal with all these new development. Such a situation, demanded for a single administration or a common ruler who would take care over the general welfare of the people in different *Raids* and villages. Hence, the *Basans* and *Lyngdohs* voluntarily came to an agreement to institute the office of Syiemship by anointing a particular clan called *Jaid Syiem*.[73] With these new developments, the institution of Syiemship evolved to look after different needs of the entire State and *Ki Khun Ki Hajar*.

---

[66] Snaitang, *Christianity and Social Change in Northeast India*, 16.

[67] The Khasis used to address their Chief or *Syiem* as *U Paiem* which means "Father King" and the people of the state as *Ki Khun Ki Hajar* which means the "children in thousands". This implies the close relationship and attachment that exist between the Chief and the people of the state.

[68] Edward Gait, *A History of Assam*, 5 th ed. (Guwahati: Lawyer's Book Stall, 1992), 248.

[69] Giri, *The Khasis under the British Rule, 1824-1927*, 17.

[70] See Lyngdoh, *Ka Niam Khasi*, 261-262.

[71] See Bareh, *The History and Culture of the Khasi People*, 41. See also Mawlong, Megaliths and Social Formation in Khasi-Jaintia Hills, 43.

[72] See Kynpham Singh, "Syiems and Durbars in Khasi Polity" in *Tribal Institutions of Meghalaya*, edited by S. K. Chattopadhyay (Guwahati: Spectrum Publications, 1985), 16.

[73] See Lyngdoh, *Ka Niam Khasi*, 259. Cf. Singh, Syiems and Durbars in Khasi Polity, 17. See also Homiwell Lyngdoh, *Ki Syiem Khasi bad Synteng*, 3rd ed., (Shillong: Desmond P. Reade Diengdoh, 2003), 1-114.

Syiemship is confined to that particular clan and only the male member is eligible or entitled to occupy the office.[74]

Being a matrilineal society, succession to the office of Syiemship does not pass to the Chief's son; rather it passes either to his uterine brother or if there is no brother it will pass to his nephew, i.e. to his eldest son of his eldest sister.[75] Although the office of Syiemship is hereditary, it is at the same time elective. The *Syiem* is elected by the *Dorbar* where membership is restricted to the founding clan or the original settlers only.[76] It is this *Dorbar* which decides who is eligible or the right heir to the throne. Nevertheless, being democratic the power or authority rest not with the Chief but with the *Dorbar Hima.* As stated earlier, the Chief cannot make decision on his own but has to consult and acquire the consent and approval of the *Dorbars.* As Nataranjan rightly puts it,

> The will of the people was sovereign not only in theory but also in practice. Rules were enforced strictly; the code of conduct emphasised that the dignity of every individual was the same in the eyes of law.[77]

Moreover, in the village set up there is no separate area reserved for the Chief but all the people, rich or poor, the nobility and the Chief live together.[78] Based on the democratic order of equality, the *Syiem* clan is not higher than other clans and neither *U Syiem* nor any member of the *Bakhraw* clan is above the other in the society.[79] Nevertheless, the people as *Ki Khun Ki Hajar* pay due respect to the Chief and always ready to render any services on his behalf.[80] The important duties of the Chief comprises maintaining law and order, peace and security, execute judgement to criminals, care for the poor, the needy, the widows, the deserted, the destitute and also seeing that justice is done to them, and the like.[81] Hence, his role as the *Syiem* is to ensure for the overall development of the people of the state including economic prosperity. L. S. Gassah observes that the Chief

---

[74] However, there is an exception if the family do not have any male members then the female has the right to occupy the office.

[75] For detail see Bareh, *The History and Culture of the Khasi People,* 42.

[76] This *Dorbar* consists of the members who represent the original clan only like the *Myntris, Basans* and *Lyngdohs.* All these members are generally known as *Myntris.* However, this *Dorbar* is not to be confused with the *Dorbar Hima* mentioned above where every citizen involved. For detail see Gurdon, *The Khasis,* 66-75.

[77] See Nataranjan, *The Missionaries among the Khasis,* 39.

[78] See Gurdon, *The Khasis,* 33.

[79] R. T. Rymbai, "The Evolution of the Hynniew Trep Polity," in *Khanasamari- U Khun U Hajar ka Ri u Hynniew Trep,* edited by Sumar Sing Sawian (Shillong: Apphira Publications, 1998), n.p.

[80] See Snaitang, *Christianity and Social Change in Northeast India,* 14.

[81] *Ibid,* 15. See also H. Onderson Mawrie, *Ka Pyrkhat u Khasi* (Guwahati: Silpi Printers, 1997), 68.

is "responsible for regulation and distribution of Jhum lands so that each family or household has a plot of land for cultivation. A Chief would not like to see his people suffer from shortage of food in normal circumstances."[82]

Khasi Religious System

There has been different interpretations regarding the Khasi religion. Based on their superiority attitude, the earlier British writers both missionaries and government officers generally classified the Khasi religion like other tribal religion as animistic, superstitious and even not equivalent to be considered as religion. Lish[83] a missionary from Serampore to the Khasis in 1832, opines that the Khasis "believe in the existence of one Supreme Being, the Creator of the world." But they also believe that, the daily affairs of humans and even their land are under the influence of divine agents or spirits or gods who reside "in the caves and jungles, or in the neighbourhood of steep mountains and rocks" the places they never approach, lest they will suffer for disturbing the residence of the deities who need to be pacified with sacrifices.[84] Lish may have confused these places with the Sacred Groves, whom the Khasis believe to be the residing places of the *Ryngkew* or *Basa,* the guardian spirit or the one who protects that area.[85] Hooker in 1854, as cited by Chowdhury in similar vein observes that Khasis are superstitious, having no religion, but believe in the Supreme Beings and in the deity of groves, caves and streams.[86] On the other hand, while Hunter considers Khasi religion as "demon-worship,"[87] Gurdon suggests that the Khasis "cannot, however, be said to worship the Supreme God" though though they ocassionally invoke God in time of trouble. For him, the religion of the Khasis may be characterized as "animism, or spirit-worship, or rather, the propiation of spirits both good and evil on certain occasion, principally in times of trouble."[88]

However, the Khasis have their own interpretation of their religion.The Khasis believe that their religion is not founded by any human persons but it is God-given from the beginning of time.[89] This is clearly reflected in the Creation

[82] L. S. Gassah, "Self-Management among Tribals in Meghalaya," in *Antiquity to Modernity in Tribal India: Tribal Self-Management in North East India,* Vol. II, edited by Bhupinder Singh (New Delhi: Inter-India Publications, 1998), 98.

[83] See John Hughes Morris, *The Story of our Foreign Mission (Presbyterian Church of Wales),* 2nd ed., (Aizawl: Synod Publication Board, 1990), 25.

[84] Lish, A Brief Account of the Khasees, 140.

[85] See Spiton Kharakor, "Ki 'Lawblei 'Lawkyntang," in *Sengkutsnem 1989, Ninetieth Year Souvenir (1899-1989)* (Shillong: Seng Khasi, 1989), 23.

[86] Chowdhury, *The Khasi Canvas,* 183.

[87] Hunter, *A Statistical Account of Assam, 218.*

[88] Gurdon, *The Khasis,* 105.

[89] See R. T. Rymbai, "Some Aspects of the Religion of the Khasi-Pnars," in *Khasi Heritage,* edited by Hipshon Roy (Shillong: Seng Khasi, 1979), 110.

Story or the myth of *U Lum Sohpetbneng.*[90] The traditional belief says that in the beginning *Ka Hukum* or God the lawgiver created the *Ramew* or the mother earth and the earth was initially covered with water. Then God created *U Ryngkew* or dry land. In the process the rivers and small streams cleanse the earth and produced soil, stones, etc. This act is symbolically believed to be the union or marriage of *U Ryngkew* and *Ka Ramew.* Then God also created other bodies like the sun, the moon and the stars above and air, fire, etc below. All creations responded well according to the design of the Creator. Then *Ka Ramew* conceived again and in her second conception giving birth to other species like the animals, the birds, the trees, the grass, plants and others which added beauty to the once barren land.

When everything came into existence, peace and prosperity prevailed, and then *Ka Ramew* felt the need of someone who will take care and look after all the creation of God. Hence, *Ka Ramew* or the mother earth beseeches God to send someone to look after the entire creation. It was because of the urgent plea of the mother earth, that God convened the *Dorbar Blei* or the Divine Assembly with the *Khathynriew Trep Khathynriew Skum*[91] or the sixteen families in heaven whom the Khasis belief, they lived together with God their creator in heaven. In the meeting, it was decided that the *Hynniew Trep Hynniew Skum*[92] or the seven families should come down to the earth and take the responsibility of caring and look after all the creations. God also planted a divine tree on the sacred mount called *U Lum Sohpet Bneng*[93] which served as a golden ladder that bridged heaven and earth, so that the seven families can have the freedom to communicate freely between heaven and earth anytime they feel necessary. It is believed that the seven families lived a very happy and prosperous life here on earth. Hence, peace and security enveloped the entire universe. God also gave them their religion and some commandments[94] to lead and guide them in their daily affairs.

It is the belief of the Khasis that their religion has no founder but it is the gift of God to them since the beginning of time. Hence, they call it *Ka Niam*

---

[90] See Junita War, "The Khasi Concept of Nature," in *The Tribal Worldview and Ecology,* edited by A. Wati Longchar and Yangkahao Vashum (Jorhat: The Tribal Study Centre, 1998), 41-43. Cf. R. T. Rymbai, "Christian Mission and the Indigenous Religion of the Khasi-Pnar" in *Religion in North East India,* edited by Sousmen Sen (New Delhi: Uppal Publishing House, 1993), 70-73.

[91] The Khasis belief that this *Khadhynriew Trep Khadhynriew Skum* or the sixteen families are living together with God in heaven. When the seven families came down to the earth the nine families remain in heaven with God.

[92] The Khasis belief that these seven families or the *Hynniew Trep* later become the ancestors of the Khasi people which include the seven sub-tribes of the Khasis namely, the *Khynriam, Pnar, Bhoi, War, Maram, Lyngngam* and the now never-heard-of Diko.

[93] *Lum Sohpet Bneng* means the Mount of the Navel of Heaven. The mountain is so called because it serves as the umbilical cord that connects heaven and earth.

[94] These commandments will be discussed later. Cf. Rymbai, "Christian Missions and the Indigenous Religion...," 69-73.

Tipbriew Tipblei or the religion which knows humans and knows God.[95] The word 'religion' in Khasi is *Ka Niam,* it is a combination of two words, one is *Nia* which means 'cause or reason' and the other word is *im* which means 'living.' Hence, from the combination of these two words we get the word *Nia-im* that is the 'living cause.'[96] God is the cause of everything, living and non living. It is out of that cause, human beings and this natural world are created.[97] Hence, everything living and non living have their source in God the Creator or *U Blei Nongbuh Nongthaw.*

Furthermore, Mawrie observes that Khasi religion is based on two important things namely *Ka Nia* and *Ka Jutang* or reason and covenant. Here, the Cause is God and reason belongs to human. It is on that Cause and covenant that human beings base their reasons, and that covers the entire relationship between God and human. If there is a breach of this covenant on humans' side then God will turn his/her back on humans. Here, there is the Khasis' saying which says *Phai lyndet U Blei.* Hence, it is the responsibility of humans to find ways and means in order to restore the broken relationship with God.[98] This indicates that the Khasis have strong belief that their religion is based on the covenant between humans and God.

Concept of God

Like all other tribals, the Khasis have a clear conception of God and God's relationship with human beings in particular and the natural world in general. For them, God is above gender or God is neither male nor female. Hence, one can address God in masculine as *U Blei* or in the feminine as *Ka Blei,* or we can even address God in plural aspect as *Ki Blei.* When the plural forms are applied to God, it does not mean that there are many Gods but only one. But it indicates the way that the Khasis address those whom they respect and honour. For instance, the way that they address their King is *Phi Ki Syiem* or you the Kings.[99] This does not mean that there are many Kings; rather it is a mark of respect and reverence paid to them.

As stated above, God is the source of everything that exists. Everything that exist both living and non-living has their origin from God. Moreover, God manifests Himself/Herself in and through the nature whom He/She has created. Mawrie observes that the expression of beauty, mystery and majesty of nature is

---

[95] See W. R. Laitphlang, "Ka Niam Ha U Khasi," *Sneng Khasi* 5/19 (December, 1981), 6.

[96] Cf. Nataranjan, *The Missionary among the Khasis,* 42.

[97] See H. O. Mawrie, *The Essence of Khasi Religion* (Shillong: Ri Khasi Press, 1981), 2-3.

[98] See Mawrie, *The Essence of Khasi Religion,* 36-37.

[99] See R. T. Rymbai, "Christian Mission and the Indigenous Religion…," 74.

but the manifestation of God's presence.[100] In other words, nature serves as the channel through which God communicates to human beings.[101]

Furthermore, the Khasis have no temples or any special place built for corporate worship. For them, God fills the heaven and earth. Hence, they can worship Him/Her anywhere or every where they find it convenient. It may be a grove, a cave, a hillock and so on.[102] All these places can become places of worship. Therefore, one can choose any site or spot for worship. The Khasis use the word '*tang*' which means 'consecrate or sanctify.' Once the place is sanctified that particular place can become a sacred place for worship. But this does not imply that the Khasis 'worship nature' as termed by outsiders, rather a particular place is being consecrated to worship God.[103] As such, the Khasi people have the freedom to worship God in any place they deemed good. The best place to worship God is at home, where all the members of the family gather together and "is in constant need of His (God) help and blessing."[104] It may be noted that this may be the reason, why the Khasi religion is regarded as the family religion.[105] Moreover, as God is the Supreme Being and His/Her presence permeates the entire creation, people can address or worship God in different aspects in accordance to their need, such as God universal, God localised and God at home.

God Universal

God universal is understood as the presence of God that covers the entire universe both heaven and earth. God is omnipresence and stands above creation. As such, they invoke Him/Her as,

- *U Blei Nongbuh Nongthaw*-God the Creator and dispenser of all things.
- *U Blei Hajrong Hatbian*-God who is above and below, the omnipresent God who fills the entire cosmos.
- *U Blei U Trai Kynrad*-God the Lord and Master of the universe.
- *U Blei U Nongsei Nongpynlong*-God the principle of growth and conservation, one who brings forth and dispenses life.
- *U Blei Shihajar Nguh*-God to whom all obeisance is due.[106]

---

[100] Mawrie, *Ka Pyrkhat U Khasi,* 5.

[101] H. O. Mawrie, *Ka Theology ka Niam Khasi* (Shillong: Ri Khasi Press, 1991), 66.

[102] Mawrie, *The Essence of Khasi Religion,* 47.

[103] Mawrie, *Ka Theology ka Niam Khasi,* 66.

[104] Rymbai, "Christian Missions and the Indigenous Religion...," 75.

[105] For detail see Snaitang, *Christianity and Social Change in Northeast India,* 29.

[106] See Pascal Malngiang, *Aspects of Khasi Religion* (Shillong: Seven Hut Enterprise, 1991), 18-19. See also Kynpham Singh, "Khasi and Jaintia Religion," 96.

God Localised

The word 'local' here refers mostly to different areas within the territorial boundary of Khasi and Jaintia Hills. As land in the context of Khasi and Jaintia Hills, is divided into a number of *Himas* or state, *Raids* and villages, God localised here means God of a particular State, *Raid* and village whom the Khasis worship in order to protect their particular place. Hence, the Khasis invoke God as,

- *U 'Lei Muluk U Lei Jaka*-God the guardian of state or *Raid.*
- *U 'Lei Khyrdop U Lei Kharai*-God the defender of their land from external invasion.
- *U 'Lei Hima Sima*-God as the protector "of the state and its people in all spheres of their life, political, economic, social, etc.
- *U Ryngkew U Basa*-God the defender of the village.[107]

God at Home or Household God

Here God universal becomes God at home, the one who is the care giver and provider of the family. Hence, God at home is often refered as,

- *U/Ka 'Lei Longspah-* God of wealth and prosperity who is the bestower of economic well being to the family.
- *U/Ka 'Lei Longkur Longjaid-* God who increases, multiplies and protects the well being of the entire clan.
- *U/Ka 'Lei Longing Longsem*-God of family the one who looks after the over all progress and welfare of the family.[108]

Belief in other Spirits

Like all other tribals, side by side with the belief in God the Supreme Being, the Khasis also believe in existense of other spirits or deities like *Ki Ksuid Ki Khrei.*[109] Mawrie maintains that the world is a living place not only for human beings but also for other spirit.[110] These evil spirits are believe to come from time to time to inflict and torture human beings through different types of suffering and

---

[107] For detail see Mawrie, *The Essence of Khasi Religion,* 42-43.

[108] *Ibid.,* 48-49.

[109] In recent past, there is an attempt from those writers who belong to the traditional Khasi religion, to consider Khasi primal religion as a monotheistic religion which is not correct. Though the Khasi people has clear conception of God, alongside their belief in God they also belief in the presence of other evil spirits. Most of their writings are based on their opposition against the missionaries' activities of conversion many people from the Khasi community into Christian faith.

[110] Mawrie, *Ka Theology jong ka Niam Khasi,* 73-74. See also Mawrie, *Ka Pyrkhat U Khasi,* 17-26.

sickness.[111] Hence, in order to get rid of these evil spirits that torment humans, they have to be appeased and propitiated through a series of sacrifices.[112] Thanzauva maintains that the tribals believe in the existence of both the benevolent and the malevolent spirits.[113] These benevolent spirits may be regarded as the aspect of God the Supreme being whom the Khasis believe to be the one who helps and protect them in times of need.[114] In the case of the malevolent spirit, he says that tribals have to offer some sacrifices to appease them. And it is because of these acts of appeasment that the missionaries regarded them as worshipping the evil. "The idea of worshipping evil spirit" states Thanzauva, "seems to have been developed by the observers, not the tribal themselves."[115]

The is, therefore, a misunderstanding with regard to the Khasi religion; with the Britishers labelling it merely as animism or demon worship or even not equivalent to be considered as religion. It is such understanding that considers primal religion like Khasi religion simply as evil, superstitious, deragatory, inferior, devoid of all good things and so on. In other words such characterization stems from the superiority attitude that sees everything non western or traditional or local as pagan, heathen and inferior possessing nothing good in them. Chowdhury maintains that the opinion formed by the British writers "were influenced more by their fixed ideas as to what religion ought to be and not what religion is." He further suggests for the need to consider the problem of religion "in an objective spirit rather than in a spirit of judgement."[116] For him, to label the Khasis as having no religion or to brand their religion as simply animistic as done by the British writers is incorrect. "Religion" he says covers their entire social fabric, it is "a way of life with them."[117] Commenting on the negative portrayal of the Khasi religion, Shobhan N. Lamare states that in today's context the term animism is understood as derogatory.[118]

Moreover, Khasi religion is not a monotheistc religion as suggested by the Khasi writers who belong to the traditional faith.[119] But our discussion above

[111] These evil spirits like *Ka Rih, Ka Duba* and many others use to come to cause harm and other calamities to humans. For detail see Chowdhury, *The Khasi Canvas,* 191-192. Cf. Nataranjan, *The Missionary among the Khasis,* 47-48.

[112] Nataranjan, *The Missionaries among the Khasis,* 47. See also Bareh, *The History and Culture of the Khasi People,* 323.

[113] Thanzauva, *Theology of the Community: Tribal Theology in the Making,* 190.

[114] Cf. Nataranjan, *The Missionary among the Khasis,* 46.

[115] Thanzauva, *Theology of the Community: Tribal Theology in the Making,* 190-191.

[116] Chowdhury, *The Khasi Canvas,* 184.

[117] Chowdhury, *The Khasi Canvas,* 188-189.

[118] Shobhan N. Lamare, *The Jaintias: Studies in Society and Change* (New Delhi: Regency Publication, 2005), 59.

[119] Rymbai opines that Khasi religion is a monotheistic religion. See Rymbai, "Some Aspects of the Religion…," 115. See also Mawrie, *The Essence of Khasi Religion,* 21-22.

implies that, it is both theistic and animistic in nature. Bareh maintains that Khasi religion is "both theistic and animistic, though in the beginning, it was apparently monotheistic."[120] But he does not give any detailed explanation on how Khasi religion shifted its belief from monotheistic to its present forms. Nevertheless, as far as Khasi religion is concerned, the fact remains that "both kinds of beliefs, theistic and animistic, exist side by side."[121]

Reverence to Ancestors/Ancestress

Paying homage to their dead ancetors/ancestress is another feature of Khasi religion. This act of reverence includes the *ai bam* or offerings of food and other materials that may taken place ocassionally as they think it necessary. Such practice is done as a mark of respect to the three progenitors of the clan namely, *U Saidnia* (the first maternal uncle), *U Thawlang* (the First ancestor) and *Ka Iawbei* (the first ancestress) of the clan.[122] The tradition tells us that each clan has their own triad from whom the clan descended, continue and flourish. For the Khasis clan or kinship relationship is very strong. In other words, there is a strong bond of attachment not only between members but to the clan itself. Hence, the triad as the founder of the clan are held in high esteem. In other words, one has to pay respect to them because it is through them "we have come into being in in this world."[123] To put it differently, we have to honour them "because they have left their marks upon the life of their descendants."[124] Bareh argues that honouring the dead ancestors/ancestress with offerings of food is connected with cremation rites and megalithic erections.[125] This indicates that there is a strong link that connects the dead and the living counterpart within the clan.[126] According to the tradition, it is the duty of every Khasi to pay respect to their dead ancestors/ancestress for the latter are there to guide and bless their descendants with good and prosperous life.[127] Consequently, no family or clan can prosper if they neglect their duty

---

[120] Bareh, *The History and Culture of the Khasi People,* 322.

[121] Chowdhury, *The Khasi Canvas,* 190.

[122] However, being a matrilineal society, among the triad the Khasis revered the *Iawbei* most. See Chowdhury, *The Khasi Canvas,* 201-202.

[123] See Maham Singh, "Nongkrem Festival," in *Khasi Heritage,* edited by Hipshon Roy Kharshiing (Shillong: Seng Khasi, 1979), 148.

[124] Bareh, *The History and Culture of the Khasi People,* 333.

[125] Bareh , *The History and Culture of the Khasi People,* 333.

[126] As stated earlier, anything wrong committed by any member, it will affect not only the person concern but the entire clan and it will even offended the triad. On the other, a good and appreciable act by any member will bring good name to the clan including the triad as the founder as well.

[127] Maham Singh, "Nongkrem Festival," 151.

towardrs their ancestors/ancestress.[128] Bareh argues that one has to appease the ancestors/ancestress for they "have stepped up to the position of supernatural beings, partners with God, having enough power to aid, assist and bless their living counterparts."[129] Commenting on the above discussion on respecting the dead ancestors/ancestress, Chowdhury argues that the Khasis "seem to share the belief with many other Austric races that the spirit of the dead ancestors [sic] participate in supernatural powers, and are capable of aiding the mortals."[130] It is the belief of the Khasis that all those who live a righteous life while here on earth, when they die they will go to God's house and enjoy eating betelnut or what the Khasis refer to as, *Bam kwai ha Dwar u Blei.*[131] In other words, it indicates that God will happily accept such a righteous person, as per his/her righteous deeds and works which he/she had done while here on earth.[132] Accordingly, being in the house of God the dead ancestors/ancestress are now in a position to help, guide and bless their descendants in different circumstances either in times of joy and happiness or in times of trouble and crisis. Hence, adoring the dead ancestors/ ancestress for Gurdon may take place occasionally in times of trouble,[133] Chowdhury argues that the Khasis will not start any new project without asking the blessing of their dead ancestors/ancestress.[134] Perhaps, it is for this reason that many writers consider these acts of reverence to their ancestors/ancestress as "ancestor worship" which is not correct.[135] Here, for the Khasis to pay homage does not mean to "worship the ancestors/ancestress" as understood by some but simply a token of remembrance. Joseph Minattur as cited by Chowdhury fairly puts it when he says,

> The Khasis do not worship the dead. The giving of food (ai bam) to the spirits of the departed ancestors [sic] is to win their favour and blessings. These spirits being in the house of God are in a position to intercede for the living before God and secure his help and protection for them.[136]

---

[128] Gurdon mentions this act of respect as an act of worship which is not correct. Cf. Gurdon, *The Khasis,* 111.

[129] Bareh, *The History and Culture of Khasi People,* 333.

[130] Chowdhury, *The Khasi Canvas,* 203-204.

[131] Those who live an unclean or unrighteous life especially those who commit serious offence like incest and other serious crime their soul is condemn to roam endlessly up to the nine layers below or *Ka Khyndai Pateng Niamra.* See S. Hayong, "The Concept of Sin in the Khasi Traditional Religion," in *Doing Tribal Christian Theology with Tribal Resources: Cultural Resources from North East India,* edited by Razouselie Lasetso and Eyingbeni Humtsoe (Jorhat: ETC Programme Coordination, 2009), 66.

[132] See Laitphlang, "Ka Niam Ha U Khasi," 8.

[133] Gurdon, *The Khasis,* 110.

[134] Chowdhury, *The Khasi Canvas,* 200.

[135] Different writers like Gurdon, Nataranjan, Bareh and others opine this act of respect as "ancestor worship."

[136] See Chowdhury, *The Khasi Canvas,* 203.

The religious teachings of the Khasis reveal two basic principles needed to be observed in their daily life. That is, besides worshipping God and invoke His/Her blessing to the well being of humans, the Khasis pay deep respect to humans and this includes respect they owe to the spirit of the dead ancestors/ancestress.[137]As stated above, the Khasis pay homage to the dead ancestors/ancestress for their blessing to the well being and welfare of their descendants. This is clearly reflected in their prayer. Hence, for the blessing of the family, God as *Ka 'Lei Longkur Longjaid* or *Ka "lei longspah* work together side by side with *Ka Iawbei.* Thus, in their prayer for different needs of the family/clan they have to invoke both at the same time. Their starting words of their prayer goes like this, "*To sngew to sngap Ko Blei Ko Iawbei*" and followed some other words.[138] Here, we see first come the address to God as *Ka 'Lei Longkur Longjaid* or so to say *Ka 'Lei Longspah* and then followed the address to *Ka Iawbei.* Both of them are belief to be caring for the need, well being and prosperity of the clan and the family. To put it differently, both *Ka Blei* and *Ka Iawbei* have special place and importance for different needs of the family/clan including economic well being and prosperity. So, for the Khasis if they are to prosper and flourish in their daily life and different enterprises, it is their duty to pay homage to their dead ancestors/ancestress.

Khasi Religious/Ethical Teachings

As stated earlier, the story of *U Lum Sohpetbneng* depicts that when God gave the Khasis their religion, he also gave the three commandments to follow as guidance in their daily life. These three commandments in particular and the religious teachings in general became the source of inspiration and foundation of their social, political, economic, and ethical behaviour. To put it differently, religion and its commandments is basically a way of life for the Khasis.[139] Its commandments has influences and permeates the entire fabric of social structure. These commandments are, *Kamai ia ka Hok, Tipbriew Tipblei* and *Tipkur tipkha.*

Kamai ia ka Hok

The term *Kamai ia ka Hok* has a very deep and broad meaning, and can not be translated in one word or one sentence. There is no equivalent term that could convey its real meaning. The word *Kamai* can be translated as "to earn by one's own effort and labour" and the word *Hok* literally understood as "righteousness." It can also be translated as justice. Hence, the term *Kamai ia ka Hok* literally means to earn righteousness.[140] It is the belief of the Khasis that human beings come into this world to labour for righteousness, or as the Khasis say, *Ngi wan*

[137] See Maham Singh, "Nongkrem Festival," 148.

[138] Mawrie, *Ka Pyrkhat U Khasi,* 9, 17.

[139] Chowdhury, *The Khasi Canvas,* 188-189.

[140] Rymbai, "Some Aspects of the Religion...," 111.

sha kane ka Pyrthei ban Kamai ia ka Hok. This indicates that God has sent human beings to this earth to toil for righteousness. Hence, there is a Khasi saying that goes *Ka Hok kaba tam ha kane ka Pyrthei* or righteousness is the most precious commodity here on earth.[141] Humans are therefore expected to live a righteous life, think righteously, act and work righteously in order to earn righteousness. In other words, it is the on-going process of striving for justice and righteousness in all our dealings and relationships. Rymbai observes that ,

> The import of this commandment is the primacy of the righteous life which *Ki Hynniew Trep* and their descendants should live throughout their lives on earth. To live a righteous life man [sic] must not only speak the truth and act fairly and justly in all his [sic] dealings with his [sic] fellowmen [sic] but should be honest in his[sic] very thoughts and wishes as well.[142]

At the same time, a person who live and act righteously at the end of his/ her life here on earth will be able to reach God's house and enjoy eating betelnut endlessly or what the Khasis refer as *Bam Kwai ha Dwar u Blei.*[143] That is, this commandment links human life here and now on earth with the afterlife. Hence, the term *Kamai ia ka Hok* has actually enveloped the whole aspect of life in the Khasi society be it social, cultural, political, economic and so on.

Tipbriew Tipblei

As in the case of the term *Kamai ia Ka Hok,* the concept of *Tipbriew Tipblei* possesses deep meaning with no equivalent term or word that could suffice its definition. The word *Tip* means 'to know', the word *briew* means 'human' and the word *Blei* means 'God.' Thus, the term *Tipbriew Tipblei* literally means to know our fellow human beings and to know God as well.[144] In other words, it signifies to be concious of our relationship with our fellow human beings and with God as well. That is, human can be conscious of God only when he/she is conscious of their fellow human beings who are the creation of God. No one can have right relationship with God if they neglect their duty towards their fellow human beings.The Khasis believe that human beings come into this world through *Ka Hok Blei* or God's righteousness.[145] From *Ka Hok Blei* two important aspect of human life emerged namely i) *Ka Hok Longbriew Manbriew* and ii) *Ka Sap Tipbriew Tipblei.*

---

[141] See S. Hayong, "The Concept of Sin…," 59.

[142] Rymbai, "Some Aspects of the Religion…," 111.

[143] See S. Hayong, "The Concept of Sin…," 65-66.

[144] Rymbai, "Some Aspects of the Religion…," 111-112.

[145] Mawrie observes that *Ka Hok Blei* includes the whole nature of God. It is the source and cause of everything that exist. It is through *Ka Hok Blei* that God reveals Himself/Herself to human beings. God's relationship with humans is based through *Ka Hok Blei.* See Mawrie, *Ka Theology Ka Niam Khasi,* 19.

Ka Hok Longbriew Manbriew means the right of human beings to become human, and that right comes from God alone the source of everything. As it come from God , human life is therefore considered precious. Each and every individual person possesses this inherent right to live as human that need to be realised, respected and protected. There is a Khasi saying that says *Ieit Ialade bad Burom ia Kiwei* or love yourself and respect others. Hence, a person can be considered as *Tipbriew Tipblei* only when he/she realise and respect the inherent rights of other fellow human beings as intended by the Divine. This indicates that one should not exploit, discriminate, oppress, or supress any one for one's own benefit or advantage.

Ka Sap Tipbriew Tipblei can be understood as the inherent or instinctive power bestowed by God to every individual to realise himself/herself as human and their relationship to their fellow humans and to God as well.[146] It is this instinctive power that enables them to be concious about their relationship with God and also with their fellow human beings. So, it is through *Ka Sap Tipbriew Tipblei* that humans are equipped to live the life of *Tipbriew Tipblei.* Rymbai observes that humans could know God only when they know thier fellow humans. For him, to know our fellow humans "connotes performance of one's duty to them, which is to be good, kind and helpful to one and all; not to cause harm or injury to anyone for one's own profit or pleasure."[147]

Jaitdkhar argues that one who does not live *Ka Jingim Tibriew Tipblei*[148] or the one who undermined or ignored this teaching, when they die, their souls will not reach God's house but are expected to roam around till they reach the nine layers down below or what the Khasis refer as *Khyndai Pateng Niamra.*[149] But the person expected to reach God's house is the one who maintain good relationship with God and fellow humans.[150] Hence, *Tipbriew Tipblei* is closely related with the concept of *Kamai ia ka Hok.* So, like in *Kamai ia ka Hok,* in the concept of *Tipbriew Tipblei* the present life of humans is connected with the afterlife. Thus, *Tipbriew Tipblei* encompassess the entire fabric of Khasis' way of living either social, political, economic, cultural and religious life.

Tipkur Tipkha

The tradition tells us that the word *Tipkur Tipkha* is one of the main commandments given by God to the Khasis. For the Khasis, all those relatives

---

[146] Mawrie, *The Essence of Khasi Religion,* 17.

[147] Rymbai, "Some Aspects of the Religion...," 112.

[148] *Ka Jingim Tipbriew Tipblei* means a life that is conscious of the relationship with God and other fellow humans.

[149] Jaitdkhar, *Ka Niam-Ki-Khasi: Ka Niam Tipbriew Tipblei,* 1.

[150] Cf. Philomena Kharakor, *Ka Kolshor Khasi kumba paw ha ka Litereshor Khasi, 1930-1940,* 115-116.

who belong to the mother's side or who descend from the same *Iawbei* or the first ancestress belong to the *Kur* or clan. At the same time, all those who belong to the father's clan are called *Ki kha.* The word *Tipkur* means to know one's own maternal relations, and *Tipkha* means to know one's own paternal relations.[151] As the Khasi society is a matrilineal society, the genealogy is traced from the mother side. Kinship or clan loyalty in the Khasi society is very strong. This indicates that a sense of attachment and belonging to the same clan or *Kur* binds all members of the same clan as a strong unit. As stated earlier, when two Khasis meet for the first time they identify themselves not only by the place to which they belong but also by the clan or *Kurs* as well. This reflects the fact how the *Kurs* or clans occupy an important place in the Khasi society.[152]

For the Khasis, it is a *Sang* or taboo to marry within the same clan. Such heinous crime is considered forbidden, sacrilegious and unforgivable before God and humans.[153] Hence, to have knowledge about one's own *Kur* is not only necessary but a must within the Khasi society. As the concept of *Tipkur* is important to the Khasi society, so it is also with the *Tipkha* or knowledge about one's own paternal relations. It is the belief of the Khasis that it is forbidden to marry with the *Bakha Trai* or the real nephew/niece of the father up to three generations,[154] for they are considered like brothers and sisters and still having blood relationship. The Khasis address the paternal grandmother as *Meikha* and their father's sisters as *Niakha.* All relatives from the father's side especially *Ka Meikha* is held in high respect.

For instance, in the earlier times when most of the relatives from both sides stay in a village, if the child is born to a couple, the couple shall not make house visitations anywhere even to relatives house, unless that child is taken first to his/her *Meikha.* This practice is done for the respect due to her, and also for the belief that she can bless the child with good health, prosperity and well being in his/her entire life's journey. This indicates that marriage for the Khasis is not only a bond that binds the couple but a tie that links the two *Kurs* or clans. Hence, the teaching related to *Tipkur Tipkha* is considered as one of the most important principle that all Khasis are expected to follow. For the Khasis any crime or sin of heinous nature, committed by a person will not only affect the person responsible for the transgression but it will adversely affect the whole clan and even the relatives from the father's side. Thus, what the Khasis fear most in their life is what they call *Ka Byrsieh.* The word *Ka Byrsieh* means a taint or stigmas that will negatively envelope the clan and the relatives from the father's side. Commenting

[151] Rymbai, "Some Aspects of the Religion…," 112.

[152] Cf. Jaitdkhar, *Ka Niam Khasi ka Niam Tipbriew Tipblei,* 24.

[153] Hayong, "The Concept of Sin…," 57.

[154] Cf. Jaitdkhar, *Ka Niam Khasi ka Niam Tipbriew Tipblei,* 24.

on the effect of *Ka Byrsieh* to the relatives of the transgressor Kynpham Singh says as he rightly puts it,

> Three sins *Ka Rem Thawlang,* disrespect shown to the father and his clan, *Ka Rem Iawbei,* disrespect shown to the female members of the clan and *Ka Rem Saidnia,* disrespect shown to the male member of the clan, are considered among the grievous sins. They are sins directed not against a person alone but against the whole clan, against *U Thawlang, Ka Iawbei* and *U Saidnia,* and against the Creator himself [sic].[155]

It is believed that *Ka Byrsieh* will not only bring shame to the concerned relatives but at the same time, it will bring misfortune and misery to the family that will adversely affect the well being and prosperity of the family members.

Hence, the above discussion reflects the fact that the religious set up of the Khasis is closely related to their economic development and prosperity. That is, for the prosperity and well being of the people, the religious teachings and practices of the Khasis need to be significantly considered.

Festivals

Festivals play an important role in the tribal way of life. Tribals express their joy and happiness through different types of festivals that have been practiced from one generation to another since time immemorial. Like other tribal groups, the Khasis have many festivals that have been celebrated since the beginning of time. These festivals take place in different seasons in different parts of Khasi and Jaintia hills. Most of these festivals are associated with the agricultural life of the people which reflect different experiences of the people within particular space and time. Mary Pristilla Rina Lyngdoh observes that these festivals are normally celebrated either "before the sowing or after the harvesting work is over." She further states that these festivals are of two types i) secular or festive dances without any religious ceremony, and ii) festivals associated with religious rituals.[156] Chowdhury on the other agrees with Rymbai[157] when he argues that "a festival, on the face of it, is a secular activity but, if we should try to trace its origin, it may end up in some religious concept."[158] However, though festivals have some religious connection they have nevertheless reflected the joy and happiness of the people. Here, we will

---

[155] Singh, "Khasi and Jaintia Religion," 103.

[156] Mary Pristilla Rina Lyngdoh, *The Festivals in the History and Culture of the Khasi* (New Delhi: Radha Publications, 2009), 68.

[157] Rymbai argues that all festivals of the Khasis though they are primarily religious, they also manifest the "fondness of the people for the gayer side of life." See R. T. Rymbai, "The Festivals of a Khasi and their influence of his Life," in *Khasi Heritage,* edited by Hipshon Roy Kharshiing (Shillong: Seng Khasi, 1979), 124.

[158] Chowdhury, *Ki Khun Khasi Khara (The Khasi People),* 246.

discuss only three of them namely, i) *Ka Shad Nongkrem* ii) *Ka Shad Suk Mynsiem* and iii) *Ka Behdeinkhlam.*

Ka Shad Nongkrem

Ka Shad Nongkrem or Nongkrem Dance also known as the *Shad Pomblang* or goat-killing ceremony, is the religious festival of the Khyrim state that takes place annually at Smit.[159] In the earlier times, this festival usually held in the late spring, generally in the month of May,[160] but at present it is held during the months of October and November after the harvest.[161] The festival is a five-day ceremony held consecutively in week days known in Khasi as *Pamtiah, Umni, Iewduh, Lyngka* and *Pynsing.*[162] Among the five days of rites and rituals, there are two important parts that need to be mentioned-one is related to *U Lei Shillong,*[163] the first ancestor and the first maternal uncle of the *Syiem* clan, while the other is related to the Supreme God. In the first part, the important ceremonies include pouring of rice beer as libation to *U Lei Shillong* or the Shillong deity for invoking his blessings to both the *Syiem* clan and the people of the state. This act of pouring the rice beer is repeated for the second and the third time respectively for invoking the blessing of the first ancestress and the first maternal uncle of the *Syiem* clan. Besides the honour and respect paid to the ancestors/ancestress, there is also sacrifice of a goat in honour of *U Lei Shillong.*

In the second part, the important ceremonies include thanksgiving dance performed as a gratitude to God for his/her blessings and protection to the state and the people. Then, prayers are offered to the Supreme God, to invoke his/her blessings upon the state and its people, and to provide the wisdom and understanding to the *Syiem* and the *Dorbar* equipping them to look after the well being and overall development of the state and its people.[164] It may be noted that while sacrifice is offered to the deities, only prayers and invocation are beseeched to the Supreme God.[165] This Festival is not a mountain worship

---

[159] The Nongkrem dance festival was originally the religious festival of the undivided Shillong state. When the state was divided into two- the Mylliem and Khyrim state the festivals remains with the Khyrim state, and was held regularly at Nongkrem the headquarter of the Khyrim state. At present, this festival held no more in Nongkrem but in Smit a village about 11 km from Shillong, the capital of Meghalaya, but it is still called *Shad Nongkrem* or Nongkrem dance.

[160] Gurdon, *The Khasis,* 155.

[161] Lyngdoh, *The Festivals in the History and Culture of the Khasis,* 73.

[162] See Singh, "Nongkrem Festival," 148.

[163] Notably, the *Syiem* of Shillong state has a mythological divine origin. According to the tradition, *U Lei Shillong* or the Shillong deity is believed to be the founder of the state. He is said to be the father of the legendary ancestress *Ka Pah Syntiew* the first ancestress of the Syiem clan. He is believed to reside in Shillong peak, hence the peak is considered sacred by the Khasis.

[164] For detail see Singh, "Nongkrem Festival," 148-153.

[165] Chowdhury, *Ki Khun Khasi Khara (The Khasi People),* 266.

ceremony[166] neither it is *Ka Shad-Nguhsyiem* or a dance in honour of the ruler or the Chief, for respect and honour here is not meant to address the *Syiem,*[167] rather prayers are invoked to God to bless and provide wisdom to the ruler for better governance. Singh observes that this festival is "a ceremony to strengthen the ties of unity between the different units of the states and above all to pray to God to give peace and contentment in the state."[168] Sukhdev Singh Chib maintains that this ceremony is "taken as a thanksgiving ceremony to God for bestowing good harvests, peace and prosperity. It is in fact a rhythmic form of prayer offered to Almighty for the well being of all."[169] In other words, it indicates the fact that this ceremony besides paying respect and honour to the ancestors/ancestress it also reflects the gratitude shown to the Almighty and invoke his/her blessing for bountiful harvest, economic prosperity and well being for both the rulers and the people of the state.[170]

Ka Shad Suk Mynsiem

Ka Shad Suk Mynsiem[171] literally means 'dance of joyful heart' or 'dance for peace of mind'[172] or 'the dance of the blissful heart'[173] held annually in Shillong during the spring season where Khasis from different parts of Khasi and Jaintia Hills come to participate. Though the festival is not a religious ceremony as in the case of Nongkrem dance, it was founded by the *Seng Khasi*[174] or the association of the

---

[166] Chowdhury observed that the religious core of this ceremony is mountain worship. Though the sacrifice is offered to *U Lei Shillong* and the hill is considered sacred it does not mean that the Khasis worship this peak, rather this peak offered a place of worship and prayer and invocation are also offered to God for the well being of the state and its people. Cf. Chowdhury, *The Khasi Canvas,* 257.

[167] This idea is suggest by Kharakor when she says that it is more fitted to call this festival as *Shad-Nguhsyiem* rather than *Ka Shad Pomblang.* See Philomena Kharakor, *Ka Kolshor Khasi Kumba paw ha ka Litereshor Khasi,* 177.

[168] Singh, "Nongkrem Festival," 153.

[169] Sukhdev Singh Chib, *This Beautiful India: Meghalaya* (New Delhi: Light & Life Publishers, 1980), 82.

[170] See Lyngdoh, *The Festival in the History and Culture of the Khasi,* 73.

[171] *Ka Shad Suk Mynsiem* is also popularly known as *Ka Shad Weiking* because it is held at Weiking ground at Jaiaw.

[172] Khongphai argues that the literal meaning of *Ka Shad Suk Mynsiem* is 'dance for peaceful mind.' See A.S. Khongphai "Shad Suk Mynsiem (Thanks-Giving Dance)," in *Khasi Heritage,* edited by Hipshon Roy Kharshiing (Shillong: Seng Khasi, 1979), 131.

[173] Kynpham Singh, "Ka Shad Suk Mynsiem (The Thanksgiving Dance)," *Sneng Khasi* 3/11 (April, 1981), 2.

[174] The *Seng Khasi* is a socio-cultural organization of the Khasis who belong to the traditional faith, was founded by sixteenth non Christian young men who met together on the 23rd November 1899 in the Brahmo Samaj Hall at Mawkhar, Shillong with the intention to foster the spirit of oneness and unity, and to preserve and protect the Khasi custom and culture from the influence of external force like the Britishers and the Christian missionaries who condemned and maligned Khasi

Khasi people who belong to the Khasi traditional faith, in order to preserve the Khasi custom and culture from external influence. Hence, this festival started as a response to the impact of westernization and conversion movement led by the Christian missionaries.[175] In 1910, *Seng Khasi* passed a resolution to organise a dance in the Weiking ground annually in order to preserve different customs and usages of the Khasi people which were passed on from time immemorial by the people. Thus, the first dance was organised by the *Seng Khasi* on the 14th and 15th of April, 1911, as part of an attempt to preserve and protect the cultural identity of the Khasis.[176] Singh has rightly puts it when he says,

> "We must know that though the dance is organised and managed by the *Seng Khasi*, it is actually the dance of the whole Khasi nation, which, we hope, will further the preservation of our customs, usages and culture and which will be held annually."[177]

Though *Ka Shad Suk Mynsiem* as a national festival started in 1911, the dance itself as a cultural practice of the Khasis was practised since time immemorial. At present, *Ka Shad Suk Mynsiem* is held for three days. While only virgin female are allowed to participate, there is no restriction for the male and any one young and old can take part. As mentioned above, *Ka Shad Suk Mynsiem* is a thanksgiving dance celebrated in the spring season in the beginning of sowing and planting. Chowdhury argues that as the festivals synchronizes with the spring season; it reflects "its association with the agricultural activity of the people."[178] The dance is being performed on one hand as a gratitude to Almighty God associated with the wellbeing of the past year, while on the other hand; it is a dance for invoking God's blessings for bountiful harvest in the coming season.[179] Hence, as the name suggest, it signifies the joy and happiness of the people that God has provided for the community's welfare and general prosperity.

---

culture and religion as something pagan, evil, heathen therefore need to be rejected. One among many of the cultural practice of the Khasis that need to be preserved is *Ka Shad Suk Mynsiem.* See Kynpham Singh, "Seng Khasi,' *Sneng Khasi* 3/10 (November, 1980), 4.

[175] The Christian missionaries during that time were the missionaries of the Welsh Calvinistic Mission or the Presbyterian Church as it is known today. They were not only involved in conversion activities but prohibited the Khasi converts to take part and attended all cultural and religious activities of the Khasis, which the founders of the *Seng Khasi* organization saw as a threat to the survival of the Khasi traditional customs and cultures that was handed down and preserves through the centuries by their ancestors/ancestress and passed on from generation to generation.

[176] Cf. Kharakor, *Ka Kolshor Khasi Kumba ka paw ha ka Litereshor Khasi,* 174. See also R. T. Rymbai, "The Festivals of a Khasi and their Influence on his Life," in *Khasi Heritage,* edited by Hipshon Roy Kharshiing (Shillong: Seng Khasi, 1979), 125.

[177] Singh, "Shad Suk Mynsiem…," 2.

[178] Chowdhury, *Ki Khun Khasi Khara (The Khasi People),* 258.

[179] Rymbai, "The Festival of a Khasi…," 125.

Ka Behdeinkhlam

The word *Behdeinkhlam* is a combination of three words, *Beh* means 'to drive,' *dein* means 'stick' and the word *Khlam* means 'plague.' Hence, *Behdeinkhlam* means to drive away the plague with sticks which affect not only humans but the crops as well.[180] This festival is a month long celebration held annually in the month of July after the sowing is over. It is usually held at Jowai, the capital of Jaintia Hills districts and in some other places of the district.[181] Though the female do not participate in the public celebration of the festival, their role at home is not to be ignored. Rymbai maintains that the role of the womenfolk is to offer sacrificial food to the ancestors/ancestress and invoke their blessing for the well being of their descendants and enable them to live a clean righteous life here below.[182] There are different rituals and sacrifices associated with the festival. Prior to the main festival, a month long preparation which includes many rituals needs to be performed such as, *Ka Dih So Pen,*[183] *Ka Knia Khang,*[184] and *Ka Knia Pyrthat*[185] and so on. While in the ceremony of *Knia Khang* God is invoked for

---

[180] Lamare, *The Jaintias: Studies in Society and Change,* 63.

[181] Besides the festival at Jowai, *Behdeinkhlam* is also celebrated in other villages like Tuber, Chyrmang, Ialong, Mukhla, Muthlong, Bapung, Pasyih, Thadmuthlong, Mukhaialong, Chamcham, Sabah, Muswang, Sohshrieh and so on. It is reported that the festival at Tuber is the biggest one having thirty *rots,* whereas the festival at Jowai have not more than ten *Rots.* However, being held in the capital of the district the festival at Jowai gets more attention from the media, government and the public. Cf. Kharakor, *Ka Kolshor Khasi Kumba ka paw ha ka Litereshor Khasi,* 179. See also Lyngdoh, *The Festivals in the History and Culture of the Khasi,* 71.

[182] It is believed that the ancestors/ancestress use to visit their descendants during the celebration to help and bless them, hence offering of sacrificial food to them as a mark of respect and reverence is practiced. See Rymbai, "The Festival of a Khasi…," 127.

[183] This ritual is a small ceremony performed before the market day in the house of the priestess. The priestess was assisted by the *Dolois, Pators* and the *Wasans* where the altar is erected and pouring liquor as libation to the four sisters who are the original settlers of the Jowai town. These four sisters are Ka Bon, Ka Tein, Ka Wet and Ka Doh became the ancestress or *Ki Iawbei* of many clans in Jowai. Hence, honour and respect is paid to them. See R. T. Rymbai, "Behdienkhlam," in *Khasi Heritage,* edited by Hipshon Roy Kharshiing (Shillong: Seng Khasi, 1979), 140. See also Lamare, *The Jaintias: Studies in Society and Change,* 64.

[184] *Ka knia Khang* is a kind of ritual where sacrifice of fowls is performed. This sacrifice is offered to the four deities believed to be the protector of Jowai town. All expenditure in this sacrifice is to be incurred by the contributions collected by the *Wasans* from the original inhabitants of Jowai, on the market day that was held after *Ka Dih So Pen* ceremony. When the collection is done, in the next day, all the *Wasans* together with the elders of the community gathered together in the priestess house, divided themselves into four groups, went in four different corners of Jowai town where the *Knia Khang* is to be carried out and prayer to the Supreme God is offered. See Rymbai, "Behdiengkhlam," 140. See also Lamare, *The Jaintias: Studies in Society and Change,* 64.

[185] *Ka Knia Pyrthat* is another ritual performed when the new moon appears. This sacrifice is performed on the top of the hill outside the town, but only the priests of Tuber, Ialong and Chyrmang participated. For one week prior to the commencement of this sacrifice, the *Dolois,* the *Wasans* and the priests must not visit their wives and have to stay in their mother's houses.

peace, prosperity and protection from all kinds of diseases in the case of *Ka Knia Pyrthat* prayer is offered to God for strength to overcome all hardship and distress in the coming year. After these ceremonies, other important activities for the festival include construction of *Rots*[186] by different localities or *Dongs,* searching for two important sacred trees called *Ka Dein-Khlam*[187] by a group of people and *Khnong*[188] by the *Khon-Raid* are being performed accordingly. The last three days of the festival are the most important and performed with much music and funfair. On the first of the last three days, the trees are taken out of the forest to the *Iawmusiang,* the local market place in Jowai where as in the next day they are taken to different localities at Jowai. On the evening of that day, "a replica of the *Dein-Khlam* is set up before every individual house at Jowai."[189] In the last day, important ceremonies are performed including *Kynti-Khnong,*[190] followed by *Ka Sympat Iung* ceremony.[191] This ceremony is a symbolic act of driving away all evil spirits that bring disease and distress to human beings. It is done by the entire male member by beating the roof of the house by bamboo sticks and strike down the small *Dein-Khlams* set up in every house the previous day. Rymbai maintains that these bamboo sticks are given to them by "the priestess praying to God to drive out evil and to bring peace and welfare to the family."[192] Chib observes that though effect of many diseases at present "has been uprooted yet the symbolic driving away of the evil spirits that cause sickness and misery continues."[193] In the afternoon is the immersion ceremony where all the *Rots* brought up by different locality and immersed at the pool of *Aitnar.* This is followed by bringing the

---

The expense for this sacrifice is borne by the income derived from the four religious lands. In this sacrifice, the priest invokes God's providence for strength to overcome the enemies and for support in time of hardship and distress in the years to come. Rymbai, "Behdienkhlam," 141. Lamare, *The Jaintias: Studies in Society and Change,* 64.

[186] These *Rots* are very tall structures made of bamboo frame and covered with multicolor paper with various design at the top prepared for immersion at the pool called *Aitnar.* The *Rots* are around ten in numbers constructed by different *Dongs* or locality of Jowai town. See Chowdhury, *The Khasi Canvas,* 220. See Also Kharakor, *Ka Kolshor Khasi Kumba paw ha ka Litereshor Khasi,* 179.

[187] *Ka Dein-Khlam* is normally a tall and straight tree cut from the forest by a group of people particularly for this festival.

[188] *Khnong* is another tree bigger than the *Dein-Khlam* tree cut from forest by one particular *Dong* known as *Khon-Raid.* This tree is considered the most sacred than the *Dein-Khlam.* Only the *Khon-Raid* have the right to carry this tree from the jungle to *Iawmusiang* and back to the locality and even to the immersion pool.

[189] See Rymbai, "Behdienkhlam," 142. Chowdhury, *The Khasi Canvas,* 142.

[190] *Kyntin-Khnong* is a kind of ceremony usually held at the premises of the priestess early in the morning of the last day in honour of the ancestress. See Lamare, *The Jaintias: Studies in Society and Change,* 65.

[191] *Sympat Iung* literally means to strike the house by the stick.

[192] Rymbai, "Behdienkhlam," 143.

[193] Chib, *The Beautiful India: Meghalaya,* 84.

sacred tree or *Khnong* to the pool by the *Khon-Raid* where everyone rushes to touch it.[194] The last ceremony is called *Datlawakor*[195] similar to a football game played between the lower and the upper region of the river Myntdu. It is believed that the region who wins the game will be blessed with a rich harvest in that year. Hence, *Behdeinkhlam* festival is a ceremony where the people of Jaintia Hills invoke God's blessing for good harvest and to drive away all evil spirits that cause hardship and miseries to the people. Lyngdoh argues that besides driving away "all evils that plague human life" the festival is celebrated "to invoke God's blessings for a bountiful harvest, and well being of the people on the whole, so that they could live happily throughout the year."[196] To put it differently, the festival is very much associated to the economic well being of the people.

The above discussion indicates the fact that for the Khasis, different festivals accordingly related to the agricultural activities of the people. They are but the reflection of what actually happen in different seasons of agricultural life of the people. Hence, celebration of the festivals held either after the sowing or after the harvest period of agriculture. It is either to offer gratitude and thanksgiving to God for the bountiful harvest in the last season or invoking His/Her blessings and care for the new crops in the next season. In other words, festivals highlight close relationship between God the Supreme Being and the people. At the same time, festivals play an important role for the economic well being and prosperity of the people.

Megalithic Culture

Megaliths have become an integral part of Khasi culture and society. Megalithic culture or the custom of erecting memorial stone is part of the worldwide phenomena that has spread to three different continents namely Europe, Asia and Africa.[197] In India, apart from Khasi and Jaintia Hills this culture is found among the Ho-Munda tribes of Chotanagpur, Mikirs, some Naga tribes, Garos and Mizos.[198] Out of the six types of megaliths[199] found in different parts of the world,

---

[194] For detail see Chowdhury, *The Khasi Canvas,* 221.

[195] *Datlawakor* is a kind of game resembles the football game. It is played in a place called Mynthong where all the player have to participate bare footed with a round piece of wood served as a ball. Simultaneously with this ceremony the *Wasan* makes a sacrifice of a fowl at the sacred grove called *Khloo Langdoh.* See Lamare, *The Jaintias: Studies in Society and Change,* 65-66.

[196] Lyngdoh, *The Festivals in the History and Culture of the Khasi,* 71.

[197] Chowdhury argues that megalithic culture possesses an intercontinental character and their distribution can be traced from Europe through Asia and Africa to Pacific Islands as far as the Easter Island and Eastern Carolinas. See Chowdhury, *The Khasi Canvas,* 52-53. Cf. Bareh, *The History and Culture of the Khasi People,* 20.

[198] See Mawlong, "Megaliths and Social Formation...," 35. See also Gurdon, *The Khasis,* 148-149.

[199] For detail see Chowdhury, *The Khasi Canvas,* 54-55.

five types are found in Khasi Hills, namely, menhirs or vertical stones known in Khasi as *Mawshynrang*, dolmens or table-stones called *Mawkynthei,* alignment or those consist in straight line in odd number three, five, seven, nine and eleven, circles and stone cists where the bones or the ashes of the dead members of the clan is kept.[200] Gurdon calls them cenotaphs or memorial stones[201] for most of them are commemorative in nature.[202] In the earlier period, megaliths were erected in different times and space with different purpose and significance. They have both socio-economic and religious significance.[203] Apart from forming part of global scenario, S. N. Rao observes a typical nature of Khasi megaliths not only for their massive concentration[204] but also for the social and ideological significance attached to them. As he rightly puts it,

> Each stone put up either for funerary or for commemorative purpose, is given a proper name in Khasi that clearly signifies their place of importance in their society. In this respect, the Khasi megaliths occupy a singular place of global importance.[205]

It is not that we agree or disagree with Rao, but the important thing that may be noted is that megaliths were erected in Khasi and Jaintia Hills with a particular purpose and significance either for the clan and the society as well. Bareh classified the Khasi megaliths into two categories, namely, ossuary and monumental stones[206] or funerary and memorial megaliths respectively. While

---

[200] The menhirs are the vertical stones standing uprightly in the ground with less than a metre to more than four metres in height and theses are found in many places in Khasi and Jaintia Hills. The dolmens are the flat slabs raised by smaller stones above the ground to a height of half metre or even less usually lay perpendicularly before the menhirs. The alignment generally erecting in odd numbers are found in Nongtalang and other places. The circles erecting in a round figure found in Nartiang. And the cists consist of square sarcophagi, composed of four large stones well fitted together and covered by a stone slab. In these cists bones or ashes of the dead relatives are kept normally in an earthen pot. For detail see Henry Yule, "Notes on the Khasia Hills and People," *Journal of Asiatic Society of Bengal* XIII/152 (1844): 618-619. Gurdon, *The Khasis,* 145-147. Cathrine-Namita Chadap Sen, *The Origin and Early History of the Khasi-Synteng People* (Calcutta: Firma Private Limited, 1981), 24-25.

[201] Gurdon, *The Khasis,* 144. The term 'megalith' was firstly adopted at the meeting of the Congress of Anthropology and Prehistoric Archaeology in 1867. See Chowdhury, *The Khasi Canvas,* 53.

[202] Mawlong, "Megalith and Social Formation...," 35.

[203] See Sousmen Sen, *Social and State Formations in Khasi-Jaintia Hills* (Delhi: B. R. Publishing Corporation, 1985), 38.

[204] But many of the megaliths in Khasi and Jaintia Hills were destroyed or buried under the ground during the great earthquake that has taken place during the year 1897.

[205] S. N. Rao, "Megalith Practice among Khasi and Naga of North East India," in *Archeology of North East India,* edited by G. P. Singh & Sen Gupta (Delhi: Vikas Publishing House Pvt. Ltd., 1991), 109.

[206] Bareh, *The History and Culture of the Khasi People,* 19.

ossuary or funerary megaliths belong exclusively to the clans, the monumental stones or memorial megaliths are either erected in honour of the clans' ancestors/ancestress or for some important events that have taken place in the society. Here, we will discuss on the two categories of megaliths namely i) megaliths related with the clan and ii) megalith related with other events in the society.

Megaliths related with the Clan

Among many megaliths erected in Khasi and Jaintia Hills, those monuments related with the clans are found in good numbers. They were erected in memory or honour of the dead ancestors/ancestress of the clan. Sen suggests that these megaliths were erected "for commemorating the dead."[207] As stated earlier, in the Khasi society the ancestors/ancestress are believed to possess the power of blessing to bestow upon their living descendants. Hence, paying respect and honour to the death relatives is the duty of every Khasi. These megaliths are often found in odd numbers either three menhirs with one dolmen or five menhirs and a dolmen and even nine and eleven menhirs with two dolmens respectively.[208] Among all the menhirs the tallest in the centre is called *U Mawkni* represents the oldest maternal uncle or *U Saidnia,* and the others both on the left and the right side are called *Ki Mawbud* or *Ki mawpyrsa* represent the brothers and nephews respectively.[209] On the other hand, if two dolmens are placed together closely, the one in the left represents the oldest ancestress or *Ka Iawbei Tynrai* whereas the other on the right represents the younger ancestress or the ancestress of the sub-clan or *Kpoh.*[210] However, this does not mean that honour and respect are paid only to the ancestors/ancestress of the maternal kin. In Khasi society relations of both the maternal and paternal sides are held equally important. Hence, honour and respect is upheld to both the maternal and paternal ancestors/ancestress.[211] Mawlong maintains that as the father played an important and significant role for the total welfare and prosperity of the family, he and his ancestors/ancestress are paid equal honour and respect. That is, in case of paternal kin or *Ki Kha,* the tallest menhir in the middle is called *U Mawthawlang* or the oldest ancestor's monument, while the others on both sides and the dolmen in front represent the male and the female ancestors/ancestress of the *Kha* relatives respectively.[212] As such, specific way of paying respect and honour to both the *Kurs* and the *Khas*

---

[207] Sousmen Sen, *Social and State Formations in Khasi-Jaintia Hills,* 38.

[208] See Gurdon, *The Khasis,* 150. Cf. Lyngdoh, *Ka Niam Khasi,* 245.

[209] See Lyngdoh, *Ka Niam Khasi,* 245-246. Cf. Sen, *Social and State Formation in Khasi-Jaintia Hills,* 38.

[210] See Gurdon, *The Khasis,* 151. Cf. Lyngdoh, *Ka Niam Khasi,* 245. Cf. Mawlong, "Megaliths and Social Formations…," 38.

[211] See Chadap Sen, *The Origin and Early History of the Khasi-Synteng People,* 25-26.

[212] See Mawlong, "Megaliths and Social Formation…," 38-39. See also Lyngdoh, *Ka Niam Khasi,* 250-251. Cf. Chowdhury, *Ki Khun Khasi Khara (The Khasi People),* 194-195.

groups by erecting the megalith is followed. So, megaliths memorial structures reflect both the *Kurs* and the *Khas* principles in the socio-economic life of the Khasis.[213] It is believed that this act of paying homage to the relatives of both sides will add blessings to the well being and prosperity to the living descendants.

Another important megaliths related with the clan is the cists or the *Mawshyieng* and the *Mawbah.*[214] After the cremation ceremony the bones and ashes of the dead relatives were usually kept in an earthen pot and deposit in the *Mawshyieng* for a particular period before transferring them to a final resting place at the *Mawbah.* It is the belief of the Khasis that, if all the rituals and ceremonies related for the dead are not performed accordingly, the dead relatives will not reach the house of God, but their spirit will roam aimlessly and cause affliction and misery to the surviving members. At the same time, if the dead relatives are given due honour by observing all the necessary ceremonies and rituals, their life will be blessed and will experience prosperity and well being here on earth.[215]

Besides the above, other important megalithic structures related to the *Mawbah* are the *Mawkjat*[216] and the *Mawlynti*[217] generally consist of three menhirs and a dolmen. These monuments were erected in certain places, where the members carrying the bones and ashes, (not the dead bodies as Sen writes),[218] spent their night during the journey to the *Mawbah* of the clan to deposit the remains of their dead relatives.[219] Mawlong suggests that since erecting these types of monuments involved extensive labour and feasting, such categories of monuments could be raised only by the so called *Jaid Bakhraw* or the founding clan having surplus wealth.[220] She further states that, claiming higher status, the

---

[213] Sen, *Social and State Formations in Khasi-Jaintia Hills,* 38.

[214] *Mawshyieng* means monuments where bones are kept. These monuments belong to particular *Kpoh* within the clan and are found in many places in the land. They are also known as *Mawkynroh* and *Mawphew.* But *Mawbah* means great ossuary or place where the bones of all the clan members are kept. Hence, they belong to the whole clan. Compare with *Mawshyieng* they are few in numbers. Hence, as many members of the clan scattered in different places they have to travel a long way for depositing the bones and ashes of the dead members to the *Mawbah.* See Chadap Sen, *The Origin and Early History of the Khasi-Synteng People,* 31-32.

[215] Chadap Sen, *The Origin and Early History of the Khasi-Synteng People,* 33.

[216] *Mawkjat* literally means 'stone of the leg' and are called so, because of the belief that the spirit of dead will sit and rest their limbs on the flat table stone.

[217] *Mawlynti* literally means 'stone of the way,' may be called as such because they are usually erected on the way where everyone can rest and sit peacefully.

[218] Sen wrongly mentions that these monuments were erected whenever they rested on their way to the *Kpep*-the stone platform where the dead is cremated, carrying the dead. See Sen, *Social and State Formations in Khasi-Jaintia Hills,* 38.

[219] See Gurdon, *The Khasis,* 150.

[220] Mawlong opines that such elaborate acts could become possible only through the surplus generated from trade especially iron, lime, etc. Though the work is normally voluntary where the workers received no payment but only food and liquor in the evening, it is only the rich could

founding clan were also expected to generously share their wealth and resources through public feasting. Also, sharing their resources for the benefit of the community "could enhance the donor's personal prestige, and that of his family and clan."[221] Yule as cited by Chowdhury states that if you ask a Khasi for the purpose that their ancestors/ancestress erected these monuments, the answer is "to preserve their name."[222] Moreover, most of the megaliths were erected on the way side, so they serve as a good resting place for the travellers. Chadap Sen rightly argues when she says,

> The megaliths were generally erected alongside roads or close to well-known routes, so as to attract the attention of passersby. Though the stones were of course sacred, there was no taboo on sitting on the dolmens. Thus, they provided comfortable resting places for the many pedestrians who travelled from village to village, often with heavy loads. This may have often been in the minds of those who decided on the sites of their family monuments, for by providing a simple public service in this way they might earn the gratitude of the travellers and thus spread the fame of the family.[223]

Besides, achieving the fame for the service done to the community, this act signifies the fact that for the tribal people the rich are expected not only to accumulate wealth for themselves, but to share their resources for the good of the community. Longchar maintains that for the tribal or indigenous people, "richness is measured not by how much one accumulates, but by how much a person shares with the members of the community."[224]

Megaliths related with other Events in Society

Another category of Khasi megaliths are those erected in remembrance or in honour of particular persons or for some important events that has taken place in the community. For instance, one could find large collection of megaliths structures with different shapes and heights near the Nartiang market to commemorate the establishment of the market there. Gurdon observes that these groups of monuments with the tallest among them 27 feet in height and 2 and half feet thick, were supposed to be erected by two men U Lah Laskor[225] and U Mar

---

perform such feasting. See Mawlong, "Megaliths and Social Formation…," 41. Cf. Chadap Sen, *The Origin and early History of the Khasi-Synteng People,* 33.

[221] See Mawlong, "Megalith and Social Formation…," 50-52.

[222] See Chowdhury, *The Khasi Canvas,* 60.

[223] Chadap Sen, *The Origin and Early History of the Khasi Synteng People,* 29.

[224] Wati Longchar, "Natural Resources: Perspectives of Primeval Traditions," *Jeevadhara* XL/235 (January 2010): 32.

[225] The name Laskor according to Gurdon is the equivalent word in Pnar dialect for the Khasi word 'Lyngskor' which means the prime minister.

Phalyngki[226] as a remembrance for the inauguration of the Nartiang market.[227] This signifies that the economic life of the Khasis is very much associated with the erection of megaliths. It may be noted that the name Mawsmai literally means the oath stone, derives from a stone monument erected in memory for the settlement of dispute between Sohra and another village. According to the tradition, war broke out between Sohra and another village situated in the present location of Mawsmai. And when "they make peace and swore to it, they erect a stone as a witness."[228] Hence, the name of that village was changed to Mawsmai.[229]

The above discussion indicates that megalithic culture has close connection with the economic life of the Khasi people. Interestingly, erection of different megalith structures does not only mean paying homage to them, but also invoking their blessings for the economic well being and prosperity of the people.

Brief Introduction on Khasi Economy

The term 'economy' is originated from the Greek word *oikonomous* which means 'household management.' The *Compact Oxford Dictionary* defines the word 'economy' as "the state of a country or region in terms of the production and consumption of goods and services and the supply of money" or "careful management of resources."[230] The word 'economy' is also defined as "the practical adjustment, organization or administration of affairs or resources, especially industrial resources" or "the management of household matters."[231] That is, economy deals with "the study of production, distribution and consumption of goods and services."[232] Land and its resources, both forest and mineral resources, serve as the main source of income for the economic life of the tribals. People survive by what the land produce. As stated earlier, the land tenure system of the Khasis indicates that land is to be shared by all members in the community. This

---

[226] The word 'Mar' in Jaintia Hills is referred to the giant with extra ordinary energy and strength who could carry anything as heavy as a big menhir single handed even to a far distance.

[227] See Gurdon, *The Khasis,* 152-153. Another version is that the establishment of Nartiang market is associated with the Jaintia King, Ram Singh II (ca 1790) who entrusted U Mar Phalyngki to construct a road and bridges to connect Jaintiapur the capital of the Jaintia kingdom with the King's summer residence at Nartiang. There are stone bridges like the one at Thlumuwi near Jarain village on the way from Nartiang to Jaintiapur. See Chowdhury, *The Khasi Canvas,* 56.

[228] See Yule, "Notes on the Khasia Hills and People," 619.

[229] See Chadap Sen, *The Origin and Early History of the Khasi-Synteng People,* 30.

[230] See Catherine Soanes and Alan Spooner, *Compact Oxford Dictionary Thesaurus & Word Power Guide* (New Delhi: Oxford University Press, 2003), 280.

[231] Allen Walker Reade, *The New International Webster Comprehensive Dictionary of the English Language* (Florida: Trident Press International, 1996), 400.

[232] John K. Roth, *International Encyclopedia of Ethics* (New Delhi: S. Chand & Company Ltd., 1996), 248.

may prove true prior to the coming of the British rule in these hills.[233] It may be noted that previously as per the customary practices of the people where land distribution is made available to all citizens, the economic condition of the people in general appears to have been accurately sufficient. Chadap Sen maintains that compare with the other parts of the country, wealth seems to be evenly distributed, for even the *Syiems* or Chiefs adopted a simple way of living with minimum demand imposed upon their subjects.[234] Here, we will discuss how the economic resources or production of the Khasi people has been managed down through the centuries or before the coming of the British rule till date. As the Khasi people were under the British colonial rule, an attempt is made to analyse the growth of Khasi economy by using the tool of Postcolonial studies.

What is Postcolonialism?

'Postcolonialism' is one of the most significant terms that has been widely debated in the arena of academic enterprise and intellectual discussion in the last few decades. Postcolonial studies maintain Leela Gandhi, "emerged both as a meeting point and battle ground for a variety of disciplines and theories."[235] It is a paradigm that has emerged due to the "desperate unequal distribution of power" and thus mostly "concerned about economic, political, cultural and social justice in the world"[236] both during and the era that followed the colonial regime. Bill Aschroft et al maintain that postcolonial theory emerges due to the "inability of European theories to deal adequately with the complexities and varied cultural provenance of post-colonial writings." They further state that European theories "emerge from particular cultural traditions which are hidden by false notions of the universal," and it is this very European ideology that is strongly question by postcolonial writings.[237]

Colonialism

Colonialism is not a new phenomenon. It is as old as human history itself. Though its beginning may be traced back to the early period,[238] here this research will

---

[233] It is important to note that, with the coming of the British rule into these hills many of the old age practices of the Khasis have been distorted like their concept of land and so on.

[234] Chadap Sen, *The Origin and Early History of the Khasi-Synteng People,* 242.

[235] Leela Gandhi, *Postcolonial Theory- A Critical Introduction* (Delhi: Oxford University Press, 1999), 3.

[236] Musa W. Dube and Jeffrey L. Staley, "Descending from an ascending into heaven: A Postcolonial Analysis of Travel, Space and Power in John," in *John and Postcolonialism,* edited by Musa W. Dube and Jeffrey L. Staley (London: Sheffield Academic Press, 2002), 3.

[237] Bill Aschroft, Gareth Griffiths and Helen Tiffin, 2 nd ed. *The Empire Writes Back* (London: Routledge, 1989), 11.

[238] It is often referred that colonialism begins from the second century onwards when the Egyptian, Babylonian and Roman Empire, etc successfully attempt to expand their empire. See

stress from the fifteenth century, the time when the European began its territorial expansion in Asia and other parts of the globe.[239] 'Colonialism' argues Loomba can be described "as the conquest and control of other's people land and goods"[240] Loomba further asserts that besides economic exploitation, the colonizers took complete domination and subjugation on the colonised by restructuring their economies and "drawing them into complex relationship with their own, so that there was a flow of both human and natural resources between colonies and colonial countries," with the maximum advantage in all spheres of activities will go to the colonial countries.[241] It is important to note that in the process of capturing and exploiting the land and economies of the third world, the colonizers eventually distorted diversity and promote a universal standard for the benefit of those in power.[242] The outcome of such practice has not only distorted the power and abilities of the colonised peoples but their role in the whole process was relegated to the periphery.

Under colonialism, colonialist ideologies, coupled with the imperialist literature compel both the colonizers and the colonised to internalise the colonial assumption of the superiority of certain peoples at the expense of the other. 'Internalising' maintains McLeod means "an effective way of disempowering people, it was also the source of trauma for colonised peoples who were taught to look negatively upon their people, their culture and themselves."[243] In other words, it is the 'colonizing of the mind.'[244] Admittedly, the third world people were forced to accept the binary opposition between self and the other, the civilised and the primitive, the west and the east, the Occidental and the Oriental and so on. Such ideologies tend to convey that the western value system contains the best, natural and the authentic way of life, while the cultural value system of

---

Walter Fernandez and Anupama Dutta, *Colonialism to Globalization: Five Centuries after Vasco da Gama* (New Delhi: Indian Social Institute, 1999), 1. See also Ania Loomba, *Colonialism/Postcolonialism* (London: Routledge, 1998), 2.

[239] The fifteenth century is regarded as the beginning of European colonization which started with the journey of Columbus (1492) and Vasco da Gama (1498) in search for new land for economic exploitation.

[240] It is important to note that colonizers not only conquered land and economy of the third world people, but also reforming the communities, involving in various activities against the native such as plundering their resources, warfare, genocide, enslavement and so on. Loomba, *Colonialism/Postcolonialism*, 2.

[241] It was reported that a gradual flow occurred from both sides. While slaves and raw materials moved from the colonized countries to the so called 'mother country,' the third world countries became a captive market for the manufactured goods of the European countries. See Loomba, *Colonialism/Postcolonialism,* 3-4.

[242] Dube and Staley, Descending from an Ascending into Heaven: A Postcolonial Analysis of Travel, Space and Power in John, 51.

[243] John McLeod, *Beginning Postcolonialism* (New Delhi: Viva Books Private Limited, 2010), 19.

[244] McLeod, *Beginning Postcolonialism*, 18.

the East is considered as having no authentic value at all, uncivilized and therefore need to be reformed.[245] To put it in Edward Said's terminology the "Oriental is irrational, depraved (fallen), childlike, different" while the European are "rational, virtuous, mature, normal"[246] The colonised is therefore portrayed as the "inverse or negative image of the colonizers,"[247] or what the west is not.

Postcolonialism

Does Postcolonialism mean a period that followed the colonial era? Or does it mean the end of colonialism? In his book, *The Bible and the Third World*, Sugirtharajah rightly ask, "Does post-colonialism, in its hyphenated form mark the end of colonization? Or in its unhyphenated form Postcolonialism, does it indicate the continued messy and complicated history, colonialism leaves in its awake?" But it is the latter that is most preferable in the arena of intellectual debate and academic discussion.[248] Postcolonialism is to be understood not just as "coming literally after colonialism and signifies its demise"[249] or it does not signify the end of colonialism, for colonialism did in fact involve not merely "geographical and political domination but also include cultural and economic structures that persist to this day."[250] In other words, it is not "about historical stages or periodization"[251] rather it is to be seen as "the contestation of colonial domination and the legacies of colonialism."[252]

The first task of Postcolonialism is to "challenge and revise dominant definition of race, culture, language and class" in the process of making the voice of the colonised people heard.[253] Postcolonialism is expected to actively contest and critically interrogate against the hegemonic attitude, imperialist thought pattern and worldview, imperial ideologies and power that still persist in different fields and spheres such as "politics, economics, histories and theological and Biblical studies.[254] Frantz Fanon as quoted by Barry argues that the main task for

[245] McLeod, *Beginning Postcolonialism*, 19.

[246] Edward W. Said, *Orientalism* (New Delhi: Penguin Books India Pvt. Ltd, 2001), 40.

[247] Gandhi, *Postcolonial Theory- A Critical Introduction*, 15.

[248] R. S. Sugirtharajah, *The Bible and the Third World* (Cambridge: Cambridge University Press, 2001), 245.

[249] Loomba, *Colonialism/Postcolonialism*, 12.

[250] Musa W. Dube, *Postcolonial Feminist Interpretation of the Bible* (Missouri: Chalice Press, 2000), 48.

[251] R. S. Sugirtharajah, *Asian Biblical Hermeneutics and Postcolonialism* (Sheffield: Sheffield Academic Press Ltd., 1999), 16.

[252] Loomba, *Colonialism/Postcolonialism*, 12.

[253] Loomba, *Colonialism/Postcolonialism*, 20.

[254] R. S. Sugirtharajah, "A Postcolonial Exploration of Collusion and Construction in Biblical interpretation," in *The Postcolonial Bible*, edited by R. S. Sugirtharajah (Sheffield: Sheffield Academic Press, 1998), 93.

the once colonised peoples in making their voices heard is to reclaim their own past. For many centuries back, the western colonialist power tended to ignore and sideline the past history of the colonised people, terming their "pre-colonial era as a pre-civilized, limbo or even as a historical void."[255] So, reclaiming their past histories means to "recover" the lost history of those who have been "hidden from history"[256] It is the lost history of the neglected or the colonised other. Nevertheless, reclaiming the past does not mean to go back to the past.[257] Nor does it means, to glorify or romanticise all things indigenous, rather it means "the past is giving back its values."[258] Hence, instead of cherishing the goodness of the past as Fanon argues,[259] a more dynamic relationship between the traditional cultural heritage and the contemporary struggle of the present day generation against the imperialist ideology is to be stressed.[260] This demand for the rediscovery and reinterpretation of the cultural treasures of the past for dynamic interaction with the ground realities of the contemporary present day struggle of the indigenous people is a must.

However, Postcolonialism does not mean to point out the crimes or drawbacks of colonialism but to contest its ideologies that have silenced the ideologies of the colonised 'other.' It also tries to make a "liberative attempt to redeem them from the distorted perspective of the west."[261] It is an attempt to reassert and reclaim the 'value and agency' of the other,[262] to put it in Simon Samuel's word, it is "a means of redemptive response to domination."[263] Postcolonialism is therefore an attempt to reclaim the dignity, identity and rights of the indigenous community or the colonised other which were being sidelined during the colonial period.[264] Hence, Postcolonialism observed Sugirtharajah, "Offer a space for the once colonised. In effect, it means a resurrection of the marginal, the indigenous and

[255] Peter Barry, *Beginning Theory: An Introduction to Literary and Cultural Theory* (New Delhi: Viva Books, 2010), 186.

[256] Loomba, *Colonial/Postcolonial*, 232.

[257] It is important to note that, down through the centuries, the colonized past history is no more the same. It is also not always feasible to recover the 'authentic root' or even to go back to the real home again. For in the process of inter-contact and inter-mingle with other, especially in a pluralistic country like India, certain changes and reforms could definitely t have taken place. See R. S. Sugirtharajah, "Postcolonialism and Indian Christian Theology," *Studies in World Christianity* 5/2 (1999): 235.

[258] Mc Leod, *Beginning Postcolonialism*, 85.

[259] See, Frantz Fanon, *The Wretched of the Earth* (Middlesex: Penguin Books, 1963), 182.

[260] Mc Leod, *Beginning Postcolonialism*, 87.

[261] M. Stephen, *New Trends in Christian Theology* (New Delhi: Serials Publications, 2009), 190.

[262] Gandhi, *Postcolonial Theory- A Critical Introduction*, 44.

[263] Simon Samuel, "A Postcolonial Historiography: Towards a Postcolonial Approach to Reading the Discourse of Colonial Subject Community," *Doon Theological Journal1*/1 (2004): 8.

[264] Stephen, *New Trends in Christian Theology*, 191.

the subaltern."[265] He further argues that, "Postcolonialism provides a location for other voices, histories and experiences to be heard."[266] However, McLeod argues that, Postcolonialism does not imply the coming of the new world or creating a new history, where all the defects and drawbacks of colonial rule has been erased but it "recognise both historical continuity and change." He further states that material realities and modes of representations of colonialism still persist today. At the same time while realising that some "challenges and changed" have been accomplished, there are still other areas that needed to be confronted.[267] Furthermore, Dube maintains that postcolonial studies are not just about history for imperialism persists in new and remarkable forms-what is now term globalization or neo-colonialism.[268] Hence, this implies that Postcolonialism is not merely about the past history of colonialism, but it sees colonialism as an active force that still persist today in the form forces of globalization or neo-colonial agencies. That is, "even in postcolonial situation, after the official end of colonialism, the struggle against oppression continues."[269] It is important to note that in the form of Multinational Corporations (MNCs), universal media and international monetary bodies, military and ideological matters, imperialism continues to persist in the so called neo-colonialism and globalization or to put it in Sugirtharajah word "a newer form of economics and cultural neo-colonialism."[270]

Fanon warns against the danger of neo-colonialism if the educated indigenous middle class "steps into the shoes of the former European settlement" for their own selfish motive and financial profit.[271] That is, these educated indigenous middle class serve against the interest and welfare of the people by allowing the Multinational Corporations (MNCs) to exploit the natural resources of the newly independent nation, thus "betraying the people's struggle." Hence, the national middle class, maintains Fanon, serves only as intermediary of the Western bourgeoisie in their mission to exploit the resources of the natives.[272] Furthermore, postcolonial studies reflect that in the inter-contact and inter-mingle between colonisers and the colonised a cultural syncretism evolved as both were "deeply altered by the colonial process."[273] Hence, a new identity or a

---

[265] Sugirtharajah, *The Bible and the Third World,* 250.

[266] Sugirtharajah, *The Bible and the Third World,* 272.

[267] Mc Leod, *Beginning Postcolonialism,* 33.

[268] Dube, *Postcolonial Feminist Interpretation of the Bible,* 48.

[269] Joerg Rieger, *Globalization and Theology* (Nashville: Abingdon Press, 2010), 28.

[270] Sugirtharajah, *The Bible and the Third World,* 247.

[271] Fanon, *The Wretched of the Earth,* 122.

[272] Fanon, *The wretched of the Earth,* 122-123.

[273] Loomba, *Colonialism/Postcolonialism,* 19.

hybridized identity is formed.[274] Referring to Said, Sugirtharajah rightly describe "hybridity" as follows,

> It is not about the melting away of the difference between us and them or East and West, or about dislodging the colonial construct of the 'other' but involve a new found independence achieve not simply by rejecting provincial, national and imperial attachment, but by working through them.[275]

Rieger maintains that the colonised are shaped by the colonial influence to such an extent that they become more like the colonizers. In such a situation, "the colonised adopt or are forced to adopt-some traits of the colonizers, including their dress, their language, their culture, and even their mannerism." He further states that "the colonized never become exactly identical to the colonizers. As they mimic the colonizers, an important difference remains." But the "colonized have little choice but to adapt if they want to survive."[276] Anti-colonialism is not new.[277] What is new in this current postcolonial study is that, it goes beyond the binaries opposition of colonialism between East and West, self and the other. That is, it does not depend on the "negation of the other" but impel us to "choose between truth and truth."[278] Hence, translating this view for our theological enterprise in the present day context Sugirtharajah rightly points out,

> In the face of a more coercive discourse which insist on a single truth, single worldview and single history, the postcolonial mode of hybridization can be seen as a more pliable and accommodative, and more willingly to incorporate dissidents.[279]

The above discussion reflects a similar situation in the context of the contemporary present day Khasi society. Looking from the economic perspective, the Khasi people experience the exploitation of their natural resources not only in the British colonial rule, but the so called neo-colonial forces continue to exploit the people with the help of the national middle class who have welcome the coming of big companies to establish their factories in the state. Hence, in an attempt to analyse the challenges experience by the Khasi people concerning their economy, there are three important things needed to be taken into consideration. Firstly, through their contact with the British colonial rule, Khasi people experience not only the exploitation of their natural resources but also their mind were colonised. Secondly, through their inter-mingling with the colonial masters a cultural syncretism has taken place. Thirdly, though the people are no more

[274] Sugirtharajah, *Asian Biblical Hermeneutics and Postcolonialism*, 16.

[275] Sugirtharajah, *Asian Biblical Hermeneutics and Postcolonialism*, 17.

[276] Rieger, *Globalization and Theology*, 28-29.

[277] Sugirtharajah, *The Postcolonial Bible*, 93.

[278] Sugirtharajah, "Postcolonialism and Indian Christian Theology," 236.

[279] Sugirtharajah, "Postcolonialism and Indian Christian Theology," 237.

under the colonial role, the remnant of the colonial regime under the forces of the so called neo-colonial power still persist in today's Khasi society.

Khasi Economy in the Pre-Colonial Period

Due to the limited sources of information, it is not easy to give an authentic profile of the Khasi economy prior to the coming of the British rule. Hence, we have to depend on the earlier writings of the British writers and other writers on the subject which could throw some light on the economic condition of the people in the pre-colonial era. Notably, prior to the coming of the British rule to North East India tribal economy was generally self sufficient. Referring to the hill tribes of Arunachal Pradesh in the Pre-colonial era, Bhattacharjee observes that, with their simple way of living and limited wants, content with their own means and modes of productions, the hill peoples were generally self-sufficient.[280] In the context of Pre-colonial economy of the Khasis, though the earlier records are not available, back in 1879, Hunter observes that even though the earlier Khasis "do not grow sufficient grain for their own subsistence, and are dependent to a great extent on imports of rice from the neighbouring districts"[281] the material condition of the Khasis during that period were prosperous.[282] That is, like most of other tribal groups, content with their simple way of living and limited wants, one could affirm that traditional village economy of the Khasis were self sufficient.[283] The most significant economic activities of the Khasis during that era were agriculture and trade.

Agriculture

Like most of the other tribes of North East India, agriculture serves as the primary occupation of the Khasi people. It is the source of their livelihood, subsistence, status, as well as their economic life.[284] As stated earlier agricultural activities among the Khasis differ from region to region. That is, different regions cultivate different crops suited to the nature of the land and the places. For them, agriculture is practiced in two ways of cultivation, i) Jhumming or Shifting Cultivation and ii) Permanent Cultivation.

---

[280] See J. B. Bhattacharjee, "The Eastern Himalayan Trade of Assam in the Colonial Period," in *Studies in the Economic History of North East India,* edited by J. B. Bhattacharjee (New Delhi: Har Anand Publications, 1994), 188.

[281] Hunter, *A Statistical Account of Assam,* 226.

[282] Hunter, *A Statistical Account of Assam,* 220.

[283] Cf. Nataranjan, *The Missionary among the Khasis,* 178.

[284] There was a tendency to regard trade as the original occupation of the Khasis. But a closer and detail studies of their economic activities suggest that while trade was one of their occupations, majority of the people during that period were engaged in agriculture. See Sen, *Social and State Formation in Khasi-Jaintia Hills,* 35.

Jhum Cultivation

Jhumming or shifting cultivation[285] through the method of 'slash and burn' is one of the traditional cultivation practised widely by the tribal of North East India since time immemorial. It has become part and parcel of their life. It is the source of their livelihood where most of the life sustaining support is derived. Thanzauva considers it as the 'back bone' of the tribal economy.[286] As for other tribal groups, the Khasis engage in Jhumming since the earlier time. Bareh maintains that the difficult and rugged terrain of certain part of the region compelled the people to adopt Jhum cultivation rather than permanent cultivation. He further states that compared with the other neighbouring tribes shifting cultivation is limited among the Khasis.[287] In the same vein, Syiemlieh suggests that the nature of the land in some region comprising the "high hills with their steep slopes and deep valleys" discourage the people for adopting terrace cultivation.[288] On the other, Gurdon observes that among the Khasis, Jhum cultivation is generally adopted by the people living in the eastern and southern parts of Jaintia Hills, Ri Bhoi and the Lyngngams in the west bordering Garo Hills.[289] That is, shifting cultivation was not followed by the entire tribe except in certain region. In the region where Jhumming is not practised the Khasis followed another method of cultivation called *Ka rep bun,* a system of cultivation on the same plot of land without destroying the forest. Accordingly, they collect some branches and grass, covered them with soil till they dry up, when they will be burned for making as natural manure. Gurdon suggests that this system "is much in advance of any system of natural manuring to be seen elsewhere in the province."[290] Rana calls it "a more advanced method of Jhumming."[291] In other words, it appears that

---

[285] The Jhumming cycle starts with the clearing of jungles in the early winter, in the month of November and allows them to dry till January or February where the entire place will be burnt with fire. The land is usually not manure but the wood ashes become the manure and no water is needed, but seeds are sown when the first rain falls. But this type of cultivation has resulted to the loss of many of the forest area in different parts of the land. Shifting cultivation does not involve the whole year working; hence members of the family are free to engage any works like coolies and others when there is no work in the Jhumming field.

[286] K. Thanzauva, *Transforming Theology: A Theological Basis for Social Transformation* (Bangalore: Asian Trading Corporation, 2002), 108.

[287] Bareh, *The History and Culture of the Khasi People,* 408.

[288] David R. Syiemlieh, "Technology and Socio-Economic Linkages of the Khasi-Jaintias in Pre-Colonial Times," in *Society and Economy in North-East India,* Vol. I, edited by Mignonette Momin and Cecile A. Mawlong (New Delhi: Regency Publications, 2004), 24.

[289] The people living in the eastern Jaintia Hills are the Biates which even today still practicing shifting cultivation and those living in the southern parts are the War people which Jhumming is rarely seen today. See Gurdon, *The Khasis,* 40.

[290] Gurdon, *The Khasis,* 39.

[291] B. S. Rana, *The People of Meghalaya* (Calcutta: Punthi Pustak, 1989), 136.

apart from shifting cultivation the Khasis followed other method of cultivation or permanent cultivation. The most important crops produced through these system of cultivations are seasonal crops like paddy, millets, kachu, maize, Job's tears, soya beans, etc.[292] The amount of production was sufficient enough to support many of the tribal families for their survival and the whole year requirements.

Permanent Cultivation

Permanent cultivation is the other type of cultivation practised by the Khasis. But there are different crops cultivated in different regions depending on the nature of land suited to particular crop. In the Pre-colonial era, the most important traditional crops were rice, maize, millets, yams, kachu, oranges, pine apples, betel nuts, betel leaves, pepper, bay leaf, etc. Among these crops, rice, oranges, betel nuts and betel leaves share the important place to the economic life of the people. To begin with, rice is the most valued crop cultivated in the valley and low level tracts where irrigated rice farming[293] could be developed such as in central and northern Jaintia, central part of Khasi Hills, and the Ri Bhoi area in the north.[294] It may be noted that wet rice farming was practised by the Khasis long before the British came to rule over these hills. Since the Pre-colonial era, irrigated rice farming or wet paddy field is used 'by means of the plough' in Jaintia Hills different from those in Khasi Hills where it is practised by means of the hoe.[295] It was suggested that Pnar people cultivated by using plough and bullock carts may be due to the influence of the Bengalee people of Sylhet region which was under the rule of the Jaintia chief for a considerable period of time.[296] Hunter maintains that there are thirteen different varieties of rice cultivated in Khasi and Jaintia Hills.[297] As stated earlier, even if variety of rice grown in the land, Khasis did not have sufficient grains for subsistence and have to import rice from the plain. Some of the reasons may be cited as i) the nature of the land in some region suited well for other production rather than rice,[298] ii) people chiefly engage themselves in trade

---

[292] See Gurdon, *The Khasis,* 40; Bareh, *The History and Culture of the Khasi People,* 409-410.

[293] Bareh maintains that rice irrigated farming of the Khasis originated from the bank of the Mekong river in Cambodia and carried on to their present abode during their migration period in search of good rice land. Bareh, *The History and Culture of the Khasi People,* 407. Many scholars and writers suggest that the Khasis migrated to their present abode from the east either from Indo-China or Cambodia and so on. See Gurdon, 18; P. K. Bandyopadhayay, *The North East Saga* (New Delhi: Publication Division, Ministry of Information and Broadcasting, Government of India, 1978), 45.

[294] Bareh, *The History and Culture of the Khasi People,* 407.

[295] See Pamberton, *The Eastern Frontier of India,* 220.

[296] See Chie Nakane, *Khasi and Garo: A Comparative Study in Matrilineal Systems* (Paris: Mouton and Company, 1967), 95-96.

[297] For detail see Hunter, *A Statistical Account of Assam,* 222.

[298] It is important to note that while areas like *Ri Bhoi* and Jaintia Hills are good for rice cultivation, other areas like *Ri War* is best suited for other production rather than rice. Hence,

activities or commercial pursuits,[299] and iii) most of the Khasi *Syiems* or Chiefs possess considerable portion of fertile land in the plain of Sylhet and also in the *duars* of Assam in the north where they engaged the plain people to cultivate rice for them. John Wiles, a collector of Sylhet once writes, "A Cosseah (Khasi) never cultivates the soil; he [sic] employs Bengalee *ryots*; he [sic] comes down at the time of harvest and carries off the produce."[300] These may be some of the reasons that the Khasis prefer to import rice rather than cultivate them. Besides rice, other traditional crops like millets, maize, kachu, yam, other roots, etc. though not making as articles for export, were the main staple food production that support the people in the entire land.[301] The Pre-colonial era testifies that the southern slope of the Ri War area produced best quality of fruits needed to be mentioned like oranges,[302] pine apples and other crops of superior quality like the betel nuts, betel leaves, pepper, etc. Most of these crops are grown extensively and produce not only for domestic consumption, rather for exporting to other places especially to the plain of Bengal. Among several fruits produced from Khasi and Jaintia Hills, it was oranges that render the name of Sylhet famous. Shumboo Chunder Dey rightly argues when he states that

> The Sylhet orange is the only fruit which combines such beauty of colour with such deliciousness of taste. It seems to me that if there is any fruit which remains (though not exactly in the same state) to relate the sad romance of the blissful Garden of Eden, it is the sweetest orange of golden hue.[303]

The fruits produced in the area were famous not only for their taste but also for the quantity and amount of production.[304] It is the custom of the Khasis that during the harvest season, persons who pass through the orange orchards can take and eat some fruits without permission from the owner, but they are not expected to take home. But this is not because of large production of fruits rather

---

people of the latter are more engage in trade activities. Cf. Bareh, *The History and Culture of the Khasi People,* 408-409.

[299] Cf. Pamberton, *The Eastern Frontier of India,* 219.

[300] W. K. Firminger, *Sylhet District Gazetteer,* III/172. Letter of John Willes, Collector of Sylhet to Earl Cornwallis, 15 September, 1789.

[301] Cf. Yule, "Notes on the Khasia Hills and People," 622.

[302] Oranges are the traditional fruits that grown extensively in the Ri war area border with the plain of Bengal now called Bangladesh. It was the main source of economy for the people of the region and considered as one of the best quality ever produced during the Pre-colonial era. As it is traditional people of the area have different way of counting the fruits. For instance, in War Jaintia the way of counting is four pieces consist of one *hali,* sixteen *halis* or sixty-four pieces comprise of one *bhar* and sixteen *bhar* consist of one *luti.*

[303] See Shumboo Chunder Dey, *Sylhet* (Calcutta: G. P. Roy & Co, 1880), 19.

[304] See H. Walters, "Journey across the Pandua Hills near Sylhet in Bengal," *Asiatic Research* 17/333 (1832): 500; Cf. Frowde, *Imperial Gazetteer of India: Karachi to Kottayam,* 261; *U Nongphira* 152 (Naiwieng, 1914): 203.

it is the customary practices of the people even during harvesting to leave one or two fruits in each tree so that the poor, birds and animals can eat some and share some of the harvest.[305] Besides oranges, other crops of significant importance are the betel nuts and betel leaves.[306] The latter two are traditionally part and parcel in the economic life of the people in the War region. A clear example could be seen with the people of War Jaintia; wherever they migrate, the two crops betel nuts and betel leaves become their main agricultural crops and the source of their income.[307] Though it is not possible to get source references on the importance of these two crops in the economic life of the people in the War region in the pre-colonial period, when the British came to these hills betel nuts and betel leaves were the two main crops that have significantly contributed to the economic well being of the people in the region since time immemorial. The Board of Revenue in 1858 reported that the two agricultural items provided the people of the area with good profit. As they rightly put it,

> This trade is carried on only by Cossyahs (Khasi) and give them good profits. The betel nut groves stretch from Cheyla (Shela) at the base of the hills. The pawn leaves (betel leaves) is cultivated principally at the base of the Jynteah (Jaintia) Hills, are considered by the natives to be of far superior quality to those grown in the plain and are in good demand.[308]

Commenting on the abundant presence of betel leaves or *paan* plantation at Syndai village of War Jaintia, Hutton observes that the people of the village depend almost entirely on betel leaves for their livelihood.[309] This finding also proves true to many villages of the War area. Hence, apart from other agricultural

---

[305] In War Jaintia dialect these left over fruits are called 'soh slow.' These fruits are left deliberately so that the poor and animals can have and take freely. See "Inspection of Limestone Quarries," *U Nongphira* 152 (Naiwieng, 1914): 204.

[306] Since time immemorial, betel nuts and betel leaves plantation in War area are important profitable crops. Allen mentions how *Paan* leaves are gathered and counted such as, one bundle or *tap* contains 160 leaves and 20 *taps* make one *Kuri.* So also betel nuts are counted as follows, 10 nuts make 1 *gai* or *Kynti,* 40 *gais* make 1 *bih* or *kani,* 16 *bihs* makes 1 *lynti.* See B. C. Allen, *Assam District Gazetteers (Vol. X), The Khasi and Jaintia Hills, the Garo Hills and the Lushai Hills* (Allahabad: Pioneer Press, 1906), 33, 77-78.

[307] The people of War Jaintia who migrated to Ri Bhoi district in the border Assam, Cachar area of Assam and in the hills of Sylhet district till today, their main source of income are from betel nuts and betel leaves plantation.

[308] See *Board of Revenue (Part II) Proceedings on Deputation,* Cherrapunjee, 25 October, 1858, 493-494.

[309] The "Syndai *paan* bari" maintains Hutton, "are irrigated by bamboo aqueducts bringing water from the nearest stream. This keeps the soil damp and the air moist and cool...." It is the general practice of the War people to split the bamboo into two equal parts, join together at one end after another to bring water even from far away streams to the betel leaves field as irrigation. See J. H. Hutton, "Some Megalithic works in Jaintia Hills," in *Journal of the Asiatic Society of Bengal,* New Series, 22/6 (1926): 341.

products, oranges, betel nuts and betel leaves serve as the main source of income that has extensively contributed to the economic well being of the people.

Trade

In the Pre-colonial era, trade essentially played a crucial role in the economy of the Khasis. Notably, trade for them are not only an important source of economy but has become part and parcel of their life. Commenting on the Pre-colonial occupation of the earlier Khasis, Sen opines that among many tribes of North East India of that time, the Khasis were perhaps the most trade conscious.[310] So also, A. C. Mohapatra argues that the Khasis were expert traders.[311] They are "keen traders and ready to earn money in any honest way."[312] Many of them are 'adventurous merchants' visiting carrying on their trade as far as Dacca and Calcutta during winter.[313] The earlier Khasis carried on their trade activities both within and outside their territories such as the plain people of Assam in the north and that of the Sylhet district in the south. Trade with their neighbours flourished in the Pre-Colonial period. But there are no genuine sources with regards to the origin and growth of the market within the hills. Syiemlieh opines that markets in the hills seem to develop at a later period,[314] that is, much later after the development of the market with the neighbouring plain people. Notably, market among the Khasis has a close link with the erection of Megalith monuments. In the earlier past, the Khasis mark the establishment of new markets by erecting megalith monuments. For instance, tradition (if that is correct) tells that the transferring of the megalith monument at the market place at Raliang to Nartiang marked the closure of the market in the former and the establishment of the new market in the latter in the last part of the eighteenth century.[315] This indicates that market at Raliang must have been developed some distant years back. However, the concept of market among the Khasis is not new, for this is expressed even in their folklores like *Ka Iew Luri Lura.*[316] A particular mentioning of *Ka Tung Rymbai*[317] an

---

[310] Sen, *Social and State Formation in Khasi-Jaintia Hills,* 35.

[311] A. C. Mohapatra, "Locational Pattern of Market in Pre and Early British Period in North East India (Khasi, Jaintia and Garo Hills)," in *Studies in the Economic History of North East India,* edited by J. B. Bhattacharjee (New Delhi: Har-Anand Publications, 1994), 165.

[312] Frowde, *Imperial Gazetteer of India: Karachi to Kottayam,* 257.

[313] *An Account of the Province of Assam and its Administration* (Shillong: Assam Secretariat Printing Office, 1903), 49.

[314] Syiemlieh, "Technological and Socio-Economic Linkages...," 31.

[315] I. M. Simon as cited by Chowdhury recites the events that connect megalith erection with the establishment of new market. For detail see Chowdhury, *The Khasi Canvas,* 56-57.

[316] For detail see Primrose Gatphoh, *Ki Umjer Ksiar* (Guwahati: Dispur Print House, 1941), 134-135 discuss in Chapter V.

[317] *Ka Tung Rymbai* is one of the important indigenous delicious dishes of the Khasis, that they use to have as one item either at home or in any important occasion. Till today, *Ka Tung*

indigenous Khasi foodstuff as an item of barter and trade in the folklore, affirms that the concept of market is indigenous to the Khasis. Interestingly, their weekly calendar is characterised by daily market commencing at regular interval of eight days.[318] Though important genuine sources related to the development of these markets within the hills is not available, it has nevertheless signified that local indigenous markets play an important role in the growth and development of the Khasi economy since the Pre-British period.

Like other tribal groups of the region Khasi relation with the Assamese people is both political and economic. Historical records highlight instances of friendly contact and commercial relations between the Khasis and Assamese people that mutually benefit both the people of the hill and the plain since the Ahom rule.[319] This could be seen in the existence of trade relations between Ahom and that of Khyrim and Jaintia respectively. Some of the important markets held at Sonapur, Gobha, Phulaguri, Hatiarmukh and so on. However, the progress and active continuance of trade activities between the two sides depends much on the peace and security that prevail between them.[320] The main items of export by the Khasis are iron, yam, honey bee wax, etc., and the import items include tobacco, dried fish, goats, cotton, silk clothes and so on.[321] Robinson maintains that it was the extensive supplies of Khasi iron which is of better quality than those produced in Assam that drove away the iron of Assam from its own market.[322] On the other

---

Rymbai is available in every market within the hills.

[318] In the earlier period when markets were yet to exist in the hills, days of the weeks is known by the daily border hats taken place in different places. So, the name of the days is known as Jaintiapur, Japlem, Lyngkhat, and so on. When the market develop in the hills, the name of the days are known according to market days that took place daily in different parts of the hills, such as Lyngka, Nongkrem, Umlong, Rynghep, Shillong, Pomtiah, Umni, and Iewduh in Khasi Hills and Khyllaw, Pynsing, Mulong, Musiang, Mushai, Pyngkat, Tymblein, and Hat. See P. R. T. Gurdon, "Notes on the Khasi, Syntengs and allied Tribes, inhabiting the Khasi and Jaintia Hills District in Assam," in *Journal of Asiatic Society of Bengal* LXXIII/4 (1904): 69. Cf. Lyngdoh, *The Festivals in the History and Culture of the Khasi,* 56-59.

[319] See Satish Chandra Kakati, *Discovery of Assam* (Guwahati: The Tribune Press, 1954), iv. See also Ramesh Chandra Kalita, *Assam in the Eighteenth Century* (New Delhi: Omson Publications, 1992), 125.

[320] For instance, in 1647, when the *Raja* of Jaintia seized an Ahom trader, as retaliation the Ahom arrested Jaintia traders at Sonapur, hence diplomatic relations ceased for 8 years till reconciliation is established between the two sides. Similarly, when the Jaintia King failed to release Tamradhvaj, the Kachari King that were under Ahom rule that time Rudra Singh, the Ahom king closed the market at Gobha which serves as the important market that supplies the need of Jaintia. See Nirmal Kumar Basu, *Assam in the Ahom Age, 1228-1826* (Calcutta: Sanskrit Pustak Bandar, 1970), 40, 60, 133. See also Lakshmi Devi, *Ahom Tribal Relations* (Guwahati: Assam Book Depot, 1968), 109, 111, 132.

[321] W. J. Allen, *Report of the Administration of the Cosseah and Jynteah Hill Territory* (Calcutta: John Gray "Bengal Hurkary" Press, 1858), 44.

[322] Robinson, *A Descriptive Account of Assam,* 35.

hand, muga silk items both raw and manufactured were imported by the Khasis not only for their domestic use but also for exporting to Sylhet.[323] Hence, though the trade was not much extensive it has nevertheless contributed to the growth of Khasi economy.

Commercial activities with the plain people of Bengal were carried on with the development of number of markets known as *Hats* in the foot hills. The important markets or *hats* held regularly on the Sylhet side as Bholaganj, Teria ghat, Pandua, Chhatak, Lyngkhat (Lakhat), Jaintiapur, Jaflong or Japlem (Jafling), Pharalbazar, Mawdon (Maodong), Ponatit, Sonapur, Molaghul and Lengjut.[324] Hunter states that these hats held at regular intervals of eight days a week to permit the traders to visit different markets alternately in rotation.[325] Thomas Fisher, Superintendent of Cachar, maintains that the hill people whom he met prefer to call themselves *Khyee* or traders.[326] Trade and commerce transactions followed barter system[327] and the entire trade was under the control of the hill people. Syiemlieh argues that the hill people export more than they import.[328] The principal items of export include iron, limestone, different fruit items like oranges, pine apples, lemons and others, cotton, silk, betel nuts, betel leaves, bay leaves or *tezpat*, honey, etc. The import items consist of rice, fish, salt, silk clothes, goats etc.[329] Iron smelting carried on extensively by the Khasis from time immemorial,[330] and iron trade considered to be of excellent quality became one of their main export items of that period. W. J. Allen reports that "the Cossyah iron is known to be of excellent quality of all purpose" is more preferred to English iron by the Bengalee blacksmith. He further states that the average quantity of

---

[323] Robinson, *A Descriptive Account of Assam,* 240.

[324] Thomas C. Watson, "Chirrapunji, and a detail of some of the Favourable Circumstances which render it an Advantageous Site for the Erection of an Iron and Steel Manufactory on an Extensive scale," in *Journal of Asiatic Society of Bengal* 3/26 (1834): 26; Cf. R. Boileau Pamberton, *Report on the Eastern Frontier of British India* (Calcutta: Baptist Mission Press, 1835), 215.

[325] Hunter, *A Statistical Account of Assam,* 241.

[326] The word *Khyee* or *Khaii* in Khasi means 'trade' and *Nongkhaii* means 'trader.' See Thomas Fisher, "Memoirs of Sylhet, Kachar and the Adjacent Districts," in *Asiatic Journal* IX (1840): 833.

[327] In the Pre-Colonial period, the use of money as a medium of trade exchange was yet to exist. There were coins minted by the Jaintia Kings since the sixteenth century, but most probably meant for private circulation not for trade exchange. See E. A. Gait, "Some Notes on Jaintia History," in *Journal of Asiatic Society of Bengal* LXIV (1895): 244. Cf. M. N. Acharya, *The History of Medieval Assam* (Guwahati: Dulla Barua and Company, 1966), 33.

[328] Syiemlieh, "Technology and the Socio-Economic linkages…," 31.

[329] See Pamberton, *Report on the Eastern Frontier of British India,* 215. Lish, "A Brief Account of the Khasis," 138.

[330] Lt. Yule reported about the widespread of iron excavation in the hills when he says, "So numerous and extensive are the traces of former excavations, that judging by the number at present in progress, one may guess them to have occupied the population for twenty centuries." See Lt. Yule, "Notes on the Iron of Khasia Hills," in *Journal of Asiatic Society of Bengal* XI (II)/129 (1842): 833.

iron exported to Sylhet annually is approximately 50,000 maunds.[331] Syiemlieh maintains that maximum quantity of iron was supplied to different markets in Bengal and the remaining ores was manufactured into spades, daos, knives, arrow heads, swords and spears.[332] Hence, iron trade has largely contributed to the Khasi economy during that period.

Other significant item of export in large quantities was the limestones. Playne observes that Khasi limestones is "unrivalled in India for its purity and general excellence and that it has been preferred before all other kinds for considerably more than a century. In proof of its purity, it may be said that analysis shows that the stone contains 96% of pure lime."[333] It is reported that it was the Mughal who were first traders of this minerals before attracting the attention of the East India Company and the British traders. "Sylhet Lime" was said to be the monopoly of the Mughal Governor of Bengal.[334] Limestone was traded mostly to the Bengal merchants at Chaatuck and Sunamgunj where it was manufactured before exporting to different markets like Calcutta, Dacca and different commercial centre of Bengal.[335] This implies that lime trade become one of the major source of income that has largely contributed to the growth of Pre-Colonial Khasi economy. Other major income generation trade activities come from different crops of good quality like oranges, betel nuts, betel leaves, pine apples, tezpat which were supplied mainly to Bengal. While Oldham reports that Calcutta and other places were exported with good quality of pine apples and oranges of Khasi Hills,[336] Lamb maintains that by 1828, besides *paan* and *tezpat*, almost the whole of Bengal were supplied with oranges from these hills.[337] Hence, during the Pre-Colonial era the whole of Bengal was supplied with Khasi iron, oranges and limestones.[338] Besides the above items of trade produce largely

---

[331] Allen, *Report of the Administration of the Cosseah and Jynteah Hills Territory,* 48.

[332] D. R. Syiemlieh, " Khasi Iron Culture and Iron Trade in the Late Eighteenth and the Early Nineteenth Century," in *Studies in the Economic History of North East India,* edited by J. B. Bhattacharjee (New Delhi: Har-Anand Publications, 1994), 245.

[333] Somerset Playne, *Bengal and Assam, Behar and Orissa: Their History, People, Commerce and Industrial Resources* (London: The Foreign and Colonial Compiling and Publishing Company, 1917), 426.

[334] See, *Report of the Administration of the Province of Assam for the Year, 1901-1902* (Shillong: Assam Secretariat Printing Office, 1902), 23.

[335] Lish, "A Brief Account of the Khasis," 138.

[336] Thomas Oldham, *Geological Structure of Part of the Khasi Hills* (Calcutta: F Carbery, Bengal Military Orphan Press, 1854), 77.

[337] Letter from G. Lamb, Dhaka, 30 April, 1828 in Foreign Secretariat Proceeding (36), 14 November, 1828, No. 3 as cited by Amalendu Guha, *Medieval and Early Colonial Assam: Society, Polity and Economy* (Calcutta: K. P. Bakchi & Company, 1991), 6. See also, Pamberton, *The Eastern Frontier of India,* 242.

[338] Saswati Biswas, "Preservation of Tribal Culture In North East India How Strong is the Non Tribal Threat," in *Tribal Studies in North East India,* edited by Sarthak Sen Gupta (New Delhi:

by the Khasis from their land there are other items like silk and cotton usually imported by the not only for domestic use but for exporting to the plain of Bengal. While the latter were usually bought from Assam and the Garos,[339] the former was generally purchased from the markets in Assam. Lindsay as cited by Syiemlieh include China silk as one items traded by the Khasis to Sylhet.[340] Does it mean that Lindsay mistook Chinese silk with the Assamese silk? However, if what Lindsay mentions is correct, it indicates that commercial connections of the Khasis like the other tribes of the region during the Pre-colonial period did not end up with the Assamese people but have largely extended as far as China on the North.[341]

For the tribals, land, besides providing space for cultivation, its forest resources supply different variety of items that serve as source of livelihood and economy to the tribal people. Forests are closely linked with the life of the tribals and play a vital role in their socio-economic life since time immemorial. Different varieties of forest products like the herbs, medicinal plants, wild fruits and edible leaves, etc., became the normal commodities of commerce for many tribal villages. Mr. L. Rynjah as cited by J. Matthew insists that forest products being the essential items for barter trade, serves as important sources of economic support for the tribal people in the earlier times. Hence, plenteous availability of different forest productions not only provide a variety of food materials for tribal people but also offers a range of opportunity and means of employment for them.[342] Indigenous handicraft made of bamboos and canes also owe its debt to forest and its resources. Some of these indigenous craft to name a few are variety of mats, trays containers, baskets of different size and designs.[343] These types of bamboo baskets are meant not only for domestic utility but also for the purpose of trade. Looking back to the situation of that time, where neither wheeled carrier nor animal were used but human labour were the only means of transportation of goods, these bamboo baskets will not only be extensively used but also they will

Mittal Publications, 2002), 23.

[339] It may be noted that the cotton grown in Khasi hills (northern part) is of inferior quality, compare with those grown in Assam and Garo Hills. Hence, apart from those grown in Ri Bhoi areas, the Khasi traders generally use to purchase from the Garos and different markets of Assam for exporting to Bengal. See Robinson, *A Descriptive Account of Assam,* 244.

[340] See Syiemlieh, "Technology and Socio-Economic Linkages…," 29.

[341] Bhattacherjee maintains that active trade enterprises between different tribes of Assam and the people of Tibet, Burma and China had taken place to a large extent in the Pre-colonial period. See Bhattacharjee, "The Eastern Himalayan Trade…," 187-205.

[342] T. Matthew, *Tribal Economy of North Eastern Region* (Guwahati: Spectrum Publication, 1980), 34-35.

[343] For detail see Chowdhury, *The Khasi Canvas*, 63-64.

be in great demand.[344] As such, trade and handicraft activities simultaneously go hand in hand. Syiemlieh maintains that these bamboo baskets were used for the purpose of exporting different goods like fruits, *tezpat,* iron and limestone.[345] If that is the case, then handicraft activities served as employment to many people of that time. Apart from these crafts mentioned above, netted pouches or bags generally made by the earlier Khasis from the fibres developed from the leaves of pine apple, formed part of Khasi dress where they used to carry "clasp, knives, comb, flint steel and betel nut box."[346] Hence, handicrafts work of the earlier Khasis play a vital role in their economic life, and serve not only for domestic utility but more significantly for trade and commercial pursuits.

Hence, though the Khasis had to import some items like rice, trade and commerce not only become the source of income generating enterprise, but also contributed largely to the growth and development of Khasi economy and their economic well being.

Khasi Economy during the British Period

The above discussion, points out that agriculture and trade are the two main sources of income that have largely contributed to the economy of the Khasis in the Pre-colonial era. However, with the coming of the British rule[347] many changes have taken place in the history of Khasi economy. It was during that era that money economy was first introduced by the Britishers. Though barter system of trade still continued side by side, money as a medium of trade exchange began to take place.[348] The advent of the British rule also brought a mixed result to the Khasi economy during that period. Though the Britishers introduce new fruits

---

[344] Watson observes that transportation was usually carried on by the Khasi porter where not only goods but even human beings were transported in baskets at reasonable charges. As most of the occupations of the Khasis did not involved a year round services, hence many people will join this labour even as part time job. See Watson, "Chirrapunji and a detail of some of the favourable circumstances…," 26-27.

[345] Syiemlieh, "Technology and Socio-Economic Linkages…," 25.

[346] Pine apple leaves were collected before the arrival of the monsoon, soaked them in water for few days, then beating them to separate the fibres through which they can make these bags. See Oldham, *Geological Structure of part of the Khasi Hills*, 77.

[347] It is important to note that it is the East India Company that has first come to these hills, but in the latter stage the entire land fell under dominion of the British rule. The British occupation to these hills started in 1826 and by the year 1835 the Britishers had successfully took control over the whole land. The coming of the British rule is considered as the first phase of globalization. This area will be discussed in detail in the next chapter.

[348] Syiemlieh observes that barter as a medium of trade exchange continue till the nineteenth century. See Syiemlieh. See David R. Syiemlieh, "Trade and Markets in the Khasi Jaintia Hills: Changed Conditions in the 19th and 20th Centuries," in *Society and Economy in North East-India,* Vol. III, edited by David R. Syiemlieh and Manorama Sharma (New Delhi: Regency Publications, 2008), 54.

and vegetables of economic importance like potatoes and pear and other fruits,[349] nevertheless they have simultaneously been able to capture trade activities that serve their colonial interest. As stated earlier, like in many places of the third world, the Britishers came to these hills not to help improving the economy of the people but to exploit it. Giri observes that the motive behind the advent of an Imperial power to these hills, was to "become the undisputed master of the hills" which could enable the British to capture trade activities and to exploit the rich mineral resources for the interest of the British.[350] Allen argues that "lime quarries of the Khasi Hills formed one of the principal attractions of Sylhet" and "lime trade drew a large number of Europeans to that district."[351] Here, we will discuss the economic condition of the Khasis during the British colonial period.

Agriculture

As discuss earlier, in the agricultural areas, both seasonal and permanent crops had contributed to the economic well being of the people. It was reported that in the first part of the twentieth century around 76% of the people were engaged in agriculture.[352] This implies that agriculture is the main occupation of the people where majority of them depend their livelihood. Though different varieties of agricultural crops were cultivated, crops with better economic and trade importance like oranges, pineapple, betel nuts, betel leaves, pepper, etc in the southern slopes of Ri War area and other crops like rice, potatoes, cotton, etc in the Central and Ri Bhoi area in the north were preferably cultivated during the era. For instance, the vast orange plantation spread from Dawki area in the east to Shella area in the west.[353] Together with the oranges trees grew the betel nut trees in "carefully kept and regularly renewed groves."[354] However, a big earthquake of 1897, cause a major setback and destroyed many agricultural crops that affected the economy of the people for quite a number of years later. It was reported that the worst affected crops were those in the southern slopes like the oranges, pine apples, betel nuts, betel leaves, tezpat, pepper, and so on.[355] Since that event took

[349] It may be noted that potato and other fruits like pear or what the Khasis called *Sohphoh Nongkhlaw* are said to be introduced to these hills by David Scott in 1830. See *Board of Revenue: Part II, Proceedings on Deputation,* 25 October, 1858, 491; See also Pamberton, *Eastern Frontier of the British Territories,* 223.

[350] Giri, *The Khasis under the British Rule, 1824-1947,* 42.

[351] Allen, *Assam District Gazetteers, (Vol. X) The Khasi and Jaintia Hills, the Garo Hills and the Lushai Hills,* 14.

[352] Frowde, *Imperial Gazetteer of India, Karachi to Kottayam,* 257.

[353] *Report of the Administration of the Province of Assam for the Year, 1901-1902,* 19.

[354] *An Account of the Province of Assam and its Administration 1903,* 25.

[355] Cf. *Report of the Administration of the province of Assam for the Year, 1901-1902,* 13.

place the agricultural profits has been reduced though they are still considerable.[356] Nevertheless, agriculture still remains one of the main sources of economy for the people.

Trade

As stated earlier, in the Pre-British period the entire trade was under the hands of the local indigenous people. All the markets in the hills as well as in the foot hills were controlled by the hill people. However, during the British period there are significant changes in the trade economy of the people. With the British colonial rule expanded and the entire land was under their dominion, the role of the Khasis with regard to the border trade also diminishes. The border *hats* which were under the hands of the Khasis earlier are no longer under their independent control.[357] The earlier discussion points out that the main intention of the Britishers were to exploit the economy of the people especially trade economy. Admittedly, under the colonial rule while few areas of trade activities were in the hands of the tribal people, trade with higher amount of profit were captured by the Britishers. That is, trade with high profit generation like oranges, lime stones, coal, etc were under the control of the Britishers whereas the rest of the commercial activities remain with the hill people. It seems correct to say that those trade activities that remain under the hands of the local indigenous people were those which do not suit the interest of the colonial ruler.

It is reported that, by the time the Khasi and Jaintia Hills fell under colonial rule trade within the land through the development of the weekly market has considerably increased to a certain extent. Available records in the early part of the twentieth century tell that a considerable proportion of the local indigenous population earn their living by travelling to different markets held weekly at different places in the district. The important commodities produced in these markets were generally include agricultural products, forest products, handicraft items, iron materials and so on, brought from different nearby villages for trading. Commenting on the market within the hills, by the middle of the nineteenth century, Oldham observes that almost every big village has a market, where all the necessary items that the local people need are available, thus making it convenient for all Khasis who are fond of visiting markets.[358] Hence, all the necessary items

[356] Allen, opines that the earthquake which occurred on 12 June, 1897 was felt over an area of 1,750,000 sq. miles, from Rangoon on the southeast to Kangra on the Northwest and seriously damage many buildings within an area of 1,45,000 sq. miles. Besides the loss of many lives it has also cause serious destruction to many agricultural crops. See Allen, *Assam District Gazetteer (Vol. X), The Khasi and Jaintia Hills, the Garo Hills and the Lushai Hills,* 34, 88.

[357] Syiemlieh, "Trade and Markets in the Khasi Jaintia Hills…," 54.

[358] See Thomas Oldham, "The Geological Structure of part of the Khasia Hills, with Observation on the Meteorology and Ethnology of that District," *The Calcutta Review,* XXVII (July-December, 1856): 87; Cf. Hutton, "Some Megalithic work in Jaintia Hills," 335.

needed for the local people both for domestic use and for exporting to different markets in the plain are available in these local markets. To put it differently, the Khasi traders generally obtained trade products from the weekly markets held at the interior of the hills, carried them down for sale to the traders of the plain either to Assam or Bengal, where they purchased necessary items needed, which are not available in the hills to be bartered or sold again at the markets in the hills.[359] Some of the important markets centres flourished during the era are Cherrapunjee, Laitlyngkot, Shillong, Jowai, and Nartiang. Notably, while till the year 1879, there were no Marwari or Jain merchants in Shillong, by the year 1908, few Marwari shops has been established in Shillong, but in the interior places the entire trade is operated by the local indigenous population.[360] "The Khasis" said the report "have succeeded in keeping nearly the whole of the trade of the district in their hands, and this in itself must be a considerable source of wealth."[361] This implies that by the early part of the twentieth century Marwari traders had already began to carry on their trade in Shillong.

But trade with Assam is not very extensive and include chiefly agricultural products and iron materials manufactured by the hill blacksmith to be exchanged with items necessary for domestic use. The total amount of this trade activity is a meagre amount of Rs. 15000 approximately.[362] Besides the above, the other trade where the Khasis engaged are potatoes, betel nuts and betel leaves and iron. It may be noted that trade on potatoes though it shows promising profit in the earlier years, there was steady decline in the export due to the presence of the fungus (Phytophthora infestans). Hence, the available statistic shows that while in the year 1881-82 around 127000 maunds were exported, by the year 1886-1887, potatoes it has come down to 104000 maunds. The decline in the export further decreased to 41000 maunds in 1887-88, and still lower in 1901-1902 where the export amounted to 37000 maunds.[363] These potatoes were exported either to Gauhati or to Calcutta by the Khasi traders.[364] On the other hand, though the trade on betel nuts and betel leaves gave the Khasis good profit in the earlier years

---

[359] See *Board of Revenue (Part II) Proceedings on Deputation,* 488.

[360] Hunter observes that by the year 1879, there was complete absent of Marwari or Jain merchants in Shillong whereas in Assam one could find these merchants even to the interior places. See Hunter, *A Statistical Account of Assam,* 241. Frowde, Imperial *Gazetteer of India: Karachi to Kottayam,* 263.

[361] See *Assam District Gazetteer (Vol. X), The Khasi and Jaintia Hills, the Garo Hills and the Lushai Hills,* 89.

[362] Some of the trade items export to Assam include yam, potatoes, honey, hoes, hatchets, knives, etc. and the import items sugar, salt, dried fish, goats, pig, silk clothes and so on. See *Board of Revenue (Part II) Proceedings on deputation,* 489.

[363] *An Account of the Province of Assam and its Administration,* 35.

[364] Some of the Khasis traders were exported potatoes to Calcutta by themselves as they realized considerable profits from such endeavours. See *Board of Revenue (Part II): Proceedings on*

with the average production of betel nuts was 300 lakhs, and that of the betel leaves amounted to 1000 lakhs during the year 1858.[365] But this trade received a major setback due to the big earthquake in the later years. At the same time, iron trade that has contributed significantly to the economic well being of the Khasis in the Pre-Colonial period, has largely diminishes in the colonial era. The main reason is the stiff competition of the English iron supplied to all markets in the region at a lower price than those manufactured by the Khasis.[366] Such act had really affected not only the commercial enterprise of the local people but also even those involved in manufacturing and smelting. Some of the remaining places where iron is still smelted during that time are Nongspung, Umphrup and Nartiang.[367] Hence, the above discussion indicates that during the colonial period, with the exception of potatoes, betel nuts and betel leaves, other trade engaged by the Khasis belong to less profit generating items. It may be due to the insignificant source of income that could be achieved from the trade that the Britishers totally leave them at the hand of the local people.

Some of the important items of trade importance that attract the interest of the Britishers are oranges, limestone and coal. In the colonial period trade on these items was entirely in the hands of the Britishers. This means that trade in orange that was one of the main sources of income to the Khasis in the Pre-colonial era, were no more within their hands. It was reported that Mr. Henry Inglis began to take leases on almost all the principal orange groves in Shella since 1829. The whole of these oranges were transported to Chattuck where a considerable amount were sold to the Bengali traders from different large markets like Sylhet and Dacca and the remaining quantity were exported to Calcutta by Mr. Inglis. It is told that Calcutta city was principally supplied with oranges from these hills. As the quality of the products is good, the supply could not meet the demand, hence there was considerable enhancement in the price of the items. In the year 1857-58, the exported quantity was amounted to 452 lakhs.[368] By the year 1901-1902, the amount of export was recorded as 74000 maunds.[369] In the year 1903-04, more than sixty million oranges were produced from the land and

---

Deputation, 492; C. S. Mulan, "Hill Tribes of Assam," in *Introducing India,* edited by K. N. Bagchi & W. C. Griffiths (Calcutta: The Royal Asiatic Society of Bengal, 1947), 123.

[365] *Board of Revenue (Part II) Proceeding on Deputation,* 488.

[366] *An Account of the province of Assam and its Administration,* 40.

[367] Allen, *Assam District Gazetteers (Vol. X) The Khasis and Jaintia Hills, the Garo Hills and the Lushai Hills,* 29.

[368] See *Board of Revenue (Part II): Proceedings on Deputation, 1858,* 493.

[369] The different in the way they give the report on the amount of oranges exported this time is not clear. While in 1858 the report were given in terms of number, in this report it is given in terms of maunds and one maunds is equivalent to 40 kgs. See *Report of the Administration of the Province of Assam for the Year, 1901-1902,* 19.

exported to the plain of Bengal.[370] As the entire trade was solely monopolised by Mr. Inglis it has badly affected the economy of the Khasis. This was against the customary practices of the Khasis that always consider for the common good and welfare of all in the community. The local people complaint that the *Soh Bam*[371] which usually given free of cost now have to be paid, which was against the custom of the people.[372]

The other trade item that was under the monopoly of the Britishers is the limestone. As in the case of oranges, trade in limestone provides the Khasis significant source of income in the Pre-colonial period. However, when this trade came under the control of the Britishers, the Khasis were denied immense contribution of this trade to their economy as well. The official report of the colonial ruler in 1903 states,

> The Government is the sole proprietor of all the quarries in Jaintia and Garo Hills and the one in Sylhet as well as four in Khasi Hills, the remainder are the joint property of the Khasi rulers or communities and the British Government, the latter administering the estate and reaping half the profit.[373]

The lime trade that was centred at Chuttuck and Sunamgunj[374] and the sole monopoly of the Mughal Governor of Bengal seems to have passed into the hands of the Inglis family towards the end of the eighteenth century.[375] By the year 1858 with the exception of some quantities of limestone obtained from the quarries of Mr. Stark and Sarkies Company, Mr. Inglis seems to have secured the entire "best situated limestone belt at the base of the hills partly under leases from the government and partly under the hills chiefs."[376] The total quantity of limestone exported from these hills by the year 1851 was amounted to 16,80,050

---

[370] Allen, *Assam District Gazetteer (Vol X),* 1906, *The Khasi and Jaintia Hills, the Garo Hills and the Lushai Hills,* 76.

[371] *Soh Bam* is referred to those oranges usually given to all the labourers to take home twelve pieces each from the best quality without paying any price.

[372] "U Mawshynrut na Nongstoin bad Rambrai," *U Nongphira* 153 (Nohprah, 1914): 218.

[373] See *An Account of the Province of Assam and its Administration,* 1903, 42.

[374] Limestone was transported from the quarries in Khasi Hills to Chattuck and Sunamganj the centre of lime trade that time by boats especially during summer when the river force is strong.

[375] Towards the middle of the nineteenth century there were disputes between some Britishers like Messrs. Duncan and Gibson and others and Mr. H. Inglis with regard to gaining control of the trade on limestone and even coal, where cases were moved to the Cherra Court. Many cases were filed by the local indigenous people for different tortures and injustices done to them by Mr. Inglis. But Mr. Inglis having the connection Colonel Lister, the then Political Agent of the Khasi Hills (being his son-in-law) won all the cases against him. It is reported that Mr. Inglis will not allow any person on his way of gaining control over the trade. So, strong and powerful was the influence of the Inglis family that they could succeed and resist against all outside opposition. See Nigel Jenkins, *Gwalia in Khasia* (Llandysul, Dyfed: Gomer Press, 1995), 249-251.

[376] *Board of Revenue (Part II) Proceedings on deputation, 1858,* 489-490.

maunds , of which 14,48,550 maunds was realised from the quarries of Mr. Inglis and 2,31,500 maunds from the quarries of Mrs. Stark and Sarkies and native merchants and the total amount of lime produced from the stone burnt was amounted to 14,71,000 maunds.[377] With the whole trade concentrated under the monopoly of Mr. Inglis the price of the lime stone was said to be excessively high. It was reported that the revenue received by the British Government varies from 13-20 thousand rupees per year.[378] Hence, extraction of the mineral resources though it brings major sources of income, the lion share of the entire trade profit goes to the Britishers not to the local indigenous population.

The other commercial commodity that was under the monopoly of the Britishers is coal. The existence of coal in these hills seems to have been brought to notice in 1815, when Mr. Stark reported to the Government about the presence of coal in the lower hills of Sylhet.[379] By 1906 coal fields were discovered in different parts of the hills.[380] It was on the 20th April, 1840, that the Government took lease from the Cherra Raja forever at a specific royalty of one rupee for every 100 maunds, while at the same time reserving the right of the local people to mine, without any disturbance from the Government. [381] But with regards to Lakadong mines there is no such lease since the Raja of Jaintia Hills resigned all claims to the land when he surrendered to the British Government in 1835.[382] Allen reports that Cherrapunjee coal fields was first operated in 1840 by Captain Lister, the then Political agents in Khasi hills who exported around 8,500 tons of coal to Calcutta. But due to the problem of transportation the operation was closed. He further states that later the field was mined by the Khasis "in a wasteful and unsatisfactory manner."[383] Oldham in 1854 observes that with the clause in the lease that prevent the Government to interfere the local people from mining, it appear that most of the coal exported from the hills were actually mined by the Khasi merchants. But they have to pay a royalty of one rupee per 100 maunds to the Government.[384] The official report tells that by the year 1858 coal trade was in the hands of Mr. Inosian of Calcutta under the Sylhet coal company. It appear that the person concern operated both the Cherra coal field and the Lakadong coal field by paying the royalty of one rupee per 100 maunds to the

---

[377] See Oldham, *Geological Structure of part of Khasi Hills*, 90.

[378] See *An Account of the province of Assam and its Administration, 1903*, 43.

[379] Oldham, *Geological Structure of Part of the Khasi Hills*, 57.

[380] For detail see *Assam District Gazetteer (Vol. X), The Khasi and Jaintia Hills, the Garo Hills and the Lushai Hills*, 1906, 28.

[381] See Oldham, *Geological Structure of Part of the Khasi Hills*, 58.

[382] Oldham, *Geological Structure of Part of the Khasi Hills*, 69.

[383] Allen, *Assam District Gazetteers (Vol. X), The Khasi and Jaintia Hills, The Garo Hills and the Lushai Hills*, 1906, 25.

[384] Oldham, *Geological Structure of Part of the Khasi Hills*, 67.

Government[385] The same reports states that while Cherra coalfields realised an average export quantity amounted to 25,000 maunds, the Lakadong coalfields till 1852 could supply an average quantity of 2,00,000 maunds.[386] But due to the difficulty in transportation the mines could not function properly in later years. Admittedly, though the right of the local indigenous population to mining is not completely restricted, as the management is totally under the Government the maximum profit goes to the Britishers rather than the local population.

Success of trade will not be possible without proper transport and communication. There existed number of important roads that connected different important place in these hills in the 1870s.[387] To enhance trade activities the Government felt the need to extend railway network to the province for the transportation of coal in different mines present at Khasi and Jaintia Hills, Garo and Naga Hills, etc.[388] In 1918-19, the eastern Bengal Railway made a preliminary engineering survey for connecting Shillong and Pandu but the traffic prospects did not show to bring any good profit, hence the work did not materialise. However, the 12 km line from the Sylhet side that linked Theriaghat and Companyganj was constructed by the Government for the transportation of trade commodities in 1883-84. Though the proposal to extent the line from Theriaghat to Cherrapunjee did not prove successful, the plain portion appears to bring occasional profit. It was reported that this line was used for passenger traffic as well as good traffic especially limestone and coal "had years of both profit and loss." But after the earthquake 1897, the line was closed for passenger traffic.[389] Nevertheless, extension of railway traffic to these hills was meant to benefit the trade activities of the Britishers not for the local indigenous population.[390]

According to the Government record, in comparison with the Assam side, trade on the Sylhet side held great importance and the average amount of exports may be estimated approximately Rs. 4,00,000 and the imports may

---

385 *Board of Revenue (Part II) Proceedings on Deputation,* 1858, 491.

386 *Board of revenue (Part II) Proceedings on Deputation,* 491, 506.

387 See Hunter, *A Statistical Account of Assam,* 58; See also S. B. Medhi, *Transport System and Economic Development in Assam* (Guwahati: Publication Board Assam, 1978), 42.

388 *The Agricultural Ledger,* Vol. 14 (Calcutta: Office of the Superintendent Government Printing, India, 1898), 4.

389 Medhi, *Transport System and Economic Development in Assam,* 86. Cf. Marbaniang, *Assam in a Nutshell,* 117. Cf. Hamlet Bareh Ngap Kynta, *The Economy of Meghalaya* (Guwahati: Spectrum Publication, 2001), 41.

390 It was reported that Babu Jeebon Roy one of the prominent Khasi trader during that time appealed for the extension of the railway traffic from Nongjri quarries to river Piyan, but his case was rejected on the ground that resolution was passed to allow only the Assam Bengal railway for operation and management of the railway to these hills not for others. See "Inspection of Limestone quarries," *U Nongphira* 152 (Naiwieng 6, 1914): 203.

be Rs. 2,00,000 respectively.[391] Hunter in 1879 maintains that the total exports during that time was Rs. 7,00,000 and the total imports had increased to Rs. 3,50,000 respectively.[392] These figures shows not only the increasing value of trade but also reflected that the hill areas exported more than what they import or so to say profit will be more for the hill people. From the government perspective, though the trade in these hills was carried on in a 'primitive' way by the simple and 'ignorant' inhabitant it was increased considerably due to the "peace and security ensured to them by the protection and political control of the British Government."[393] However, though the success of trade was achieved from the period, it may be pointed out that as the important exported commodities that yield high profit were in the hands of the Britishers, the major chunk of trade profit generated benefit more to the Britishers rather than the local indigenous population.

The Middle Class

During the British era another class of people developed called the middle class. This class is related neither to agriculture nor to trade but held great importance in the economic sphere of the people especially in the later period. Downs observes that the coming of British colonial rule led to the influx of many outsiders in the form of administrators, clerks, soldiers, merchants, technicians and missionaries who offer a new standard of living particularly in the urban areas and administrative centres.[394] At the same time many new offices and educational institutions were gradually established especially in the administrative headquarters at Shillong. For the tribal people this standard of living with new job opportunities in due course become the most sought after, especially by the educated class. Hence, when education began to gain ground in the hills,[395] many educated people were joining in different job opportunities offered by the new set up. Bareh maintains that many educated Khasi people were working in different capacities in and outside Shillong.[396] However, this new class played an important role in the history of the community in the later period.

Khasi Economy in the Post-Independent Period

The above discussion shows that in the British colonial period many of the important sources of income that generated high profit to the people were under

---

[391] *Board of Revenue (Part II) Proceedings on Deputation,* 1858, 489.

[392] For detail see Hunter, *A Statistical Account of Assam,* 236.

[393] *Board of Revenue (Part II) Proceedings on Deputation,* 1858, 488.

[394] F. S. Downs, "Christianity as a Tribal Response to Change in North East India," *Missiology* VIII/4 (October, 1980): 408-409.

[395] Hunter, *A Statistical Account of Assam,* 246-248.

[396] Bareh, *The History and Culture of Khasi People,* 397.

the control of the colonial ruler. The controlling of different sources of income has significantly affected the economy of the Khasis. With the departure of the colonial master, the Khasis like other tribal groups of North East India are now under the independent India. With the achievement of Independence in 1947 and the partition of the country into India and East Pakistan and later Bangladesh many changes had taken place in the economic life of the tribal of North East India in general and the Khasis in particular. On one hand, the transfer of power to the Indian national leader means that tribal people are facing a new system of administration. On the other hand, trade activities and trade relations between the hill people and their plain counterparts which had been established since the Pre-colonial era was severely affected. Detailed below, an attempt is made to discuss the economy of the Khasis in the Post-independence period.

Impact of Partition

The partition of the country in the Post-Independence era has badly affected the economy of the Khasis. Khasi and Jaintia Hills which had served as trade route between Assam and Sylhet, all of a sudden is converted into a landlocked region. For the Khasi people who experienced economic prosperity through their interaction with their counterparts in the plain since time immemorial closing the border means halting the main source of their economy. The sudden closure of many border markets severely affected both import and exports of different goods and services that has left a large section of the population without proper employment.[397] With the closure of the border *hats,* important agricultural crops like oranges, betel nuts, and betel leaves which were in great demand earlier in the plain of Bengal, now facing a dearth of suitable markets for exporting. This has brought untold misery to the Khasi people who have to find some other routes for exporting their goods. With no proper road communication within these hills and no trade facilities available most of these crops worth lakhs of rupees were left to rot in the fields.[398] Hence, the sudden closure of border trade that has immensely contributed to the economic well being of the people has in no time "reduced the population from a position of prosperity to one of near-poverty."[399] Moreover, it signifies that import items like rice, fish, clothes, etc. are no more available for the people especially those living in the War region that depend mostly from the plain

[397] Border markets provided employment not only to the traders but also to the coolies and daily wage labourers that has involved certain bulk of the population.

[398] There was an attempt to revive the border trade, through the negotiation between India and Bangladesh, but the re-opening of some market in 1970-71, could not continue. Hence, these markets were closed again after a brief period. L. S. Gassah, "Effects of Partition on the Border Marketing of Jaintia Hills" in *Marketing in North-East India,* edited by J. B. Ganguly (New Delhi: Omsons Publications, 1984), 66.

[399] I. M. Simon, *Meghalaya District Gazetteers: Khasi Hills District* (Shillong: Art & Culture Department, Meghalaya, 1991), 64.

of Sylhet for these items. Hence, the people in these hills have to depend for many important necessary items needed from the supplies from the main land India.

Agriculture

The Census of India 1951 shows that the percentage of population depends on agriculture in the United Khasi and Jaintia Hills District is 67.7 %.[400] Besides, reports show that in the Post-Independence era about 20.24% of the population still engaged in Jhumming[401] especially concentrated mostly in Lyngngam area in the west, Ri Bhoi in the north and Saipung area in Jaintia Hills. This reflects that majority of the Khasi population are still engaged in agricultural activities. There have been some changes in the agricultural production of the Khasi people in the Post-Independence period. That is, some crops that contribute immense wealth to the local indigenous people in the earlier times experienced a sudden decline since then people attempted to cultivate many other crops in different parts of the region. The orange productions in the War region which had been an important source of economy to people, has gradually diminished due to the widespread attack of blight in the entire area of the region.[402] Hence, the main crops produce in this hills which contributes in the growth of economy of the local indigenous population in the aftermath of independence consist of betel nuts, betel leaves, brooms, *tezpat*, potatoes, different varieties of fruits and vegetables, rice, ginger, etc. Some agricultural products like brooms, *tezpat,* potatoes and ginger are purchase by the Marwari wholesalers from the farmers in Shillong where they will be exported outside the State. Whereas, the rest of the items found their way for marketing either to different weekly markets held in different corner of the land or transported to the state capital Shillong. However, even though many new agricultural crops are being introduced in these hills the outcomes in many of the cultivated crops do not yield good results as earlier. This has badly affected the economy of the people.

Trade

As stated earlier, with the effect of partition, trade with the Sylhet region which flourished in the early period and served as good source for economic growth, was no longer made possible in the Post-Independence era. But trade activities ceased to continue not only with Sylhet but also with Assam. Since the closure of the border trade with the Sylhet region now in Bangladesh, North Eastern region in

[400] B. B. Vaghaiwalla, *Census of India, 1951,* 106.

[401] B. B. Dutta, "Tribal Development in Khasi-Jaintia Setting" in *Tribal Demography and Development in North East India,* edited by J. Matthew (Delhi: B. R. Publishing Corporation, 1990), 59.

[402] This is the report of I. M. Simon based on the Khasi Hills region only. But the infection of this disease on the orange plantations affects the entire area of cultivation both in the Khasi hills and Jaintia hills region. See I. M. Simon, *Meghalaya District Gazetteers: Khasi Hills District,* 64.

general and Khasi and Jaintia hills in particular has become a landlocked region. Hence, one could assume that with regard to trade activities in the region there appear to be more import than export during this period. With no industries or factories like food producing unit and other necessary items needed for human consumption exist in these hills, so almost everything has to be imported from outside the states. The Post-Independence era testifies that non tribal merchants like the Marwari and others whose number were insignificant in the early part of 1900s, has gradually increased and control almost the entire trade activities both as wholesalers and retailers in the capital city of Shillong and even find their way to carry their trade activities in small towns.[403] Hence, all the goods and commodities imported from outside and to be supplied to different corners of the land are under the control of the non tribal wholesalers and stockists who generally fixed the price of all the items according to their own conveniences. As the non tribal merchants control most of the trade, hence exported agricultural items like potato, broom, *tezpat,* ginger to name a few have to pass through their hands, as they also serve as middle men for the transportation of these commodities outside the state. These non tribal merchants not only purchase the items from the farmers but they are the one who fixed the price of all the commodities. Hence, in most cases these wholesalers and stockists generally buy the things at throw away prices especially the perishable goods as the local indigenous farmers have no other alternatives but to hesitantly accept what have been fixed by the former.[404] In the Post-Independence era, different weekly markets still continue to exist in different corners of the land. As stated earlier almost in all the markets, the entire trade is within the hands of the local indigenous people. Today in many market places side by side with the weekly market, permanent trade activities began to be established. Nevertheless, since almost all of the essential commodities needed for marketing in different local market have to be purchased from the non tribal wholesalers, the major amount of the profit goes to the non tribal merchants not to the native traders. The outcome of such a situation is that tribal trade which has earlier been the source of economic prosperity is now shattered and insecure.

In the Post-Independence period, in a landlocked region like Khasi and Jaintia Hills with little trade linkages with the outside world, land and its resources is the only economic entity that is worth to bementioned. Coal trade which has been carried on since the British period is another commercial item worth mentioned. Coal trade in this period is entirely operated by the local Khasi

---

[403] It may be noted that with the exception of meat shop and trade in betel nuts and betel leaves non tribal merchants control the entire trade at Shillong. Today non tribal traders are found in good numbers even in small town like Jowai, Khliehriat, Lad Rymbai, Nongpoh, Byrnihat and other areas.

[404] Cf. Gassah, "Effects of Partition...," 67.

traders.[405] Coal mining at present concentrating in Bapung area and Shkentalang area of Jaintia Hills, Shahlang and Borsara area of West Khasi Hills and a small extent of mining is carried on in Cherrapunjee area. However, coal mining though it generates employment to many people, the unscientific and unscrupulous mining operation by using the traditional 'rat hole' method brought irreparable damage to the entire environment.[406] Since the last few decades volume of coal trade has considerably increased where thousands of trucks are engaged daily for transporting of coal either to Guahati in Assam or to Bangladesh.[407] But coal trade though it has immensely contributed to the growth of economy of the local people, this trade is concentrated only on certain pockets whereas majority of the population do not benefit by the trade but have to be content with the limited economic facilities.

Forest plays an important role in the economic life of the tribals. Many of the forest products become the source of living for the tribals. At the same time, the above discussion depicts that, in a landlocked region like the Khasi and Jaintia Hills, land and its resources become the most important economic source to the people. Hence, for the tribal people like the Khasis, forests become the most precious commodity that has immensely contributed to their economy. However, in the last few decades commercialization of forest that was unheard of in the earlier times began to take place. Hence, with the increasing demand for timber materials in other parts of the country many of the erstwhile lush green forest cover became asource of maximum monetary profit for some section of the people. It is reported that every day about 40,000 ft. of saw logs are exported outside the state. This means that an average of 5 hectares of forest is commercialised every day.[408] So, a large number of saw mills developed in different parts of the region. No doubt commercialisation of forests provides job opportunity to many local people, but at the same time it has destroyed much of the forest cover in the region. This situation moved the Supreme Court to pass an interim order to ban all types of commercialisation of forests in the region.[409] However, such type of blanket ban on the trade that provided employment to many local indigenous

[405] However, in the recent past some non tribal merchants also started to take interest in this flourishing coal trade.

[406] It is important to note that due to this unscientific mining the whole environment is damage like sinking of land, landslides, loss of paddy fields and so on. See Henry Lamin, *Economy and Society in Meghalaya* (New Delhi: Har-Anand Publications, 1995), 110.

[407] See Bareh, *The History and Culture of Khasi People,* 430.

[408] See, F. S. Suchiang, *Meghalaya Eco-Resource Development Project (A Report),* 1994, 26-31.

[409] It may be noted that the Supreme Court order is passed due to the Public Interest Litigation filed by the Khasi Student Union at the Gauhati High Court pleading for a 10 years moratorium ban on all kinds of timber trade. See "KSU Moves High Court on Forest Protection," *The Shillong Times* 6 June1981, 1. See also "KSU Demand for Moratorium on Timber Trade," *The Meghalaya Guardian,* 27 June 1996, 1.

people without the provision of any alternative job facilities resulted in many people facing starvation especially those who reside in the West Khasi Hills. Hence, many people left their villages and migrated to the capital city of Shillong in search of employment. With no other alternatives, those who remain in their villages despite the Supreme Court ban on timber trade after few years resorted to other activities like charcoal burning which again resulted to the loss of forest. The charcoal produced by this section of population, besides being sold in different markets as fuel for many families in the region, the maximum quantity is exported to different industries at Byrnihat.[410] It is said that the amount of forest destroyed through charcoal burning is more severe than timber trade for even the small trees are not spared. This implies that tribal economy and forest economy are closely related and cannot be separated. Hence, the above discussion portrays the fact that commercialisation of forests though it serves as source of livelihood to many people, it has nevertheless threaten their own survival leaving them with future economic insecurity.

The Middle Class

As stated earlier, besides agricultural and trading class, another class developed in the economic category of the Khasis. This class of people consists mainly those who are serving in different institutions and departments of the Government. In the Post-Independence era under the Government of Assam there were 581 tribal employees serving in different department of the government of Assam.[411] With the creation of the state of Meghalaya, and the addition of many departments for the smooth functioning of the governmental activities, many members of the population joined government jobs, this class keep on increasing. It may be noted that it is this class who implemented all the policies and schemes of the government. In the Post-Independence era, with the agricultural productions not yielding good profit as in the earlier times, the government workers appear to be better off in comparison with those who are engaged in agriculture. At the same time, as the salaries are well paid, many among the tribal population both urban and rural population opted for government job. Hence, many among the tribals especially in the rural areas tend to ignore agriculture in search of well paid job in the government offices. The outcome of such a practice has badly affected the role and importance of agriculture in the economy of the people.

---

[410] See "Kylla thlen bamduh ki Kharkhana Byrnihat ia ki Khlaw ka West Khasi," *Mawphor*, 6 October, 2009, 1.

[411] Dhiren Bhagawati, *Meghalaya: Issues and Legacies of its Early Years* (Guwahati: D V S Publishers, 2007), 95.

Conclusion

The above discussion highlights the Khasi setting with regard to their traditional social, political, religious and cultural life of the people. It also discusses on the economy of the Khasi people in the Pre-Colonial, Colonial and the Post-Independence period. It may be noted that the social, cultural, religious and political life of the people play an important role in the growth and development of their economy. The research found that though the people have to import rice from outside the economy of the people was nevertheless self sufficient. Looking by the standard of that time, with their simple way of living and limited wants, their life seemed to be self sufficient. Agriculture and trade, the two main important economic activities of the people not only provided enough source of livelihood, but also contributed adequate support to the economic well being of the people. Nevertheless, with the coming of the British and later the non tribal merchants many of the important sources of economy of the local indigenous population were taken away from them. Admittedly, Britishers did not come to this part of the world to help improve the economic life of the people, but to exploit and extract the rich economic resources of the land to the maximum. It may be noted that to expand the horizon of their empire, the colonial ruler not only capture the natural resources of economic importance, but also brought along with them non tribal people to serve their interest. This in turn has adversely affected the economy of the indigenous population. By the time the colonial rule came to an end, the economy of the land was in a deplorable state. Hence, in the post independence era, the people have to depend heavily on the financial support of the central government. Consequently, at the time when the economy of the local indigenous population is weak, the advent and impact of the present phase of globalization does not help in the recovery of the economic condition of the tribal people; rather make their problem worse and render them more impoverished from what they had been earlier.

Chapter 2

Globalization: An Overview

Before the coming of British colonial rule with their simple way of life the Khasi people who are living in this part of the world perhaps have sufficient source of income to support their day to day life. The entire social, political, cultural and religious life of the people has made significant contribution to the growth and development of their economy. However, with the advent of the British coupled with the sudden influx of the non tribal merchants most of the important sources of tribal economy were exploited. Hence, Khasi people who were economically sound prior to the coming of the British colonial rule, now have to depend almost entirely on the financial assistance of the central government. In this chapter an attempt is made to study the history of globalization and how it has affected the economy of different sections of population in different parts of the globe. Using the tool of Postcolonialism, the researcher will try to investigate how the two phases of globalization: the colonialist globalization and the present day globalization affected almost the entire fabric of the people and society of the Third world, and also its agencies, culture, and world view and so on. At the same time not to forget the emergence of the two powers: the US and the USSR in the post war globalization with their attempt to capture the world and overtake each other in the aftermath of the Second World War. "For Postcolonialism," maintains Rabecca Todd Peters "globalization is a new form of colonialism that is re-inscribing dependency and control over politically weak and economically impoverished countries." She further states that "proponents of Postcolonialism are largely people in poverty, the disenfranchised, those who feel that their traditions and cultures are being destroyed by the neocolonial practices of the dominant form of globalization and their allies."[1] In addition they see globalization as the

[1] Rabecca Todd Peters, *In Search of the Good Life. The Ethics of Globalization* (New York: Continuum International Publishing Group, 2004), 139.

forces that destroy not only their traditions and culture but their livelihood as well. Hence, "globalization is representing the familiar threat of colonialism in a new, sophisticated, and highly seductive package that promises wealth, possessions, and comfort, but that remains neo-colonialism nonetheless."[2]

Globalization

Globalization is one of the oft-quoted and widely used terms in contemporary debate and discussion. It has become one of the major phenomena that has penetrated and encroached upon different aspects of human life and daily activities, regardless of national borders, geographical area or territorial boundaries. Globalization is a process which steadily arose during the last few decades of the present era, and whether people like it or not, they cannot stay away or isolate themselves from its realm. No country or section of citizens can remain outside the ambit of this dominating force.

Today, the issue of globalization has received considerable attention in the arena of academics, social, political, economic, cultural, information technology and other disciplines of human enterprises. Globalization means different things to different people. The supporters of globalization who propagate and benefit from the process, deem it as the only option that could raise up and improve the living condition of the people to a large extent. For them there is no alternative (TINA)[3] that can transform the society apart from the process of globalization. Whereas to the majority of the world population, who are extensively being neglected and marginalized, the lower strata of the social ladder, understand this process as the alarming movement that threaten their very existence and survival.

Hence, different scholars interpret this complex phenomenon differently. For some, globalization is seen as a complex of inter-related process that has taken place in different parts of the global arena. In his book *The Consequences of Modernity* (1990), Anthony Giddens as quoted by Dasgupta and Kiely define Globalization as "the intensification of worldwide social relations which link distant localities in such a way that local happenings are shaped by events occurring many miles away and vice versa."[4] In the same vein, Medury says, "Globalization refers to the multiplicity of linkages and interconnections between the states and societies, which make up the present world system. It describes the process by which events, decisions and activities in one part of the world come to have significant consequences for individual and communities in quite distant parts

---

[2] Peters, *In Search of Good Life: The Ethics of Globalization,* 141-143.

[3] The word TINA is first coined in 1980 by Margaret Thatcher the then Prime Minister of Britain. For her, globalization is the only process that could help the world from the financial problem. See R. V. Mathias, "Publisher's Note," in *The Dynamic and the Impact of Globalization- A Subaltern Perspective,* M. Victor Louis Anthuvan (Madurai: Amirtham Publications, 2006), viii.

[4] Samir Dasgupta and Ray Kiely, "Introduction" in *Globalization and After,* edited by Samir Dasgupta and Ray Kiely (New Delhi: Sage Publications, 2006), 25.

of the globe."[5] "Globalization" argues Arthur is understood as "the inter-related complex of processes, industrial, economic, technological, cultural and cognitive, which have resulted in regional boundaries (whether of family, class, religion or nation), is being rendered permeable to distant influences." "Permeability" for him means what happens in one part of the globe has considerable impact even to distant places.[6]

On the other hand, there are those who see globalization as a uniting movement that could merge the entire world into one single unit. A. A. Shaikh subscribes to this view when he argues, "Globalization is a process of economic, social, cultural and political integration of the countries of the world. It aims at connectivity, closeness, togetherness and interdependency. It is a phenomenon of unification. Its essence is integrated world with single order."[7] Contrary to this understanding, some portray globalization not as an integrating force but a powerful movement fragmenting the world into many factions. Commenting from the economic aspect of globalization C. T. Kurien as quoted by Razu observes, "If 'globalization' means the coming closer of the national economies of the world, then this is not happening. On the contrary, they are getting more distanced. The gap between the North and the South has increased and in terms of trade, since the 1980s national economies have become more isolated."[8] In other words it signifies that "the world has become more differentiated, more insecure, more fragmented along with growing gaps in social and economic inequality."[9] Furthermore, there are others who define globalization both as an integrating

---

[5] Uma Medury, "Changing Complexion of Public Administration in the Globalization Era: Some Emerging Issues," in *Globalization: Myth and Reality,* edited by Govind Prasad and Anil Dutta Mishra (New Delhi: Concept Publishing Company, 2004), 49.

[6] He further elaborates this view when he maintains that destruction of rainforest in Brazil may lead to protests in London, Tel-Aviv or Brisbane, or purchase of computers in Vancouver will affect employments opportunities in Philippines and Korea, or the financial crisis in Asia will have an impact on the livelihood of whelk fishermen in Wales, that agricultural decisions which will massively shape the environment and economy of Kenya or Bolivia are made in boardrooms in London and New York, that capital will be transferred to areas of the world where workers' rights and incomes are low, so that profit may be maximized and so on. For detail see Chris Arthur, *The Globalization of Communications: Some Religious Implications* (Geneva: WCC Publications, 1998), 3.

[7] A. A. Shaikh, "Globalization: Its Clashes, Contents and Discontents," in *Globalization: Myth and Reality,* edited by Govind Prasad and Anil Dutta Mishra (New Delhi: Concept Publishing Company, 2004), 69.

[8] I. John Mohan Razu, "Towards an understanding of the phenomenon of Globalization: An attempt," in *Globalization,* edited by Rose Mary Vishwanath (Bangalore: Verba Network Service, 1998), 2.

[9] Saroj Malik, "Contradictions and Challenges of Globalization: Need for an Alternative," in *Globalization: Myth and Reality,* edited by Govind Prasad and Anil Dutta Mishra (New Delhi: Concept Publishing Company, 2004), 38.

process as well as dominating force that serve the interest of the developed nations. Mishra rightly express this view when he argues,

> "In a positive sense, it is used to describe a process of increasing integration into the world economy. In other words, it means the expansion of economic activities across national boundaries. It is also used to prescribe a strategy of development based on a rapid integration with the world economy and view it as salvation. In other words, globalization is a process associated with increasing economic openness, growing economic interdependence and deepening economic integration in the global economy. In the negative sense, it is seen as domination by developed nations over developing nations.[10]

The above discussion clearly indicates that globalization is understood differently by different people. In other words, it highlights the complexity of the process of globalization and the way how it is defined. On one hand, globalization is viewed as a movement that enhances oneness, unification, integration, interconnection and interdependence of the world economies for the benefit of humankind. On the other hand, the process of globalization serves the interests of the developed nations in their attempt to exploit the resources of the Third World nations that has widened the gap between the rich and the poor nations. In the midst of diversity of understanding on the concept, the UNDP (United Nation Development Program) Report defines globalization not only as a movement that enhances economic opportunities but also as a powerful force that neglects and discriminates the poor and the marginalised. This is rightly reflected in their statement as quoted by Upadhyay in the following words.

> Globalization expands the opportunities for unprecedented human advance for some but shrinks those opportunities for others and erodes human society. It is integrating economy, culture and governance but fragmenting societies. Driven by commercial market forces, globalization in this era seeks to promote economic efficiency, generate growth and yield profits. But it misses out on the goal of equity, poverty eradication...[11]

Hence, it is clear that, the issue of globalization contains no single description but multifaceted and diverse description. Here, in this research the main emphasis will be on economic globalization and not to distinctly deal with different dimensions of globalization. The writer will critically analyse the process of economic globalization, both its positive and negative contribution to human society particularly the tribal communities. It is an attempt to evaluate whether globalization benefits human societies or not. Who are the beneficiaries from this

[10] Anil Dutta Mishra, "Globalization: Concept and Nature," in *Globalization: Myth and Reality*, edited by Govind Prasad and Anil Dutta Mishra (New Delhi: Concept Publishing Company, 2004), 5.

[11] Vandana Upadhyay, "Globalization and Development in North East India," in *Globalization and Development Dilemma*, edited by M. C. Behera (New Delhi: Mittal Publications, 2004), 33.

process? How far this system has improved the living condition of the poor and marginalised in different parts of the globe?

Genesis of Globalization

It is not easy to trace back to the genesis of globalization. But one thing is clear that the process of globalization is not a new phenomenon that has developed in the recent past but it has a long history behind it. Balasuriya observes that the process of globalization originates when "one breaks the boundaries of his or her own world and interact/influence the other." He further argues that, it may be a war fought between nations, or the knowledge system where one interacts with the other, or trade relations between different nations, and so on. All these events contribute to the growth and development of globalization.[12] In the same vein, Patrick while stressing on the recent episode of globalization, opines that its roots can be traced back "in the distant past when trade and commerce moved out of one territory to another, transcending the natural barriers of sea and mountains."[13] That is, the origin of globalization started when one nation began to move out of its geographical or territorial boundaries either to have dominion or to establish trade relations, etc. with the other nation in other part of the globe. Whatever the case may be, globalization developed in different periods of space and time with diverse sets of worldviews, ideologies, interests, institutions, practices and the like. Nevertheless, different scholars have different opinion about its origin and development. To put it differently, scholars suggest different period and dates with regards to the origin and growth of globalization in different phase of history. For some scholars, globalization begins in the fifteenth and sixteenth centuries, with the territorial exploration of Columbus (1492) and Vasco da Gama (1498) respectively in order to 'discover new lands.'[14] On the other hand, others seem to propose that the process of globalization started with the establishment of the early Egyptian, Babylonian, Greek, and Roman Empire and so on.[15] The

---

[12] Tissa Balasuriya, *Globalization and Human Solidarity* (Thiruvalla: Christava Sahitya Samithy, 2000), 7.

[13] Gnana Patrick, "Empowering Modernity and Ambivalent Globalization: A Perspective of the Indian 'Social' Minorities," *Jeevardhara* XXXIV/199 (January, 2004): 42.

[14] Prof. T. K. Oomen of Jawaharlar Nehru University, New Delhi advocates that globalization begins with the sea voyage undertaken by Columbus, Vasco da Gama and Captain Cook the founding fathers of the New World in the sixteenth century. See T. K. Oomen, "Globalization and Structural Change: Historicity and Implications," *Religion and Society* XLI/2 (June, 1994): 16. See also P. Maria Joseph Christie, S. J. , "Conflict of Values in the Globalized Era," *Satya Nilayam* 10 (August, 2006) : 2. So also, historian Robbie Robertson suggests that globalization begins with Columbus' journey in 1492. See Greg Buckman, *Globalization: Tame it or Scrap it?* (Bangalore: Books for Change, 2004), 6.

[15] Manoj Sinha, "Globalization and Consumerism: A Study of its Impact," in *Globalization: Myth and Reality*, edited by Govind Prasad and Anil Dutta Mishra (New Delhi: Concept Publishing Company, 2004), 188. See also, A. Wati Longchar, "Globalization and Indigenous People:

above explanation highlights that globalization commenced when "one breaks the boundaries of his or her own world and interact/influence the other." Its main emphasis is for territorial expansion or trade activities. While the former developed and flourished within particular space and time, the latter still continue to dominate and influence the world today, carried on by the rich nations over economy of the poor nations.[16]

Phases of Globalization

The growth and development of globalization can be traced back to the distant past. Though scholars differ in mapping out its history, they all agree that globalization developed in different phases at different time. J. H. Dunning opines that globalization started in the early part of the sixteenth century developed into five different phases.[17] But other scholar like Longchar[18] categorises these phases into four different stages. On the other hand, some like Oommen[19] and Arun[20] who propose for three major phases of globalization, which begin with the territorial exploration of the European travellers to discover new land. It may be noted that, though the starting period on the process of globalization between Dunning and the latter two scholars is same, Dunning identifies five important stages of globalization, while the latter proposes only three major stages. Nevertheless, in this research an attempt is made to discuss three important phases of globalisation-the Colonialist Globalization, the Post world War Globalization and the Present Day Globalization. This attempt does not mean to undermine or

---

Challenges for Doing Theology in Asia," in *Tribal Theology: A Reader,* edited by Shimreingam Shimray (Jorhat: Tribal Study Centre, 2003), 185.

[16] In the earlier period exploitation of the economy of the poor nations was carried on by the colonial forces, but today exploitation of the economic resources of the poor nations or the third world countries is done by the so-called neo-colonial forces like the MNC or TNC.

[17] For Dunning globalization contains five different phases namely Mercantile Capitalism and Colonialism (1500-1800), Entrepreneurial and Financial Capitalism (1800-75), International capitalism (1875-1945), Multinational Capitalism (1945-1960), and Globalizing Capitalism (1960-1990). See I. Mohan Razu, "The Symbiosis between Poverty and Globalisation: A Need for a Critique from Political Ethics," *National Council of Churches Review* CXX/10 (November, 2000): 880.

[18] Longchar suggests four important stages that have taken place in the process of globalization. See Longchar, "Globalization and Indigenous people...," 185.

[19] Oommen identifies three major stages in the process of globalization. The first stage began with the sea voyage of the European travellers to find out new land. The second phase was marked by the development of two major powers- USA and USSR blocks, attempting to dominate the world, and the third is the present phase of globalization, which started after the collapse of the USSR block.See T. K. Oommen, "Globalization and Structural Change: Historicity and Implications," *Religion and Society* XLI/ 2 (June, 1994): 16-22.

[20] Arun categorizes three important stages in the process namely, the colonialist globalization, the post world war globalization and the modern phase of globalization. See Joe Arun S. J., "Taming the Global Demagogue I," *Vidyajyoti Journal of Theological Reflection* 66/ 6 (June 2002): 419-431.

ignore the importance of the Egyptian, Greek, Babylonian and Roman Empire. It may be noted that globalization during that era had its own significant value and importance with its respective growth and progress within that particular space and time. But as the main emphasis of the research work is within the Indian context and also the present economic globalization, hence it is more appropriate to begin with the colonial period.

Colonialist Globalization

The expedition of Christopher Columbus in October 1492 to Americas and Vasco da Gama in May 1498 to India "marked the beginning of colonialism."[21] To put it differently, it may be considered as the important landmark in the process of Globalization. It is referred as the first phase of globalization. It is reported that, Columbus on hearing about the enormous richness of Asia, commenced his sea voyage in search of new land. After five weeks journey they instead reached Bahamas, and named the place San Salvador meaning the 'Holy Saviour.'[22] With the same intention, Vasco da Gama reached Calicut in India in search of the richness of Asia.[23] These two significant events coupled with the successive exploration of Europeans to different parts of Asia, Africa and America resulted in the exploitation of the world trade and colonization of different areas of the globe by the colonial power. In other words, it demonstrates the beginning of economic subjugation and political domination of the western Imperial power upon the countries of the Third World. Oommen opines that the vision for migrating from the Old World to the New World stems from the ideology advocated by Thomas Hobbes that people from the former have the right to migrate to any unoccupied space available in the latter without disturbing or depriving the 'natives' of their material possessions.[24] He further states that with such mind set, there emerged two sets of migrations- the settler and the colonial countries.[25] But in both cases, the main target was to exploit the natural resources available in the newly occupied region. Rangriz terms this period as the 'extensive' or 'widening' phase

---

[21] Walter Fernandez and Anupama Dutta, *Colonialism to Globalization: Five Centuries after Vasco da Gama* (New Delhi: Indian Social Institute, 1999), 1.

[22] On their arrival in the wrong place, the followers of Columbus plundered the gold and silver found in that island. Arun, "Taming the Global Demagogue I," 424.

[23] Fernandez and Dutta, *Colonialism to Globalization: Five Centuries after Vasco da Gama,* 1.

[24] Thomas Hobbes, the English political philosopher once advocates that it is not wrong for the people of the thickly populated old World to migrate and settle in the thinly populated region of the new World for their livelihood. See Oommen, "Globalisation and Structural Change...," 16.

[25] The settler countries are referred to those countries with sparsely populated region where the colonizers gradually became the permanent citizens of that country like the United States of America, Latin America, Canada, and Australia. Those countries with thickly population like in Africa and Asia became the colonial countries. See Oommen, "Globalisation and Structural Change...," 16-17.

of globalization that connect the whole world economically. He further states that under the colonial economic relationship trade relationship was confined between the national economies at the centre and the underdeveloped economies at the periphery. But in most cases the colonies were "serving as sites for the extraction of natural resources" and also "as kept markets for the manufactures of the North Atlantic powers."[26] It is reported that, in one of the Imperial meeting in 1890s, the infamous British colonizers Cecil Rhodes eventually remarked,

> We must find new lands from which we can easily obtain raw materials and at the same time exploit the cheap labour that is available from the natives of the colonies. The colonies (will) also provide a dumping ground for the surplus of goods produced in our factories.[27]

With the intention to exploit the raw materials and cheap labour, the colonialist ruler went on exploring new lands and the Third World countries, with their abundant wealth and natural resources became the target areas for subjugation and exploitation. It may be noted that, in their mission to search for new land trade monopoly was the primary concern while territorial expansion was secondary. Simultaneously, the third world countries besides providing cheap labour and abundant raw materials for the colonial ruler had indirectly become the main source that contributed towards the growth and development of Industrial Revolution in the European countries.

Exploitation of Resources

The most significant intention of the colonialist travellers was the mission to take advantage of different resources like the raw materials, cheap labour available in the colonies and so on. With this vision in mind, the western colonial forces went searching for new land and plunder the rich natural resources and cheap labour forces of the third world countries.

Exploitation of Raw Materials

One among several policies of the colonial ruler was the policy to exploit the raw materials cheaply available in the colonies to sustain the increasing demand of the Industrial Revolution in Europe. It is reported that, by 1800s, the European colonization[28] was able to capture most of the "fertile and mineral rich areas of the Americas and the Pacific," took control and exploiting of the raw materials, thus equipping them to sustain the increasing demand of the emerging Industrial

---

[26] Hassan Rangriz, "Globalization: The Nature and its Dynamics," in *Globalization: Myth and Reality,* edited by Govind Prasad and Anil Dutta Mishra (New Delhi: Concept Publishing Company, 2004), 26.

[27] Arun, "Taming the Global Demagogue I," 424.

[28] The important colonial forces operated during the period were the British, French, Dutch, Spaniards, Portuguese, Germans and so on and in the later period it also included the Americans.

Revolution in Europe.[29] In similar line, Oommen reveals the same situation happened in Asia and Africa where raw materials were extracted from the colonies to support the demand for the same in different industrial sectors of Europe.[30] By the year 1914, many regions with abundance natural resources in different parts of the world became the principal suppliers of raw materials for industrial demand in Europe.[31] Dadabhai Naoroji as quoted by Desai argues that the construction of Indian railways by the colonisers was to help facilitate "the movement of raw materials from the interior parts of India to port towns with a view to supply them to expanding industries in England."[32]

Admittedly, to sustain the emerging needs of the Industrial Revolution, the colonial rulers even went to the extent of changing the economies of the colonies into main "supplier of cheap raw materials and capital." Besides, legal structure with regards to land, natural and mineral resources "had to be changed to suit the colonial needs."[33] This is what Loomba argues that the colonizers went to the extent of changing the economy of the colonies by "drawing them into complex relationship of their own."[34] A striking example is noticed during the eighteenth and nineteenth centuries, a particular phase when colonial rule prospered to a certain level, British rulers purposely invested in cash crop plantations like cotton and indigo, the chief essential raw materials highly required and demanded for the growth of the textile industries in Liverpool and Manchester.[35] Dutt maintains that it was the commercial policy of the British colonial rule "to make the Indian people grow raw produce only, in order to supply material for the looms and factories of Great Britain."[36] It was reported that Indian cotton was first exported to England in the year 1790, and by the year 1827, the total export of cotton from India to England was 68 million lbs. But the Indian cotton faced stiff competition

---

[29] Buckman, *Globalization: Tame it or Scrap it?*, 7-8.

[30] Oommen, "Globalisation and Structural Change...," 17.

[31] Tirthankar Roy, *The Economic History of India, 1857-1947,* 2nd ed. (New Delhi: Oxford University Press, 2006), 3.

[32] S. S. M. Desai, *Development of Indian Economic Thought* (Bombay: Himalaya Publishing House, 1981), 66. It is reported that railway line in Central India and the road between Dharwad and Karwar in Karnataka was constructed with the purpose of facilitating the transport of cotton to England. S. R. Ramaswamy, *In the Woods of Globalization* (Bangalore: Sahitya Sindhu Prakashana, 1995), 171.

[33] Fernandez, *Colonialism to Globalisation: Five Centuries after Vasco da Gama*, 41.

[34] Loomba, *Colonialism/ Post Colonialism*, 2.

[35] Jetti A. Oliver, "Recolonization, Globalization and the Role of the Church," in *Globalization: A Challenge to the Church,* edited by P. Jagadish Gandhi and George Cheriyan (Chennai: ACISCA, 1998), 4.

[36] For instance, as early as 1769, the Directors of the East India Company encouraged the manufacture of raw silk in Bengal and discouraged that of silk fabrics. See Romesh Dutt, *The Economic History of India,* vol. I, (New Delhi: Publication Division, 1989), xxii, 168.

from American cotton which is of better quality, and by the year 1827 the total export from America was 294 million lbs.[37]

However, with the occurrence of Civil War in America, export of raw cotton rose from 10,203,470 to 18,779,040 million sterling in 1863- 64 to 37,573,637 in 1865. But when peace returned to America it fell down again to 11,746,184 million in 1877.[38] Eventually, with their exploitative mind set, the colonial ruler went to the extent of shifting the market for purchasing the raw materials wherever they could achieve maximum gains and profit."It is now evident" says Abraham that "the industrial development of the west would not have been possible without the cheap raw materials and labour from the colonies."[39] Had it not been for the vision to manipulate the economic resources of the colonies, the colonial ruler could have invested either in developing the industrial sector or in improving the irrigation facilities to increase agricultural products or even to some other crop plantation badly needed for the basic need of the people.

Market Captivity

It is reported that prior to the British colonization process, India seemed to be more advanced than Britain with regards to some areas related to trade activities, superior quality of manufacture and textile product like spices,[40] textile products like clothes, etc.[41] For instance, in 1560s British merchants came to India for selling their clothes, but found their materials unmatched to the superior qualities of Indian products. Hence, they have to return back after purchasing quality Indian clothes.[42] Textile export products from India kept flooding the British markets during those periods, had threatened the very existence of the cotton textile manufacturers in England, because of their quality materials.[43] It is said that woollen manufacturers from England strongly pressurized the government to prohibit the entry of printed cotton goods from India but to import only the

---

[37] It is said that America produced the best cotton for the Lancashire looms. See Dutt, *The Economic History of India,* vol. I, 179-180.

[38] Dutt, *The Economic History of India,* vol. 2, 241-242.

[39] K. C. Abraham, "Globalization and Liberative Solidarity," in *Globalization and its Impact on Human Rights,* edited by Mathews George Chunakara (Thiruvalla: Christava Sahitya Samithy, 2000), 137.

[40] In the earlier time, British were importing different items from Asia mostly for consumption in their domestic market. Later textile goods replaced some items like spices and so on. See Avinash Jha, *Background to Globalisation,* 2000, Reprint (Mumbai: Centre for Education and Documentation, 2001), 30.

[41] Thomas Munro highly appreciated the excellent quality of Indian Shawl to that of the English in which the one he used for seven years, but found not much different in the clothes after long period of use. See Dutt, *The Economic History of India,* Vol. 1, 171, 197.

[42] For detail see, Ramaswamy, *In the Wood of Globalization*, 166-170.

[43] Besides cotton goods, India also exported raw jute, raw silk, silk piece-goods, saltpetre, indigo, rice, wheat, tea, opium, and so on. Ramaswamy, *In the Woods of Globalization,* 170.

plain white cotton clothes required for printing and dying with western styles and designs.[44] What followed was that England prohibited the entry of all important goods produced by its local factories like the Indian cotton and silk fabrics. "She would have none of these beautiful and cheap fabrics" says Dutt rather "preferred to consume her own inferior and more costly stuffs."[45] It is said that during 1695-1700, the British parliament passed a law that prohibited the entry of Indian clothes in England.[46] With the ban on the entry of Indian export products, Indian trade received a major setback and its growth and development began to diminish.

As stated earlier, the massive exploitation of raw materials from the colonies[47] at throw away prices provided a major boost to the manufacturing factories in Europe. The result is that the western countries re-exported the manufactured goods to the colonies' markets and selling them at exorbitant prices. Hence, colonies markets were transformed into 'captive market' for the finished manufactured products of the western countries.[48] To put it differently, "India should be retained as a market for British exports."[49] Abraham terms this practice as "double exploitation."[50] To make this vision possible, British imposed two main commercial policies for exploiting the market of the colonies. Firstly, the tariff policy of the government favours the British manufactured goods at the expense of Indian export products. With regards to tariff policy, the government of British India imposed prohibitive tariffs on manufactured goods exported from India to England, while the same was generally relaxed for the flow of British merchandise to India.[51]

Admittedly, while the manufactured goods imported from England were nominally charged with a paltry duty of 2 and half per cent, the export goods of India to England was imposed with heavy duties ranging up to 400% on their value.[52] Secondly, the colonies have to be connected with railways lines for the

---

[44] Jha, *Background to Globalisation,* 31.

[45] Dutt, *The Economic History of India,* vol. 1, 198.

[46] Though the sale of Indian clothes was banned during that period, Indian clothes were still reaching England through the black market and that prompted England to make a policy for destroying the textile industries of India. See Ramaswamy, *In the Woods of Globalization,* 170-171.

[47] For instance, England received raw cotton items both from America and India.

[48] Fernandez, *Colonialism to Globalisation,* 41.

[49] B. R. Tomlinson, *The Political Economy of the Raj (1914-1947): The Economics of Decolonization in India* (Cambridge: Cambridge Commonwealth Series, 1979), 27.

[50] Abraham, "Globalization and Liberative Solidarity," 138.

[51] It is reported that the Lancashire cotton manufacturers were able to pressurise and convince the "Secretary of State to force the Government of India to impose a countervailing excise on Indian cotton manufacturers when a general tariff of 5 per cent was imposed in 1894." See Tomlinson, *The Political Economy of the Raj (1914-1947),* 15, 27.

[52] Dutt, *The Economic History of India,* vol. 1, 193.

purpose for expanding the market of the British manufactured goods.[53] Naoroji as cited by Desai, maintains that besides exploiting the raw materials for the demand of Industrial Revolution in Britain, the construction of Indian railways "opened up Indian markets for British goods." It is most discouraging that large extension of railway system did not "give rise to a flood of satellite industries' as happened in other developing countries.[54] It instead helped the movements of British capitalists to penetrate deeper into the interior of India[55] as well as manufactured goods from one place to another. Tomlinson argues that the improved transport system in the form of railway projects through British investment did help to facilitate the increasing market of the "Lancashire goods" and other "British metal manufactures and engineering products."[56] Hence, development of railways helps to promote the interest of the colonial ruler in keeping the market of the colonies under captivity rather than the native.

Dutt argues that in the year 1813, Calcutta exported to London two millions sterling of cotton goods whereas by the year 1830 it had to import two millions sterling of British cotton manufactures. He further states that the import of British cotton twist which started in 1823, rose from 121,000 lbs in 1824 to 4,000,000 lbs in 1828.[57] Similarly, "export of cotton clothes drop sharply after 1800, and import of machine-made cloth and yarn expanded."[58] It is also reported that import of cotton clothes from England had increased tremendously from 8.18 lakhs yard in 1814 to a massive 5.18 crores yards in 1835.[59] Hence, due to the exploitative commercial policy of the British, a textile exporting country like India in the former years had to depend one fourth of its textile needs from England by 1850.[60] By the year 1913, India had to import more than 3000 million yards of cotton piece-goods which amounted to "one third of India's total imports and over half her imports from Britain" in the same year.[61] In such a changing situation, western manufactured goods gradually began to penetrate different regions of the country and capturing the Indian market thereby compelling the

---

[53] As stated earlier, another purpose for introducing railway projects in India, besides enhancement of trade activities was for the free movement of British troops from one place to another when crisis arise, so that peace will be prevailed in India under the British rule.

[54] See S. S. M. Desai, *Development of Indian Economic Thought,* 66.

[55] See Amiya K. Bagchi, "The Great Depression (1873-96) and the Third World: With Special Reference to India," in *India and the World Economy: 1850-1950,* edited by G. Balachandran (Delhi: Oxford University Press, 2003), 158-159.

[56] Tomlinson, *The Political Economy of the Raj, 1914-1917,* 5.

[57] Apart from cotton manufactured goods, India also imported woollen goods, copper, lead, iron, glass, and earthenware. Dutt, *The Economic History of India,* vol. 1, 193.

[58] Roy, *The Economic History of India, 1857-1947,* 61.

[59] Ramaswamy, *In the Woods of Globalization,* 171.

[60] Ramaswamy,*In the Woods of Globalization,* 171.

[61] Tomlinson, *The Political Economy of the Raj (1914-1947),* 2.

colonies to largely depend on western manufactured products. In turn, the growth of the local trade production slowly diminished.

De-Industrialisation

With the vision to monopolise trade and commerce related activities, apart from keeping the market of the colonies captive, the next step was to restrain the growth and development of the native manufactures setup. Hence, regions like South Asia that have substantial and promising manufacturing capability, need to be de-industrialised.[62] The colonial rulers attempt all possible ways and means to promote British industries at the expense of Indian industries. In other words, the commercial policy of the British colonial ruler was to make India totally dependent on the manufactured goods of the British. While Oommen traced back the beginning of de-industrialisation, to the period where the manufactured goods from British, were imposed to flood Indian markets under the patronage and support of the colonial rule,[63] Dutt asserts that it was the peculiar commercial policy of the Colonisers which is the main cause. This policy for Dutt, included forcing "Indian artisans to work in the Company's factories; commercial residents were legally vested with extensive powers over villages and communities of Indian weavers; prohibitive tariffs excluded Indian silk and cotton goods from England; English goods were admitted into India free of duty or on payment of a nominal duty"[64] and the like. All these factors contributed to the disappearance of manufacture factories in India. For instance, "it became the official policy of England to destroy the Indian textile industry and other similar industries" like iron industries in order to manipulate the industrial capabilities of India under their control.

Ramaswamy maintains that in the eighteenth century around 10,000 small furnaces were operated in different parts of India. However, the colonisers imported tonnes of iron goods from England to Indian markets ruining the industrial base and capabilities of the Indians.[65] Similarly, as early as 1769 the Director of the East India Company made an order that it is mandatory for all the silk-winders to work in Company's factories;[66] anyone who refused to comply with the order would face severe punishment. The outcome of such an order not only restricted the production of silk and cotton goods but the people of India who used to export these materials to the different market in Asia and Europe in

[62] Fernandez, *Colonialism to Globalization: Five Centuries after Vasco da Gama,* 41.

[63] Oommen, "Globalisation and Structural change...," 17.

[64] Dutt, *The Economic History of India,* vol. 1, xxiii.

[65] Ramaswamy, *In the Woods of Globalization,* 170-172.

[66] It is important to note that, prior to the establishment of the colonial rule; manufacture industries provided employment to large number of Indian population. For example, millions of women earned their livelihood as labourers in weaving related works such as spinning, dyeing, tanning and so on. See Roy, *The Economic History of India, 1857-1947,* 65.

the earlier years "began to import them in increasing quantities." Eventually, while the value of cotton imported to India in 1795 was 717 pounds, it rose to 31,943 pounds in 1805 and again increased to 108,824 pounds in 1813.[67] Admittedly, in such a situation, not only the export trade of India began to decline but also the skill and knowledge of the workers with regards to the trade began to disappear. Oommen maintains that "in the process the local arts and crafts died and along with them the traditional craftsmen and artisan."[68] It is regrettable that the native's arts and skills in the manufacture trade not only disappear but the loss was never replaced by any new industries. Dutt argues that the extinction of indigenous industries and manufactures compelled large portion of population, to shift to agriculture as the last resort.[69] Eventually, it was estimated that before importing cotton cloth from Britain around 4-5 millions of Indian population were engaged in hand spinning industry, but by the end of the nineteenth century numbers of peoples who lost their employment was more or less the same.[70] Consequently, with the vision to exploit the economic resources of the colonies, the colonisers not only destroyed the industrial capabilities of the natives, but also pushed the people to the ever increasing agricultural activities. This has not only restricted the employment opportunity of the local indigenous population but the entire economy of the colonies was relegated to the periphery.

Monopolisation of Human Labour

Simultaneous with the exploitation of raw materials from the colonies, another vital policy of the colonial rule was the monopolisation of the human labour of the colonies. Colonialist globalization witnessed the threefold flow of human labour both within the colonies itself and to other parts of the Empire in accordance with the interest of the colonial rulers. Firstly, human labours were shifted from one part of the country to other region of the country as cheap labourers, to realise the maximum profit for the companies of the colonial rulers. For instance, the cheap labour force from the tribal and Adivasi communities from Chotanagpur area of Central India, were transported to different tea gardens in Assam as low paid workers to suit the intention of the colonisers. Commenting on the prevailing living situation of the Indian labourers recruited in different tea gardens in Assam during that period, Dutt argues that they were not only working without adequate protection but also "cease to be free men and women after they have once signed their contract."[71] Secondly, cheap and unskilled labours from India were transferred

---

[67] Dutt, *The Economic History of India,* vol. 1, 168-169.

[68] Oommen, "Globalisation and Structural change," 17.

[69] Dutt, *The Economic History of India,* vol. 2, 241. See also Desai, *Development of Indian Economic Thought,* 163.

[70] Roy, *The Economic History of India, 1857-1947,* 65.

[71] Dutt, *The Economic History of India,* vol. I, xxvi, 245.

to other parts of the British Empire as per the colonial designs for more profit. Colonial era testified the flow of Indian labours to different colonies namely West Indies, Mauritius, South Africa, Burma (Myanmar), Malaysia and Fiji indentured by the British colonial rulers "to exploit the resources of these countries for the benefit of the Britain."[72] Thirdly, in other region like Africa one could witness the 'massive deportation' of cheap and unskilled human labours as slaves to be utilised in several plantation farms of the colonisers. Szentes rightly argues when he terms such practice as "depopulation of the continent, the removal of its main productive force, human manpower, and the loosening and breaking up of the cohesive forces of local societies."[73] This is what Loomba perceives as "complex relationship" between the colonisers and the colonies that resulting in the twofold flow of both human and raw materials for the interest of the colonial regime. The outcome of such an unjust affair, has not only destabilised the main productive force of the colonies, but restricted and pushed back the weak economy of the colonies to the periphery. To put it differently, human labours from the colonies were exploited to the maximum to serve the interest of the colonisers.

Economic Drain

Besides the exploitation of raw materials and that of human labour, the colonial era also exhibited severe manipulation of the financial resources of the colonies by the colonial power. Dutt maintains that prior to the coming of the East India Company, whether under the wise or the foolish ruler the "proceeds of taxation flowed back to the people and fructified their trade and industries." With its exploitative mentality, the East India Company considered India as the fertile ground for plantation in which all the proceeds will be exacted and remitted to Europe. To make its mission success, all the important employment with high position and better paid jobs were set aside for European personnel "seeking a lucrative career in the East."[74] Szentes argues that these personnel were surplus labour of the developed capitalist countries, migrated to the colonies for the mission to exploit the peripheries' economy in the form of "skilled labour, technicians, foremen and administrative personnel required by investments in the periphery, not to speak of the colonial administration's personnel and the

[72] "Indenture" here is referred to the formal agreement or contract that bind the Indian labourers to work for the colonial rulers. See James David, "Globalisation: Past, Present and Future," in *Dimensions of Globalisation,* edited by James David and John Desrochers (Bangalore: Centre for Social Action, 1998), 17.

[73] Tamas Szentes, *The Transformation of the World Economy. New Directions and New Interests,* (London: Zed Books Ltd, 1988), 40.

[74] Dutt, *The Economic History of India,* vol. I, xxv.

army."[75] In 1858 when the reign of the East India Company[76] was transferred to the British Crown, the commercial policy of the colonisers did not change. Hence, most of the economic resources of India were diverted to suit the colonial interest. Scholars term this system of exploitation as "Economic Drain."[77] In his "preface" on the Book *England's Debt to India,* Lajpat Rai says, "Whatever India has paid and still pays to England in money or in goods, without receiving an equivalent in money or in goods, is the drain."[78] Commenting on the total value of exports and imports of India during the year 1835 to 1872, Naoroji as cited by Chaudhury maintains that Britain had transferred 500 million pounds for her income.[79] He further states that while surplus from the export trades were entirely exacted by the Europeans, during the same time imports were also overpriced by 10%. Hence, between the years 1883-92 the national earnings appropriated by the European, amounted between 20 million pounds and 30 million pounds, a sum total greater than the annual averages of export surpluses of 17 million pounds in the 1870s.[80] The above amounts comprise what Naoroji considers as the economic drain, an act that has impoverished the already weak economy of India. This points to the fact how national wealth was exploited by the colonial rulers which at the same time pushed back the national economy to the periphery. Naoroji says, "This, then, is the way the treasure goes, and poor British India gets all the abuse-insult added to injury. The candle burns not only at both ends but at all parts."[81]

Referring to the exploitation of Indian wealth in terms of revenue, Dutt asserts that from 1891-92 to 1900-1, a period of ten years of Queen's rule; the entire revenue collected amounted to 647 million sterling. That is, including the proceeds from railways, irrigation works and all other sources the average

---

[75] Szentes, *The Transformation of the World Economy,* 52.

[76] Trade monopoly of the East India Company came to an end in 1833 but it was until 1858 that the reign of the Company was abolished.

[77] See Sunanda Sen, "Tributes and Transfers from Colonial India," in *India and the World Economy, 1850-1950,* edited by B. Balachandran (New Delhi: Oxford University Press, 2003), 121-123. Cf. K. N. Choudhury, "India's International Economy in the Nineteenth Century: A Historical Survey," in *India and the World Economy, 1850-1950,* edited by B. Balachandran (New Delhi: Oxford University Press, 2003), 54.

[78] Lajpat Rai, *England's Debt to India,* xxxiii, cited by Shiva Chandra Jha, *Indian Economic Thought: Mahatma Gandhi to Indira Gandhi* (New Delhi: Deep & Deep Publications, 1990), 64.

[79] The above amount according to Naoroji also includes railway loans which could not be properly regarded as drain has to be deducted. But even then, the exhaustion of national economy has been substantial. Cf. K. N. Chaudhury, "India's International Economy in the Nineteenth Century: A Historical Survey," in *India and the World Economy, 1850-1950,* edited by G. Balachandran (New Delhi: Oxford University Press, 2003), 57.

[80] Cf. Sen, Tributes and Transfers from Colonial India, 123.

[81] Dadabhai Naoroji, *Poverty and Un-British Rule in India* (London: 1901), 177, 233 as cited by Sen, Tributes and Transfers from Colonial India, 123.

collection annually is 65 million. But if one looks to the amount spend as salaries and other administrative expense in England considered as Home Charges within ten years is 159 million, with an annual average of nearly 16 million sterling. Hence, Dutt maintains that one fourth of the revenue obtained from India is annually transmitted to England, and if we add the Home Charges spent in India the total amount drain out of Indian resources will go beyond 20 million. He further states that "the richest on earth stoops to levy this annual contribution from the poorest" in which "those who earn 42 pounds per head ask for 10s per head from a nation earning 2 pounds per head."[82] Looking from the context of that time, if the amount remitted every year to England is more than 20 millions sterling, the drain of national wealth outside the country is substantial. In a Chapter on Romesh Dutt (1848-1909), Desai argues that there is nothing to be proud of, with regards to the increase of revenues in India, which extracted the source of livelihood of the poor people for "it does not mean increase of prosperity but only an oppressive increasing taxation on the food supply of the poor."[83] Such a situation led to the impoverishment of the Indian economy to a large extent. The outcome of this practice not only diminishes the trade potentiality of the colonies but it also did not benefit trade activities of England either. For if bilateral trade between countries is to flourish both the partner countries should be able to contribute substantially in the exchange process if not on equal terms. To put it differently, trade activities could have definitely improved and developed to a certain extent if India is wealthy and prosperous. Dutt argues that such practice besides being unable to contribute to the growth of the British trade activities, at the same time "drains the life blood of India in a continuous ceaseless flow." As he rightly puts it,

> For when taxes are raised and spent in a country, the money circulates among the people, fructifies trade, industries and agriculture, and in one shape and another reaches the mass of the people. But when the taxes raised in a country are remitted out of it, the money is lost to the country forever; it does not stimulate her trades or industries, or reach the people in any form.[84]

It may be noted; the annual total Land Revenue collected in the year 1900-1 was 17 and half millions sterling, while the total expenditure on Home Charges which include interest on Indian debt, railways, civil and military charges, etc.

---

[82] Romesh Dutt, *The Economic History of India,* vol. 2 (New Delhi: Publication Division, 1989), x -xi.

[83] Desai, *Development of Indian Economic Thought,* 168. Dutt also reveals how heavy taxes were levied on the peasantries, the farmers, as well as to the small clothes manufacturers. As he says, "The miserable clothing of the miserable Indian labourer, earning less than 2½ day was taxed by a jealous government." See Dutt, *The Economic History of India,* vol. 2, vii.

[84] Dutt, *The Economic History of India,* vol. 2, xi.

in the same year was almost equally at 17 million sterling.[85] Moreover, between 1877 and 1900, the Public Debt had increased from 139 million to 224 million sterling.[86] The said amounts speak of how national wealth was remitted out from the country to serve the interest of the colonial rulers for achieving maximum profit.

Nevertheless, for the promoter of colonial interest, all the expense spent during this period was actually meant for the development of India. Participating in the debate on the drain of national wealth, McLane divided the Home Charges into two categories- the economic payments and the political payments. Economic payments for him comprise interest on railways, permanent debt, stores and so on. It amounted to 10,386, 989 pounds in the year 1901-02 which he says "any independent country might take in the early stages of industrial development and railway building." Political payments include military, administrative, civil charges, pensions, etc. This comes to 6,981,666 pounds in the same year, which "India could not presumably have paid as an independent country."[87] Hence, such amount spent during that period benefitted India to a large extent in the form of good administration she received from Britain. Commenting on how India benefited from the service rendered by England, Strachey as cited by McLane opines,

> The payments made by India are the result and the evidence of the benefits which she derives from her connection with England. In place of constant anarchy, bloodshed, and rapine, we have given her peace, order, and justice; and if our Government were to cease, all the miseries which she have been saved would inevitably and instantly return. Her payments in England are nothing more than the return for the foreign capital in its broadest sense which is invested in India, including as capital not only money, but all the advantages which have to be paid for such as the intelligence, strength, and energy on which good administration and commercial prosperity depend.[88]

On the other, nationalist writers like Dutt argues that the great mistake in this case is that, though the entire expenditure on the Public Debt is met on the revenue extracted in India,[89] it appears as if the "whole Indian Debt represents

---

[85] Dutt, *The Economic History of India,* vol. 2, xi.

[86] The increase in the amount was mainly due to the construction of railways and the Afghan war. See Dutt, *The Economic History of India,* vol. 2, xii.

[87] Cf. John McLane, "The Drain of Wealth and Indian Nationalism at the Turn of the Century," in *India and the World Economy:1850-1950,* edited by G. Balachandran (New Delhi: Oxford University Press, 2003), 76.

[88] See John Strachey, *India: Its Administration and Progress,* 1903, 195, cited by John McLane, The Drain of Wealth and Indian Nationalism at the Turn of the Century, 70-71.

[89] Dutt, *The Economic History of India,* vol. 2, 243. See also B. R. Tomlinson, "Britain and the Indian Currency Crisis, 1930-2," in *India and the World Economy, 1850-1950* (New Delhi: Oxford University Press, 2003), 248.

British Capital" that have "sunk in the development of India."[90] For them, the intention behind construction of railways in India is not to bring development to the Indian people, but to exploit the resources of India. Wacha as cited by McLane argues that while some railways were constructed to help the military, other were built at the request of British manufacturers with the intention to exploit the Indian markets, "thereby hastening the de-industrialization of India and converting her into a producers of raw materials only."[91] Furthermore, construction of railways in India during that period asserts Dutt is "beyond the pressing need of India and her resources."[92] Dutt further goes on to say that if both Britain and India benefitted in establishing the British Empire in India, the entire amount of expense should be contributed by both the nations. It is grave injustice that India alone should bear the entire cost of the expenditure, incurred in England right from the salary of top official to that of the fourth grade employees.[93] Moreover, besides the expenditure on the service operated by the Government of British Empire in India, it may be pointed out that maximum numbers of the employees are Europeans.[94] As most of the important jobs were reserved for the Europeans, it is impossible for the educated Indian to obtain employment in different capacities of the British Government in India. Naoroji termed the omission of Indians in the employment set up as "moral drain." For him, the recruitment of Europeans in different job opportunities where qualified and competent Indians are available is nothing more than "stunting the capabilities and intelligence of the Indians."[95] Dutt argues that annually the amounts of ten millions pound were remitted to the British Government as salaries of the Europeans officers in India. The outcome of such situation was "a continuous Economic Drain from India, which has increased in volume with the lapse of years, and has impoverished an industrious, peaceful, and once prosperous nation."[96]

The problem of Economic Drain was not only addressed by the nationalist writers but even the sincere English writers of the early years understood the

---

[90] Dutt, *The Economic History of India,* vol. 2, xi.

[91] D. E. Wacha, *Indian Railway Finance,* 1912, cited by John McLane, The Drain of Wealth at the Turn of the Century, 78.

[92] Dutt, *The Economic History of India,* vol. 2, xii.

[93] Dutt even suggests that India will have to pay for the administration in India and Great Britain will pay the Home Charges. See Dutt, *The Economic History of India*, vol. 2, xi-xii, 271.

[94] As stated earlier, most of the jobs available in the different departments of the Government of British India were reserved for the surplus employees from Europe who were seeking lucrative job in the East.

[95] Dadabhai Naoroji, *Poverty and Un-British Rule,* (1901), 56-58, cited by McLane, The Drain Wealth and Indian Nationalism at the Turn of the Century. 84. It may be noted that McLane cited from Naoroji, to response to his work on 'moral drain.'

[96] Dutt, *The Economic History of India,* vol. 1, xxvi, 271-272.

gravity and severity of such a practice. Elsewhere realising the intensity of the practice, in 1838 Martin once wrote,

> For half a century we have gone on draining from two to three and sometimes to four million pounds sterling a year from India, which has been remitted to Great Britain to meet the deficiencies of commercial speculations, to pay the interest of debts, to support the home establishment, and to invest on England's soil the accumulated wealth of those whose lives have been spent in Hindustan. I do not think it possible for human ingenuity to avert entirely the evil effects of a continued drain of three or four million pounds a year from a distant country like India, and which is never returned to it in any shape.[97]

Similarly, commenting on the seriousness of the drain of wealth from India to the Great Britain, Shore rightly comments, "The Halcyon days of India are over; she has been drained of a large proportion of the wealth she once possessed; and her energies have been cramped by a sordid system of misrule to which the interest of millions have been sacrificed for the benefit of the few."[98]

The above discussion exhibits the massive drain of national wealth from India to Great Britain. As stated earlier, with the vision to achieve maximum profit, the colonial ruler went to a certain extent to exploit the wealth and economic resources of the colonies. Their coming to India was not meant to develop the country but to loot and plunder its rich resources. For instance, constructions of railways was not meant to help improve the living conditions of the people, rather to open ways and means for monopolisation of trade activities and extension of other related commercial business. Hence, what followed from this, is the massive remittance of the national wealth to Great Britain that has not only impoverished the economy of India but relegated it to the periphery. Oommen rightly argues when he says that with the departure of the colonial rulers "what they left behind were impoverished economies."[99]

Colonisation of the Mind

Apart from exploitation of colonies' resources, another facet of colonisation that left deep mark in the psyche of the Third World people is the colonisation of the mind. With the exploitative mentality 'to loot and plunder,' the colonisers were able to conquer not only territories and economies of the colonies but the mind of

---

[97] Montgomery Martin, *Eastern India* (London, 1838), Introduction to vols. i and iii as cited by Dutt, *The Economic History of India,* vol. I, 272.

[98] The honourable John Shore was one of the best of the Bengal administrators in the 1830s and he wrote his own observation in his thoughtful work on India. F. J. Shore, *Notes on Indian Affairs,* vol. ii (London: 1837), 28, as cited by Dutt, *The Economic History of India,* vol. I, 273.

[99] Oommen, Globalisation and Structural Change: Historicity and Implications, 17.

the Third World people.[100] Said's work *Orientalism* describe the bipolarisation of the world persisting between the Occidental and the Oriental or the Self and the Other. Orientalism opines Said can be referred as "corporate institution for dealing with the Orient." He further elaborates it to mean "making statements about it, authorizing views of it, describing it, by teaching it, settling it, ruling over it: in short, Orientalism as a Western style for dominating, restructuring, and having authority over the Orient."[101] This notion that divides the world between the Self and the Other, has twofold effects; it describes the dominating attitude of the West on the Third World people and the acceptance of the latter on what has been imposed and labelled against them. In other words, it indicates how the West were able and succeed in its mission to subjugate not only the wealth and territories of the Third World people but also their mentality making them feeling inferior and lesser than the West. Fanon reveals how the colonial 'masters' succeeded in making the colonized person not only "to admit the inferiority of his[sic] culture" but also "in the last extreme, the confused and imperfect character of his[sic] own biological structure." This attitude of systematic negation of the other person imprinted a confused state about their own personhood to ask "In reality, who am I?" He further state that, "The defensive attitudes created by this violent bringing together of the colonized man [sic] and the colonial system form themselves into a structure which then reveals the colonized personality."[102] Looking from the postcolonial perspective on the relationship between the colonisers and the colonised and vice versa, Nandy as cited by Brar terms this relationship as that of an 'intimate enemy.' In this relationship" says Brar "much before the enemy is recognised as enemy, its values, beliefs and norms are internalised by the victims, so that the more the victims opposes the enemy, the more its acts like the enemy itself..."[103] Consequently, colonial imperialism left a deep imprint in the psyche of the Third World people. The mind is therefore colonized in European thought, worldview, outlook, cultures, history, method of education and the like. With the impact of western education imparted by the colonial machinery, people of the Third World are trained to adopt everything western at the expense of the local indigenous way of living. To put in Patrick's words, "Indian in blood and colour, but English in taste, in opinions, in morals and in intellect."[104] People from the Third World, began to perceive things from the western perspective, ignoring

---

[100] Ambrose Pinto, "Vasco da Gama: Culture, Colonization and Globalization" in *Social Action* 49/3 (July- September, 2000): iv.

[101] Said, *Orientalism,* 3.

[102] Fanon, *The Wretched of the Earth,* 190, 200.

[103] Bhupinder Brar, "Theorising Transitions: Post-Coloniality, Post-Socialism and the Coming Age of Globalization," in *Interpreting Globalization: Perspectives in International Relations,* edited by Rajen Harshe, (Jaipur: Rawat Publications, 2004), 103.

[104] Patrick, Empowering "Modernity and Ambivalent Globalization," 35.

and looking down at the traditional values as inferior, primitive, devoid of good things, backward, underdeveloped and so on.[105] Accordingly, "everything western has come to be hailed as modern and progressive."[106] For instance, anything western contains the best quality and need to be achieved. People are ready to obtain whatever things produced from the west, ignoring the traditional stuffs even they are of the same or better quality. That is, the minds of the natives were prepared for a global economic phenomenon.

The above discussion reveals that with the vision to "loot and plunder" the colonial rulers went on to exploit the colonies and accumulated enormous amount of wealth. This has resulted in the growth of Industrial Revolution in several European countries dominated by the British. As a result the Britishers became richer and "London overtook Amsterdam as the dominant financial centre of the world."[107] The domination of Britain on the world capital market continued till the First World War.[108]

The Post War Globalization

The second phase of globalization started with the end of the Second World War.[109] This phase testified the emerging growth of the two super powers attempting to overtake each other in the aftermath of the Second World War. These two blocks are the capitalist democracies based on market economies[110] led by the USA and the socialist one party system which developed into command economies under

---

[105] I. Wati Longchar, "The Need for Doing Tribal Theology," in *An Exploration of Tribal Theology,* edited by I. Wati Longchar, (Jorhat: Tribal Study Centre, 1997), 9.

[106] M. A. Oommen, "Globalization and Decolonization: The Contemporary Challenges," in *Globalization: A Challenge to the Church,* edited by P. Jegadish Gandhi and George Cherian (Chennai: Association of Christian Institutes for Social Concern in Asia, 1998), 16.

[107] It may be noted that at the beginning of the nineteenth century, Amsterdam became the most significant and influential global capital centre in the world followed by London. However with the massive wealth Britain could accumulate through the Industrial Revolution, London replaces Amsterdam as the Global financial capital of the world. Britain then could invest heavily in machinery, factories and other infrastructure like new railways, roads and ports, etc. See Buckman, *Globalization: Tame it and Scrap it?,* 19.

[108] The First World War popularly known as the Great War was taken place from 1914 till 1918 had greatly affected the World economy.

[109] The Second World War that took place in 1939-1945 is often considered as one of the major periods in the economic transition of the entire world.

[110] Market based economies has its roots from Adam Smith who belief that if economies is left to the market, wealth would be distributed equally among the citizens. See Adam Smith, *The Wealth of Nations,* Vol. I, Reprinted (London: J. M. Dent and Sons LTD, 1960), 15-56. See also Dogan Gocmen, *The Adam Smith Problem: Human Nature and Society in the Theory of Moral Sentiments and The Wealth of the Nations* (London: Tauris Academic Studies, 2007), 97. See also Victor V. Claar & Robin J. Klay, *Economics in Christian Perspective: Theory, Policy and Life Choices* (Illinois: IVP Academic, 2007), 47.

the leadership of USSR.[111] In the case of the former, Oommen maintains "market played a central role in economic development" where as for the latter the state has taken the central role "as the agency which plans economic development and inspires social transformation."[112] In the post war scenario, the global international trade activities and relationship differed greatly from that of the previous era. The colonial globalization exhibited the process of unjust transfer and shifting of natural and human resources from the colonies to the metropolitan or developed countries. This resulted in the gradual transformation of the Western countries as the epicentre of international trade activities and simultaneously relegated the colonies to the periphery. But in the Post war globalization, one could see the emergence of two great powers competing against each other, striving to monopolise trade and commerce related activities or to gain control over the entire world affairs.

The Hegemonic Position of the United States

As stated earlier, colonial era portrays the dominating leadership of Britain in the global arena that continued till the Great war. By virtue of its technological supremacy and industrial advancement coupled with improved financial institutions, Britain maintained its ultimate position as the global leader. However, despite the fact that London retained its position as the leading financial centre till 1914 based on Gold Standard,[113] the pivotal role of Britain as the world leader gradually began to decline.[114] With the outbreak of the Great War, the hegemonic position of Britain as the international power had critically deteriorated. Consequently, it indicated the demise of the dominating position of Britain in the international market and trade related activities which simultaneously validated

---

[111] Prasad Mathew, "Free India Today: In the Context of Globalization," *National Council of Churches Review* CXVIII/8 (September, 1998): 581,

[112] Oommen argues that both the system have their own drawback. While the free market ideology of the capitalist group failed to protect the interest of the weak, the poor and the marginalised, in the socialist economies inspirations and motivations for individuals and groups is lacking. See Oommen, "Globalization and Structural Change," 17.

[113] Notably, world trade was carried on during that period by the establishment of a complex multinational payment based on Gold Standard. 'Gold Standard' is generally referred to the system of converting national currency into gold. This does not mean that the country has to pay their entire business transaction in terms of gold, but it means that long term international imbalances could be settled with gold. See Buckman, *Globalization: Tame it or Scrap it?*, 20.

[114] The diminishing of British power seemed mainly due to the emerging industrial and financial strength of USA, coupled with the gradual growth and development of other countries like Germany, France and Japan. See Stephen Gill and David Law, *The Global Political Economy* (Baltimore: The John Hopkin University Press, 1989), 130.

the place of the United States as the emerging leader with regard to the global trade and other world affairs.[115]

The occurrence of the Great Depression[116] and later the outbreak of the World War II, had severely obstructed the flow of capital and trade affairs. Many countries view this crisis as great hindrance that could bring devastated effect not only for their respective countries but also on the growth and development of the entire global trade and capital. As such, it raised serious doubt and major concern from several nations with regards to the prospect of world economy. On the other side, it offers favourable opportunity and ample scope to the US to exert its influence as the emerging major leader concerning trade and other global affairs. With the impact of Great Depression still fresh in the mind of several nations, coupled with the effect of the world war where the economic position of many countries terribly shattered,[117] serious effort to rebuilding the war torn countries need to be taken into consideration. Many nations were looking forward for the rebuilding and reconstruction of not only their damaged infrastructure within their countries but even their shattered economies in the aftermath of the war. Hence, most countries had to rely on the US for financial assistance operated through the Marshall aid,[118] in order to reconstruct their shattered nations. To state differently, the US remained the key figure in the process of rebuilding the Post War capitalist order. Gill and Law rightly comment when they say,

> In 1945, the United States found itself in a uniquely strong position, much surpassing that of Britain at the height of its power in the nineteenth century. With half the world's GNP, over three quarters of the world reserves and a technological lead in most manufacturing industries, the United States was well placed to induce cooperation in other countries. All of the former

[115] In the Pre war period, global economy relied mainly on British capital whereas in the Post World War global economic dependence shifted to US capital.

[116] Great Depression is understood as a time of crisis in the capitalist world which started with the collapse of US stock-market in October 1929. It is important to note that in the Post World War II the world economy no longer rely on British capital but on the US capital. It is said that the withdrawal of US capital led to the eruption of Great Depression. "Depression" says Jha "describes a state of economy when people remain unemployed while the factories remain closed persistently. There are no new investments either since profits are not expected." For detail see Jha, *Background to Globalisation,* 51-52. See also Buckman, *Globalization: Tame it or Scrap it?,* 21-22.

[117] The World War II not like the First World War had seriously affected the flow of global trade. Its impact to the world in general and Europe in particular was devastating. Generally, there were "acute shortages that resulted in high inflation and low economic growth, which depressed the world trade." See Buckman, *Globalization: Tame it or Scrap it?,* 10.

[118] The Marshall aid was named after George Marshall, the then US's secretary of state. It was generally granted financial assistance to West European countries in 1947-52. See Brojendra Nath Banerjee, *Globalisation: Rough and Risky Road* (New Delhi: New Age International (P) Limited, Publishers, 1998), 390.

imperial powers were devastated by the war and needed American support for their post-war reconstruction efforts.[119]

With its strong position in different sphere related to global affairs the US attempted all efforts to exert its dominion and influence the entire globe. Jha maintains that the Second World War offered "an opportunity for the US elite to carve out a plan of world dominance with the rest of the developed world as junior partner."[120] Interestingly, at the initiative of the US as the hegemonic leader, 44 countries[121] assembled at Bretton Woods[122] in July, 1944. The main purpose of this conference was to "erect a new framework for the post-war global economy – a stable, corporate international monetary system, which would promote national sovereignty and prevent future financial crisis."[123] In other words, it means an attempt to find ways and means how to reorganise and reconstruct the world economy in the aftermath of the war. However, critics observe that the main intention behind the conference was to promote the interest of the developed country especially the US.[124] Gilpin maintains that the the US' efforts for the creation of a stable and prosperous international economy stemmed from the belief that they "had a vital stake in a prosperous economy." Hence, the establishment of the Bretton Woods system indicated the shift in the American thinking[125] to enlarge the horizon of its dominion and expansion of its trade activities in the global sphere. Some of the important issues developed in the conference were:

Firstly, with the pressure and influence mounted from the US side, the conference seriously considered the issue of decolonisation as the inalienable right of the colonies for self determination and self rule. It may be noted that in the process of decolonisation, Britain with numerous colonies worldwide had

---

[119] Many countries like Germany, Japan and other countries of Western Europe severely affected by the war, had to rely on America for financial assistance in their effort to reconstruct their country as well as national economy. For the purpose of helping them, Marshal Aid happens to be the main source of support. However, communist countries opted not to accept such aid and preferred to stay away from the US's embrace and financial assistance. See Gill, *The Global Political Economy,* 140.

[120] Jha, *Background to Globalization,* 55.

[121] Actually, out of the total 55 countries in the world that time, these 44 countries were in the club of non-communist countries under the leadership of the US. The communist countries choose to dissociate themselves from the domain of the US. See Jha, *Background to Globalisation,* 56. See also, Cf. Rangriz, "Globalization: The Nature and its Dynamics," 26-27.

[122] Bretton Woods is a small resort village in New Hampshire, US.

[123] See Ellwood as cited by Arun, "Taming the Global Demagogue I," 427.

[124] This view stem from the fact that though many countries attended the conference with the exception of Britain and France, it was the US who took major decision. Countries from the Third World were just the keen observer having no voice in the entire process of discussion. See Rangritz, Globalization: The Nature and its Dynamics, 27.

[125] Robert Gilpin, *The Challenge of Global Capitalism: The World Economy in the 21st Century,* (Princeton: Princeton University Press, 2000), 55.

maximum to lose, whereas the US with less colonies has nothing much to lose. Hence, US pressure for decolonisation stemmed from its hidden agenda of "better access to markets, minerals, materials and foreign investment opportunities" for its firms in several former colonial empire of Britain and France spreading in the different region of the Third World.[126] In other words, with its superior position in the aftermath of the War, the US had already developed well thought plan for expanding the horizon of global dominance and monopolising the world trade and world economy to serve its own interest. It is reported that in the early 1950s the US export trade was at its peak where "a full third of all the world's exports came out of the country."[127]

Secondly, the conference resolved to work out on the establishment of some basic norms and institutions that would promote exchange rate, stability of post war international money order and trade liberalisation. As many among the countries faced severe economic and financial crisis, the conference felt the necessity of framing some rules and guidelines necessary for the smooth functioning of the post war liberal monetary order. A prominent economist John Maynard Keynes from British standpoint suggested creating "a specific international currency (the bancor) which would eventually become the main reserve currency."[128] But his suggestion was bluntly rejected by the powerful America. The US with its technical lead and economic influence obtained the better advantage than the others.[129] The agreement was resolved to establish "a system in which there will be free movement of goods between countries with the American dollar as the international currency."[130]

For the reconstruction and recovery of the shattered global economy, two apex bodies were established in 1945 to man the financial irregularities that could occur in the world arena. These financial institutions are the International Monetary Fund (IMF) and the World Bank (WB) and later another financial institution-General Agreement on Tariff and Trade (GATT) was established with their headquarter at US.[131] The role of the IMF was expected to provide emergency

---

[126] Gill, *The Global Political Economy,* 142.

[127] Buckman, *Globalization: Tame it or Scrap it,* 10.

[128] Jha, *Background to Globalisation,* 56.

[129] Szentes observes that in the post war scenario, with the economies of many European countries were shattered, most of the qualified scholars immigrated to the US thereby indirectly help that country gained the most advantage than the others. See Szentes, *The Transformation of the World Economy,* 60. With better salaries and facilities coupled with wider recognition for research work many scientists and engineers the so called 'cream of the society' not only from Europe but from different countries of the Third World immigrated to USA that has further strengthened its position in comparison to other countries. See Jha, *Background to Globalisation,* 63-64.

[130] Arun, "Taming the Global Demagogue I," 427.

[131] The British had high hope that the headquarter of these financial institutions be based at London and even stake claim for the same. However, their desire was out rightly rejected by the

loans to countries facing sudden financial crisis in order to promote financial stability. The WB on the other hand, was supposed to grant long term loans for reconstruction of the economy of the countries badly ruined by the Second World War. The GATT was expected to "set rules to remove competitive trade barriers and global trade policies."[132] With the establishment of these institutions, national economies as well as the free movement of trade were expected to make good progress in the near future. Ramaswamy critically observes that from their inception "these institutions were champions of world market."[133] With its intention of economic exploitation and market expansion the US could exert its influence thereby designed the role of these institutions in such a way that they could serve its own interest. Notably, prominent economist Keynes cautiously made strong remark that permitting the free movement of "commodities and capital might pave the way for gradual instability and inequalities."[134] However, with its financial supremacy and economic influence, the US paid no attention to his opinion but rather went ahead to implement its proposed agenda. Accordingly, the policies and the functioning role of all these institutions in the post war scenario were largely influenced by the dominating leadership of the US.[135] Even in the latter years these institutions proved to be more beneficial in serving the interest of the few rich and affluent nations.

In sum, the compelling situation of the early part of the twentieth century had considerably weakened the position of Britain as the global leader, which at the same time validated the emergence of the US as the dominating global power in the world arena. With the outbreak of the World War II and its aftermath, the US with its strong economic and financially sound background, moving far ahead of others thereby became the favourable replacement as the hegemonic leader that could reconstruct and support the weak economy of the world.

Secondly, the atmosphere at the Bretton Woods reveals that though many countries attended the conference it was the US who could influence the entire proceedings and decision making process. The other countries like those from the

---

US on the ground that US deposited maximum share of capital investment. It is said that US Chief negotiator, Henry Dexter White stated that the US had contributed much more money than any country, so the head office of these institutions should be based at any place selected by the US. See Buckman, *Globalization: Tame it or Scrap it,* 24. (Detail discussion on these institutions will be done in the latter section).

[132] Arun, "Taming the Global Demagogue I," 428.

[133] Ramaswamy, *In the Woods of Globalization,* 51.

[134] Ramaswamy, *In the Wood of Globalization,* 51.

[135] The earlier activities of the IMF in the earlier part of the post war era was limited due to the financial supremacy of the Us, which could provided enormous financial assistance to many Western European countries on its own. On the other hand, WB during the same period granted loans mainly to the Western European countries. It was only in the 1950s that the WB began to provide financial support to less developed countries.

Third world were unable to make their presence felt. In other words, these poor countries from the Third World not only seemed to be voiceless in raising their concerns but also indirectly submitted themselves to the hegemonic leadership of the US.

Thirdly, the agreement to choose the US dollar as the international currency and the establishment of the three financial bodies with the headquarters at US, had strengthened the role of the US as the undisputable leader, to be in charge of rebuilding the stability of the world economic order. In other words it provided an ample scope for the US to expand its trade activities and have dominion of the entire affairs of the world.

The Hegemonic Position of the USSR

The post war scenario reveals that besides the growing domination of the US, over the 44 countries attended at the Bretton Woods conference, the USSR appear to be another global super power emerging in the global arena. The communist countries mostly from Eastern Europe out-rightly withdrew themselves and stayed away from the Bretton Woods conference. Under the leadership of the USSR they preferred building up and reconstructing their economies outside the ambit of US controlling circle.[136] There are two main reasons[137] that the USSR Block declined to accept the US embrace.

Firstly, it appeared that like the USA, the USSR also possessed large bulk reserve of natural resources that favoured "the capacity for relative self sufficiency." Hence, there is ample scope for the USSR to emerge and developed into well balanced super power in the global context. Secondly, the USSR entirely rejected the acceptance of the Marshal Aid on the ground that the US had hidden designed agenda not precisely for economic empowerment of Europe but mainly to hinder the growth of Communism and restrict the growth of USSR as the major super power, so that it can expand its market without any obstruction. To put it differently, the acceptance of this kind of financial assistance facilitated a welcome gesture for the US economic expansion to capture the entire communist region of Eastern Europe embraced by the USSR. It may be noted that The USSR hegemony consolidated its controlling power over a large part of Europe containing around 8% of world population under its domination.[138]

It the late 1940s, it was plainly clear that USSR had intensified its development programme competing with its chief rival-the US. Furthermore,

---

[136] Jha, *Background to Globalization,* 58.

[137] See, Gilpin, *The Challenges of Global Capitalism,* 58. See also Gill, *The Global Political Economy,* 140-141.

[138] Joseph Stiglitz, *Globalization and its Discontent* (New Delhi: Penguin Book India (P) Ltd, 2002), 133.

the Soviet Union[139] had traditionally obtained absolute commanding control and ownership rights, in its co-producing ventures with other countries with better equipment, for maximum penetration not only to Eastern European countries, but also to several less developed and Third World countries.[140] By the year 1970, Soviet Union economy was qualitatively transformed and USSR became not only the second largest economy in the global sphere but had accomplished in elevating "a military form of industrialization" compatible with that of USA.[141] Nevertheless, with its supreme power and dominance, Eastern European countries became more and more dependent on Soviet leadership for the improvement and development of their economies.[142] From trade related activities to other forms of economic transformation, the continuing support and assistance of the mighty Soviet became unavoidable for these countries.

To sum up, though USSR dominating control governed only 8% of the global population, with its advance transformed economy and networking trading companies worldwide, its trade activities and export capability was not limited within the parameters of the Eastern Europe but penetrated and covered to several countries of the south. This revealed the craving ambition for enlarging the sphere of its domination to different parts of the globe.

Secondly, the voluntarily unwillingness of the Soviet Block to come under the embrace of US, indicated the appearance of not one but two super power emerging and competing for global domination. For sometimes, it has restrained the single manipulation of the US in the overall affairs of the world. In short, it expressed the phase of bipolarization[143] of the globe where the two major super powers attempted all efforts for the expansion and intensification of their supremacy.

The Cold War Context

The post war era testified the emergence of two super powers-the USA and the USSR not only in terms of economic advancement but also in the competitive strength of military power and arms race in the so called 'cold war' period.[144]

139 Soviet Union and USSR are used here interchangeably as they both refer to the same.

140 Soviet Union had its own transnational enterprises by the year 1970, operating a network of Banks and trading companies worldwide, essentially developed for promoting Soviet exports of energy, raw materials and arms to the less developed countries and the Third World. Cf. Gill, *The Global Political Economy,* 306-321.

141 Gill, *The Global Political Economy,* 302.

142 It is clear that USSR attempt all efforts to keep these countries under its dominance making them more dependent on its assistance and support in many areas of developmental programmes.

143 Stalin terms this division of the world economy as the "two system" i.e. the command or communist economies and the capitalist economies of the free world. See Gilpin, *The Challenge of Global Capitalism,* 52.

144 This area will not be discussed here because it is beyond the intention of the research work.

After the USSR block isolated itself away from the US domain, the US block proceeded forward to garner all possibilities to confront and contain the progress of the communist regime. The US moved ahead against all odds to promote its keen interest of getting better "access to markets, materials and foreign investment opportunities" in the Third World countries especially in Asia, Africa and Pacific.[145] On the other hand, in the late 1940s the USSR deepened its development enterprises in different areas. Its economic performances have considerably improved, its trade expansion and export network system were competent enough to penetrate different corners of the globe, and the Soviet regime had been strengthened to a larger extent. The two super powers venture out to capture all opportunities of containing the world economy and international trade. Eventually, the two super powers involved themselves to granting aids to different countries especially those from the south in their pursuit for global dominance.[146] The less developed countries as well as the Third World countries have no other option but to associate and attach themselves with either of the block. To intensify its territorial dominance the US and its allies pursued their "political campaign and economic blockade against the communist countries" which prompted to the formation of CMEA (Council for Mutual Economic Assistance) in 1949 under Soviet leadership[147] with the purpose of strengthening economic cooperation, interdependence in trade relationship and other related matters. This aggressive competition[148] between the two rivals block came to an end with the collapse of Berlin wall in 1989 and the disintegration of USSR in 1991,[149] with the subsequent overthrow of the communist regime in Eastern European countries. With the collapse of the Communist Regime the US became the only super power left to man the economic activities and other affairs in the global arena.

In sum, the Post World War context testified the transition of the world affairs from the colonialist globalization to the stage of bipolarization of the world. Accordingly, whereas the colonialist globalization exposed the massive gross exploitation of the economic resources of the colonies by the colonial master, the Post World War globalization portrayed the fierce competition of the two super powers attempting to capture and dominate the entire affairs of the world. In other words, while trade exploitation was the hallmark of the first

---

[145] Gill, *The Global Political Economy*, 141.

[146] Gill, *The Global Political Economy*, 142.

[147] The members of the CMEA were East Germany, Czechoslovakia, Bulgaria, Poland, Romania, Hungary, Cuba, Mongolia, Vietnam and the USSR. See Gill, *The Global Political Economy*, 312-313.

[148] The aggressive competition of the two super powers not only in the economic sphere but also in arms race had threatened to jeopardize the stability and security of the entire globe in the so called 'cold war' became the major concern of every nation.

[149] Gilpin, *The Challenge of Global Capitalism*, 16.

phase of globalization, military supremacy and trade expansion was the distinctive feature of the second phase.[150] The less developed countries and the Third World countries had no other choice but to rely on the much needed support frequently provided by these two world powers. Rangritz considers the Post World War globalization as the "intensive and deepening phase of globalization"[151] where every country tend to seek for better economic and political cooperation though it was largely under the leadership of the two super blocks. The intensive phase of globalization in the aftermath of the war largely intensified and strengthened the interdependence among various countries of the world.[152] The formation of trade organizations for better trade relationship like the CMEA and others are the glaring examples where trade related activities and economic interdependence became vitally deepened.

The Present Day Globalization

The collapse of the Berlin Wall and the disintegration of the Soviet Union turned out to be an important milestone in the history and the process of globalization. The two important events situated the world into another phase or period in the history of globalization-The Present Day Globalization. Accordingly, the two episodes not only sealed the end of bipolarization of the world but facilitated forward movement in the process of globalization in the contemporary present day world. In fact, it is often referred as the "triumph of capitalism over communism"[153] which "open out a wide range of expansion for western business"[154] or place the entire globe "under new hegemon once again."[155] These series of events had rapidly hastened the pace of the entire process of globalization that has immensely altered different aspects of the global scenario. In its report entitled, "The world has changed" the UNDP Human Development Report has therefore said,

> Over the past decade dramatic events have changed the global political order-the end of the Cold War unleashed a wave of global political integration. The fall of the Berlin Wall in 1989 and the end of the cold war removed political

---

[150] The two super powers attempt all possible effort to gain control not only for trade expansion but for military superiority and arm races competition at a break-neck speed with no amount of limitation.

[151] Hassan Rangritz, *Human Resource in the Globalized World* (Delhi: Abhijeet Publications, 2004), 141.

[152] Razu, "Towards an Understanding of the Phenomenon...," 6.

[153] Arun Kumar Singh, "Globalization, Sovereignty and Human Rights," in *Globalization: Myth and Reality,* edited by Govind Prasad and Anil Dutta Mishra (New Delhi: Concept Publishing Company, 2004), 134.

[154] Jha, *Background to Globalization,* 112.

[155] Amar Gunnam, "Globalization, culture and Development: An Economist's Perspective," in *Globalization and the Changing Scenario of Culture Interaction,* edited by N. Joy Kumar Singh (Imphal: Centre for Manipur Studies, 2007), 4-5.

> and economic barrier-bringing more that 400 million people in Eastern Europe and Commonwealth of Independent States (CIS) and almost 1.3 billion people in China and the Viet Nam into the world of global contacts and communications. Ideas and information began to flow freely as countries lifted censorship, travel restrictions and prohibitions on political parties and civil society organizations. And foreign investment poured into China, Viet Nam, Poland and Russian Federation- as did Mc Donald's, Hollywood Movies and CNN real-time global news.[156]

The above quotation reveals how the current phase of globalization is different from the previous phase. The bipolarization of the globe in the previous phase set a series of barriers between the two blocks that restricted the smooth flowing of economic and trade related activities. In other words, flow of trade and commerce were almost confined within one block as number of restrictions and prohibitions were implemented between the arch rivals. But the case is different in the current phase of globalization. Driven by the ideologies of neo-liberalism,[157] the proponents of globalization positively see the current stage of globalization as a process of integration in the sphere of cultures, values, mindsets, international monetary order, trades and global economic activities and so on. For them, globalization besides uniting the globe into one single unit, is the only process that could make the world prosperous. Coupled with the support of the media and technological advancement, the forces of globalization have penetrated every nook and corner of the world. There is no area or section of population that remain isolated and stay outside the process of the forces of globalization.

For the promoter of globalization, this trend has positively contributed to the betterment and benefit of the entire globe, whether western or non western, the First or the Third World. Thomas Friedman terms this current phase of

---

[156] Singh, "Globalization, Sovereignty and Human Rights," 134.

[157] Neo-liberal economics is a branch of neo-classical economics process by the agencies of globalization. The term "neoliberalism" is developed by the most prominent figure Milton Friedman and the Chicago School. It is reported that both neo-classical economics and neo-liberal economics focus mostly on "markets, economic growth in GDP terms, considered only business corporation, consumer is the king, support export oriented production at the expense of local or regional self-reliance, etc." See Peter Suderbaum, *Understanding Sustainable Economics: Towards Pluralism in Economics* (London: Earthscan, 2008), 125. See also Rabecca Todd Peters, *In Search of the Good Life: The Ethics of Globalization* (New York: Continuum International Publishing Group, 2004), 39-41. Modern neo-classical economics is the product of the eighteen century British utilitarian philosophy and the ideology of the Enlightenment thinking. "Neo-classical economists view humans as individuals isolated from one another, their main occupations being production, consumption and distribution of goods." See Robert R. Gotfried, *Economics, Ecology and the Roots of Western Faith: Perspective from the Garden,* (Maryland: Rowman & Littlefield Publishers, Inc, 1995), 4. See also Andrew Henley, "Work and Unemployment," in *Christianity and the Culture of Economics,* edited by Donald A. Hay and Alan Kreider (Cardiff: University of Wales Press, 2001), 118.

globalization as the Globalization 3.0.[158] Globalization 3.0 for him has its unique and distinct feature. It is different from the previous phase of globalization not in the sense that it has shrunk the world into a tiny size or global village; rather it has empowered "the individuals to collaborate and compete globally." So, all the cities of the Third World, like Bangalore and others could reap the same benefit as that of New York and others in the western affluent countries. This is what he means when he says that the world is flat.

Conversely, the critics maintain that the current phase of globalization has brought more harm than good to the present day world. It has not only polarized the world between the rich affluent countries and the poor countries, the developed and the under developed, the First and the Third world, but within the country, citizens are divided between the privileged few and the marginalised class, the rich and the poor or to put it in the Marxist's terms "the haves and the haves-not." The present day globalization is therefore nothing but the replication of colonialism. Whereas the colonial era testified the exploitation of the colonies economic resources by the colonial master, in the current phase of globalization in the name of free trade the Third World countries are being exploited by the so called G7 countries in general and the USA in particular through number of corporate agencies like the MNCs/TNCs.[159] The process of globalization has therefore equipped the few rich affluent countries taking the centre place at the core of economic affairs leaving the Third World countries at the bottom line of economic prosperity and development, and within the countries the population are divided between the few rich privilege groups and the majority poor and marginalised group.

De-territorialisation

Motivated by the ideologies of neo-liberalism, the forces of globalization today have infringed and encroached upon every terrain of the globe irrespective of territorial and geographical boundaries or region. In the wake of economic liberalization and free trade expansion, General Agreement on Tariffs and Trade (GATT) which later converted into World Trade Organization (WTO) framed rules and regulations to remove trade barriers and hurdles that may obstruct the free flow of trade and other trade related activities. In other words, all controls and measures that constitute barriers to the entry of the import goods should be done away with.[160] With this, international movement of trades, services, technology

[158] Thomas Friedman, *The World is Flat* (London: Penguins Books, 2006), 9-11.

[159] In the colonial era, the western imperialist powers like Britain and other European countries not only exploited the economies of the colonies but also took major course of decision with regards to the future of the colonies. Today most of the global economic decision were generally taken by the G7 countries- the US,UK, Canada, Germany, France, Italy and Japan in general and mostly the US in particular.

[160] Biplab Dasgupta, *Globalization* (New Delhi: Sage Publications, 2005), 20-21.

and goods could easily move either from country to another or one corner of the globe to another without much interruption. To put differently, this can be obtained only if "national boundaries cease to inhibit the flow of goods and capital. That means the control over this flow by nation states should be reduced and even eliminated."[161] Scholars term these practices as 'de-territorialisation.'[162] De-territorialisation here is understood that by virtues of trade liberalization and free transferring and relocating goods and technology to any destination deem preferable, geographical territorial boundaries are easily erased and deleted. The forces of globalization like the Multi National Companies (MNCs) and Trans National Companies (TNCs), supported by the Bretton Woods Institutions (BWIs) generally derecognised and overstepped national or territorial boundaries, when resolving any decisions with regard to trade expansion, when and where to invest, what to produce, where to market their products and so on. With the vision on maximum proceeds, their main focus is chiefly on global profit achievement and their interest cannot be limited or confined within the border of one specific national territory. Mishra maintains that, with new technological developments financial transactions are capable of moving easily across multiple national borders at a great speed unmindful of the rules and regulations of the sovereign nation states. To put it differently, globalized economy became increasingly non-territorial.[163]

Diminishing Role of the State

With the purpose of generating maximum profit through trade liberalization, the current process of economic globalization not only de-recognised and ignored geographical national state boundaries but even the role generally played by sovereign state has been adversely affected. With the increasing influence of the MNCs/TNCs in the economic affairs, the function of the state usually taking the centre stage in all aspect of societal and public governance, is now forcefully relegated and push to the back seat in the entire economic dealings. The state is not in a position to decide what to produce, how much to produce and where to market all the products, for all these decisions rest with the MNCs/TNCs. In the name of free trade and economic liberalization, the corporate agencies went to the extent of monopolising the entire economic policies of different countries which in turn resulted to the "erosion of national sovereignty and narrowed the

---

[161] John B. Cobb Jr., *The Earthist Challenge to Economism: A Theological Critique of the World Bank* (New York: St. Martin's Press INC, 1999), 28.

[162] Arun, "Taming the Global Demagogue I," 428-429.

[163] Pramod Mishra, "Globalization poses new challenges to South-South Solidarity," in *Globalization: Myth and Reality*, edited by Govind Prasad and Anil Dutta Mishra (New Delhi: Concept Publishing Company, 2004), 373.

ability of the government...."[164] With the "policy-making capacity" of the state eroded, the state is left with no option but to adopt the policies prepared and approved by the corporate agencies.[165] In such a situation, the role of the state is diminished and the entire "economic management should be left to the market." It is the market that determines and dominates the economy both at the national and global level. It is believed that "any intervention by the state-in the form of controls, subsidies, selective protection, etc. would distort price" henceforth will obstruct the free flow of trade, thus restraining the growth of economy.[166] That is, any interference of the state in the development and expansion of the free market economy is viewed with suspicion. Hence, the capabilities of the state in taking major decision with regards to the present day economic activities are being curtailed and narrowed down. This idea stems from the belief that the sovereign nation state is an outdated institution with limited capabilities to fairly deal with ample and diverse increasing needs of the contemporary complex global scenario. In other words, the market system is far better than the state in satisfying the craving desire of the people. Participating in the debate Medury defines the market theory in the following,

> ...the government is less efficient than the markets over providing services to individuals. The market firms due to competition and profit motive make a more effective use of given resources than the government agencies, which lacks similar incentives. Also individuals can choose the services they want from the market, subject to their income, whereas the government provision of services leaves them with little or no choice.[167]

This indicated the fact that in the current liberalisation of economic system, most of the function of the sovereign state as the institution that look after different needs and welfare of the citizens is being restricted by the so called 'market system.' With the increasing number of the countries from the South[168] opted for trade liberalization on one hand and major economic policies and decisions being taken by the forces of globalization on the other, the position of the national state in the entire economic affairs is gradually deteriorated. Mishra rightly commented when he says that "the capacity of sovereign nation-states to protect their domestic economies and citizens is diminished by the global economy." That is, the wealth

---

[164] Mishra, Globalization: Concept and Nature, 6. Cf. Prakash Sarangi, "Role of the State in an Era of Globalization," in *Interpreting Globalization- Perspectives in International Relations,* edited by Rajen Harshe (New Delhi: Rawat Publications, 2004), 200-201.

[165] Martin Khor, *Rethinking Globalization: Critical Issues and Policy Choices* (London: Zed Book, 2001), 11.

[166] Dasgupta, *Globalization,* 21.

[167] Medury, Changing Complexion of Public Administration in the Globalized era, 53.

[168] The term 'south' is another word use for the Third World countries or less developed countries, so also the term 'North' is referred to the developed and First World countries.

of the state is being created not within the jurisdiction of the national government but "at the global level, outside the control of national governments and domestic public policies."[169] In the contemporary present day global economic policy reforms, sovereign state is compelled to discard many of its roles in the economic sphere in favour of the market. Rangritz states that the emergence of 'supra national' borderless global economy, that embraced and integrated numerous local economies in a single global system, has not only altered the economic set up at the national level, but is converting national government into municipalities.[170] If the role of the state in economic affairs is rapidly eroding, that means the state now has only limited functions for the welfare of its citizens. To put it differently, in the changing scenario of economic reform both at the national and global level, the decreasing and declining function of the state does not create anything healthier for the good and the welfare of the citizens.

Growing Disparities

It cannot be denied that the current phase of globalization provided several facilities and opportunities for the enhancement and smooth development of life. The recent advancement of technology and communication system has indeed made human life easier and faster in many aspects.[171] These progress and development provided by the process of globalization proved to be beneficial and helpful in different capacities. However, detail analytical studies on this progress and achievement from the perspective of the Third World one may "look at this process with apprehension."[172] Side by side with the progress and splendour offered by the process of globalization one could witness poverty and scarcity that envelope the other side of society. This growing disparities and contradictions demonstrated during the current stage of globalization compel many to critically assess and scrutinize this process with suspicion. Commenting on the unequal proceeds offered by the present phase of globalization, Khor maintains that globalization is "a very uneven process, with unequal distribution of benefits and losses."[173] That is there are only few countries that enjoy maximum benefits in the expansion of trade and economy, whereas many countries could share only minimal and scanty profits.

The *Human Development Report* revealed that there are wide and growing disparities between the countries of the North and those of the South and the rich and the poor both between and within the countries, since the acceleration

---

[169] Mishra, "Globalization Poses New Challenges…," 373.

[170] Rangritz, *Human Resources in the Globalized World,* 136.

[171] Shimreingam Shimray, "Globalization Process and Tribal People," in *Tribal Women and Globalization,* edited by Narola Imchen (Women Studies Center, 2008), 6.

[172] Abraham, "Globalization and Liberative Solidarity," 139.

[173] Khor, *Rethinking Globalization,* 16.

and intensity of economic globalization has taken place. The Report of 1992 estimated that 20% of the world's population in the developed countries could possess 82.7% of the entire global income, but the 20% people living in poorest countries could hardly share the benefits of 1.4% from the world's income.[174] Again, in the Report of 1995 it is revealed that the North with its population of just about one-fifth in the world "consumes 70% of the world's energy, 75% of its metals, 85% of its wood and 60% of its food."[175] Furthermore, with the globalization of economics in the last few decades the 20% of the worlds poor have not benefit much in the process. For instance, their share in the world trade is only 1%, and in the financial market is merely 0.2%. Simultaneously, though more than three-fourth of the world's population live in the developing countries, but they could enjoy the benefit of only 16% of the world's income whereas the riches 20% could possessed around 85% of the global income.[176] Similarly, the *Human Development Report 1999* of the United Nations Development Fund (UNDP), released in London on 12th July 1999 confirmed the growing disparities between the rich and the poor both between and within the countries in the process of globalization. It is reported that in 1960 the 20% of the world's people in the rich countries possessed 30 times the income than the poorest 20%, whereas by the year 1997 it has increased to 74 times higher. At the same time, the wealth of the 200 richest peoples in the world is more than the combined income of 41% of the world population. So also, the top fifth of the world's people in the richest countries enjoy 82% of the increasing export trade and 68% of foreign direct investment whereas the bottom fifth barely more than 1%.[177] The above facts and figures testify the widening gap that has arisen not only between the countries of the North and the South but most significantly the growing disparities between the rich and the poor both between and within the countries of the world. It is indeed an encouraging scene with regards the success story of some of the developing countries like Brazil, India and China in the contemporary global economic reform today.

By the year 2005, these countries "produce more than 50% of the world's total output in terms of purchasing power parity" and their contribution to the export trade rose from 20% in 1970 to 42% in 2005 with the promising growth

---

[174] Khor, *Rethinking Globalization,* 17.

[175] M. P. Joseph, "Denying Life: Theological Meaning of Globalization," *National Council of Churches Review* CXVI/7 (August, 1996): 456.

[176] M. P. Joseph, "Denying Life: Theological Meaning of Globalization," 461. See also M. A. Oomen, "More a Moral Crisis than a Development Dilemma: An Examination of Some Issues of Globalization," in *Globalization and SAP: Trends & Impact- An Overview,* edited by Ajit Muricken (Mumbai: Vikas Adhyayan Kendra, 1997), 89.

[177] Vimal Tirimana, "Moral Theological Implications of Globalization from a Third World Perspective," *Vidyajyoti Journal of Theological Reflection* 65/4 (April 2001): 288-289. Cf. Joseph E. Stiglitz, *Making Globalization Work* (London: Penguins Books, 2006), 57.

of 6% during those three consecutive years in comparison to the growth of only 2.4% in the developed countries.[178] Similarly, the growth rate of China in the 1980s was averaged at 9.3% annually and the growth rate increased to 10.1% in 1990-96 per annum.[179] As far as the Gross Domestic Product (GDP) growth rate is concerned, economic progress of some of Third World countries like India look promising, whereas the social sector such as poverty, health, education, etc. tells a different story.[180] It is reported that China had 26.1 million people living in absolute poverty and it is also possess 18% of the world's poor[181] where as India is a home of 40% of the world's poor and 260 millions of its people are living Below Poverty Line (BPL).[182] Admittedly, while the GDP of these countries reflects the promising growth rate, it nevertheless reflects "the distribution of the benefits of economic growth among various sections of the population."[183] Hence, though globalization through the development and advancement of technological facilities provided diverse opportunity to the present day generation of the population it has nevertheless created increasing disparities not only between the developed and developing countries but within the countries the gap between the rich and the poor keep on widening.

Global Competition

One of the important features of economic globalization is the practice of competition. Simultaneous with the promotion of market economy or trade liberalization economic globalization also endorses fierce competition between countries and within countries. This trend is explicitly noticed not only in the area of international trade and commerce but in every aspect of global arena. The critics of globalization points out that in the market of global competition it is always the powerful and competent competitors who have the capability to capture the entire facilities and opportunities at the expense of the weak and incompetent contenders. For instance, this type of globalization has equipped the G7 countries to exploit all ways and means to keep the Third World countries under their domination.[184] To put it differently, the forces of globalization in spite of their

---

[178] P. Maria Joseph Christie, "Conflict of Values in the Globalized Era," *SNC Journal of Intercultural Philosophy* 10 (August, 2006): 3.

[179] Paul Hirst and Grahame Thompson, *Globalization in Question* (Cambridge: Polity Press, 1999), 155.

[180] This area will be discussed in the next Chapter.

[181] Xavier Jeyaraj, "An SEZs with a Difference," *Social Action* 58/3 (July-September, 2008): 273.

[182] Christie, "Conflict of Values in the Globalised Era," 10.

[183] Preeti Sampat, *Economic Globalization Today: Resource Book* (Bangalore: Books for Change, 2003), 10.

[184] Geetha Menon, "New Colonialism and the Campaign against Foreign Debt: A Woman's Perspective," in *Globalization,* edited by P. Jagadish Gandhi and George Cherian (Chennai:

promise for free trade and equal opportunities to participate in the economic affairs, have instead created huge inequalities both between and within countries. According to the *Human Development Report 1996,* it is clear that within three decades of that period only 15 countries experience high growth. At the same time, while 89 countries their conditions were worse than ten years earlier, among the developing categories, a number of 70 countries their average income were less than in the 1960s and 1970s.[185] That is, the idea of global competitiveness based on unequal terms of trade helps to facilitate only the rich and affluent countries whereas the poor and less developed countries are not only being left out in the process but they are excluded and pushed down to the periphery. Simultaneously, within the country the poor and marginalized communities are being neglected and unmatched in the race for competition. To put it in Darwin's word "the survival of the fittest." This trend will leave the poor countries of the Third World and the poor sections within countries more impoverished and marginalized. Patrick maintains that the Third World countries like India will find their "interests and development plans sidelined or marginalized" in the global competition whereas the poorer sections within the countries found themselves "being left out in the race for competition."[186]

Promote Individualism

Besides encouraging the spirit of competition, the process of globalization has generally offered ample scope and opportunities with considerable prospect for individual to enhance themselves and freely move forward in the arena of economic prosperity. Patrick observes that "globalization has accentuated the process of individuation."[187] The process of individuation for him means that the contemporary globalised world offered a space for the individual with unlimited possibilities to freely promote himself/herself. These opportunities are presented equally to all sections of population including the poor and marginalized communities like the Dalits and the tribals.[188] That is, with diverse job and employment opportunities on one hand and unlimited scope for self reliance and self sufficiency on the other, there is great advantage for the individuals to attain better future. It cannot be denied that the globalized era offered different opportunities and wider scope for every individual person to strive forward in the economic arena. But the ground realities prove otherwise.

Association of Christian Institutes for Social Concern in Asia, 1998), 21.

[185] Khor, *Rethinking Globalization,* 17.

[186] Gnana Patrick, "Empowering Modernity and Ambivalent Globalization" *Jeevardhara* XXXIV/99 (January, 2004): 49-50.

[187] Patrick, "Empowering Modernity...," 43.

[188] For him, even the Dalits who have some assets to invest can obtain high qualifications and high post in the market of employment which is the positive contribution of the process of globalization.

Analysing this view from the perspective of the poor and the marginalized, it can be said that this trend of individuation has immensely facilitated the selected few and the rich affluent sections, the so called elites[189] that has emerged in every societies to exploit and captured every possibilities and facilities of better life. To put it differently, all the economic facilities offered by the globalised era are beyond the means and the reach of the maximum number of population who are socially and economically marginalised. The selected few could employ all possible means to extract the economic facilities for their own benefit and economic betterment at the expense of other individual belong to the socially and economically poor and marginalised sections. In this case, there is no tendency of sharing the economic resources rather a person intends to accumulate to the maximum without any limitation. So, the more the person able to acquire and possess for himself and herself, the more their dignity and position in the society will be recognized and noticed. As such, poor individuals belonging to the less income and marginalised groups find themselves relegated to the margin of economic and social life. This trend is quite contrary to the practice of collective and communitarian way of living that present in many traditional societies of the Third World like the tribals and others. In the traditional societies like the tribals the individual or one single accumulation of wealth by any person is not encouraged or approved rather the ethics of sharing and partaking together the economic resources prevails. Thanzauva rightly puts it when he argue, "The sense of community is so strong that they give priority to their community in their thinking and actions rather than to their individual personal needs."[190]

The Process of Industrial Development

Another important feature in the process of the present phase of globalization is the process of industrial development. Most of the former colonies in the Third World are rich in natural and mineral resources. Since their independence many former colonies trail the path of development by opting for the process of industrialization. Joseph sees this venture of former colonies for industrialization as the "context of the emergence of new form of globalization." He further elaborates this view when he says that "the ideology behind their industrialization venture was informed by their determination to participate in the global process, but with

---

[189] It may be noted that in the present day globalised era even among the marginalized communities of the Third World there emerged the elite section of population but their percentage is insignificant and invisible, but the maximum numbers of the population are poor. These so called elites of the society mostly exploited all the economic facilities and opportunities offered in today society.

[190] K. Thanzauva, *Theology of Community: Tribal Theology in the Making* (Bangalore: Asian Trading Corporations, 2004), 143.

independence."[191] Since the former colonies are newly independent nation, most of their ventures were the imitation of the path already trod by the advanced western industrial nations. For the developed countries this commitment by the former colonies suits their interest to impose their dominating tendencies over the latter. Joseph terms the process of globalization as the venture "to thwart the striving of former colonial nations to seek an independent course of development."[192]

Though the colonial rulers no longer possess political control over the former colonies, the remnant of colonialism is revealed through the forces of the so called neo-colonial power evolving in the form of corporate agencies like the MNCs/TNCs. Hence, the advocates of globalization or corporate agencies attempted all efforts to insist for the rapid growth and development of diverse forms of industries in different regions of the globe, especially in the former colonies or the Third World countries where resource materials are easily available for the same, unmindful of the threat and deteriorating consequences done to the environment. For obtaining unlimited profit in short period the corporate giants like the MNCs/TNCs do not hesitate to invest crores of rupees for any project provided the area is potentially viable to generate huge amount of profit. To this situation, the 1980s testify the investment by the corporate giants to the development of industrial areas in the forms of Special Economic Zones (SEZs) particularly in the Third World countries. SEZs define Raj and Roy as the "regions within a country that have economic laws more liberal than the country's typical economic laws. They are usually used by developing countries to attract investment and serve as enclaves of economic freedom for business located within them."[193] That is, SEZs offered numerous legal relaxation and economic advantage to the investor in addition to concessional rate on the propose land for industrial development most often at the expense of the local inhabitants like the small farmers and others.[194]

For greater economic advantage, the advocates of globalization could venture all available efforts to make their vision realized. In due course the worst sufferers are the local citizens of the proposed area, not to mention about the environmental disaster that such project will cause to the ecological surrounding, once the commencement of the so called developmental activities began to take place. It is plainly said that the process of globalization with the aim for maximum economic exploitation could transform particular space into towns or small towns

---

[191] M. P. Joseph, "Foreword- Towards a theological critique of globalization," in *Globalization and Human Solidarity*, by Tissa Balasuriya (Thiruvalla: Christava Sahitya Samithi, 2000), 8.

[192] Joseph, "Towards a theological critique of globalization," 8.

[193] SEZs were first developed in China in the 1980s and later spread to different countries like Brazil, India, Iran, Jordan, Kazakhstan, Pakistan, the Philippines, Polami, Russia, Ukraine, etc. See J. Felix Raj and Samrat Roy, "SEZs: Broken Promise in West Bengal," *Social Action* 58/3 (July-September, 2008): 283.

[194] Arun Kumar, "Socio-economic Aspects of SEZs," *Social Action* 58/3 (July-September, 2008): 235.

into big cities within short period. A clear example is the case of Shenzhen of China which developed from a small town of merely less than 20,000 inhabitants in 1977, to a large city with high industrial inputs exceeding 20 billion dollars by the year 1998. Looking on the growth rate of the city within short period is highly commendable and encouraging, whereas the other side of a story depicts that Shenzhen is suffering from rapid environmental disaster, with alarming increase of crime rate, exploitation of labour especially migrant labourers, etc.[195] Hence, driven by the ideologies of neo-liberals, the process of globalization under the controlling power of the so called neo-colonial power, continuously plundered and raped the earth resources. Such venture caused alarming destruction not only to different sections of local population like the small farmers but also resulted to severe damage to the entire natural ecological surrounding in which the quality of life is under threat.

Worldview of Globalization

Globalization is no more a theoretical concept but a practical reality that has permeated the entire dimensions of human way of living. Whether human society agrees to its principles or differs to its ideologies, it is here and remains in our midst against all odds. It has come with striking worldview and great assurance of better future that has extensively influenced the world especially the under developed and developing countries of the Third World.

The Question of Modernity

One of the most important worldview of globalization is its endorsement on the process of modernity. It is said that globalization promotes the flow of modernity. 'Modernity' for Joshi would simply understood as "industrialization," or to be more accurately viewed as "technology, inventions, mass production and innovations."[196] In other words, it can be defined as progress and development where the world can be transformed into modern progressive world. With this vision in mind, the advocates of globalization make all efforts to explore different ways and means to remodel the entire globe into a well developed modern world. For them, if the world is to be progressively developed there is no alternative (TINA) except to follow the path of globalization. The TINA factor plays the vital role here and is forcefully imposed to the Third World countries, as they make efforts to transform their weak economies into well modern developed economies. To achieve this end, the earth natural resources are being exploited and subjugated at an alarming rate in the process of building a new modern and progressive world. The outcome of such a practice is that, the sustainability of

---

[195] Jeyaraj, "An SEZs with a Difference," 272-273.

[196] S. L. Doshi, *Modernity, Postmodernity and Neo-Sociological Theories* (Jaipur: Rawat Publications, 2006), 15.

the earth natural resources in general, and the Third World economic resources in particular are being ignored and sidelines. To put it differently, the process of transformation of the globe into a modern and developed world is carried on at the expense of the Third World countries.

World as Economic Entity

It may be noted that the rationale behind derecognizing nation-state boundaries on one hand and the integration of global economy on the other, is to accumulate and obtain maximum profit in a short span of time. The ideology of 'maximum exploitation' or 'to loot and plunder' is nothing but the replication of the vision very much prevalent in the colonial mindset. Under such circumstances, the world is reduced "to the status of economic territories to be exploited by transnational capital, without any accountability or obligation to the nation-state."[197] The concept of the world as 'sustainable entity' is replaced by 'economic entity,' with the capability to serve the desire and interest of human beings. For the neo-colonial forces the entire earth and its resources, are designed to fulfill the wants and desire of the present day generation. Here, the earth is perceived as separate entity, detach from other entity like God and human, a notion well understood and preserved in the traditional understanding since the early period. Nature is therefore understood as a self enclosed structure, having no value and worth in itself, separated from both God and human.[198] The value of the earth and its resources is being ignored and looked down. For the advocates of globalization the value of the earth is considered only in its capability to generate maximum profit. Quoted from the modernization school of thought,[199] Joseph sees the distance of civilization from nature. That is, anything associated or linked to nature is often looked down as primitive, whereas those things opposite to nature are considered as modern. Such perception not only disrobed nature of its spirituality, but generally deemed it as a spiritless flesh to be subjugated to the maximum.[200] The same idea of subjugating the earth resources that stem from the colonial principle is being carried on by the advocates of globalization, to loot the earth resources for the benefit of the corporate agencies. It is argued that the so called neo-colonial or capitalist mindset to accumulate maximum profit at short period without considering the needs of the future generations is the root cause of ecological disaster and ecological imbalances especially in the context of the Third World. Earth resources are being exploited and misused to meet the

[197] Ajit Muricken, "Globalization-Overview," in *Dimension of Globalization,* edited by James David and John Desrochers (Bangalore: Centre for Social Action, 1998), 10.

[198] H. Paul Santmire, *The Trivial of Nature* (Philadelphia: Fortress Press, 1985), 133.

[199] The two schools of thought here is referred to the Sociological School of Marion Levi and Economic School of W. W. Rostow.

[200] Joseph, "Towards a theological critique of globalization," 15.

increasing demand of consumerism.[201] With the pressure of global competition, there is a tendency to exploit the earth at alarming rate without considering for the consequences.

Human Beings

The forces of globalization view human beings as economic beings detached from the soil and nature around, whom globalization can exploit to the maximum for unlimited profits. Human beings and human life itself has lost its value in the process of globalization. Joseph has rightly pointed out how the forces of globalization venture out to exploit human beings, in different ways and different capacities.[202] Firstly, human beings have been easily converted as consumer beings by homogenizing of their taste. Secondly, bodies of women are not only converted as commodities in the consumerist market, but their entire being became the puppets at the interest of the market.[203] Thirdly, people and their creative capabilities are being "reduced to objects for production and growth." Fourthly, in the process of globalization the few rich and affluent section "play snake and ladder with the lives of millions of poor and marginalised" in which the quality of life is being distorted at the behest of the expanding consumerist market. That is, to promote the free flow and expansion of market the quality of human life has not only been ignored but converted into commodities to be exploited. It may be noted that today, countries with large population like China and India[204] comprising 40% of the world populations, which till the last few decades, have been negatively considered as expendable and hindrance to development, are now positively perceived not only for their large labour force but also as the potential market capable of generating maximum profit as well.[205] Since human beings are considered as economic beings, the forces of globalization often referred to human beings in terms of figures or percentage, not as essential beings having their respective value and worth. In most of the annual economic reports and fiscal reports with regards to the progress and economic activities, human beings

---

[201] Longchar, "Globalization and Indigenous People," 190.

[202] Joseph, "Towards a theological critique of globalization," 9-14.

[203] It is important to note that in the process of exploiting the beings of human life to the maximum, women's body are being continuously misused by the corporate agencies through different advertisement for promoting diverse brand of their products right from a small item like bathing soap to other higher profit making business like car and so on without taking into consideration with regards to the dignity and respect of their beings.

[204] Today, China the most populous country in the world is home to more than 1.3 billion of the world's people and India the second largest country in terms of population has more than 1.04 billion people.

[205] Christie, "Conflict of Values in the Globalized era," 3-4.

are calculated in terms of data, numbers, and percentage.[206] With this system of calculation being followed, the value or quality of human persons as essential beings is undermined.

God

How does globalization understand the role of God? What is the place ascribing to God in the entire affairs of global economic liberalization? The critics of globalization expound that 'money' and 'market' replace God in the process of globalization. Joseph terms this new religion as "money theism"[207] where money takes the central stage in the overall affairs of the globe. Divinization of money resulted in the rapid subjugation of both humans and nature for wealth accumulation. The intrinsic relationship that binds together God-Human-Nature largely upheld in the early period, is now fractured and shattered. The role of God as the creator of everything that exists in this planet, is being ignored and sideline in the process of globalization.

Market-The Answer

Another important world view of globalization, is their portrayal of market as the criterion to help solving the fate of economic problems. Hence, market occupies the central core in the sphere of development activities. As stated earlier, with the role of the state in different sphere of activities is being curtailed, the entire economic affair in the global arena is left to the market. Market is perceived as the only answer that could solve all the problems of economic development.[208] So, all human resources and natural resources are directed towards the market. Driven by the neo-liberal ideologies, the proponents of globalization believe that it is none other than the market that could transform and develop the economy of the Third World countries. To promote the growth of market, the corporate giants invested millions of capital through advertisement for marketing their manufactured products. Nevertheless, looking from the postcolonial context, this market factor that lays great emphasis on the flow of international trade, is the agenda appropriately designed to serve the interest of the developed countries, through the agencies of the corporate bodies. That is, market is perceived not only as the channel for the expansion of their economic domination, but most importantly to help them dump and promote their finished products for maximum

---

[206] J. V. Raghavendra Rao, "Globalization, Dalits and Social Justice," in *Globalization and Social Justice,* edited by P. G. Jogdand, Prashant P. Bansode and N. G. Meshram (Jaipur: Rawat Publications, 2008), 181-183.

[207] Money Theism for him has its own concept of the divine, priesthood, rites, liturgies, missionaries, theologians, modern Churches and cathedrals. See Joseph, "Towards a theological critique of globalization," 11.

[208] Martin Khor, *Globalization & The Crisis of Sustainable Development,* 2nd ed. (Penang: Third World Network, [2001], 2002), 18-19.See also Muricken, "Globalization-Overview," 12.

profit. The entire plan was to exploit the economy of the former colonies or the Third World countries. As a result, they did not take into consideration the basic needs of the local indigenous population.

Admittedly, market has really equipped the corporate companies to accumulate unlimited wealth but it could not help the poor getting rid of their economic problems. Market has instead hampered their aspiration for improving their economic status and left the people more impoverished and marginalised than ever before. In the context of free market system the only people who counts are those "who have goods to sell and money to buy."[209] That is, the so called market economies not only ignored the poorer sections of the society, but also denied their rightful share in the entire economic affairs. In the words of Oommen, this market economic system "excludes the so-called poor, or less endowed, the property less or anyone without exchange entitlements from participating in the market."[210] Hence, the entire market set up, is suitably designed to satisfy the aspiration of the rich and affluent section of population, while excluding those who have no share to participate in the market.

The Issue of Economic Integration

It may be noted that for the advocates of globalization "global economic integration represents a vehicle for significant welfare enhancement."[211] It indicates a big anticipation that globalization has the capability to raise the living standard of the entire world population. For them, global economic integration involves twofold economic advantages. On one hand, it will help the free flow of goods, services, capital and even labour forces between countries of the world, while on the other; it will remove the barrier for direct foreign investment to improve the economies of the Third World countries. This will not only help facilitate the Third World countries to get access to international market for exporting their goods, but simultaneously lead to the enhancement of the economic condition of different countries. By integrating their economies with the global economic system, the Third World countries have nothing to lose but everything to gain from the free market system.[212] Furthermore, integrating their economies with the North is the process of modernizing their economies. So, joining the global arena indicates free from economic isolation that could enable them to share the benefit of global economic achievement.[213] With such great expectation, the promoters

[209] Longchar, "Globalization and Indigenous People," 187.

[210] M. A. Oommen, "Globalization and Working Towards Alternative Development Paradigms," in *Globalization and its Impact on Human Rights*, edited by Mathew George Chunakara (Thiruvalla: Christava Sahitya Samithy, 2000), 54.

[211] Rangritz, *Human Resources in the Globalized World*, 183.

[212] Stiglitz, *Making Globalization Work*, 4.

[213] Vikas Adhyayan Kendra, "The Myth of Globalization," in *Dimensions of Globalization*, edited by James David and John Desrachers (Bangalore: Centre for Social Action, 1998), 42.

of globalization succeed not only to pressure the Third World countries to open their economies, but also to impose their own pattern of trade, removing trade restrictions, while at the same time exploiting the entire economic resources of the Third World without no limitation. Looking from the postcolonial context, the vision of economic integration is the ideology firmly rooted in the colonial dogma, serving as the impelling force to the colonizers to monopolize the economies of the colonies.[214] To state differently, the process of global economic integration is nothing but the sinister design of the forces of globalization to capture and loot the economic resources of the former colonies.

Agencies of Globalization

Economic globalization today operates through different agencies that help facilitate its smooth running to different nook and corner of the globe. These agencies serve as the main channel for the promotion and expansion of its jurisdiction. There are no areas or regions that remain outside the realm of its domination. In the colonial times, domination and subjugation of the colonies was directly carried on by the colonial regime. But in the present day context, globalization expanded its jurisdiction through different agencies or the so called neo colonial forces. These agencies of globalization can be discussed as under.

The Bretton Woods Twin

As mentioned in the previous section, the historic conference at Bretton Woods held in July, 1944 resulted to the establishment of the two important institutions popularly known as the Bretton Woods twin, to man the smooth running of the entire global economy in order to save the world from the recurrence of any untoward financial crisis. With the Great Depression that shook and rattled the economy of the entire western world fresh in the memory of the participating countries, the conference resolved to make all efforts finding ways and means to prevent the occurrence of any such crisis in the near future. To maintain the stability of the global economy, the conference resolved to promote liberalization of the global trade and economy that could enable the free movement of goods and services to different parts of the globe. It was with these purposes in mind that the two agencies- the International Monetary Fund (IMF) and the World Bank (WB) came into existence.

The International Monetary Fund (IMF)

As stated earlier, the occurrence of Great Depression in 1930s, coupled with the outbreak of World War II had greatly affected the growth and development of world's economy in general and the stability of the national economies in particular. To prevent the recurring of another economic crisis as well as to

[214] Kendra, "The Myth of Globalization," 42.

maintain the stability of the global economy the IMF was established in 1945. The primary function of the IMF was to provide emergency financial assistance to any countries facing sudden economic crisis so as to maintain economic stability. That is, the IMF is expected to help facilitate "short-term stabilization of countries experiencing balance of payment difficulties."[215] It was hope that the IMF will be able to prevent the outbreak of another global depression.[216] With the deteriorated economy of many western countries, the role of IMF in maintaining the stability of world economy became the utmost important. However, the earlier activities of IMF were partially restrained due to the financial supremacy and influence of the US, which could provide enormous financial assistance to several countries through its Marshal plan in the post-war reconstruction era.[217] By 1970s the economic position of several countries had been considerably improved, financial aids of the IMF were no more necessary for most of the western countries.[218] Since then, the functions of the IMF not only confined within the location of the Third World countries, but its importance in providing financial assistance to these countries grown extensively.

Admittedly, the IMF not only shifted its function from the First World to the Third World but even its role as the World body diminishes.[219] This is what Dasgupta terms as "a radical deviation from the original concept behind the creation of the IMF."[220] In other words, though the operation of the IMF was shifted to the poor countries of the Third World, most of its function were influenced and controlled by the developed countries or the G7. Hence, Third World countries are once again experience the process of re-colonization in the forms of domination of advance countries upon their weak economies. It is said that with the influence of the developed countries, the IMF will not provide

---

[215] Buckman, *Globalization: Tame it or Scrap it?,* 51.

[216] Stiglitz, *Globalization and its Discontents,* 12.

[217] It may be noted that in the post-war reconstruction US with its high resources could extend its financial assistance to many countries particularly the European countries that were severely devastated during the outbreak of the World War II. See Gill, *The Global Political Economy,* 143.

[218] The last time where the developed countries took IMF loan was in 1975 when Italy and UK asked for financial assistance from the IMF. In the following years, the developed countries found other way of funding their financial deficits from the global capital market. Dasgupta, *Globalization,* 34.

[219] Though, the IMF functions within the realm of the less developed countries, since the major chunk of financial contribution to the IMF in those era was funded by the rich countries, it is the rich countries that have dominating control over the IMF activities. It is said that G7 countries secured nearly half of the voting right in the IMF, thus automatically became the commanding authority over all the affairs of the organization. Their quota in the IMF is linked to their contribution to the organization. So, even if the quota is going to be revised it favours the rich countries.

[220] Dasgupta, *Globalization,* 34.

its financial assistance to any countries unless the concern countries "engage in policies like cutting deficits, raising taxes, or raising interest rates that lead to the contraction of the economy."[221]

Hence, with diverse regulations and conditions imposed by the IMF on those countries facing financial crisis, instead of improving their economic status with loans provided by the IMF, their position seemed to be even worse than before.[222] Jha observes that by providing loan to countries to overcome their earlier debt, the poor countries were put up in a situation where they are more open to external investment and imports. In turn, before the poor countries realized the gravity of the situation, they were burdened with heavy debt. These conditionalities that come along with loan in the form of Structural Adjustment Programmes, not only intensified the access of IMF to national economic policies but also changing these policies to be more open to world market system.[223] That is, in providing financial loan to those countries facing crisis, the IMF not only failed to stabilize the situation but sometimes make the situation worse by putting these countries under the bondage of heavy debt. Oommen terms these funding policies of these agencies as a new "form of domination and colonization." Commenting on the increasing amount of debt experience by many Third World countries he further said that "old colonialism, despite its exploitation, was not a period of persistent public debt," but in the present day context, with the active operation of the so called neocolonial forces, a developing country like India is "moving towards a high foreign debt watermark of $100 billion."[224]

Many of the critics of globalization view this situation as the failure of the IMF. It is reported that, the IMF not only failed in keeping the purpose of its original conception to maintain financial stability in the national economy, it also failed in its new venture too. Apart from deviating from providing emergency financial help to the nations facing financial crisis, the IMF extended its services to offer "ten year extended fund facilities since 1974 and structural adjustment loans since 1986,"[225] but in many cases it failed in its mission. Stiglitz maintains that the IMF is not able to accomplish in many of its new mission. As he rightly puts it,

---

[221] Stiglitz, *Globalization and its Discontents,* 12-13.

[222] For instance, many poor countries of Africa found that their economic status not only failed to improve but became worse after achieving financial assistance from the IMF. See Ramaswamy, *In the Woods of Globalization,* 63, 65.

[223] Jha, *Background to Globalization,* 109. One among several conditions employed by the IMF through the Structural Adjustment programme as precondition for loans is reduction in employment despite rise in production. See Walter Fernandes, "Globalization, Liberalization and the Victims of Colonialism," in *Globalization and its Victims,* edited by Michael Amalados (Delhi: Vidyajyoti Education & Welfare Society/ISPCK, 1999), 10.

[224] Oommen, "Globalization and Decolonization...," 15.

[225] Dasgupta, *Globalization,* 34.

> The IMF has made mistakes in all the areas it has been involved in: development, crisis management, and in countries making the transition from communism to capitalism. Structural adjustment programs did not bring sustained growth even to those, like Bolivia, that adhere to its strictures....[226]

In sum, though the role of IMF was to help those countries facing financial crisis, with the influence of the developed countries it has placed many directions and conditions on those countries received loans from its sources. Most of these conditions are created to help the developed countries expand their trade monopoly and exert their domination over the Third World economy. To put it differently, the role of the IMF therefore largely served the interest of the developed countries, rather than helping to improve and recover the weak economies of the Third world countries.

The World Bank (WB)

Another important twin institution the WB, designed and established in 1945 with the purpose of granting long term loan "through specific project loans"[227] for the reconstruction of the economies of those countries severely affected by the World War II . The earlier activities of the WB in providing long term loans in the Post War era concentrated mainly in rebuilding the badly suffering and shattered economies of major capitalist countries. It was only in 1950s that the WB began to extend its financial assistance by funding other less developed countries of the South.[228] Since then, it had substantially financed the weak economies of the Third World countries of Asia, Africa and Latin America. Most of its activities, were concentrated in providing financial loans to profit oriented projects like power generation, transport, etc.[229] However, with the emergence of integrated global capital market, developed countries with good credit ratings, did no more depend from the WB for funding their required projects. Only the poor countries with low credit having no other sources to finance their projects approach the WB for financial assistance.[230] Though the functions of WB concentrated mainly within the sphere of the less developed countries, its entire activities are carried on under the control and influence of the G7 countries. It is the developed countries that give directions and guidelines for the implementation of diverse schemes and policies of the WB. By 1980s the WB stepped beyond its primary activities of funding specific projects to financing broad based programmes in the form

---

[226] Stiglitz, *Globalization and its Discontents,* 18.

[227] Buckman, *Globalization: Tame it or Scrap it,* 51.

[228] GIl, *The Global Political Economy,* 144.

[229] Arun, "Taming the Global Demagogue I," 428.

[230] Dasgupta, *Globalization,* 34.

of Structural Adjustment Loans (SALs) particularly to the poor countries.[231] But like the IMF, the WB also imposed number of directions and conditions, for the less developed countries seeking its help which directly favours the expansion of free trade manipulated by the rich affluent countries. Under the SALs the countries approaching for loans had experienced two significant areas of disadvantage in their new venture.[232] Firstly, the SALs for the poor countries indirectly facilitated to promote the expansion of world trade, manipulated by the rich countries at the expense of the poor countries. Hence there is the reverse flow of capital from the Third World countries to the western industrialized countries. Secondly, under SALs, the WB persuasively convinced the poor countries to opt for total privatization thereby reducing the power of the native government. The outcome of such a situation is that, the state policies of the native government were disregarded, the value of their currencies were devalued, Third World people have to produce export-oriented crops at the expense of necessity food crops, privatization even the public services like health and education and so on. All these practices were done to promote the interest of the developed nations at the cause of the poor countries of the Third World. In other words, the WB programmes instead of providing economic remedy to the poor countries of the world, had in turn made their economic situation bad.

Structural Adjustment Programme (SAP)

The Structural Adjustment Programme (SAP) is referred to those policies designed by the WB and IMF, that have been implemented and imposed upon the Third World countries. Any countries approaching for fund have to accept some conditions and directions prescribed by the agencies of globalization in the form of SAP, which include restructuring and reorganizing their economies to suit the demand of either the IMF or the WB. According to the standpoint of the advocates of globalization, SAP has the capability to bring "rapid industrialization, transfer of technology, with availability of credit and foreign aid as loans, grants and investment."[233] In other words, for the advocates of globalization, SAP could able to promote the easy flow of both financial help and technological assistance that could bring rapid industrial and economic development to the Third World countries. In order to achieve and reap the benefit of global economic advantage the concern country need to strictly adhere to the roles and regulations imposed by the IMF and the WB. These include among many, the liberalization of trade, deregulation of economy, privatization of public undertakings and financial

---

[231] The WB started providing SALs but it began on this venture only when the IMF which already undertaking in this area gave its approval. Once the IMF approved, the WB imposed conditions in that country began operating.Stiglitz, *Globalization and its Discontents,* 18.

[232] Ramaswamy, *In the Woods of Globalization,* 53.

[233] Balasuriya, *Globalization and Human Solidarity,* 34.

institutions so as to provide favourable atmosphere for the process of globalization to develop and flourish. In other words, it means removing all barriers or restrictions that could hinder or obstruct the free flow of capital and economic related activities.

Hence, in order to satisfy the requirement of those conditions set up by the global funding agencies, the concerned country need to go many steps further such as to "spends less by cutting back government expenditures, social services and economic investments so that the resources can be placed elsewhere."[234] This means that, to serve the interest of the global funding agencies the country has to adhere to all conditions and ignore different developmental activities, generally implemented for the good and welfare of its citizens. Commenting on the impact of varied forms of conditions imposed by the twin agencies on the economy of the poor countries Biplab Dasgupta argues that "the conditionalities accompanying their loans now shape the economic policies of the poor recipient countries that have virtually no influence over the decision-making process of the twin agencies."[235] The tragedy is that, even though the countries strictly followed the prescribe conditions imposed by the Bretton Woods institutions; there appeared no evidence to achieve desirable growth.[236] On the contrary, SAP brings more harm than good to the growth and development of countries' economy especially the Third World countries. That means, adhering to the imposed guidelines of SAP, has instead affected the entire economy of the concern country. A classic example in this aspect is the case of Bolivia which experience economic crisis despite following the conditions imposed under SAP.[237] It is said that many countries of the Third World, that have opted for trade liberalization under SAP had noticeably experience increasing erosion in the market share of many local industries, closing down of many industrial units, depriving ample employment opportunities as well as the gradual drop of state revenue. This aspect was revealed by the African group of nations at Doha Round of negotiation and also shared by many poor countries of the Third World.[238] This signifies the anguish and agony of the poor countries over the negative impact of free trade system on the weak economy of the poor Third World countries. To put it differently, SAP are designed to facilitate the economic domination of the developed countries, upon

---

[234] Mathews George Chunakara, "Globalization and its Impact on Human Rights," in *Globalization and its Impact on Human Rights,* edited by Mathews George Chunakara (Thiruvalla: Christava Sahitya Samithy, 2000), 96.

[235] Dasgupta, *Globalization,* 34.

[236] Biplab Dasgupta, *Structural Adjustment, Global Trade and the New Political Economy of Development* (New Delhi: Vistaar Publications, 1998), 116.

[237] For detail see Stiglitz, *Globalization and its Discontents,* 18.

[238] The African countries that share this concern are Kenya, Mozambique, Nigeria, Tanzania, Uganda, Zimbabwe and Zambia which also supported by India, Egypt and Brazil. See Jawara, *Behind the Scene at the WTO,* 25-26.

the poor countries without taking any consideration the need for the improvement of the economy of the latter.

In sum, initially in their original conception both IMF and WB were established with different assignment, to function in two distinct areas of operation. But in course of time, the two institutions became closer in their endeavors and dealings with different issues. For instance both the organization engaged in funding SALs to countries, particularly the poor countries of the South. With the market mantra of the 1980s becoming part of the Washington consensus,[239] the operation of these two agencies became more intensified especially in the context of the Third World countries. With this shift in policies, the former distinction between the roles of the twin is being eroded. In addition, members of the WB are mandatorily bound to be members of the IMF also.[240]

Secondly, despite the entire operation of the IMF and the WB is carried on among the Third World countries, the two agencies are led by the representatives of the G7 countries. Hence, the twin is compelled to serve the interest of the G7 countries in general and the US in particular. In the present day context, most of their funding projects in the Third World are operating with the intention to promote the agenda of the G7 countries or expanding the trade activities of the North. The end result is that these two institutions had failed to produce promising result for economic improvement to many countries of the Third World they are rending their financial assistance. In the words of Stiglitz,

> The two institutions could have provided countries with alternative perspectives on some of the challenges of development and transitions and in doing so they might have strengthened democratic process. But they were both driven by the collective will of the G7 ....[241]

Looking from the postcolonial context, the twin institutions are nothing, but the agencies of neocolonialism that served the interest and mandate of the rich and affluent developed countries in the process of exploitation of the Third World economies.

---

[239] The free market mantras of the 1980s became part of the new Washington consensus- a consensus between IMF, WB and the US treasury about the right policies for developing countries which signaled a radical different approach to economic development and stabilization. However, it is said that the economic policies that developed in the Washington Consensus which emphasized on market liberalization and introduced in the developing countries do not suit in the context of developing countries. The manufactured products of the developing countries cannot in any way compete with the imported products of the advance industrial countries. The outcome of these policies led to the extinction of many weak industries in the Third World countries. See Stiglitz, *Globalization and its Discontents,* 16-17.

[240] Dasgupta, *Globalization,* 36.

[241] Stiglitz, *Globalization and its Discontents,* 14.

The World Trade Organization (WTO)

Another agency that help facilitated the expansion and domination of globalization or the so called neo-colonial forces is the WTO. While the WTO came into being in 1995, for about five decades, world trading system was regulated under the directions of General Agreement on Tariffs and Trade (GATT) established in 1947. The main objectives for the formation of GATT were "to reduce tariff rates, to reduce and eliminate the non-tariff barriers, to eliminate the quantitative restrictions and to settle the disputes among the contracting parties."[242] In other words its main intention was to regulate "world trade and determining the quantum and direction of trade flows."[243]

In its original concept GATT was a forum staged for different countries, debating and negotiating on trade related issues with the purpose of reaching to agreements on different tariffs and trade activities. But formulation of GATT Agreement, reflected the exclusive interest of the so called powerful and affluent countries that have dominated different international forum, without taking into consideration the need and aspiration of the poor and developing countries.[244] Between these periods, GATT multilateral trade negotiations were held for nine rounds.[245] It was in the tenth round of GATT's meeting held at Marakesh, Morroco in 1994 that led to the formal establishment of WTO in 1995.[246] With the formation of WTO, GATT as a trade accord was converted into a membership organization, constituted of 146 members' country and covering more than 98% of the global trade. The WTO is more powerful than GATT as it is "wider in its coverage, deeper in its penetration and more effective in implementation of the agreements."[247] The WTO is therefore expected to set rules for the removal of trade barriers and promote free flow of trade activities. Nevertheless, the WTO does not frame rules and conditions like the WB and the IMF, but offer a forum where trade negotiations and agreements will be discussed and dealt with accordingly. It is believed that the WTO is a democratic agency, as it follows the UN pattern of one country one vote that was generally different from the Bretton Woods institutions. Theoretically, it was established as a democratic

---

[242] Anthuvan, *The Dynamics and the Impact of Globalization- A Subaltern Perspective,* 28.

[243] Dasgupta, *Globalization,* 48.

[244] It is said that although many poor and developing nations became part of GATT, when the Dunkel Draft was finalized it was done with the mutual agreement of the US and Western European countries. Moreover, any countries opposed the GATT agreement it will not only branded them as untouchables but also invited the wrath of the US and other international financial institutions. See Ramaswamy, *In the Woods of Globalization,* 70-73.

[245] Fatoumata Jawara and Aileen Kwa, *Behind the Scene at the WTO* (London: Zed Books, 2003), 8.

[246] Jawara, *Behind the Scene at the WTO,* 8-10.

[247] For the differences between GATT and WTO, See Anthuvan, *The Dynamics and the Impact of Globalization,* 31-32, 35.

agency but in practice many Third World countries complained and accused that, most of the important agendas discussed as well as the resolutions were largely dictated and monopolized by the so called powerful and affluent countries, with no concerns for the opinion of the poor and developing countries. Hence, even though the developing countries constituted two third of the membership, it does not restrict the developed countries from dominating and manipulating the entire proceedings of the WTO affairs.[248]

The Uruguay Round[249] of negotiations for the purpose of promoting the easy flow of global trade goes beyond the purview of GATT system, by embracing new areas like agriculture, intellectual property rights, services, trade-related investment measures and so on.[250] These new endeavour besides open more prospects; it also granted more power to the successor of GATT-the WTO. According to the agreements that evolved during that round of negotiation, WTO became powerful organization with supreme authority on decision making that served against the interest of the South. With this existing agreement, the WTO possess the authority to alter different policies of the state to fall in line with its interest. Any countries that refused to comply with the dictum of the WTO will not only experience removal of trade sanction on its export materials, but also will be isolated in the global arena. Admittedly, the poor countries with no other option have to adhere to the authority of WTO. Commenting on the growing domination of WTO on the poor nations of the Third World, Khor argues that "many domestic economic policies of developing countries are therefore being made in the WTO negotiations rather than in parliament, bureaucracy or cabinet at the national level."[251]

With the new area it has ventured, the WTO has offered more space to the powerful rich countries of the North as well as the so called neo-colonial forces, not only for free trade expansion but also to intensify their dominion over the poor countries of the South. This reflects the colonial mindset of "looting and plundering" every aspect of the former colonies' economy, leaving the poor and developing countries at the margin of the economic development. That is, all the new ventures it has taken were designed to equip the countries of the North to get free access to different economic resources of the Third World. In sum, driven by the collective agenda of the rich nations, different policies of the WTO

---

[248] Jawara, *Behind the Scene at the WTO,* 20.

[249] The Uruguay Round (1986-93) is the eighth and the last round of GATT before the formation of WTO. It may be noted that each round of negotiations was followed by an agreement that continued for some years and before it came to an end another round of negotiation was taken place till the Marrakesh Agreement. In this manner GATT progress from one round to another and in each round barriers of trade were remove thereby resulted to the easy flow of goods around the globe. See Dasgupta, *Globalization,* 49.

[250] Khor, *Rethinking Globalization,* 13.

[251] Khor, *Rethinking Globalization,* 13.

could not help, rather piled up more problems to the already fragile situation of economic and social realities of the poor countries of the South. In other words, free trade system adopted by the global economic bodies has rather enslaved the poor countries than freed them.

The Role of MNCs/TNCs

The MNCs/TNCs seem to be the most powerful and dominant agencies, that further deepened the intensity of the process of globalization, or the so called neocolonial forces to every nook and corner of the globe. Anthuvan traces the origin of these corporate bodies to colonial era began in the 17th century.[252] With the integration of national economies and liberalization of trade, the fast expanding role of the MNCs/TNCs has been noticed in different facets of global economic affairs. These corporate bodies have recently become the major actors and prominent forces in the world economy, with the capability to reframe and restructure the whole set up of world trade system and global economic activities. It is said that in the 1990s there are about 37,000 large MNCs/TNCs (with 1, 70,000 affiliates) operating in different parts of the globe, with the top 300 industrial corporations not only capturing 70% of the total FDI but also controlling over 25% of the world's stock of productive assets.[253] By the year 2003, there were 65,000 MNCs along with 850,000 subsidiary and branches, operating in different parts of the globe with their annual turnover accounted for $20,000 billion.[254] Moreover, the Revenue collection of one of the bigger corporate companies is much higher than the Gross Domestic Product (GDP) of some countries combined together.

A classic example is that, "in 2004, the revenues of US car company General Motors were $191.4 billion, greater than the GDP of more than 148 countries." On the other, by the end of 2005, "US retailer Wal-Mart's revenues were $285.2 billion, larger than the combined GDP of sub-Saharan Africa."[255] With such huge amount of treasure in their coffers, these corporate institutions are not only rich but powerful. Accordingly, with the colonial vision to loot and plunder lively in their plan, these corporate bodies attempt all efforts to invest extensively any amount at any space and time; they deem it fit to garner maximum but unlimited profits. Their main objective for investing on any projects, especially in the poor

---

[252] For him, multinational companies in the form of trading companies started in the colonial period. For instance, the Hudson Bay Company, the East India Company, the French Levant Company to cite few examples. See Anthuvan, *The Dynamic and Impact of Globalization- A Subaltern Perspective,* 11.

[253] I. Mohan Razu, "Globalization, TNCs and the Exploitation of the Poor," in *Globalization: A Challenge to the Church,* edited by P. Jegadish Gandhi and George Cheriyan (Chennai: Association of Christian Institute For Social Concern in Asia, 1998), 29.

[254] Anthuvan, *The Dynamics and the Impact of Globalization: A Subaltern Perspective,* 81.

[255] Stiglitz, *Making Globalization Work,* 187-188.

countries of the Third World, is to exploit the market and economic resources of the concern country, not to bring any sort of developmental activities to the local situation. Even the big countries found themselves unmatched to compete with the dominant power of these corporate giants. If the nation-states make any efforts to levy taxes or regulate the flow of their services against their prescribe norms, they threaten to shift and move away to any place they consider better.[256] The free market mantra advocated by the global powers, is not regulated or administered by the national government but by the so called neo-colonial forces like the MNCs/TNCs. It is these corporate giants who decide and determined all affairs of international trade and economies.

With the aspiration for unlimited profit, they have the capability and mandate to decide not only for the growth and development of global trade but also what and what not to produce, what the people need, where and when to market their goods without considering the concern of the nation-states. Whatever they decide, happen to be the norm and mandate that need to be accepted and followed irrespective of its consequences. Nevertheless, their free role to expand trade activities does not help, but proved detrimental and disastrous to many poor countries of the Third World. Admittedly, if even the big countries found themselves below par, unmatched with the powerful corporate giants with the command of the rich powerful corporate giants, the poor and powerless countries of the Third World have no alternatives except to adhere and accept the conditions imposed by these corporate giants. In other words, they are left with no other option but to open and mutely witness their market and economic resources being exploited by the corporate bodies. The end result is that, the situation of the poor countries of the South will be more impoverished and fragile incapable of moving out of their periphery's condition.

Culture of Globalization

The growing intensification and influences of globalization to different nook and corner of the globe, has generally created a globalized culture or the cosmopolitan culture. This trend has rapidly invaded and integrated people from different walks of life and different corners of the world, unifying them into one monoculture-a globalized culture. With the intention for unlimited gains globalization venture out to find all ways and means to create cosmopolitan culture that would be readily agreed to accept and consume without any hesitation different but costly items produced and promoted by the so called neo-colonial forces or the corporate companies. With the influences of globalization looming large and penetrating different sections of population, people nowadays are more cosmopolitan in their outlook, likes and dislikes, ways of living and so on. This integration of culture, lifestyle, consumption pattern and other modes of cultural nuances

[256] Stiglitz, *Making Globalization Work,* 188.

are experienced more rapidly in the present day context. The devotees of this cultural homogenization believe that global interrelations and interconnections is the only alternative to raise cultural standard and uniformity.[257] Admittedly, looking from the postcolonial context globalization can be depicted as the "latest phase in the long story of an expanding Western cultural hegemony,"[258] that has simultaneously led to "a near total denial of civilization and cultural diversity." [259]

Schuurman states that people's favour for cosmopolitan culture resulted in the erosion of national cultural identity.[260] To put it differently, the emergence of western cultural imperialism involves undermining of local culture and practices, while at the same time forcefully imposing western dominant culture and its inherent values upon the local indigenous culture. With the world rapidly shrinking into a global village coupled with the impact of information technology, massive inflow of western lifestyle, consumption patterns and other modes of western cultural value have become more apparent in today's society. Hence, western imperialist culture or cosmopolitan culture due to global integration is rapidly being experienced in many societies of the Third World countries.[261] In the present day context these experiences is witnessed in the emergence of consumerist culture, globalization of taste, language and mind of the people. Nevertheless, though globalized culture brought some positive changes[262] in the context of the Third World it has indirectly contributed to the gradual erosion of local indigenous and traditional culture.

The Emergence of Consumerist Culture

The present day consumerist culture is nothing but the cultural invasion and expansion of the western imperialist culture imposed upon the culture of the people of the Third World countries. Consumerist culture as one aspect of the global culture developed in America in the twentieth century and now become the fast emerging adopted culture in many societies of the Third World countries today. Accordingly, before the countries of the Third World realized the influence and impact of the western consumerist culture, it already became part and parcel

---

[257] Frans J. Shuurman, Globalization and Developmental Studies: Introducing the Challenged," in *Globalization and Development Studies,* edited by Frans J. Shuurman (New Delhi: Vistaar Publications, 2001), 35.

[258] John Tomlinson, "Vicious and Benign Universalism," in *Globalization and Development Studies,* edited by Frans J. Schuurman (New Delhi: Vistaar Publications, 2001), 45.

[259] Razu, "Towards an Understanding of the Phenomenon of Globalization," 6.

[260] Schuurman, "Globalization and Developmental Studies…," 9.

[261] Razu, Towards an Understanding of the Phenomenon of Globalization, 6.

[262] But most of the positive changes like communication facilities, transport and others are enjoyed mostly by a small section of rich people whereas the majority of poor people who neither have the capacity of getting access to these facilities nor the purchasing power to different consumerist items these changes have no meaning for them.

of their daily living. Consumerist culture does not simply mean mere interest in consumption rather "consumption becomes the main form of self-expression and the chief source of identity."[263] This indicates that the person's identity is based on the capacity to acquire things or his/her ability to consume. So, the more a person can acquire or possess the higher will be his/her status and position in the society would be. Consumerist culture is therefore the culture of the rich and the powerful.

As stated earlier, the process of globalization not only divides the world countries between the rich and the poor, but also within the country between the rich and the poor sections. Hence, globalization is an association that unites the rich and affluent people of both the rich and poor nations. That is, consumerist culture promoted by the forces of globalization is the culture of the wealthy and prosperous section of the world population, both from the rich and the Third world countries as well. With the influence of information technology and mass media, capitalism has transformed individuals into consumer entities, by capturing and diverting all their aspirations and desires towards acquiring the things produced by the corporate companies. With different varieties of branded imported consumer goods dumping by the developed countries in different markets of the Third World countries, individuals having the purchasing power are now compelled to earn more to be able to possess every new items selling in the market-new clothes, new shoes, new kitchen wares, new cars and so on.[264] In a consumerist society, people who are respected and held in high esteem are those who have the capability to purchase more and possess new things available in the market. However, this trend created a wide social disparity between the rich and the poor, the affluent and the marginalised sections or to put in Marxist term 'the haves and have-nots' and the like. The poor section of the population with no purchasing power and means to achieve things are relegated to the periphery. Such a situation leaves a deep imprint not only on the psyche but on the whole life and being of the marginalised poor people of the Third world countries.

Globalization of Taste

With the motive to capture and exploit the market of the globe in general and the Third World in particular, the forces of globalization or the neo-colonial forces make all effort to homogenize the taste of the world population. A growing trend towards globalization of taste is being experienced by all sections of population even to the remotest corner of the globe. To homogenize the taste of global citizens, the forces of globalization set certain standard to change the food habit of the

---

[263] James David, "The Backlash against Globalization," in *Dimension of Globalization,* edited by James David and John Desrochers (Bangalore: Centre for Social Action, 1998), 32.

[264] Saroj Mallick, "Contradictions and Challenges of Globalization: Need for alternatives," in *Globalization: Myth and Reality,* edited by Govind Prasad and Anil Dutta Mishra (New Delhi: Concept Publishing Company, 2004), 41-42.

people, by offering different varieties of food items which are completely different from the local indigenous food products available since time immemorial. The so called 'Macdonaldization' is rapidly expanding and penetrating to different region of the globe, not only in the urban set up but in the interior rural areas as well. This trend is being experience today in the form of standardization of taste in favour of fast food items, soft drinks, and many different varieties of modern food stuffs originated from the western countries.

Admittedly, the so called western cuisine or fast food culture has rapidly replaced many traditional local indigenous food items in many parts of the Third World countries. People nowadays prefer to have a sandwich, hamburger or pizza instead of samosa, dosa, and puri, or some soft drink items like coca cola, pepsi, miranda and others in place of coconut water or *lebu pani* the food items generally used by the Indians for centuries. That is, people nowadays tend to favour on variety of western foodstuff items at the expense of the local traditional cuisine and other indigenous food items. The trend of homogenizing of taste has not only substituted the consumer's taste but has rather "dominate the creativity and character of local and national cultures."[265] To state differently, substituting the consumer's taste simply means not merely replacement of taste but it indicates the growing loss of indigenous skills, creativities, expertise, and proficiency that has severely affected the growth and development of knowledge on the local traditional products.

Using the influence of information technology and mass media as the vehicle to promote homogenization of taste, the forces of globalization extended this trend not only on various food items, but also in other luxuries consumers' goods like expensive cars (Toyota, Mercedes, etc.), different electronic gadgets, dress materials like Levis jeans, Reebok, Nike sports items, and many other imported but luxuries items that have penetrated and found their places in different local markets of the Third World countries. Joseph argues that the core objective of these mass productions is not the demand of consumption but the aspiration to obtain maximum gain and profit, that can be exploited through the neo-colonial forces that have spread their coverage to different regions of the globe. He goes on to elaborate that to convert this vision to reality consumers are bred "for the mass products by homogenizing their taste."[266] Hence, young people from around the globe have many things in common to share and experience which is not the case of their older generation in the earlier period.[267] Globalization of taste

---

[265] Joe Arun, "Taming the Global Demagogue II," *Vidyajyoti Journal of Theological Reflection* 66/7 (July, 2002): 531.

[266] Joseph maintains that these neo-colonial forces have the power to regulate the entire process of mass production by integrating others into this system of market. See Joseph, "Towards a Theological Critique of Globalization," 9.

[267] Chunakara, "Globalization and its Impact on Human Rights," 99.

has recently become the emerging trend created by the so called neo-colonial forces at the expense of the local indigenous culture and traditional practices. This is nothing, but the imposition of the western culture and practices, upon the indigenous culture in the process of homogenizing the taste for maximum profit. Admittedly, this trend leaves deep harmful impact on the psyche and being of the poor sections in the Third World who in no way have the capability and means to adopt such life style. Whereas the rich and affluent section of population may welcome this new development as progressive and beneficial, the marginalized poor section without any purchasing power and capacity, this new shift in life style is not only expensive but generally beyond their reach, with their meager poor income. Eventually, they are left with no option but to submit to their fate.

Globalization of English Language

With the vision to capture the economies of the colonies, British Imperialism in the colonial era also made all attempt to spread their language to different parts of the globe. As the British territories covers many areas in different continents, English language has better advantage than the other language, therefore became the most used language in the colonial period. Consequently, even after the colonial rule came to an end, English language became the lingua franca of the entire globalized world. It is said that today, the language is used and spoken by more than 1.5 billion people around the globe, whereas 350 million people use it as their mother tongue, while the rest as second language.[268] This reflects the importance of English as a global language that serves as a medium of communication in diverse capacity in different parts of the globe. Accordingly, English language happen to be the language of literature, education, info-age, call centers, computer, internet- the language that contains all knowledge and information in different fields and disciplines.[269] Other developed countries like Japan and Germany today become the fast growing countries, even to surpass the US in different fields of developmental activities, but their language is rapidly being invaded and overcome by English.[270]

With the aspiration to capture the global economy the forces of globalization exploit the importance of English language, making use of it as a channel for acquiring maximum profit. In other words, English has become the most important commodity, like other commodities, required for different purposes in the global arena. That is, a person who can communicate and write in English has better prospect in terms of employment opportunities and other business related activities. Similarly, a person who can speak English is often regarded as modern

---

[268] V. Khrishna Rao, "Globalization Unleashed English Tsunami," *Indian Currents* (11-17, December 2006): 35.

[269] Friedman, *The World is Flat,* 6, 22-24.

[270] Rao, "Globalization Unleashes English Tsunami," 35.

civilized, having a better standard of living, whereas a person who can speak only his/her mother tongue is generally considered as backward, primitive, uncivilized and so on. This implies that English is the language of the educated, the powerful, the higher up and so on, making used by the so called neo-colonial forces as a vehicle to exploit diverse means of economic opportunities for unlimited gains. Nevertheless, with the growing influence and global use of English, the local indigenous vernaculars are being restricted or confined to regional or local domestic context.[271] Consequently, globalization of English though generally offering better employment opportunities, it has nevertheless contributed to the erosion of local vernaculars in different parts of the globe.

Globalization of the Mind

Another significant feature of the culture of globalization is the globalization of the mind. Globalization of the mind is not a recent phenomenon but has its roots in the colonial era. The mind which were colonized during the colonial era, are now being globalized and restructured with cosmopolitan outlook, worldview, lifestyle and understanding. People are now more cosmopolitan in their way of looking at things, thought pattern, taste, and so on. The forces of globalization or neo-colonial power directed the entire process of thought and understanding towards accepting the western norms and values, as the only way of achieving higher standard of living with the promising prospect of better future. That is, western value systems are the only way that could help facilitated or contributed towards the better welfare of humanity. Even Nehru the notable freedom fighters during the Independence era opted for western system of development of modernization and industrialization against the Gandhian model of *Swadeshi.*[272] For him, it is only the western system of development that could lead towards a self sufficient and prosperous India. To state differently, Western imperialism and influences eventually left deep impact on the psyche and mind of the people of Third World. Having captured the mind of the Third World people, globalization forcefully re-imposed the imperialist culture on the life of the people. To make their motive successful, the neo-colonial forces employ the role of media as the instrument to reach and capture every nook and corner of the globe. In other words, with the growth and advancement of the information technology and mass media, transmission of western cultural values and practices into the life situation and practices of the Third world people is taking place at a rapid rate.

With the advancement of science and technology, the potentiality of mass media is competent enough to convert and transform the mind of the people

[271] David, "The Backlash against Globalization," 33.

[272] For Nehru if India wanted rapid development in all aspects, western model of modernization and industrialization must be adopted. Gandhi on the other hand, wanted to strengthen and developed manufactured based or cottage industries, the strength of Indian economy and occupation of majority Indians. See Ramaswamy, *In the Woods of Globalization,* xxv.

making them more cosmopolitan in their outlook, behavior and way of life. Advertising agencies based in affluent capitalist countries promote western ideal and western lifestyle as the norm or standard of better living. This trend is not limited or confined to the young or older generations but has also impinging and laid deep influence even to the small children of tender age. Small children these days are bombarded with 'thousands of television ads' inflicting their tender minds to go after western food items like Cadbury chocolates, soft drinks and the like.[273] Before the child could learn something about his/her own cultural values and practices he/she is learning about western ideals and lifestyle. With peoples' mind are globalized anything imported and promoted by the so called neo-colonial forces or agent of globalization is often hailed as ideal and modern. That is, anything produced or manufactured from the west is considered to be of best quality needed to be acquired without second thought. People of the Third World are after western imported materials at the expense of local indigenous stuffs. Such a situation enables the forces of globalization to extensively exploit the Third World people without any limitation. In turn, this trend not only weakens the economy of the Third world country but simultaneously relegated them to the periphery without any hope for improvement in the near future.

Conclusion

The above discussion reveals different stages of globalization-the colonialist, the post world war and the present phase of globalization. Using the tools of Postcolonialism the study reflects how the first phase of globalization i.e the colonialist globalization exploited the resources of the colonies and the Third World countries. With the vision for unlimited gains colonialist globalization went on to monopolize the economic resources of the colonies for maximum profit. The second phase of globalization shows the emergence of two super powers attempted to exert their dominating control of the entire globe. However, with the collapse of the socialist group the entire globe is now under the new phase of globalization. This is generally dominated by the so called neo-colonial forces or the forces of globalization, in their attempt to exploit and monopolize the earth resources at an alarming rate unmindful for the damage done to the environment. Hence, the present phase of globalization is nothing but the replication of the colonialist globalization. The so called neo-colonial forces are so rich and powerful and their operation for maximum profit resulted to name a few-the diminishing role of the state, erasing of the national borders, and the growing disparities not only between the rich and poor nations but within the countries widening gap between the rich and poor citizens keep on increasing. Though the promoters of

[273] Jainarain Sharma, "Consumer in the Globalized world," in *Globalization: Myth and Reality*, edited by Govind Prasad and Anil Dutta Mishra (New Delhi: Concept Publishing Company, 2004), 200.

globalization promise to bring a better and prosperous world, the ground realities proved otherwise. The study reflects that the process of globalization help facilitate and equip the few rich privileged and affluent sections of the world population to climb up in the social ladder whereas simultaneously relegating the marginalized poor sections to the periphery without any hope for economic improvement in the near future. That is, the process of globalization could not help to improve but adds more complications and problems to their already delicate and impoverished economic situation of the poor people especially to the Third World countries like India.

Chapter 3

India and Globalization

The process of globalization is not a new phenomenon but it manifests itself into different phases. It is important to note that there is close similarity between the first phase and the present phase of globalization. To put it differently, the present day globalization is just a reproduction of the colonialist globalization wherein the so called neo-colonial forces like the MNCs/TNCs become the major players in the scene. Moreover, even though globalization offer great promise for better world and better opportunities open to all sections of world population, the ground reality proved otherwise. In reality, it is only the selected few and the privileged sections that could enjoy the benefits offered by the process of globalization, whereas the poor and the marginalized sections that could not matched in the competition process are generally relegated and pushed to the periphery. Here, an attempt is made to examine the role of globalization in the context of the contemporary Indian society beginning from the New Economic Policy in 1991. In other words, this section will try to explore whether different sections of Indian population benefit from the present phase of globalization.

The Independence Scene

After two centuries of domination, the colonial rule finally came to an end and India achieved its independence on the 15th of August, 1947. As stated earlier, the economic drain that flew out of India over the years, through different ways of colonial exploitation put India in vulnerable position of economic hardship and insecurity. The colonial rule had finally come to an end, but millions of the country's population experienced poverty, homelessness, hunger, starvation, malnourishment, ill health, diseases, illiteracy, and so on. Referring to the pitiable situation of India that time, Brojendra Nath Banerjee rightly states when he says,

> Britain had left behind canals and roads and railways, universities, a dedicated civil service. India could not feed itself and was virtually without industry; its people were overwhelmingly illiterate, frozen in the grip of the caste system and at 350 million people already beginning to be dangerously overcrowded.[1]

The challenges the new independent country posed to the nationalist leaders seemed to be immensely great. With the vision to develop the new independent country, different views emerged to make Indian economy catch up with other progressive and developed countries. People of India were divided between different economic thought of the two prominent leaders of the country-Mahatma Gandhi and Pandit Jawaharlal Nehru. Both views seemed to have important aspects that could help improve the existing and impoverished Indian economy that could generally benefit the entire Indian population.

Gandhian Model

Gandhian approach of economic development is based on the indigenous model of *Swadeshi*[2] where each village is self-sufficient. For Gandhi, if India is to progress and achieve economic prosperity in the near future, developments need to begin from the village community level. His vision for the new independent India, argues Satish Kumar is "but a confederation of self governing, self reliant, self employed people living in village communities, deriving their right livelihood from the products of their homesteads."[3] In other words it indicates, "a revival of the village economies of the past, relying on local self-sufficiency to the extent possible and catering to the basic necessities of the people."[4] The main emphasis of the Gandhian model was on the scientific development of agriculture and improvement of the small and cottage industries where different sections of

[1] Brojendra Nath Banerjee, *Globalisation: Rough and Risky Road,* (New Delhi: New Age International (P) Limited, Publishers, 1998), 21. According to 2010 data from the United Nations Development Programme, an estimate 37.2 per cent of Indians live below the country's national poverty line. See http://wikipedia.org/wiki/Poverty_in_India (5 Oct 2012).

[2] C. T. Kurien, *Global Capitalism and the Indian Economy,* (New Delhi: Orient Longman Limited, 1994), 31. The word *Swadeshi* is understood as 'local self sufficiency.' It comes from the Sanskrit word *swa* means 'own' or 'self' and *desh* means 'country'. So, *Swadeshi* means 'one's own country.' The *Swadeshi* movement as part of Indian independence movement is an economic strategy intent to eradicate the British colonial rule and improving the economic condition of the local population. Some of the strategies of the *Swadeshi* movement include boycotting the British manufactured goods and work for improving the domestic manufactured products as well as manufactured technique. That is, to make the country self-sufficient and self-reliance without depending from foreign assistance. See http://en.wikipedia.org/wiki/swadeshi-Movement. (3.10.2011).

[3] Satish Kumar, "Gandhi's Swadeshi- The Economics of Permanence." See http://caravan.squat.net/ICC-en/Krrs-en/ghandhi-econ-en.htm (3 Oct 2011).

[4] Kurien, *Global Capitalism and the Indian Economy,* 31. Cf. I. G. Patel, *Glimpses of Indian Economic Policy: An Insider's view,* (Oxford: Oxford University Press, 2002), 1.

population would be benefitted. It is a dream of Gandhiji that a new independent country would strive forward in different spheres of development so that the well being and total welfare of every section of population become a reality.

Nehruvian Model

On the other hand, Jawaharlal Nehru's firm commitment in building a strong independent nation both socially and economically if not militarily, is witnessed in his famous speech "Awake to Freedom" on the eve of Independence Day, the 14th August, 1947 at the parliament where he emphasised on the urgent necessity to abolish poverty, illiteracy, ignorance and the like. Emphasising on the great task ahead that a new independent country has to take in the process, Nehru addressed,

> That the future is not one of ease or resisting but of incessant striving so that we might fulfil the pledges we have so often taken and the one we shall take today. The service of India means the service of the millions who suffer. It means the ending of poverty and ignorance and diseases and inequality of opportunity. The ambition of the greatest man of our generation has been to wipe every tear from every eye. That may be beyond us but so long as there are tears and suffering, so long our work will not be over.[5]

Nehru perceived that the urgent task ahead for the new independent country to undertake as it step towards the process of development are "rapid agricultural and industrial development...rapid expansion of opportunities for gainful employment, progressive reduction of social and economic disparities, removal of poverty and attainment of self reliance..."[6] For him, the development strategies needed for the new independent country like India is of twofold. He strongly believed that the best way to improve the economic position of India would be to follow the system of central planning of development as well as adopting western model of heavy industrialization. Like Gandhi he saw the great task ahead would be to build up a strong nation that could help raising the living condition of millions of the country's population. But unlike Gandhi, he also favoured the western forms of industrial development. For him, industrial development is necessary to make India find its significant place in the context of modern world. He further believes that if foreign investment is allowed in the industrial sector, it will make India not only find its place in the modern world

[5] This is an extract from the famous speech of Nehru where he stressed on the "Tryst with destiny" a couple of minutes before India's achievement of freedom from the British colonial rule. See "Awake to Freedom" (Nehru's speech, August14, 1947), as cited in Banerjee, *Globalisation: Rough and Risky Road,* 28.

[6] "Statetment of Industrial Policy, July 24, 1991," in *Liberalisation and Globalization of Indian Economy (Volume I),* edited by K. R. Gupta (New Delhi: Atlantic Publishers and Distributors, 2000), 190.

but also help enlarging its knowledge in the sphere of technology. As N. Jayapalan rightly puts it, "Nehru made it plain that he wished to encourage foreign capital investment in the industry not for its own sake but because of the industrial and technical knowledge it would bring with it."[7] For Nehru big industries like "steel plants, washeries and barrages" are but "the temples of modern India."[8] They are the important means that could facilitate building a strong and developed nation which in turn will be capable of raising the standard of living of the millions in the country. At the same time, as a prominent nationalist leader, influenced by the Soviet Union's system of planning, Nehru became more inclined towards planned development and state control over the economic sectors. To put it differently, the main approaches of Nehruvian model was based on "large scale industrialization, central planning, the application of advanced technology and huge capital investments" and the like.[9]

Mixed Economy

With the attainment of freedom, when Nehru became the first Prime Minister of independent India, the Gandhian model of development was surpassed by Nehruvian model of economic development. The initial phase of Independence witnessed different strategies employed by the government in its attempt to help the nation engaged in different developmental sectors. After the nation became a republic in 1950, India adopted a development pattern based on the mixed economy, where the public enterprise as well as private enterprise co-exist side by side.[10] In other words it indicates a combination of "both capitalism and socialism with central planning and implementation through five-year plans."[11]

---

[7] N. Jayapalan, *Economic History of India: Ancient to Present Day,* 2nd edition, (New Delhi: Atlantic Publishers & Distributors (P) Ltd, 2008), 277.

[8] See Dhulasi Birundha Varadarajan, "Impact of New Economic policy on Foreign Trade," in *Liberalisation and Globalization of Indian Economy (Vol. I),* edited by K. R. Gupta (New Delhi: Atlantic Publishers and Distributors, 2000), 176. Though, Nehru had strong commitment towards transforming India into a self reliance independent country, his economic policies was hampered by the sudden partition of the country which has taken place simultaneously with the achievement of independent. It is said that the partition of India besides many problems, also brought about the unexpected split in the economic resources of India. See "Economic Policies of Jawaharlal Nehru," www.mapsofindia.com/personalities/nehru/economic-policies:html (4 Oct 2011).

[9] See www.istr.org/conferences/bankok/WPVolume/Kumar.Mauday.pdf (4 Oct 2011).

[10] Right after the achievement of freedom, Prime Minister Nehru along with the statistician Prasanta Chandra Mahalanobis stressed the importance of both public and private sectors towards maintaining the growth and development of the India's economy. See "Economic History of India" at http://www.indohistory.com (6 Oct 2011).

[11] The Five year planning programme was based on the USSR's model of development. See George Cherian, "Globalization- A Conspiracy of the Rich against the Poor," in *Globalization: A Challenge to the Church,* edited by P. Jegadish Gandhi and George Cherian (Chennai: Association of Christian Institutes for Social Concern in Asia, 1998), 69.

The important features of mixed economy observes George Cherian include the involvement of,

> Public and private sector in industry, cool attitude towards foreign investment, protection of domestic market, state intervention over market economies, etc. It was based on the concept of welfare state and the state took care of the welfare of the poor up to a certain extent, regarding food, agriculture, education, health, housing, etc through subsidies and other welfare measure.[12]

It is believed that in a democratic country like India, a mixed economy where both the public and private sectors are simultaneously involved coupled with different five year planning system could have the capability to achieve considerable and desirable growth and development in the years to come. It may be noted that the Indian economic policies in the early independent period underlined firm commitment towards creating "congenial encouraging environment for the growth of private industry, protecting the Indian industry from foreign capital and protecting millions of poor from starvation."[13] To achieve these objectives, the state strongly committed towards public investment in the form of infrastructural facilities like development of transport and communications, major irrigation projects, etc. on one hand and promoting Indian industrialization by protecting Indian industrialists from excessive foreign competition on the other.[14]

These commitments were enshrined and emphasised clearly in the Directive Principles of State Policy of the Constitution. Thus, besides protecting the national economy of the new independent country from the many challenges that may come from external forces, the state also pledged firm commitment towards the good and welfare of the citizens especially the poor and the marginalised. It is believed that employing these vital economic policies, coupled with congenial atmosphere toward growth and development, will not only place India in the path of developmental process but simultaneously help improving the living conditions of the millions of citizens from the weaker sections. It is plainly visible that the chief objective of the government during the post-independence era was "growth with equity," abolition of poverty, and equitable distribution of wealth and prosperity to all sections of the population. Consequently, economic growth and social justice are expected to go hand in hand. To state differently, the economic policies of the nation was against the "concentration of wealth and means of production" in the hands of the few but economic resources are to be evenly distributed to all. Gupta and Sarkar maintain that with these main objectives gained prominence during the period, "the Indian economy came

---

[12] Cherian, "Globalization- A Conspiracy...," 69.

[13] See VAK Team, "The New Economic Path- Trends and Impact" in *Globalisation and SAP: Trends and Impact- An Overview,* edited by Ajit Muricken (Mumbai: Vikas Adhyayan Kendra, 1997), 152.

[14] Kurien, *Global Capitalism and the Indian Economy,* 32.

to operate within a framework of regulations and controls."[15] For instance, the Industrial Policy Resolution of 1956 stated that even if the industrial activity was earmarked under the domain of private sector, the state should ensure that the motive behind industrial growth do not meant exclusively for private profit but should be directed in conformity with social purpose. Accordingly, important segments that include "defence production, communications, power, steel and fertilizers" besides making "provisions to determine in broad terms what will be produced" entirely rest with the state.[16] The role of public sector in the developmental programmes gain maximum attention and "the government intervention in economic activities increased beyond limit."[17]

Nevertheless, despite serious effort made by the government towards accelerating better economic growth and development the outcome was far from satisfactory. It is reported that the actual GDP of India during that period signifies a constant growth rate or the so called Hindu growth rate[18] of just about 3.5% per annum.[19] Such rate of growth neither helps the country in the pace of developmental process nor able to raise the living condition of the marginalised poor as expected. Citing several reasons[20] for the low economic growth of India

[15] It is important to note that the economic policies of the post-independence era earmarked "certain reservation of specified industries for the public sector to enable it to reach certain heights in the economic ladder, prevention of economic concentration," and the like. Besides, the government as the decision-makers engaged variety of policies and control instruments to influence investment decision in the private sector such as "regulation of industrial capacities, a system of industrial licensing, import controls, prices and distribution controls." See S. P. Gupta and A. K. Sarkar, "Economic Reforms and Growth," in *Liberalisation: Its Impact on the Indian Economy*, Volume I, edited by S. P. Gupta, (Delhi: Macmillian India Limited, 1993), 57.

[16] VAK Team, "The New Economic Path- Trends and Impact," 152.

[17] V. N. Attri, "Liberalising the Indian Economy," in *Liberalisation and Globalization of Indian Economy*, Volume I, edited by K.R. Gupta (New Delhi: Atlantic Publishers and Distributors, 2000), 32.

[18] The so-called Hindu rate of growth was coined by Rajkhrishna to refer to the actual slow growth of Indian economy during the 1960s and the 1970s. See R. N. Ghosh and R. Gabbay, "Prospects of the Indian Economy: The 1990s and Beyond," in *Sustainable Development: Human Resources, Gender and Environment*, edited by R. N. Ghosh, R. Gabbay and K. C. Roy (Delhi: Atlantic Publishers and Distributors, 1999), 235.

[19] See R. Nagaraj, "Growth Rate of India's GDP, 1950-51 to 1987-88; examination of Alternative Hypothesis," *Economic and Political Weekly*, 25/26, (June 30, 1990): 1396. www.jstor.org/pss/4396440 (7 Oct 2011)

[20] For Bhagawati several among many reasons for India's low growth rate are- India's turned inwards begin with a balance of payment crisis, overvaluation of currency, lacking of good literate workers, inefficient public sector enterprises and so on. For detail see Jagdish Bhagawati, "The Design of Indian Development," in *India's Economic Reforms and Development: Essays for Manmohan Singh*, edited by Isher Judge Ahluwalia and I. M. D. Little (New Delhi: Oxford University Press, 1998), 24-34. Besides the above, some other reasons for the low growth rate may include over-population, impact of Caste ridden society, corruption, and the like. While Ramanjaneyulu argues that licensing and controls as the main causes, Gupta opines that it is corruption as well as inefficiency and slow

during the post-independent era, Bhagawati maintains that India began its economy in 1950s with "high growth rates, openness to trade and investment, promotional state, social expenditure awareness, confidence that poverty would be seriously dented by growth, macro stability" with great expectation of high growth rate, but by 1980s it ended up with "low growth rate, closure to trade and investment, a licence-obsessed, restrictive state, inability to sustain social expenditures, loss in confidence in the efficacy of growth in reducing poverty, macro instability, indeed crisis..."[21] It may be noted that by 1980s, the economic policies adopted by the government of India expected to be progressive and balanced where "the state playing a predominant role, was neither balanced nor sustainable."[22] Despite the strong commitment to bring high growth rate as well as better welfare to different sections of population, coupled with the good support of the constitution the outcome is far from satisfactory. On the contrary, Indian economy in the post-independent era not only had a constant growth rate, but also faced deep economic crisis.

The Crisis

By 1980s it was plainly clear that the economic policies adopted by India in the post-independent era have not only failed to improve the economic status of the country but is also incapable to raise the living conditions of the marginalised poor. To put it differently, the aspiration and hope of the nationalist leader, coupled with different strategies and efforts could not succeed in bringing the desired result. India is not only left behind in the process of world economic progress but its entire economy underwent serious problems. By the beginning of the 1990s, India's economic position faced a deep crisis. Scholars give different reasons that have gravely affected India's economy and led to this serious economic crisis. Chandra *et al* suggest three major weaknesses of India's economic policy that made India to experience this major crisis. These include over protection through import restrictions which resulted in "inefficiency and technological backwardness in Indian industries;" "inward-oriented development" that make

---

moving of the Indian politician and bureaucracy compared to those of the developed countries. See M. Ramanjaneyulu, "Pros and cons of Indian Economic Liberalisation," in *Liberalisation and Globalization of Indian Economy,* Volume I edited by K. R. Gupta (New Delhi: Atlantic Publishers and Distributors, 2000), 17. See also K. R. Gupta, "Liberalisation and Globalisation of Indian Economy," in *Liberalisation and Globalization of Indian Economy,* Volume I, (New Delhi: Atlantic Publishers and Distributors, 2000), 5.

[21] Bhagawati, "The Design of Indian development," 34-35.

[22] Pushpa Bisht, "India under Globalization: Facing an Unequal World," in *Globalization: Myth and Reality,* edited by Govind Prasad and Anil Dutta Mishra (New Delhi: Concept Publishing Company, 2004), 95. It is believed that the failure of economic growth and development in India was attributed to the failing of the Nehruvian model of economy based on the socialism which involved the role of the government in almost every sphere of economic productions. For detail see Ghosh and Gabbay, "Prospects for the Indian Economy...," 236.

India slow to adjust to "changes occurring in the international situation and world capitalism" especially in the 1960s-70s; and the emergence of regional political imperatives with "strong articulate demand on state resources" and so on.[23] It may be noted that here it is more of internal rather than external factors. On the other hand Dasgupta maintains that some of these causes that bring India to this crisis include heavy foreign debt,[24] changes of economic policies to cater the needs of the rich affluent sections of population,[25] and the outbreak of gulf war.[26] He rightly argues when he says,

> The crisis of 1990-91 was prompted by the following: (a) the repayment need for the 1981 IMF loan, (b) the large size of the private international bank loan, coupled with rising fiscal deficits that created uncertainties about loan repayment, (c) the Gulf crisis of 1990, that led to the sudden and massive escalation of the oil import cost, the disappearance of $2-3 billion of annual remittance from Indian workers in Kuwait, Iraq and other Gulf countries, and the heavy cost of airlifting of Indians residing in Kuwait, and (d) the heavy speculative outflow of NRI (non-resident Indian) funds held in India- up to $1 billion- within a short time to East Asia.[27]

It may be noted that the crisis that affected India's economy during that era derive both from the internal as well as external factors. The outcome of such a situation brings more harm than good to the weak economy of the poor country like India. In case of the latter, the sudden outbreak of Gulf war brought unexpected financial expenditure that resulted to severe economic burden and misery to the weak economy like India. Though the effect of the war was worldwide felt, to a poor country like India the impact has been more serious than expected.

In the case of the former, the impact is of threefold. Firstly, the excessive protection of the indigenous manufacture industries without taking into

[23] For detail see Bipan Chandra, Mirdula Mukherjee and Aditya mukherjee, *India After Independence, 1947-2000,* (New Delhi: Penguin Books, 2000), 357-361.

[24] It is reported that in 1981, to bail the country out of the financial problems, Indira Gandhi the then Prime Minister of the country applied for financial assistance of $5billion from the IMF in the form of structural adjustment loan (SAL) with certain conditions laid by the IMF that has badly affected India's economy and burdened the whole nation with heavy foreign debt.

[25] The mid 1980s witnessed the changed policy decision of the Indian government to developed industries that produced domestic consumers' products like refrigerator, television, video, washing machine, and the like with the loan burrowed from private international banks which in turn led India facing severe economic crisis.

[26] The outbreak of Gulf war in 1990, not only led to the massive increased of oil price but also caused India billion dollars for shifting Indian workers in Kuwait and Iraq back to India. This had seriously affected the low economic position of poor country like India.

[27] Dasgupta, *Globalisation: India's Adjustment Experience,* 17. Cf. Mohan P. Shrivastava et al., "Relevance and Incidence of Globalisation in Indian Economy" in *Liberalisation and Globalisation of Indian Economy,* Volume III, edited by K. R. Gupta (New Delhi: Atlantic Publishers and Distributors, 1999), 84-85.

consideration different changes taken place in the global world and the demand in the international situation make Indian industries backward and incompetent to adapt to the different changes occurring in the global arena. P. Gupta and A. Sarkar observe that "the regulatory policy has led to structural rigidities; preventing the economies from reaching a higher growth path... regulatory framework should be progressively relaxed in response to the dynamic changes taking place and to attain the objectives of the economic policy."[28] Secondly, the SAL obtained from the IMF with certain conditions needed to be adopted instead of facilitating towards the growth of India's economy kept the country under the bondage of heavy foreign debt. Thirdly, the changed policy objective of India to develop industries that cater to the needs of the rich with borrowed money from private international banks not only added miseries to the existing bondage of foreign debt, but it is for the first time that India resolved to produce consumers goods to satisfy the needs of the elite section of the society. Hence, there is a sudden shift of focus from helping the marginalised poor that gained prominence during the post-independent era towards catering to the needs that suit the rich affluent section of the society at the expense of the less privilege section. In other words, it is a deviation from the concept of welfare state towards a more open economy which in turn forces the country into the bondage of IMF debt trap.[29] However, the outcome in both the cases has seen India undergone the process of deep and severe financial crisis besides many other related problems.

Commenting on the impact of the crisis to the India's economy during the period Ramanjaneyulu argues that different but serious problems like "large trade deficits, huge foreign debt, sharp decline in the external value of rupee, low economic efficiency, recession" have resulted in "fiscal and external imbalances, inflation, chronic unemployment" and so on.[30] Chandra et al maintain that by the end of 1980s the "fiscal and balance of payment situation" led the country experience heavy bondage of debt both domestic and foreign debt. As they rightly put it,

> Total government (centre and state) domestic debt rose from 31.8% of GDP in 1974-75 to 45.7% in 1984-85 and 54.6% in 1989-90. The foreign debt situation also rising from $23.5 billion in 1980-81 to $37.3 billion in 1985-86 to $83.8 billion in 1990-91. The debt service ratio which was still a manageable 10.2%in 1980-81 rose to a dangerous 35% in 1990-91.[31]

---

[28] Gupta, "Economic Reforms and growth," 58.

[29] Cherian, "Globalization- A conspiracy...," 69.

[30] Ramanjaneyulu, "Pros and Cons of Indian Economic Liberalisation," 16.

[31] Chandra et al, *India after Independence, 1947-2000,* 363. According to the report, India's external debt climbed 6.6% to $326 billion by September-end from 306 billion at the beginning of the current financial year 2011-2012. See http://timesofindia.indiatimes.com/business/india-business/Indias-external-debt-rise (5 Oct 2012)

Hence, the above data reflects the deteriorating situation of India's economy that led the country to mounting debt, both domestic and foreign debt. Pandey observes that "the mounting burden of borrowings, both domestic and foreign, brought the economy to the brink of insolvency in the early 1991."[32] If the government debts soar higher within few decades, the foreign exchange reserves of India were not in a good position either. It is reported that despite the loan available from the IMF, the foreign exchange reserves of India during the same period dropped down from $5.85 billion in 1980-81 to $4.1billion in 1989-90 and it come down again to $2.24 billion in1990-91. With the intensity of the crisis looming large the government promptly compelled to "sell 20 tonnes of gold to the Union Bank of Switzerland in March 1991 to tide over the crisis."[33] This crisis indicates not only the deterioration of India's economy, but even the foreign exchange reserves of India were in a bad state. With this new and difficult circumstances taken place, the new government under Narasimha Rao as the Prime Minister and Manmohan Singh as the Finance Minister, found that the government has the capability "to import only for a few weeks, and did not even have the capacity to import for one month or beyond."[34] To help solve the crisis and rescue the country from further economic bankruptcy, Prime Minister Narasimha Rao and Finance Minister Manmohan Singh had to look elsewhere for financial assistance. It is said that the IMF/WB which had bailed out the country from financial bankruptcy in 1981, once again came to rescue the country, but demanded that the country open up its economy to the outside world and adopt some structural adjustment programmes.[35] The outcome of such a situation is that India began to open up to globalization in the form of New Economic Policy.

India Opens up to Globalization

After decades of regulatory and excessive protection coupled with the occurrence of severe economic crisis of 1990-91 that cruelly affected the entire nation,

[32] Shridhar Pandey, "Liberalisation, Globalisation and the state in Indian Economy" in *Liberalisation and Globalisation of Indian Economy*, Volume III, edited by K. R. Gupta (New Delhi: Atlantic Publishers and Distributors, 1999), 64.

[33] Chandra et al, *India after Independence, 1947-2000,* 364. See also Naina Shaik Mohamed, "Impact of Globalization: India and Canada," in *Globalization: Myth and Reality*, edited by Govind Prasad and Anil Dutta Mishra (New Delhi: Concept Publishing Company, 2004), 275.

[34] Dasgupta, *Globalisation: India's Adjustment Experience,* 18.

[35] Joseph Fonseca, "The Globalization of Business- an Ethical Inquiry: With Special Reference to India," in *Jeevardhara* XXVI/156, (November, 1956): 425. It is important to note that, to obtain the loan from the IMF/WB India had to agree at certain conditions and regulations prescribed by the two bodies which had really affected on the recipient country. See Bisht, "India Under Globalization: Facing an Unequal World," 95. Cf. Kurien, *Global Capitalism and the Indian Economy*, 101. For Instance, India could apply for a loan of $ 2.3 billion from the IMF only when it began fulfilling certain conditions imposed by the IMF. See Dasgupta, *Globalisation: India's Adjustment Experience,* 18.

India is left with no other option but to open its economy to the outside world. Eventually, though India joins the process of economic globalization in the summer of 1991 through important economic reforms, a glimpse of economic reforms can be traced back in the mid sixties with some vital expansion in the seventies.[36] But the economic policies of these two decades could not bring the desired growth as well as improving the living condition of the marginalised poor.

When Indira Gandhi came back as the Prime Minister in 1980, she consciously realise the need of economic growth. Therefore, she was strongly determined to bring major changes in the economic policies of India. It was felt that if India is to achieve sustainable growth as well as to abolish poverty, many of the controls and regulations that were imposed as prevention and protection of India's economy from the invasion of the outside forces need to be removed. In other words it indicates "a shift from administrative regulations to a process of liberalization."[37] This effort attempted by Indira Gandhi, was generally carried on during the Rajiv Gandhi era,[38] and was further intensified with the commencement of the major economic reforms in the 1990s under the New Economic Policy of the government of India.

New Economic Policy

As stated earlier, the grim financial crisis that led to the brink of economic collapse compelled India to join the process of economic globalization by introducing a sequence of economic reforms that commenced from July 1991.[39] The entire

[36] The emergence of Indian economic reforms can be referred back to the 1960s with "the introduction of export incentives" though it failed to continue for a longer period. The reforms of mid seventies onwards seemed to be concentrated in "the area of industry, technology upgradation, domestic trade, taxation and finance" with the chief motive to build up "industrial growth and domestic competitiveness." For detail see Gupta, "Economic Reforms and growth," 58-60.

[37] When Indira Gandhi came back to power, her main concern was to bring economic growth as well as to illuminate poverty. Hence, these were clearly spelled in the Sixth Five Year Plan (1980-85). In order to achieve this goal, the economy of the country need to be reformed by relaxing all restrictions and control that had been imposed in the earlier decade. For detail see Kurien, *Global Capitalism and the Indian Economy*, 93-94.

[38] It is reported that the economic reforms followed by Rajiv Gandhi (1985-90) could not bring improvement as desired. The balance of trade deficit, increased rather than decreasing. It is also affirmed that during the seventh plan the receipts on invisible account decline from Rs.19, 070 crores to Rs. 15,890 crores. See Narendra Prasad, "Efficacy and Impact of a decade of Economic Reforms on the Indian Economy," in *Economic Reforms in India,* edited by Bishwa Nath Singh, Mohan Prasad Srivastava, Narendra Prasad (New Delhi: APH Publishing Corporation, 2003), 112.

[39] It may be noted that, Prime Minister Narasimha Rao together with the then Finance Minister introduced a series of reforms by revoking the existing economic policy which stressed on the socialist pattern of development coupled with the absolute control of the government in all spheres of economic production. See Shridhar Pande, "Liberalisation, Globalisation and the State in Indian Economy," in *Liberalization and Globalization of Indian Economy,* edited by K. R. Gupta (New Delhi: Atlantic Publishers and Distributors, 2002), 8.

process of economic reforms is generally known as New Economic Policy (NEP). It may be noted that the entire structure of the New Economic Policy is based on different conditionalities and regulations of the Structural Adjustment Programmes (SAP) imposed by the IMF and WB.[40] Though the government initially claim that the framework of the NEP is prepared "indigenously without any prompting from outside"[41] a deep look into the structure of the NEP mirrored the deep influence of the IMF and WB, as well as certain structural adjustment to different conditionalities strictly prescribed by these two bodies. Scholars like Shrivastava sees the process of economic reforms comprises of different sets of measures which include the "short-term stabilisation measures, the medium-term structural adjustment programme, and the second generation reforms of the present day."[42] Chandra *et al* perceive the reforms not only as an attempt to free the economy from the absolute control of the government, but also as an effort to enhance the capability of Indian economy to competitively and positively involve in the process of economic globalization. As they rightly put it,

> The process of reforms started in 1991, involved an immediate fiscal correction, making the exchange rate more realistically linked to the market (Rupee devalue about 20%), liberalization of trade and industrial controls like freer access to imports, a considerable dismantling of the industrial licensing system and the abolition of MRTP, reform of the public sector including gradual privatization, reforms of the capital markets and the financial sector, removing a large number of restrictions on MNC and foreign investment and welcoming them particularly FDI and so on. In short, it was an attempt to free the economy from stifling internal controls as well as equip it to participate in the worldwide globalization process to its advantage.[43]

---

[40] VAK Team, "The New Economic Path...," 155.

[41] It is reported that to solve the financial crisis of the country that time, the government was bailed up by the IMF loan of $2.3 billion but only after agreement to certain conditions imposed by the IMF. Hence, though the NEP was prepared prior to the signing of the IMF conditionalities, it was all done with the intention to help facilitated easy availability of the IMF loan. See Dasgupta, *Globalization: India's Adjustment Experience,* 18-20.

[42] While the former stressed the need of "devaluation of the Indian Rupee, drastic fiscal compression and credit squeeze and continuation of severe import controls" the middle measure comprises different reforms such as "trade reforms, exchange rate reforms, reforms in industrial policy, capital market reforms, reforms in financial policy, tax reforms, public sector reforms" and the like. On the other hand, the latter advocated the importance of joining the process of "liberalisation, globalisation, and marketisation" with the intention to allow the market to replace the state and public sector to a maximum extent. See Mohan Prasad Shrivastava, "A Decade of Globalisation, Liberalisation and Economic Reforms in India: An Assessment," in *Economic Reforms in India,* edited by Bishwanath Singh, Mohan Prasad Srivastava and Narendra Prasad (New Delhi: APH Publishing Corporation, 2003), 75-76.

[43] Chandra *et al, India after Independence, 1947-2000,* 366.

In sum, the entire package of economic reforms can be shortly recapitulated as liberalisation, privatisation, and globalisation. With the existing economic policy followed on socialist pattern of development has been sidelined, liberalisation, privatisation and globalization or the LPG model have become the new slogan of economic development. It is believed that the LPG model will largely benefit a poor country like India as "it would accelerate productivity, employment and workers' wages and also a greater accumulation of wealth through product exports and so on."[44] They are enlisted as the only strategies that could help and bail out the economy of the nation in the ongoing economic crisis during that period.

Liberalisation

As stated earlier, in the context of economic globalization, the concept of liberalisation implies that the state's role in the entire economic affairs is generally minimized to a large extent. The entire economic supervision and management is expected to be left to the market. To give a free hand to the market indicates that "all controls and regulations, as also measures that constitute barriers to entry, should be done away with."[45] To put in other words, it implies "scrapping of the undesirable restrictions, controls and licensing over investments, imports and production."[46] "Liberalisation measures" opines Kalirajan "aimed at eliminating structural and institutional rigidities which are a drag on economic performance, promoting export growth and attracting greater flow of FDI."[47] It is believed that eradicating the existing restrictions and controls will not only help the free flow of goods and services but also improve the economy of the country. Hence, if the country wants to improve its economic position, its economic policies need to be flexible. The outcome of such practice compels the state to "take a back seat in economic matters." Any attempt to assert controls and restrictions in the process of marketisation will obstruct the flow of global trade "thus hindering economic growth."[48] Consequently, in the new economic set up, it is the market which plays a greater role in the entire affairs of economic growth and development.

---

[44] J. V. Raghavendra Rao, "Globalization, Dalits and Social Justice," in *Globalization and Social Justice: Perspective, Challenges and Praxis,* edited by J. G. Jogdand, Prashant P. Bandsode, N. G. Meshram (Jaipur: Rawat Publications, 2008), 160.

[45] Dasgupta, *Globalisation: India's Adjustment Experience,* 21.

[46] Ramanjaneyulu, "Pros and Cons of Indian Economic Liberalisation," 16.

[47] Kalippa Kalirajan, "Liberalisation Strategies and Poverty Reduction in India" See www.eastasiaforum.org/2010/09/06/liberalisation- strategies-and-poverty-reduction-in-india/ (28 Oct 2011).

[48] Dasgupta, *Globalisation: India's Adjustment Experience,* 21.

Privatisation

Alongside liberalisation, another important component of the NEP in 1990s is privatisation.[49] The word privatisation is "fundamentally concerned with the transfer of assets or activities from the public to the private sector."[50] To put it in different words, it is the shift of ownership of certain public enterprises or agencies from the operation of public sector to the domain of private sector. "Public ownership" maintains Dasgupta "should be allowed only in cases of natural monopolies and strategic industries, such as in defence and research establishments, and should not be allowed to become a drain on the state's resources."[51] For instance, while in the sphere of industrial sector, the number of areas reserved for public enterprises declined from 17 to 8 sectors,[52] on the other, 20% of the government share holding in public sector units was offered to "mutual funds, financial institutions and the general public."[53] So also, it was found that not long after the privatisation policy was implemented "13 public enterprises and 21 hotels owned by the government have already been privatized."[54] Nevertheless, beside the above there is an attempt to convert some other sectors like the power sector which were under the public domain to the private sector.[55] Hence, most of the important assets and services formerly under the public sector are now being privatised. Those who support the New Economic policy advocate that privatization of all these sectors apart from helping them to improve their

---

[49] It may be noted that privatisation was first adopted by the UK government in the latter part of the 1970s. By the year 1991, it is reported that the UK government had completely transferred the ownership of all the public sector to the private sector. See Saroj Gupta, "Privatisation in India" in *Liberalisation: Its Impact on the Indian Economy,* edited by S. P. Gupta (New Delhi: Macmillan India Limited, 1993), 90.

[50] Collyer asserts that though this definition contains much truth in it, in reality it is only one dimension of privatisation which concern mostly on financial transaction and exchanges. Tran M. Collyer, "Theorising Privatisation: Policy, Network Analysis and Class," in *Electric Journal of Sociology*, 2003, www.sociology.org/content/vol7.3/01_collyer.html (28 Oct 2011).

[51] Dasgupta, *Globalisation: India's adjustment Experience,* 21.

[52] These areas comprised mainly to four important sectors namely "essential infrastructure goods and services, exploration and exploitation of oil and mineral resources, technology development and building up of manufacturing capability in vital areas and manufacturing of product based on strategic considerations." See Madhuri Srivastava, "Globalisation of Indian Economy: Direction and Challenges" in *Liberalisation and Globalization of Indian Economy,* Volume I, edited by K. R. Gupta (New Delhi: Atlantic Publishers and Distributors, 2000), 118.

[53] C. S. N. Raju, "New Economic Policy and GATT" in *Liberalisation and Globalization of Indian Economy,* Volume I, edited by K. R. Gupta (New Delhi: Atlantic Publishers and Distributors, 2000), 126.

[54] Anil Dutta Mishra, "Globalization: Concept and Nature," in *Globalization: Myth and Reality,* edited by Govind Prasad and Anil Dutta Mishra (New Delhi: Concept Publishing Company, 2004), 15.

[55] Banerjee, *Globalisation: Rough and Risky Road,* 5.

competency and competitiveness will also fetch "much-needed funds for reducing the fiscal deficit."[56] Whereas others see that such an attempt is not only directed towards concentration of wealth in the hands of few, but also view it as a process of removing various forms of public services formerly offered by the government for public needs.[57] Hence, the process of privatization is viewed with suspicion. This indicates that while the process of privatization will benefit only a small section of population, simultaneously it will seriously affect the weaker section of the society especially the poor and the marginalised.

Globalization

The other major constituent of the New Economic Policy of 1991 is globalization. Globalization here means opening up the country's economy and effectively integrating it with the global economy. Globalization is generally understood as market oriented pattern of development "designed to generate culture of competition and to promote high efficiency in production, technology transfer, mutual sharing of fruits of research and development and to take to such measures which may remove the evils of closed sheltered economy involving inefficiency, low productivity, obsolete technology"[58] and the like. The advocates of the New Economic Policy of 1991 believed that allowing the Indian economy to participate and integrate with the global economy will not only generate free flow of goods and services but also generally benefit it in the long run. It indicates the philosophy of doing away with the existing system of controlled and sheltered economy and situates the economy in the process of global competitiveness. To integrate the national economy with the global economy besides enhancing its growth and development, it will also transformed and equip it into a more efficient and competent economy in the global arena. It is expected that such an attempt will "improve efficiency of production through infusion of competitiveness amongst the Indian traders and producers." At the same time, it will simultaneously bring "improvement in quality, productivity, efficiency and cost effectiveness, which would in turn, boost up exports and foreign exchange earnings and steer our economy out of the present crisis."[59] Hence, the country has nothing to lose but many things to gain in the process.

---

[56] Dasgupta, *Globalisation: India's Adjustment Experience,* 21.

[57] Vimal Tirrimanna, "Moral Theological Implications of globalization from a Third World Perspective," *Vidyajyoti: Journal of Theological Reflection,* 65/4 (April 2001): 298-299.

[58] S. K. Patel and R. C. Talati, "Globalisation of the Indian Economy" in *Liberalisation and Globalization of Indian Economy,* Volume I, edited by K. R. Gupta (New Delhi: Atlantic Publishers and Distributors, 2000), 86.

[59] Siddharth Shastri, "Globalising the Indian Economy: A Disastrous Move" in *Liberalisation and Globalization of Indian Economy,* Volume I, edited by K. R. Gupta (New Delhi: Atlantic Publishers and Distributors, 2000), 36-37.

It has been commonly understood that through this major shift in the national economic policies and new economic venture Indian economy is being globalised.[60] For those who strongly support this shift, feel that with the introduction of economic reform programmes such as "relaxation of government controls over production, investment and prices in the domestic economy and progressively opening up of the Indian economy to foreign trade, capital and technology"[61] India will achieve sustainable and higher growth rate in all round economic development. Nevertheless, the critics of the reform policies pointed out that with the commencement of the NEP and India joining the process of economic globalization, the country tends to move away from the traditional socialist pattern of economic development that have been implemented since the time of independence. This shift in the economic policies of the country, instead of facilitating towards the growth and development of a sustainable economy, could benefit only a small section of population. Whereas the vast majority of population especially the poor and the marginalised have been left out in the process of economic development. To be precise, the earlier valued concept of "development with equity" as well as vision of social and economic justice with special consideration for the poor and marginalised is being ignored and sidelined. Suresh Mane maintains that with the declaration of the New Economic Policy (NEP) "the long cherished constitutional goals of growth with justice, equity, social responsibility and accountability" is swiftly replaced by "liberalisation, privatisation, globalization, efficiency, marketability and competitiveness leaving marginalised sections without safety nets."[62]

Indian Economy: Post-reform Era

The implementation of different reforms programmes[63] under the New Economic Policy of 1991 portrays that after many decades of control and restriction, Indian economy has eventually joined the process of economic globalization. This departure from the existing economic policy and joining the global economy

---

[60] Khrishna Mohan Prasad, "Changing economic Scenario and Globalization of Indian Economy" in *Liberalisation and Globalisation of Indian Economy,* Volume 3, edited by K. R. Gupta (New Delhi: Atlantic Publishers and Distributors, 1999), 181.

[61] Mishra, "Globalization: Concept and Nature," 14.

[62] Suresh Mane, "Constitutional Dimensions of Social Justice in the Era of Globalization," in *Globalization and Social Justice: Perspective, Challenges and Praxis,* edited by J. G. Jogdand, Prashant P. Bandsode and N. G. Meshram (Jaipur: Rawat Publications, 2008), 216. See also VAK Team, The New Economic Path...," 155.

[63] Under the New Economic Policy different reforms have taken place in different spheres of economy. These reforms are introduced through different policies such as new trade policy, new industrial policy, new banking and finance policy, Public sector, agricultural sector, and so on. For detail see Dasgupta, *Globalization: India's Adjustment Experience,* 22-26. See also S. P. Gupta, "Introduction: Recent Economic Reforms and Their Impact" in *Liberalisation: Its Impact on the Indian Economy,* edited by S. P. Gupta (Delhi: Macmillan India Limited, 1993), 7-10.

marked a great milestone in the economic history of the country. It has been more than two decades since India joined the process of economic globalization and its influence and impact has been greatly visible and witnessed in certain areas. For the supporters of globalization such a step will create diverse opportunities for enlarging and enhancing economic ventures in the long run. It may be noted that the business families, the industrialists, and the upper middle class families perceived this integration as a positive step taken by the national government.[64] Hence, they wholeheartedly supporting and backing the move as it offered them ample scope and prospects for a better economic future. On the other hand, for the weaker sections especially the small farmers, the poor and marginalised this economic step taken by the government did not seem to bring any promising future that could positively improve their economic status and condition of living. For them, all the advantages brought by the process of globalization seems to benefit the selected few, whereas the weaker sections will be sidelined and overlooked in the entire business enterprise.[65]

As there have been diverse views and opinions concerning the manner in which India opened up to economic globalization, so also different perceptions and understanding emerged with regards to the consequences brought by economic globalization within this period. Though the adherents of globalization listed diverse benefits that the country achieved by joining the process of globalization, the critics who are not subscribe to the above ideology lamented over certain disadvantages and loses brought down by the process of globalization to the economy of the country. This implies that the process of economic globalization could not promote equal benefits to different sections of the population. Mishra argues that, "globalization is very uneven process, with unequal distribution of benefits and losses."[66] Here, in the following an attempt is made to analyse both

---

[64] For instance, for the big business families like the Birlas, the Tatas and others, the process of economic globalization is an important step taken by the government that help facilitated them in their attempt to develop their growing economic enterprises. See Michel Chossudovsky, *The Globalization of Poverty: Impacts of IMF and the World Bank Reforms,* (Penang: Third World Network, 1997), 127. A number of industrialists under the umbrella of Confederation of Indian Industries (CII) saw this move as a good platform for international competition. See VAK Team, "The New Economic Path…," 156. So, also the upper-middle class people the process of globalization come as a boon. Hence they welcome globalization with open arms, for it brings advance consumer goods, latest model of imported automobiles, European cosmetics and fashions and so on. See "Unrestricted Globalisation: Boon or hazard?" http://india_resource.tripod.com/globalization.html (5 Oct2011). Cf. K. N. Panikkar, "Globalisation and culture-1," in *Globalisation and SAP: Trends & Impact- An Overview,* edited by Ajit Muricken (Mumbai: Vikas Adhyayan Kandra, 1997), 80.

[65] Saroj Malik, "Contradictions and Challenges of Globalization: Need for an Alternative" in *Globalization: Myth and Reality,* edited by Govind Prasad and Anil Dutta Mishra (New Delhi: Concept Publishing Company, 2004), 40.

[66] Mishra, "Globalization: Concept and Nature," 12.

the advantages and disadvantages received by the nation and its people on joining the process of economic globalization.

Globalization: Benefits to India

It cannot be denied that the process of globalization offered different economic opportunities to the country as well as its people. Integration of economy with the global economy seems to imply that Indian economy will gain to the maximum and this will help the country surging ahead towards better economic growth and development. Within these two decades of integration there have been certain areas of growth in the economy of the country.

Growth of Indian Economy

It has been noticed that since the integration of the country's economy with the global economy, India is one among the fastest growing economy in the world. India's economy which had a constant growth rate of 3% in the seventies, coupled with the severe financial crisis that pushed the economy to the brink of collapsing in the 1990s, is recently growing at a very fast pace. It is reported that the GDP growth rate has consequently increase from 5.6% in 1990-91 to 7.8% in 1996-97,[67] and it has stepped up to 8.5% in 2006, 9.0% in 2007 and 7.8% in 2008.[68] The post-reform scenario portrays that Indian export and import transaction has been surging considerably within these two decades. It is important to note that while the exports increased from US $18 billion in the year 1990-91 to US $27 billion in 1994-95, the imports transactions rose up from US $28 billion to US $31 billion respectively during the same period.[69] With this rapid increased in the country's economy, the GDP position of India in the world economy rose from the 8th position in 1991 to fourth largest economy by the year 2001in terms of "purchasing power parity basis."[70] Similarly, with the total business transaction amounting to $3.3 trillion, India is the world's fifth largest economy in the world next only to EU, US, China and Japan.[71] The above figures mirrored an

---

[67] Chandrasekaran Balakhrishnan, "Impact of Globalisation on Developing countries and India," http://economics.about.com/od/globalizationtrade/l/aaglobalization.htm (4 Oct 2011). See also Mohan Prasad Shrivastava, "A Decade of Globalisation, Liberalisation and Economic Reforms in India: An Assessment," in *Economic Reforms in India,* edited by Bishwa Nath Singh, Mohan Prasad Srivastava, Narendra Prasad (New Delhi: APH Publishing Corporation, 2003), 81.

[68] Kimberly Amedeo, "India's Economy," See http://useconomy.about.com/od/worldeconomy/p/India_economy.htm (4 Nov 2011).

[69] R. N. Ghosh and R. Gabbay, "Prospects of the Indian Economy: The 1990s and Beyond," in *Sustaining Development: Human Resources, Gender and Environment,* edited by R. N. Ghosh, R. Gabbay & K. C. Roy (Delhi: Atlantic Publishers and Distributors, 1999), 240.

[70] Balakhrishnan, "Impact of Globalization on Developing countries and India."

[71] See Amedeo, India's economy, http://useconomy.about.com/od/worldeconomy/p/India_economy.htm (4 Nov 2011).

encouraging trend with positive improvement in the history of Indian economy in the post-reform era particularly the macro-economic sector.

Opportunities to Indian Companies

As stated earlier, the Indian capitalists accepted the process of globalization as a positive step towards better economic venture that offer good platform for both national and international competition. Prior to the economic reforms most Indian companies invested small capital in their business transactions with limited capacity of production. In the post-reform period many of the Indian companies "have gone in for enlarging the capital base and production capacity substantially."[72] Eventually, level of competitions both in national and international arena have largely encouraged most of the big companies to make their presence felt in the field of global economy. It is interesting to note that many of the big companies in India have been able to capture the opportunities of global competition "by investing in new technology and production methods and raised their production standard."[73] For most of the big companies, globalization appears to be a boon that offered unlimited option not only to enhance their production capacities but also equip them to emerge as major economic global player. Notably, the post-reform economic scenario has witnessed how the process of globalization facilitated some big Indian companies emerged as Multinational Companies themselves by enlarging their business transactions across the globe.[74]

Employment Opportunities

For the supporters of globalization, the present day generation has varieties of employment avenues and job opportunities than the earlier generation. With the advent of globalization, one could witness the increasing numbers of industries operating different business enterprises through the involvement of the MNCs/ TNCs in number of areas like "cell phones, automobiles, electronics, soft drinks, fast food" which in turn created new avenues in different parts of the country.[75] Simultaneously, with the booming software service and information technologies sector growing at a rapid rate, coupled with the growing number of English speaking people job opportunities for the Indian youth are plentiful.[76] Hence, for the IT literate personnel employment opportunities are abundant. Besides

---

[72] VAK Team, "The New Economic Path...," 157.

[73] Jyoti Malhotra, "Globalization and the Indian Economy," www.indiastudychannel.com/ resources/74993-globalization-indian-economy.aspx (5 Nov 2011).

[74] Some of these big Indian Companies are Tata motors (automobiles), Infosys (IT), Ranbaxy (medicine), Asian Paints (paints) and so on. Malhotra, "Globalization and Indian Economy."

[75] Malhotra, "Globalization and Indian Economy."

[76] It is interesting to note that due to the presence of number of English medium schools, together with using English as the medium of education in many places, India has a vast number of English speaking populations among several developing countries. See "Unrestricted Globalization-

employing 1.4 million workers IT sector earnings have increased from 150 million dollars to 24 billion dollars in 2005-06.[77] It is said that since India joined the process of globalization large numbers of job are being outsourced to India offering vast number of employment opportunities to the country's population. This is due to time zone that India have, in comparison to US and Europe added major advantage to India. For instance, series of works sent in the evening from US to India can be finished during the day in India, which not only save time but increased delivery speed to their customers back there in US. Comparatively, with the amount of money spend less in India for the same type of work if done in US, most of the western companies preferred India as their outsourcing destination.[78] Hence, the advent of outsourcing industry proved to be a boon to many people seeking for employment opportunities.

Foreign Investment

One of the main objectives of the New Economic Policies in particular and integration to global capitalist system is to attract foreign investment in different areas of economic development. It is the belief of the advocates of economic reforms that foreign investment, besides having the capability to bring the desire level of economic growth and development to the country concern will also "generate employment, reduce income inequality and poverty."[79] To put it differently, the inflow of foreign investment to the country is important as it is expected to help contribute towards the better welfare of the population especially the weaker sections like the poor and the needy. There are two forms of foreign investment, namely the Direct Foreign Investment (FDI) and the portfolio investment. While the former is referred to the "investment of foreign capital into new productive activity which may or may not lead to an increase in exports" the latter is understood as those types of investments where "foreign capital purchasing the shares of existing Indian companies to claim a share of the profits and exercise control in the sphere of production."[80] With the Indian economy being opened to

---

Boon or hazard?" in *South Asian Voice,* http://india_resource.tripod.com/globalization.html (5 Nov 2011).

[77] Rao, "Globalization, Dalits and Social Justice," 179.

[78] It is reported besides saving the time that the company preferred India as they have to spend less amount of money for Indian people are satisfied with lesser salaries compared with the works in US. In reality what the people earned through outsourcing job is far better than what they are getting elsewhere in other agencies in India. See "The Benefit of Job Outsourcing to O2I," www.outsourcing2india.com/why_india/articles/job-outsourcing-to-india.asp (7 Nov 2011).

[79] Govind Prasad, "Globalization and Foreign Direct Investment: India and Canada" in *Globalization: Myth and Reality,* edited by Govind Prasad and Anil Dutta Mishra (New Delhi: Concept Publishing Company, 2004), 253.

[80] VAK Team, "The New Economic Path...," 161.

the global economy,[81] post-reform era witnessed the increasing trend of inflow of the foreign investment into the country within these two decades. It is reported that while in the year 1990-91 the FDI inflow to the country was amounted only to $97 million, by the year 2002-03 the total amount of inflow rose to $2256 million. At the same time, whereas in the year 1990-91in terms of portfolio investment the total inflow is about $6 million, by the year 2002-03 the total inflow has increased up to $386 million. Simultaneously, while the number of FDI approved in the year 1991 was 289, the amount approved was Rs. 534 crores and the actual inflow of FDI was RS. 351 crores, by the year 2002 the number of FDI approved has increased to 1966 and the amount approved of FDI was Rs.11140 crores, whereas the actual inflow of FDI during (January-August) of the same year has increased to Rs. 21286 crores.[82] Nevertheless, compared with other developing countries like China and others, the percentage that India share to the total world FDI is meagre. It is found that in the year 2001, while China could attract up to $46.8 billion which formed 6.4% of the total share percentage in the world, India could attract only $3.4 billion forming only a paltry of 0.5% of the total share in the world.[83] However, whatever the case may be there is an increasing inflow of the foreign investment into the country since the integration of the country's economy with the global economy. For those who support the process of globalization this inflow indicates the increasing investment for the growth and development of the Indian economy. In other words, it is a great achievement to the economy of the country within a short span of time. But the critics of globalization maintain that such an inflow is nothing but the "invasion by MNCs" to exploit the resources of the country.[84] Kalirajan argues that though the foreign investment did not directly contribute towards poverty elimination, it has nevertheless "influenced the structural changes in the economy, particularly with respect to promoting industry."[85]

The above discussion indicates that integrating the Indian economy with the process of globalization has indeed brought certain economic benefits to the country and some section of the Indian population. The gloomy days

---

[81] It may be noted that liberalization of Indian economy by removing series of controls and restrictions was done with the intention of attracting massive flow of foreign investment. See Kalipa Kalirajan, "Liberalisation Strategies and Poverty Reduction in India," www.eastasiaforum.org/2010/09/06/liberalisation-strategies-and-poverty-reduction-in-india/ (28 Oct 2011).

[82] Prasad, "Globalization and Foreign Direct Investment…," 261.

[83] Prasad maintains that the main reasons for this failure among many include anti-export bias of our foreign trade policies, lacking of good infrastructure, lack of government commitment and credibility, uncertainties of coalition government and so on. For detail see Prasad, "Globalization and Foreign Direct Investment...," 256, 262-263.

[84] This will be discussed in detail later. See VAK Team, "The New Economic Path…," 157.

[85] Kalirajan, "Liberalisation Strategies and Poverty Reduction in India," www.eastindiaforum.org/2010/09/06/liberalisation-strategies-and-poverty-reduction-in-india/ (28 Oct 2011).

of the pre-reforms period that has pushed the economy of the country to the brink of collapse has finally become a matter of the past. Indian economy has rapidly achieved certain level of growth and it is considered as one among the fastest growing economy today in the arena of global economy. The promoter of the New Economic Policy believed that joining the global economy besides facilitating the growth and development of the country's economy, will help share the benefits to the entire sections of population. To be precise, the benefits of growth and development attained by the country will trickle down to different strata of population which in turn aiding in raising the living conditions of the poor and the marginalised.

However, analysing the post-reform economy of India from the perspective of the poor and the marginalised, one could say that joining the process of economic globalization though it help India achieved certain growth, has benefitted only a small section of the population.[86] It is only the rich and the privileged few that have reaped the benefit of economic globalization, whereas the weaker section of population has been left out in the ladder of economic development. Commenting on the challenges of economic globalization to the Indian economy in the post-reform era Einhorn argues,

> Since the dark days of 1991, India has come a long way. It has healthy foreign exchange reserves (despite high levels of domestic debts), a booming software and services export market, and a bourgeoning knowledge economy. Clearly India has tremendous potential to benefit from globalization but challenges confronting India are daunting and substantial.[87]

Hence, it is vividly clear that despite Indian economy is growing to the certain extent, the sharing of benefits and losses caused by the process of economic globalization to the people of India are uneven. For the million poor and marginalised the benefits of the entire economic progress and development are still a distant dream.

Disadvantages of Economic Globalization

As stated above, though globalization offered a series of advantages to the country's population, it is indeed enjoyed only by small section of the population. Besides the ample scope and opportunities that have largely benefitted the society, there are also scores of disadvantages that come along with the process of globalization. These sorts of drawbacks are experienced mostly by the weaker sections of the society.

---

[86] Despite the growth of Indian economy, actually it is only a small section of population that are really benefit from the process like the capitalist, big business family, the upper middle class and so on.

[87] See Jessica Einhorn, "Millions of Indians Awaits Benefits of Globalization" in www.yale.edu/content/millions-indians-await-benefits-globalzation (3 Nov 2011).

The Entry of the MNCs/TNCs

The integration of national economy with the global economy offered a crucial opportunity to the MNCs/TNCs to enhance their territory for obtaining maximum profit. For the supporters of globalization the coming of the MNCs/TNCs will bring growth and development to the Indian economy by bringing new technology and capital investment. In reality this is not the case. It is important to note that the main objective of these companies is not to bring development to the region rather to exploit the available resources for quick and maximum profit. In other words these corporate giants are not "development agencies" but they are "profit seeking organisation."[88] Coming to a country like India they could earn threefold profit.

Firstly, they could exploit the cheap labour force readily available for recruitment in their new enterprises established in the country. India is well known for its cheap labour available in different capacities. It is reported that coming to India the MNCs/TNCs could utilised a bulk of "trained, skilled and relatively inexpensive labour such as low-cost engineering talent,"[89] as well as cheap unskilled labour force for manufacturing consumers' goods to be sold back at high cost.[90] Hence, for the corporate giants who are looking for minimum investment for maximum profit this offered a good bargain to quickly enlarge their earnings.

Secondly, India offers a big market for commercialising the consumers' goods produce by their firms due to its expanding westernized highly rich and middle income class population. With a huge middle class population estimated at 170 million[91] and crazy after foreign and imported goods reaching at their door step, the corporate giants make them the target of exploitation. To capture the big Indian market the MNCs/TNCs largely entered in different capacities of productions, thereby replacing the small local industries in producing different consumers' goods. Ramaswamy argues that the intention of the corporate giants to exploit the market of the country is witnessed in their attempt to enlarge their amount of production right from toothpaste up to the readymade garments. The

---

[88] See "Perspective on Trans-National Companies" in www.grips.ac.jp/csids/perspectives/perspective03.pdf (15 Nov 2011).

[89] Besides the above it is said that the Japanese MNCs in India depend on "local sourcing for 77% of their inputs, as compared of 50% in China." See Matthew Emde, "An Analysis of the Effects of the MNCs on India since Liberation," www.arts.usask.ca/economics/skjournal/sej-2nd/sej2-emde.pdf (15 Nov 2011).

[90] VAK Team, "The New Economic Path…," 162.

[91] It may be noted that these middle income class population is half the population of USA and is much higher than the population of many countries. Hence, India offers a big market to the giant companies for diverse types of their products. See Vincent Fernando, "Faber: India's Middle Class will soon be larger than Americas" www.articles.businessinsider.com/2010-02-15/markets/30074431_1_rupees-population-vehicle-sales (15 Nov 2011).

classic example is the case of Hindustan-Lever which operated a total transaction of Rs, 14,000 crores in 1990 alone. Out of this total amount, this company achieved Rs.1,400 crores from soaps and detergents, Rs.200 crores from toothpaste and tooth powder and so on.[92] This indicates that besides the ability to accumulate huge profits, the corporate giants were able to penetrate and capture different areas of productions which can be easily operated by the local firms.

Thirdly, besides succeeding on their mission to exploit the intensive market, the MNCs/TNCSs do not have to invest huge amount, as the country offered "large export subsidies and other facilities in the name of earning foreign exchange by promoting exports."[93] With the intention to attract huge FDI the government do away with all restrictions that could hinder the MNCs/TNCs from establishment of their firms in the country. This indicates that the corporate giants are free to set up their firms for manufacturing and marketing of "consumer goods like colour television, VCR, cars, washing machines, refrigerators, etc" without any hindrance or obstruction.[94] With such a welcoming atmosphere, the corporate giants attempt all efforts to establish their firms within the country as manufacture base for export to global market. That is, they not only focus on the magnitude of Indian market but intend to make "India their production base for international markets."[95]

Hence, within these two decades with numbers of FDI approvals keep on increasing, one could witness large number of diverse MNCs/TNCs entering into the country to exploit every sector of the Indian economy.[96] According to the World Investment Report 2009, published by the United Nations Conference on Trade and Development (UNCTAD) altogether there are 3,057 MNCs operating in India which include 815 country based and 2,242 foreign affiliates.[97] All these companies established their firms with the motive to exploit the economy of the country for quick profit. To achieve their objectives these companies come either to set up "wholly owned new undertakings or been taking over Indian companies

---

[92] Ramaswamy, *In the Woods of Globalization,* 104-105.

[93] Thomas Sebastian, *Globalization and Uneven Development: Neo-colonialism, Multinational Corporations, Space and Society,* (Jaipur: Rawat Publications, 2007), 207.

[94] Ramaswamy, *In the Woods of Globalization,* 155.

[95] VAK Team, "The New Economic Path...," 157.

[96] Citing from the *Fortune Magazine,* Sebastian reveals that large number of MNCs/TNCs has already made their strong presence in different sector like banks, commercial and savings, chemicals, computers, office equipments, electronics and electrical equipments, food consumer products, food production, industrial and farm equipments, household and personal products insurance, motor vehicles and parts, pharmaceuticals, scientific, photo, control equipments, and so on. See Sebastian, *Globalization and Uneven Development: Neo-colonialism, Multinational Corporations, Space and Society,* 186.

[97] See "Number of MNCs in India" www.numberof.net/numberofmncsinindia/ (14 Nov 2011).

with 5% equity stake."[98] Sebastian maintains that most of the MNCs/TNCs entered the country in the post-colonial era through collaboration programmes set up with the existing established local venture, "fully making use of the existing facilities and networks of the local partner" for joint production.[99] In this joint venture the Indian party usually function as junior partner under the scheme designed by the MNCs/TNCs. While this collaboration undertaking carries on for certain period, in due course the MNCs/TNCs partner "slowly and steadily raises the stake and ends up buying the entire stake of the local partners."[100] In other words, despite the claim of the supporters of New Economic Policy that the inflow of MNCs/TNCs will come along with new forms for technology and technological knowledge, it is clear that most companies are here not to "bring new technology and new production but merely take over existing ones or things already being done."[101] A classic example is the case of Parle company where its owner Ramesh Chauhan surrender his company to the giant company Coca Cola a US based soft drink MNCs.[102] It is reported that from 2004 to 2009 the number of Indian based MNCs declined by nearly 50% whereas the numbers of foreign affiliates increase by 90%.[103] This implies that in due course many of the Indian companies surrender their ownership status to the foreign company. So, what follows is that besides capturing the entire venture the corporate giants continue to exploit all the available economic resources without any amount of limitation.

Sebastian perceives the contemporary role of the MNCs/TNCs in the Third World context as nothing but "a strategy of international capital under its neo-colonial operation." He further states that in the present neo-colonial context, the gradual growth of India's industrial set up with the assistance obtained from foreign collaboration programmes does not "lead to a break from colonial dependence." On the contrary, "the Indian economy got more and more

---

[98] These companies come from different countries like US, Europe, Japan, South Korea, etc. Some among these companies are General Motors and Daewoo (automobiles), Whirlpool and Swedish MNCs (White goods sector), Carier and Aircon, etc. (air-conditioning), Ericsson AT&T, etc. (Telephone, cable and telecommunications), Japanese and South Koreans (electronics goods) and the like. See VAK Team, "The New Economic Path...," 157.

[99] For instance, while "Kiloskar produce the smaller horse power diesel engines, its major partner Cummins produce the larger horse power engines. In chemical and petrochemical plants, the central pressure vessels were supplied by the MNCs, while the simple to fabricate parts were supplied by the Indian firms." See Sebastian, *Globalization and Uneven Development: Neocolonialism, Multinational Corporations, Space and Society,* 181.

[100] Sebastian, *Globalization and Uneven Development: Neo-colonialism, Multinational Corporations, Space and Society,* 181.

[101] Mahesh Prasad, "India: TNCs muscling into Cottage Industry Sectors," www.twnside.org.sg/title/tnc-ch.htm (15 Nov 2011).

[102] Prasad, "India: TNCs muscling into Cottage Industry Sectors."

[103] Number of MNCs in India www.numberof.net/numberofmncsinindia/ (14 Nov 2011).

integrated into the operation of capital from the imperialist countries."[104] What follows is that, with the integration of India's economy to the global economy coupled with the removal of various controls and regulations, exploitation of the country's economic resources by the MNCs/TNCs became more intensified and deepened without any restraint or limitation. The transfer of political administration from the colonial rulers to the local nationalists' personnel has instead made the pathway easier for the international capital to assert its increasing dominion over the national capital. To state differently, in the name of bringing growth and development to the country's underdeveloped economy through the smooth flowing of FDI, the national political administrators make all efforts to see that there are no hindrances that could obstruct the operative role of the MNCs/TNCs. Sebastian argues that it is indeed "become more efficient, as the exploitation is done now with the consent of the ruling class."[105] Fanon assert that the political representatives of the newly independent country instead of helping for the growth of the local economy have become the agents of the corporate giants for exploiting the rich economic resources of the state.[106]

As stated earlier, one of the main motive of the coming of MNCs/TNCs was not to bring development but to accumulate maximum profit within short period. So, while the corporate giants could extract maximum profit, only a tiny section of population could share little benefits from the operation of these big companies. Those who could share the benefits are mostly those who are employed by these companies to make their vision materialise whereas the poor and marginalised are completely left out from sharing any sort of advantages. Hence, the inflow of MNCs/TNCs to the country instead of raising the living condition of the poor and marginalised make their situation even worse than expected. Some of the disadvantages brought by the process of globalization are listed below.

Firstly, with the new economic reforms offered welcome atmosphere for the inflow of FDI to India, the MNCs/TNCs have aggressively entered into the country to exploit the available opportunities for big profits. Prasad maintains that the corporate giants are moving into the country with the motive of taking over "the well-managed Indian companies and to muscle their way into consumer goods sectors where suppliers are small and cottage industry producer." Citing the example of Pepsi Global Foods and Beverage Company[107] in its move to capture

[104] Sebastian, *Globalization and Uneven Development: Neo-colonialism, Multinational Corporations, Space and Society,* 182.

[105] Sebastian, *Globalization and Uneven Development: Neocolonialism, Multinational Corporations, Space and Society,* 182.

[106] Fanon, *The Wretched of the Earth,* 122-123.

[107] Pepsi Foods is the US TNC Pepsi-Coca Cola company operating in India.

small Indian cottage industry snack food manufacturers of "Bikaner Bhujia,"[108] he argues that though the Pepsi denying it, fears aroused among the bhujia workers that the company intend to patent the snack food under its brand name "Pepsi Namkeen" to restrict the local indigenous manufacturers to produce and market their product.[109] A recent study by National Commission for Women on the "Impact of WTO on Women in Agriculture"[110] reveals how the local indigenous cottage industries of Bikaner facing stiff challenges from the MNCs like the Pepsi. The report provides many example how the "indigenous know-how is now being exploited by MNC bent on monopolizing the traditional markets" thus undermining the local producers and labelled their products as of inferior quality.[111] Notably, after a long struggle with numerous copycats in September 2010, Indian Patent Office confirms the Geographical Indication right to the local manufacturers of Bikaner under the brand name Bikaner Bhujia.[112]

Whatever may be the case, with the ability to produce huge volume of goods backed up by powerful and massive advertisement on one hand, coupled with smart and attractive packaging products flooding the market on the other, the impact on the local manufacturers would be disastrous.[113] It is reported that with attractive packaging of their products the corporate companies are selling their stuff at a price much higher than the local products. Despite the price of the MNCs/TNCs products are much higher than the local products; the westernized urban middle class people influenced by the globalised cosmopolitan culture are ready to pay any amount for the foreign goods, thus making the giant companies accumulate maximum profit.[114] This implies that the cosmopolitan culture created by the process of globalization or neo-colonial forces has deeply influenced or ingrained in the psyche of the middle class population who are ready to pay anything for the imported goods or goods with foreign trademark produced

---

[108] Bikaner Bhujia derives its name from Bikaner town in the western state of Rajasthan. It is a salted spicy snack food, a kind of cottage industry that provides employment to 2.5 million people in the area. See N. P. Chekutty, "The Whole World's Bhujia" www.indiatogether.org/2005jul/eco-bikaner.htm#continue (15 Nov 2011).

[109] Prasad, "India: TNCs muscling into Cottage Industry Sectors."

[110] The study was prepared by the New Delhi-based Research Foundation for Science and Technology.

[111] Chekkutty, The Whole World's Bhujia, www.indiatogether.org/2005/jul/eco-bikaner.htm#continue (15 Nov 2011).

[112] See www.en.wikipedia.org/wiki/Bikaneri_Bhujia (15 Nov 2011).

[113] Chekkutty, "The Whole World's Bhujia."

[114] Gopal Agarwal the President of Bikaneri Bhujia Kutir Udyog Bachao Sangar Samity (Save Bikaneri Bhujia Cottage Industry Struggle Committee) reported that while the local manufacturers were selling Bikaneri Bhujia at Rs.40 per Kg and the potato chips at Rs. 60 per Kg during that time, the TNCs were selling the same at Rs. 75 and Rs. 240 per Kg respectively. See Prasad, "India: TNCs muscling into Cottage Industry Sectors."

by the MNCs/TNCs ignoring the local products even if they are cheaper and more affordable prices. If this is the case, the MNCs/TNCs not only succeed in capturing the entire market, but many of the original manufacturers will be driven out of their business thus leaving thousands of the dependent families cut off from their source of livelihood.[115] Simultaneously, one could witness massive diverse products of manufactured goods produce by these corporate giants flooding in different grocery shops of the country, thereby preventing the spread of local products though selling at cheaper and affordable prices. Besides these consumer goods produce by the MNCs/TNCs are generally beyond the reach of the weaker section of the society especially the poor and the marginalised group.

Secondly, to make their case more attractive, these corporate giants come with a big promise to help the country's economy by generating and creating employment opportunities to numbers of unemployed youth of the country. But these promises are never kept. A classic example is the case of Pepsi who entered India during the Punjab problem, with the promise to generate employment to the unemployed youth of Punjab in order to take them away from the path of terrorism that was highly influenced the young generation in Punjab that time. Among several commitments promised by the Pepsi Company include creating "employment for 50,000 nationally, including 25,000 extra job for Punjab, 7.4% of total investment in food and agro-processing, export of 50% of total production, non use of foreign brand names in domestic sales, etc."[116] Looking into the promises made by this big company, one could agree that the intention of establishing this project was to generate economic growth and development to the country in general and Punjab in particular. But in reality the case is different. Though the Pepsi Company claimed to have generated indirect employment to 26,000 people like vendors, etc, the official report illustrated that the real figure of employment shows that the company has directly employed only 783 people in 1990-91, 909 people in 1991-92, and 2,400 in 1996 which is just 3% of its promise.[117] As they are profit seeking organisation they would attempt all possibilities to increase their earnings even at the expense of the local population. Looking from the post-colonial perspective, such a practice is nothing but a replication of the colonial subjugation of the economic resources of the local people. In other words, it brings to the present day context the historical memories of how the rich resources of the country being subjugated and subdued by the British East India Company in the colonial era.[118] While the local people anticipated that the coming of MNCs/TNCs will bring essential development to the area, at the end of the day, it is only these corporate giants, who could

[115] Chekkutty, "The Whole World's Bhujia."

[116] Cherian, "Globalization- A conspiracy...," 71.

[117] Cherian, "Globalization- A Conspiracy...," 71.

[118] Prasad, "India: TNCs Muscling into Cottage Industry Sector."

extract maximum benefits using the resource of the local area, whereas the local population could share little benefit through these kinds of project. Hence, the coming of MNCs/TNCs besides reducing the employment prospect of the local people on one hand, and exploiting the economic resources of the local people on the other, it does not help to bring much difference to the living condition of the people especially the poor and the marginalised.

Special Economic Zones

With India joining the process of globalization, combined with the intention to attract FDI for economic growth and development, Special economic Zones (SEZs) Act based on China model was passed in 2005. With the passing of the SEZ Act the government make all effort not only to offer welcome atmosphere to the corporate companies for FDI in the country, but also "to impart stability to the SEZ regime."[119] Mr. Murasoli Maran the then union Minister of Commerce and Industry as cited by Dohrmann once comments that SEZs are "our best dream projects" and they are the "magnet and glue - (a) magnet to attract FDI and glue to identify and bind strategies that will benefit a large number of people and organisations."[120] With this in mind the main objectives of the SEZ Act are- a) generation of economic activity b) promotion of exports of goods and services c) promotion of investment from domestic and foreign sources d) creation of employment opportunities e) development of infrastructure facilities.[121]

It is clear from the standpoint of the government that establishment of SEZs will not only bring the free flow of investment but also will create employment opportunities to different sections of the nation's population. Hence, to instil confidence of the SEZs enterprises particular area is set aside as "foreign territory for the purpose of trade operations, duties and tariffs" coupled with different economic laws that are more liberal than the existing country's laws, for attracting more FDI and infrastructure development.[122] Nayak maintains that SEZ is understood as "a demarcated area of land especially for trade, owned and operated by a private company. It enjoys exemption from custom duties, income tax, sale

---

[119] Though the SEZs Act was passed in 2005, it is reported that way back in 1965, India was the first country in Asia to realize the importance of Export Processing Zone (EPZ) model for promoting exports when the first EPZ established in Kandla, Gujarat. In similar vein, to promote the engine of economic growth under the neo-liberal capitalist framework, "a comprehensive draft SEZ Bill was passed on May, 2005 by the parliament and received Presidential assent on the 23rd June, 2005." See "Special Economic Zones in India" by the Ministry of Commerce and Industry, http://www.sezindia.nic.in/about-introduction.asp (29 Nov 2011).

[120] See Jona Aravind Dohrmann, "Special Economic Zones in India- An Introduction," 62. http://www.asienkunde.de/articles/a106_asien_aktuell_dohrmann.pdf (15 Nov 2011).

[121] Ministry of Commerce and Industry, Special Economic Zones in India.

[122] It is reported that with the passing of SEZ Act large number of private Industrial Township have come out covering several thousand acres of land in different parts of the country. Dohrmann, "Special Economic Zones in India...," 62.

tax and service tax."[123] The favourable atmosphere offered by the country has resulted to the rapid rush of corporate bodies to establish their SEZs enterprises in India. Accordingly, as of March, 2008 there were 206 SEZs operating in India with the total investment amounted to the tune of Rs. 69,000 crores including Rs. 54,000 crores of FDI, thereby providing employment to 98,000 workers and exported goods and services to the tune of Rs. 52,000 crores.[124] By the month of February, 2010 out of the formal approval of 571 SEZs approximately covering the area of 67,680 hectares, 348 SEZs have been notified and a total of 105 have already started exporting. Similarly, during the financial year 2008-09 there has been rapid increase of total export amounted up to Rs. 996,890 million showing an increase growth rate of 50% from the previous year. Notably, the first three quarter of the financial year of 2009-10 again reveals an increase growth rate of 127% within that period.[125]

Looking on the rapid increase of direct investment in different parts of the country in the SEZs area as well as the sudden growth of export goods, one may argue that establishment of SEZs enterprises brought positive growth and development to the economy of the nation. However, a closer look from different aspects on the growth and development of SEZs regime discloses that this is only one side of the story. Besides the small section of population who are getting employment, it is the corporate bodies who received the maximum advantages within a short span of time at the expense of the weaker section of society especially the poor and the marginalised.

It is generally believed that the establishment of the SEZs will bring development to the area. That is, local people are often made to believe that once the area developed into township the advantages will trickle down to the entire surrounding areas. The establishment of the SEZs come along with forced acquisition and grabbing of the land, resulted not only to the loss of farm lands, dwelling home and other properties but also led to the displacement and dislocation of the entire people of the area. Hence, the establishment of SEZs often invite stiff opposition from the local people which sometimes resulted to

---

[123] The main difference between the earlier Export Processing Zone and SEZ is that "the former is just an industrial enclave while the SEZ is an integrated township with fully developed infrastructure. It includes restaurants, housing and apartments, gymnasiums, clubs, multiplexes, shopping malls, schools, business centre and swimming pools." See Arun Kumar Nayak, "SEZs and Displacement," *Social Action* 58/3 (July-September, 2008): 258-259.

[124] See Kannan Kasturi, "SEZs: Engine derailed?" www.indiatogether.org/2009/jan/eco-Sezbust.htm (29 Nov 2011).

[125] Vidya Bhushan Rawat, Namidi Bharath Bhushan and Sujata Surepally, "The Impact of Special Economic Zones in India: A Case Study of Polepally SEZ," (A Paper presented at the International Conference on Global Land Grabbing, on the 6-8, April, 2011, Social Development Foundation, New Delhi, August 2010).

even the abandoning of the entire project.[126] A case study conducted by Rawat et al demonstrates that with the establishment of the Polepally SEZ[127] covering an area of 1000 acres, the three villages Polepally, Gundhagadda Thadda and Mudireddipally had indeed lost 693, 300 and 150 acres of their land respectively, in which Polepally alone 339 families lost their land. Besides, though the packages of compensation in the forms of repayment and rehabilitation are promised, they rarely reached the affected people on time. At the same time, "such compensation even paid in full, is woefully, inadequate to the loss of land and non-land assets, the loss of livelihood opportunities and the disruption of traditional rural lives."[128] Moreover, most of the farmers who received compensation hardly know any skills or activities besides agriculture thereby making them invest their money in other business or new activities is a distant dream, hence the amount of money compensated to them is not properly utilised.[129]

Grabbing the land from the local people has definitely affected not only the farmers, but also the landless and non-farms workers that live in the area. The latter will be the most affected groups in the entire process. Kumar argues that these groups of people which "traditionally integrated into the farm economy, would be completely at sea without much capital. Such people would constitute about half of the population of the villages and can only add to the ranks of the unemployed"[130] Eventually, it is true that the coming of SEZs created some jobs and employment opportunities but maximum number of jobs are for high-skilled and semi-skilled workers.[131] Hence, most of the jobs available in these new

[126] For instance, the people of people of Nandigram in West Bengal made strong resistance to the establishment of Nandigram SEZ, a joint venture project initiated by the West Bengal government and the Salim Group from Indonesia meant for a chemical hub covering an area of 14,000 acres of land within the parameter of 29 different villages. Likewise, the farmers of Jamnagar, Gujarat in 2006 move the Supreme Court to raise their voice against the selling of 10,000 acres of land for the SEZ to be establishment by the Reliance Infrastructure. See Dohrmann, "Special Economic Zones in India...," 73. See also Xavier Jeyaraj, "An SEZ with a Difference," *Social Action,* 58/3 (July-September, 2008), 273.

[127] Polepally is situated on the National Highway 7, a distance about 96km from Hyderabad in Andhra Pradesh, with the neighbor villages of Mudireddipally and the tribal village of Gundlagadda Thanda. The area is home mostly to the weaker sections of society like the ST, SC, Muslims and other backward castes people. It was in 2005 that the establishment of SEZ has started in the area where the land is taken away from the villagers and allocated to a number of pharmaceutical enterprises for manufacturing pharmaceutical products.

[128] The study also found that even though the eviction process commenced way back in 2004-05, till April 11, 2010 the housing colony promised to the affected villagers has not been constructed. Rawat et al, "The Impact of Special Economic Zones in India...."

[129] Arun Kumar, "Socio-economic Aspects of SEZs," *Social Action 58/3* (July-September, 2008), 236.

[130] While the farmers will at least get some kind of compensation, the landless and non-farm people are not entitled to receive the same. Kumar, Socio-economic Aspects of SEZs, 237.

[131] Kumar, "Socio-economic Aspects of SEZs," 237.

enterprises are usually captured by the urban skilled workers, leaving the poor marginalised rural and unskilled workers outside the arena of job competition and be satisfied with few menial job. Commenting on the misery of the affected people, Rawat et al maintains that "while their land resources were directly taken away for the SEZs, families saw other assets that remain in their possession like cattle and farm implements, lost their value."[132] In the name of national interest, not only their lands are being grabbed but also the sources of livelihood are taken away from them.[133] To put it differently, the establishment of SEZs instead of raising the living condition of the people in the area make the lives of vulnerable section or the marginalised poor more impoverished than earlier. The slogan of the government that the benefits will trickle down to different layers of the society contains no substance to the life experience and daily struggle of the weaker sections. Admittedly, though the area within the SEZs Townships is well developed with latest infrastructure available, the entire areas outside the boundary of the SEZs Township remain the same as underdeveloped as before.[134]

Geographical Concentration of Wealth

Elsewhere, it is mentioned that the process of globalization creates disparities between the centre and the periphery. The opening up of the country's economy to the global economy with the aim to evenly share the benefits to diverse sections of population, does not seem to bring equal distribution of wealth neither between different regions nor different sections of population. With the vision to obtain easy and quick profit MNCs/TNCs make all effort to invest in a place where transport and communication system assist them to achieve their goal. Bose asserts that prior to the economic reforms taking place, the central government attempted every effort to encourage private enterprises to invest in "no industry" and "backward" districts with the aim of creating "balance regional development" by providing "a series of fiscal incentives, concessions and subsidies"[135] so that development can evenly shared in different parts of the nations. However, with the economic reforms being implemented, combined with the welcome atmosphere to the MNCs/TNCs gaining momentum the concept of "balance regional development" became a thing of the past. Most of the MNCs/TNCs will set up their projects only in a place where good network of road transportation and good telecommunication system is easily available. For instance, the Japanese are investing in a model town of Gurgaon and the Singaporeans are investing in a technology park near Bangalore unmindful of

---

[132] Rawat et al, "The Impact of Special Economic Zones in India...."

[133] Nayak, "SEZs and Displacement," 260.

[134] Cf. Kumar, "Socio-ecnomic Aspects of SEZs," 238.

[135] Ashish Bose, "Globalization, Migration and Urbanization," in *Religion and Society* XLI/2, (June, 1994): 30.

the pressure created to the already populated cities.[136] On the other hand, these giant companies will established their firms in the backward areas only if the natural resources are easily available and at a very much cheaper rate.[137] Hence, the concept of centre-periphery, urban-rural, developed-underdeveloped is very much prevalent in the present phase of globalization. As most of the employment opportunities in these different projects are exploited by the educated urban rich and middle class, the concentration of wealth is also urban centric. Sebastian maintains that the global accumulation of wealth in India is mainly concentrated within a few metropolitan cities like Mumbai, Delhi, Kolkata, Chennai, Pune, and Bangalore and the like. On the other hand, region wise distribution of these giants company reveals that western region have 42.21%, southern region have 27.25%, eastern region have 16.3% (mostly West Bengal) and northern region 12.23%. Whereas the states in the heartland belt of India[138] as well as the North Eastern Region[139] have little to share of the benefits, thus occupy insignificant place in the whole scheme of things mapping by the process of globalization.[140] This indicates that developmental activities in general and accumulation of nation's wealth in particular are concentrated in some regions and mostly urban centric. Whereas other backward region especially the interior and rural areas are being neglected in the course of many developmental project and activities in the process of present day globalization. This implies that most of the rich sections of the nation's population are concentrated in urban areas leaving the marginalised poor to struggle for their daily living in the poor interior rural areas. The present form of neglecting the rural areas, considering them as periphery in the present concept of development left deep negative impact on the people of the area. With no proper employment opportunities available in the rural areas, most of them migrate to the urban areas and are compelled to live in the increasing number of slums in sub human conditions.

Impact on Social Sector

As stated earlier, globalization not only creates division between rich and the poor countries of the world but within countries it divides the population between the rich and the poor. Though India is considered as one of the fastest growing

---

[136] It may be noted that states like Madhya Pradesh which can accommodated numbers of projects are being ignored due to its poor transport and communication system. See Bose, "Globalization, Migration and Urbanization," 31-32.

[137] For instance, the MNCs/TNCs are flooding the mineral rich states like Orissa and Jharkhand because of the presence of many precious materials for different industrial set up.

[138] These states include Bihar, Jharkhand, UP, Uttaranchal, MP, Chhattisgarh, Rajasthan, Orissa, and AP.

[139] The North Eastern States are Assam, Arunachal Pradesh, Nagaland, Manipur, Mizoram, Tripura, Meghalaya and Sikkim.

[140] Sebastian, "Globalization and Uneven Development...," 200.

economy in the world in the recent decades, the benefits attained in the process do not trickle down to the lower strata of the society especially the poor and the marginalised. Interestingly, besides the rapid growing of India's economy, India has many richest persons in the world. The report available released by the Forbes Magazine in October, 27, 2011 shows that out of 1210 billionaires in the world today. 50 of them are Indian.[141] Likewise, another report shows that the total combined wealth of 55 Indians is estimated at USD 246.5 billion (close to 11 lakh crores rupees). Similarly, the rich persons in India are rapidly increasing since India joins the global economy. The same report reveals that India has 62000 households who have combine income worth Rs. 250 million and it is expected that these rich Indian households will rise to 219,000 in the next five years.[142] This indicates that the new economic reforms have significantly benefitted a meagre section of the 1.1 billion Indian populations. However, this indicates only one side of the story, for majority of the weaker section of population are living in a very poor condition.

The National Planning Commission of India officially claims that the percentage of people living Below Poverty Line (BPL) has gradually decline from 36% in 1993-94 to 27.5% in 2004-05 i.e. 28.3% for rural and 25.7% for urban population.[143] However, this system of estimation based on income without taken into consideration other aspects related to poverty such as shelter, health care, transportation, etc was severely criticised in the Indian press as "ridiculously low" and astounding.[144] This has prompted the government to select the Tendulkar committee in 2008, which submitted its report in November 2009. Based on the Tendulkar methodology of calculation that include the amount spend on food, education and health care, and the amount of monthly income raised, while the percentage of urban BPL population remains the same at 25.7% that of the rural had increased from 28.3 to 41.8%. Likewise, the BPL population in the entire

---

[141] See http://www.zimbio.com/Mukesh+Ambani/articles/uPPuHIivy7w/Top+50+Richest+Person+India+List+Forbes+World (28 Nov 2011).

[142] See Arun Prabhudesai, "How India's Rich spend & invest their money" http://trak.in/Tags/Business/category/indi-business-news-everything-you-want-to-know-about-india/what-are-indian-people-how-do-they-live-what-i (27 Nov 2011).

[143] This official calculation of poverty in India reported by the Planning Commission based on the methodology recommended by the Lakdawla Committee (1993) that was in used since 1973-74. It was used as a method to estimate the magnitude of poverty based on the "per capita consumption level" and "associated with a commodity bundle that yielded a specified level of calories which was then thought to be appropriate for rural and urban respectively." See "Press Note on Poverty Estimates." http://planningcommission.nic.in/reports/genrep/Press_pov_27Jan11.pdf (28 Nov 2011).

[144] Excluding other factors, the National Planning Commission estimates that a monthly income of about Rs. 356 per person for rural and Rs.539 per person for urban would be sufficient enough for required diet per head. See Carl Haub and O. P. Sharma, "What is poverty, Really? The case of India" www.prb.org/Articles/2010/indiapoverty.aspx (21.11.2011).

country which was estimated at 27.5% in 2004-05, was increased to 37.2% an addition of 100 million people more.[145] This indicates that the amount of developmental activities are urban centric, thus creating a huge gap between the urban and rural population. Likewise, based on the required amount needed to spend for each person in today's context, one could argue that the number of poor people calculated is still meagre. According to the report of World Bank calculation about 41.6% of India's population live below $1.25 per day and 75.6% of the population live below $2 per day that rightly indicates the magnitude of poverty in India today.[146]

Moreover, though the Planning Commission claims that 37% of the country's population are living below poverty line (BPL), the new study conducted by the Oxford Poverty and Human Development Initiative using the Multi-dimensional Poverty Index (MPI),[147] reveals that about 55% of the 1.1 billion population or 645 million are living under poverty. This implies that one-third of the world's people find their home in India. According to this new system of calculation 421 million of Indian poor people are living in eight North Indian and East Indian state,[148] and the number is more that the 410 million poor living in the 26 poorest African countries. This new study also reveals that only 31% are access to improve sanitation system in 2008, 350 million or about 35% of India's population has food insecurity consuming less than 80% of the total energy requirements, more than 1.5 million children suffer from malnourishment and 43% of children are under weight and so on. The new study also demonstrates that poverty is very high among the weaker section of population in which 81.4% of Scheduled tribe,

---

[145] The amount of monthly expenditure per person was raised to Rs. 447 for rural and Rs. 579 for urban people. See Haub and Sharma, What is Poverty, Really? The case of India; See Press Notes on Poverty Estimates. See also "How Poverty is calculated in India" http://business.rediff.com/slide-show/2010/apr/21/slide-show-1-bcrisis-how-poverty-is-calculated-in-india.htm (21 Nov 2011).

[146] Haub and Sharma, "What is Poverty, Really? The case of India."

[147] The MPI was developed in 2010 by Oxford Poverty and Human development Initiative and the United Nations Development Programme. It attempts to assess the intensity of poverty, thereby analysing beyond the income based to include all factors that affected human life. This covers the entire household level as well as income assets such as "child mortality, nutrition, access to clean drinking water, sanitation, cooking fuels, electricity, and years of schooling and child enrolment. A person is considered poor if he/she is deprived in at least 30% of the Weight Indicators." Hence, it is more precise and comprehensive ways to assess different levels of poverty. This new system is said to replace the existing Human Poverty Index that has been used by UNDP's annual Human Development Report since 1997. See Arun Kumar, "Half of India's Population lives below the Poverty line," www.wsws.org/articles/2010/aug2010/india-aoz.shtml (21 Nov 2011).

[148] These States are Bihar, Chhattisgarh, Jharkhand, Madhya Pradesh, Orissa, Rajasthan, Uttar Pradesh and West Bengal.

65.8% of the Scheduled Caste and 58.3% of Other Backward Class are living in extreme poverty.[149]

Accordingly, as developmental programmes are more urban centric, economic globalization not only creates disparities between the centre and the periphery and the urban and rural but the gap between the rich and the poor is widened. To put it differently, economic policies adopted in the post-economic reforms in line with economic globalization facilitated wealth accumulation of small privilege few rich section of population at the expense of the marginalised and rural poor population. Hence, with not much employment opportunities and facilities available to them, the poor sections especially from the rural areas migrated to the cities and ended up living in the increasing slums areas in different cities under sub-human condition devoid of all forms of securities. It may be noted that in every city of the country one could witness the increasing number of slums that spread in every available space of the city for constructing their poor dwelling place. As per the government statistic about 60% of the population of Mumbai forming roughly 7 million people are living in slums.[150] On the other hand, Bangalore the silicon valley of India considered as the symbol of India's development has paradoxically witness the alarming growth of slums in the 1990s from 444 slums in 1991, with a population of 1.12 million, to 743 slums in 1998-99, with a population of 2.2 million, forming about 20% of the city's population.[151] Moreover, the Times of India reported that the percentage of slums population had rapidly increased from 23% in 2001 to nearly 30-40% of the city current population living in appalling sub-human condition.[152] Ironically, while Bangalore is considered as the fastest growing cyber city of India, but just within the parameter of the city, millions of its population are excluded from the advantages offered by the process of globalization. Hence, even though the government claims that integration of the country's economy with the global economy will bring inclusive growth to all sections of population the ground reality proved otherwise.

---

[149] See Kumar, "Half of India's population lives below the poverty line." See also "Poverty in India, http://en.wikipedia.org/wiki/Wiki/Poverty_in_India (20 Nov 2011).

[150] See Eric Follath, "The Paradox of Mumbai: Slums, Stocks, Stars and the New India," www.spiegel.de/international/spiegel/0,1518,469031,00.html (29 Nov 2011). See also "Slums," www.macalester.edu/courses/geog61/espencer/slums.html (29 Nov 2011).

[151] Sebastian, *Globalization and Uneven Development: Neo-colonialism, Multinational Corporations, Space and Society,* 262.

[152] Sunitha Rao R, "Every 3rd B'lorean lives insub-human slum," *The Times of India,* Bangalore, March, 17, 2011, http://articles.timesofindia.indiatimes.com/2011-03-17/bangalore/29137890_1_slum-population-slum-dwellers-urban-poverty (29 Nov 2011).

Agriculture

Down through the centuries, agriculture occupies an important place in the Indian economy and has been considered as the backbone of Indian economy. It is said that about 70% of the country's population depend on agriculture for their livelihood,[153] thereby providing employment to 60% of the total workforce in the country.[154] Indian economy, observes Singh "continues to be predominantly an agrarian economy in terms of population dependency and labour force proportion even after more than five decades of independence."[155] Besides providing employment opportunities to millions of Indian population, agriculture has also supplies raw materials for building up the growing Indian industries.[156] To put it differently, the growth of agricultural sector is vital for the impending growth of the entire economic scenario of the nation. Nevertheless, with concerted efforts concentrated more on Industrial development since independence, the importance of agriculture to the country's economy is being neglected by the policy makers.[157] The less attention paid to agriculture by the policy makers which the critics term as "anti agriculture" bias has adverse impact on the growth and development of agriculture.[158] With the exception of the Green Revolution period (despite all its side effect done to the environment) that has transforming India from a "begging

[153] M. A. Oomen, "Transnational Capital, GATT/WTO and the crisis of National Sovereignty: The Case of India" in *Globalisation and SAP: Trends and Impact- An Overview,* edited by Ajit Muricken (Mumbai: Vikas Adhyayan Kendra, 1997): 36.

[154] Y. D. Pujari, "Socio-Economic Impact of Globalization on Indian Agriculture" *Golden Research Thought* 1/IV (October 2011) http://aygrt.net/oct/2011/Economics%20_GLOBALISATION_ON_INDIAN_AGRICULTURE.aspx (3 Dec 2011).

[155] Gajendra Singh, "Globalization and its Impact on Indian Agriculture," in *Impact of Globalization on Development,* edited by Meenu Agarwal (New Delhi: Deep and Deep Publications (P) LTD, 2008), 245.

[156] Agricultural products like cotton, jute, oilseeds, sugar cane, etc., are some of the items that contributing to the growth of industries. See V. M. Rao, "Agriculture since Independence," in *Dimensions of Globalisation,* edited by James David and John Desrochers (Bangalore: Centre for Social Action, 1998), 97.

[157] It may be noted that the First Five year Plan (1950-51) adopting Harrod-Domar model are primarily concentrated on investment in "irrigation, power and other infrastructure for accelerating drowth," but with the introduction of Nehru-Malanobis model of development in 1956 more emphasized is given to the development of heavy industries. See "The State of Food and Agriculture 1995," produced by Economic and Social development Department, www.fao.org/docrep/v6800e/v6800EOD.htm (5 Dec 2011).

[158] Ashok Gulati, "Indian Agriculture in an Open Economy: Will it Prosper?" in *India's Economic Reforms and Development: Essays for Manmohan Singh,* edited by Isher Judge Ahluwalia and I. M. D. Little (New Delhi: Oxford University Press, 1998), 122. Cf. G. Thimmaiah, "Impact of Trade Liberalization on Indian Agriculture," in *Economic Reforms in India,* edited by Bishwa Nath Singh, Mohan Prasad Srivastha and Narendra Prasad (New Delhi: APH Publishing Corporation, 2003), 136-138.

bowl to a bread basket"[159] one could witness a gradual decline in the growth and development of the agricultural sector. In other words, though the agricultural GDP grows more than 3% per year during the era of Green Revolution that has overtaken population growth, this momentum could not be maintained in the 1990s, and rather it reveals a down sliding trend.[160]

Ironically, the integration of national economy with the global economy coupled with the introduction of different reforms programmes in the 1990s failed to recognise the place of agriculture in the growth and development of the country's economy. What follows is that though agriculture being "the biggest sector in terms of employment and income generation," once again has "remain outside the purview of the reform package initiated in early 1990s."[161] Hence, in comparison with other sectors like industry and service sectors, agriculture failed to receive proper attention of the policy makers.

It is reported that India signed the GATT treaty on the 15th April, 1994 at Marakesh, Morocco, and also became the founding member of WTO, a new world organisation replacing GATT, but consigned to implement diverse regulations of GATT.[162] As founding member, India is expected to strictly follow different the directions and conditions imposed by the WTO thereby restructuring its trade policies both domestic as well as international to suit the requirement of WTO. With the agricultural sector for the first time being included under the purview

---

[159] Green Revolution was first introduced in India in 1963 by Dr. Norman Borlaug the "father of Green Revolution." With the adoption of Green Revolution started in Punjab and later spread to other states, using the high-yielding variety (HYV) seeds, chemical fertilizers, pesticides and irrigation, India experiencing food security and poverty reduction especially in Punjab. It may be noted that in the mid- 1960s India has to import lot of food grains from outside, but by 1970s India has generally become self sufficient in food grains. It is reported that "between 1967-68 and 1970-71 food grain production rose by 35%. Net food import fell from 10.3 million tons to 89.5 million tons over the same period. Food availability increase from 73.5 million tons to 89.5 million tons over the same period. Food availability continued to increase sharply to 110.25 million tons in 1978 and 128.8 million tons in 1984 and food stock had crossed the 30 million tons by the mid eighties." Bipan Chandra, Mirdula Mukherjee, Aditya Mukherjee, *India After Independence, 1965-1991,* (New Delhi: Penguin Books, 2000), 354. However, the excessive use of chemical fertilizers and pesticides left deep negative impact on the quality of the soil and fertility of the land. It is said that the once fertile land has now become barren and unfit for cultivation. Punjab once considered the model of Indian agriculture "now is beset with disease soils, pest infested crops, water logged desserts and indebted and discontented farmers." See Vandana Shiva, "The Green Revolution in Punjab," http://livingheritage.org/green-revolution.htm (1 Dec 2011). See also "The end of India Green Revolution?" http://news.bbc.co.uk/2/hi/south_asia/4994590.stm (1 Dec 2011).

[160] See Ramesh Chand, "Effects of Trade Liberalization on Agriculture in India: Commodity Aspects," www.uncapsa.org/publication/wp45.pdf (5 Dec 2011)

[161] Singh, "Globalization and its Impact on Indian Agriculture," 244-245.

[162] Meenakshi Sharma and Roona, "Globalisation and its Implications for Indian agriculture," in *Impact of Globalization on Development,* edited by Meenu Agarwal (New Delhi: Deep & Deep Publications (P) LTD, 2008), 24.

of the new treaty, members' country were obliged to streamline their policies in line with the WTO demand which covers four main areas. These areas include a) Lowering domestic support to agriculture, b) Replacing all non-tariff barriers (NTBs) by bound tariff rates and eventually slashing down even tariff barriers, c) Providing access to markets of each member country and d) Lowering export subsidies in agricultural trade.[163]

For the supporters of globalization, integration of agriculture with the global market will automatically enable all member countries to have equal opportunity to improve their economy in general and agricultural sector in particular.[164] But the critics maintain that, for a country like India where the agricultural sector is under the domain of "million peasant households most of which comprise tiny land holdings," liberalisation of this sector would bring more harm than good to this sector. Despite diverse opinion arose with regards to the opening of agriculture to the global market, India proceeded ahead "towards liberalise trade environment."[165] What follows is that, India makes all effort to quickly reframe all its policies to immediately meet the WTO conditionalities. That is, quantitative Restriction (QR) on imports was generally deleted and exports are being exposed to global trade. So, with the exception of few commodities both imports and exports are open to global market competition to be exploited by private parties. The National Agricultural Policy (NAP), presented in the parliament in July, 2000 speaks volume of these. That is, the clauses like conservation of bio-diversity, liberation of agricultural research, liberation of domestic market, integration of agricultural trade in the global system, enabling lease of land for agri-business, accelerating the growth of agribusiness" and many others is but a reflection of the "WTO-sponsored strategy of integration of Indian agriculture with the global market."[166]

For a country like India, where agriculture provides employment to maximum people and millions of the population depend on it for their source of livelihood, recognising the importance of agriculture is vital for the growth and development of the country's economy. Nevertheless, due to the negligent attitude of the policy makers and its failure to receive due attention like other sectors, the growth and development of agriculture keep on decreasing with limited hope of proper success. Hence, while the country's economy recorded a rapid growth scenario from 5.8% in 1990-91 to 7.8% in 2008-09, agricultural sector experiences a down sliding trend of growth. It is reported that from 1951-91, the share of agriculture in the nation's GDP has sharply declined from 56%

---

[163] "The Impact of New Economic Policy on Agricultural Sector," Chapter V, www.shodhganga.inflibnet.ac.in/bitstream/10603/604/11/11_chapter5.pdf (3 Dec 2011).

[164] The impact of New Economic Policy on Agricultural Sector.

[165] Cf. Chand, "Effects of Trade Liberalization...."

[166] "The Impact of New Economic Policy on Agricultural Sector, (Chapter v)," 171.

to 32%[167] and it has again came down to 20.6% by the year 2006.[168] Similarly, in contrast to other sector the growth rate of agricultural sector reveals a diminishing trend from 4.69% in 1991 to 2.6% in 1997 and further down 2.3% in 2005-06.[169] The following table shows the growth rate of agriculture in comparison to other sector since 1984-85 till 2008-09.

Year	1984-85	2002-03	2004-05	2005-06	2006-07	2008-09
Agriculture	35.2	26.5	21.7	20.5	17.8	18
Industry	26.1	22.1	21.6	21.9	26.6	22.00
Service	38.7	51.4	56.7	57.6	57.4	60.00

Economic Survey of 2008 & 2009 (% of GDP).[170]

The above table indicates that while other sectors like the service sector make rapid growth, agriculture the backbone of India's economy keep on decreasing. The implementation of the NEP and integration of the economy with the global economy seems to make no difference to agricultural sector. It has instead made the condition worse than earlier. If the integration of the country's agriculture with the global agricultural business and exposing the nation's agriculture to global competition badly damage the opportunities to bring the expected growth to this sector, the most sufferers in the process will be the poor and the weaker section of the society in general and the small farmers in particular who depend entirely on agriculture for their livelihood. Some among the many major challenges of globalisation on this sector are listed below.

Firstly, integration of agriculture with the global trade business does not help this sector where millions peasants belong to small marginalised farmers or landless farm workers. It may be noted that to strictly abide to the diktat and conditionalities prescribe by the WTO, India began phasing out considerable number of subsidies usually offered to the poor farmers with regards to fertilisers, pesticides, water, electricity, etc that has hit hard the fate of the marginal farmers. It is reported that under the liberation policies subsidies on pesticides were reduced by two third by the year 2000. Likewise, while the farmers in Maharashtra spent only Rs. 90 per acre prior to the liberalization era, now they have to spend between Rs. 1000 and Rs. 3000 making an increase of 1000% to 3333%. Simultaneously, there is a hike of 300% in case of fertilisers and the farmers in Andhra Pradesh

[167] Gulati, "Indian Agriculture in an open Economy: Will it Prosper?," 122.

[168] "Impact of Globalization on Indian Agricultural sector" http://www.ssmrae.com/admin/images/168d52131d54abe17f22e88f58d21327.pdf (5 Dec 2011).

[169] Besides the growth rate is already slow down, coupled with the monsoon failure, it is reported that the growth rate of agriculture in 2002-03 was 1.1% and in 2004-05 was 0.7%.

[170] Pujari, "Socio-Economic Impact of Globalization on Indian Agriculture."

have to pay an electricity tariff that has increased by five times from 1998-2003.[171] Such a sudden hike in different items makes the farmers to suffer the most. With financial assistance through Banking and public credit system not easily available due to series of rules and procedures to be followed,[172] poor illiterate farmers often turned to private money lenders for loans at higher rate of interest sometimes as high as 24% per month.[173] Such a helpless situation has pushed many farmers into a debt trap. Chossudovsky maintains that cutting down of different subsidies coupled with the increasing prices of other agricultural inputs has indeed "pushing a large number of small and medium-sized farmers into bankruptcy."[174] Such a situation has compelled many farmers to take the extreme step of committing suicide. It is reported that while by the year 2000 farmer suicide forms 12% of the total suicide in the country,[175] in the year 2003 alone more than 17,000 farmers committing suicide across the country.[176]

Secondly, prior to the liberalisation of economy the farmers from all over the country usually obtained their seeds from the government institutions through the well regulated market at a cheaper rate. However, with liberalisation Indian seeds market was open to corporate sectors that run agribusiness like the Monsanto, Cargill, Pioneer seeds and the like to enter into the Indian seeds market without any restrictions.[177] With the passing of the New Seeds Policy in 1998 and different restrictions were relaxed, seeds market was captured by different MNCs for commercialising their expensive "genetically modified seeds" at a higher price beyond the purchasing capability of the marginal and small scale-farmers.[178] For instance, prior to the liberalization era, farmers of Andhra Pradesh usually spent only Rs.70 for cotton seeds per acre, whereas by 2005 after the closing down of

---

171 See "Globalization Impact on Indian Agricultural Sector," http://wiki.answers.com/Q/Globalisation_impact_on_Indian_agriculture (7 Dec 2011).

172 Jogdand et al, *Globalization and Social Justice,* 180.

173 "Globalization Impact on Indian Agricultural Sector."

174 Chossudovsky observes that more that 70% of rural households are small marginal farmers or landless farm workers constituting around 400 million populations. See Chossudovsky, *The Globalization of Poverty: Impacts of IMF and World Bank Reforms,* 128. See also Jogdand et al, *Globalization and Social Justice,* 180. Cf. Ramaswamy, *In the Woods of Globalization,* 9, 20.

175 It is reported that officially a total of 25,000 people committing suicides by the year 2000, unofficial figure puts it as 1,00,000 people committing suicide across the country. See "Globalization Impact on Indian Agricultural Sector."

176 Somini Sengupta in the New York Times, 19, September, 2003 highlights the miserable condition that led to the suicide of 17,000 people. See Amitabh Pal, "Indian Farmers Bear the Brunt of Globalization," www.progressive.org/mag_apb091906 (8 Dec 2011).

177 "Globalization Impact on Indian Agricultural Sector."

178 Pal, "Indian Farmers bear the brunt of Globalization."

Andhra Pradesh State Seeds Development Corporations (APSSDC)[179] and other organisation the cost of seeds increased to Rs.1000, an increase of 1428%. Likewise, the price of "genetically modified pest resistance seeds like Monsanto's Bt (*Bacillus thuringiensis*) cotton costing Rs. 3200 or more per acre a hike of 3555%."[180] Such a situation facilitated the interest of the MNCs/TNCs to monopolise the seeds market at the expense of the marginalised and poor farmers. Shiva maintains that the liberalization of the seed sector demonstrated that "pollinated seed varieties which can be saved and replanted are replaced with hybrid seeds which must be purchased every year from the corporations." She further states that "Farmers are compelled to buy costly hybrid seeds and chemicals that they cannot afford."[181] This reveals that liberalization of the seeds sectors not only help to expand the market of the MNCs/TNCs but enhance their capability to exploit the nation's farmer at will. In other words, integration of the agricultural sector with the global market instead of helping the farmers, bring more misery to their already deteriorating situation by leaving them at the hands of the corporate agribusiness bodies.

Thirdly, for the promoters of globalization, integration of agricultural sector to global trade business will provide equal opportunity to all WTO member countries to improve their agricultural sector. But the ground reality seems to prove the other way. Post-liberalization period witness the entry of MNCs/TNCs into the agricultural sector where farmers are compelled to alter crop pattern away from food base crops in favour of other exported oriented cash crops. A large area of cultivation under staple food crops is being substituted by export related cash crops. To state differently it implies a sudden shift of focus from agriculture to agri-business. This model seems to be good for the western country but not for a country like India where agriculture is not only forms the major sources of livelihood but it is somewhat a way of life.[182] Shifting from agriculture to agri-business marked a radical changed imposed upon the farmers from the earlier concept of food security to producing other exported crops suited the interest of the corporate agribusiness giants. This implies that it is the MNCs/TNCs who decide what to produce and what not to produce.[183] Hence, farmers were encouraged to cultivate tomatoes instead of wheat, flowers in place of rice,

---

[179] It is reported that adhering to the deregulation guidelines of the IMF, 14 of the 24 units of the APSSDC's seed processing units were close down in 2003, leaving the fate of the farmers at the hands of the corporate agribusiness bodies.

[180] "Globalization Impact on Indian Agriculture Sector."

[181] Vandana Shiva, *Globalization's New Wars: Seed, Water & Life Forms* (New Delhi: Women Unlimited, 2005),15.

[182] While in the developed countries only 2% of population depend on agriculture, in the developing countries about 60%-80% of population depend on agriculture for their livelihood. See The Impact of New Economic Policy on Agricultural Sector, 159.

[183] The earlier understanding was that the country could export only when there is a surplus and import when there is food deficit, but now the idea of export and import would depend on

and so on. A classic example of this shift is witness in Kerala where "vast tracts of forest and paddy fields have been converted into rubber, coffee and coconut plantations."[184]

At the insistence of the corporate agribusiness giants, Indian agriculture based on growing multiple varieties of traditional crops is suddenly shifted to growing other export oriented monocultures crops. It is an irony argues Shiva that the MNCs/TNCs used the word "diversification" for the promotion of monocultures crops.[185] Admittedly, for the corporate giants, it is making quick profit that matters more than food security. Hence, they will make all efforts to convert the mixture based agricultural crop patterns of the country into some kind of export oriented monocultures crops that suit their interest. A clear example is the case of McDonald's which prefers particular variety of potato called Russet Burbank because of its bigger size at the expense of a multiple varieties of Indian potatoes in different sizes and taste for their food ventures.[186] Likewise, in recent years number of farmers in different parts of the country went into big protest against the attempt of the corporate giants to introduce certain kind of genetically modified brinjal called Bt Brinjal, an effort that will seriously affected and even lead to the extinction of different varieties of brinjal available in the country. If this attempt is successful it will not only help the corporate giants to exploit the market but also led to the extinction of multiple varieties of brinjal available in the country.

Moreover, with the removal of different Quantity Restrictions (QR) under the export and import regulations, coupled with the growing expansion of agribusiness market, different agricultural products are imported and find their ways to different markets of the country thereby "making India the dumping ground for cheap, subsidised agricultural products...."[187] With no more restrictions imposed, different varieties of cheap imported agricultural goods flooded the Indian market, thus pushing the price of different local agricultural products like cotton, pepper, etc. It is reported that while the price of cotton crashed to more than 60% since 1995, other crops like pepper from Kerala which earlier cost at Rs. 27,000 per quintal in 1998, come down to Rs. 5,000 in 2004 a decline of 81%.[188] This indicates that free exposing of agricultural sector to international global trade arena besides destabilising the prices of agricultural products has

---

the decision of the agencies of globalization. See Brojendra Nath, "Globalization of Agriculture," *Religion and Society,* LXI/2 (June, 1994), 53.

[184] "The Impact of New Economic Policy on Agricultural Sector," 173.

[185] Shiva, *Globalization's New Wars: Seed, Water & Life Forms,* 19.

[186] Shiva, *Globalization's New Wars: Seed, Water & Life Forms,* 19-20.

[187] Soon after becoming the member of WTO, India makes all efforts to phase out Quantity Restriction from 1429 items from 1st April, 2000 to 1st April, 2001, "The Impact of New Economic Policy on Agricultural Sector," 174.

[188] The report shows that nearly 50% of suicides among Kerala's farmers come from pepper producing district. See "Globalization Impact on Indian Agricultural Sector."

pushed many farmers to bankruptcy that even led to suicides. Thus altering the agriculture sector to agribusiness while it helps the MNCs/TNCs to capture the market has brought nothing positive to the farmers, but instead added more misery to the small and marginal farmers.

Fourthly, besides the above, another area of concern for the critics of globalization is the patent on life forms like seeds and plants. With the agreement on Trade Related Intellectual Property Rights (TRIPS) signed at Marakesh it is clear that not only the entire world market is covered by "a single system of international patents," but also patent rights were extended to life forms or agricultural items like seeds and plants.[189] It may be noted that the Indian Patent Act 1970 forbid any sorts of patenting on agriculture and other life forms. However, with the amendment done in 2002, patent to agricultural items like seeds and plants are allowed.[190] As stated earlier, once the patent is registered to any items in any country, it becomes the sole property of that firm. Any kind of research wanted to be carried on by any nations or organisation needs to get the permission of that firm. Hence, with the signing of the new GATT agreement, Indian agriculture will not only open to the global world but also become vulnerable to be manipulated and captured at the hands of the mighty MNCs/TNCs for their respective profit motive.[191] Shortly after the Murakesh agreement, important agricultural items that were formerly belonging to the indigenous Indian population are being captured under the monopoly of the corporate giants. For example, while the medicinal neem items normally used by many Indian families since time immemorial is patented by the US firm W. R. Grace, turmeric is under different firms from US, Germany, and Indonesia. Likewise Basmati rice is captured by another US grain corporation called Cargill and Continental Grain.[192] With all these agricultural items falling under the monopoly of the corporate giants, their value and importance that has served and catered to the needs of the million Indian people for centuries now lie at the hands of these corporate bodies. Hence, patenting of important agricultural items like neem, turmeric and basmati has not only affected the economy of the Indian farmers but also violated the inherent right that the Indian population possessed on these items since time immemorial.

---

[189] It may be noted that prior to the signing of GATT agreement on April, 1994 and the launching of the WTO in January, 1995 different countries have their own patent laws. But at Marakesh the whole world is ruled by one international patent law. At the same time, prior to Marakesh patent rights were confined to things like machine and medicines but it was after signing the TRIPS that life forms like seeds and plants are also included. For detail see Dasgupta, *Globalisation: India's Adjustment Experience,* 78-92.

[190] Shiva, *Globalization's New Wars: Seed, Water & Life Forms,* 58.

[191] Nath, "Globalisation of Agriculture," 59.

[192] For detail see Shiva, *Globalization's New Wars: Seed, Water & Life Forms,* 93-104.

Hence, the above discussion reveals that integration of the Indian agriculture to the global trade business does not bring any positive contribution to different sections of population especially the marginal and small-scale farmers. This implies that the real beneficiaries on the entire process are the corporate giants like the MNCs/TNCs. Different agricultural policies adopted by the government favours the interest of the MNCs/TNCs leaving the fate of the millions of farmers at the hands the corporate giants. As it is said,

> Instead of addressing this issue in a serious manner, the National Agricultural Policy tries to worsen the situation by advocating for corporate control of Indian agriculture, withdrawal of subsidies to the farmers and its redirections to the corporate, open market for all agriculture goods to be dumped on Indian soil at the cost of Indian producers, bio-diversity conservation to facilitate intellectual property Rights for seed companies and gene giants at the cost of the farmers who will lose their rights to save the seeds and the Indian researchers who will be denied to do independent research to breed new varieties and so on.[193]

Conclusion

The above discussion reveals that right after independence, India followed a planned economy based on Russian model with certain restrictions to protect the economy from outside influence. It is believed that this economic model will not only help improve the growth of the country's economy, but will also benefit and help improve the living condition of different sections of population. However, with the country facing economic crisis that affected the entire country in the 1990s, India restructured its economy by implementing the New Economic Policy based on the Liberalization, Privatisation and Globalization or the so called LPG model. There is high hope by the policy makers that integrating the economy with the economic globalization besides raising the economic status of the country, will also gradually improve the economic condition of different sections of population. Hence, by joining the process of economic globalization, India has nothing to lose but many things to achieve in the process. However, though the country achieved rapid economic growth within a short period, the ground realities show a different story. That is, the process of globalization benefitted only a small section of population, whereas the majority poor and marginalised are further relegated to the margin of economic development. The above discussion shows that the process of globalization does not provide equal distribution of profits and losses to different section of population. And the worst affected groups are the vulnerable and weaker section of the population like the Dalits and the tribals.

---

[193] "The Impact of New Economic Policy on Agricultural Sector," 170.

Chapter 4

The Challenges of Globalization to Tribal Economy: Khasi Perspective

The previous discussion gives us a brief discussion on how India opened up to the globalized world after long time of protecting and safeguarding its economy. It can be said that integration of Indian economy with the global economy though it helps improve the economy at the national level, on the other hand, it could not raise the living conditions of the millions of Indian from the grip of poverty. In other words, the process of integration of Indian economy with the global economy could benefit only a tiny section of population, whereas large section of population, the poor and the marginalized could not draw much benefit in the entire process. The worst sufferers in the entire process are the vulnerable sections like the dalits and the tribals. This brings enormous challenges to the economic life of the vulnerable marginalized communities like the dalits and the tribals. In this chapter an attempt is made to discuss the challenges of globalization to the tribal economy based on the Khasi context. Using the tool of Postcolonialism the researcher will attempt to see how colonialist globalization and neo-colonial forces brought certain challenges to the economic life of the tribal people.

Challenges of Globalization to Tribal Economy

Like any peoples group in other parts of the globe, tribal people of the North Eastern Region in general and Khasi people in particular are not free from the challenges posed by the process of globalization. Since globalization has no boundary, its forces have entered different parts of the globe and there is no region or space that remains isolated outside the ambit of its dominating force. Notably, though India achieved its Independence in 1947, its people especially the poor and marginalized like the Dalits and the Tribals are "yet to achieve economic independence."[1] Nevertheless, till recently,[2] majority among the tribal people of the region and the Khasis as well are not aware of the invasion of the forces of globalization that have permeated and penetrated every nook and corner of the region. Commenting on this regard Thanzauva rightly observes when he points out that tribals of North Eastern India are the most unprepared group for the challenges brought by the process of globalization.[3] This particular argument seems to prove right in the context of the Khasi people of Meghalaya. That is a majority among the Khasi people are not aware how their entire life situation in general and their economic life in particular is being affected by the process of economic globalization. This chapter attempts to investigate the challenges posed by globalization to the economic life of the Khasis. However, to have a comprehensive understanding of the intensity and magnitude of the challenges caused by the process of globalization to the economic life of the Khasi people today, it is necessarily important to first have a brief relook on how the economy of the Khasis is shaped in its encounter and contact with the colonial rule or the commonly understood as the first phase of globalization.

Challenges of the Colonial rule to the Economic life of the Khasis

As stated earlier, the colonial master[4] came to India with the motive to exploit the rich economic resources like trade and other rich mineral resources available in this part of the world rather than to bring development to the people of India. With this same intention the colonial rulers extended their rule to this part of the region. Giri maintains that the primary motive behind the advent of the colonial master to these hills was "to become the undisputed master of the hills."[5] The coming of the British colonial rule marked not only the first entry of the foreigners into the land, but also the native people were for the first time introduced into the process of modernization. Nevertheless, this first encounter had instead brought mixed bearing on their simple tribal way of life especially their economic life.[6] In other words, this encounter with colonialist globalization had adversely affected the whole life situation of the tribal people and has simultaneously brought enormous challenges to the economic life of the tribal people.

[1] Peters, *In Search of a Good Life: The Ethics of Globalization,* 43.

[2] It was only when their land and sources of livelihood are being destroyed by the neo-colonial forces or the forces of globalization that they realized the intensity and danger of the invasion of globalization.

[3] Thanzauva, *Transforming Theology: A Theological Basis for Social Transformation,* 114.

[4] It may be noted that it was the East India Company who first came to this region for the purpose of trade activities and later the ruling power was taken over by the British government.

[5] Giri, *The Khasis under the British Rule: 1824-1947,* 42.

[6] Nataranjan, *The Missionary among the Khasis,* 91.

The Process of Modernization

Deriving from the Latin word *modernus*, the word modernity[7] came to be understood as a "significant break from traditional values."[8] Kant as cited by Norris maintains that "modernity" signifies "a break with tradition."[9] This implies how the traditional society that was associated with agriculture or depend its economy on land undergo a significant changes in the context of modernity where people tend to look beyond agriculture for other occupational activities offered in the modern society like, factories, offices, etc. Anthony Giddens rightly defines modernity as quoted by S. L. Doshi when he describes,

> A prime feature of industrial societies today is that, a large majority of the employed population work in factories, offices or shops rather than agriculture. And over 90% of people lived in towns and cities, where most jobs are to be found and new job opportunities are created.[10]

The above quotation reflects a departure from the simple agrarian society to a complex urban context where diverse and new opportunities are to be found. Though the percentage of people living in urban areas may vary from one country to another and may be much different from what Giddens has estimated, the fact remains that majority of the people prefer to live in urban areas where the employment opportunities are in abundance. Hence, modernization as a process is a global phenomenon that affects every society. Modernization[11] can be explained as transformation of society from rural agrarian set up to a secular, urban and industrial society. This is what happened in the context of tribal people and the Khasi people as well. The earlier discussion pointed out that with the advent of colonialist globalization, a new class of people the middle class emerged that has connection neither with trade nor agriculture. Srikant observes that after five decades of violent confrontation with the colonial master, "the native hill

---

[7] The era of modernity or the modern period is usually referred to an era that began from 1650s to about 1950s. It is said to be superseded by the so called post modern era that was probably began since 1960s. See Roger E. Olson, *The Story of Christian Theology* (Secunderabad: OM Books, 1999), 540.

[8] Catherine Soanes, Alan Spooner and Sara Hawker, *Compact Oxford Dictionary, Thesaurus, and Word Power Guide,* Indian edition, (New Delhi: Oxford University Press, 2003), 575.

[9] Christopher Norris, *The Truth about Post Modernism,* (Oxford: Blackwell Publishers, 1993), 61.

[10] S. L. Doshi, *Modernity, Post Modernity and Neo-Sociological Theories,* (Jaipur: Rawat Publications, 2006), 15.

[11] Modernization besides its many features is closely linked with industrialization. As society being modernized, the individual becomes increasingly important, gradually replacing the family, community and so on. Division of labour, characteristics of industrialization is also applied to institutions which become more highly specialized. Instead of being governed by tradition or custom, society comes to be governed according to abstract principles formulated for the purpose. Traditional religious beliefs often decline in importance and distinct traits are often lost. See http://encyclopedia2.thefreedictionery.com/modernization (8.2.2011).

tribes started reconciling themselves to the changes that have been thrust upon them and started exploring the possibilities of development within the constraints imposed by colonial rule."[12] But their contact with the colonial ruler brought significant changes to their entire life situation including their economic life. Srikanth further argues that one among several changes that emerged during the period is the emergence of the middle class. As he puts it,

> From within each of the tribes, there developed a middle class, which had their base neither in land nor in business. This class comprised newly educated members working in modern professions and closely associated with the church. Access to modern education and interaction with the British officials and the missionaries gave them knowledge about the world around and implanted in them new ideas and aspirations.[13]

It may not be totally true that this class is closely associated with the church, as many of them were members of traditional faith. However, one cannot deny that this class hold significant role in the context of the tribal people till today. In the present context, in the midst of the diminishing trend both in agricultural and trade activities, it is the middle class population or the salaried workers that have better source of economic survival among the tribal people. It may be noted that white collar job or modern employment opportunities, are the most sought after job among the unemployed youth in the tribal society. Young people are more keen to work in government offices rather that engaging themselves in agriculture and trade activities. Hence, with the government unable to create much employment avenues, many of the young people remain unemployed. The trend of ignoring agriculture which still formed majority of people depending on it, for their survival, will leave deep impact on the economic life of the people today and in the near future. This therefore brought tremendous challenges to the economic life of the tribal people in the long run.

However, it may be noted that in the process of shifting from traditional society to modern society, tradition is weakened and fractured and its impact is witnessed in many areas of life including agrarian set up, religious practices, feudal system, social and political set up and so on.[14] As stated above, the coming of British colonial rule or the colonialist globalization made the tribal people to have their first experience of what happened to the outside world, and the process of modernization. No doubt, the process of modernization/colonialist globalization in the first place, seems to bring important positive consequence(s) to the welfare and social well being of the tribal people. For instance, it introduces

---

[12] H. Srikanth, "British Colonialism and the Hill Tribes of Composite Assam" in *Man and Society: A Journal of North East Studies* 6 (Spring, 2006): 102.

[13] Srikanth, "British Colonialism and the Hill Tribes...," 102.

[14] S. L. Doshi, *Modernity, Post Modernity and Neo-Sociological Theories,* (Jaipur: Rawat Publications, 2006), 15-20.

good educational institutions, new model and well-built concrete houses, new material goods, better mode of transportation and communication, different job opportunities and so on.[15] All these new facilities have been well served for the betterment and welfare of the native indigenous people. Nevertheless, colonization/modernization led to the diminishing of many of the traditional religious and cultural values. Many of the customary practices and the traditional good qualities of the tribals like hospitality, communitarian life, hard work, honesty, simplicity and the like have been replaced by corruption, immorality, insincerity, individualism, materialism, and so on. Tribals are being made to believe that, to be modern means to get rid of everything traditional, which are considered "devilish, irrational, inhuman, inferior, backward, primitive and so forth."[16] So also to add from the above, among the Khasi community respect for elders, respect for women, respect for life, social etiquette, moral principle like *Kamai ia ka Hok, Tipbriew Tipblei, Tipkur Tipkha,*etc are gradually losing their value and importance among the people.[17] Hence, tribals began to feel inferior of their own cultural values and customary practices, whereas, considered everything western as the best and the norm. Such perception are deeply ingrained and cemented in their psyche that makes them to perceive that "West is the best" and anything western should be set as the standard necessitated to be followed. To put it differently, their minds are being colonized making them to judge everything from the western perspective at the expense of the rich tribal cultural heritage. As such, tribal traditional value like respect for the land, forest, and the entire natural environment has gradually deteriorated. The unity and interconnectedness of God, human and nature is broken.[18] Tribal people, who were the keepers of nature, now have turn out to be the exploiter of natural resources. Land which was held in high respect now lost its value and reverence. People tend to be more keen to adopt materialistic culture at the expense of soil centered way of living. Everything is now perceived as existing for the wellbeing of human persons. This was in contrast to the earlier practices of the tribals which have high regard for the

---

[15] Snaitang, *Christianity and Social Change in Northeast India,* 48-49.

[16] A. Wati Longchar, *The Tribal Religious Traditions in North East India,* (Jorhat: Eastern Theological College, 2000), 162.

[17] Barness Mawrie, "Khasi Society and the Impact of Modernity: Challenges to Identity and Integrity," in *Tribes of North East-India: Issues and Challenges,* edited by Brinchi K. Medhi, R. P. Athparia and K. Jose (New Delhi: Omsons Publications, 2009), 187.

[18] In the process of modernity human takes the centre stage and other realities like God and the nature are being ignored. Nature is being portrayed to be existed for the benefit of human. With human reasoning power was accorded prime importance, it is belief that the more knowledge human could gather the more powerful they will be. Descartes argues that knowledge could enable human to dominate and exert control over nature. See Richard. A. Young, *Healing the Earth,* (Nashville: Broadman and Holman Publishers, 1994), 45.

natural environment. In turn it has deeply affected and poses enormous challenges to the economic life of the tribals.

Exploitation of Economic Resources

Exploitation of economic resources of the indigenous people, not political rule[19] remains the primary motive of the British colonial rule. To serve their colonial interest the British administration avoided direct rule over the Khasis and left the internal affairs almost entirely at the hands of the *Syiems*. However their relationship with the colonized people here, first through the Agreements or Treaties[20] and later through the Sanads[21] was clear indication of maintaining their supremacy over the land and local indigenous population. Though the colonial ruler made an agreement to respect the custom of the people many of their activities were against the customary practices of the local people. For instance, with the introduction of the Sanads the colonial government "recognized only the *Syiem* and the *Syiem* alone as the head of the state subject to the control of the District Commissioner and completely ignored the recognized existence of the *Dorbar*."[22] For the Chief this act of bypassing the *Dorba*r is wrongly understood as equipping them with higher status.[23] Hence, they began to overlook the importance of the *Dorba*r and neglecting the right of the people or *Ki Khun Ki Hajar*. Such a wrong perception led to a series of conflict "between the *Syiem* and the *Dorbar*, the *Syiem* and the people, and consequently between the people and the British government."[24] From the colonial ruler's perspective recognizing the Chief implies the easiest way to get access to the economic resources of the land as the Chief was just a nominal head

[19] Since the beginning it was extraction of economic resources rather than political administration that was the priority of the colonial master. It was only in the later stage that political control was established in the colonized territory. See Sharmila Das Talukdar, *Khasi Cultural Resistance to Colonialism,* (Guwahati: Spectrum Publications, 2004), 28.

[20] For instance, to cite one example the Treaty that was signed between the East India Company and Dewan Singh Raja, Chief of Cherapunjee together with the *Myntris* on the 10th September, 1829 states that the company will protect their territory, respect the customs of the people, and help each other in case of war and conflict and so on. The relationship through the Treaty continued till 1859 and it was in 1877 that the Agreements were completely withdrawn by the colonial ruler. See Mills, *Report on the Khasi and Jaintia Hills, 1853,* 45.

[21] The Sanads were first introduced in 1859. With the total abolishment of the Treaties in 1877, the Sanads remains as the only means that connected the Chief and the British colonial rulers. See V. Venkata Rao, "The Khasi Political System- The Syiemship," in *Tribal Institution of Meghalaya,* edited by S. K. Chattopadhyay (Guwahati: Spectrum Publications, 1985), 44.

[22] Kynpham Singh, "Syiem and the Durbar in Khasi Polity," in *Tribal Institution in Meghalaya,* edited by S. K. Chattopadhyay (Guwahati: Spectrum Publications, 1985), 25.

[23] Actually in the Sanads all the power of the *Syiem* is being curtailed for he has to submit himself under the authority of the District Commissioner. See Sir Keith Cantlie's, *Notes on Khasi Law* (Shillong: Chapala Book Stall, 2008-2009), 143.

[24] Singh, "Syiem and the Durbar in Khasi Polity," 26.

already submitted under the commanding control of the colonial government. This was clearly spelt out in different conditions inserted within the Sanads that was imposed upon different Chiefs. Some of the conditions mentioned in the Sanads include the freedom of the colonial government to establish civil and sanitaria, cantonments and posts in any part of the land rent free, to handover all the natural resources like lime, coal, etc to the British Government, freedom of the British government to sale or lease the waste lands, and so on.[25] This indicates that though the chief is recognized as the head of the state, is but a nominal head without any authority and his rule should not by any means obstruct the interest of the colonial government. To state differently, the colonial government do not wish to burden themselves with the internal affairs of the natives as long as they do not clash with the interest of the colonial interest of exploiting the economic resources of the land. From the colonial perspective, these endeavors seemed to serve the purpose and the interest of the colonial government. But for the native people all these efforts besides imposing untold suffering to the native, it has brought massive challenges to the economic life of the people.

Land

According to the colonial perspective, land and its resources have no value. This perception may perhaps find its root in the modern period where land and its resources have virtually lost its value and worth. Its value and worth lies in its ability to serve for the good and welfare of human beings.[26] Kant as cited by Gunton even goes to the extent of declaring that the "scientist has to torture nature to extract her secret."[27] With the mindset to exploit land and its resources, the colonial ruler found this part of the region rich in natural resources suited their colonial interest. But their role over this region brought tremendous pressure and challenges to the entire economic life of the Khasis and the concept of land in particular.

Firstly, according to the traditional customary practices and usage, land belongs to the people not to the Chief or *Syiem*. The *Syiem* or Chief does not own land but the sole authority on land rest with the people. However, with the advent of the British rule to these hills this system of land ownership has undergone significant changes. To suit their sinister design for extracting the economic resources of the land without any difficulty the colonial ruler went against the customs of the native recognizing the Chief as the sole authority over the land not the people.[28] Henceforth, any matters regarding land, the Britishers deal directly

---

[25] For detail see Cantlie, *Notes on Khasi Law,* 143-145.

[26] H. Paul Santmire, *The Travail of Nature,* (Philadelphia: Fortress Press, 1985), 133-134.

[27] Colin E. Gunton, *The Triune Creator* (Cambridge: William B. Eerdmans Publishing Co., 1998), 127.

[28] See Bhagawati, *Meghalaya: Issues and Legacies of its Early Years,* 45.

with the Chief not with the people of the state as the real owner. As stated above, with the Chiefs already lost their authority over land and its resources through the Sanads, this indirectly means that the entire land and its resources had become the property of the colonial government. Thus, this practice besides violated the old age custom and usage that the Khasis followed since time immemorial, it has also brought series of complications and diverse internal problems to land relation of the Khasis in the later period.

Secondly, as stated earlier, prior to the coming of the Britishers land revenue system was unknown to the Khasis either in the *Ri Raid* or *Ri Kynti* land. When the Britishers transferred the headquarter of the province from Cherapunjee to Shillong, they came into certain agreement with the Chief of Mylliem for acquiring considerable plot of land for the need of the new capital.[29] The Britishers started issuing pattas and imposing revenue to the land holders within their jurisdiction.[30] For the native people where land belongs to the people and is to be shared by all in the community such new system is against the customary practices of the people. However, this new way of looking at the land as a commodity for sale in order to gain good profit, started gaining ground in the mind of the native population. Fernandez maintains that "land, which is another component of their identity ceases to be their sustenance and becomes a commodity.[31] Bhagawati observes that the "original concept of community ownership of land prevailing in the tribal society has given place to feudalistic patterns of land control during the colonial rule."[32] This new system of imposing revenue was soon followed by the *Ri Kynti* owners to those people who purchase land from them that is either to Khasis and non Khasis as well. The Report of the Land Reforms Commission puts it

> The self-assumption by *Ri Kynti* owners of a right to impose land revenue on a Khasi has been question as anti-custom. After the advent of the British, Khasi *Ri Kynti* owners have started to issue periodic leases or pattas to Khasis to whom they have disposed of the land on payment of the full value of the land at the time of the sale or transfer.[33]

This has also opened up the way for selling the *Ri Kynti* lands in which in most cases only the rich could afford to buy. With the material culture influencing the mind of the people, coupled with the gradual diminishing loss of respect for

---

[29] See Kynpham Sing, "Khasi Hills and Jaintia Hills up to 1874," in *Tribal Heritage,* compiled by Hipshon Roy Kharshiing, (Shillong: n.p., 1979), 54.

[30] Bhagawati, *Meghalaya- Issues and legacies of its Early years,* 47. Cf. Rymbai, "The Pattern of Landholding of the Khasi-Pnars," 191.

[31] Walter Fernandez, "Tribal Identity, Customary Law and Modernisation in Northeastern India," *Tribes of North-East India: Issues and Challenges,* edited by Brinchi K. Medhi, R. P. Athparia and K. Jose (New Delhi: Omsons Publications, 2009), 372.

[32] Bhagawati, *Meghalaya: Issues and Legacies of its Early Years,* 50.

[33] For detail see *Report of the Land Reforms Commission for Khasi Hills,* 20.

the land there are instances even misusing the community land for the purpose of one's own benefit. On the other hand, these practices have left many people landless. To put it differently, traditional customary practices like respect the value and importance of land, is gradually being ignored for short term temporary monetary benefits. Today, in the era of globalization the tribal society usually known to be an egalitarian society gradually turning into class society, and there is wide gap between the rich and the poor people among the Khasi people. It may be noted that the rich people[34] and middle class people[35] in the Khasi society especially those in the urban areas like Shillong, Jowai, Nongstoin, etc make all attempts to buy land either in urban areas or from the poor people of rural areas[36] making the cost of land beyond the reach of many.[37] This practice has generally converted many people both in the rural and urban areas landless. For the Khasis like other tribal groups where land and nature are inseparable from their way of life, the consequences of such practices have been severe. Such act has adversely affected not only the system of land tenure system, but in due course, it has disturbed the entire economic life of the Khasis.

Trade

As stated above, the coming of the British to this region has tremendously brought significant changes to different life situation of the people, especially their economic life. Among several sources of economic life that has deeply affected by the coming of the colonial rulers, are trade activities. The Pre-colonial era witnessed dynamic and successful trade relations between the Khasis and the plain people of Bengal or the Sylhet people. It may be noted that the two significant trade items among the many that the town of Sylhet got its name famous were oranges and lime. The so called "Sylhet oranges" and "Sylhet lime" are in fact the trade commodities produced by the Khasi people from the hills of Khasi and Jaintia since the Pre-colonial era. With the motive to exploit and plunder, all resources of economic importance in this part of the world, the volumes of commercial goods and trade activities operated between the hill people and the plain people of Bengal attracted the interest of the British colonial ruler. Commenting on the exploitative and plundering mentality of the British colonial ruler Srikanth rightly puts it when he says that "the British took a keen interest in the administration of the hills inhabited by the Khasi-Pnars and Garos in view of their strategic location

[34] The rich people here is referred not only to the urban rich but also to the rich people living in the rich coal belts of the land like Jaintia Hills, Borsara, Shahlang and other places.

[35] The middle class people are mainly concentrated in the urban areas making every effort to capture all available facilities and opportunities at the expense of the poor and rural people.

[36] For instance, most of the lands in the fertile Ri Bhoi District are now purchased by the rich people of Shillong for establishing of their farms.

[37] For detail see "Rich tribals' land-deal spree hits poor hard," *The Shillong Times,* 28 June 2007, 1.

and commercial significance."[38] But the coming of British colonial rule left deep negative impact on the flow of trade activities that has not only obstructed the entire progress and development of trade activities of the Khasis but also adversely affected the skills and trade potentialities of the Khasis.

Firstly, as stated earlier, one cannot deny that the colonial ruler introduced some of the new agricultural items of economic importance like potatoes, pear, beets, cabbages[39] and so on that have greatly benefitted the economic life of the people in some areas of the Khasi society till today. Nevertheless, other trade items of greater economic value like oranges, lime, coal, sillimanite and so on were gradually captured by the Britishers especially Mr. Hary Inglis at the expense of local population, thus leaving the local native people those trade activities of less economic value.[40] With the support achieved from the colonial government for the expansion of trade activities, the colonial traders took control almost the entire trade that were previously under the hands of the native traders.[41] In other words, getting maximum control over trade activities had not only denying the native population of getting access to different varieties of trade items but also badly damaged the economic sources of the local native. For instance, as the maximum trade on lime[42] was under the monopoly of Mr. Hary Inglis, even the local native traders have to buy limestone from his company for lime production.[43] At the same time, to achieve maximum profit the Inglis Company exported the entire supply of sillimanite to Calcutta and England thus ignoring the need of the native people usually depended on this material to sharpen their agricultural

---

[38] H. Srikanth, "British Colonialism and the Hill Tribes of Composite Assam," *Man and Society: A Journal of North East Studies* III (Spring 2006): 90.

[39] Nataranjan, *The Missionaries among the Khasis,* 133.

[40] With the exception of Mrs. Stark, Sarkies & co almost the entire trade activities were under the monopoly of Mr. Hary Inglis. See Thomas Oldham, *Geological Structure of part of the Khasi Hills,* (Calcutta: F Carbery, Bengal Military Orphan Press, 1854), 54. It may be noted that Mr. Hary Inglis control almost the whole trade activities during those time. With his family connection to Colonel Lister the then Political Agent in the Khasi Hills as his father-in-law, Mr. Inglis could able to stand even the strong competition of other European traders. For detail see B. C. Allen, *Gazetteer of the Khasi & Jaintia Hills Garo Hills Lushai Hills,* (Delhi: Gian Publications, 1905), 16-17.

[41] It is reported that with the exception of prominent Khasi personnel like Babu Jibon Roy involved in trade activities during that time, the colonial traders took monopoly and captured of the entire trade activities from the hands of the native local people. Cf. Allen, *Gazetteer of the Khasi & Jaintia Hills Garo Hills Lushai Hills,* 21.

[42] It is reported that towards the end of the eighteenth century lime trade seems to have been captured by the Inglis family and remain under their monopoly for quite many years. See Allen, *Assam District Gazetteers (Vol X) The Khasi and Jaintia Hills, The Garo Hills and the Lushai Hills,* 15.

[43] See Thomas Oldham, "The Geological Structure of part of the Khasi Hills, with the observation on the Meteorology and Ethnology of that District," *The Calcutta Review,* XXVII (July-December, 1856): 90.

tools like knives and daos. This indicates that in the process of exploiting the economic resources of the native people to the maximum, the colonial ruler not only captured trade activities from the hands of the local people but also denied the birthright of the native on their natural resources. That is, the local people were denied access to those important economic items and trade activities in their own land. Moreover, for the Khasis any attempt to monopolise things meant for common usage and sharing by all the people in the society for one's own personal benefit, is categorically term as anti custom and against the norm of the society.[44] Hence, taking control and monopoly of trade activities by the colonial rule, besides denying the sources of livelihood to the native people, had also challenged the customary practices followed by the Khasis from time immemorial.

Secondly, as trade relations between the Khasis and the plain people of Bengal, extensively flourished during that period, one could notice the presence of different markets or *hats* at the foot of the hills. It may be noted, that the Khasi people not only possessed commanding control over these border market or border *hats* but also many among the tribal people earned their livelihood through different means from these border *hats*.[45] However, with the British administration extended to these hills area, the Khasi people found that the border *hats* are no more under their independent controls. Hence, the Khasi merchants were denied access not only to some economic items of greater economic importance, but also there appeared many restrictions that hindered the smooth flowing of trade as imposed by the colonial ruler. These badly shattered the source of livelihood of those local people depended on these market on one hand, which at the same time deeply affected the economic life of the Khasis on the other.

Thirdly, for better transportation of the mineral resources, railway line was constructed by the company of the colonial ruler which was extended from Companygunj up to Theria Ghat.[46] This railway line served as transportation route for mineral resources especially lime stones,[47] but this railway line was unfortunately destroyed by the great earth quake of 1897 and subsequent flood.[48] After the great earthquake, another railway line by the name Dwara-Ichamati railway was run by the private company of the colonial ruler for transporting mineral resources. But when Babu Jibon Roy, the prominent Khasi leader of that

[44] See "U Mawshynrut na Nongstoin bad Rambrai," *U Nongphira,* 153 (Nohprah, 1914): 218.

[45] The presence of these border markets had largely help the Khasi people not only through exchange of different goods through barter system, but many earned their living as porters or transporting goods even human persons who are old, sick and so on. See Wastson, Chirrapunji and a detail of some of the favourable circumstances which render it an Advantageous site for the Erection of an Iron and Steel Manufactory on an extensive scale, 26.

[46] See "Inspection of Limestone Quarries," *U Nongphira* 152 (Naiwieng 1914): 203.

[47] See *An Account of the Province of Assam and its Administration,* (Shillong: Assam Secretariat Printing Press, 1903), 43.

[48] "Inspection of Limestone Quarries," 203.

time, involved in trade activities made an appeal to Mr. Henry Cotton, for the construction of railway line from Nongjri quarries up to Piyan river, his petition was turned down on the ground that a memorandum of understanding was signed by the colonial government with the Assam-Bengal Railway company, not to give permission to any company for they will extend their railway operation up to Gauhati in the near future.[49] But the question remains, that for the private company of the colonial people permission was allowed but not for the local indigenous people. Giri maintains that in the colonial era, the developmental process whether it is construction of railway lines, or the construction of sanatoriums and summer resorts all serve for the motive of colonial interest.[50] This is a clear indication of the colonial mindset, who did not want to see the progress made by the local indigenous people.

Fourthly, as stated earlier among different tribal groups of that time, the Khasis were the most trade conscious communities in the region. The Khasis were not only able to control trade activities within these hills, and the border *hats* in the foothills, but also many among them were prominent and adventurous merchants who travelled as far as Dacca and Calcutta for trade activities.[51] However, the coming of the British administration to this part of the world not only captured trade activities from the hands of the Khasis, but witnessed the beginning of gradual influx of different people from outside the region to this part of the land. With Shillong gradually emerging as the capital of the Province[52] as well as the headquarter of the armed forces, the colonial ruler also brought many people with them for diverse purpose required in different government enterprises and other related activities of that era. Mathur maintains that the British colonial ruler brought many workers from East Bengal for employment in Government offices, educational activities, and trade and so on.[53] It is said that besides those working in administration, the government even encouraged immigration of different sets of people from different skills and background to work like traders, merchants, and the like for diverse need necessary in building the emerging township. Hence, this period witnessed "several Bangalees, Assamese and Marwaris coming and settling in Shillong as bureaucrats, professionals and businessmen."[54] To put it differently

[49] "Inspection of Limestone Quarries," 203.

[50] Pabitra Giri, "Implications of New Economic Policy for Development of North-East India," in *Globalization and North East India,* edited by Bimal J. Deb, Keya Sengupta and B. Data Ray (New Delhi: Concept Publishing Company, 2008), 39-40.

[51] *An Account of the Province of Assam and Its Administration, 1903,* 49.

[52] It is important to note that it was in 1874 that the British government declared Shillong as the Provincial capital of Assam. See L. Gilbert Shulai, *Ka Shillong: Naduh Ka Snem 1863* (Shillong: Riwar Offset Press, 1998), 1.

[53] P.R.G. Mathur, *Khasi of Meghalaya: A Study in Tribalism and Religion* (New Delhi: Spectrum Publications, 1980), 10.

[54] Srikanth, "British Colonialism and the Hill Tribes...," 93.

all these attempts automatically enabled "to assist them in extending further the horizon of their empire."[55] This has eventually resulted to the large influx of people from outside the region to this part of the land.[56] Such a changing scenario brought severe challenges to the entire tribal way of life especially their economic life. With the entry of different batches of traders from outside the region to these hills, traders from the tribal communities argues Bareh "seem to have been seized with fear in entering competitions with new entrants who had come to take up jobs like wholesalers, stockist, and retail dealers in an emerging situation."[57] What followed is that in course of time people from outside the region began to take control almost the entire trade in these hills that has automatically, not only affected employment opportunities but also brought immense challenges to the economic life of the indigenous tribal population of the land.

But one may ask how can the Khasis who were the most trade conscious communities among the tribal groups in the region that time "have been seized with fear" by the coming of the traders from outside the community and the region as well? How it happened that the Khasis who seem to have a commanding controlled over trade activities prior to the colonial era did not have the courage to face trade competition coming from outside? How trade activities slipped out of their hands and were captured by the non tribals? The answers to these questions are of threefold. In the first place, though the Khasis had complete control of trade activities in the pre-colonial period, the case is different when the colonial rule is extended to this part of the region. As stated earlier, the colonial merchants, coupled with the strong support of the colonial administration could not only capture all the important trade items that were confined to the hands of the indigenous people, but also to suppress the promising native traders involved in trade activities. Hence, with the important trade resources being taken away from their hands, the native traders were left with no option but to remain confined in petty trade of low economic profit.

Moreover, it is important to note that even though the Khasis were considered as expert traders, almost all their trade items were among the natural resources produced within the land. But even these trade items were taken away from their control by the colonial merchants. When the Marwaris entered the land they introduced different trade items like house building materials of different kinds, various kinds of kitchen wares, dress materials and the like brought from outside the region mostly necessary for the emerging capital of Shillong, which were almost all new to the Khasi traders.[58] That is, while on one side trade activities in

---

[55] Bareh Ngap Kynta, *The Economy of Meghalaya,* 59-60.

[56] It is reported that while the population of Shillong was only 4000 souls in 1881 it has slowly increased to 26,536 people in 1931. See *Census of India 1931,* Volume III, 32.

[57] Bareh Ngap Kynta, *The Economy of Meghalaya,* 60.

[58] Interview with Toki Blah on the 12th May, 2011.

which the native people were experts were already captured by the colonial rulers, again trade items brought by the Marwari merchants were new to the Khasis. Hence, trade activities were gradually slipped away from the local indigenous people and remained under the control of Marwari merchants.

Furthermore, when the colonial rulers entered these hills, besides exploiting the economic resources of the local indigenous population they also introduced not only the written language but also new system of education to the people of the land. It followed that the educated literate personnel were more preferred in different job opportunities or the so called "white collar job" in different offices newly emerging in the new capital at Shillong. At the same time those persons working in different offices newly established in the capital were considered as "riewdonburom" literally gentleman/woman or persons obtaining higher status and respect in the society.[59] This seemed to set a new trend for the Khasi people, who preferred to choose for education rather than getting involved in trade activities. In course of time the Khasi people forgot everything about trade whereas at the same time, traders from outside the region captured the entire trade activities in these hills.

De-industrialization

Another important objective of the colonial ruler in their attempt to exploit the economic resources of the people is de-industrialization. As stated earlier, with the motive to suppress the economy of the colonies, the colonial master made all effort to dismantle the indigenous skills and potentialities of the native population in the area of industries. Prior to the coming of the British colonial rule iron industry formed one of the main sources of economic life of the Khasis. The iron produced by the Khasi is not only of "excellent quality" but also it was exported in big quantities.[60] Lt. Yule description confirmed this when he reported on the extensive areas of iron excavations in these hills. In his words, "so numerous and extensive are the traces of former excavations, that judging by the number at present in progress, one may guess them to have occupied the population for twenty centuries."[61] The other report of the government put it this way, "its great extension in the former times is evidenced by the remains of the smelting furnaces which covers the surface for many miles from the brow of the hill below Cherapunjee as far as north as Mylliem and beyond. The slag from these working supplied a considerable portion of the metal for the cart road between Chera and Shillong."[62] The intensity and magnitude of its quantities, no doubt,

[59] Interview with Toki Blah on the 12th May, 2011.

[60] Allen, *Report of the Administration of the Cosseah and Jynteah Hills Territory*, 48.

[61] Lt. Yule, "Notes on the Iron of Khasia Hills," 833.

[62] See *An Account of the Province of Assam and Its Administration, 1903*, 40. See also Robinson, *A Descriptive Account of Assam*, 226. For detail see also Thomas Oldham, *Geological Structure of Part*

speak volumes of its extensive widespread in different areas of the hills. To put it differently, it is nothing wrong to say that this industry could not only provide employment opportunities to many people but is also one of the main sources of economic life of the Khasis. However, with the British administration being extended to this part of the land, this important industry of the Khasis received a major setback. With the motive to exploit the market in the region, the colonial ruler not only introduced and supplied iron goods imported from Manchester to different markets within the hills, but also sold them at cheaper rate than those furnished and manufactured by the native people in Khasi hills.[63] Hence, strong competition from the British iron supplied in large quantities, together with the support obtained from the administration not only suppressed the growth and development of iron trade but also demolished the indigenous iron industries of the native people. To wipe out this traditional iron-smelting industry, developed by the local people since time immemorial, could have far reaching effects on the economic life of the people. On one hand, destroying this traditional industry, that served as significant economic resources to the native people points out not only to the rapid decline of iron trade among the natives but also it implies the gradual loss of arts, skills and proficiency related to the industry, that had been developed and passed through the centuries. Srikant maintains that "colonialism destroyed the traditional economic base of the native communities and replaced the age-old political and social structures by new institutions and practices compatible with the interests of the new rulers."[64] Further, such a situation could affect the employment opportunities of the local indigenous population that could render many people without job.

The Role of the Church/Christianity

By the time the Welsh Presbyterian Mission started its mission work in these hills in 1841,[65] the entire land was under the dominion of the British colonial rule.[66] Though the objectives and agendas of the Welsh Mission and the colonial rulers

of Khasi Hills, (Calcutta: F Carbery, Bengal Military Orphan Press, 1854), 70-75.

[63] See *An Account of the Province of Assam and its Administration,* 40.

[64] Srikant, "British Colonialism and the Hill Tribes...," 79.

[65] Prior to the coming of the Welsh Calvinistic Methodist Church or commonly known as the Presbyterian Church of Wales in 1841, it was Krishna Pal from the Serampore Mission who first started doing mission works among the Khasis in 1813 but the for some reasons the work was abandoned in later years. For detail see B. L. Nongbri, "Serampore Mission in North East India with Special Reference to Khasi Hills (1813-1835): A Historical Survey," *Indian Theological Journal* 2/2 (July December, 2008): 38-48. See also J. F. Jyrwa, *Christianity in Khasi Culture,* (Shillong: K. J. P. Assembly Press, 2011), 90-93.

[66] By 1835 the whole land was under the dominion of British colonial rule. It was on the 11th February 1835 that Colonel Lister (then Captain Lister) was appointed as Political Agent of the Khasi Hills with Cherapunjee as the headquarter. See A. J. M. Mills, *Report on the Khasi and Jaintia Hills, 1853,* (Shillong: North-Eastern Hill University Publication, 1985), 1.

intent to be different, for convenient sake their cooperation in many areas like security and education[67] was clearly visible during their entire course of their stay here in these hills. That is, while the motive of the colonial ruler was to exploit the economic resources of the people, the main purpose of Christian mission was to convert the native people into Christian faith. Looking back to the ministry of the Christian Church, no one could deny the immense positive contribution rendered by the Christian church towards the welfare of the native people. Their valuable services in terms of literature, education, health and social services have largely contributed towards the uplift of the status and standard of living among the local indigenous people.[68] Their attempt to raise the living condition of the local indigenous population is highly appreciated and commendable. That is, had it been not for the missionaries' dedicated ministries, things would have been different for the local indigenous people today. Nataranjan argues, "With the contact of different religions and civilisations in the Khasi Hills, new ideas crept into general social life. A new Khasi civilisation has emerged, in the sense of a fairly advanced culture, with a blend of the old and the new."[69]

Nevertheless, despite their dedicated services towards uplifting of the living condition of the native people, their attitude towards tribal culture and customary and religious practices is predominantly negative. The missionary educational system made the local indigenous population to understand that everything western is superior, true and universal expression of reality. In contrast anything of tribal culture and religious practices are considered pagan, devilish, heathen, and satanic and therefore need to be discarded. Such negative perspective towards their own culture, besides making the tribal people to feel culturally inferior, it also made them to accept anything western as the norm need to be followed. Hence, if the British colonial ruler could succeed in colonising the mind of the tribals, the missionaries intensified the problem through their educational and social ministries.[70] To state differently, the mind of the natives were prepared for a global economic phenomenon. Moreover, to be converted to Christianity or

---

[67] It is reported that with the visit of Judge Mills of Calcutta in 1853 and witnessed the educational activities started by the Welsh Mission, in the following year the colonial government began to extend its help to the Welsh Presbyterian Mission by supporting a monthly grant of five pound for the need of mission's schools. It is said that this was the first grant made by the government towards educational purpose run by religious organization and this marked the beginning of the co-operation between the Welsh Presbyterian Mission and the colonial government. See John Hugh Morris, *The Story of our Foreign Mission (Presbyterian Church of Wales),* Reprinted, (Aizawl: Synod Publication Board, 1990), 30-31.

[68] For detail see Snaitang, *Christianity and Social Change in North East India,* 65-120.

[69] Nataranjan, *The Missionary among the Khasis,* 96-97.

[70] It may be noted that while the British colonial rulers concentrated mainly in the urban areas, it is the missionaries who travelled and stationed in every nook and corner of the land for establishing their mission activities. As such, they could carry out their purpose anywhere they think necessary and needed for to enlarge their objective.

to accept the Christian faith strictly means to stay away or abandon all kinds of traditional cultural and customary practices. That is the person concern is expected to sever ties and dissociate himself/herself from anything related with his/her culture which the missionaries considered as pagan, superstitious and derogatory and so on. The person who is a member of the church is expected to strictly observe the following condition.[71]

- He/She has to abandon and discard all pagan practices and rituals.
- To abstain or restraint from doing any work on the Sabbath, that is, Sunday.
- They should have good knowledge of all the Christian teachings.
- They should live according to the teachings of the gospel.

If anyone overstepped the imposed conditions, he/she will have to face disciplinary action like suspension from the church membership or even face excommunication from the church.[72] With such strict rules imposed by the church, any person converted to Christianity is expected to renounce all connection with tribal cultural practices. Such restrictions left deep impact on the local indigenous people. In his comparative study on the impact of colonial rule between the native Indian communities in Canada and the native tribal communities in the hills of the then Assam now North East India, Srikanth points out that in contrast to the missionaries' activities here in the hills of the then Assam, in Canada the Christian missionaries made an attempt to "bring up the native children in residential schools by taking them away from their native environment and forcing them to learn the English language and the English way of doing things."[73] But what Srikanth failed to see is that though the Christian missionaries in the hills of the then Assam attempted to learn the native language, developed the local script and literature, and educating the people which are indeed commendable acts, they have nevertheless introduced the so called "mission compound areas"[74] in

[71] S. Evans, "Ka Jingpyniaid Balang," in *Ka Centenary History Ka Balang Presbyterian ha Ri Khasi-Jaintia naduh, 1841-1940,* edited by D. Ropmay, 110-111.

[72] For example, any persons happened to attend cultural festivals or functions will have to be suspended or even excommunicated from the church. It may be noted that many of the festivals of the Khasis are in reality dances usually perform to offer thank and gratitude to God for the good harvest in the season. That is, while *Ka Shad Sukmynsiem* means giving thanks to God for the good harvest in the previous year and also to invoke God's blessings for the next sowing, *Ka Behdiengkhlam* means to invoke God for good harvest and protection of the crops as well as for the well being of the people. They are therefore not simply ordinary function but very much connected to the way of life of the tribal people.

[73] Srikanth, "British Colonialism and the Hill Tribes…," of Assam, 110.

[74] The "mission compound" areas introduced by the missionaries in different villages and towns exist even today. One could witness these "mission compound" in different villages and town like Shillong, Mairang, Jowai, Sohkha, Shangpung, and so on.

many villages and towns that still exists today. While the concept of the "mission compound" is generally meant to help the new converts, escape the persecution from relatives opposing their new found faith, which was the case then, on the other hand it also isolated the new converts who now stay separately from the old environment so as to enable them to renounce all things related with the traditional culture which the missionaries termed as pagan. This proved to have far reaching effect on the entire life and worldview of the new converts in particular and the Khasi people in general. For the tribal people, their rich cultural practices are part and parcel of their life. It is their way of life. Such prescribed conditions to renounce all traditional cultural practices mean being cut off from their roots. Nevertheless, with the better facilities with regards to health, education as well as social activities, the Christian missionaries were able to win over the hearts and minds of the local native population. Srikanth rightly observes when he puts it,

> By winning over the hearts and minds of the natives, the Christian missionaries succeeded in pacifying the native anger against the colonial rule and help the natives reconcile to the changes introduced by the British in the Hills.[75]

Furthermore, the evangelical theology introduced by the missionaries wrapped in western ideologies and developed in a distant land, stressed more on salvation of human soul or personal conversion, and also emphasized the second coming of Christ. It reflects a spirituality that places the human person above everything including the created world. In other words, it is a theology detached from nature. This type of theology separated from the real life situation of the tribal community seemed "other worldly, anthropocentric and detached from the soil."[76] At the same time, it makes the people to perceive that this world is not our home and all the worldly things have no value at all. The entire material world will one day be destroyed. If this world is not our home and has no value there is no need to take care of it. Such perception that ignores the present day struggle of the people, besides making the people longed for the 'other world,' has also led them to perceive that their life has nothing to do with the created world. Hence, for the tribal people whose way of life is closely connected with land and nature, this type of understanding besides uprooting the tribals from their traditional cultural practices it, has also caused severe blow to their economic life. Commenting on the close connection of the tribal economy and the forest resources Thakur and Thakur as cited by Pohsngap maintains that tribal economy

---

[75] Srikanth, "British Colonialism and the Hill Tribes…," 111.

[76] A. Wati Longchar, "The need for doing Tribal Theology," in *Tribal Theology: A Reader*, edited by Shimreingam Shimray (Jorhat: Tribal Study Centre, 2003), 3.

and forest economy cannot be separated, the moment they get separated it will cause severe blow to both.[77]

As stated earlier, for the tribals land and the natural environment are the source of their economic life. This makes them not only to pay deep respect and reverence to the nature but also to have close relationship with the mother earth. But with their minds being colonized in western thought and outlook tribal people began to look down on their own cultural heritage and ignore many rich traditional customary practices. Looking at things from the western perspective they perceived their own culture as inferior with no valid expression of reality. What followed is that tribal people were alienated from their own roots. Now they began to see the natural earth as having no value where they can do whatever they like to it. Hence, their close relationship with the mother earth or *Ka Mei Ramew* got fractured. But for the tribals whose main sources of income come from the land and natural resources this has dealt a deep blow to their economic life. Tribal ancestral parents clearly understood the interrelationship between people and the natural environment that surround them. But with the influences of modernization, westernization, secularization and of late globalization, today's tribal generation has ignored their rich cultural heritage, thus looking at the natural world as having no value but something to be exploited and subjugated for the benefit of human species at the expense of other creation.

In sum, the above discussion testifies the fact that for the tribal people, land and its resources are the only important sources of their economic life. But the entry of the British colonial masters to this part of the land brought enormous challenges to the entire life situation of the tribal people especially their economic life. With their main motive to exploit the rich economic resources of the colonies, British colonial rulers could succeed not only in exploiting the resources of the people but also to capture and colonise their hearts and minds. Thus ignoring their rich cultural heritage tribal people began to look at things from the western perspective, eagerly adopting material culture losing their respect for the value and importance of land, and so on. Moreover, the coming of Christian missionaries with their mission activities, though they have largely contributed towards uplifting the living condition of the Khasis, with their negative attitude towards tribal cultural practices, their role in extending the colonial ideologies is quite visible thus making the problem far reaching. The outcome of all these, besides alienating the tribals from their roots, it has left deep impact on land their only source of economic life. Commenting on the impact of colonial rule to the life situation of the tribal people, Biswas opines that "with the departure of the

[77] L. Pohsngap, "Ecology and Tribal Culture," in *Ecological Challenge and Christian Mission,* edited by Krickwin C. Marak and Atul Y. Aghamkar (Deldi: CMS/ISPCK, 1998), 152; See also M. N. Karna, "Socio-Economic Aspects of Ethnic Identity in North-Easter India," in *Liberalization and India's North East,* edited by Gurudas Das and R. K. Purkayastha (New Delhi: Commonwealth Publishers, 1998), 233.

British not much was left of tribal culture to be preserved."[78] Biswas talks about tribal culture here could be applied to the impact of colonial rule on the economic life of the tribal people. Though there is truth in her statement, I however tend to disagree with the other part of her argument. Her point is that the tribal people have lost almost everything due to the colonial rule, and the non tribal people have no role to play in the diminishing trend of tribal culture and economy. In other words, non-tribal people are neither a threat to tribal culture nor to tribal economy. In her words, "the (tribal) people do not realise the fact that rising poverty and unemployment are totally unrelated with the presence of the common non-tribal people."[79] It is true that colonial rule had done much damage to both tribal culture and their economic life. But what she fails to see is that the increasing influx and migration of non-tribal people which began from the colonial period till today to Khasi and Jaintia Hills cause serious threat to both the culture and economy of the small tribal community like the Khasi. Looking at the growth and development of Khasi economy, one could agree that throughout its entire history, the Khasi economy had suffer double exploitation-once at the hand of the British colonial rule and now at the hand of the non-tribal merchants.[80] To state differently, besides colonial exploitation that resulted in the vulnerability of the Khasi economy, the situation of the Khasi economy become worst today as all trade activities now lie in the hands of the non-tribal merchants.

Post-Independence Scene

As stated earlier, prior to the coming of the British colonial rule the economy of the Khasis was generally self sufficient. But with the advent of the colonial rule coupled with severe exploitation of the economic resources, one could witness a diminishing trend in the economy of the Khasi people. By the time of the departure of colonial rule the condition of the economy was in a very bad state. In, general, in the post independence era, with different changes taking place there is not much improvement in the economic life of the people in these hills. This has resulted in big challenges to the economic life of the people. In order to have a comprehensive understanding about the different challenges faced by the Khasi people during this era two important areas need to be taken into consideration- i). Economic resources derive from the land and ii). Central Funding.

---

[78] Saswati Biswas, "Preservation of Tribal Culture in North East India- How Strong is the Non-Tribal Threat?" in *Tribal Studies in North East India,* edited by Sarthak Sengupta, (New Delhi: Mittal Publications, 2002), 22.

[79] Biswas, Preservation of Tribal culture in North East India- How Strong is the Non-Tribal Threat?, 30-31.

[80] In the present day context almost the entire trade activities both wholesale and retail is control by the traders from the non-tribal communities.

Economic Resources Derived from the Land

The post independence era testifies a very discouraging situation in the economic life of the Khasi. As stated earlier many of the economic resources derived from the land have been captured and taken away from the hands of the native. On one hand, the Khasis already lost major trade activities in the foothills at the hands of the British colonial ruler, while on the other in urban areas like Shillong and other places trade activities was already captured and control by the Marwari merchants. This has badly affected the economy of the local indigenous population.

Firstly, as stated earlier the partition of the country made the matter worst. The sudden sealing of the border and closing of the entire business transaction indicates that the people lost both the import and export trade activities. As stated earlier, since there was neither proper transportation nor proper commercial centre to market their crops worth lakh of rupees were left rotten in the field. By the time people found ready market for their crops, all business activities was already controlled by the big Marwari merchants who not only control the market, but fixed the prices for different items at will.[81] In most cases, the local farmers had to sell their crops at a throw away prices that has bring neither any proper benefit to their labour nor help them to have a secured future.[82] Moreover, as the entire trade activities both wholesale and retail are in the hands of the non-tribal traders all the money derive from the land do not circulates within the land, but flow outside the state. This has caused severe impact on the growth of the native people's economy. In addition, the increasing influx and migration of non-tribal people with their efforts to capture all available opportunities in trade activities resulted to the deteriorating situation of trade activities among the local indigenous population.

Secondly, till today agriculture still forms the main occupation of majority of population.[83] But in the last few years, with the increasing population that put pressure on land, agriculture that used to provide large economic benefit to the people does not produce income as it usually did a couple of decades back.[84] However, with the lack of appropriate attempts to make proper study and investigation to find out the causes in order to revive its growth and development

[81] Interview with Mrs. Eltis Muktieh, a business woman on the 24 May, 2012.

[82] Interview with Emoral Marsing, a businessman on the 25 May, 2012.

[83] Utpal Kumar De, "Human Development and the Management of Natural Resources: Some Basic Issues," in *Human Development-Experience of North East India,* edited by Kiran Sankar Chakraborty and Gurudas Das (New Delhi: Akansha Publishing House, 2007), 37-38.

[84] It may be noted that agricultural activities have failed to produce benefit to the people as was the case few decades back. For example, oranges that used to provide ample benefits to the people especially in the War area have died down except in few areas like Mawphu. See I. M. Simon, *Meghalaya District Gazetteer: Khasi Hills,* 64.

by the government,[85] many people face huge losses and gain no income that is usually derived from this section. There is a Khasi saying which says, *Nang rep Nang syrdep* which means the 'more you toil the poorer you remain.' It portrays the pathetic situation of the farmers or those who depend on agriculture for their livelihood. Though agriculture still occupies an important place in the economic life of majority of the people, it has nevertheless failed to provide desired economic benefit to the people.

Thirdly, as stated earlier forest served as one of the main sources of income for the tribal people. However, in the last few decades with the influence of modernization, westernization and even globalization, commercialization of forests that were unheard for in the olden days were widely practiced in the land. However, the earlier blanket ban on timber trade[86] (though it was a timely and right decision) which had provided employment to many people, without providing any other alternatives proved costly to both people and the environment. Nongbri argues that for the tribal of North East India, agriculture and forest are closely interlinked. Hence to restrict the farmers from using forest resources is to violate on his/her rights to livelihood. The impact on the local people is therefore immeasurable. Some of the affected areas among many include 5,396 persons involved in wood base industries, 500 shops were forced to close down, large scale unemployment, high incidents of school drop outs, and the like.[87] Many among those people, who had lost their job in timber trade, saw mills, etc turn to "shifting cultivation, charcoal burning and even removing and selling the bark of trees, practices that are no less (if not more) destructive to the environment than the felling of trees."[88] It is reported that charcoal burning which is ecologically

---

[85] Notably, all the agricultural scientists were trained in the agricultural Universities located in the plain areas with the system of research suited the crops growing in the plain areas. The universities that concentrate on the way to develop mountain agriculture are lacking. Hence, most of the attempts to revive agriculture in this hill region seem to be incapable to bring desire and meaningful result. Discussion with Toki Blah 12th May, 2011.

[86] See "KSU moves HC on forest protection," *The Shillong Times,* 6 June 1996, 3; See also "KSU demand for moratorium on timber trade," *The Meghalaya Guardian,* 27 June 1996, 4. Cf. "Controversy over KSU move for moratorium on timber trade," *The Meghalaya Guardian,* 6 June 1996, 1.

[87] It is said that 16 villages around Kynrud areas in West Khasi Hills where 85% of the total population depend on forest related activities for livelihood are badly affected. See Tiplut Nongbri, "Impact of the State Logging Ban in Meghalaya, India," in *Globalization and Indigenous Peoples in Asia,* edited by Dev Nathan, Govind Kelkar and Pierre Walter (New Delhi: Sage Publications, 2004), 151-152.

[88] Nongbri maintains that many persons are making their livelihood by peeling off the bark of the *jalawan* (*leatsea glutinosa*) and other varieties of trees and selling them to Marwari businessmen for a paltry of Rs. 2-6 per kilogram. The Marwaris businessmen in turn supply it to pharmaceutical firms in South India for making incense and medicine the practice which are so harmful to the forest in particular and the entire environment in general. Nongbri, "Impact of the State logging Ban in Meghalaya," India, 154.

destructive is generally and increasingly done by the people of the areas in order to supply to the emerging industries at Byrnihat.[89] It is said that the number of trees that vanished due to charcoal supplies, far outweigh that of timber trade because even the small trees also were not spared for the same purpose. If this practice is not checked, it will soon lead to the loss of maximum forest cover in the land that will result to the loss of rich bio-diversity and other forest resources.[90] Thus, the presence of different industries and factories in the land owned and managed by the non-tribal entrepreneurs not only resulted in the exploitation of the economic resources of the native people but also denying the local indigenous population diverse job opportunities.[91] This has greatly challenged the economic life of the local native people.

Central Funding

As stated earlier, tribal economy that was self sufficient prior to the coming of the colonial rule has to depend on financial support provided by the government in the form of grants. Thanzauva maintains that it is the failure of *Jhum* cultivation as the main cause of economic dependence.[92] But in the context of the Khasi people with its rich resources, besides the failure of agriculture both permanent and *Jhum* cultivation, it is the lost of trade coupled with the impact of partition that resulted in economic dependency on the central government.

Firstly, it is true that crores of rupees was annually invested by the central government to this region. Most of the financial assistances from the central government are generally intended to bring development to different sections of population especially at the grass root level. But due to severe corruption practices in different capacities[93] and spending mostly on unproductive purposes, the intended amount not only failed to reach to the grass root level but also incapable to bring meaningful and desired development to the land. It is reported that "crores of rupees pumped into these states by the central government are being spent mostly

[89] Almost all the factories or industries at Byrnihat are run by the non-tribal people and at the same time almost all the workers employed are the non-tribal people coming from outside the state. See "Kylla Thlen bamduh ki karkhana Byrnihat ia ki khlaw ka West Khasi," *Mawphor,* 6 October 2009, 1, 5.

[90] See "Ap ka jingma ia ki kynbat dawai ba la jan syllen lut ki khlaw," *Mawphor*, 1 December 2009, 1, 5.

[91] Most of the employees in different factories at Byrnihat are people from the non-tribal communities.

[92] Thanzauva, *Transforming Theology: A Theological Basis for Social Transformation*, 107.

[93] Peter Haokip, "Major Challenges Faced by the Tribals of North East India," in *Tribes of North East India: Issues and Challenges,* edited by Brinchi K. Medhi, R. P. Athparia and K. Jose (New Delhi: Omsons Publications, 2009), 82-83.

on unproductive purposes, benefitting a handful of politicians and bureaucrats."[94] To put it differently, with the influence of westernization, modernization and of late globalization, tribal people that were known for simplicity, honesty and hard work are now after quick temporary monetary benefit. What follows is that central funding assistance financed by the central government is unable to fulfil the intended purpose but also failed to be utilised in proper way.

Secondly, the developmental activities employed by the central government in tribal areas using the so called "top-down" model does not fit well in the context of the tribals.[95] Most of the planning is done at the top level perhaps without proper survey and analysing the need of the area concerned. That is, what is planned at Delhi is generally implemented here, perhaps without taking into consideration the needs of the people in general and the relevance of the projects to the area concerned. Therefore the tribal people besides having no knowledge on those particular projects, they also have no role to participate in the entire process of developmental activities. The outcome of such practices often led to the failure of maximum developmental schemes meant for the people in different areas. Though the state being considered as "special category state" received the grant of 90% of its plan allocation from the centre due to its weak internal resource base, and the state government has to contribute only 10% of the total amount, most of the developmental schemes failed to bring the desire result.[96] Moreover, with the weak planning board at the state, besides the planning section at the district level are poorly staffed, most of the fund allocated to the state from the central government are under-spent and generally have to be returned to the centre.[97] This has badly affected the developmental activities in the entire state. To state differently, the developmental efforts seem to be neither suited to the area concerned, nor is able to bring any changes to the economic condition of the people. The whole concept of bringing development close to the people that was also always the slogan usually used by different government agencies do not seem to have meaningful outcome. Hence, in many cases in the interior and rural areas, one could witness many abandoned government buildings[98] meant for different

---

[94] H. Srikanth, "Liberalization and Development of India's North East: Learning from Experience," in *Liberalization and India's North East,* edited by Gurudas Das and R. K. Purkayastha (New Delhi: Commonwealth Publishers, 1998), 162.

[95] Shreeranjan, *Perspectives on Development in Meghalaya* (Shillong: A Publication of State Institute of Rural Development (SIRD) Meghalaya, 2001), 44.

[96] P. Nayak and E. D. Thomas, *Human Development and Deprivation in Meghalaya* (New Delhi: Akansha Publishing House, 2007), 75-76.

[97] Gurudas Das, *Structural Change and Strategy of Development Resource- Industry Linkages in North East India* (New Delhi: Akansha Publishing House, 2005), 102.

[98] For instance, one could see these abandoned buildings left uncared like Gramsevak quarter, Soil conservation building, irrigation building at Sohkha, failed hospital project building at Lamin, etc., and many building left in ruins in different corners of the land. It indicates the fact that large

developmental schemes generally remain unutilised or left in ruins for the failure of the developmental schemes which are meant to reach the people of the area. This point to the fact that though large amount of financial investment is being spent in different capacities and crores of rupees sanctioned for different projects, such efforts could not improve the living condition of the majority of people in the land.

Thirdly, it may be noted that most of the developmental activities implemented by the government are urban centric. There are hardly any developmental projects that reach the rural or the interior areas. Those projects or schemes that reach the rural areas are mainly those that do not function properly or projects that could not help raise the living conditions of the people especially the poor. This has created great disparities in the economic and social life of the urban and rural areas. The outcome of urban centric development enables the urban population to enjoy diverse kinds of facilities and opportunities, thus leaving the rural population at the margin of economic advantage. Among those who benefitted from this system of development are mostly the so called middle class people comprising a small section of population working as government servant or serving in different capacities within the government. Whereas those who could not share the economic benefits of this system include majority of the population, the poor and marginalised living at the periphery or the margin of economic development.

To sum up, the post-independence era testifies the diminishing trend in the economy of the majority of native tribal population. Among several reasons, the loss of trade activities, the inability of agricultural sector to bring the needed source of income, impact of partition, coupled with the failure of series of developmental schemes meant for the uplift of the people at the grass root level, resulted in the weakness and insecurity of the native local economy. What follows here is that poor people from the rural and interior areas rushed to the urban centre in search of livelihood to support their family. According to the report conducted by the National Sample Survey Organisation (NSSO) it is found that while India has recorded a decline in migration of tribal people from the villages to the urban areas, Meghalaya recorded the migration of 3.8 percent, next only to Arunachal Pradesh (4 per cent) when compared to the whole country.[99] It is reported that out of a total 80.58% of the tribal population in Meghalaya, 55.36% are found in the urban areas.[100] This demonstrates the fact that there is an increasing rush of

amount of financial involvement but failed to bring meaningful development to the people of the area.

[99] See "Migration of tribals higher in Meghalaya," *The Shillong Times,* 17 June 2010, 1, 5. See also, Eugene D. Thomas, *Poverty and Rural Development in Meghalaya (India)* (New Delhi: Akansha Publishing House, 2004), 30-31.

[100] Mawrie, "Khasi Society and the Impact of Modernity...," 185.

the indigenous people to urban centre in search of livelihood. At the same time, since most of them do not have the required skill and expertise in any kind of job, they end up in doing petty jobs like daily wage labourers, hawkers, housemaids, etc with no social or economic security. With the urban life being quite expensive, instead of improving their living condition, they rather have to live in sub human conditions, even worse than their rural life. But those who remain in their villages with not much alternative left for their survival began to loot and plunder whatever available natural resources. Today with most of the economic resources could not bring meaningful assistance to enhance their livelihood, besides some economic sources are no more accessible to them, the tribal people tend to exploit and destroy all natural resources available to them.[101] For instance, one could witness number of orchid sellers moving around in Shillong city with loads of orchid plants extracted from different forest of the land to sell in the city. This practice besides resulting in the loss of some rare and endangered species it has also disturbed the rich bio-diversities of number of plant species in the entire natural environment. These points to the fact that in the post–independence era, with the exception of a tiny section of middle class that enjoy government salaries, majority among the population have weak and insecure economy. It is reported that about 45% of the people in Meghalaya fall Below Poverty Line (BPL) in the year 1993-94.[102] This percentage has climb up to 48.90% in the year 2002.[103] Churchill rightly comments when he argues, "with the exception of the government employees and the few influential contractors, the whole populace of the region is reeling under poverty. There is no infrastructural development, no income generating institutions and no room for self-employment. In fact, it resembles a third world within the fast developing country of India."[104] Hence, when the economic life of the tribal people is insecure and weak, the coming of the present day globalization brings great challenges to the entire economic life of the people.

The Challenges of the present day Globalization to Tribal Economy

It may be noted, when the tribal economy already become insecure and weak, the advent of the present day globalization bring more harm than good to the economic life of the tribal people. It is often argued that the present phase or

---

[101] See, "Development and Displacement at Kalinga Nagar," 21.

[102] It is said that while poverty in India dropped by 6.7 per cent between 1987-1988 to 1993-94, in the North Eastern region poverty has increased from 40% to 46% during the same period. Shreeranjan, *Perspectives on Development in Meghalaya*, 78.

[103] Directorate of Economics & Statistics, *Statistical Hand Book Meghalaya, 2008-2009* (Shillong: Government of Meghalaya, 2009), 29.

[104] Laishram Churchill, " India's LEP and the North East: A Study on Environmental Impact," in *Look East Policy & Polemics and Perspectives,* edited by Thingnam Kishan Singh (New Delhi: Concept Publishing Company, 2009), 74-75.

present day globalization has its roots in the colonial period. It is but the replication of the colonialist globalization. Whereas the first phase of globalization or the colonialist globalization portrayed the fact how the colonial master went on to exploit the resources of the colonies without any amount of limitation, the present day globalization makes all efforts to penetrate every nook and corner of the Third World countries, to extract the economic resources in order to obtain quick profit within a short span of time. In the name of TNCs/MNCs or the so called neo-colonial agencies, globalization today tend to erase all national borders to plunder all available economic resources of the Third World countries. The earlier discussion portrays that globalization not only divide the countries of the world between the rich and the poor or the First World and the Third World, but within the countries it divides the population between the rich and the poor. Hence, in the context of the tribal people in Khasi Jaintia, one could witness the exploitation of resources is twofold. First, it is being carried on by the TNCS/ MNCs and the second it is done by the big companies run by the rich people in India. In other words, with the single window agency in operation, tribal people in Khasi Jaintia suffer from double exploitation. Hence, besides many challenges posed by the present day globalization, tribal people in Khasi Jaintia continue to suffer due to extraction of their economic resources both at the hands of TNCs/ MNCs and those big companies control by the rich section of the population in the country. It is important to note that in the name of bringing development to the people the government has implemented a single window programme to allow the big corporate bodies to come for investment here and establish their plants in any part of the land. According to the government perspective, the coming of these giants companies means ushering development to the state. That is, besides developing the area it will automatically create diverse kind of job avenues besides direct and indirect employment opportunities to the unemployed persons of the state. The state in general and the local indigenous people in particular, have nothing to lose but many things to gain through the investment of these giant companies. With this understanding in mind the government made some relaxation to the rules and regulations, to allow the TNCs/MNCs and other big companies to come and invest in any part of the state. Hence, within these few years these giant companies enter the land and began to exploit the rich resources of the tribal people.

The Role of TNCs/MNCs

The earlier discussion points out that for achieving maximum profit within short period, the so called neo-colonial agencies overstep all national geographical boundaries where ever suited their interest. It may be noted that most of the areas or region inhabited by the tribal people like Jharkhand, North Eastern Region, etc are rich in natural and mineral resources. In the context of the Khasi Jaintia region, plenty available of rich mineral resources like coal, lime stones, etc attracted different forms of big companies like the TNCs/MNCs to enter and extract economic advantage to the maximum. With the New Economic Policy (NEP) of the Government of India became fully operated in 1991, this has opened up the opportunity for the TNCs/MNCs to establish their firms in any parts of the country including the North Eastern Region and Meghalaya as well.[105] For example, with the green signal from the government, one could witness the entry of TNCs/MNCs or the so called neo-colonial agencies like the Lafarge Umiam Mining Pvt Ltd[106] to this region to extract the rich limestone resources of the region. It may be noted that Lafarge Company does not intent to bring investment to the state; rather its main motive is to plunder the lime stones resources plentifully available at Nongtrai village in order to feed its cement company already established at Chhatak in Bangladesh. It is said that Lafarge depends entirely on the Shela-Nongtrai area for the supply of lime stones to feed its company there. Hence, every day thousands tons of lime stones from the forest are unscrupulously extracted and transported by this company to Bangladesh through the 17 km conveyor belt passing through the fertile agricultural land.[107] While the people of Nongtrai or the land owners welcome the project as something that bring development to the area,[108] majority of the people in the area perceive this project will bring more harm than good to the people and the entire surrounding environment.[109] Taking this wanton destruction of the natural environment as a threat to both human and the fragile eco-system in the area the Shela Action Committee (SAC)[110] filed the Public Interest Litigation (PIL)

---

[105] B. Datta Ray, "North East India in the Context of New Economic Policy," in *Globalization and North East India,* edited by Bimal J. Deb, Keya Sengupta, and B. Datta Ray (New Delhi: Concept Publishing Company, 2008), 2.

[106] Larfarge Umiam Mining Pvt Ltd is a joint venture between Lafarge S. A from France and Cementos Molins from Spain. This TNC/MNC has also established its own cement plant at Chhatak, Bangladesh known as Lafarge Surma Cements Ltd which depends mostly from Shela-Nongtrai area for the supply of lime stones. See "Hukum ka Supreme Court ban sangeh tih Mawshun ia ka Lafarge na Shela-Nongtrai," *Mawphor,* 6 February 2010, 1.

[107] See "MPHRC cries hoarse over Lafarge's Project," *The Shillong Times,* 26 October 2007.

[108] Those who support the project, that is the Nongtrai people, argue that the Lafarge Company has brought different developmental activities in the village which includes health care, education, drinking water, footpath, bathing place, toilet and others. See "Kyrshan sa ka shnong Shela ia ka Lafarge," *Mawphor,* 12 April 2010, 1, 5.

[109] It may be noted that the two groups from Shela area- one who support the project and the other under Shela Action Committee who are against the project and even filed the PIL to the Supreme Court that led to the closing of the company for some period of time. Besides other NGOs who are fighting against the operation of Lafarge include Meghalaya People's Human Rights Council (MPHRC), Khasi Student Union (KSU), Federation of Khasi Jaintia Garo People (FKJGP), Civil Society Women Organization (CSWO), Hynniewtrep National Youth Front (HNYF), and many others. See "NGO to move PM against Lafarge," *The Shillong Times,* 15 May 2010, 1, 5.

[110] The Shella Action Committee is an association of the local people in Shella area formed in 2007 to protest against the illegal exploitation of lime stones by the Lafarge Company. See "Hukum

to the Supreme Court that led to the closing of the company for sometimes.[111] Besides exploiting the mineral resources of the local people for supplying to its firm outside the country at Chhatak, Lafarge now make all efforts to capture and plunder the local natural resources to the maximum by setting its cement industries at Lama in *Elaka* Lakadong[112] and also at *Elaka* Nongkhlieh.[113] Many people who are concerned for the well being of local people and preservation of the eco-system perceived this as a threat to both the native people and the surrounding environment.

Big Companies

The earlier discussion points to the fact that globalization not only divided the countries of the world between the rich and the poor, but within the country it divides the population between the rich and the poor section of the population. And this happened within the tribal society itself. The tribal society that earlier witnessed to an egalitarian society is now moving towards a class society, where the rich and the poor classes are rapidly appearing. What follows is that in most of the local tribal areas, one could observe not only the big TNCs/MNCs exploiting the resources of the tribal people, but also by the rich section in the country at the expense of the poor and marginalised tribal communities. In the context of the tribal people of Meghalaya, the rich non tribal sections, in collaboration with the politicians and a tiny rich and powerful section of the tribal population, are moving forward to capture every possibilities to exploit the rich natural resources which the state possess. Blah rightly points out to this aspect when he states, "The wealthy, the powerful, the politicians of this generation connived together to dispossess the poor, the marginalised and the silent majority of their rights through a plea that whatever they were doing is for the good of the very people they were actually exploiting."[114] In recent years one could see the mushrooming of different companies to this part of the country to begin their projects especially in the mineral rich district of Jaintia Hills. For instance, the government has generally approved the establishment and setting up of different cement factories[115] by giant

sangeh tih Mawshun ka SC ia ka Lafarge ha Shella," *U Nongsain Hima,* 5 February 2010.

[111] But it seems that the Supreme Court ruling goes in favour of the Company. See "Hukum ka Dupreme Court ban sangeh tih Mawshun ia ka Lafarge na Shella-Nongtrai," *Mawphor,* 6 February 2010, 1, 5.

[112] "Maham ka JYF ia ka Sorkar bad JHADC ban ai NOC ia ka Lafarge," *Mawphor,* 14 May 2008, 1.

[113] See "Sushma moved against Lafarge," *The Shillong Times,* 15 November 2010, 3.

[114] Toki Blah, "The MAA and its PIL- the untold story, *The Shillong Times,* 17 August, 2006, 4.

[115] Some among many companies that have established their firms include Adhunik Cement Ltd, Cement Manufacturing Company Lumshnong (CMCL), JUD Cement Pvt Ltd, Green Valley

companies at Lumshnong areas within the radius of just fifteen kilometres.[116] Besides many more companies are in the process of setting up their plants in different parts of the land. Almost all these projects are owned by the outsiders. But the moot questions arose on how the government allowed these companies to come in big numbers in a small area? What is the logic behind the policy of the government to agree to the entry of these corporate bodies in the first place itself? What prompted the government to give its approvals to these corporate bodies? Does the government take into consideration the need of the native people in its nod to accept the establishment of these industries? What about the social and local equity in the entire process of the so called development? What will be the impact to the entire eco-system due to the establishment of these companies? Is there any guarantee that the coming of these giant companies to the area will help to improve the living conditions of the people? How will these projects affect the economic survival of the native people? Are the needs of the people taken into account when giving the approval to these companies to set up their plants?

It is true that Meghalaya in general and Jaintia Hills in particular is rich in natural and mineral resources like coal, lime stone. But the coming of these companies in large number will bring more harm than good to both the local native people and the environment as well. Most of these cement companies both TNCs/MNCs as well as big national corporate bodies are said to be illegally located in the forest land, thereby destroying the entire surrounding environment including forests, lands, flora and fauna. Though there are different objection and complaints for the same, till today these companies carry on their activities without any limitation. However, their advent to this region brought enormous harm rather than bringing development to the local area.

Impact of these Giant Company on People and Land

As stated earlier, the motive of all the companies when they enter any areas was to exploit the economic resources at faster rate without any restriction or hindrance. Hence, their agreement either with the national or state government portrays their sinister designs that could benefit them at any cost without any concern for the local people or the natural environment. Though the government, both the national and the state government usually make tall claims that the entry of different companies would bring development to the local area, in reality it is often proved otherwise. To state differently, the advent of these big companies cause great negative impact to the people as well as the environment.

Industries, Hills Cement Pvt Ltd, Meghalaya Cement Ltd, Amrit Cement, Topcem, Star Cement, etc. See "Mining activities threaten Jaintia Hills people," *the Shillong Times,* 5 June 2008, 1.

[116] Blah, "The MAA and its PIL- the untold story," 4.

Alienation of Tribal Land

The history tells us that since the time they joined the Indian union through the Instrument of Accession[117] at the time of independence, tribals of North Eastern Region in general and tribal of Meghalaya in particular was kept under particular protection within the Sixth Scheduled of the Indian constitution.[118] According to the Sixth Scheduled and the Meghalaya Land Transfer Regulation Act 1971, land belonging to the indigenous Khasi population cannot be transferred to the non-tribals.[119] In addition, those among the non-tribals who possess some plot of land in Khasi Jaintia,[120] if they want to sell that particular land or property they are supposed to sell it only to the tribal people not to the non-tribals. This implies that tribal lands and properties are supposed to obtain special protection in the laws of the land. Nevertheless, to attract the investment of the big companies like TNCs/ MNCs the government of Meghalaya made some adjustment and relaxation in the Meghalaya Land Transfer Regulation Act 1971, to enable the big companies to buy land and started their industries in any part of the state. A classic example is the case of the Lafarge Company at Shela area. The local people generally raised a complaint against the company for acquisition of land belonging to the local indigenous population through unfair means according to the Sixth Scheduled of the constitution. But the State Government in 2001 made some relaxation of the Meghalaya Land Transfer Act to enable the Lafarge to acquire land for its project.[121] Such an action done by the State Government like giving no objection certificate (NOC) to this company made those people who spearheading the anti Lafarge Movement to put the blame to the government for functioning against the interest and welfare of the local indigenous population.[122] This what John Cobb Jr states that the political power sacrifice to the impersonal market.[123]

Moreover, with the motive to attract Foreign Direct Investment (FDI) the State Government seems to make all efforts to see that there is no hindrance or

---

[117] Instrument of Accession can be referred to the MOU between the Government of India and the Khasi Chiefs when the latter join the Indian union.

[118] But it is important to note that though the tribals of North East India were under the protection of the Sixth Scheduled, in the case of the Khasi people of Meghalaya since the time of British rule large number of non-tribals already began to migrate to this land in the form of traders, arm and military forces, office workers, etc.

[119] See "Shella panel-IFC talks on Lafarge project inconclusive," *The Shillong Times,* 9 May 2008, 1, 5.

[120] Many of the non-tribals possessed some land in and around Shillong that began during the time of the British colonial rule till today.

[121] See "Shela panel-IFC talks on Lafarge project inconclusive," *The Shillong Times,* 9 May 2008, 1, 5.

[122] See "Lap ka MoEF ba shukor ka Lafarge bad Sorkar Jylla ia ka Sorkar Kmie," *Mawphor,* 14 July 2007, 1, 5.

[123] Cobb Jr., *The Earthist Challenge to Economism: A Theological Critique of the World Bank*, 57.

hurdle for this giant company to operate its project. In other words, the action of the State Government give the impression to the people that it is more concerned for the good and interest of the neo-colonial forces at the expense of the local natives. In the era of globalization, where the agencies of globalization attempt to convert every property or asset into commodity to exploit, land becomes the most precious asset for the corporate bodies. Though the Chief Minister, Dr. Mukul Sangma elsewhere states that "industrialists/entrepreneurs etc would be allowed to buy or lease only as much land as is needed and not in excess," with their rich resources there is no regulations or conditions that could hinder the giant companies from getting any amount of land or property they deem fit for maximum extraction of economic profit.[124] Commenting on the efforts of the local educated class who take sides with the forces of neo-colonialism, Fanon rightly term this as "betraying the people's struggle." Elsewhere, Fanon warns against the danger of neo-colonialism if the educated middle class for their own self interest, act on behalf of the neo-colonial forces by allowing the TNCs/MNCs to exploit the natural resources of the native people. For him, the national middle class who rule over the state are just the "agent" or "intermediary" of the western bourgeoisie in their attempt to exploit the economic resources of the native people without any amount of limitation.[125] To state differently, the present day globalization offers an arena for the rich and powerful both in the First World and the Third World to collaborate and join together for the common mission of exploiting all the available economic resources of the Third World people without taking into account the damaged done to both the environment and the majority poor and marginalised.

It is reported that Lafarge Company, a "multinational cement giant has indulged in gross violation of the law of the land by mortgaging tribal land at Nongtrai and Shela to six foreign banks" for getting a loan of US$ 135 million to run this big project without the knowledge of the land owner.[126] It is said that the company has taken on lease of the said land to be renewed every 35 years,[127]

[124] See Patricia Mukhim, "When market triumphs politics," *The Shillong Times*, 29 April 2011.

[125] See Fanon, *The Wretched of the Earth*, 122-123.

[126] The names of six foreign international Banks are Asian Development Bank (ADB), Deutsche Inves-titions und Entwicklungsgevellschaft, European Investment Bank (EIB), International Financial Corporation (IFC), Arab-Bangladesh Bank (ABB), and Standard Charter Bank (SCB) of Bangladesh. See "Cement Giant Violated Law of Land: KSU," *The Shillong Times*, 26 May 2006. See also Hukum Ka Supreme Court ban sangeh tih Mawshun ia ka Lafarge na Shela-Nongtrai.

[127] Interview with the Nongtrai Focus group on the 1 May 2012. The members are B. Lyngdoh (Headman), T. L. Rapmai and T. Shabong.

and also bought around 150 hectare for its project.[128] But the question is how the tribal land which has legal protection can be allowed to be mortgaged outside the country and that too without the knowledge of the land owner? What will be the impact of this deal to the welfare and security of the local native in the near future? What are the benefits that the local indigenous people obtain through this land deal? Whatever the case may be, the truth remains that once the lands are taken on lease or sold to these companies, the local people have no more access to these lands.

Furthermore, with regards to the Lumshnong area, it is reported that, at the allurement of the company through its agents, most of the local people were selling their land at throw away prices.[129] With the minds of the people already globalised, they have no problem to sell their land even at low price.[130] However, the people of the area found that after selling their land to the companies, that is, the land which they were associated with since time immemorial, it is no more accessible to them. Being alienated from their land the situation of the poor people is worse than before. It is regrettable but true, that people who are associated with the natural surroundings for centuries back are now totally cut off from the entire areas. Hence, their whole experiences through their association with these places will also gradually disappear. What the people lose therefore is not simply their land and the resources for economic life, but their entire experiences and relationships they have with the land that has been brought down through the centuries. Cobb rightly comments when he states,

We are constituted by our relations. Very important among these relations are those to our own bodies. These are part of the natural world. Through our bodies and even more directly we are related to other parts of nature. Who we are, what we are, is affected not only by our human communities but also by the broader natural environment. Relations to other living things are important, especially to children. The landscapes of the places we call home shape our sense of reality and of belonging. Hence, the deterioration of our natural surroundings

---

[128] See "Kput kylla ka Lafarge ia ki trai shnong Shella da ka ujor sha Supreme Court," *Mawphor,* 19 May 2011, 1,7.

[129] It is said that the villagers at Lumshnong were selling their land to the companies at Rs. 70 per square feet. In comparison to the market price of the land especially in the industrial areas this price is very insignificant, for the companies can dig deep down as long as the mineral resources are there. Discussion with Mr. R. Khonglah the then Headman of the village at his residence on the 15. 9. 2007.

[130] It is reported that "Local people sell their land to such companies through a local person who is close to the company concerned or in the name of the local director of a company." See "Mining activities threaten Jaintia Hills people," *The Shillong Times,* 5 June 2008, 1.

not only reduces the resources of economic life, it directly impoverishes our experiences.[131]

Destroying the Cave System

The state of Meghalaya in general and Jaintia Hill District in particular have number of beautiful cave system[132] and some are among the longest even in Asia. But the coming of these big companies to this part of the land besides setting up their plants nearby these cave system will definitely disturb the entire cave system. With the sincere efforts and dedicated services of the Meghalaya Adventures Association (MAA),[133] Meghalaya has been placed on the world map of speleologists, where speleologists all over the world visited the beautiful cave system of the state. For instance, the famous Narpuh Reserve Forest is the home of number of caves like the Krem Kotsati-Um Lawan (21.5 kms) considered one of the longest cave in whole of Asia.[134] However, the indiscriminate mining activities of both coal and lime stones in this area has threatened the very existence and presence of the cave system of the state. This has prompted the MAA to file the Public Interest Litigation (PIL) to the Supreme Court for the same.[135] But in its hearing on the 1st September 2010 the Supreme Court dismissed the case on the ground that the petitioner's advocate was absent, and at the same time that the apex court was satisfied with the expert committee set up by the government for the protection of the caves.[136] A similar complaint was lodged by none other than the Leader of opposition, Lok Sabha, Sushma Swaraj against the proposal to establish

---

[131] John B. Cobb, Jr., "Marx and Whitehead," http://www.religion-online.org/showarticle.asp?title=3359. (8.7.2009).

[132] MAA in its petition to the Supreme Court define Cave as "the unique creation of nature and integral to environment and human-animal-plant existence. Their destruction will result in un-assessable loss to humanity and will certain lead to a catastrophe, the implication of which would be immeasurable." The petition further states that caves "where the human eyes and ears could not reach yet, have such bio-diversity with variety of creatures existing and hence endangering this cave life would be lethal to the life visible on earth and in water…It takes 15-20 million years to form a natural cave." See "Caves may remain in history only," *The Shillong Times*, 31 October 2007, 3.

[133] The Meghalaya Adventures Association (MAA) was formally established in 1990 with the main purpose of exploring and preserving the numerous cave systems in the state. Since its formation, MAA have generally identified around 1000 caves existing in different part of the state. Within few years from then, Meghalaya has become the hottest caving destination in the world where Speleologists from all over the world keep exploring the beautiful cave system of the state. See Blah, "The MAA and its PIL- the untold story," 4.

[134] See "JAC demands end to Lafarge operations in State," *The Shillong Times*, 21 August 2008, 1. See also Brian D. Kharpran Daly, "The Shameful Plunder," *The Shillong Times*, 28 May 2011, 2.

[135] Blah, "The MAA and its PIL- the untold story," 4.

[136] But those who know the reality consider this as a flaw, as the integrity of the expert committee in this case is questionable, for they are the same people who constituted the single window agency with the attempt to make all efforts to give necessary clearances to many cement

a cement company at Elaka Nongkhlieh in Jaintia Hills District by Lafarge India Private limited. The company has proposed to set up a 1.1 mn tonne cement plant by undertaking mining activities in the area within Nongkhlieh Elaka.[137] Elaka Nongkhlieh is located between two reserve forest at Narpuh and Saipung, and the whole area is famous for its natural cave system of about 118 cave passages, stretching across 148 km including the Krem Laitprah stretching over 31 km and one of the longest in the Indian sub-continent.[138] Nevertheless, the coming of different companies to this area has disturbed the entire area including the cave system. Though the tourism and economic prospective of these cave system are yet to be realised, these caves are the rich heritage and real treasure that could help building up the economic life of the people of the area in the near future.

Loss of Natural Resources

As stated earlier, most of these cement companies are said to be illegally located in the forest land, which is against the rules and regulations laid by the ministry of environments and forest. Besides, there are others like the Lafarge India Private Limited at Elaka Nongkhlieh situated in the crucial areas where the sources of livelihood derived. Nongkhlieh area is located between or part of the two reserved forest-Saipung and Narpuh Reserved Forest. The proposed mining site surrounded by forest and lies adjacent to the *Pynthor Le-Tein* the most fertile valley in Jaintia Hills considered to be the rice bowl of the people. It is also the originating sources of four main rivers namely Umpyoi, Lukha, Kupli and Letein rivers.[139] Hence, if the project is implemented it will be great set back not only for the people in the area, but also to the entire environment. In short, it will affect not only human species but the entire surrounding will be disturbed that will result to the untold misery to all living species in the near future. Recently, there appeared strong objections and complaints for the same from different quarters by different NGOs, political parties and others against the establishment of these companies, but till today these companies carry on their activities without any limitation. But the coming of large number of companies to this part of the region resulted not only to the alienation of tribal lands but also to the rapid exhaustion of raw materials. It is reported that the companies bought the land from the local people at low prices and began to exploit the earth resources at a faster rate than expected. At the same time, with the single window clearance of the government in operation and the large number of them presence in the small area, it is but

---

companies and the quarries to carry on their works. See Brian D. Kharpran Daly, "The Shameful Plunder," *The Shillong Times* 28 May 2011, 4.

[137] Mining activities are supposed to be operated at Synrang Nohkso, Khim Pynam, Umrap, Langchrieh to Korsati (Lumsorman) within the Elaka Nongkhlieh.

[138] See "Sushma moved against Lafarge," *The Shillong Times,* 15 November 2010, 3; Amarjyoti Bora, "Mine –rape" *The Shillong Times,* 8 March 2009, 3.

[139] See, "Sushma moved against Lafarge," *The Shillong Times,* 15 November 2010, 3.

natural to have strong competition in every sphere of their activities. Hence, it appears that time and again, each of these companies tends to increase the capacity of their production. For instance, while the government statement states that production capacity of the Cement Manufacturing Company Ltd (CMCL) will be 900 TPD (Ton Per Day), the Annual Report of 2006-07 portrays that CMCL has actually produced 508150 MT or 1540 TPD when calculating 330 working days. The report further states that the capacity of production will soon increase to 1800 TDP which is double of the production limit.[140] This means the wanton extraction of the earth resources which resulted in the fast disappearing of the minerals and economic resources from the land.

It is reported that the famous Narpuh Reserve Forest the largest reserve forest and home of rich bio-diversity as well as rich mineral reserve in the state is the worst affected.[141] Looking on the intensity and magnitude of wanton mining activities of the mineral resources, one could suggest that it will not take much time for the earth resources to finish. The outcome of this trend of exploitation is deplorable. What will happen to the land and the native population after the entire economic resources are exhausted. No doubt, after all the available resources are exploited these companies owned by the outsiders will be leaving, but what is left for the native people is barren and depleted land unfit for any vegetation or any other purpose. To state differently, these companies will attempts all available opportunities to extract the resources, and by the time the land is returned to the original owner, it will be a devastated and ruined land that has lost all value of economic purpose. Furthermore, besides the rapid loss of the mineral resources, it also causes rapid environmental damage like loss of agricultural activities,[142] deforestation, extinction of flora and fauna, diminishes the quality of air and water, and so on. It is reported that rapid extraction of the earth resources for quick profit has damaged the water resources where the villagers depend for centuries for drinking water.[143] Due to the massive construction works for the Adhunik Cement Ltd and discharge of fuel from the plant which is only two kms from the source of water supply of the Lumshnong village, "the water has become muddy and greasy and is unfit for consumption."[144] This is risky as it will cause

---

[140] See "Caves may remain in history only," *The Shillong Times,* 31 October 2007, 3.

[141] It is reported that Narpuh Reserve Forest with the total area of 94 Square kilometer has high ecological value. Chowdhury who has done systematic research on this forest found that the forest is home of 400 different Birds, 120 Mamals that includes 37 different kinds of Bats, 30 kinds of Carnivores, 7 different kinds of deers, and 30 different kinds of squirrels. See Russell Nongrum, "Hato ka khlaw Narpuh kan kut tang ha ka khana pateng?" *Mawphor,* 10 May 2002, 1, 5.

[142] Prior to the coming of the company agriculture especially rice was the main occupation of the villagers. See "Mining threaten Jaintia Hills people," *The Shillong Times,* 5 June 2008, 1.

[143] See "Cement cos threaten J Hills environment," *The Shillong Times,* 20 September 2008, 1, 5.

[144] The Lumshnong Student Association argues that "discharged of fuel from different machines used for the construction of the plant were released in nearby streams thereby polluting

serious health hazards and danger to the life of the native people depending on this source for water supply. The people of Lumshnong area now experience the scarcity of water and even demanded the companies to arrange an urgent supply schemes for the village, in which the companies have sponsored drinking water supply to the village twice a day during those time,[145] but later on it stopped supplying the same to the village.

Furthermore, the local people made complaints that with the massive exploitation of the earth resources and the discharge of fuel by the cement companies all the rivers situated in the nearby areas are affected.[146] The recent change in the water colour of the Lukha river that first happened on the 18th February 2007, which at the same time destroyed and killed thousands of aquatic life like fishes and others is small example of the misery experiences by the local people and the natural surroundings.[147] This has badly affected the sources of livelihood to many poor people usually get fresh fish from this river since time immemorial. Commenting on the intensity of the loss of local people due to the operation of this project, Dympep rightly argues when he said that "If our forest, water and unique institutions are destroyed by corporations and backed by international institutions, it is deplorable."[148]

As stated earlier, in a land lock region like North East in general and Meghalaya in particular, land and its resources are the only economic resources worth mentioned. Hence, ruthless exploitation of the natural resources of the tribal people besides affecting the entire eco-system has badly affected the economic life of the people in the entire area. At the same time, while the people and the eco-system are severely affected, the maximum benefit in the whole operation goes to the companies. Blah argues that under the liberal industrial policy of the State government "each cement factory will enjoy the benefits of a tax holiday, subsidy on power, subsidy on transport and subsidy on employment of locals. Production is practically free."[149] That is, while people and environment

---

the water sources." See "Cement plant pollutes drinking water," *The Shillong Times,* 4 July 2007, 1.

[145] The two companies namely Adhunik Cements Ltd and Cement Manufacturing Company Lumshnong are said to have sponsored water supply for sometimes to the Lumshnong village. See "Mining activities threaten Jaintia Hills people," *The Shillong Times,* 5 June 2008, 1.

[146] Some of the rivers got affected due to the effluent discharged by CMCL at Lumshnong area are Um Mutha, Um Soo and Lukha. See "Cement cos threaten J Hills environment," *The Shillong Times,* 20 September 2008, 1, 5.

[147] See S. D. Laloo, "Hato ki bor sorkar ki la shimkhia shisha ban buddien?," *Mawphor,* 27 March 2007), 1, 5. Cf. "Lap ka WKHSU ia ka jingma ia kid oh um na ka karkhana sain nar," *U Nongsain Hima,* 18 January 2010, 1, 7.

[148] Dino Dympep is the Secretary General of the Meghalaya People Human Right Council (MPHRC). See "MPHRC Cries hoarse over Lafarge's Project," *The Shillong Times,* 26 October 2007, 1.

[149] Toki Blah, "The MAA and its PIL- the untold story," 4.

suffer the brunt of the greedy and ruthless exploitation of the entire surrounding, these corporate giants keep on multiplying their profits without any maximum limit. Commenting on the increasing amount of benefits extracted by these giant companies Blah further rightly argues,

> Approximately two MT of limestone convert to one MT of cement. Market Rate of limestone is Rs. 200/MT. With all the above subsidies taken into account the cost of production of cement comes to approximately Rs. 900 per MT, cost of labour included. It is sold in the open market at approximately Rs. 4000 per MT and for a 100 MT capacity plant; it comes to Rs. 3, 10, 000 per day. On that very day the local who once owned the land where the limestone came from gets Rs. 200 or 0.02 per cent of the profit.[150]

If that is the case, considering the case of one company like the CMCL with its capacity production of 1800 TPD the amount of profits accumulated by the company through exploitation of the resources of the land worth million rupees per day. With number of companies mushrooming in the area, the amount of money and economy drain outside the land is beyond one could estimate. Looking from the perspective of the local people one could say that the amount of profit obtained by the local people through the entire process is almost nil. Hence, for the tribal people whose land and resources have been taken away from them apart from losing their source of livelihood, this trend seems to disturb and hamper the entire eco-system making it unhabitable in the near future. Such act not only destroys the earth resources, but it has also broken the delicate balance of the whole eco-system. Commenting on the damaged done by the corporate giants to the entire surrounding environment Churchill fittingly argues, "it has been a glaring truth that these private investors are always indifferent to the negative environmental impacts brought about by their commercial ventures. In their basic motive underlined by maximization of profit they fail to secure the environmental interests."[151]

In other words, the entire process instead of bringing development to the people has made their economic condition more impoverished than before, in which not only their economic resources are being plundered but also even their once peaceful habitat has been disturbed. That is, with the exception of a small section of population that might have been benefitted from this process, one cannot deny that the system has threatened the security and economic survival of the majority of the people. Butola rightly comments when he says that exposure of North Eastern Region to the process of globalization will lead to depletion of resources, loss of hereditary rights over their natural environment which will lead to disempowerment of the people. "Disempowerment" for him means "loss of their rights over the use and preservation of their environment in its complete

[150] Toki Blah, "The MAA and its PIL- the untold story," 4.

[151] Churchill, "India's LEP and the North East...," 78.

biodiversity. Once, the tribals are alienated from their natural environment then the objective bases of their social activity, art, culture and popular science, etc. too will lose its significance and meaning."[152] Hence, the loss of the people in the entire process will be immense. This does not mean saying "no" to development. But people need development that could help improving the living conditions of the poor and marginalised besides doing justice to the earth and its resources. To state differently, development should protect and not damage and alienate the habitat.

Employment Opportunities

As stated earlier, from the government perspective the advent of these giant companies is to bring development to the area. It is also natural for the companies to claim that their projects will bring both direct and indirect employment to the local people. Direct employment means that the educated local people will be directly recruited in different capacities in accordance with their qualifications. Indirect employment means that the establishment of these companies will also simultaneously generated other types of employment like tea stalls, restaurants, fruit stalls, and so on. In their agreement with the people of the area prior to the establishment of their plants the company's management make tall claims that 60% of the different job available in the company will be given to the local population especially to the unemployed youth of the area. It is said that though the company entered the area with the big promise of bringing development to the area, in comparison with the amount of profit that the company obtained through this project, the benefits that the local people share is almost nil. It is reported that almost 100% of the employees in this projects are non local,[153] thus denying the local indigenous people ample scope of employment opportunities. Today it is found that the employment opportunities to the local people in different cement companies are very slim as these companies brought both skilled and unskilled labourers from outside the states. In their statement sent to Dr. Donkupar Roy the then Chief Minister of the state in 2008, the Joint Action Committee against Alienation of Tribal Lands in Meghalaya[154] complaint that "the cement companies had violated agreements to provide 60 per cent job opportunities to local communities by employing people from outside the state while the locals

[152] B. S. Butola, "Structural Adjustment and the Politics of Recognition and Redistribution in the North Eastern Region of India," in *Liberalization and India's North East,* edited by Gurudas Das and R. K. Purkayastha (New Delhi: Commonwealth Publishers, 1998), 83.

[153] "Cement Giant violated the law of the land," 1.

[154] The meeting conducted by Joint Action Committee Against Alienation of Tribal Lands in Meghalaya (JACAATLM) is attended by different NGOs which include Jaintia Forum of Biodiversity, KSU Jaintia Hills, Shella Action Committee, Hynniew Trep National Youth Front (HNYF), Khasi student Union (Lumshnong Unit), Lumshnong Student Union, Meghalaya Indigenous People Forum, and affected land owners from Shella, Tynger and Sohbar.

were exploited in the form of cheap labour and low wages."[155] The main reason that the companies' management state was that, the tribal people is not qualified for different jobs available in the project. In the process of globalization poor tribal people find themselves unfit and their labour skills unmatched to different modern technique system. Hence, they suffer major setback in availing lucrative job opportunities offered by these corporate bodies. But even in different vacancy available where the local people are qualified, the Companies prefer the non-local at the expense of the native people.[156] Apart from direct employment one could say that even in indirect employment, shops that emerged near the project area belong mostly to the people from outside the state. This indicates that the recent changes in the tribal society not only affected the source of livelihood of majority poor people but it will also hinder the growth and development of tribal economy. Hence, the coming of different projects to the tribal areas instead of helping to raise the living conditions of the people, it will rather push them further to the margin of economic ladder.

Who Benefitted in the Entire Process?

The above discussion illustrates that employment opportunities for the unemployed youth of the state is significantly low. If that is the case one may ask, who benefitted through the establishment of different companies in the land? It may be noted that among the local people, those who will gain from the entire process are only small section of population. In other words, those who will be benefitted are small section of elites besides those who have property to sell. Commenting on the benefits to be obtained by those who have property to sell as well as the giant companies at the expense of the common people, Daly has rightly express, "the rich coal barons will only get richer and the cement factory owners even wealthier leaving the poor peasants and farmers destitute."[157] On the other hand Srikanth maintains that

> A section of elites closely associated with the liberalization process no doubt gets some benefits. But majority of the indigenous people will be exposed to the problems of land alienation, displacement, proletarianisation and unemployment. Due to lack of social commitment, the private capital mercilessly plunders the natural wealth and creates serious ecological problems in the region."[158]

---

[155] See "JAC demands end to Lafarge operations in State," *The Shillong Times,* 21 August 2008, 1.

[156] "Maham Ka JYF ia ka Sorkar bad JHADC ban ai NOC ia ka Lafarge," *Mawphor,* 14 May 2008, 1, 5.

[157] Brian D. Kharpran Daly, "The shameful plunder," *The Shillong Times,* 28 May 2011, 4.

[158] Srikanth, "Liberalization and Development of India's North-East...," 164.

So what the local people gain in the entire process are only short term monetary benefits that will not last, besides irreparable destruction done to the natural surroundings. Though the government and the companies claim that the coming of different companies to the land is to bring development to the people, the ground reality shows a different story. On the contrary, almost the total profit in the entire process goes to the company. In other words, while the process benefits few people, the overall development of the people is not the target. The entire process can be termed as, "people around the development" rather than "development around the people."[159] That is, people are being made poor in an environment abundant in natural resources. To state it differently, despite having rich deposits of different mineral resources the state of Meghalaya is still considered one among the poorest state in the country. The Meghalaya Human development Report, 2008 states that according to the Human Development Index (HDI), Meghalaya found to be one among the poorest state in the country. The report states that the position of Meghalaya shows a decline from 21 in the year 1981 to the position of 24 in 1991 and further down to 26 in 2005, among the 35 states and Union Territories.[160] This implies that developmental activities implemented by the government do not help raising the living condition of the people especially the poor and the needy. In the era of globalization there is a tendency that the big corporate bodies will go anywhere they deem fit to establish their firms in order to extract maximum benefit within short span of time. This point to the fact that the companies do not come to certain areas to bring development, rather to exploit the economic benefit of the land without taking into account the damage done to the local indigenous population and the surrounding environment as a whole.

Impact of Coal Trade

As stated earlier, in a land lock situation like North East India, with less trade linkages with the outside world, land and natural resources are the only capital worth to be mentioned. At the same time, in the era of globalization where the demands for raw materials are much more than in any period of history, exploitation of raw materials will be more severe than expected. This is appropriately true in the context of the rich mineral resources area of Khasi Jaintia Hills of Meghalaya. The significant area where coal mining is done in huge quantities in Khasi Jaintia

---

[159] Giri, Implications of New Economic Policy for Development of North-East India, 40. See also P. C. Dutta and B. C. Pradhan, "New Economic Policy and Development in NER of India," in *Globalization and North East India,* edited by Bimal J. Deb, Keya Sengupta and B. Datta Ray (New Delhi: Concept Publishing Company, 2008), 193.

[160] See "Wan shadien ka Meghalaya ha ka Human Development Index," *U Nongsain Hima,* 28 October 2009, 1, 7.

is witnessed in Jaintia Hills, Borsara and Shahlang areas.[161] Though coal mining in Jaintia Hills started in the 1970s, the intensity and magnitude of coal trade is carried on in large volume in the 1980s.[162] In the present day context, Meghalaya has produced more than 6 million tons of coal annually.[163] Most of these raw materials are either exported to mainland India through Assam or outside the country to Bangladesh.[164] The increasing demand for the raw materials both inside as well as outside the country, coupled with the desire of the present day generation for quick and maximum benefits, one could witness rapid exploitation of mineral resources that left deep impact both on the economic life of the people as well as the entire surrounding environment.

Firstly, as stated earlier in Meghalaya in general and Khasi Jaintia in particular land belong to the people. But in the era of globalization where the cost of land is very high, the rich section of the population capture every opportunity to purchase land in different parts of the state thereby leaving the majority poor and marginalised, landless. This is aptly true in the case of rich coal belt areas of the state. Hence, mining activities as well as trade related activities on coal are almost entirely under the hands of the rich local traders. However, with stiff competition from the world market, the selling prices of coal have come down from $46 to $25 per metric ton, coal business that used to fetch maximum benefits to the traders could not provide appropriate benefits to the local traders as it was few years back.[165] Nevertheless, with the volume of trade increasing, rich local traders could obtain quick profit within short span of time. On the other hand, looking on the ground realities of the entire business transaction, the entire benefit in the whole process is not equally shared by different sections of population. In other words, it is only the small rich section of the population that are benefitted, whereas the majority poor and marginalised could hardly share the profits generated by the trade.

---

[161] In the case of the former mining activities started four decades back, in the latter two it is a recent phenomenon. As stated earlier, coal mining in Khasi Jaintia is not a recent phenomenon. It started since the colonial era in Cherapunjee and other areas though not in large volume as it is today. But it is in these few decades that coal trade is done in maximum quantity.

[162] See S. C. Katiyar, "Impact of Coal Mining in Jaintia Hills," *Eastern Panorama* (December, 1997): 38.

[163] The above mentioned quantities also include the amount of coal trade being carried on in the entire state of Meghalaya including Garo Hills areas. See C. F. Lyngdoh, "Meghalaya needs a mining policy," *The Shillong Times,* 21 April 2008, 4.

[164] Hence, one could observes that every day thousands of trucks plying on the roads for exporting the raw materials either to Beltola, Assam or Tamabil, in the Bangladesh border that generally cause much inconvenience to the general public due to the traffic jams always happening in these days.

[165] It is reported that the price of coal come down due to the lower price offered by other countries in the international market namely Korea, Australia and Indonesia. See Bareh, *The Economy of Meghalaya,* 227.

Secondly, looking by the intensity and large volume of coal trade being carried on in the land, one may assume that coal related trade activities could offer maximum number of employment opportunities in different capacities to the local people. But if one paid a visit to different mining areas in the land, one could witnessed that maximum number of those involved in coal mining activities are generally non local. C. F. Lyngdoh a retired mining engineer maintains that a standard colliery in India that produced 10,000 tonnes per months could generally provide employment opportunities to around 400 persons per day including clerical, technical and operative staff. He further states that despite Meghalaya produced 6 million tonnes per year that could normally employed 20,000 people[166] the number of the local indigenous people working in the coal mines are very less. Lyngdoh states that the two main reasons for this are:[167]

> i). The coal mines are very unsafe so that local people do not like to risk their lives working in these coalmines in spite of highly lucrative wages. ii). The mine owners prefer to employ cheap migrant labourers because if there is a fatal mine accident[168] the dead miner can be easily forgotten (even his body need not be retrieved) and nobody raises questions about the dead miner whose name and address even is not known or registered.

Hence, despite the highly paid wages in this trade the local people prefer to avoid risking their lives rather than work in unsafe conditions. This indicates that employment opportunities for the local indigenous people in the mining areas are very rare. On the other hand, the inclination towards employing the migrant labourers has rather attracted large number of immigrant population to enter the mining area in search for employment. This has resulted in the heavy influx of migrant people[169] that has not only outnumbered the local indigenous

---

[166] This number do not include thousands of truck drivers and handymen that are daily involved in transportation activities in and around the mining areas as well as those who transport the raw materials from the mining places for export to either Assam or Bangladesh.

[167] C F Lyngdoh, "Meghalaya needs a mining policy," *The Shillong Times,* 21 April 2008, 4.

[168] Lyngdoh argues that the accident often taken place as there is lack of safety standards. As he rightly puts it, "Naturally there will be frequent roof fall or caving in accidents in our coal mines. But the identity of the victims is not known because there is no system for registering the workers, while this is statutorily required in the Mine Act." See, Lyngdoh, "Meghalaya needs a mining policy," 4.

[169] It may be noted that besides the labourers from the mainland India, the influx of migrant labourers from Bangladesh and Nepal keep on increasing. At the same time, with the lack of rules and regulations that could prevent the entry of migrant labourers, one could witness heavy influx of outsiders to the land. Hence besides resulting to the rapid changing of the demographic structure of the state, it will also left deep impact to the economic life of the people. Recently the state has adopted the working permit system called Three Tier ID Card System to help checking the presence of the illegal migrant labourers, but it yet to be implemented practically. See "Thaw Committee ki Sengbhalang bad RS ban dawa pyntrei noh ia ka ILP bad Work Permit," *Mawphor,* 8 May 2011, 1, 7. Cf. "Govt expresses reservations on ILP," *The Shillong Times,* 20 May 2011.

population, but also alters the entire demographic balance of population in the land. The classic example is the Lad Rymbai market where the non-tribal traders not only control the entire trade, but also maximum numbers of the population are non-tribal.

Thirdly, the unscientific and haphazard extraction of the mineral resources using the outdated system of "rat-hole method" brought severe destruction and ecological imbalance to the entire eco-system. With the Mining Policy[170] of the government is yet to be passed by the government, coupled with the absence of rules and regulations that could provide vital suggestion to the mine owners, all the mine owners could do whatever they deem it fit to achieve maximum profit. Hence, ruthless exploitation of the earth resources caused serious danger to humans as well as the surrounding environment. It is reported that all the important rivers and streams in and nearby the mining areas have been highly contaminated with acidic water that flows from unscientific coal mining as well as careless dumping of coal in the areas. Such a careless attitude by those involved in coal related activities has not only polluted and damaged the water resources making them unfit for human consumption but also destroys diversities of aquatic life living in these rivers centuries back.[171] The unscientific mining, besides damaging the sources of many streams and rivulets that led to the disappearance of many streams, it has also caused serious hardships and miseries to the entire population as safe drinking water is not available, thereby causing injurious health hazards to the entire population in the area.[172] At the same time, it is reported that while in many major rivers like Myntdu, Kupli, Umsuwai, Thwai Kungor in Jaintia Hills that have their sources of origin in the mining area, the colour of the water has generally changed and aquatic life has disappeared since the 1980s the time when mining activities reach at certain height. In other rivers like Waikhyrwi, Wailong, Wah Kwai in Jaintia Hills, the impact of coal mining is happening in recent times. For instance, few decades back many among the inhabitants of Psadwar village, a

[170] It is important to note that till today the State Government has yet to pass the Mining Policy. With the absence of the essential Mining Policy the impact of unscientific mining operation in the state would be fatal. Hence, without the proper Mining Policy the authority of the state over the mining activities cannot go beyond collecting revenue. See Den Syiem, "Hato ka jingtih dewiong ha Meghalaya ka long be-ain," *Mawphor,* 21 January 2010, 1, 5.

[171] See Sanio Siangshai, "Coalmines threaten life in Jaintia Hills," *The Shillong Times,* 20 August 2007. 3. See also "Unscientific mining activities polluting water, environment," *The Shillong Times,* 12 June 2004, 3. See also, M. H. Mohrmen, "Kylla Bih sa ka wah Kwai, duhjait sa ki dohum," *Mawphor,* 20 January 2010, 1, 5; Se also K. L. Tariang, "Sustainable water resources in Meghalaya," *The Shillong Times,* 5 November 2010, 2. See also "Rare phenomenon behind fish death in J Hills," *The Shillong Times,* 4 June 2007, 1.

[172] It is said that due to the unscientific mining using the age old system of "rat-hole method" many streams and rivulets have been dried up. Besides as the water bodies is highly contaminated with acid people of the area has to buy water for drinking making untold sufferings to the poor and marginalised section of the population.

village lying on the bank of Myntdu River in the border Bangladesh earned their livelihood by selling fish from the Myntdu River. It is regrettable but true, that due to the impact of coal mining, today no form of aquatic life is present in the river anymore.

This ruthless exploitation of the earth resources has not only damaged the water resources but also adversely affected food grain production in the state especially paddy. It may be noted that Meghalaya is a food deficit state. It can produced only 3.3 lakh metric tons out of the 4 lakh metric tons needed for the entire population.[173] With the impact of coal mining food insecurity faced by the people will be severe. In his report at the Assembly meeting, E. C. Bamon the then Agriculture Minister of the state, narrates how coal mining proved hazardous to the means of livelihood of the people especially agriculture. He states that paddy cultivation has been seriously affected due to the shifting economic pursuits of the people from agriculture to coal mining. It is reported that in Jaintia hills alone wanton mining activities resulted to the loss of 41, 513 hectares of land generally used for paddy cultivation. That includes the loss of 16, 926 hectares in 2004-05, 12,293 hectares in 2005-06, and 12,294 hectares in 2006-07.[174] This indicates that thousands hectares of paddy fields are being converted every year to coal mining.

Fourthly, another serious problem cause by coal mining is land degradation. Land degradation resulted to soil erosion, siltation in nearby streams and paddy fields, landslides, sinking of the earth etc. In fact, most of the land surrounding the mining areas remains barren. It is found that the cultivated field in the valleys are largely affected by the run-off water during rainy season which carry large amount of dissolved toxic elements thereby contaminated the fertile cultivated land. As a result, after few years land became unviable for cultivation and has to be abandoned by the farmers. The soil testing conducted in the area found that the soils of the abandoned field are highly acidic unfit for any vegetation.[175] Besides, if one paid a visit to the mining areas one could witness the ugliest face of the earth surface that has severely affected the landscape of the area. That is, one could witness that in many places the earth has been sinking and crack has been occurring in some of the earth surfaces. Lamin rightly pointed out when he refers to this,

> There are, for instance, eight sinking places within an area of 20 acres in the village. The sinking of the land occurs after the mining of coal because the supporting pillars below the ground are removed and shifted to new places.

---

173 See "Mining depletes food grain production in state," *The Shillong Times,* 30 September 2008, 3.

174 See "Coal mining affects paddy cultivation," *The Shillong Times,* 8 November 2008, 1.

175 L. Boral and T. Lyngdoh, "Degradation of Eco-system due to Coal mines," in *Forest: A Global Perspectives,* edited by S. K. Majumdar (Pennsylvania: Academy of Science, 1996), 461.

> There are more than 25 cases of landslides during 1984-89, according to the report of the headman of the village[176]

This indicates that unscientific mining operation has not only caused alarming threat to human life but the whole environment has been affected and degraded. Recently, a report came in both the electronic and print media about the sudden crack of the earth surface in the area around Sohkymphor market that has cause grave danger to all living beings. This has compelled the village council to enforce strict rules and regulations not to allow any mining done within the parameters of the village. Nevertheless, whatever may be the case; it is vividly clear that maximum damage and destruction has already been done to the environment, and it will take centuries for the earth to regain its strength and well being.

If this is the case, the impact of coal mining activities has not only put serious alarm to the food security of the people, but it has also brought serious challenges to the economic life of the people, not to mention about alarming threat to the health of the people in the entire surrounding of the mining areas. That is, for achieving maximum profits through short term monetary benefits within a short period, the people not only shift their economic pursuits but they are doing this at a faster rate without taking into consideration the needs and birth right of the future generation. This seems to convey that the present day generation wants to finish all the resources that our ancestral parents have consciously preserved at the expense of the sons and daughters of future generation. In short, it reflects the ungrateful attitude of the present day generation to the vast heritage left behind by our ancestral besides grave injustice done to the future generation.

Cutting Down of Public Subsidy

The earlier discussion portrays that for the purpose of integration of national economy with the global economy, India as well as other countries have to follow the Structural Adjustment Programmes (SAP), designed and imposed by the so called agency of globalization on the less developed countries like the Third World countries. According to the prescribe conditions of the SAP, the national government is expected to "spend less by cutting back government expenditures, social services, and economic investments so that the resources can be placed elsewhere."[177] Needless to say that the pressure from the WB, IMF, WTO and others institutions of globalization coupled with formulated policies and conditions like "reduction of expenditure in social sectors, cut down in employment and

---

[176] H. Lamin, *Economy and Society in Meghalaya,* (New Delhi: Har Anand Publications, 1995), 110.

[177] Matthews George Chunakara, "Globalization and its Impact on Human Rights," in *Globalization and its Impact on Human Rights,* edited by Matthews George Chunakara (Thiruvalla: Chritava Sahitya Samithy, 2000), 96.

government subsidies, etc" had adversely affected the tribal people.[178] So, what is decided at the global level has its impact not only at the national level, but also to different region of the country thereby adversely affecting the grass root level. This entails that the government both at the centre and the state tend to surrender number of its responsibilities usually managed by the public sector, to the private sector without taking into account its adverse affect on the marginalised poor and the needy. For the people of Meghalaya where more than 40% of the populations are living Below Poverty Line (BPL) the entire situation is fatally deplorable. It is true that the government today employ different schemes for social justice like the National Rural Health Mission (NRHM), the Sarve Siksha Abhiyan (SSA), and the Mahatma Gandhi National Rural Employment Guarantee Scheme (MGNREGS), etc for helping the people especially in the rural areas. But the critics of this schemes opine that the motive behind implementing these programmes are mostly based on political gains rather than helping raising the living condition of the poor and the marginalised section of the society. Jacob[179] maintains that most of these programmes are "employed to mitigate the effect of structural violence and as a vote-winning strategy rather than as a commitment to up lift the poor." He further makes his point clear when he states,

> The national health budget was reduced to 0.9% of the GDP in the 1990s. Although, the United Progressive Alliance was voted to power on its promise of raising it back to 2-3%, this is yet to materialise. The ruling class (read politicians, administrators and their corporate partners) seems to employ social justice project to soften democratic opposition to its capitalistic ideas of development. These schemes seem to be measures to prevent open revolt by the poor, rather than solutions to produce an egalitarian society. However cross underfunding of such schemes ensures the success of capitalistic ventures, thus increasing privatisation and running down the public sector.[180]

If one make a sincere analytical study of these programmes one could find that such projects could hardly make any difference in the uplift of the living conditions of the vulnerable section of the society. For instance, the execution of MGNREGS in Khasi Jaintia Hills demonstrated that this scheme was implemented without proper analytical study of the need of the tribal people in this part of the country. What is planned in Delhi is generally executed in all the regions of the country irrespective of its relevance to the need of the people in the area. It may be noted that such programmes implemented to provide daily wage

---

[178] P. C. Dutta and B. C. Pradhan, "New Economic Policy and Development in NER of India," in *Globalization and North East India,* edited by Bimal J. Deb, Keya Sen Gupta and B. D. Dutta Ray (New Delhi: Concept Publishing Company, 2008), 217.

[179] Professor K. S. Jacob is on the Faculty of the Christian Medical College, Vellore.

[180] See K. S. Jacob, "Capitalism: Regulate, Rework, Transform," *The Hindu,* (Kochi) 22 January 2011, 12.

labour to the people-instead of initiating schemes that could help the local people standing on their own feet-could hardly capable to raise the vulnerable living condition of the people. To state differently, it will give them short term meagre monetary benefit rather than bringing lasting solution to their age old helpless socio-economic condition of their life. Hence, this cannot help them come out of the bondage of poverty. At the same time, people from War area complaint that since the implementation of these schemes daily wage labourers prefer to work under this scheme rather than working as daily wage labourers in the betel nut fields, thus affecting the agricultural activities that the people of the area depending on centuries as their source of livelihood. Moreover, implementation of the schemes totally funded by the central government at the grass root level, where most of the villagers lack basic knowledge and required experience in financial management bring more harm than good to the local people of the area. This has resulted to the misusing of the money by those in authority at the village level responsible for the betterment and welfare of the villagers like the headmen and other important members. It may be noted that number of corruption cases have been committed by the members of the different village committees in many places are reported both by the electronic and print media.[181] In general, these schemes seem to bring more complications to the already vulnerable situation of the rural people instead of solving their poverty related problems.

Privatization

As stated above, in the era of globalization where the national government has to adhere to the diktat of the agencies of globalization, one could witness that the government both at the centre and the state level tend to surrender most of their duty and responsibility at the hands of the private sectors. This has proved to be true in the case of the state of Meghalaya where the government is moving forward to privatise the power sector and the health sector to big companies from outside the state. In the case of the former, Meghalaya in particular and North East India in general has huge potential to generate thousands megawatts of hydro electric power that has attracted the attention not only of the state government but also the corporate companies to exploit the rich power resources that the region could offer. It is reported that the Indian Government has identified 168 sites in the entire region as potential sites for mega dams capable of producing hydro electric power.[182] Most of the state government in North East India are moving forward

[181] A series of corruption cases has been reported like in Nongrim-Nongladew, Jongksha, and other places where those in authority at the village level misusing the fund meant for the wages and other related expenditure for the schemes. See Shobha SV., "Ostracised for Demanding Information," *Open* (24 October, 2011): 27. See also "Job card holders deprived of their rights, public funds misappropriated." *The Shillong Times,* 5 April 2012.

[182] See Sushanta Talukdar, "Protect people in downstream of hydel projects: AASU," *The Hindu* (Kochi), 5 August 2009, 22; See also "Dams displacing human habitat in NE," *The Shillong*

to sign MOUs with the private firms for generating electric power through the mega power project.[183] This has led to strong opposition from different NGOs on the grounds that construction of big dams would automatically submerge many villages that would render thousands people homeless.

In Meghalaya, way back in December 2007, the state government resolved to hand over five power projects to private companies against the mounting opposition from different sections of the population.[184] Moreover, several NGOs and different sections of the local indigenous population lodge a strong complaint against the government agreement on the power deal terming this deal as controversial, mortgaging the state resources and total sell out of the people of the state to the corporate giants.[185] Due to the strong protest the state government Meghalaya Progressive Alliance,[186] the coalition government of that time scrapped the deal on the controversial power project. But when the Meghalaya United Alliance came back to power again, the government rolled back its decisions which had been scrapped earlier to hand over the power generation projects to the big companies from outside the state with the motive to have joint venture programmes with the state government through the agreement of Built Operate Transfer (BOT). That is, the companies will operate for sometimes and after 40 years the projects will be returned back to the government.[187]

According to the State Government's perspective, the coming of big companies would not only bring huge investments to the state, it will also bring lots of developmental activities to the area as well as creating ample scope of employment opportunities to the local indigenous unemployed persons of the state. For instance, according to the MOUs signed with the companies for the Kynshi power projects,[188] the companies have to provide 90% of job available to

---

Times, 23 August 2004, 2.

[183] See "NE govts suffer epidemic of MOUs with pvt Cos," *The Shillong Times,* 3 May 2008, 1, 5.

[184] These power projects are Kynshi Stage I, Kynshi Stage II, Myntdu-Leshka Stage II, Umngot and other. See "Scrap Cabinet decision on power projects: FKJGP," *The Shillong Times,* 8 January 2008, 1.

[185] See "KSU rally peacefully, office picketing from today," *The Shillong Times,* 8 January 2008, 1; See also "Scrap Cabinet decision on power projects: FKJGP," *The Shillong Times,* 8 January 2008, 1.

[186] It may be noted that Meghalaya has three different governments within these five years term.

[187] See Patricia Mukhim, "Is this Mukul's last ditch efforts to save the power deal," *The Shillong Times,* 16 January 2008, 1, 5; See also "Rai ka Cabinet ban aiti ia ka Kynshi Project sha ki company, buh teng shwa ia ka Myntdu-Leshka," *Mawphor,* 22 December 2009, 1, 5.

[188] The then State Government Meghalaya United Alliance (MUA) under the Chief Minister Mr. D. D. Lapang resolved to hand over the Kynshi Stage I and Kynshi Stage II both above 100 MV to two giants companies namely, Athena Private Ltd and Jaypee Group from New Delhi. See "Lapang nod to power projects," *The Telegraph* (Guwahati), 22 December 2009.

the local unemployed youth of the state with the salary at par with the government, an engineering college to be established by the companies for the region, 1% of the total investment amounted to Rs. 7000 crores for developmental activities in and around Kynshi area, 2% free electric power to be given to the state, 30% of construction works to local contractors, besides students completing their engineering courses, ITI, polytechnic will be absorbed into different job capacities and host of many other promises.[189] Looking on the agreement one could suggest that local indigenous people will achieved lot of benefit through the coming of these projects. But experiences with different cement companies setting up in the state tell us that promises by the so called giant companies are good only in paper. The companies tend to ignore all the promises besides not respecting the sentiments and needs of the people in terms of employment opportunities and developmental activities to the local areas. Instead once the companies get settled not to mention about violation of the agreements, they will attempt all efforts to ensure getting maximum benefit at the expense of the local people. This is true with the Kynshi project where the Athena Pvt Ltd began its work without adhering to the agreement signed with the local people. This has prompted the local people to force the company to discontinue its work till the earlier agreement is respected and implemented.[190] Hence, with their strong financial position it is clear that the companies will not follow the signed agreement but will move forward to make all efforts to exploit the economic resources of the state for quick profit, without taking into account the rights and needs of the local indigenous population. Such acts will not only affect the sources of livelihood of the local people but will also bring new challenges to their entire economic life.

The State government is also moving forward to privatise the health sector especially in the rural areas. It is said that in December 2008 the State Government entered into agreement with some NGOs from outside the state for the management of the health sector in the rural areas through the Public Private Partnership. As per the agreement, a Jharkhand based NGO Citizen Foundation took over the management of some health centre like the Kynrud PHC, Myriaw PHC, Ichamati PHC and Nongkhlaw CHC which till recently been serving the rural people through government subsidised rate that has greatly benefit the poor people.[191] It is also reported that the government is planning to hand over the entire health sector in the rural areas to different NGOs in the near future. According to the government sources, handing the entire management of

---

[189] See Patricia Mukhim, "Is this Mukul's last ditch effort to save the power deal" *The Shillong Times,* 16 January 2008, 1, 5; See also "Rai ka Cabinet ban aiti ia ka Kynshi Project sha ki kompani, buh teng ia ka Myntdu-Leshka," *Mawphor,* 22 December 2009, 1, 5.

[190] See "Ba thok u CM pynsangeh ki trai khyndew ia ka Kompeni ban sdang Kynshi Project," *Mawphor,* 4 June 2010, 1.

[191] See "NGO-run hospitals fare poorly," *The Shillong Times,* 13 May 2010, 1.

the health sector to the NGOs will certainly bring better health care and other health related facilities to the rural populace.[192] Nevertheless, the people found that the services rendered by these centre is far better when they were under the management of the government. Some of the drawbacks of these centres these days are shortage and irregular supply of medicine, irregularity of salaries to different workers and so on.[193] If this is the case, the handing over of these health centres to NGOs from outside the state will bring lot of hardship and miseries to the poor and marginalised people of the rural areas who do not get access to better health facilities present in the urban areas. In turn, withdrawal of government duty and responsibility on social services will badly affected the economic life of the vulnerable section of the society like the poor and marginalised.

Impact of Consumerist/Cosmopolitan Culture

As stated earlier, in the era of globalization one could witness the emergence and invasion of the consumerist or cosmopolitan culture that has been penetrating every nook and corner of the North East India and among the Khasi people as well. One of the important features of consumerist or cosmopolitan culture is the globalization or homogenization of taste. The so called "Macdonaldization" is witness in standardization of taste in favour of fast food items and cool drinks is spreading very fast especially among the urban folks. People tend to be fond of eating western cuisine like pizza, hamburger, diverse types of ice cream, cool drinks rather than the traditional food items like *putharo, pumaloi,*[194] and the like. The growing interest in western food items may lead to the extinction of the traditional food items and together with that the existing knowledge and skills in the trade.

With the influence of mass media, the so called globalization of taste does not confine to food items but also occur in terms of dress code, music and others. Young people today irrespective of financial background opt for more expensive luxurious dress items like Levi jeans, Reebok, etc the trend that spread all over the world. But for the tribal people where majority of the people are Below Poverty Line (BPL) this emerging consumerist culture tend to be a financial burden to many poor families. Moreover, with their minds being globalised young people today prefer Hollywood culture and western music but shy away from traditional music and dances. Mawrie observes that a Khasi youth today seems to perform more western music and dances at the expense of traditional music and dances. He further goes on to say that "a Khasi youth today will know more of western culture

[192] The then Minister in Charge of health department maintains that the government is planning to hand over the entire health sector to the NGOs in the near future. See "Yn phah pyniaid noh ha ki Sengbhalang ia baroh ki PHC ha ka Jylla: Dr. Pariong," *U Nongsain Hima,* 15 December 2008, 1, 7.

[193] See NGO-run hospitals fare poorly, 1.

[194] *Putharo* and *pumaloi* are two traditional food items of the Khasi made of rice powder.

than his own. This is a very unhealthy development because it will gradually lead to loss of one's own culture which will ultimately result in the loss of identity itself."[195] In similar vein, Phrangsngi Pyrtuh sees the influence of western culture as a danger that will lead to the extinction of Khasi Culture. As he rightly puts it,

> The rate at which our young generations opt out from their own culture (because its not cool and old) and adopt this free flowing western-influence culture is escalating to such an extent that it may soon become a dominant culture. If this happens, we will see mass voluntary abdication of the Khasi culture in favour of the "free floating" western culture.[196]

Hence, western consumerist culture poses great danger to small communities like the Khasis. Similarly, with the motive to exploit the market for maximum profit, the agencies of globalization have invaded the region through different luxurious goods of diverse kinds and brands. Today if one visits any cities or towns in the region he/she could witness different varieties of imported foreign goods available in different market of the region.[197] With their minds globalised, coupled with the influences of information technology and mass media, tribal people are eagerly aspiring to possess every type of imported goods sold in the market be it electronic gadgets, kitchen wares, clothes, sports materials and the like without a second thought. Commenting on the present trend develop among the tribal people, Mukhim has rightly pointed out when she says,

> One problem with us tribes is that we have based our aspirations on a western acquisitive model which is not sustainable. We mimic what we see on television. We want homes with Italian tiles; bathrooms with Jacuzzi baths; a bar that's much better than one you would see in an American middle class home; a kitchen with the latest gadgets advertised on TV and then a TV set that's like a cinema screen size.[198]

In today's globalised era, the rich section welcome this trend with open arms as it offers them with latest gadgets and new imported goods at their door steps. But this is different with regards to the poor sections of the society. It may be noted that the standard of living followed by the rich sections of the society is beyond the means and the reach of the vulnerable sections of the society. In a tribal society, where the practice of communitarian life is still followed in different capacities this is clearly visible in their day to day dealings. For instance, in any tribal functions like the marriage ceremony, Christmas festival and other

---

[195] See Barness L. Mawrie, "Electic culture: Its repercussions," *The Shillong Times,* 18 May 2011, 4.

[196] Phrangsngi Pyrtuh, "The Amnesiac Khasi Culture," *The Shillong Times,* 6 April 2009, 4.

[197] These days large number of foreign goods are flooded into the urban centers of North East Region like Gauhati, Shillong, Dimapur, Aizawl and so on.

[198] Patricia Mukhim, "When market triumphs politics," *The Shillong Times,* 29 April 2011, 4.

social functions one could see wide disparities between the rich and the poor sections of the society. With the materialist culture has rapidly spread among the tribal people, many among the poor people today tend to avoid different social functions as they could not afford the luxurious life style emerging in today's tribal society. To state differently, the marginalised poor section of population find it beyond their reach even to buy necessary dress materials needed for such related functions. Similarly, is the case with many marriages celebrated today. The amount of money involved and lavish spending to celebrate a marriage ceremony by the rich people today is so huge; thereby making the poor people to shy away from ecclesiastical marriage ceremony performed in the church. Hence, this trend besides dividing the tribal population between the rich and the poor, the haves and the haves-not has further pushed back the marginalised poor section to the margin of social hierarchy. Pyrtuh maintains that "globalization impacts small indigenous communities like ours more than it does others. It signifies a race to the finish where only the fittest survives."[199] The outcome of this trend left deep negative impact on the psyche of the poor people who can in no way afford to adopt such increasing standard of living and luxurious lifestyle.

Look East Policy

The political and economic history of India tells us that since the colonial era and even after Independence, India's foreign and economic policy was always turned towards forging trade relationship with the west[200] rather than with the East Asian countries. Despite developing some kind of international relations with the South-east Asian countries like the Bandung Conference of Afro-Asian Nations (1954) and even Non Alliance Movement (NAM), India never make any serious attempt to strengthen its economic relations with the South-east nations.[201] At the regional level, for quite a long time India's foreign policy has been confined within SAARC circle in general and Pakistan centric in particular.[202] In the Cold War era when the bi-polarisation of the entire globe between the two super powers- the USA or the Western Block and the USSR or the Eastern Block, India had a closer ties with the USSR. But the collapse and disintegration of USSR, India loss not only a close friend that supports her in any circumstances but also loss

[199] Phrangsngi Pyrtuh, "Whither our Culture?" *The Shillong Times,* 22 October 2008, 4.

[200] It may be noted that prior to the colonial era India strong trade relations has been always towards the west. This continue even after the achievement of Independence.

[201] Thingnam Kishan Singh, "India's Look East Policy: Origins and Conceptualization," in *Look East Policy & India's North East: Polemics and Perspectives,* edited by Thingnam Kishan Singh (New Delhi: Concept Publishing Company, 2009), 1. See also Indu Prakash Singh, "Fine-tuning foreign policy with ASEAN," *The Shillong Times*, 31 January 2008, 4.

[202] Konthoujam Indrakumar, "Mapping India's Look East Policy: Shifting Alignments," in *Look East Policy & India's North East: Polemics and Perspectives*, edited by Thingnam Kishan Singh (New Delhi: Concept Publishing Company, 2009), 20.

of market for its exported goods.[203] With the capitalist model remaining the only alternative, the entire world economy was restructured and streamlined along the scheme designed by the western capitalist countries under the leadership of the US and supported by the agencies of globalization like the WB, IMF and WTO. The severe crisis faced by India in 1990s, coupled with the pressure from global economic system compelled India to open its economy and adopted the policy of liberalization, privatization and globalization. India began to realise that confinement within the parameter of SAARC will not help improve its economic status. To put it differently, such a situation necessitated India to look beyond SAARC and tend to look towards its eastern neighbours. Hence, there is a paradigm shift in India's foreign policy and it was against this back drop that India adopted the so called Look East Policy (LEP). The Indian Government "embarked on a programme of free market restructuring at home and sought new markets and economic partners abroad."[204] Look East Policy did not arise in a vacuum, but it is the result of India's open to global economy or neo-liberal economic reforms thereby joining the global liberal economic and free market system.[205]

But the moot question is, why India all of a sudden turning towards the east? What prompted India to adopt the Look East Policy? Among several reasons that compel India to look to the east, one could agree that the first thing is not merely the aspiration of having trade engagement and economic relations with the South East Asian nations and even Asia–Pacific region, but it reveals "India's desire for greater competition with and containment of China."[206] The point to be noted here is that India does not like to see that China have complete control over those nations, that may even led to the capturing the entire Indian ocean in its fold. Similarly, the post Cold War era saw Asia-Pacific region lying at the important location not only in terms of economic advantage but even with

[203] In the Cold War era India followed a policy of mixed economy and closed market with certain restrictions. The erstwhile Soviet Union was the prominent financial support for India's economic development. With the collapse of USSR this strong bond of relationship also vanished. See Indrakumar, Mapping India's Look East Policy: Shifting Alignments, 26.

[204] It may be noted that apart from regional integration like SAARC and ASEAN, there are other sub-regional grouping like BIMSTEC (Bangladesh, India, Myanmar, Sri Lanka, Thailand Economic Cooperation) started in 1997 out of Bangkok Declaration and the Ganga Mekong Cooperation (GMC) launched in July 2004 by the Vientiane Declaration and the members are India, Myanmar, Thailand, Cambodia, Laos and Vietnam and many other such attempts. See Ashok Kumar Ray, *Revisiting North East India in the Era of Globalization* (New Delhi: OM Publications 2007), 214-215.

[205] Indrakumar, "Mapping India's Look East Policy...," 27.

[206] Indrakumar, Mapping India's Look East Policy...," 20. See also Lokendra Arambam, "Globalization and Cultural Encounters: The Manipuri Perspective," in *Globalization and the Changing Scenario of Cultural Interaction (Manipur Experience),* edited by N. Joykumar Singh (New Delhi: Akansha Publishing House), 33.

regards to emerging geo-political importance. Indrakumar rightly pointed out when he argues,

> Indeed world geo-politics has shifted from Europe to the Asia-Pacific region. For obvious reasons, the 21st century belongs to this region in general and Southeast Asia in particular. The end of the Cold War saw the emergence of the new security dynamics in the Asia-Pacific region.[207]

At the same time, the growth and development of the ASEAN countries' economy in recent years not only attracted the attention of the globalised world but also added to the importance of the region in the world economic arena. It is reported that,

> Between 1993 and 1996 exports between ASEAN countries expanded from US$ 43 billion to almost US$ 80 billion in 1996, representing an annual growth of some 28%. In 1996, of 28.6 million tourist arrivals in ASEAN, 40 per cent came from within ASEAN. ASEAN has become a major economic player with Gross Domestic Product of US$ 737 billion and a total of US$720 billion. In 2002 EU was ASEAN's second largest export market and third largest trading partner after the USA and Japan.[208]

The above statistic reveals the growth and expansion of economy of the ASEAN countries not only with the outside world, but even among themselves. The growth of their economy coupled with the strategic geo-political location they occupy facilitated the important place they grasp in the process of expanding the horizon of free market system in today's global arena.

Look East Policy and North East India

The North Eastern Region[209] of India is a land lock area covering an area of 2, 55,083 sq. Km. While the entire area is connected to Indian mainland by a narrow breath of land covering just 20 sq. Km commonly known as "chicken neck" or "Siliguri neck," it has 4825 km of international border with Bangladesh, Bhutan, Myanmar and China.[210] In other words, the region shares 98% of its border with

---

[207] Indrakumar, "Mapping India's Look East Policy...," 37.

[208] Hidam Predamanda, "India's Look East Policy and the Political: An Interrogation into the Survey of the 'Global' in Manipur," in *Look East Policy & India's North East: Polemics and Perspectives,* edited by Thingnam Kishan Singh (New Delhi: Concept Publishing Company, 2009), 213.

[209] The North Eastern Region consist of the seven sister states comprising Assam, Arunachal Pradesh, Nagaland, Manipur, Mizoram, Tripura and Meghalaya and recently Sikkim was added as the eight brother.

[210] Konthoujam Indrakumar, "Imagining the North East through Look East Policy: Towards a Contextual Understanding," in *Look East Policy & India's North East: Polemics and Perspectives,* edited by Thingnam Kishan Singh (New Delhi: Concept Publishing Company, 2009), 58-59.

neighbouring countries and only 2% with mainland India.[211] For many decades the whole area was neglected in terms of development infrastructure, thereby suffers economic disabilities due to the step motherly treatment rendered by the central government.[212] Since the colonial era the region was generally considered as a "frontier region" thereby occupies less importance place in the eyes of the Indian Government.[213] The so called "frontier region" inherited from the British colonial legacy, resulted to the common belief that despite the entire region need to be militarily defended, economically it has nothing much to contribute to the strength of Indian economy. It is said that the core of Nehru's Policy with regards to North Eastern Region was that, the North Eastern tribal people are economically backward therefore needed great deal of assistance from the centre.[214] In other words, they have to depend mostly from the central government for financial help. Indrakumar appropriately argues when he states, "as such for the Indian State it is not economic considerations but political and strategic compulsions that force it to hold on to the North East."[215] He further states that the contemporary economic history of the region demonstrates that the ruling elites of the nation continue the colonial policy of extracting the raw materials of the region in order to serve the interest of the metropolitan capitalists. Hence, even after more than six decades of achieving independence the region, still remains a "dependent periphery." Today one could witness the exploitation of the raw materials of the region like oil and natural gas in Assam, coal and lime stone in Meghalaya mostly for the economic advantage of the capitalists of the mainland India.[216] Notably, the postcolonial

---

[211] B. P. Muktieh, "Role of Financial Institutions and Banks," in *Look East Policy: Impact on Northeast India,* edited by Charles Reuben Lyngdoh and Merostar Rani (New Delhi: Akansha Publishing House, 2008), 50.

[212] See R. L. Wali, "New World Disorder and India's Market Driven Reforms," in *Liberalization and India's North East,* edited by Gurudas Das and R. K. Purkayastha (New Delhi: Commonwealth Publishers, 1998), 37. Cf. Apurbananda Mazumdar, "Globalization and Regional Imbalance: Prospects of North-East India in a Super-Colonial World order," in *Liberalization and India's North East,* edited by Gurudas Das and R. K. Purkayastha (New Delhi: Commonwealth Publishers, 1998), 62. Cf. Partha S. Ghosh, "Challenge of Governance and Globalization A Case Study of India's North East," *Man and Society: A Journal of North East Studies* 2/1 (Spring 2005), 33-34.

[213] See G. P. Prasain and E. Nixon Singh, "Globalization and FDI in North East India," in *Globalization and North East India,* edited by Bimal J. Deb, Keya Sengupta and B. Datta Ray (New Delhi: Concept Publishing Company, 2008), 148.

[214] Ray, *Revisiting North East India in the Era of Globalization*, 179.

[215] For detail see Indrakumar, "Imagining the North East through Look East Policy...," 59.

[216] Today not only the capitalists of the mainland India are exploiting the resources of the region, but even the TNCs/MNCs make their presence felt. See Indrakumar, Imagining the North East through Look East Policy: Towards a Contextual Understanding. The North East is dependent from the central government and mainland India in the sense that bulk amount of goods come from the mainland India and there are signs of underdevelopment in different parts of the region.

India at the dawn of independence continue the policy of the colonial rule by turning their backward areas as peripheries or internal colonies for exploiting their natural resources in order to support the industrial projects of the metropolitan. Hence, North East India with its rich mineral resources fit in well in this scheme. The region became the supplier of raw materials though "without distributive benefit to the states of northeast."[217] The end result is that the entire region suffer underdevelopment syndrome thereby further relegated to the periphery. To state differently, the peripheral situation not only led to the dependence of the region to the core/centre but make the region remain less competitive thereby further exposing it to exploitation.[218] As stated earlier, though the region is different from the mainland in many aspects, all developmental activities employ in the region either under the North Eastern Council (NEC) or different schemes from the Central Government are generally meant or relevance for the main land India rather than for the region. Hence, they have failed to bring the desired results.[219] To state differently, the developmental model employed in the mainland India must not be imposed in the region as "it is important to study the region from the social perspective taking into consideration their costume, culture, tradition and ethnic complexity."[220] Such an attitude not only led to the isolation of the areas from the main land India, but also affected the entire development activities in the area making it remain an underdeveloped region till today.

In such a situation, how will India's Look East Policy help to improve the economic condition of the region? What will be the impact of LEP to the people and the region once implemented? There are speculations that LEP launched in 1992 paved the way for regional trade co-operation with the eastern neighbour such as Bay of Bengal Initiative for Multi-Sectoral Technical and Economic Cooperation (BIMST-EC), and Mekong-Ganga Cooperation (BMG).[221] It is believed that Look East Policy if properly implemented will enormously benefit the North Eastern States because of its strategic geographical location and the

---

For detail see also Tanmay Bhattacharjee, *Political Economy of North East India* (Silchar: Published by the Author, 2004), 73-77.

[217] Ray, *Revisiting North East India in the Era of Globalization,* 194-195.

[218] Gurudas Das, "Liberalization and Internal Periphery: Understanding the Implications for India's North-East," in *Liberalization and India's North East,* edited by Gurudas Das and R. K. Purkayastha (New Delhi: Commonwealth, 1998), 142.

[219] Cf. Gorgy Chakravarty, "Economic Policy and the North East Looking Beyond Neo-Classical Praxis," in *Globalization and North East India,* edited by Bimal J. Deb, Keya Sengupta and B. Datta Ray (New Delhi: Concept Publishing Company, 2008), 180.

[220] Ajailiu Niumai, "Development and Discontent Meet in the North East: Perspective on India's Look East Policy" in *Look East Policy & India's North East: Polemic and Perspectives,* edited by Thingam Kishan Singh (New Delhi: Concept Publishing Company, 2009), 56. See also M. N. Karna, *Socio Economic Aspects of Ethnic Identity in North-Eastern India,* 230.

[221] Muktieh, "Role of Financial Institutions and banks," 48-49.

whole region will become a producing and exporting region to both South Asia and ASEAN countries. "Look East Policy" cited Wanswett "envisages the northeast region not as the periphery of India, but as the centre of a thriving and integrated economic space linking two dynamic regions with a network of highways, railways, pipelines, transmission lines crisscrossing the region."[222] In his keynote address, Jairam Ramesh also stresses on the need of improving the infrastructure like roads, trading centres, land custom stations, power and the like required for promoting trade and other related business activities.[223] Hence, besides being India's gate way to the east, Northeast India will be the centre of dynamic trade and business activities connecting the two important regions.[224] The ASEAN countries will offer "big opportunities for India's trade and the North East may take advantage particularly in areas of horticulture, floriculture and medicinal herbs."[225] At the same time, the region has rich resources in tea, oil, natural gas in Assam, lime stone, coal, and uranium in Meghalaya besides the entire region is considered to be a bio-diversity hot spot. Moreover, the region has the potential to produce enormous power resources up to the tune of 70,000 MV comprising 30% of the total requirement of the country.[226] With this in mind the Central Government has identified about 168 mega hydro electric project in different parts of the region.[227] Hence, it will offer great prospect for the development of the region. But the moot question is whether the region will really benefit through the implementation of this policy? Looking deeper into this policy adopted by the Central Government several important points need to be taken into account.

Firstly, a proper analytical study of this policy reveals that the core concept of the LEP was to restrain and hinder the expanding control of Chinese trade activities, rather than any attempt to develop the long time neglected area of the North Eastern Region. It may be noted that LEP reflects not only an attempt of India to open up to its east neighbours, but it is a great endeavour engaged by

[222] D. Wanswett, "Welcome Address," in *Look East Policy: Impact on Northeast India,* edited by Charles Reuben Lyngdoh and Merostar Rani (New Delhi: Akansha Publishing House, 2008), 3.

[223] Jairam Ramesh, "Keynote Address," in *Look East Policy: Impact on Northeast India,* edited by Charles Reuben Lyngdoh and Merostar Rani (New Delhi: Akansha Publishing House, 2008), 8-9.

[224] For details see Amiya Sarma and Bhupen Kumar Sarma, "India's Look East Policy: Economic Possibilities for the Northeast," in *Look East Policy: Impact on Northeast India,* edited by Charles Reuben Lyngdoh and Merostar Rani (New Delhi: Akansha Publishing House, 2008), 44-45.

[225] Niumai, "Development and Discontent Meet in the North East…," 49.

[226] Indrakumar, Imagining the North East through Look East Policy: Towards a Contextual Understanding, 58. See also Amalesh Banerjee, "Reform and Inclusive Growth of North East Economy," in *Globalization and North East India,* edited by Bimal J. Deb, Keya Sengupta, B. Datta Ray (New Delhi: Concept Publishing Company, 2008), 123.

[227] Talukdar, Protect People in downstream of hydel projects: AASU, 22.

the Central Government to have economic and trade relationships both bilateral and collective relations with the ASEAN countries. Nevertheless, on formulating this noble policy "the Government of India did not consult the people of North East who will get most affected."[228] It may be noted that once the project is implemented the indigenous people as well as the surrounding environment will be greatly affected, influx of migrant and immigrant from the mainland India as well as nearby countries that will not only bring discontentment to the region but also change the entire demographic structure of the region. Hence, people participation in the entire process is not only required but a necessity. But ignoring the voice of the people in the region raise certain doubt whether this huge endeavour will generate certain benefit to the economic life of the people.

Secondly, as discussed above it is clear that North East India are lacking in many respect in terms of infrastructure and industrial development necessary "to generate vibrant economic growth."[229] At the same time, with the exception of constructing high ways like Tamu-Kalewa-Moreh road[230] and East West corridors[231] by the Central Government, most of the North Eastern States are not yet prepared to extract the benefits that LEP will generate in the near future. This raised certain doubts and suspicions that the entire region will still remain a weak link by the time the project is fully implemented. In other words, the region will be still handicapped in many respects making it incapable to compete and exchange trade related activities with its neighbour. Whereas most of the ASEAN countries especially the Asian Tigers like Thailand, Malaysia, Indonesia and Singapore are highly developed in comparison to the North Eastern Region. Churchill maintains that the ASEAN countries, "have forged quite ahead, taking their dignified places among nations of the world."[232] Hence, it will generally be the completion of the unequal. Commenting on the certain drawbacks that the North Eastern Region expected to achieve with regards to the implementation of LEP Indrakumar precisely maintains,

> The region will certainly experience, to use the phrase of Indian Prime Minister, 'a seamless web of trade and ties.' Within this 'seamless web of trade and ties' the North East Region (NER) forms the weakest link because of its relative deprivation in the infrastructure and industrial development in the primary, secondary and tertiary sectors. The absence of white paper on the overall economic policy of the region in connection with ongoing Look East Policy makes it all the more difficult to assess the prospect of the

---

[228] Niumai, "Development and Discontent Meet in the North East...," 51.

[229] Indrakumar, "Imagining the North East through Look East Policy...," 69.

[230] Indrakumar, "Mapping India's Look East Policy...," 35.

[231] An East-West corridor is a four lane road connecting India from the western part to the North Eastern part of the country.

[232] L Churchchill, "India's LEP and the North East...," 74.

> region *vis-a-vis* LEP. However, from the present infrastructural and industrial backwardness, one can only visualize that the NER has become a part of the global free trade regime and will remain a periphery due to its inadequate industrial and infrastructural base necessary for any competitive economy.[233]

Thirdly, with the handicap of infrastructure and under development, coupled with the unpreparedness of the North Eastern states to reap the would-be benefits generated by implementing LEP, one can only be sceptical that the entire region will become only the corridors or thorough fare for the exchange of goods and services or the free flow of trade regime between the mainland India and the ASEAN countries.[234] If that is the case, it is certainly clear that LEP has instead offered increasing opportunities to the TNCs/MNCs to capture the entire business and trade activities pushing the local indigenous population margin of economic advantage. Commenting on the role of TNCs/MNCs in the present day neo-liberal context Churchill maintains that even the Central as well as the State government will become just collaborators to the corporate giants of the agencies of globalization. As he rightly puts it, "the people as well as the governments will be highly tempted and motivated to favour the MNCs and private investors as a result of the acute poverty and absence of employment opportunities."[235]

Look East Policy and Khasi People

The above discussion points to the fact that there are certain doubts whether the LEP brings any genuine benefits to the indigenous population of the region. This is aptly true in the context of the Khasi people. As it is for other states of the region, till today the state of Meghalaya is yet to prepare anything worth mentioning for reaping the would be benefits offered by the LEP. This seems to indicate that the state is indifferent to the economic advantage offered in the entire process of LEP. As stated earlier, in the context of the Khasi people trade activities in the state is entirely under the control of the Marwaris. The presence of Marwaris with their efforts to extract and siphon off the maximum economic benefits from the indigenous population makes the local people's economy weak, thereby refraining from any dynamic competition in trade arena. Das maintains that the region suffers not only from the exploitation and siphoning off most of the region economic resources, but even the central funds made available to different states of North East, "the lion's share of it goes to buy goods and services from the core areas adding little to the local productive capacity."[236] The glaring

---

[233] Indrakumar, "Imagining the North East through Look East Policy...," 70-71.

[234] Cf. Giri, "Implications of New Economic Policy...," 44. Cf. Ghosh, "Challenge of Governance and Globalisation...," 50-51.

[235] Churchill, 'India's LEP and the North East...," 81. Cf. Churchill, "Implication of New Economic Policy...," 49.

[236] Das, "Liberalization and Internal Periphery...," 142-144.

truth is that huge economic drain where economic resources are siphoned off and transferred outside the state by the Marwaris renders the indigenous economy weak and unstable. Indrakumar confirms this situation is also true, with regard to many states in the region. He states,

The contemporary economic reality of the region is characterised by the fact that '*marwaris*' and other non-indigenous inhabitants are holding and controlling its economy. Along with foreign as well as domestic immigrants they play the role of a 'parasite class' in the regional economy in the sense that they consume and siphon off huge amount of wealth in the form of profit accrued from business and as labour wages.[237]

Moreover, as stated earlier though the state is rich in mineral and natural resources the people are generally poor and the presence of BPL people keep on increasing. In the era of globalization where survival of the fittest is a stark reality, majority of the local people with their poor condition are not in a position either to compete or to reap the benefits offered in the entire process of LEP. The whole economic benefits will be captured by the corporate giants like TNCs/MNCs and that of the metropolitan capitalists. Notably, with the presence of number of Cement Companies already began to exploit the economic resources of the land, total implementation of LEP will offer enormous blessings to them to expand and enlarge their business activities to the readymade market of the ASEAN countries. In turn, this will result to the maximum exploitation of the indigenous' mineral resources thereby causing irreparable damage not only to the source of livelihood of the local people but also to the entire surrounding environment. The moot question is how the Khasi economy able to survive the test of time when LEP will be totally implemented. It is regrettable but true, with many drawbacks, there is not much advantage worth mentioning to be expected for the region in general and Khasi people in particular in the entire course of LEP operation. Rather what will be left to the region and Khasi people as well will be depleted environment, an environment that had already lost its value to balance the entire eco-system. Hence, there is nothing wrong to conclude that the entire course of LEP function will instead bring huge challenges to the economic life of the Khasis.

Conclusion

The above discussion shows that the advent of the British colonial rule or the first phase of globalization brought tremendous impact to the economic life of the Khasi people. Firstly, its negative attitude towards tribal culture and practices brought enormous changes to the whole life situation of the Khasi People. Secondly, its successful mission to exploit the economic resources of the local natives had severely affected the growth and development of Khasi economy. Moreover, in the postcolonial era when India achieved its independence, coupled

[237] Indrakumar, "Imagining the North East through Look East Policy...," 67.

with the impact of partition the situation is not better for the tribal people. The development activities implemented by the central model using the "top-down" model do not help improving the living condition of the people. At the same time the increasing presence of the Marwari merchants that has captured the entire trade activities from the local people has rendered their economy insecure and weak. At the time when the tribal economy is insecure and weak, the coming of present phase of globalization makes the things no better for the local people. Globalization has rather brought more complications to the already insecure economic life of the people. To state differently, globalization besides damaging the surrounding environment through its attempt to exploit the economic resources of the native people for unlimited quick profit, it has also divided the tribal people between the rich and the poor thereby pushing major chunk of population to the margin of economic life. In the era of globalization it is only a tiny section of population who are benefitted whereas majority of the people are relegated to the periphery. This resulted to serious challenges to the survival of the Khasi economy in general and the marginalised poor tribal people in particular. Such a situation demands serious and authentic response from the theological point of view. It is believed that appropriate response suited to the struggles and problems presently experienced by the tribal people will certainly help not only to correct the drawbacks of the present phase of globalization, but also enable to provide some practical suggestion for the good and betterment of the economic life of the people.

Chapter 5

An Indigenous Khasi Tribal Theological Response

Our discussion in the preceding section illustrates the challenges caused by the process of globalization on the economy of the tribal people. The advent of the present phase of globalization has brought more harm than good to the already weak economy of the tribal people. Driven by the economic aspect of neo-liberal ideologies, globalization today affects the entire fabric of human community. As stated earlier, the present phase of globalization not only divides different countries between the rich and poor, but within the country divides the population between the rich and the poor, proposes a consumerist culture that tend to the needs of the affluent section in the society at the expense of the marginalised poor, and damage the source of livelihood of the local people and the like. The previous discussion, illustrates that in the context of the Khasi people, one could witness rapid exploitation of the earth resources, not only by the corporate giants like the TNCs/MNCs but also by the big companies managed by the rich section of population from mainland India. Besides damaging the delicate balance of the entire ecosystem, the present day globalization has also divides the tribal people between the rich and the poor section. Despite big claims promised by the advocates of globalization, the ground reality portrays that it is only a tiny section of population that are benefitted, whereas a bulk of tribal population is being demoted to the margins of economic life with little or no hope of a better future. Such a situation entails adequate and earnest response taking into consideration various problems faced by the tribal people in their daily struggle for livelihood and economic survival. An indigenous tribal theological response is not only an attempt to pin point or to spot the short comings and disadvantages of the present phase of globalization rather it aims to propose and address different steps and practical suggestions for the improvement of the living conditions of the majority poor and the marginalised section of population.

Revisiting the Meaning of Economy and Ecology

The word "economic" and "ecology" are closely related. Both the terms originated from the same Greek root word *oikos* which means "household." In other words both deal with the *oikos* or household. One is the *nomos* or the "rule of the households;" and the other is the logos or "structure of the household."[1] The word ecology was first coined by Ernest Heckel in 1870 from the Greek word *oikos* which means "household" or "habitat" and *logos* which mean "study." P. D. Sharma defines ecology as "the study of the structure and function of eco-system" or "the study of structure and function of nature."[2] Robert R. Gottfried defines ecology as "the body of knowledge concerning the economy of nature- the investigation of the total relations of the animals both to its inorganic and its organic environment; including, above all, its friendly and inimical relations with those animals and plants with which it comes directly or indirectly into contact."[3] Hence, the term ecology may be defined as the science of human and non-human habitation, the interaction and interrelationship of different organisms living together and depending on the eco-system for their survival.

As stated in Chapter I, the word "economy" is etymologically rooted from the Greek word *oikonomous*. This is a combination of two Greek words *oikos* which means household and *nomos* meaning law and order. That is, *oikonomous* etymologically is referred to the ordering and managing the household.[4] Thus maintenance of livelihood and life in general is the primary purpose of economy.[5] This vision of managing and maintaining life is rapidly challenged by the process of globalization in the last few years.[6]

"Economics" maintains Rasmussen "means providing for the household's materials and service needs and managing the household well."[7] He further states

---

[1] John B. Cobb Jr., *Sustainability: Economics Ecology & Justice* (New York: Orbis Books, 1992), 56.

[2] P. D. Sharma, *Ecology and Environment* (Meerut: Rastogi Publications, 1995), 52.

[3] Gottfried, *Economics, Ecology, and the Roots of Western Faith: Perspective from the Garden*, 11.

[4] Brian Griffiths, *The Creation of Wealth: A Christian Case for Capitalism* (Illinois: InterVarsity Press, 1984), 111. See also Ninan Koshy, "Issues and Challenges facing the Indian Churches in the Twenty-First Century," in *National Council of Churches Review* CXX/7 (August, 2002): 668.

[5] M. P. Joseph, "Denying Life: Theological Meaning of Globalization," in *National Council of Churches Review* CXVI/7 (August, 1996): 465.

[6] Martin Robra, "People's Struggle for Life are a source of inspiration for an enriching spirituality," in *National Council of Churches Review* CXXII/1 (January-February, 2002): 7.

[7] Larry L. Rasmussen, "Creation, Church and Christian Responsibility," in *Tending the Garden: Essay on the Gospel and the Earth,* edited by Wesley Granberg-Michaelson (Grand Rapid: William B. Eerdmans Publishing Company, 1987), 116.

that economics means the law (*nomos*) of the household (*oikos*). This is understood as "arranging those societal systems which provide for the material well being of all the planet's members and abiding by the rules of the ecosystems upon which each and every economic system is utterly dependent."[8] Sen argues that "economics is not solely concerned with income and wealth but also with using these resources as means to significant ends, including the enjoyment of long and worthwhile lives."[9] In similar vein, economic development does not simply mean the improvement of the country's economy; rather it has to be understood as the enhancement of the economic potentialities of the people, in which every member of the nation possesses the capabilities to achieve better standard of living. "Economic development" states Chellakan is "therefore cannot be seen just in terms of growth in income and output; it also consists in improving the human capabilities to choose the kind of lives people want to live."[10] According to Rasmussen the term economic has a theological meaning; it is part of the divine economy in which the entire creation is expected to enjoy healthy atmosphere and share life abundantly.[11] To put it differently, the main purpose of economics is to improve and develop the welfare of the entire household where each and every member could enjoy life in its fullness.

This is contrary to the present understanding of the term as understood by the modern neo liberal economics where the earth and its resources are meant exclusively for the good and betterment of richer human communities at the expense of the poor and creation. To be precise, in the process of globalization the ground realities illustrate that not all among the human community are benefitted in the process. It is only the rich and the selected few that could exploit all the facilities and economic advantages offered in the process of globalization, where as the poor and marginalised section is pushed to the margins of economic life with hope for better living seems to be a distant dream. At the UN Conference on Environment and Development held at Rio de Janeiro in 1992, popularly known as the Earth Summit it was felt that the present pace of "economic progress benefitting a segment of human population, was not necessarily compatible with the health of the earth." That is, the current speed and intensity of economic development is not compatible with the great economy of earth's complex eco

---

[8] Larry L. Rasmussen, "Theology of Life and Ecumenical Ethics" in *Eco-Theology: Voices from South and North,* edited by David G. Hallman (Geneva: WCC Publications, 1994), 118.

[9] Amartya Sen, "The Economics of Life and Death," *Scientific American* (May, 1993) 18 cited in *Earth Revealing Earth Healing: Ecology and Christian Theology,* edited by Dennis Edwards (Minnesota: The Liturgical Press, 2001), 21.

[10] Amal Raj Chellakan, *Eradicating the Poverty and Empowerment of the Poor* (Delhi: ISPCK, 2007), 290.

[11] Rasmussen, *Creation, Church and Christian Responsibility,* 116.

system.[12] For a long time the earth and its resources have been exploited without limitations, which benefitted only a small percentage of human population leaving the maximum number of marginalised poor people to struggle for livelihood and economic survival. Such a situation needs to be profoundly addressed taking into consideration not only the needs of human community but also other non human species as well as the health of the entire inhabited earth.

Who are the Poor?

"Poor" and "poverty" tend to be the most discussed terms in the present era of globalization. A new understanding of these terms in the contemporary context, need to be vividly redefined. In her article, "Liberation Theology in the Twenty-First Century" Kwok Pui Lan rightly argues when she states, "Are the labels First, Second, Third, and Fourth World still relevant? Who are the new rich and new poor in today's economy, in which the First World exists within the Third World, and the Third World within the First World?"[13] As stated earlier, with the rapid onslaught of globalization backed up by neoliberal ideologies, the country's population is divided into rich and the poor. This enables small and tiny section of population in every society to capture all economic benefits and economic facilities at the expense of the poor. Notably, the standard of living of the rich section of population in the Third World is much developed and far better than many people in the more developed countries. Hence, there is a need to redefine the term poor in today's context. Economically, poor is understood as deprivation of certain basic necessities of life that include food, shelter and clothing.[14] But today, the poor are to be understood not only as those who are deprived of the economic means for better living, rather those who are also the victims of political, social, cultural, religious and sexual discrimination and deprivation.[15] "People are poor" asserts M. P. Joseph, "because they are underdeveloped. The poor lack skills, lack capital and they lack power. Their GNP and per-capita level is miserably low. While 'civilized modern countries' maintain a high per-capita income and a high level of GNP, the poor uncivilized people have nothing to

---

[12] Anne M. Cliffoed, "From Ecological Lament to a Sustainable Oikos," in *God's Stewards: The Role of Christians in Creation Care,* edited by Don Brandt (California: World Vision Publications, 2002), 52.

[13] Kwok Pui Lan, "Liberation Theology in the Twenty-First Century," in *Opting for the Margins: Postmodernity and Liberation in Christian Theology,* edited by Joerg Rieger (Oxford: Oxford University Press, 2003), 72.

[14] K. C. Abraham, *Liberative Solidarity: Contemporary Perspectives on Mission* (Thiruvalla: Christava Sahitya Samithi, 2001), 50.

[15] Josey James Thamarassery, *Church Sign and Sacrament of Unity* (Kottayam: Oriental Institute of Religious Studies, India, 2009), 451-452. For detail, see also Chandran Paul Martin, "India Case Study Paper on Christianity, Wealth and Poverty," in *Christianity, Wealth and Poverty,* edited by Chandran Paul Martin (NCCI/ISPCK, 2004), 206-207.

show in the economic graph."[16] Commenting on the situation of the poor in the era of globalization Felix Wilfred accurately argues when he says, "the poor are told in many words that they are not wanted; that they are a burden and that they are simply redundant. The whole atmosphere seems to be charged with the spirit of eugenics and the philosophy of survival of the fittest. The concrete way of expressing it, is to exclude the poor from every sphere."[17] This reflects the condition of the victims, the under privileged, and those who are outside the ladder of economic development. Gutierrez rightly argues that to be poor means being deprived of food, clothing, housing, healthcare, education, denial of human dignity, personal freedom and so on.[18] He further states that,

> This led to the claim that the poor person is 'insignificant' a person who is considered a 'non person' someone whose full rights as a human being are not recognized. We are talking about persons without social or individual weight, who count little in society or in the church. This is how they are seen or more precisely, not seen, because they are in fact invisible in so far as they are excluded in today's world.[19]

This description is well suited to the context of the majority of the tribal people in India who are exploited and discriminated in different capacities and spheres of life. In this thesis, poor people are referred to as the tribal people of India in general and the Khasi people in particular, who are excluded, discriminated and denied of their rightful share in the process of today's economic globalization. They may be specifically defined in the Hebrew term as *ebyon* or the one who is lacking something; or in the Greek term *ptochos* which means to have literally nothing.[20] Here below the discussion will be on the resources from the tribal traditional heritage.

Mapping the Resources from the Traditional Tribal Heritage

The above discussion illustrates that the main purpose of economics is the well being and prosperity of all members of the earth community or the *oikos*. Such perception is well understood by our tribals' ancestral parents. Our ancestral parents have profound understanding that the well being of human community

---

16 M. P. Joseph, "Where is your Sister/Brother?" Carbon Civilization Defiles Faith in God," in *A Christian Response to Ecological Crisis,* edited by Thomas Samuel and Mathew Koshy Punnakadu (Thiruvalla: Christava Sahitya Samithi, 2009), 81.

17 Felix Wilfred, *Asian Dreams and Christian Hope* 2nd edition (Delhi: ISPCK, 2003), 47-48.

18 Gustavo Gutierrez, *A Theology of Liberation* (Maryknoll: Orbis Books, 1973), xxi.

19 Gustavo Gutierrez, "The Situation and Task of Liberation Theology Today" in *Opting for the Margins: Postmodernity and Liberation in Christian Theology,* edited by Joerg Rieger (Oxford: Oxford University Press, 2003), 97.

20 K. C. Abraham, *Transforming Vision: Theological-Methodological Paradigm Shifts* (Thiruvalla: Christava Sahitya Samithy, 2006), 139.

largely depends on the health and well being of the entire eco-system. Rymbai argues that our ancestral parents are divinely inspired to realize that the well being and security of human community and that of other members of the *oikos* cannot be viewed in isolation.[21] They all together constitute the wholeness of life. Each and every member of the *oikos* possesses intrinsic value and worth therefore need to be respected. They make all efforts to preserve the entire environment around them and see that nature and its resources are not to be misused and the balance of the eco-system is not disturbed. They clearly understood that disturbing the balance of the cosmos means destroying the source of livelihood and economic survival. Their farsightedness enabled them to preserve the source of livelihood on one hand while at the same time maintaining the balance of the eco-system on the other. Hence, it is not wrong to admit that the present day generation survives with the resources that have been preserved by our ancestors/ancestress down through the centuries. Here in the following an attempt is made to bring out important insights from the traditional tribal heritage as a response to the challenges brought by the process of globalization to the economic life of the tribal people.

Theological Insights of Tribal Ethical Norms

It may be noted that tribal people in general and different tribal groups in northeast India in particular have different social-ethical norms that have guided their communities in different capacities and circumstances down through the centuries. For instance, the concept of *sobaliba*[22] of the Ao Nagas and also the concept of *tlawmngaihna*[23] of the Mizos are some among the many ethical norms practiced by the tribals. For the Khasis, among others practices the ethical teaching of *tipbriew tipblei* as well as the concept of *kamai ia ka hok* are the two important social ethical teachings practiced by the Khasis since time immemorial As discussed earlier, in the era of globalization the poor and marginalised section are not only excluded from the mainstream of the economic ladder, but are also denied their rightful share in the earth's economy. In such a situation, important insights from the traditional tribal cultural heritage that are liberative and life

[21] Cf. R. T. Rymbai, "The Traditional Ecological Concepts of the Khasi-Pnars," in *The Tribal Worldview and Ecology,* edited by A. Wati Longchar and Yangkahao Vashum (Jorhat: The Tribal Study Centre, 1998), 15.

[22] *Sobaliba* of the Ao Nagas is a socio-ethical norm of self sacrifice that include honesty, integrity, social etiquette, and the like. For details see A. Wati Longchar, "Interaction Between Gospel and Culture among the Nagas," in *Encounter Between Gospel and Tribal Culture,* edited by A. Wati Longchar (Jorhat: Tribal Study Centre, 1999), 53-55.

[23] *Tlawngaihna* is a socio-ethical principle of the Mizos which means resistance of being helped by others where an individual put the common interest of the community before his/her respective personal interest. For details see Thanzauva, *Theology of the Community: Tribal Theology in the Making,* 152-164. See also M. Kipgen, "*Tlawngaihna* and Christianity" in *Encounter between Gospel and Tribal Culture,* edited by A. Wati Longchar (Jorhat: Tribal Study Centre, 1999), 56-73.

affirming seem to bring viable resources in an attempt to address a different option that may be able to help improve the economic and living condition of the marginalised poor section of the society.

Re-discovery of the tribal concept of Tipbriew Tipblei

The earlier discussion, testifies that the concept *Tipbriew Tipblei* has encompassed the whole gamut of Khasi thought and deeds whether social, economic, political and religious spheres. The term generally means to be conscious of our relationship with God the Divine being and other fellow humans as well. To be conscious of our relationship with God signifies to have good relations with our fellow beings. A person cannot claim to have good relation with God unless it is reflected through his/her daily dealings with their fellow humans. It has both horizontal and vertical aspect. This consciousness is inherently ingrained into the psyche of human beings by the divine. This consciousness enables one to recognize the intrinsic right of each individual to live a fully human life as intented by the divine that need to be cherished, respected and protected. As this right is bestowed upon human beings by God, humans are expected not to exploit, abuse, oppress, or discriminate other fellow beings for one's own benefit or personal advantage. To put it differently, each and every person has the right to live as a full human being, but not at the expense of others. Some among the diverse implications of the concept *tipbriew tipblei* are:

- To be conscious of their beings as the creation of the Supreme Being or *U Blei Nongbuh Nongthaw.*
- To maintain good relationship with the creator and realized the presence and guiding principle of God in their daily life. For the Khasis recognition of the presence of God in the individual personal life is best expressed in the concept of *Ka Rngiew.*[24]
- To recognize the value and worth of other people as creation of *U Blei Nongbuh Nongthaw* or God the Creator with respect and dignity.
- To recognize that each individual is bestowed with an inherent right to be equal member of the community. This right must not be trampled or abused for one's own advantage or personal benefit.

---

[24] The term *Ka Rngiew* is referred to as a kind of spiritual cover that encompass the individual right from the time of birth till death. It may be comparable with the Biblical concept of *Imago Dei.* For details see Dondor Giri Nongkhlaw, "That elusive Niamkur (Clan Religion) of the Hynniewtrep Geographical Landscape," in *Indian Theological Journal* 1/1 (Jan-Jun, 2007), 57-61. See also S. Hayong, "The Concept of Sin in the Khasi Traditional Religion," in *Doing Tribal Christian Theology with Tribal Resources: Cultural Resources from North East India,* edited by Razouselie Lasetso and Eyingbeni Humtsoe (Jorhat: ETC Programme Coordination, 2009), 55-56. See also Ladbasuk Lyngdoh, "Life after Death in Khasi Religion and Resurrection in the Bible," in *Garnering Tribal Resources for Doing Tribal Christian Theology,* edited by Razouselie Lasetso (Jorhat: ETC Programme Coordination, 2008), 276.

- To have good relationship with other fellow beings in the community.
- To live a decent, respectable and honorable life.
- To manage and maintain the wellbeing and security of the family in a proper way.
- To be able to educate and bring up their children in the right path.
- To be able to enrich and develop the inherited property handed down by our ancestors/ancestress for the well being of the family and the entire clan as well.[25]
- To be loyal to his/her family as well as the *Kur* or clan, be an example to the younger generation as well as provide important advice and valuable suggestion for better living.
- To be ready to work for the common good and better welfare of the clan in particular and the community in general.
- To be kind and helpful to the sick, the aged, the poor, the marginalized through sharing the resources with all those in need.
- To avoid causing harm or injury to any fellow beings human and non human.
- To be sensitive to the need of others as in the case of sharing the community land. For instance, as the community land is to be shared equally by all members, the person who is *tipbriew tipblei* will not cultivate more than necessary for him/herself so that others also can have share in it.[26]
- To realize and recognize the value and dignity of mother earth and pay deep respect towards nature and other creations.
- To understand one's duty and responsibility towards nature and the surrounding environment. As tribal people have close relationship with nature the person who is *tipbriew tipblei* is aware of the right of other creations and makes all efforts to do justice to the mother earth and different creatures living around.
- To find different ways and means to prevent the mother earth from any act of domination, oppression and exploitation in different capacities. As the mother earth is created by God the person who is *tipbriew tipblei* will not be happy to see any sort of subjugation taken place in any part of the entire natural surroundings.

In sum, in their daily life experience, a person who is considered as *tipbriew tipblei is* the one who looks after the well being of his/her family, has good relationship with others in the community and live a good and honourable life.

---

[25] Discussion with Sumar Sing Sawian on the 2nd May 2012.

[26] It is important to note that the earlier tribal practices with regard to the community land was that any member of the community can occupy any plot of the community land for cultivation but they have to see that the right of occupancy for other members must not be trampled or violated.

To put it differently, *tipbriew tipblei* means to be good, kind hearted, helpful, caring, accommodative, honest, sincere, hard working, trustworthiness, integrity, loyalty, incorruptibility, reliability, sensitive to the need of others, ready to share the resources with the needy and so on. Mawrie maintains that these characteristics are expected to be reflected in the family, among the *Kur* or clan, as well as in the society or community in general.[27] On the other, human could possess these characters only if he/she has right relationship with God. Hence, humans who are *Tipbriew Tipblei will* not like to see that their neighbors are suffering, victims of injustices, victims of poverty, discriminated, exploited, oppressed and the like. But they would be happy to see that everyone in the community lives a happy, prosperous and healthy life, free from all injustices. To put it simply, it is a life in its fullness.

Tipbriew Tipblei in Today's Context

As stated above, the concept of *Tipbriew Tipblei* has a reservoir of important teachings and ethical code of conduct that has guided the Khasi people down through the centuries. Nevertheless, with the influence of external forces that have crept the Khasi societies in particular and tribal communities in general like colonization, Christianization, and most recently the present phase of globalization, the importance of this principle is almost lost if not completely gone in the present day lives of the Khasi people. The earlier discussion demonstrates that one of the most important conditions of the western missionaries to those Khasis who came to accept the Christian faith is to abandon and renounce all traditional cultural and religious practices they use to follow. The Christian church established by the missionaries was not in a hurry to enroll the people as members of the church unless they were generally satisfied with their conduct and behavior.[28] The church believed that anything associated with cultural and religious practices are pagan or evil hence needs to be discarded. Hence, all the new converts need to cut off all attachment and connections with different traditional cultural and religious practices including important ethical principle like *tipbriew tipblei.*[29] Looking from the postcolonial perspective such perception

[27] Barnes L. Mawrie, *Introduction to Khasi Ethics* (Shillong: DBCIC Publications, 2005), 22-24.

[28] For instance, missionary William Lewis place the condition that before accepting the converts as members of the Christian church there will be a trial period till the church is fully satisfied with their way of living. See S. Evans, "Ka Jingpyniaid Balang- Church Organisation," in *Ka Centenary ka Balang Presbyterian ha Ri Khasi Jaintia naduh 1841 haduh 1940,* edited by D. Ropmay (Shillong: Literature Committee ka Assembly, 1940), 84.

[29] With the introduction of mission compound the new convert were not only separated from their kith and kin, but also totally detached and isolated from anything traditional that the missionaries term as evil. It may also be noted that one aspect of the introduction of the mission compound, was to avoid any sort of persecution that may happen to the new converts from their relatives. But separation of the new converts from the community they had been brought up

is nothing but the product of colonial mindset that sees everything non western as the other, inferior, evil and devoid of all good things. Even when the western missionaries handed the management of the Christian church to the local indigenous leaders, the church still followed the policies of the missionaries that ignored and disregarded the value and importance of traditional cultural heritage like the ethical principle of *tipbriew tipblei.*[30] This turned out to be a big setback to the entire tribal community. The Christian church till today generally ignores different important traditional cultural heritage without taking into account the important role they played in transforming the Khasi society down through the centuries. Hence, one could witness the disappearance of this important teaching in different aspect of people's life be it social, economic, political, religious and so on. Commenting on the role of *tipbriew tipblei* in the economic life of the people in today's context, Gasah argues that the dynamic impact of this principle was largely experienced and practiced in the earlier time, before they have any contact with the outside world. In those times, population was still less, land for cultivation was available in plenty, there was no competition and no pressure on land. But this is not the case today; with the influence of the outside forces this principle is practically disappearing in the daily life experiences and practices of the Khasi people.[31] Hence, there is a need to rediscover and reinterpret this ancient wisdom to make them more relevant and meaningful in the present day struggle of the Khasi people.

Tipbriew Tipblei versus Globalization: Theological Implication

The principle of *tipbriew tipblei* illustrate a well and profound relationship to both our fellow human beings and to God. As stated earlier, humans are expected to have good relationship with other fellow beings only if they have good relationship with God their creator. This ethical teaching may be comparably equivalent with the biblical commandment which says, "You shall love your God with all your heart" and "You shall love your neighbor as yourself." (Math 22: 37-39). Matthew states that when the Pharisees asked about the greatest commandment among the law, Jesus replied was to "love God with all your heart" is the great and first and the second is to "love your neighbor as yourself." He also says, "On these two commandments depend all the law and the prophets" (v. 40). This will be generally understood if one places it in the context of the Ten Commandment of Exodus (Ex 20:1-17). In the Ten Commandments it is clearly seen that the first

---

make them slowly forgetting different cultural practices and traditional ethical norms by adapting themselves to different conditions set up in Christian teachings.

[30] Notably, all the new converts are expected to be new persons and strictly followed Christian teachings with no more attachment or connection with any traditional customary religio-cultural practices.

[31] Interview with Dr. L.S. Gassah, Professor and Dean of the Department of Political Science, NEHU, Shillong on the 3 May 2012.

four commandments deal with individual's relationship to God, while the latter six commandments talk about human relationship to one other in the society. It connotes that a person who loves God as well as his/her neighbor will not love other god apart from *Yahweh*, will not steal, will not kill, will not commit adultery and so on. The main thrust of this principle portrays that a person will not do anything that could hamper or damage the relationship of either to God or his/her fellow beings. It entails the spirit of holistic recognition of the interrelatedness and interdependence of all realities that affirms the importance and value of life both living and non living. Hence, it offers space to the weak, the defenseless, the poor, the deprived, the marginalised and those who are pushed to the margin of social and economic life.

The biblical mandate to love God and our neighbor is well ingrained within the concept of *tipbriew tipblei*. Hence, an active engagement of these two dynamic principles will not only be able to challenge the dominant forces of globalization promoted by the neo-liberal ideologies but will also have the potential to address the immediate problems generally experienced by the marginalised poor in their daily life struggle for livelihood and for better living condition. It entails the need for a new awareness in our way of theologizing. To state differently, the main task of the theology of *tipbriew tipblei* is to actively engage in critical analysis of the worldview, the agencies, the culture and the oppressive structure of neo-colonial forces that make all efforts to strive for unlimited profit without limits. At the same time, it will keenly involve in its commitment towards paying sufficient attention to the victims of this oppressive structure, that is, the underside of the society in their attempt to wrestle for their survival, 'the other,' as well as the problems faced by the natural environment around. Longchar maintains that "theology has to take the stand for the victims of hegemonic structures of oppression and other dominant powers."[32]

The previous discussion illustrates that the present day society testifies how the agencies of globalization together with the rich and powerful section of the country's population make every effort to extract all the available earth's resources for quick and unlimited profit. This is nothing but the replication of colonial mindset being carried on by the so called neo-colonial forces.[33] Driven by the spirit of neo-liberalism and the option for unrestricted accumulation of wealth, the corporate giants and powerful sections today "do not know when to say enough."[34] For them, the earth and its resources are merely commodities

[32] Wati Longchar, Indigenous Peoples and Christian Theology, *Indian Theological Journal* 2/1 Jan-June, 2008): 19.

[33] In this thesis the term neo-colonial forces and neo-liberal are meant for the same, hence they are used interchangeably in the thesis.

[34] W. S. Annie, *Globalization and Women's Subsistence Labour: A Third World Theological Perspective* (Bangalore: BTESSC/SATHRI, 2009), 79.

meant to satisfy the unlimited want of the wealthy and powerful. In the process of achieving their goal, their action largely caused severe injustices to both the defenseless poor section of population and the nature. Their motive is "to loot" and "to plunder" and have no concern for the well being of the poor like the tribals and dalits as well as the mother earth. Both the poor as well as nature have to bear the brunt of the unlimited wants of the powerful sections that can control everything with their big amount of capital. This is very true in the context of the tribal people in general and Khasi people in particular.

Here, theology of *tipbriew tipblei* critically questions the neo-liberal ideology of maximum exploitation that does not bring anything good either to the human community or to the mother earth. Theology of *tipbriew tipblei* perceives this action as deviation from the intended purpose of the divine that sees the mother earth and it resources as good. It sees that the starting point of of the world's problem today is because of humans' greed trying to capture more resources than what necessary for him/her. This necessitates the ideology of use and not misuse of the earth resources. The Genesis narrative portrays that when God placed human in the garden "to till it and keep it," God also said "You may freely eat of every tree of the garden (Gen 2: 15-16)." This signifies that humans can share the bounty of the earth resources but at the same time calls for responsible action to use not to misuse this opportunity. Accordingly, misusing this God free given opportunity will not bring good consequence. And this is what the theology of *tipbriew tipblei* portrays.[35] Hence, it is in tune with the Gandhian philosophy that "the earth has enough for man [sic] need but not for man's [sic] greed."[36] A person who is *tipbriew tipblei* will not use or occupy more than what he/she needs. This indicates that even if there are possibilities to achieve maximum profit with regards to wealth and property they will not do so at the expense of other fellow beings. To state differently, it is against the spirit of this principle to acquire what

[35] The Khasis believe that any irresponsible act that affects others will bring shame and misfortune not only to the person concern but to the entire clan. The Khasi saying goes, "*U im kum uba khlem kur khlem jaid*," which means he/she lives as if he/she has no relatives or clan. A person who is *Tipbriew tipblei* will therefore make all efforts to abstain from doing anything that violates or abuse the rights of other fellow beings. See H. Onderson Mawrie, *The Essence of Khasi Religion,* (Shillong: Ri Khasi Press, 1981), 9.

[36] According to eco-feminism both women and the mother earth are victims of the patriarchal mindset that perceived them as inferior and object of exploitation. Hence, the suffering of women and the mother earth are one and the same. Eco-feminism as a term was first used in 1974 by the French writer Francoise d'Eaubonne, with the purpose to explore "how the domination of women is interconnected with the domination of nature by stressing the links, historical, biological and experiential, between women and nature." See Astrid Lobo Gajwala, "Making a Path to the Womb: Eco-Feminism and its Implications," in *Ecological Concerns: An Indian Christian Response,* edited by Joseph Mattam and Jacob Kavunkal (Bangalore: NBCLC, 1998), 54-55. See also J. Patmury, "Ecofeminism, Ecojustice and Ecospirituality," in *Theology of our Times* 6 (August 1999), 57- 59.

is rightly not ours.[37] Keeping this principle intact, theology of *tipbriew tipblei* strongly challenges the worldview of the neocolonial forces that have no concern for the poor and mother earth.

Theology of *tipbriew tipblei* challenges the motive of neo-colonial agencies for acquiring unlimited profit that offers no space for the poor and marginalised. This exploitative ideology serves as the instrument to enhance accumulation of wealth by small minority while leaving the majority poor more impoverished than before. Hence, it is "pro-rich," "pro-powerful," taking comfortable stand on the side of the "haves." In reality, different programmes developed by the process of globalization or the so called neo-colonial agencies, their motives, practices, facilities, consumerist culture and the like are meant exclusively for the benefits of the rich affluent section not for the marginalised poor. To put in Marxism term, it means for the "haves" not the "have nots" or the underside of the society. Longchar maintains that in the era of globalization, the status of the individual is purely based on what the person possesses or acquires, and the marginalised poor who have no property to sell or capital to invest, are exclusively left outside the economic ladder.[38] They are the "outcaste" of today's global economic development. The poor are not only ignored rather they are nowhere within the programmes of the contemporary economic globalization. Commenting on the plight of the poor in the present day era of economic globalization, Wilfred rightly affirms this view when he says that "We are moving towards *amnesia of the poor*-the forgetfulness of the poor-and their exclusion at all levels....But today, the worst thing happening with globalisation is that the poor are told in many words that they are not wanted; that they are a burden and that they are simply redundant."[39]

This is very true in the context of the marginalised poor section or the underside of the society whose presence have been sidelined and their voices have not only been ignored but silenced by the neo-colonial forces. Admittedly, the comings of different big companies to the Lumshnong areas make the local indigenous people lost their voices concerning the well being of the indigenous people, the society as well as the natural environment around them.[40] Poor people like the tribals and the dalits found that they are not only excluded but forcefully alienated and detached from their birth right. Their land, forest, air, water, etc that were freely available to them few decades back are now no more under their

---

[37] See Jeebon Roy, *Ka Kitab ba Batai Pynshynna shaphang U Wei U Blei* 2nd ed. (Shillong: Ri Khasi Press, 1979), 34. See also Singh, "Khasi and Jaintia Religion," 107.

[38] Longchar, "Globalization and Indigenous People...," 188.

[39] Wilfred, *Asian Dreams and Christian Hope: At the Dawn of the Millennium*, 47.

[40] Interview with Brian Gympad, a villager at Lumshnong on the 17th May, 2012.

possession but taken away from them by the neo-colonial forces.[41] Hence, neo-colonial philosophy is nothing but the replication of the social-Darwinism theory "survival of the fittest" in the field of economic global competition.[42] That is, the capable will survive whereas the rest will perish. This is contrary to the principle of *tipbriew tipblei* where the focal point of concern is the equality and justice of every member in the community. In this context, theology of *tipbriew tipblei* makes efforts to understand the plight of the poor, listen to their stories and struggles and make their insignificant voices heard in the contemporary debate for human survival as well as the survival of the mother earth. To state differently, it indicates to journey together in solidarity with the excluded, people who have lost their importance in their struggle for better living condition and striving towards realization of their true humanness. Commenting on taking sides with the margins David N. Field maintains,

> Our pilgrimage to the margins is not the journey of lone travelers; rather it is a process of acquiring new conversation partners as we enter into dialogue with victims and the abandoned. It is a process of listening to their reflection on God's action, the articulation of their response in faith and praxis, and their critique of our faith, praxis and theology. Such conversations are always bound up with the complexities of power relations and inequalities of the resources.[43]

Though the above quotation is based from the Euro-African perspective, it nevertheless indicates that taking sides with the margins means to be in solidarity with the victims and the excluded as they struggle against oppressive structures and exploitation of their sources of livelihood. Besides taking sides with the margins, theology of *tipbriew tipblei* critically challenges the oppressive structure of neo-colonial forces promoted by the ideologies of neoliberalism that offer no space for the underside of the society. Hence, it commits itself towards realizing the causes that led and lead to the massive poverty and inequality of the contemporary tribal societies while at the same time creating a proper platform for the margins to raise their voices and concerns. "Economic neoliberalism" argues Gutierrez is seen not only as "being ineffective in ending poverty but even being one of the causes of

---

[41] For instance, in the Lumshnong area where the mushrooming of big companies in the last few years not only the land and water was exploited and damaged, even the air they breathed is so much polluted that may cause serious health hazard to all the people in the surrounding area. Interview with Rangbahduh Khonglah former village headman of Lumshnong on the 17th May, 2012.

[42] See Wilfred, *Asian Dreams and Christian Hope: At the dawn of the Millennium*, 21. See also Annie, *Globalization and Women's Subsistence Labor: A Third World Theological Perspective,* 93.

[43] David N. Field. "On (Re)Centering the Margins: A Euro-African Perspective on the option of the poor," in *Opting for the Margins: Postmodernity and Liberation in Christianity,* edited by Joerg Rieger (Oxford: Oxford University Press, 2003), 60.

poverty."[44] It will rather increase the plight of the poor rather than help to solve their problems. Theology of *tipbriew tipblei* insists for restructuring the oppressive structure to give space for the unheard, the lost voices of the marginalised poor. It is not merely creating a level playing field that opens the opportunities for all to excel in the field of competition. Creating a level playing field may not help. This situation may still offer the fittest to recapture all the facilities of better living that will further weaken the impoverished condition of the poor. But it goes beyond that, towards recognizing the value, the dignity, the rights and equalities of the marginalised poor or the other, so that justice will prevail in the society. For "without equality there is no justice."[45]

Being carried away by the ideologies of neo-liberalism, neo-colonial forces proceed forward to exploit all available opportunities without taking into consideration the plight of the poor. The story of the rich young man, who came to see Jesus, portrays that it is not only difficult but impossible for the rich to share their resources with the poor and the needy. Matthew reported that when Jesus asked him to go and sell his property and distribute his treasure with the poor, he went away sorrowful for he has great possessions. (Math 19:21-22). Legrand argues that "Money, or economic reality, gets its value not by being accumulated but by being given."[46] This metaphor reflects the attitude of the corporate giants today that are not sensitive to the plight of the poor. In this context there is no room for sharing the resources with those who are in need. This is against the spirit of *tipbriew tipblei* that do not like to see their neighbor suffering from any kind of injustices.

For the tribal people in general and Khasi people in particular, being rich convey different meaning. Traditionally, the people who are considered rich are simply not only those people who could accumulated large portion of wealth, rather they are those people who share their wealth with the needy. In the context of the Khasi people, there are two important terms that normally describe the word "rich."[47] These are the term *riewspah* and *riewbha.*[48] The former may be referred to the wealthy person who has immense wealth and property, due to his/her hard work, sincerity, or dedication towards improving their economic life and well being. It does not signify obtaining wealth and property through unfair

[44] Gutierrez, "The Situation and Tasks of Liberation Theology Today," 100.

[45] Gutierrez, "The Situation and Tasks of Liberation Theology Today," 100.

[46] Lucien Legrand, "Jesus and Jesus' Movement in a Globalized World," in *Theology of Economics in the Globalized World: Indian Approaches,* edited by Jacob Para ppally & Antony Kalliath (Bangalore: Indian Theological Association, 2010), 82.

[47] The *English Khasi Dictionary* translated different terms for the word "rich." These are *riewbha, riewspah, kyrhai, seisoh, and phyrnai.* These literally means good person, wealthy person, abundance, prosperous, and bright respectively. See Nissor Singh, *English Khasi Dictionary* (New Delhi: Mittal Publications, 2010), 442.

[48] Discussion with Ladbasuk Lyngdoh on the 30th June 2012.

means or any sort of corruptible behavior. The latter is to be understood in more conceptual sense. It can be defined not only as having large possession of wealth and property, but also as kindness, generosity, kindheartedness, hospitality, willing to share with others, and the like. It indicates that a person can be considered *riewbha* only if he/she has bighearted qualities and willing to freely share his/her resources with his/her neighbor and all those who are in need. A person who is *riewbha* is generally sensitive to the needs of others thereby voluntarily eager to help them in different circumstances. Singh defines it as "rich in humility."[49] In a sense, a person who is *riewbha* is often considered as *tipbriew tipblei* and is well respected in the society. This quality is well illustrated in the folktales concerning good friendship that developed between *u riewbha* and *u baduk*[50] or the rich and the poor man. The story tells that, despite their different status in terms of economic possession, the rich person never look down upon the poor man but share his wealth and resources with him in different situation. Longchar rightly argues when he states,

---

[49] Kynpham Singh, "Khasi and Jaintia Religion," in *Khasi Heritage,* edited by Hipshon Roy (Shillong: Seng Khasi, 1979), 107.

[50] The story tells that once upon a time there lived a rich man by the name *U Nik Mahajon* and a poor man name *U Shing* and his wife name *Ka Lak* who became closed friend. Though he was rich and prosperous, the former never look down upon his friend but treated him as equals. Actually, they have nothing in common in terms of wealth and property. However, whenever the poor friends visited him, the rich often treated them well and even share his resources with the poor friends to carry back home. After a long time, the poor man thought that it will be good and proper for him to invite his friend to have meal with them. When their friend visited them, he was warmly welcome by the family. The poor man asked his wife to prepare meal for the quest, but sadly there was nothing in the house, not even a morsel of grain left. His wife went asking from their neighbors, but as they were equally poor they have nothing to help her. Sadly she came back home empty handed and told her husband that she was getting nothing. Overcome with shame and sorrow, both the husband and wife killed themselves. The rich man after waiting for so long went inside to see what has happened to his friend that he didn't come out even after a long wait. But he was shock to see two dead bodies, and understood the reason; that his friend and his wife killed themselves as they have nothing to offer him. The rich man felt that his entire wealth is of no use to him as he had lost his close friends. So, the rich man also took the extreme step and killed himself. Towards the dawn, the thief entered that very house, but as he was dead tired as soon as he get in he fell asleep and could wake up only when it was bright morning. But he was stunned to see three dead bodies there. Then he was telling himself if people caught me here they will blame me not only as a thief but also as a murderer. So, it is better that I will kill myself than facing the punishment, so he also killed himself. God in heaven has witnessed the entire incident, therefore he created from the four dead bodies as follows; the rich man as *kwai* or betel nut, the poor man and his wife as *tympew* and *shun* or betel leaves and lime respectively and the thief as *duma* or tobacco. That is, this is done with the purpose that both the rich and the poor can equally share their hospitality to each other. See Barness L. Mawrie, *The Khasis and their Natural Environment: A Study of Eco-consciousness and Eco-spirituality of the Khasis* Reprinted (Shillong: Vendrame Institute Publications, 2009), 54-55. See also Nongkynrih, "Death in a hut," in *Around the Hearth: Khasi Legends,* 34-40.

> In modern understanding 'rich' means the one who accumulates 'wealth,' but in indigenous understanding, the one who gives everything for the sake of others is called 'rich.' In other words, one's richness is measured not by how much one accumulates, but by how much a person shares with the members of the community.[51]

Sharing of wealth by the rich to the poor is not uncommon among the tribals especially in the earlier times. To cite an example, let me mention about the customary practices of the people of War Jaintia during the harvesting season with special reference to oranges and betel nut cultivation. This custom is largely practice by the Khasi people in different parts of the land depending on the diverse type of cultivation they cultivate in their respective areas.[52] In the case of the latter, during harvesting of the betel nut people do not pick up or gather all those nuts that fell on the ground with the purpose that the poor people will come and collect them as a way of sharing their economic resources with those in need. In the case of the former, diverse way of sharing is normally practice by the people. First, during the orange season, people who pass through the orange field can pluck some oranges for eating there without taking permission from the owner. However, they are not expected to take home any fruit for it is against the custom of the land. Second, it is the customary practice of the Khasi people to leave two or three oranges in each tree at the time of harvesting, so that the poor people and even the wild animal can have their share in the harvesting products. Third, every day during the harvesting period, the owner of the orange field generally use to provide twelve pieces of oranges of the best quality, apart from the smaller pieces, to all the labourers who have labored the whole day to take with them back home. All these practices are done not because the fruits are plenty; rather it is to follow the custom of the land where sharing the resources with the neighbor is a norm and a voluntarily practice rather than by compulsion.

However, with the influence of the outside forces like secularization, colonization, modernization and most recently the contemporary phase of globalization, many of these noble concepts have been distorted in the life and practices of the Khasi people.[53] Hence, there is a need to rediscover and reinterpret the spirit of sharing making it relevant to the contemporary struggles of the present day society. In other words, this noble concept could well help the people to understand their roots and prevent them from the onslaught of neo-liberal

[51] Wati Longchar, "Natural Resources: Perspectives of Primeval Traditions," in *Jeevardhara* XL/235 (January, 2010), 32.

[52] Discussion with Pynskhem Lawrinniang from Nongum area on the 28 June 2012.

[53] For instance, in the case of betel nut owner nowadays they become suspicious when people entered their field, and at the same time the poor people when they enter the fields may tend to take more than what actually was provided to them.

ideologies promoted by the forces of globalization or the so called neo-colonial dynamics.

The biblical narrative portrays that the practice of sharing is not unfamiliar to the Israelite community especially during the time of the judges. The story of Ruth (Ruth 2:1-23) tells us that Ruth, a Moabite, and her mother-in-law Naomi were greatly benefitted from the left over grains gathered in Boaz's field during that particular harvesting time. Boaz's request to Ruth not to glean to other people's field,[54] illustrates the fact that, sharing of the left over grains to the poor and needy was generally practiced by the rich section as a means of extending their help to the weaker section of the society. This implies that the rich and affluent section has to be sensitive to the needs of the weaker section.

Tribal spirit of sharing is one aspect of the theology of *tipbriew tipblei*. Tribal notion of sharing is contrary to the ideologies of neo-liberalism practices in the contemporary era of globalization where the rich section of population seems to capture and exploit all facilities of economic importance for acquiring enormous amount of wealth. It is completely against capturing all economic benefits by the rich for their own selfish interest without taking into account the inherent rights and essential needs of the weaker section of the society. Theology of *tipbriew tipblei* not only demands strong challenges to the unlimited greed of the rich sections, but also advocates the necessity of re-defining the concept of "rich" in line with the tribal understanding of *riewbha*. To state differently, the "rich" in the context of the theology of *tipbriew tipblei* is not to be understood merely as *riewspah* or having enormous amount of wealth and property, but it will also connote the notion of *riewbha*. That is, to be hospitable and sensitive to the needs of others especially the weaker section in the community. Consequently, it demands for the need to be inclusive, accommodative, generous, kindhearted, charitable, and so on. This realization must not be forced upon or imposed from outside but it has to come from within. It has to start from the heart of the person. Hence, it entails the necessity for radical *metanoia* on the part of the rich. To be specific, tribal spirit of sharing could well provide better alternatives against the neo-liberal ideologies of unlimited benefit by the affluent section of the society.

Tipbriew Tipblei: A Paradigm for Liberation

As stated earlier, the principle of *tipbriew tipblei* signifies to know or be conscious of our relationship with God and our fellow human beings. To know or be conscious of our relationship with fellow beings connotes to respect their rights, dignity, beings, and so on as persons created through *Ka Hok Blei* or divine righteousness. This ideology emerged from the realization that all created beings

[54] It may be noted that Boaz made an appeal to Ruth, not to glean in others' field was mainly due to the fear that she may be molested by men in those field. Cf. R. Daniel Premkumar, *Bonding with Mission: Faith Activism in Local Congregation* (Chennai: Inter Church Service Association, 2008), 86-87.

are the handiwork of *U Blei Nongbuh Nongthaw* or God the creator. To disrespect or dishonor any beings is to disregard or ignore the very work that the creator has made. The Bible portrays God as the God who is always on the side of the poor and vulnerable section. God is not only listening to the cry of the poor, but the deliverer of the poor from the bondage of slavery, the defender of their inherent rights that have been taken away from them. Gutierrez strongly argues when he states that "to know God is to do justice." He further states that "To know Yahweh" in this context means "to establish just relationships among persons, it is to recognize the rights of the poor."[55] *Tipbriew tipblei* affirms that one can do justice to others only if they know God and have right relationship with God the creator of everything that is. It portrays a balance of relationship to both God and neighbor. Hence, it proposes equality, justice, liberty, and respect to all beings, irrespective of status, position, possession, or gender in our daily dealings.

In the context of economic globalization, where the forces of neo-colonialism intend to capture the entire land and resources of the tribals, the issue of justice is not only important but a necessity. For the poor tribals, taking away their land means not only exploiting their economic resources but destroying their source of livelihood. This is sheer injustice. What the poor tribal people need is a not merely charity activities,[56] rather the protection and defending of their inherent rights as humans, including their right to economy or right to livelihood in their struggle for survival. In the present day context there emerged a glaring call for a globalization with a more human face. Stiglitz rightly states that we need to "make globalization fairer, and more effective in raising living standards, especially the poor. It is not just a question of changing institutional structures. The mindset around globalization itself must change."[57] But the moot question is can there be a globalization with a more human face? Will the attempt to change institutional structures and the mindset of the exploiters enable to create a just and participatory space where the marginalised and vulnerable poor section of the society find the rightful place? It may be noted that poor people need far more than that. The

[55] Gutierrez, *A Theology of Liberation*, 110.

[56] Discussion with the Focus Group at Nongtrai reveals that the local indigenous people received Rs. 10 per ton from the lime stones from the Lafarge Company. Besides providing jobs to around 100 persons as daily wage labourers, the company also provides sponsorship to the newly established schools, mobile health clinic, weaving centre, village foot path, etc. This is quite a small amount in comparison to the profit extracted by the company from the area on the 11th May 2012. Similarly, in the context of Lumshnong area there is no investment by the companies, worth to be mentioned. Besides providing daily wage labourers to the some local people, constructing the village foot path, occasional help for the village in terms of financial requirement and the like, investment of the company to the welfare of the village is very minimal. Discussion with Brian Gympad a villagcr on thc 17 May 2012.

[57] Stiglitz, *Globalization and its Discontents,* 247.

current situation demands that poor people require the recognition of their right as fully human created in the image of God or the *Imago Dei.*

Theology of *tipbriew tipblei* deliberately demands for the recognition of these rights bestowed upon the individual through *Ka hok Blei* or divine righteousness. Recognition of these rights implies restraining from violating and abusing them. The right of being humans is not possessed by the oppressors, the exploiter, the powerful, or those who control the sources of livelihood, rather it is the birth right bestowed equally to everyone including the exploited, the oppressed, the other. Mawrie maintains that humans are expected not to infringe or abuse the rights of other fellow beings. Any attempt to trample the rights and integrity of another person may amount to insulting the divine who bestowed them on every individual person.[58] In this context, theology of *tipbriew tipblei* proposes a community of equals where the worth, dignity, and the rights of the other are not only respected, but also protected and preserved. Such a situation entails freedom from all the oppressive structures, devoid of all injustice, inequalities, discrimination and subjugation. It simply means a step towards an inclusive community where each and every individual have proper place in the *oikos* of God.

Re-Defining the Tribal Concept of Kamai ia ka Hok

As stated earlier, *Kamai ia ka Hok* literally means to earn righteousness. The Khasis believed that God sent them to this world to strive for justice and righteousness. Humans are therefore expected to be just and righteous in their thoughts, words and deeds. Rymbai maintains that any attempt to neglect this ethical standard means to disregard the very purpose which the divine intended for humanity.[59] Here, to be just and righteous is not only an ideal, but it indicates to be manifested and practiced in all their daily dealings and transactions concerning their relationship with other fellow human beings in order to earn righteousness. Hence, the concept is relational. Like *tipbriew tipblei*, this principle also has both vertical and horizontal aspects. It has its source from God of justice and need to be manifested and practiced in relation to other fellow humans. *Kamai ia ka Hok* is a process that a person can practice in his/her entire lifetime so that they can earn righteousness at the end of the journey. Gassah further explains this when he said that *Kamai ia ka Hok* is to be accumulated bit by bit throughout the entire life.[60] Sawian argues that humans cannot take anything with them to God's house or *Ka Ing U Blei* but only *Ka Hok* or righteousness.[61] It suggests

---

[58] Mawrie, *Ka Theology Ka Niam Khasi*, 23-24.

[59] R. T. Rymbai, "U Hynniew Trep bad la ka Niam," *Seng Khasi Souvenir* (Shillong: Seng Khasi, 1986), 12.

[60] Discussion with L.S. Gassah on the 3rd May, 2012.

[61] Discussion with Sumar Sing Sawian on the 2nd May, 2012.

an on-going process of toiling for justice in different capacities that could help facilitate the bridging of right relationships with others in the community. So, there is no room for exclusion or discrimination; all form parts of the all-embracing community. It is believed that *Kamai ia ka Hok* is one of the main commandment[62] that God gave to human beings at the beginning of time. The story of *U Lumsohpetbneng*[63] depicts that as long as the people keep the dictum beside the other two commandments intact, they will prosper and experience harmonious way of living. But the moment they break the commandments and turn away from God their life will be in peril.[64] The ethical principle of *Kamai ia ka Hok* has therefore influenced the entire fabric of Khasi daily experiences whether it is economic, social, cultural, religious, political and so on. Some of the implications of this principle can be discussed in the following.

- To be hard working, sincere and committed to one's own duty and responsibility.
- To be able to stand on one's own feet, enrich and develop our God given talent in a manner that is worthy and commendable. In short, to live with dignity and honour.[65]
- To be just and fair in all business affairs and transactions either as buyers or sellers.
- To avoid any attempt for encroachment into the land of our neighbour and other fellow beings or any sort of intrusion beyond one's own boundary.[66]

---

[62] Other main important commandments are *Tipbriew tipblei* and *Tipkur Tipkha.* All the three commandments are meant for building an inclusive community where the value, rights, dignity and integrity of each individual person is well maintained.

[63] The story of *U Lumsohpetbneng* is already discussed in Chapter I.

[64] This understanding is well illustrated in the story of *U Lum Diengiei* which reveals how human beings experience chaos and spiritual crisis. The Khasis describe this situation as *Ka Phai Lyndet u Blei* or God has turned his back on human beings. Another story of *Ka Krem Lamat Latang* reveals how humans' spiritual crisis has reached its climax. It is only through genuine repentance on the part of human beings that God turn his face to humans again and therefore reestablished the covenant with human beings. The Khasis perceived this as *Ieng Rangbah u Briew, ap Jutang u Blei* which means humans stand with matured understanding about reestablishing his relationship with God, and God is watching over human whether he would be able to abide by the covenant or not. See Mawrie, *The Essence of the Khasi Religion*, 24-30; 31-39. When God satisfied with the act of repentance on the part of human beings, God who is not happy with humans to remain in sinful condition came down to forgive human beings. This act is what the Khasis term as *Hiar Ka Hok Blei Kdum* which means God's righteousness came down for human forgiveness. See Mawrie, *Ka Theology jong ka Niam Khasi,* 20. See also Hayong, "The Concept of Sin…," 64-65.

[65] Discussion with Dr. Bajubon Kharlukhi on the 2nd May, 2012.

[66] For instance, according to tradition in War Jaintia area, when there is any division of land or buying new land people used to erect boundary stones with *Ka duwai ka phirat* or some sort of prayer for God's blessings and in the presence of some witness. These boundary stones are

- To make all efforts for accomplishing the best in life through one's own sweat and righteous means rather than to achieve freely without any hard work.[67]
- To abstain from taking bribes and monetary benefit or any sort of profit either in cash or in kind that are against the norm of ethical principles.
- To strive forward for doing justice and righteousness in different capacities and in all spheres of life and in matters related to our relationship with the other fellow human beings.
- To attempt for mending broken relationship, strife, and other ways and means that has distorted the flow of life.
- To attempt all possibilities and opportunities in striving towards upholding the common good, the well being and better welfare of humanity and the community at large.
- To be committed towards defending and protecting the rights, dignity, equality and integrity of humanity especially the vulnerable section of the community.[68]
- To be ready to participate and toil for eradicating all forces of injustices, oppressive structures, abuse, and the like that damage the peace and security of humanity and the society.
- To strive forward for building a just, participatory, and inclusive community-a community of equals-liberated from all clutches of injustices, exploitation, oppressions, discrimination and other kinds of oppressive structure.

In a nutshell, *Kamai ia ka Hok* possesses a large pool of ethical principles that could be helpful for establishing a solid foundation in interpersonal relationships and building a just participatory and inclusive community where each individual is respected, valued and recognized. It promotes justice, equality, fairness, equal opportunities and liberation. Hence, it could serve as an important tool towards the enhancement and emancipation of all sections of the population especially the weaker section in the community. Nevertheless, as it is the case of other commandments like *tipbriew tipblei*, with the impact of the outside forces like secularization, modernization, westernization and of late the current stage of

---

considered sacred and people are not expected to remove them or even to step their feet or walk over these stones. The tradition says that it is a taboo to remove these stones for one's own selfish interest and there is fear that something bad will happen to the person concern or their families of those who violate this restriction. Hence, any act of encroachment or intrusion to the neighbours land is often referred as *Khynnium Shiniang*, and is against the norms and sanction of the society, therefore must be condemned by the entire community. Discussion with Mr. T. D. Khonglah on the 7 July 2012.

[67] Discussion with Sumar Sing Sawian on the 2nd May 2012.

[68] Jeebon Roy, *Ka Kitab ba Batai Shynna shaphang U Wei U Blei,* (Shillong: Seng Khasi, Reprint, 1979), 30.

globalization the importance of this ethical principle *Kamai ia ka Hok,* is slowly diminishing in the present day life of the Khasi people. There is urgent necessity to re-capture and re-interpret this ethical concept in the present day Khasi society as they struggle against the so-called neo-colonial forces promoted by the neoliberal ideologies. Re-discovering this important concept will not only help the present day society, but also could correct the pitfalls committed by the present phase of globalization.

Kamai ia ka Hok Versus Globalization: Theological Consideration

In the process of globalization promoted by the ideologies of neo-liberalism, theology of *Kamai ia ka Hok* provides certain alternatives not only to correct the weakness of economic globalization, but also to enhance the value and dignity of life especially that of the underside of the society. As stated earlier, two important Khasi sayings need to be discussed in this regard. First, the Khasis used to say *Ngi wan sha kane ka Pyrthei ban kamai ia ka Hok* which literally means, 'we come into this world to labour or toil for righteousness.' This reveals that God sent the people into this world to strive for righteousness in all their dealings. To state differently, humans need to make an effort to have right relationship with God their creator, as well as with their fellow beings. Toiling for righteousness here include recognizing and respecting the right of even the least among God's creation. The second saying goes, *Ieit ialade bad Burom ia kiwei* or love yourself and respect others. It implies that a person can respect other beings only when he/she has self respect first. These two sayings sprang from the idea that having sent to this world by *Ka Hok Blei* or divine righteousness, every person has his/her respective right to live as full human beings, without any exclusion or discrimination.

Firstly, it is clear that, the mushrooming of different companies at Lumshnong area was not meant to help developing the surrounding areas, rather they were attracted by the rich resources of the area for accumulating unlimited profits.[69] In the process, they destroy even the agricultural land like paddy field and others that lie close to the mining areas. To cite one among many instances, is the case where the Amrit Cement destroyed the agricultural land of two ladies from Chehruphi for they did not submit to the pressure of selling their agricultural land to the company.[70] For capturing all available opportunities for wealth accumulation, the

[69] Rangbahduh Khonglah asserts that these companies before they came to the areas for establishing their firms had already made their home work by exploring through the maps of Geological Survey of India. They know even about the different locations where the lime stones are found in abundance which are not much familiar to the local people. Discussion with Rangbahduh Khonglah, the former headman of the Lumshnong village on the 17th May, 2012.

[70] The KSU Narpuh Circle lodge the complaint against the Amrit Company for destroying the agricultural fields of these two namely Hunmon Dkhar and Tiplang Lamare for they do not succumb to the pressure of the company to sell their agriculture land to the companies. See

rich sections care less for the plight of the poor tribals. Despite repeated claims that globalization creates space for the others, the ground realities proved that there is no room for the poor in the present global economic system.[71] In this context, theology of *Kamai ia ka Hok* challenges the worldview and practices of the neo-colonial forces that do not take into consideration the suffering and struggles of the impoverished poor, rather exploited even the sources of livelihood of the marginalised poor. Singh rightly points out, "Do not acquire what is not rightly yours, be it cowrie or gold. The sin is same."[72] As stated earlier, according to the tradition, the rich people in Khasi society are often referred as *riewspah* and *riewbha*. The rich people even if they have large possession of wealth, they also have the spirit of sharing and caring for the impoverished poor. Here, caring and sharing their wealth with the poor is part and parcel of *Kamai ia ka Hok.* This means that the daily wage workers working in the field of the rich people are not harassed, discriminated, exploited, or oppressed in any manner. Both the employers and the employees are guided by the principle of *Kamai ia ka Hok.* While in the case of the former caring for the less privileged is a process to earn righteousness, in the case of latter laboring honestly means to toil righteously in order to earn righteousness. This not only advocated building up good relationship between the employers and the employees, but it reveals a process of establishing a harmonious society where the rights, values, worth and dignity of each person is recognized and respected.[73] *Kamai ia ka Hok* not only speak and recognize the presence of *Ka Hok Blei* or divine righteousness in the individual person, but also realized that the person's rights, values, talents and dignity are bestowed upon by *Ka Hok Blei.*[74] Hence, it is against the divine mandate to ignore, violate and trample the rights of the poor and marginalised.[75]

Secondly, the earlier discussion testifies that for the Khasis it is a taboo to capture other people's land or field. The erection of the boundary stones to demarcate the boundary line with the neighbour's field is always done with *Ka Duwai Ka Phirat* or sort of prayer to God to bless the field and the owner as well. Once this act is done, it becomes *Ka Hok Ka Riti*[76] or the right of the person

---

"Sngewkhia ka KSU ba thombor ka Amrit Cement ia ki Jaka Rep," *Mawphor*, (Shillong) 14 November 2011. http://www.mawphor.com/ (14.11.2012).

[71] Frtiedman opines that the present phase of globalization provides equal opportunities to all individual to collaborate and compete in the global arena. See Thomas Friedman, *The World is Flat,* 9-11.

[72] Singh, "Khasi and Jaintia Religion," 107.See also Jeebon Roy,*Ka Niam Ki Khasi* Reprinted (Shillong: Ri Khasi Press, 2009), 38.

[73] Discussion with Ladbasuk Lyngdoh on the 30 June 2012.

[74] Mawrie, *Ka Theology ka Niam Khasi,* 21-23.

[75] Gutierrez, *A Theology of Liberation,* 110.

[76] The *Khasi English Dictionary* translated the term *Ka Hok ka Riti* as the legal customs or established customs. See Nissor Singh, *Khasi English Dictionary* (New Delhi: Mittal Publications,

concern or the clan, confirmed through the established or unwritten legal customs of the land. It is also prohibited to extend or enlarge even an inch of one's own field by capturing other neighbour's land for one's own selfish interest.[77] Hence, once the boundary stones are erected they should remain ever as witnesses to the demarcation of land by the two owners. In War Jaintia dialect tampering the boundary line or capturing other's person field for one's own selfish interest, it is called as *Khynnium Shiniang*. It is an act that is done against the established norms of the community, therefore believed to bring misfortune or bad consequence to the persons as well as the entire clan. Mawrie precisely observes that while the individual concerned has the natural right to protect his/her own land through *Ka Hok ka Riti,* on the other they have to respect the right of others over their land or property, even the least among the community. He further states that any kind of manipulation or capturing the neighbour's land will bring bad impact to the person, the family, and the clan thereby affecting the image of the entire community.[78]

Thirdly, the Khasis believed that this right is given by God to each individual. If the persons recognized this inherent right bestowed by God to every person either rich or poor they will not despise or reject any one in any sphere of life. Mawrie affirms that we have to respect the right of other persons as we respect our own rights.[79] *Kamai ia ka Hok* entails that each individual is expected to be on the side of the margins, those who are not counted in the economic ladder, the other or the underside of the society. It is against discriminating, excluding, exploiting the other or even capturing their sources of economic life.[80] It sends a strong message to the neo-liberalism ideologies, that discrimination or exploitation the poor and needy is not only depriving them of their rights as humans, but it is against God's intent that all should experience and enjoy full humanness as God's creature in God's image or *Imago Dei*. The earlier discussion reveals that the term *Imago Dei* may be considered as closely similar or equivalent to the Khasi concept of *Ka Rngiew*. The concept of *Ka Rngiew* illustrates that each individual is under the spiritual cover of the divine. Giri further elaborates this perception when he states,

> This divine or spiritual cover encompasses a person right from the moment he or she is born and will always encompass and dwell, deep in the heart and mind or in the conscience of a person as long as he or she live righteously and earn livelihood righteously (*Kamai ia ka Hok).* Living righteously and

---

Reprinted 2010), 174.

[77] Cf. Roy, *Ka Kitab ba Pynshai shaphang U Wei U Blei,* 34.

[78] Mawrie, *Ka Theology Ka Niam Khasi,* 28.

[79] Mawrie, *Ka Theology ka Niam Khasi,* 24.

[80] Roy, *Ka Niam jong ki Khasi,* 39.

earning livelihood righteously (*Kamai ia ka Hok*), is believed to have come from *Ka Hukum Blei* or the divine decree.[81]

Hence, *Kamai ia ka Hok* suggests that any kind of discrimination that push the marginalised poor to the margin of economic life is not only against the intent will of God but also an insult to the divine being who is the source of justice and righteousness.

Fourthly, in the process of globalization promoted by the ideologies of neo-liberalism for unlimited profit, the rich affluent section does not care for anything but 'money' or wealth accumulation. This is what Joseph term as "money theism"[82] where money takes the place of God, in the entire process. The outcome of such a perspective, lead to the subjugation of both human and the earth resources for wealth accumulation even through unfair means. It leads to the success of a tiny section and make the condition of the poor more impoverished than before. Theology of *Kamai ia ka Hok* challenges such perspective that strive for wealth accumulation at the expense of the other or the impoverished sections. It speaks against obtaining wealth without any hard work. The Khasi saying *Kamai da ka umsyep la jong* or 'earn through your sweat' signifies that laziness, unfair accumulation of wealth, and unfair distribution of wealth is against the principle of *Kamai ia ka Hok.* Laitphlang appropriately argue that the wealth earned through one's hard work or honest means is like a continuous blessings that last for posterity, where as the wealth achieved through unfair means will bring disgrace to the owner.[83] According to tradition, the Khasis believed that wealth begotten through corruptible ways will not last long for it is against God's decree. But that which is earned through hard work gradually multiplies and continues to prosper for generations.[84] The traditional ethical teachings also tell us that it is forbidden to preserve or mix together the corrupted money achieved through unfair means with the hard earned money, for it will bring misfortune to the well being and prosperity of the family. Besides, the elders also forbid any one, to make such earnings as financial support for the need and welfare of their descendants.[85] In tune with this aspect, Singh fittingly asserts, "Money gained other than by one's own just effort is unclean. Stolen money, bribe and gambling

---

[81] But *Ka Rngiew* will be gradually diminished from the person concern if he or she committed sin or *Sang.* Nevertheless, it can be recovered and regain through a sort of sacrificial ceremony known as *Ka Ksan Rngiew* or that a person concern be justified again. See Giri, "That Elusive Niamkur (Clan Religion)...," 58.

[82] Joseph, "Towards a Theological Critique of Globalization," 11.

[83] W. R. Laitphlang, "Ka Niam Ha U Khasi," *Sneng Khasi* 5/19 (December, 1981): 8-9.

[84] Discussion with Sweetymon Rynjah on the 30th April 2012.

[85] Sib Charan Roy Jaitdkhar, *Ka Niam Ki Khasi- Ka Niam Tipbriew Tipblei,* (Shillong: Ri Khasi Press, Reprint, 1966), 50-51. See also Mawrie, *Ka Theology Ka Niam Khasi,* 30.

money bring misfortune, misery and poverty to the house."[86] Hence, theology of *Kamai ia ka Hok* challenges not only about the discrimination and oppression of the impoverished section of the society, but also speaks against the ideology of neo-liberalism of unlimited profit that led to the subjugation of both humans and the nature.

Re-visiting the Eco-spirituality of the Khasis

"Eco-spirituality" maintains Cummings "draws attention to the cosmos as a place of God's self revelation." That is "eco-spirituality studies our relationship to God as it develops in the context of our relationship with the cosmos in its totality."[87] In simple description, it indicates the interconnectedness and interrelatedness of God, human and nature. This is well fitted to the tribal world view which understand the inseparable relationship that unite God, human and nature. According to tradition, the tribal ancestral parents clearly understood that human beings cannot be separated from nature and environment around them. That is, if humanity is to survive here on earth the health and well being of the entire natural environment must also be preserved. Rymbai fittingly argues on this aspect when he states, "Our ancestors were divinely inspired to know that trees cannot live without land, nor can life remain without trees."[88] Admittedly, in accordance with the educational standard of the present day setting, one may say that our ancestral parents were not literate. Nevertheless, their teachings handed down orally for generations, with regards to the well being of humanity in particular and the health of the natural environment in general have reservoir of good teachings that could help heal the wounded and suffering earth due to humans' greediness. All these important teachings illustrate their close relationship and attachment with the natural surrounding around them including other species like birds and animals. These important teachings are well revealed in their myths, folklores, folktales, dances, festivals, songs, etc. Different tribal groups have different tales and stories to tell to successive generation which emphasize the unity, harmony and peaceful co-existence between human beings and other creations of God. Some among many of these stories of the Khasi people are the Creation story,[89] *Ka Iew Luri Lura* or 'the market of all living creatures' and *Ka Krem Lamet Latang* or 'the Cavern.'

---

[86] Singh, Khasi and Jaintia Religion, 107.

[87] Charles Cummings, "Exploring Eco-Spirituality," http://www.spiritualitytoday.org/spir2day/894113cummings.html (8.2.2011).

[88] R. T. Rymbai, "The Traditional Ecological Concepts of the Khasi-Pnar," in *The Tribal Worldview and Ecology*, edited by A. Wati Longchar and Yangkahao Vashum (Jorhat: Tribal Study Centre, 1998), 15.

[89] The detail of the Creation Story is already discussed in the Chapter I (point 1:4. Khasi Religious System).

Ka Iew Luri Lura.[90]

Tradition tells that *Ka Iew Luri Lura* or the market of all living creatures was the first market in the land of the Khasis. The market was established by human beings where in all humans and animals participated. It is believed that during this period all living creatures have no common language for communication. It was in that market through the initiative of human beings that all living creatures arrived at the decision that human language should serve as the medium of communication. As an act of gratitude to human beings, all living creatures had unanimously agreed to make human beings as their ruler. In turn, some of them like the cow, the goat, the pig, the dog, the cat, the hen, etc made a decision to stay with and serve human beings. The market happened once and continued for two days. Every creature brought its own goods for marketing. In the same way, a dog also brought *Ka Tung Rymbai* i.e. a kind of delicacy made of soya beans and some indigenous spices, which has a putrid smell. When other animals passed through her stall the peculiar smell of *Ka Tung Rymbai* repelled them. So, all animals mockingly booed at her, snatch away her basket, threw it to the ground and trampled it under their feet. Dejected and battered, in such a helpless situation, the dog went seeking the help of human beings and lodges a complaint against all wild animals. But human beings turned down her appeal on the ground that humankind did not want to provoke enmity between his/her servant and other wild animals. When justice was denied to her, since that time, the dog had a grudge against all wild animals, that somewhere she will get her revenge, against the wild animals by smelling their foot prints.

Ka Krem Lamet Latang or the Cavern[91]

Ka Krem Lamet Latang or the cavern depicts the story that there was a time when all living creatures including human beings spoke one language and lived together in unity and harmony. Accordingly, a dance festival was arranged and all the creatures arrived there to participate in grand costume and splendid attire. The festival continued for the whole day until all were tired and were about to leave the ground, when the sun and the moon the two siblings, arrived there to participate in the dance. Actually, there was nothing wrong in their way of dancing, but everyone was mocking and laughing at them, disapproving their dance, for it is not morally right for the brother and sister to dance together. Overcome with shame the sun ran away and hid herself in the caverns. With her withdrawals the entire universe was enveloped with thick darkness. Hence the entire world was in chaos. Human beings and all other creatures once again convene a meeting to select someone among them, who is fit enough to meet the sun and ask her

---

[90] Gatphoh, *Ki Umjer Ksiar,* 134-135.

[91] See Mawrie, *The Essence of Khasi Religion,* 6-7. See also Nongkynrih, *Around the Hearth: Khasi Legends,* 8-15.

forgiveness and who could convince the sun to come back again and give its light to the world. After a lengthy deliberation they select a rooster, dressed him grandly and send him for that task. Having impressed the sun with his humility, the sun gave her assurance to come back and give light to the earth. As a mark of her return, the sun asks him to crow three times, so that it will remind her of her assurance to return and give its light to the world. It is believed that to this day the rooster has to crow every morning three times at regular intervals before the sun shed its light to the world.

The above stories reveal that:

- Though human beings are entrusted with the role of stewardship over the entire creations of God, it is also implied that there is unbroken relationship between the mother earth and God.[92]
- The mother earth has its own value and worth in its relation to its creator. Its also acts as co-creator of God by giving birth to other species like the trees, plants, animals, birds, etc.
- There was a time when human beings and all God's creation were at peace with God and with each other-a time where the Khasi called the *sotti juk* or the golden age. It is a time where contentment and prosperity prevailed among all God's creations.[93]
- It also underlines the belief that all creatures are relatively interconnected and interdependent on each other which entails peaceful co-existence among all God's creation.
- Each and every creature are equal and has its own importance, dignity and respect, and all creatures have their respective share to contribute to the good and well being of the entire world community.
- There is close and intimate relationship between God, human and nature.

Tribal People and Land/Nature

Traditionally, for the tribal people, nature plays an important role in their life. The entire natural surrounding not only offers them space for living, but also provides them vital source of livelihood. Tribal peoples, especially those in rural areas for many of their essential needs depend on the nature around them. These include firewood, house building materials, wild fruits and vegetables, edible roots, medicinal plants, and so on. If one pays a visit to any tribal market place like Shillong, Jowai, or elsewhere he/she could witness different varieties of wild fruits and vegetables available in different seasons. With organic food materials

[92] The first four points are taken from the creation story that has been discussed in the Chapter I (point 1:4. Khasi Religious System). See also (S.Hayong, "The Khasi Concept of Ecology," *Indian Theological Journal* 2/1 (Jan-June, 2008): 88.

[93] Hayong, "The Khasi Concept of Ecology," 88.

rarely available in today's era, these wild natural fruits and vegetables become more important food items for the tribal peoples. This enables the tribal people not only to depend on natural resources for their source of living, but also to have close relationship and attachment with the nature around them.

As they have a close relationship with nature, their whole life system and thought pattern is embedded and influenced by nature. They vividly understand that human life and natural surrounding cannot be separated. "It is on the lap of nature that human's span of life is enfolded."[94] In short, human beings have a kinship relationship with nature. Nature is like their relative. Many among the Khasi people have their clan names from the natural species. For instances, one could noticed clan names based on animals,[95] fruits,[96] vegetables,[97] flowers,[98] trees,[99] and the like. This illustrates the ground realities of the closeness and attachment of tribal people with nature. For the tribal people, the experience about the reality of life, in their long term association with nature, shape their worldview and provides them with ample ways of understanding the importance and value of other creations. It is this kind of relationship that makes the tribal to have deep respect and value the importance of nature. Hence, any attempt to damage or spoil this relationship means self destruction. To put it in different words, to destroy nature and its resources is also to destroy this relationship. It is like inviting trouble and misfortune not only to oneself but to the entire humanity and non human creations.

Land/Nature as Mother

For the tribal and indigenous people, land/nature is the first and foremost importance in their life. "Land is life," declares Nirmal Minz.[100] Land is the primary sources of livelihood. It is from the land where all the sustenance for living derives. Human beings survive by what the land produce. For the tribal, land/nature is like their mother. Generally, they call it mother earth. The Khasis

---

[94] Hayong, "The Khasi Concept of Ecology," 91.

[95] There are clans names based on animal like *Tham* (Crab), *Shrieh* (Monkey) and so on.

[96] Some clans take their name from fruits like *Sohiong* (Khasi Cherry), *Sohlang* (small wild fruits), *Sohliia* (Small sour fruits with a rough outside), *Sohmat* (a kind of Citron), *Sohshang* (a sour red fruits), and others stated with fruit or *soh* like *Sohkhlet* and so on. See *Khasi English Dictionary*, 207-210.

[97] Those clan who are taken their names from vegetables are *Sohkhia* (Cucumber), *Pathaw* (Pumkin), *Rymbai* (Khasi bean) and so on.

[98] There are some clans that take their name from *syntiew* or flower or in short *tiew* like *Kharsyntiew, Tiewsoh, Tiewmon, Tiewphor, Tiewdop* and so on.

[99] There are also clans taken their names from trees or *dieng* like *Diengdoh, Diengngan,* and so on.

[100] Nirmal Minz, "Tribal Perspective on Ecology," in *Tribal Worldview and Ecology,* edited by A. Wati Longchar and Yangkahao Vashum (Jorhat: Tribal Study Centre, 1998), 4.

call it *Ka Mei Ramew*, *Ka Mei* means 'mother' and *ramew* means "ground" or *terra firma*.[101] As stated earlier, *Ka Mei Ramew* is the creation of God the creator or *U Blei Nongbuh Nongthaw*. The term *Nongbuh Nongthaw* has a deep and profound theological meaning. H.O. Mawrie argues that the term *Nongbuh* indicates the one who plan or design. Whereas the term *Nongthaw,* is understood as the one who creates or the cause of everything that exist. Hence, this term connotes that God made his design before hand and later created all that exist.[102] Barness L. Mawrie further elaborates this view when he states,

> *U Nongbuh* means a designer, one who sets everything in an ordered motion. The Khasis believe that the orderliness and harmony that exist in the universe is the intelligent design of the Creator. *U Nongthaw* on the other hand, means creator, thus signifying God as the omnipotent Being who is the cause of everything that has been created.[103]

He further states that even though the Khasis do not define clearly the idea of *creatio ex-nihilo,* its entire conception is there. In its actual sense, the word *thaw* means strictly to create out of nothing. It differs from the word *shna* or to make which connotes to make something out of the already existing materials.[104] This points out to the fact that *Ka Mei Ramew* has its close attachment and connection with God its creator. In short, whether humans exist or not, *Ka Mei Ramew* has its own value and worth in the sight of its creator. Another term used by the Khasis for the mother earth is *Ka Meirilung Ka Meirisan.* This literally means a mother who nurtures and takes care of anything young and tender and looks after them even when they have grown up. In short, nature as mother is one who nurtures and fosters the growth of life here on earth. Barness L. Mawrie accurately states that even though the Khasis "do not deify mother earth like the Greeks who address her as goddess *Gaia,* they uphold her with utmost respect and honour." He further elaborates this view when he says that their respect of the mother earth is exemplified in their prayer to the mother earth at the beginning of the sowing season appealing for her blessing to have good crops, as well as during the harvest time when they give thanks to the mother earth for the bountiful harvest. Similarly, prior to the cutting of a tree for some important needs, the Khasis normally use to say *Ka Duwai ka Phirat* or prayer seeking the permission of the mother earth.[105]

---

[101] Singh, *Khasi English Dictionary,* 171.

[102] Mawrie, *The Khasi Millieu,* Reprinted (New Delhi: Concept Publishing Company (P) LTD., 2010), 29.

[103] Mawrie, *The Khasis and their Natural Environment,* 35.

[104] Mawrie, *The Khasis and their Natural Environment,* 35-36.

[105] Mawrie, *The Khasis and their Natural Environment,* 145. H. O. Mawrie, *Ka Theology Ka Niam Khasi,* 67.

As stated earlier, the creation story portrays that *Ka Mei Ramew* also acts as co-creator with God by giving birth to other creations like animals, birds, plants, trees, grass, etc., which are the source of life sustenance. The earlier discussion also depicts that tribal people depend much of their needs from house building materials to medicinal materials from the *Ka Mei Ramew*. Being dependent on nature for sustaining their life, tribal people pay deep respect and reverence to the mother earth. In the Khasi matrilineal society,[106] the mother is held in high esteem and reverence. The mother is the one who supports, nurtures, and looks after everything necessary for life sustenance. To state differently, *Ka Mei Ramew* like a mother which support the flow of life is revered and paid deep homage and respect. Humans survive by what the mother earth provides for their daily living.[107] Thanzauva maintains that "Just as a baby is sucking the milk from its mother, human beings are sucking the milk of the earth in various ways."[108] The survival of human beings and other creatures depends on the health and well being of the mother earth. It is only if the people are taking the health of the earth into consideration that humans as well as other species can survive on this planet earth.

Land Gives Identity

For the tribal people, land is not only the source of livelihood but it is something that gives them identity and personhood. To have land means to have identity. For the tribal people, there is a difference between those who have land and those who do not have. There is a Khasi saying which says, *Ki lah ialong Briew mynta,* which literally means "now they have become human." This is a saying which is usually referred to those people who were very poor earlier, either having no land or no proper dwelling house. But now they are living a good and prosperous life. Hence, to be landless means having no proper identity or personhood. As land gives identity to the people, the tribals used to identify themselves by the place to which they belong. For them, it is land as a place that gives them identity. Chowdhury maintains that prior to the coming of the Britishers the Khasi normally identified themselves as natives of particular villages, that is, *U Nong-Mylliem* (a resident of Mylliem village), or *U Nong-Sohra* (a resident of Sohra Village) and so on.[109] Whenever two Khasis meet for the first time they will first introduce themselves not by their names but by the place or village to which they belong.[110] This

[106] According to the matrilineal setting, both the family or clan name and the family property belong to the mother and pass on through the daughters.

[107] Hayong, "The Khasi Concept of Ecology," 94.

[108] K. Thanzauva, *Theology of Community: Tribal Theology in the Making,* (Bangalore: Asian Trading Corporation, 2004), 219.

[109] J. N. Chowdhury, *Ki Khun Khasi Khara (The Khasi People),* 6.

[110] Cf. Thanzauva, *Theology of Community: A Theological Basis for Social Transformation,* 226.

indicates the fact that a person is very much attached to his/her native place. In other words, their personal identity is bound up with the place where they have been brought up. As land gives them identity, prior to the coming of the British colonial rule, selling of land is unheard of among the Khasi. For instance, when the Britishers needed land for establishing their capital at Sohra, the Sohra state did not sell land to them, rather gave the land in exchange with some portion of British land in the plain of Sylhet.[111] According to the traditional belief system in War Jaintia, selling of land especially the inherited land or *Ka Nongtymmen*[112] is strictly prohibited.[113] If there is a necessity for selling such land they will do so only within the clan itself.[114] According to the Khasi traditional belief system, selling the inherited land or *Ka Nongtymmen* is regarded as selling one's own identity.[115] To state differently, it may be referred as inviting misfortune not only to those involved in selling but it will adversely affected the future generations of the entire clan or the family.

Land/Nature is the Gift of God

Like all tribal groups, the Khasis believed that land is the gift of God from the beginning of time. As it is the gift of God,[116] land is to be shared by all in the community. Every family has the right to occupy it. In other words, having received it freely as the gift of God, humans have the right to use but not to misuse it. Any attempt to misuse land or nature can be regarded as insulting God the owner and giver. As it is the gift of God it is the people who own the land not the chief or *Syiem.*[117] Land belonged to the people or the community not the chief. Prior to the coming of the colonial rule, there is no land revenue or land tax paid by the people to any authority or to the chief. As stated earlier, the land tenure system of the Khasis,[118] illustrate that all families in the community could enjoy the benefits and share some portion of it.

---

[111] Giri, *The Khasis under the British Rule: 1824-1947,* 51-52.

[112] *Ka Nongtymmen* is often referred to the inherited land or property that were handed down for generations and passed on to their kith and kin.

[113] Discussion with Rev. W. Jungai on the 17 July, 2010.

[114] Discussion with Minsah P. Hayong on the 17 July, 2010.

[115] Hayong, "The Khasi Concept of Ecology," 94.

[116] R.T. Rymbai, "Evolution of Modern Khasi Society," in *Khasi Heritage,* edited by Hipshon Roy Kharshiing (Shillong: Seng Khasi, 1979), 64.

[117] Hayong, "The Khasi Concept of Ecology," 94.

[118] According to the land tenure system of the Khasis land can be classified into two categories. i) *Ri Raid* land or land belongs to the community and ii) *Ri Kynti* land or the land that belongs to particular clans, inherited from their ancestral parents.

Land/Nature is Sacred

For the tribal people, land and the entire nature is sacred. The creation account of the Khasis depicts that the creation of land is the handiwork of God.[119] It is God who gave to the *Hynniew Trep Hynniew Skum* or the seven families to look after the land and all other God's creation. Since it is the handiwork of God, land is sacred. Mawrie affirms that God reveals himself/herself in and through the nature. The "beauty and splendour of nature and this world that God has made, the broad expanse and greatness of the universe with the sun and the moon and the myriad stars on the firmament, so regulated in their respective courses," all these reveal the wisdom and incomparable power of God.[120] As God reveal him/herself in and through nature, the world of nature is therefore sacred. Rymbai further elaborates this view when he says,

> The Khasi-Pnars have no temples, churches or synagogues. God, the Creator of all fills heaven and earth. Every bit of ground is therefore sacred and no particular part and portion of it can be considered as holier than the other....So, God can be worshipped alone in one's own house[121] or in the open-anywhere, so long as the worshipper is clean in his [sic] heart and takes care not to defile by evil deeds the places where he [sic] performed his [sic] worship. The Khasi-Pnars are in the habit of saying that men should not desecrate mother earth by iniquitous action.[122]

The above quotation indicates the sacredness of land and nature where everyone ought not to defile it by any wrong action. Hence, the Khasis use to select particular site or space marked by a stone, rock, groves of trees, etc., as a place of worship. In this particular aspect, the Khasi use the word *tang* which means consecrate. And once the particular spot is consecrated, that place is considered as worship place. But without seeking the permission of God that very place cannot be considered as sacred. Once a particular site is consecrated, "the area around the site becomes the hallowed ground."[123] This does not mean that the Khasis worship the natural object or 'spirit worship' as termed by outsiders,[124] but it indicates that, that very spot is consecrated to worship God. Hence, it became a place of worship. In sum, the entire land and nature is considered sacred. This indicates that land and nature offer a place of communion between God and people, where

119 War, "The Khasi Concept of Nature," 41.

120 Mawrie, *The Khasi Milieu,* 27-28.

121 Home is considered as a place of worship. Hence, Khasi religion is also usually considered or referred as a family/clan religion.

122 Rymbai, "Some Aspects of the Religion of the Khasi-Pnars," 114-115.

123 Mawrie, *The Essence of Khasi Religion,* 15, 47.

124 See Gurdon, *The Khasis,* 105.

God can commune with the people who worship him/her. To state differently, there is a connecting thread that bind together God, human and nature.

Nature as Medium of Communication

For the tribal people in general and Khasi people in particular, nature is not only a place where God can commune with the people, but it also serves as a medium of communication. That is, nature serves as a vehicle where humans can communicate with fellow humans, as well as with God the Creator. It is the belief of tribal people that nature communicates to people in different ways and at different circumstances. In his poetry *Ka Meirilung,* Soso Tham addresses,

> *Sa shisien pat kin win ki khlaw,* (Once again the forest will roar)
> *Sa shisien pat kin khih ki maw;* (Once again the rocks will move)
> *Kum kiwei pat ki sngi kin mih,* (Like other time the days will come anew)
> *Da kumwei pat ka ri kan ih;* (In a new way the land will turn)
> *Lada ngi don ki shkor ban sngew,* (If we have ear to listen)
> *Aiu ka kren ka Mei-Ramew.* (What the mother earth has to tell).[125]

The above quotation reflects that nature communicates to the tribal people in diverse ways for helping human beings cope with the situation in different circumstances. For the tribal people, all of God's creation whether living or non living things has different stories to tell for the benefit and welfare of the people. Ramsiej precisely asserts when he states that all creations on earth like the mountains, the rivers, the trees, the rocks, etc not only possessed the scenery that exhibit the beauty and splendour of nature, but they have something to inform and enlighten the later generation with regard to the social and cultural life of the people.[126] Each of them has different stories that reflect the living condition and life experience of the people at some particular point of time.[127] It is these sort of stories passed on in oral tradition that reflects some knowledge about the religio-cultural and socio-economic life of the people. In the same vein, Mawrie further explains this view in the context of Khasi people when he states that the Khasis live in nature and the nature lives in them, with the nature they move walk and talk. Nature also communicates with human beings and shapes their thought pattern.[128] Hence, nature and human beings have a close and intimate relationship. The earlier discussion points out that God also manifest or communicate Himself/Herself to human beings through the vehicle of nature. The beauty and splendour of nature with all creations running its own course is nothing but the

---

[125] Soso Tham, *Ki Sngi Barim U Hynniew Trep* (Shillong: Ri Khasi Press, 1987), 37.

[126] K. D. Ramsiej, *Ka Mariang ha U Khasi* (Shillong: Bonsen Press, 1992), 53-54.

[127] For instance, *U Lumdiengiei* or Diengiei peak tells us about the spiritual crisis that has taken place in the life of the people because of the impact of sin after the end of the *sotti* ***Juk*** or the golden era. See Mawrie, *The Khasis and their Natural Environment*, 34-35.

[128] Mawrie, *Ka Pyrkhat U Khasi,* 78.

revelation of the presence of God in the universe.[129] Nature has therefore offered a place where human beings could reach to and communicate with their creator. Mawrie further made it clear when he affirms that nature served as a medium of communication where one can send his/her petitions or supplications to God for their diverse needs. But this does not mean that tribal people worship nature, rather it implies that as nature manifests the presence of God, so also it becomes a sacred place where humans could communicates and reach to his/her Creator.[130] This indicates that there is close intimate and interrelationship that connect God, human and nature.

Tribal People and Forests

Forests occupy a major place in the life of the tribal people. The tribal ancestral parents have deep wisdom with much awareness that forests not only provided fuel for cooking or timber and grass for house building rather they also supply pure air and clean water. This enables them to have abundant knowledge about forests. They also pay deep respect to them and make all efforts to preserve and protect them. The Khasis like other tribal groups, since time immemorial developed the idea of forest conservation, for they understand that different creations cannot live without forest but have to depend on forest resources for their various needs.[131] Rymbai maintains that Khasi ancestors/ancestress foresee the importance of conserving and preserving forests not only for life sustenance, but also to maintain the ecological balance of nature and environment. As he rightly puts it,

> There must, therefore, always be a sufficient green cover of trees for mother earth to maintain balance of nature, in order to provide human with his/her basic necessities for sustaining life-not only wood for building and domestic use, but also for pure air and water.[132]

Accordingly, for the benefits of the later generations and also for maintaining the balance of the eco-system, our ancestral parents preserved different types of forests in different parts of the land. Ancient forests can be generally classified into two categories-i) Sacred Groves and ii) Other Reserved forest.

Sacred Groves

Like many traditional societies, sacred groves are part and parcel of the religio-cultural life of the Khasi people. The idea of conserving the sacred groves among the Khasis originated since time immemorial. Nevertheless, it may be noted

[129] Mawrie, *Ka Pyrkhat U Khasi,* 5.

[130] Mawrie, *Ka Theology ka Niam Khasi,* 66-67.

[131] Hayong, "The Khasi Concept of Ecology," 95.

[132] Rymbai, "The traditional Ecological Concepts of the Khasi-Pnars," 17.

that sacred groves are not found in Khasi-Jaintia alone, but it is the customary practices of the primal societies to protect and preserve these types of forests.[133] In India the origin of preserving the sacred groves can be traced back even before the Vedic Age.[134] It is believed that in the past, each village has their respective sacred groves. Today, there are only 79 sacred groves in different parts of Khasi-Jaintia Hills and the area of each individual sacred groves differ between 0.01 ha and 900 ha.[135] Sacred Groves have been closely linked with different aspects of tribal life like social, cultural, and religious and so on. This could be noticed with the existence of numerous monoliths near the site where the sacred groves are situated. There are different varieties of rites, rituals and religious ceremonies associated with these forests.[136] These forests are found mainly in areas where non Christians reside.

In most traditional societies, sacred groves are preserved since time immemorial for the belief that they are the dwelling place of the deities. In Khasi Jaintia Hills, sacred groves are kept for the belief that they are the abode of *U Basa* the guardian spirit of God. Hence, they are considered sacred.[137] The concept and sanctity of life within the parameter of the sacred groves are well preserved. Similarly, felling of trees or even cutting the branches, killing or hurting any kind of animals or birds within the domain of the sacred groves is strictly prohibited.[138] Even while hunting any animals or chasing a snake, once they enter inside the sacred groves they are left undisturbed. This perception is correlated with the conviction that these groves are the residing place of the guardian spirit of God. Hence, any sort of action that violates these norms will hurt the sentiment of the deity, thereby inviting unnecessary penalty from the deities who looks after these forests.[139] Consequently, besides providing safe haven for the peaceful co-existence of all living creatures, these virgin forests also served as a rich biodiversity and sanctuary for diverse kinds of rare and endangered plants and other species like

---

133 In India sacred groves are found in Chotanagpur area, Marwar, Ajmer, Bikaner area of Rajasthan, and Bastar region of Madhya Pradesh. See P. S. Ramakhrishnan, "Conserving the Sacred for Biodiversity: The Conceptual Framework," in *Conserving the Sacred: For Biodiversity Management,* edited by P. S. Ramakhrisnan, K. G. Saxena and U.M. Chandrasekhar (New Delhi: Oxford & IBH Publishing CO.PVT.LTD., 1998), 4.

134 Ramakhrishnan, "Conserving the Sacred for Biodiversity…," 4.

135 B.K. Tiwari, S. K. Barik and R. S. Tripathi, "Sacred Groves of Meghalaya" in *Conserving the Sacred: For Biodiversity Management,* edited by P. S. Ramakrishnan, K. G. Saxena and U. M. Chandrasekhar (New Delhi: Oxford & IBH Publishing CO. PVT. LTD., 1998), 255-256.

136 Hayong, "The Khasi Concept of Ecology," 96.

137 L. H. Pde, *Ka Law Lyngdoh bad ka Knia Phodsohlang* (Shillong: Kaiser Mussinghoff Schuetz, 1994), 10.

138 Hayong, "The Khasi Concept of Ecology," 96.

139 Hayong, "The Khasi Concept of Ecology," 96.

orchids.[140] Moreover, as most of these sacred groves are located in the catchment areas, they also help protect the source of major rivers besides maintaining the quality of water downhill.[141] Hence, the presence of sacred groves not only provides pure air and clean water, but also maintains the balance of the entire eco-system.

Other Reserved Forests

Apart from the sacred groves, there are other types of forests that were preserved by the Khasis down through the centuries. The function of these forests is totally different from that of the sacred groves. These reserved forests comprise *Ki Law Adong* (prohibited forests) and *Ki Law Shnong* (Village forests). These types of forest are kept aside for the the needs of the community and the needs of different families with in the *Raid* or the village. In the case of the former, felling of trees is permitted with certain restriction, in case a family faces misfortune like loss of their house due to natural calamities and other causes, as an act of helping them to rebuild their houses. In the case of the latter, members of the village are permitted to cut down trees, for different needs like firewood, timber for house building and the like. Hence, with regards to the sacred groves, it is strictly forbidden to use any forest materials, whereas in other reserved forests using of forest materials are allowed with certain restrictions. This reflects the wisdom of the ancestral parents in their way of understanding not only for the needs of the individual families but also the needs of the entire eco-system.

God-Human-Nature Continuum

For the tribal people the entire cosmos and its habitat is the creation of God. They are one and indivisible. They are aware that the whole universe and everything here on earth and up there in the sky are interrelated and interconnected.[142] As stated earlier, the story of *Ka Krem Lamet Latang* of the Khasis portrays that the sun and the moon even came to participate in the dance festival arranged during the time when all creatures spoke one language or what the Khasis term

---

[140] Tiwari held that the sacred groves are home of "so rare and endangered plant species and as many as 514 species representing 340 genera and 131 families were present in these forests." See Tiwari et al., Sacred Groves of Meghalaya, 256.

[141] For Instance, the sacred groves at Shillong peak, is situated in the area where eight main rivers and streams originated and supply drinking water to number of villages and parts of Shillong city. See Tiwari et al., Sacred Groves of Meghalaya, 256.

[142] Different tribal groups have different myths and stories with regards to human relationship with the heavenly bodies like the sun, the moon, the stars, etc. See Yangkahao Vashum, "The Stars are our relatives: Tribal/Indigenous People's Stellar Theology" in *Doing Tribal Christian Theology with Tribal Resources: Cultural Resources from North East India,* edited by Razouselie Lasetsoe and Eyindbeni Humtsoe (Jorhat: ETC Programme Coordinator, 2009), 178.

as *sotti juk* the golden age[143] All creations both living and non living, animate or inanimate, have close relationship with their creator and the natural environment that surround them. For them, God, human and nature cannot be separated. This intrinsic and symbiotic relationship of God-Human-Nature implies that all realities are interconnected, interrelated and interdependent on one another. This sort of relationship is not in hierarchical order where one group is above the other. At the same time, it does not indicate anywhere about the primacy or superiority of human beings over the other species. Thanzauva maintains that this type of relationship is not to be understood as that of "vertical and horizontal relationship" but in terms of a "circle in which all are parts of the whole community."[144] In other words, it implies that in a circle "there is no beginning or end" but different parts are integrally connected and have equal value.[145] There is a thread of interrelationship that connecs and binds together all forms of reality. Each and every being have their own dignity and worth in their respective space and environment. They have specific role to play for the smooth functioning of the entire eco-system that need to be recognized, cherished and appreciated. Tribals believe in a democracy of life where even a small and tiny creature like an ant, have equal rights and respect like an elephant does.[146] All creatures either big or small have something to contribute to the good and well being of life. Therefore any attempt to obstruct or restrict the flow of life means insult against the orderliness of life in the entire eco-system. Commenting on this holistic view of reality Vashum rightly argues,

> There is no distinction between sacred and secular, physical and spiritual, earthly and heavenly. All together, constitute the wholeness of life. If one is affected all other also affected. According to this vision of life, all forms of life are interrelated to one another and they all constitute an organic unity.[147]

Hence, according to tribal worldview there is no dichotomy that separated sacred and secular, holy and profane, all form the holistic aspect of reality. All creations living and non-living, big and small are organically related and intrinsically interconnected to each other. Hence, if one is affected the entire eco-

---

[143] Mawrie, *The Essence of Khasi Religion,* 6-7.

[144] Thanzauva, *Theology of Community*, 199.

[145] A. Wati Longchar, "A Critics of Christian Theology of Creation," in *Doing Theology with Tribal Resources,* edited by A. Wati Longchar and Larry E. Davies (Jorhat: Tribal Study Centre, 1999), 73.

[146] J. War, "The Khasi Concept of Nature," in *Religion and Society* 42/3 (September 1995): 57-58.

[147] Yangkahao Vashum, "A Thankhul Myth of Creation: Implication of a Holistic view of Human Right," in *The Tribal Worldview and Ecology,* edited by A. Wati Longchar and Yangkahao Vashum (Jorhat: Tribal Study Centre, 1998), 37.

system is affected. At the same time any attempt to exploit or misuse the earth resources is tantamount to self destruction.

Tribal Eco-Spirituality in Today's Context

The above discussion, illustrates the eco-spirituality of the tribal people as perceived by the ancestors/ancestresses. It clearly reflects their wisdom in understanding the importance of preserving nature not only as a source of livelihood, but also in maintaining the balance of the entire eco-system. Nevertheless, with the influence of the outside forces such an understanding gradually diminishes in the present day tribal society. In other words, with the impact of colonization/modernization, Christianization and most recently by the present phase of globalization, the relationship between the present day tribal people and nature has undergone significant changes. With their mind being colonized and globalised the present day tribal society lost its respect and care for the nature and environment. Nature and its resources are no more perceived as valuable sources that sustain life, but merely as commodities to be exploited for attaining quick profit.[148] Such a perception has not only destroyed the sustainable sources of livelihood but also damaged the delicate balance of the eco-system that has been preserved by our ancestral parents since time immemorial. Basaiawmoit argues that the present day tribal society tended to extract the entire earth resources that has been preserved by our ancestors/ancestress for quick and maximum profit without taking into consideration the needs and natural right of the future generation.[149] Admittedly, having been influenced by the material/cosmopolitan culture proposed by the present phase of globalization, the present day tribal people tend to ignore the ecological/economic wisdom of our ancestors/ancestress thereby damaging not only the sources of livelihood but also threaten and put at risk the well being of the other members of the cosmos at a faster rate than expected. Hence, if the process of globalization is to be corrected ancient ecological/economic wisdom of the tribal people need to be seriously taken into consideration. This does not mean to go back to the past but to make use some of the available resources that have the potential to counter the ill effects of globalization in the process of building up a good, healthy and participatory community. To state differently, traditional tribal ancient wisdom that are liberative, life affirming, inclusive and accommodative offer other alternative not only for harmonious relationship but specifically for economic survival of the tribal people.

---

[148] Notably, in the present era of globalization only a small section of the tribal community together with the big companies making all efforts to extract the natural resources of the land that has threaten the survival of the entire human life and the environment around at great risk. The worst sufferers are the marginalised poor and vulnerable section of the society.

[149] Interview with Rev. Dr. P B M Basaiawmoit on the 9th May 2012 at his residence.

Tribal Eco-Spirituality versus Globalization: A Theological Reflection

The above discussion on the eco-spirituality of the tribal people reflects a deep and profound ecological wisdom of the ancestral parents. However, with the influence of the outside force land that has been home of the tribals for many centuries has been exploited and misused. The earth and forest resources that have been the life sustenance of the tribals are being destroyed. Hence the whole life and ecological relations is under threat. In the 1980s, the propagators of globalization used the famous dictum, "There is no alternative (TINA) to globalization." Nevertheless, a closer look into the tribals traditional way of life reveals that there are ample resources from the tribal traditional value system that can provide alternatives. This entails the necessity to recapture and reinterpret the ecological wisdom of our ancestors/ancestress that could benefit not only the human community but also could contribute to the health of the entire nature and environment. It is believed that reinterpretation of the eco-spirituality of the tribal people will not only correct the pitfalls of globalization but also has the capability to instill in the mind of the present day tribal society to strive towards a better life without ignoring the health of the eco-system.

Tribal Concept of Nature: A Theological Reconsideration

As discussed earlier, the ancient wisdom of our forefathers/mothers are in tune with the well being of human as well as that of nature. But the present day tribal society with special reference to the Khasis has lost their respect and reverence for nature. With their mind being colonized and globalised, land and natural resource turn into commodities to be exploited.[150] Nature has lost its value and worth bestowed by its creator. Its value and worth lies only in its potential to serve for the good and welfare of human community.[151] Hence, for the advocates of globalization land has no value at all. The natural world ceased to be considered and has lost its value and importance.[152] Such ideology that ignores and disregards the importance of nature has its root in the enlightenment period.[153] The enlightenment thinkers believed that through reason and empirical research,

---

[150] For instance, though the government allowed a maximum of 2 million tons per year for the Lafarge Company to extract the limestone for its cement company at Chattak, people of Nongtrai want to increase it to 3 million tons for quick profit. (Discussion with the Nongtrai Focus group at Nongtrai on the 11 May, 2012). On another occasion, Wansalan Hayong a truck driver usually transporting the limestone from War Jaintia area to Bangladesh once told the researcher that limestone mines meant for exploitation. There is no use to let them undisturbed but has to be mined for quick profit. (Discussion with Wansalan Hayong at Sohkha on the 18 May, 2012.

[151] H. Paul Santmire, *The Travail of Nature* (Philadelphia: Fortress Press, 1985), 133-134.

[152] Cobb Jr., *The Earthist Challenge to Economism: A Theological Critique of the World Bank*, 36.

[153] The term "Enlightenment" is referred to the European intellectual and cultural movement of the seventeenth and eighteenth century. Scholars define enlightenment as the "Age of Reason," or "The Age of Critique" where human reason take the centre stage. See E. Sreedharan, *A Text Book*

humans have the capacity to control and comprehend the universe. Human reasoning power is potentially capable to "pluck the mystery of the universe" and lead people into a happy and blessed future.[154] Kant even went to the extent of declaring that the "scientist has to torture nature to extract her secrets."[155] Driven by the ideologies of neoliberalism, the process of globalization takes steps ahead in capturing all available opportunities for attaining quick profit. In the process not only are the impoverished poor being pushed to the periphery but the entire nature has been damaged and fractured. Hence, theology of nature from the tribal perspectives provides some viable alternatives in an attempt to recapture the importance of land and nature in the present era of globalization.

The Concept of Mother Earth

As stated earlier, like many tribal groups, the Khasis called the mother earth as *Ka Mei Ramew* or ka *Meirilung Ka Meirisan.* Both these concepts illustrate the importance of mother earth not only as source of livelihood, but also as the one who takes care, nurtures, fosters and brings up the entire creation. This indicates that role of the earth as mother always endeavors to promote and foster the flow of life. Like a mother who is always concerned for the well being of her children the mother earth constantly rears and nourishes the growth and development of all God's creation. From the tiny plants to the big animals, all share one's own respective and particular space within the bosom of the mother earth. Hence, it is accommodative, life affirming, nourishing, supporting and provides everything that is needed to sustain the growth of life and existence. Hence, there is no room for disrupting the flow of life and existence. Having recognized the role of mother earth in nurturing life through their intimate relationship with her, tribal people held the mother earth in high regards and reverence. This is contrary to the neoliberalism ideologies promoted by the present phase of globalization who perceived the earth and its resources as commodities to be exploited for quick profit. Theology of mother earth challenges such mentality of subjugation not only because it is pro-rich or pro-powerful, but more importantly because of the unlimited wants of human greed that desires to finish all the earth resources at the expense of the future generation. It is such a mentality that threatens not only the life of humanity but the entire eco-system. To be specific it is against the smooth flowing of life especially the vulnerable sections of the earth community. If one takes the earth as mother he/she would certainly pay deep homage and respect to her rather than unmindful exploiting its entire resources for one's selfish motive.

---

of Historiography (New Delhi: Orients Blachswan Private Limited 2009), 107. See also Christopher Norris, *The Truth about Post Modernism* (Oxford: Blackwell Publishers, 1993), 65.

[154] Sreedharan, *A Text Book of Historiography,* 107.

[155] Colin E. Gunton, *The Triune Creator* (Cambridge: William B. Eerdmans Publishing Co., 1998), 127.

Concept of Stewardship

Against the backdrop of economic globalization driven by neo-liberalism ideologies of unlimited profit that has destroyed the mother earth and its resources, tribal theology of nature advocates nature as the gift of God. Here, being the gift of God implies that humans are entrusted with the role of "stewardship" with regards to all God's creation. The creation story of the Khasis portrays that when everything that came into existence was made in order, peace and prosperity prevail, the mother earth beseech the Creator God to send someone to take care and look after all creations. It was because of the urgent plea of the mother earth that God convened the heavenly council or the *Dorbar Blei* with *Ki Khathynriew Trep Khadhynriew Skum* or the sixteen families. At the heavenly assembly, it was decided that the *Hynniew Trep Hynniew Skum* or the seven families will have to come down and perform the role of "Steward." "Stewardship" here is not earned by humans but it is the gift of God. Being the "steward" of God there are two important things involved here. First, they are free to communicate with God the Creator. Second, they are free to use but not to misuse the earth resources. Being the stewards chosen by God, humans have to be creative, inventive, innovative, productive, fruitful, and committed to the task entrusted to them. The task entrusted to them entails not merely doing for the sake of livelihood, rather it demands firm commitment in performing their duty and responsibility towards transforming nature into a better place to live in. It connotes against misusing the earth resources for one's own selfish gain at the expense of others. Citing from M.M. Thomas, Annie maintains that "human beings are created not as a finished products but to become." Hence, "human creativity in the transformation of nature is the divine vocation of humans."[156] If it is a divine vocation, humans are expected to be honest, sincere, careful, vigilant, attentive and genuine to the task entrusted to them.

Land is Life

For the tribal people, land is life. As stated earlier, selling of land especially the inherited land or *Ka Nongtymmen* is deemed as selling one's own identity.[157] But with the impact of the outside forces,[158] all these beliefs are things of the past. In today's context where the forces of globalization have penetrated every nook and corner of the globe, lots of changes have taken place in people's perception

---

[156] Annie, *Globalization and Women's Subsistence Labour: A Third World Theological Perspective,* 91.

[157] Cf. Sngi Lyngdoh, *Ki Riti-Khyndew ba la buh u Longshwa-Manshwa jong ka Ri Bhoi* (Shillong: Ribhoi *Dorbar*, 1965), 5.

[158] As stated earlier, with the impact of colonization, modernization, westernization, Christianization as well as the present phase of globalization lot of changes have taken place in the life and practices of the tribals in general and Khasi people in particular.

on land. Two among several changes will be discussed here. First, in the process of globalization, people are divided between the rich and the poor, the urban and rural, and the haves and the haves-not. Hence, a tiny section of the rich section tended to purchase whatever land available not only in the urban areas for economic purpose[159] but even in the rural areas for establishing their farm house.[160] Boff argues that, "A minority owned the best land; the poorest land was left for the majority who, in order to survive, has to exploit and exhaust the soil, thereby, causing deforestation and disrupting the natural equilibrium."[161]

Second, with the price of land increasing rapidly on one hand and the influence of cosmopolitan or material culture on the other, people are tempted to sell their land even at the expense of their sources of livelihood.[162] By the time they realize their mistake, they are already alienated from their land. Being alienated from their land means they have lost their identity and lost their personhood. Moreover, as their sources of livelihood are cut off, the living conditions of the tribal people is transformed into a sub-human one. Hence, "The ownership of land and alienation from land" argues Minz "has theological implications for the tribal."[163]

Tribal theology of land challenges the practices of neo-colonial forces that led to the exploitation of both humans and nature. It advocates the necessity to recapture and reinterpret the importance of land as source of life and identity for the present day struggles of tribal people. In his article "The Challenge of the Old Testament Prophets to Economic Structures," Thondiparambil rightly argues that there are two types of theological reflections that need to be taken into consideration-the first legislative and the second prophetic.[164] In the case of the latter, it is regrettable but true that the Church in Khasi Jaintia Hills till today is indifferent and does not take any initiative to respond to the daily struggle of the people especially the poor and the needy. Commenting on the attitude of the Church in Khasi Jaintia, Kharlukhi affirms that the Church confines itself only

---

[159] In the urban areas people rich people buy land for things related with commercial profits and advantages.

[160] For instance, even it is clearly stated in the clause no. 6 of the Ri Bhoi Land Tenure System that "no land can be bought or sold in the Bhoi area," today maximum areas of land in the Ri Bhoi region are bought by the rich section of Khasi people especially from the urban areas to establish their farm house. Cf. Lyngdoh, *Ki Riti-Khyndew ba la buh u Longshwa-Manshwa jong ka Ri Bhoi,* 16.

[161] Leonardo Boff, "Social Ecology: Poverty and Misery," in *Eco Theology: Voices from South and North,* edited by David G. Hallman (Geneva: WCC Publications, 1994), 241.

[162] Discussion with Presbyter Gympad from Lumshnong at his residence in Shillong on the 21 May 2012.

[163] Minz, "Tribal perspectives on Ecology," 4.

[164] Joseph Thondiparambil, "The Challenge of the Old Testament Prophets to Economic Structures" in *Theology of Economics in the Globalized World: Indian Approaches* edited by Jacob Parappally & Antony Kaliath (Bangalore: Indian Theological Association,2010), 41.

within the four walls of the church building and has failed in its prophetic mission of standing against diverse kind of injustices that is affecting every fabric of the society.[165] To state differently, helping the impoverished poor and uplifting the standard of living of the vulnerable section of the society does not seem to be the agenda of the Church.[166]

With regards to the former, tribal land and nature need strong legal protection both from the state and central government. It may be noted that most of the land inhabited by the tribal people are rich in mineral resources.[167] So, it is the same with the Khasi people of North East India. As stated earlier, in the era of globalization where rapid race for competition is taking place, one could witness the increasing number of big companies that come to establish their cement companies especially in Jaintia hills.[168] These companies are not only rich and could invest big amount of capital, but also receive lots of incentives from the state government.[169] Hence, unless strong legal protection given to the tribal land and people, not only the people will suffer but the entire area will turn into a desert. Basaiawmoit argues that the state needs to urgently legislate a strong Act, not only to curb the exploitative policies of the big and corporate giants, but also in order to safeguard the right of the indigenous people as well as the entire environment.[170] On the other hand, Blah maintains that the current Industrial Policy of the State government has many loopholes. Hence, he calls for "an urgent need to review and re-design the industrial policy" with important points that need to be included. And these important points are,

- Social Responsibilities of private companies.
- Ecological Responsibilities of Private companies.
- The State government does not promote industries which extract resources at the cost of the future generation, and where the social-ecological threat is more than short term benefits.[171]

---

[165] Discussion with Dr. Bajubon Kharlukhi one of the prominent Church Elders in Shillong on the 2nd May, 2012.

[166] The Church till today collecting special fund for the poor and the needy but it is only a temporary or occasional help when needs arise, but not a long term involvement for improving their standard of living.

[167] For instance, tribal areas of Jharkhand are rich in mineral resources that attracted big and corporate companies to rush for establishing their firms there.

[168] But other companies like Lafarge companies came only to extract the mineral resources from Nongtrai areas for feeding its cement companies at Bangladesh.

[169] As stated earlier, after deducting the royalties and Meghalaya Value Added Tax (MVAT) to the tune of 39.87 crores to the state government, Star Cement is still earning a profit of 97.88 crores. See "Cement Cos in M'laya adopt extractive, exploitative Policy," *The Shillong Times* 26 July, 2012.

[170] Discussion with Basaiawmoit at Mawpat on the 9 May, 2012.

[171] Toki Blah, *Good Governance for Transformation and Development of Meghalaya* (Shillong: ICARE, 2007), 13.

The above discussion highlights the fact that there is a pressing need for strong laws that could safeguard both the indigenous local population and the entire nature and environment from the rapid exploitation of the neo-colonial forces.

Sacred Groves Model

As stated earlier, with the aim to achieve maximum profit in a short span of time the process of globalization goes on to exploit the earth resources at faster rate than expected. This resulted in the imbalance in the eco system. In such a context, the sacred groves provide a relevant model to preserve the deteriorating condition of nature. In the sacred groves all creations, both living and non-living have their own dignity and respect as God's creation. All creations live together as a family in a peaceful atmosphere of unity and harmony. This harmony is maintained properly and never once disturbed even till a century back. The earth's resources are free from any sort of exploitation and damage from the outside forces. Hence, the conception of the importance, dignity, and respect of all creations resulted in ecological balance in the entire eco-system. To state differently, recognition of the value and importance of each creation is necessary in order to save the earth from further destruction. All these understanding is well fitted and well kept within the vicinity of sacred groves till today.

Redefining the Concept of Harmonious Relationship

In the present day era of globalization where the ecological crisis has threatened humans' life and the entire eco-system, the concept of harmonious relationship need to be re-defined. According to the tribal worldview everything is essentially interrelated to each other. That is, tribal worldview portrays the unity and integrity that link together God, human and nature. Hence, the entire earth and its resources are considered sacred. Nevertheless, with the influence of outside forces in the present day era, this understanding has increasingly diminished and ignored if not totally abandoned among the tribal people. Nevertheless, the spirit of harmonious relationship can be witnessed within the parameter of the sacred groves till today. As stated earlier, the belief that the presence of *U Ryngkew U Basa* or the deity make the people to consider them as sacred and holy. This has enabled the people to maintain the sanctity and sacredness of these groves without any interruption till today. It may be noted that though the entire surrounding becoming barren and desolate, sacred groves remain as a living symbol of the unity and integrity of the entire reality like God, human and nature. It is within the domain of sacred groves that harmonious relationship of all things that exist is vividly portrayed. To state differently, different kinds of plants, trees, grass, flora and fauna share their respective space without disturbing each other within a safe environment. To state differently, each and every creation has its own dignity and respect within the groves. Hence, peace, security and harmony prevailed and all creations share and experience a secured and safe environment without any disturbance.

In the present day situation where the earth and all creations are facing the danger and threat of ecological crisis, redefining the concept of harmonious relationship is not only a must but a necessity. According to the tribal tradition, though the sacred groves are set aside as sacred, in actuality the entire earth and its resources are considered sacred. The belief that God manifests him/herself in the earth means that God is integral part of the entire creation. Hence, God's presence cannot be limited within specific location.[172] But God's presence is manifested by the entire creation. This means each and every creation has its own dignity and respect. If human beings realize the dignity and worth of the created order as a whole, they will not misuse but use them wisely with utmost care and concern. In any attempt to strive for harmonious relationship, recognition of the value and worth of other creations must be taken seriously. It is therefore a call to rediscover and "affirm our interrelatedness with nature and commit ourselves to honour the integrity of creation."[173] Rediscovering our interrelatedness with other creations is nothing but to realize our duty and responsibility towards them. It is therefore an urgent call to realize our responsibility to the entire eco-system and this should be expressed in real *metanoia*. According to David C. Scott *metanoia* or conversion here means "that we discover the finitude of nature as a balance of elements which together harmonize the support of life for all parts of the community of creation."[174] Harmonious relationship could be made possible only when we begin to realize, recognize, and appreciate the value and worth of other creation.

According to the creation account of the Khasis, when God sent the *Hynniew Trep* or the seven families to take care of the earth and other creation, the entire creation experienced peace, security, and harmony. The creation narratives portray that this sort of harmonious relationship could be made possible only when they have close relationship with God and other creation. The moment they disobey God's commandment and turn away from God the relationship is broken and humans and other creation experienced misery and gloom. In similar vein, the creation account of Genesis reveals that as long as Adam and Eve, the first humans obey God's commandment there is peace and harmony in the entire Eden garden. But the time they broke God's instruction they began to realize that peace, security and harmony began to fade away in their midst. Hence, if harmonious relationship is to be experienced, right relationship with God and

---

[172] R. D. Mawia Ralte, "An enquiry into the Divine, Human, Nature Relationship in the North East Indian Primal Religious Traditions and Its Contemporary Relevance," in *Sathri Journal: A Journal of Contextual Theology* VI/1 (April 2012): 78.

[173] K. C. Abraham, "Theological Response to Ecological Crisis," *Bangalore Theological Forum* XXV/1 (March, 1993): 13.

[174] David C. Scott, "Some Reflection on a Theological Response to Ecological Crisis," *Bangalore Theological Forum* XXV/1, (March, 1993): 21.

other creation need to be rediscovered. Here, the concept of *Tipbriew Tipblei* or the biblical mandate to love God as well as our neighbour have to be taken seriously into consideration. The concept of *Tipbriew Tipblei* is therefore not to be limited within the domain of humans but has to be included the nature and environment as well as our neighbour.

Earth is our Home

Another important characteristic of the sacred groves is that it offers a safe and secure home or dwelling place to all of God's creation. In the present day theological debate, a new way of looking at the earth emerged. That is, the whole natural environment is not only a place where each one can simply share a space, but the earth is considered as home for all God's creation. It is the *oikos* of God or a big family of all God's creation. Notably, with the development of science and technology supported by "exploitative economic system" to achieve "unlimited material progress" the earth as our home suffers to the maximum.[175] As it is a home, all members are responsible and accountable to its well being. This indicates that each and every component either living or non-living, in some way or the other contribute to the health of the *oikos* of God. To state differently, each member both living and non-living things has a role to play in making it more habitable and accommodative, so that all can share the joy and happiness offered by their dwelling place. Such was an atmosphere one could find within the ambit of the sacred groves. Commenting on the new way of looking at the mother earth Joseph rightly argues,

> Our relationship with the earth should be informed by an emotional attachment that we have towards our home. When one starts to dismantle the window frame solely for economic gain, that action not only amounts to the abuse of membership of the household, but also is an act of violence against the rights of other members to have a protective environment.[176]

He further asserts that a home is and should be a place that sustains life, allow its members to blossom freely, welcome new life and foster the continuing flow of life. At the same time, a home is a place that strengthens the bond of relationship to all its members without allowing anyone to feel as strangers.[177] This implies that all components within the *oikos* of God need to reconsider the importance and worth of each member, thereby strengthening the bond of brotherly and sisterly relationship so that the earth becomes a better place or home for all God's creation. Robra et al demonstrates that "earth was meant to

---

[175] M. P. Joseph, "Where is your Sister/Brother? Carbon Civilization defiles Faith in God," in *A Christian Response to Ecological Crisis,* edited by Thomas Samuel and Mathew Koshy Punnakadu (Thiruvalla: Christava Sahitya Samithy, 2009), 74.

[176] Joseph, "Where is your Sister/Brother?...," 74.

[177] Joseph, "Where is your Sister/Brother? ...," 74.

be home for all living creatures, existing in different spaces but linked to each other in a web of relationships. The human community is placed within the wider community of the earth, which is embedded in God's household of life."[178] This entails that all members need to be treated as equals. Hence, exploitative or abusive relationship by one member to any of the constituents either living or non-living has to be ridden off, so that each and every one will be able to enjoy the welcome atmosphere and secure environment.

Theology of Conservation

An understanding of harmonious relationship within the *oikos* of God gives way to a new rediscovery of the inherent system of conservation. This is vividly revealed in the ideology of conservation of the sacred groves by our ancestors/ ancestress. As stated earlier, Rymbai affirms that "Our ancestors [sic] were divinely inspired to know that trees cannot live without land, nor land can remain without trees."[179] This indicates their wisdom to understand that the earth is the system that supports life. It is against the ideology of neo-liberalism promoted by the agencies of economic globalization which portray the earth and its resources as commodities to be exploited for maximum profit. For them, the well being of humanity lies in their capability to preserve the natural surrounding around them, because, all creations are integrally related and inter-dependent on one another. Hence, they made all efforts to preserve the environment so that all forms of life can flourish and blossom within a secured atmosphere. Commenting on the need to preserve the natural environment Rayan rightly argues when he states,

> To live and act is to breathe the air, to drink some water, to eat fruits, roots, seeds, leaves, etc. We depend on the minerals, plants, animals, these depend on a thousand cosmic, physical, chemical, magnetic factors, forces processes and interaction.[180]

The above quotation reveals the importance and worth of each and every part of the earth resources. They are meant to be used, not to be misused for economic exploitation as practiced by the neo-colonial forces or the agencies of globalization. Hence, they are supposed to be preserved not for the sake that they are useful to human beings, rather because they have the capability to contribute to the health of the entire eco-system. In the present day era of globalization where the earth and its resources are left at the mercy of neo-colonial forces, the ethics of conservation as revealed in the sacred groves model need to be

---

[178] Martin Robra, Deenabandhu Manchala and Sarah Anderson-Rajarigam, "Affirming Life for the Disregarded Many," in *Earth Habitat: Eco-Injustice and the Church's Response,* edited by Dieter T, Hessel and Larry L. Rasmussen (Augsberg: Fortress Press, 2001), 87.

[179] Rymbai, "The traditional Ecological Concepts of the Khasi –Pnars," 15.

[180] Samuel Rayan, "Ecology and Faith: The Mystery of the Earth" in *National Council of Churches Review* CXI (October, 1991): 1281.

reconsidered. Notably, while the ancestors/ancestress of the tribals are able to preserve and protect the life of the sacred groves intact as virgin forests without any disturbance, they also conserved other forest for the needs of the community like *Ki Law Adong* or the restricted forests. With regards to the latter, it reflects their well thought vision for the urgent needs of the members of the community that may arise from time to time. Whereas in the case of the former, it reflects their wisdom to clearly understand the need for maintaining the balance of the eco system thereby became the safe havens for the flora and fauna to exist in peace and harmony. Here we see the ecological wisdom of the ancestors/ancestresses to preserve the harmony of life between humans and the natural environment. To state differently, it implies a deep thought on the unity of reality or the interrelatedness and interdependence of God-Human-Nature continuum.

Moreover, sacred groves not only help to maintain the fertility and quality of the soil or help preventing soil erosion rather they have the potential to provide pure air and pure drinking water to many villages. Notably, most of the sacred groves are located in the catchment areas the origin of major rivers or perennial streams. For example, the sacred groves at Shillong peak are situated in the areas where eight main rivers and streams originated and supply drinking water to numbers of inhabitants living downhill.[181] In short, in the sacred groves model, the balance of the environment is realized. Theology of conservation challenges the vision of neo-colonial forces that strive forward for unlimited economic profit by damaging not only the source of livelihood but also in destroying the delicate balance of the whole eco-system. The well being of the community largely depends on the health of the natural surroundings. Hence destroying the natural surrounding amounted not only to damaging the source of livelihood rather it implies destroying one's own self. In other words, it is an insult to the community as a whole and to God the Creator of everything that exists.

Holistic View of Reality versus Globalization

The essential element of tribal worldview is the presence of holistic view of reality. In the era of globalization where the dichotomy between the sacred and secular, holy and profane, God and the world became prevalent, tribal holistic view of reality offers other alternatives in saving the mother earth from further destruction. The holy-profane dichotomy that is widespread in the present era in the tribal society is not basically developed from the tribals,[182] but has its origination in the modern period.[183] Modern thinker like Rene Descartes, mathematically divided the reality

---

[181] For detail see Tiwari et.al., "Sacred Groves of Meghalaya," 256.

[182] Ralte, "An Enquiry into the Divine, Human, Nature Relationship...," 73.

[183] But modern period does not developed in a vacuum. Some important significant movement that contributed to its development are Renaissance Movement, Deism and Enlightenment period. Renaissance Movement stress more on social justice by giving more emphasized on the primacy of human beings at the expense of other realities like God and Nature. See S.L Doshi, *Modernity,*

into different parts like human mind (*gognitio*) and physical things (*Extentio*) or the material things. For him, the sum total of each part of reality resulted in the whole reality itself.[184] Vanhoozer argues that for Descartes "human subjectivity acquires foundational status, the doctrine of God becomes an implication of some aspect of man [sic]."[185] On the other hand, Gunton see the danger of Descartes' separation of God from the world, which he argues as influenced by the Deists. That is, if God is found necessary just to "regulate the order of the universe" God's service may not be necessary for the continuous involvement in the overall affairs of the universe, except when the universe has some defects.[186] When such view on reality emerged, the unity of God-Human-Nature got fractured. With the process of globalization gaining momentum this dichotomy is being widened to the maximum extent. Hence, as the world is separated from both God and human in modern age, the world is viewed as a commodity to be exploited for maximum economic profit. The outcome of such practice led to the crisis to the entire eco-system that has threatened the life of both humans and the mother earth.

This is against the tribal understanding of the holistic view of reality. For the tribals all realities are interconnected and interdependent on one another. They are not fragmented entities or the sum total of different unit that have no connection at all; rather they are intrinsically or organically interrelated and interdependent to one another. They are one and constitute the wholeness of life. As they are interrelated with each other, if one is affected the other also will suffer. Commenting on the holistic view of reality Nirmal rightly describes it when he states,

> The *Oikos* therefore, is an intricate nexus of several such ecosystems. The ecosystems are both small and large; microscopic as well as macroscopic. Not only eco-systems but also organisms could be divided into micro-organisms

---

Post Modernity and Neo-Sociological Theories (Jaipur: Rawat Publications, 2006), 15. See also John W. Riggs, *Post Modern Christianity,* (Harrisburg: Trinity Press International, 2003), 56. Richard A. Young, *Healing the earth* (Nashville: Broadman and Hallman Publishers, 1994), 142. Deism is another movement that upheld human reason as the only way of discovering truth and separated the connection of God with nature who stay away from the affairs of the earth. See Stanley J. Grenz and Roger E. Olson, *Twentieth Century Theology,* (Secunderabad: OM Books, 2004), 23. See also Roger E. Olson, *The Story of Christian Theology,* (Secunderabad: OM Books, 1999), 519. Enlightenment is another movement that upholds the importance of human reason, ignoring the place of God in the universe. E. Sreedharan, *A Text Book of Historiography,* (New Delhi: Orients Blackswan Private Limited, 2009), 107. See also Paulus Mar Gregorious, *A Light too Bright: The Enlightenment Today* (Albany: State University of New York Press, 1992), 33. Grenz and Olson, *Twentieth Century Theology,* 17.

[184] Young, *Healing the Earth*, 45.

[185] Kevin Vanhoozer, "Human Beings, Individual and Social," in Golin E. Gunton, *The Cambridge Companion to Christian Doctrine,* (Cambridge: Cambridge University Press, 1977), 159.

[186] Colin E. Gunton, *The Truine Creator* (Cambridge: William B. Eerdmans Publishing Co., 1998), 126-127.

> and macro-organisms. The important thing to remember is that the eco-systems are organismically related to each other. They affect each other and are mutually affected by each other. Environment influences organisms and is also influenced by the organisms that are its inhabitants. The *Oikos* therefore, presents a picture of mutually inter-related, inter-dependent, indwelling and inter-penetrating eco-systems.[187]

The above quotation fit well to the tribal understanding of the wholeness of life and unity of all reality. Hence, any attempt to cause injury to any parts of the *oikos* will affect the entire system of the cosmos. That is, "what harms one, harm all."[188] In the era of the present phase of economic globalization where severe exploitation and domination of the earth resources takes place the outcome will be greatly disastrous. This is what Nirmal called "ecological sinfulness or cosmic sinfulness of humans."[189] Hence, "the pattern of domination and exploitation can only lead to the silencing of nature and ecological death of both nature and humans. The new perspective affirms our interrelatedness one to another and to nature."[190] In the present day contemporary theological debate, God's existence is not perceived apart from the earth but present in everything that exist. This is true in the context of tribal theology. Tribal theology affirms the unity of all reality. Nirmal asserts that God is organismically related to His/Her creation, to His/Her cosmos.[191] In similar vein process thought also speaks against the dichotomy of reality like God and the world, holy and profane, and so on. Nalunnakkal affirms that "Process thought does not dichotomise between the 'living' and 'non-living' in a sharp manner, but only differentiates them in terms of degree of novelty.[192] Cobb and Slettom maintain that God is "persuading everything from the level of sub atomic particles to human beings to make choices that encourage the well-being of creation."[193] For the tribals, all God's creation have their own value and worth as God's creation. As they are God's creation they have their own worth in God's sight and also have close intimate relationship with God their Creator. So, mistreating them will not only affect them but also affect their intimacy with God and even God. Such ecological wisdom of the ancestral parents, need to be

---

[187] A. P. Nirmal, "Ecology, Ecumenics and Economics in Relation: A New Theological Paradigm," in *National Council of churches Review* CXI/3 (March, 1991): 883.

[188] John B. Cobb Jr and Jeanyne B. Slettom, *The Process Perspective: Frequently Asked Questions about Process Theology,* (St. Louis Missouri: Challice Press, 2003), 1.

[189] Nirmal, Ecology, "Ecumenics and Economics in Relation...," 884.

[190] K. C. Abraham, "A Theological Response to Ecological Crisis," in *Eco Theology: Voices from South and North,* edited by David G. Hallman (Geneva: WCC Publications, 1994), 70.

[191] Nirmal, "Ecology, Ecumenics and Economics in Relatio...," 884.

[192] George Matthew Nalunnakkal, *Green Liberation: Towards an integral ecotheology* (Delhi: ISPCK/NCCI, 1999), xviii.

[193] Cobb Jr and Slettom, *The Process Perspective: Frequently Asked Questions about Process Theology,* 1.

recaptured and reinterpreted for the benefit of both humans and the mother earth. If globalization is to be corrected the value and inter-relatedness of all reality need to be taken into consideration.

Panentheism

In the present day era, where the onslaught of globalization is moving swiftly, panentheism provides another model to save the earth from further destruction. Panentheism sees everything in God and "God is seen as all pervading and the ground of all being."[194] Keitzer argues that with the inadequacy of the two model, viz., the transcendental model that laid strong emphasis on God as the wholly other and the immanental model or pantheism which see that all is God and God is all, the dipolar model or panentheism seems to be the most adequate model of God. He further states that "the meeting point of these two extreme views seen to me the tribal concept of God."[195] In short tribal concept of God that emphasizes on panentheism is the most acceptable concept of God. This view is well illustrated by John Cobb in the following words:

> God's standpoint is all-inclusive, and so, in a sense, we are parts of God. But we are not parts of God in the sense that God is simply the sum total of parts or that the parts are lacking in independence and self determination. God and the creatures interact as separate entities, while God includes the standpoint of all of them in his omnispatial standpoint. In this sense God is everywhere, but he is not everything. The world does not exist outside God or apart from God, but the world is not God or simply part of God. The character of the world is influenced by God, but it is not determined by God, and the world is in turn contributes novelty and richness to the divine experience. This is Pan-en-theism.[196]

He further states that panentheism differs from both theism and pantheism. With regards to the former as it lay great emphasis on "the mutual externality of God and the world," where as in the case of the latter as it is "understood to be the identification of God and the world."[197] In other words, "whereas pantheism identifies God and the world in some way, panentheism denies that God and the world are identical, they are interdependent, a claim that distinguishes

---

[194] Renthy Keitzer, "Tribal Theological Trend in North East India" in *Tribal Theology: A Reader,* edited by Shimreingam Shimray (Jorhat: Tribal Study Centre, 2003), 46.

[195] Keitzer further states that while the Semetic religion such as Christianity, Islam and Judaism stress on the transcendency of God, the Hindus stress on the immanency of God. See Keitzer, "Tribal Theological Trend...," 47.

[196] John B. Cobb Jr, "The World and God," in *Process Theology,* edited by Ewert H. Cousins (New York: Newman Press, 1971), 164-165.

[197] Cobb Jr., "The World and God," 165.

panentheism from theism."[198] The above quotation is fitting in the tribal concept of God. For the tribals, God is not only the wholly other but he/she is very much immanent in the world. In other words, the entire earth as the creation of God, manifest the presence of the divine. Mawrie argues that it is through nature that humans communicate with the divine. This does not mean that the tribals worship nature; rather it indicates that God manifests Himself/Herself through creation.[199] Referring to the presence of God both in the above as well as below so to say the omnipresence of God in the entire universe the Khasis used to address God as *U Blei hajrong hatbian* or 'God who is above as well as below.'[200] This implies that God manifests Himself/Herself in the entire creation.

Gregory of Nyssa (335-395 AD) maintains that the wisdom and power of God is portrayed through creations. It is through the beauty and majesty of the created things that human could experience the presence of God. God, he argues is the most beautiful as well as the Supreme Good, so all things that are beautiful and good have their source from the divine. Hence creation as a whole that reflects the majesty of the divine are closely related to God the Supreme Good.[201] This realization that God is present in the universe means that the earth is sacred and sacramental. In other words it transcends the sacred-secular, holy-profane dichotomy proposed by western worldview by bringing together into a single holistic view of the unity of all realities. According to the tribal worldview all realities are holistic, so if "one is affected, all are affected."[202] Citing from the creation narrative of Genesis 1:1 where God's spirit was "brooding over the waters" Nalunnakkal maintains that panentheism is biblical.[203] Sacredness of the earth here means that creations are considered sacred not only because God declares that they are good but also because God is present in the entire creation.

If God is present in the earth, any effort to abuse or exploit the earth resources and other creation and its resources for unlimited growth and quick profit is nothing less than an insult to the divine. To state differently, it is hurting the divine who is present in the universe. John Cobb Jr., maintains that "God fully suffers with those who suffer and rejoice with those who rejoice. In Whitehead's word, God is the fellow sufferer who understands."[204] For Process Theology, God

[198] Ronald H. Nash, "Process Theology and Classical Theism," in *Process Theology,* edited by Ronald H. Nash (Michigan: Baker Book House, 1987), 14.

[199] Mawrie, *Ka Theology Jong Ka Niam Khasi,* 66.

[200] Mawrie, *Ka Theology Jong Ka Niam Khasi,* 66.

[201] William More and Henry Austin Wilson, *Select Writings and Letters of Gregory of Nyssa* (Michigan: William B. Eerdmans Publishing Company, 1988), 399.

[202] Keitzer, "Tribal Theological Trends...," 47.

[203] See George Mathew Nalunnakal, *Green Theology: Towards an Integral Ecotheology* (Delhi: ISPCK/NCCI, 1999), 249.

[204] John B. Cobb Jr, "Christology in 'Process-Relational' Perspectives," in *Word and Spirit-A Monastic Review-8: Process Theology and the Christian Doctrine of God,* edited by Santiago Sia

participates directly in the sufferings of the world and "becomes the victim of injustice and oppression rather than an aloof king."[205] John Cobb further states that all these sufferings of God seem to be revealed by and incarnate in Jesus.[206] The prologue of John's Gospel tells us about the *Logos* which is none other than God who performs different activities and identifies with all creation. "It is this *Logos*" affirms John Cobb "which had been at work in all creatures that became flesh in Jesus."[207] This indicates that the suffering of God in His/Her participation with the experience of the world is well manifested in the incarnated Jesus. To state differently, "Jesus was not an anomaly or alien in the universe and planetary life, but was the incarnation of the divine *Logos* and wisdom, present in greater or lesser degrees in all humans and planetary life."[208]

Tribal Theology may not go to the extent of saying that God participates directly in the experience and suffering of the world and humans. But their belief that God manifests Him/Herself through the universe or God is present in the world speaks volumes that any sort of oppression or exploitation to any creation is an act of insulting the Creator who enjoy in the goodness of creation. According to the tribal worldview, since God is present in the universe the entire creation is considered sacred. In today's contemporary theological debate, the world is no more perceived as "economic entity for unlimited growth" as understood by the advocates of globalization, rather it is viewed as the created world which is sacred and need to be respected by human.

Development

The term development has become an important and most discussed term among the Third World people especially the marginalised and vulnerable sections of the population like the tribals. Rongsen argues that "development as a term never exists in a vacuum." He further asserts that the term development could achieve its true meaning only when one relates it to a specific context. Hence "all development concepts are contextual."[209] Granberg and Michaelson as cited by Rongsen defines development as "to de-envelop, to unseal, to open, to free, or to remove what prevents from moving out for freedom and advancement."[210] "Development" asserts Rongsen, therefore means to "change from good to better, from less to

(Petersham: St. Bede's Publications, 1986), 92.

[205] C. Robert Mesle, *Process Theology: A Basic Introduction* (Missouri: Chalice Press, 1993), 75.

[206] John B. Cobb Jr., "Jesus and Christ in Process Perspectives" in *Handbook of Process Theology*, edited by Jay McDaniel and Donna Bowman (St. Louis: Chalice Press, 2006), 35.

[207] Cobb, Christology in Process-Relational Perspectives, 82.

[208] Bruce G. Epperly, *Process Theology: A Guide for the Perplexed* (London: T&T Clark International, 2011), 64.

[209] M. Rongsen, *Development and Ecology* (Delhi: ISPCK, 1999), 1.

[210] Rongsen, *Development and Ecology*, 1.

more, from known to unknown, for the sake of a new and better life."[211] Defining the term development in the present era of economic globalization, White and Tiongco state that the term today rarely speaks about the relationship of the poor to non-poor rather it connotes about moving from 'traditional' to 'modern' society, the growth of national income, industrial expansion, increasing availability of public utilities and so on. They further state that the term development,

> Suggest growth, progress, improvement, something to be desired. Development is therefore about values. Put cruelly, this means that in the conventional view the "advance' north is not only richer, but also morally superior to the 'backward' south. Economic growth, material accumulation and western-style modernity are the ideals to be desired, by countries and individuals.[212]

The above quotation truly expresses the contemporary understanding of the western advanced countries on the term development in western perspective. It indicates that the Third World Countries are poor, backward, illiterate, underdeveloped, or the other and are in need to follow or adopt the western model of lifestyle and advancement. That is, to be developed means to adopt or accept the western standard of living. On the other hand in his book *Development as Freedom,* Amartya Sen defines development as "a process of expanding the real freedoms that people enjoy."[213] Such an understanding of development is contrary to the present usage and perception of the term development that associates it with the growth of Gross National Product (GNP), science and technological advancement, industrialization, or in terms of economic perspective alone. Thamarassery maintains that

> This perspective of development as advancement of freedom corrects the often found tendency to define development in terms of economy alone. It is often a fallacy to associate development with economic progress. Real development goes far beyond economic benefits.[214]

The above quotation testifies that development must not be measured in terms of the growth of national economy or economic progress alone. But it must go far beyond economic development to include the entire aspect of human life. It also goes beyond achieving the basic need of the individual person of food, clothing and shelter. It entails the need to remove all barriers that enslave and keep humans under bondage as they are striving towards obtaining full humanity. In

---

[211] Rongsen, *Development and Ecology,* 2.

[212] Sarah White and Romy Tiongco, *Doing Theology and Development: Meeting the Challenge of Poverty* (Edinburgh: St. Andrew Press, 1997), 9.

[213] Amartya Sen, *Development as Freedom* (New York: Anchor Books, 1999), 3.

[214] Josey James Thamarassery, *Church Sign and Sacrament of Unity* (Kottayam: Oriental Institute of Religious Studies, 2009), 62.

sum, it speaks about transforming the persons and the society, free from any sort oppressions, suppressions, discrimination, exploitation, exclusion, and experience the fullness of life. Hence, it is people-centred development that opens the opportunities and prospects to everyone irrespective of caste, creed, and gender and so on while at the same time removes all barriers that prevent individual persons to become and experience true humanness. In short,

> ...the goal of development is not economic growth as an end in itself. The goal is full human development which involves ecological, social, ethical, cultural and spiritual as well as economic dimension. Economic activity is to be seen as a means to human development in this wider sense.[215]

Development of Tribals in the Indian Context

As stated earlier, the concept of development is based on the western perspective where the Third World countries have to "catch up" and follow the footsteps of the First World. This is made applicable even within the country in their attempt to bring development to the weaker section like the tribals. Thanzauva affirms that the "Indian intellectuals and policy makers maintained a doubled standards in applying 'Catch up' policy to tribals." That is, while they totally disagree with the term to be used in their dealings between the Third and the First World or the North and the South, the same is followed in their policies with regard to the vulnerable sections of the country.[216] The developmental activities of the Government of India, implemented in the tribal areas using the "catch up" policy and "joining the mainstream" policy[217] do not fit well in the tribal context. The concept of "catch up" as described by Thanzauva contains a dominant ideology since its origination. It indicates that some communities are more advanced and far ahead than the tribals in many respects. Hence, they are the role model for the tribals to follow. To achieve this goal, tribals have to catch up with the advanced communities in the "race for social, political and economic prosperity" through the implementation of series of Five year plan of developmental activities.[218] Longchar further elaborates this view when he states that,

> In the dominant "catch up" model, the sole criterion of judging human society is economic. It undermines the cultural and moral aspects of human society

[215] Steven C. Rockefeller, "Global Interdependence, the Earth Charter, and Christian Faith," in *Earth Habitat: Eco-Injustice and the Church's Response,* edited by Dieter T. Hessel and Larry L. Rasmussen (Augsburg: Fortress Press, 2001), 112.

[216] Thanzauva, *Theology of Community: Tribal Theology in the Making,* 47.

[217] A. Wati Longchar, "The Need for doing Tribal Theology," in *Tribal Theology: A Reader,* edited by S. Shimray (Jorhat: Tribal Study Centre, 2003), 3. See also A. Wati Longchar, *The Tribal Religious Traditions in North East India: An Introduction* Reprinted (Jorhat: Published by the Author, 2000), 163.

[218] Thanzauva, *Theology of Community: Tribal Theology in the Making,* 46.

> and projects the image of western society as a goal for civilization. When this 'catch up' theory is applied to human society, the logic is very clear. The more we are developed industrially, the higher we are up the ladder. The tribal people are industrially backward and therefore are considered inferior.[219]

Looking from the context of the tribal people one may say that while the high class/caste Indian people have taken the centre stage, the low class people like the Dalits and tribals are being pushed to the periphery. "Peripheries" defines Reid "are inhabited by an unconnected scatter of powerless, low status and poor people, whose skills and knowledge are undervalued, even when recognized by the bearers of modernity."[220]

Top-Down Model

Together with the 'catch up' theory the Indian government implemented the 'top down' model of development. "In top-down planning methods" maintains Grainger "state officials draw up plans at a national level which must be complied with at lower levels by regional and local governments."[221] In the context of the tribal people of North East India, it means everything is decided from Delhi, for the development of the tribal people and thereafter implemented in the tribal areas. Hence, tribal are not only ignored in the decision making but also not allowed to participate in the entire development activities. Thanzauva rightly argues when he states that "People become objects or recipients, not the subject of development."[222] The outcome of such practice is that a maximum number of development activities in the tribal areas became failure. As stated earlier, many of the buildings constructed by the government meant for brining development to the rural areas are rarely used or remain unutilized till they collapse. The result is even after the eleventh Five Year Plan (2007-2012), maximum number of people especially in the rural areas remains poor or many of them are even worse off than before.[223]

Bottom-up Model

With certain limitation and failure occurred with the 'top-down' approach, there is increasing requirement to search for alternative like 'bottom-up' approach. Defining the bottom-up model, Grainer states that this model is participatory

---

[219] Longchar, *The Tribal Religious Traditions in North East India: An Introduction,* 162.

[220] David Reid, *Sustainable Development: An Introduction Guide* (London: Earthscan Publications Ltd, 1995), 78.

[221] Alan Grainger, "The Role of Spatial Scale and Special Interactions in Sustainable Development," in *Exploring Sustainable Development: Geographical Perspectives,* edited by Martin Purvis and Alan Grainger (London: Earthscan Publications Limited, 2004), *78.*

[222] K. Thanzauva, *Transforming Theology: A Theological Basis for Transformation* (Bangalore: Asian Trading Corporation, 2002), 104.

[223] This is according to my own experience in my village at Sohkha.

in approach where people in particular targeted area in which development is to take place "participate actively in planning and implementation." Hence, it is a two way sharing of information both from the national level and the local targeted area level. He further states that this approach "should also lead to better implementation of a policy or project, because local people will be more enthused about something that they have helped to plan... and may assist in implementing it themselves."[224] It is believed that with the improved connection that links the national and local level this approach may not only encourage participation but it will evolve a sense of duty and responsibility to those whom developmental activities is implemented. Hence the "state planners" observes Grainer "do not just consult people at lower spatial levels, but also evolve management responsibility to them."[225] Grainer maintains that the problem with this approach is that, experience with it is not only new and limited,[226] but it does neither "provide solution to all problems that have long plagued planning" nor it can "guarantee sustainable development."[227]

Contemporary Development and Tribal People

With India opening up to globalization and the implementation of the New Economic Policy in 1991, the condition of the tribal people in general and Khasi people in particular became worse and more impoverished than before. Longchar maintains that the New Economic Policy "continues to benefit only a few privileged minority leaving more than 600 million people with a survival crisis...Such development efforts have not liberated the tribals from economic bondage."[228] As stated in Chapter IV, (point 4.4, The challenges of the present day globalization to tribal economy), the implementation of Single Window Agency by the Government of Meghalaya resulted in the mushrooming of numbers of big cement companies to exploit and extract the entire mineral resources of the land. With the co-operation and help of few handful of local people these corporate giants seem to make all efforts to finish up all the resources within a short span of time.

For the tribal people with less exposure to the outside world, the coming of these big companies seems an opportunity to bring development to their

---

[224] Alan Grainer, "The Role of Spatial Scale and Spatial Interactions in Sustainable Development" in *Exploring Sustainable Development: Geographical Perspectives,* edited by Martin Purvis and Alan Grainer (London: Earthscan Publications Limited, 2004), 78-79.

[225] Grainer, "The Role of Spatial Scale and Spatial Interactions...," 79.

[226] The Philippines' government has taken such approach to environment management since the late 1990s.

[227] Grainer,"The Role of Spatial Scale and Spatial Interactions...," 79.

[228] Longchar states that the success of this policy is that it helps the middle class people to have a sense of superiority while the tribal people are looked down as inferior in all respect. See Longchar, The Need for Doing Tribal Theology, 4.

underdeveloped local areas.[229] With their mind being colonized and globalised, land which is well respected earlier, now become a commodity for obtaining quick and temporary profits. Hence, they sell their land to these companies at a throw away price,[230] without even thinking for the next and future generation. Basaiawmoit argues that today we are living with the resources that have been preserved by our ancestral for generations but now we are trying to finish everything without thinking for the needs of future generations.[231] Now the people of Lumshnong areas not only lost their land,[232] but also became alienated from their precious land that they were associated throughout their life time. Now as their lands belong to the companies they cannot even pay a visit, for the several conditions and restrictions imposed by the companies. Hence, people became alienated from their land within their own place. What remains for them now is only their own dwelling house. Patricia Mukhim maintains that before these big and corporate companies came to the land they already did their homework by studying the strength and weakness of the tribal communities and capitalized the weakness for their own advantage. For the tribal people who are not only un-prepared for globalization and also not adapted to the industrial culture, the impact of globalization will be more disastrous. Notably, the government neither has a proper policy nor the time to evaluate or monitor the work of these companies, the companies could do anything to exploit the entire resources for maximum profit at a faster rate than expected.[233]

With more and more companies entering the land, it is not wrong to say that each company will make all efforts to compete and overtake the other, in terms of large production and obtaining huge profit. This is what Cobb Jr describes as 'rat race.'[234] Hence, with the unscrupulous mining taking place at a faster rate, land and its resources are being destroyed without mercy. The local people now look at their precious land with painful heart but they cannot do anything now.[235] If this is the case, it will not take long for the entire natural resources to be exhausted and the whole land to become a desert. Tribal theology speaks against

---

[229] Discussion with Presbyter Gympad from Lumshnong, who is staying now at Shillong on the 21 May, 2012.

[230] In the year 2000 when the companies first came to the area people were selling their land at Rs. 7 per sq. metre. Today at present it depends on the quality of lime stones, i.e., from Rs. 30 up to Rs. 140 accordingly. Discussion with Rangbahduh Khonglah former headman of Lumshnong on the 17 May, 2012.

[231] Discussion with P.B. M. Basaiawmoit on the 9 May, 2012.

[232] While some of their lands are agricultural land and jhumming land, other lands are forest area. Discussion with Brian Gympad on the 17 May, 2012.

[233] Patricia Mukhim is presently the editor of the daily newspaper *The Shillong Times* and also involved in many social activities in different capacities. Discussion with her on the 16 May, 2012.

[234] Cobb Jr., *The Earthist Challenge to Economism: A Theological Critique of the World Bank,* 1.

[235] Discussion with Brian Gympad on the 17 May, 2012.

such development that have been displacing and uprooting the indigenous people from their own habitat, with which they have been associated down through the centuries. Exploiting their natural resources not only destroy and damage their economic resources but also wipe out their inalienable right from their land and resources. Commenting on the plight of the indigenous people in today's era of globalization Longchar argues,

> The indigenous people's movements are all cries for justice; they speak aloud of the demand claiming the right to land and resources. Because, in the name of development, progress and tourism, the inalienable rights of indigenous peoples over land and resources have been forcibly taken away....People have been uprooted, dislocated and evicted from their ancestral homes, land, mountains and rivers are being polluted, and forest lie wasted. People's sacred areas have been destroyed, and this has resulted in disconnection, with their culture and spirituality.[236]

The above quotation is well fitted in the context of tribal people today. But this does not mean to say 'no' to development, but people need development that are community based or people friendly. Commenting on the mushrooming of cement companies at Lumshnong areas, Patricia Mukhim rightly argues that this is not the kind of development that people need. Tribal people need developments that are more human, more balanced or development at their own pace not to be decided from outside.[237] In short, development activities must be planned in such a way that they protect, rather than to alienate from the habitat. For the tribal people who live so close to nature, to detach and isolate them from their natural surroundings, will prove to be more harmful and disastrous. To put it bluntly, this will not only tear down their sources of livelihood, rather their entire experience with the natural surrounding will be demolished. John Cobb Jr states that,

> Through our bodies and even more directly we are related to other parts of nature. Who we are, what we are, is affected not only by our human communities but also by the broader natural environment. Relations to other living things are important, especially to children. The landscapes of the places we call home shape our sense of reality and of belonging. Hence, the deterioration of our natural surroundings not only reduces the resources for economic life, it directly impoverishes our experiences.[238]

---

[236] Wati Longchar, "The Continuity of Indigenous People in Today's World," in *Theologizing Tribal Heritage: A Critical Re-Look,* edited by Hrangthan Chungi (Delhi: ISPCK, 2008), 70-71.

[237] Discussion with Patricia Mukhim on the 16th May, 2012.

[238] John B. Cobb Jr, "Marx and Whitehead" http://www.religion-online.org/showartcle.asp?title=3359 (8.7.2009).

Whither Sustainable Development?

The above discussion reveals that economic exploitation and environmental degradation goes hand in hand. In the present era of globalization, the way that natural resources are ruthlessly extracted especially the non-renewable ones, implies that it will not take long for these materials to be exhausted thereby turn the mother earth into a desert. This is true in the context of Khasi people. Besides, since 1960 there is a growing and rising of myriad problems such as "environmental degradation, food shortage, population growth, unhealthy living and immoral society"[239] affecting the entire globe especially the Third World countries. Such a situation entail the need to reconsider the ideologies behind exploiting the earth resources especially the non-renewable ones. With ecological crisis looming large and merciless exploitation of natural resources becoming a threat to future generation, an increasing and urgent need arise for a sort of development that would benefit the people in the long run. With this in mind, the World Commission on Environment and Development (WCED) popularly known as the Bruntland Commission Report 1987 propose 'sustainable development' as the answer to the contemporary ecological crisis.[240] According to the Brundtland report,

> Sustainable development is development that meets the needs of the present without compromising the ability of future generations to meet their own needs. It contains within it two key concepts: The concept of "needs," in particular the essential needs of the world's poor, to which overriding priority should be given; and the idea of limitations imposed by the state of technology and social organization on the environment's ability to meet present and future needs.[241]

The above definition includes two main concerns. It embraces the main concern for the concept of 'needs' especially the essential needs of the poor and the concept of limitation in using the earth resources so as it will not affect the future generation. To state differently, it implies improving the quality of human life while living within the carrying capacity of supporting ecosystem and

---

[239] T. V. Muralivallabhan, *Dimensions of Sustainable Economic Development* (Nooranad: UNMA Publications, 2005), 57.

[240] The report gets its name from Gro Harlem Brundtland the then Prime Minister of Norway who was the Chairman of the commission. See Ulaganathan Sankar, "Introduction," in *Environmental Economics,* edited by Ulaganathan Sankar (New Delhi: Oxford University Press, 2001), 13. But the term "sustainable Development" was first coined by the United Nation Conference on the Human Environment (UNCHE) held at Stockholm in 1972. See Chris Patten, "Governance" in *Respect for the Earth: Sustainable Development,* edited by Chris Patten et al., (London: Profile Books Ltd, 2000), 4.

[241] Felix Wilfred, "Eco-Justice: Expanding the Horizons for a Common Future," in *Jeevardhara* XL/235 (January 2010): 12.

improving and maintaining the well-being of people and ecosystem.[242] Notably, environmental degradation not only threatens human existence but also challenges humanity to search for new way of living. The concept of sustainable development entails the necessity to challenge the dominant process of neocolonial ideologies on development that ignore the important of preserving the earth.[243] It demands that earth resources need to be used wisely in such a way that it is not harmful to the health of the mother earth and also not to compromise with the requirements of generations to come.

It is believed that sustainable development provides a healthy model in preventing the further onslaught of the deteriorating ecosystem. It speaks more about proper management of the earth resources, and suggests the wise use of resources based on optimum level and satisfaction, rather than maximum level, and the restoration of the degraded resources and so on.[244] According to the resource paper of the Presbyterian Eco-justice Task Force, sustainability necessitates humans to relate to the realm of nature by respecting its integrity thereby paving the way for smooth functioning of the eco-system in which "the earth's beauty and fruitfulness may be maintained and kept sufficient for human sustenance, and life may continue also for the non-human species."[245] Hence, to reach the goal of sustainable development "environmental protection needs to constitute an integral part of development process and cannot be considered in isolation from it."[246] Accordingly, if humanity is to survive on the planet, development process and environmental protection must go hand in hand.

Looking on the concept of sustainable development, one may argue that proper implementation of the Commission Report will enable to help improve the wise use of the earth's resources, which will in turn help the future of humanity in the long run. But now even 25 years after the Commission Report came into existence, the condition of the natural environment goes from bad to worse.

---

[242] The above quotation is taken from the Preamble of the Earth Charter issued on March, 2000. The original proposal to create the Earth Charter is to be found in *Our Common Future* the 1987 report of the UN World Commission on Environment and Development (UNWCED) with the purpose to clarify fundamental principles on environment protection and sustainable development. For detail see Steven C. Rockefeller, "Global Interdependence, the Earth Charter, and Christian Faith," in *Earth Habitat: Eco-Justice and the Church's Response,* edited by Dieter T. Hessel and Larry L. Rasmussen (Augsburg: Fortress Press, 2001), 112.

[243] Cf. Sarah White and Romy Tiongo, *Doing Theology and Development: Meetings the Challenge of Poverty* (Edinburgh: Saint Andrew Press: 1997), 154.

[244] Muralivallabhan, *Dimensions of Sustainable Economic Development,* 58.

[245] For detail see "Keeping and Healing the Creation" A Resource Paper prepared by the Presbyterian Eco-Justice Task Force; Issued by Committee on Social Witness Policy, Presbyterian Church of USA, 63.

[246] M. K. Prasad, "Ecology, Science and Sustainable Development," in *Ecological Concerns: An Indian Christian Response,* edited by Joseph Mattam and Jacob Kavunkal (Bangalore: NBCLC, 1998), 40.

Muralivallabhan maintains that the process had begun even 20 years before the implementation of the Commission Report. Notably, since then "more than 130 countries had created new environmental agencies, more than 180 international agreements and several thousand environmental NGOs" came into existence. Nevertheless, despite many efforts to save the environment from the impending future disaster, the global environmental condition remains critical.[247] In such a situation many questions arise, is there anything wrong with the concept? Or is the implementation of the concept not up to the mark? Or are there still limitations within the prescribed conditions related to the Commission Report? Whatever may be the answer the real fact is clear that despite all attempts, the situation of mother earth is still threatened and at risk. Hence, in the era of globalization where greed for maximum profit which lead to the extraction and exploitation of more and more of the earth's resources, needs to be corrected on one hand and if the future of humanity is to be safe, we need to go beyond sustainable development.

Beyond Sustainable Development

As stated above, "sustainable development" is that sort of development that meets the needs of the present contemporary generation without affecting the ability of the future generations to meet their own needs. The concept of sustainable development stems from the understanding that there is "limited to growth" as against unlimited growth. Though the concept of sustainable development emphasizes on limit to growth, it does not put strong challenges to the so called neo-colonial forces or the agencies of globalization from exploiting the earth and its resources. To state differently, even after twenty years that the concept is widely discussed and implemented in different capacities, and many countries have formed environmental agencies to correct the mistakes done, exploitation of the earth resources merely for economic gain has gone from bad to worse. The Harare Assembly of the World Council rightly puts it when it argues,

> Sustainable development, a concept prominent in international fora, still leaves powerful forces of globalization in command and does not question the underlying paradigm of continuous and unlimited progress and growth.[248]

It may be noted that such conception is still not free from anthropocentric connotation. This view is well elaborated in Nash's words when he says that "Sustainability implies the preservation of biodiversity, but primarily on anthropocentric grounds, for the sake of the well-being of future human

---

[247] Muralivallabhan, *Dimensions of Sustainable Economic Development,* 58.

[248] Martin Robra, Deenabandhu Manchala and Sarah Anderson-Rajarigam, "Affirming Life for the Disregarded Many," in *Earth Habitat: Eco-Injustice and the Church's Response,* edited by Dieter T. Hassel and Larry L. Rasmussen (Augsburg: Fortress Press, 2001), 86.

generations."[249] Wilfred maintains that the prevailing "concern here seems to be the survival of humanity which is not possible when the environment is damaged, or the resources of nature are over exploited."[250] At the same time it does not offer space for eco-justice. Eco-justice here implies the well being of all human kind irrespective of gender, class or race living on a thriving earth. This indicates that justice to human beings is inseparable from and intimately connected with justice in the entire social order. In short, "eco-justice means justice to all of God's creation."[251] Gibson argues,

> On a thriving earth, human well being is nurtured not only by the provision of those material necessities but also by a way of living within the natural order that is fitting: respectful of the integrity of natural systems and of the worth of non human creatures, appreciative of the beauty and the mystery of the world of nature.[252]

Nature is not to be seen simply as "an instrument for the present and future human well being and progress, but as having value in itself."[253] It may be noted that the value of nature is not to be seen in its ability to serve the unlimited wants of humans, rather its value lies in its relation to God its Creator. The Genesis account reveals that God declares that all creations are good in His/Her sight. The goodness that God bestowed in all creations indicates that whether humans exist or not, all creations are good in their association with their creator. Hence they have their own value and worth in God's sight. To state differently, other creatures can exist without human beings, but humans cannot exist without the other creations. For the tribal people, the value and importance of the mother earth is to be seen not only in its capability to provide source of livelihood rather it is God's given right to all creations. The Khasis considers all creations both living and non living as having value and worth in themselves. This recognition stems from the belief that it is God who breathes life in all living creatures i.e., *uba pyrsad mynsiem ha ki jingthaw baroh.* At the same time, the earth and all creations are the handiwork or design by the Creator or spring forth from *U Blei Nongbuh Nongthaw.* Hence, they never see the well being of humans apart from the well being of other creations. Everything are interlinked and interrelated to each other. Hence, human relationship with other creations in the eco-system is dignifiedly determined and perceived by mutual respect and interdependence.

---

[249] James A. Nash, *Loving Nature: Ecological Integrity and Christian Responsibility* (Nashville: Abibgdon Press, 1991), 64.

[250] Felix Wilfred, "Eco Justice…," 12.

[251] "Keeping and Healing the Creation," 2.

[252] William E. Gibson, "Eco-Justice: New Perspective for a time of Turning," in *For Creation's Sake: Preaching Ecology and Justice,* edited by Dieter T. Hessel (Philadelphia: The Geneva Press, 1985), 25.

[253] Wilfred, "Eco-justice…," 12-13.

Lukas Vischer observes that we should not use sustainable development merely for correction small ecological problems. "Economic activities" he argues must be directed by "the recognition of scales of exploitation" and "sustainability must be supplemented by the notion of sufficiency." He further states that "we need ecological ethos. Not a set of rules but an attitude of respect for God's gift of creation."[254] The most important concern in the contemporary debate today is about the recognition that humans are not above creations but part of creations. Hence, other creations need to be respected and recognized for their own inherent rights they obtained from the Creator. This perception is well reflected in the preamble of the Earth Charter which says,

> By affirming respect for 'earth' as well as 'life in all its diversity' principle I invite respect for the planet as a whole and for all the different systems that sustain the biosphere, including those that make up the geosphere, atmosphere, and hydrosphere, oceans, rivers, grasslands and mountains as well as trees and wolves warrant respect. In addition, the principle of respect for life applies to relations with persons as well as to relations with other life forms.[255]

The Health of the Earth/Community

The present paradigm of development does not take into consideration the health of the earth or the eco-system. Driven by the ideologies of neo-liberalism for maximum profit and unlimited growth, agencies of neo-colonial forces make all efforts to extract raw materials of the natural world at a faster rate than expected. In the process, they cause irreparable damage to the entire natural environment thereby making the whole ecosystem sick. It may be noted that the well being of the eco-system resulted in the well being of humanity as well as other creations. So, also a sick environment leads to the untold misery and suffering of the entire human and non human creation. Commenting on the challenges and impact of the present day development paradigm to the earth including human, White and Tiongco assert,

> As we see our impact on the world we also reevaluate our place in the world. The search for better ways to relate to our environment is inseparable from the search for a better society. In this sense, environment destruction is not only a threat to our way of life, but also a challenge to find new ways of living. Encountering material 'limit of growth' calls into question both the

---

[254] Lukas Vischer, *Listening to Creation Groaning* (Geneva: Centre International Reforme John Knox, 2004), 29.

[255] Rockefeller, Global Interdependence, the Earth Charter and Christian Faith, 113.

> dominant strategies for development and the values and assumptions on which they are built.[256]

The above quotation indicates that the health and well being of the natural environment is inseparable from the health of the human community. Looking on this aspect, Process Theology emphasizes that the common good or the health of the community also "include the non human natural world and not just something of instrumental value to human beings, but of intrinsic value." Contrary to the ideologies of neoliberalism most Process thinkers "treat the non human natural world not as externalities but as integral to economic activity."[257] For them, human beings are part and parcel of the non human natural world. Hence, they affirm the necessity for "a free, democratic, participatory, just and sustainable community in a non anthropocentric way affirming the intrinsic value of the constituents elements of the non human natural world."[258] A healthy eco-system will positively contribute to the health of all its members both humans and non human. John Cobb clearly states that,

> We are parts of natural communities, or if we prefer, eco-systems. Our personal health and well being are bound up with the health and well being of these communities or ecosystems. If we view economic development in terms of its contribution to the health and well being of human communities and natural ecosystems, we will not seek increased production as such as the goods in itself. We will instead decide, community by community, whether economic growth is needed, and where it is, what form it can take that will strengthen the community as a whole and benefit the natural environment as well.[259]

The above quotation stands against the ideologies of neoliberalism that proposed unlimited growth at the expense of the vulnerable section of population and the natural environment as well. A healthy community will not allow any of its members to be exploited or excluded, but all should enjoy their life in a healthy atmosphere. A healthy community is, therefore, a community that "cannot allow any of its members to be homeless, undernourished, or without education or medical care. The first requirement on its economy is to meet needs of this sort."[260] He further states that a community will be healthy only when its members are free

[256] Sarah White and Romy Tiongco, *Doing Theology and Development: Meeting the Challenge of Poverty* (Edinburg: Saint Andrew Press, 1977), 154.

[257] Leslie A. Murray, "Politics in Process Perspective" in *Handbook of Process Theology*, edited by Jay Mc Daniel and Donna Bowman (St. Louis: Chalice Press, 2006), 224.

[258] Murray," Politics in Process Perspective," 225.

[259] See John B. Cobb, Jr., Marx and Whitehead http://www.religion-online.org/show article.asp?title=3359 (8.7.2009).

[260] John B. Cobb Jr., A Theology of Enjoyment for a Post Capitalist Life http://www.religion-online.org/showarticle.asp?title=3544 (8.7.2009).

to develop their individual qualities and creativity. "Communities can encourage such individual creativity only when obtaining the necessities of economic survival does not dominate the lives of the people."[261] Commenting on the development of Earthism[262] in its attempt to protect the world from further destruction Cobb Jr., maintains that the Earthists "see the health of the earth, including human in habitants, as supreme importance. Instead of dominating the earth, the economy should serve the well being of the system as a whole." He further states that "Earthists typically seek the regeneration of natural systems and focus attention on those human beings who live most intimately with these systems. The health of these systems improves the livelihood of those who live in and from them..."[263] This indicates that the health of human communities and the health of non human communities cannot be separated but must go hand in hand. Notably, this does not mean that we say 'no' to development and developmental activities, but that development should be community based. Developmental activities must contribute to the health and well being of the community rather than exploiting them for unlimited economic growth. Hence, economic activities must be planned in such a way that it will help in improving the living conditions of the people and not damage their sources of living.

Biblical and Theological Contribution

Creation Account

The Biblical narratives present a vivid picture about the natural environment and all that exist as God's creation. Nature is not a separate entity rather an integral part of God the creator. This indicates that "this relationship is one of dependence and that every existing thing depends upon God for its existence."[264] God is the source and origin of everything that exist. As God created them, nature and the entire environment are within the realm of God's care. The entire nature and environment has its source and origin from God, and God's manifest Him/Herself through every creation in different capacities. As the earth is created by God, it belongs to God and God alone. But it is given to humans as a 'trust' for use and not for misuse and abuse. In many places of the biblical narrative God declares and affirms that the earth belongs to Him/Her. The Leviticus proclamation of God saying "The Land is mine" (25:23), and the Psalmist declares that "the earth

261 Cobb, "Marx and Whitehead."

262 Earthism developed due to innumerable protest against the degradation of the earth and the destruction of human communities that live closest to it. These protests constitute a new global forcesthat challenge economism. Earthism is not simply a set of ideas but a new paradigm, a different way of being in the world, in short, a new religion. See Cobb Jr., *The Earthist Challenge to Economism: A Theological Critique of the World Bank,* 35, 168.

263 Cobb Jr., *The Earthist Challenge to Economism: A Theological Critique of the World Bank,* 38.

264 J. Habgood, "Creation," in *A New Dictionary of Christian Theology,* edited by A. Richardson and J. Bowden (London: SCM Press Ltd., 1983), 129.

is the Lord and its fullness thereof" (Ps. 24:1) shows that the earth inherently belongs to God, humans has no right to exploit and abuse any part of creation. This is contrary to the ideology of neoliberalism promoted by the agencies of globalization which perceive the earth merely as productive ground to exploit for unlimited profit. Biblical concept of creation not only declares that the earth belongs to God but challenge all oppressive forces that abuse and mistreated the earth creation.

Creation Concept of Goodness

The concept of goodness is one of the important themes in the creation narrative. The creation account reveals that after each and every creation God saw that they are very good (Gen 1: 3-25). The goodness of creation underlines that creation is the handiwork of God, and its beauty was designed according to God's will. Irenaeus of Lyons (130-200 AD) strongly affirms that it is God alone who is the author of everything that exist, therefore the world and all creations "abides in subjection to God."[265] Nevertheless, the term goodness here does not convey that the creations are good in themselves, rather they are considered to be good by virtue of their standing in appropriate relationship with their Creator.[266] Augustine of Hippo (354-430 AD) affirms that the world was created in the beginning in order, beauty and goodness by the good Creator. The world for him is essentially good for it is the handiwork of God who is himself/Herself good.[267] Gregory of Nyssa maintains that creation "mirrors within its extraordinary intricacy, magnitude and inscrutability the incomprehensibility and majesty of God."[268] It may be noted that while God spent five and half days for the creation of other creatures, it took God only half a day to create human beings; the creatures of his own image and likeness. This seems to suggest that even though humans are created in God's image, the rest of the creatures have special place and value in God's sight. To state differently, other creations have their own value in their association with their Creator whether humans exist or not. God is not merely the God of history (Ps 103) but also the God of nature (Ps 104).[269]

This implies that, what God says to be good is not to be subjected to human exploitation and destruction. Theology of creation advocates the necessity to recognize the value of other creations as intended by the Creator, i.e., not to

---

[265] G. L Prestige, *God in Patristic Thought* (London: SPCK, 1952), 45.

[266] L. Osborn, *Guardian of Creation* (Leicester: Appolos, 1993), 86.

[267] F. Cayre, *Manual of Patrology and History of Theology,* First Volume, Translated by H. Howitt (Paris: Desclee & Co, 1927), 676.

[268] David Bently Hart, "The Miror of the Infinite: Gregory of Nyssa on *Vestigia Trinitatis*" in *Re-Thinking Gregory of Nyssa,* edited by Sarah Coakley (Malden: Blackwell Publishing Ltd., 2002), 118.

[269] V. Devasahayam, "Biblical Perspective on creation: Some Reflection Text Gen 2: 4-17, Rom 8: 18-25," in *Towards an Ecological Worldview,* edited by B. Benjamin (Nagpur: NCCI, 1990), 61.

damage and exploit them merely for unlimited economic profit. They are simply not commodities to satisfy the increasing desires of humans but creation with their own value and worth demand respect from human species. Notably, the Genesis creation account portrays that God enjoys and take pleasure in the company of His/Her non human creatures. God is pleased with them and admires them so as to consider them good and lovely. Nash observes that "God is pleased, satisfied, even delighted with the result of the creative process (Ps. 104:31) because they correspond with divine extension and expectation." He further states that "Divine valuation, however are not solely or even primarily anthropocentric." The earth is not meant mainly for humans, rather the entire creation including the non human creature like the animals and other species are good and blessed with fertility to "increase and multiply (Gen 1:22; 8:17)."[270] The call to be fruitful is not limited within the human community but extended to non-human creatures also. The Noah episode indicates that God desire to save not only the human species but also to save the other non human species as well. (Gen 7-8). This reveals that "humanity must coexist with nature in a symbiotic relationship of mutual fruitfulness."[271]

Besides, "nature acts as co-worker, the bridge who receives His/Her word and co-parents life."[272] The notion that nature participates as co-creator with God demonstrates that nature as God's partner gave birth to other creatures like trees and animals. Genesis narrative depicts that while God says "let there be light," God did not utter the same words with regards to trees and animals. Rather God says, "Let the earth bring forth vegetations, animals" etc (Gen 1:24). The earth here is as good as to be co-creator with the divine. She is dignifiedly honored even to participate in the mission of God's creative and dynamic action. As stated earlier, the creation narratives of the Khasis also portrays that the earth not only give birth to soil and stone but also to animals, birds, trees, plants and grass.[273] It indicates that the mother earth entered into a respectable vocation with God as co-creator of all the non human species. Creation thus becomes a joint venture in a wondrous partnership of God and the earth. It portrays a deep and intimate relationship between God and the earth. The notion of the goodness of creation discloses that nature is organically related to its creator. Hence, one cannot merely conceive God apart from His/Her creation. It thus signifies the importance and value of creation in God's sight. If globalization is to be corrected, the dynamics of

---

[270] James A. Nash, *Loving Nature: Ecological Integrity and Christian Responsibility* (Nashville: Abingdon Press, 1991), 98-99.

[271] Robert P. Meye, "Invitation to Wonder: Toward a Theology of Nature," in *Tending the Garden: Essay on the Gospel and the Earth,* edited by Wesley Grandberg-Michaelson (Gran Rapids, Michigan: William B. Eerdsmans Publishing Company, 1987), 48.

[272] S. Rayan, "Theological Perspective on the environmental Crisis," in *Religion and Society* XXXVII/2 (June, 1990): 26.

[273] War, "The Khasi Concept of Nature," 41-42.

the biblical concept of goodness need to be reconsidered and reinterpreted in the context of the present day tribal society today. This will surely assist and facilitate the tribals in their contemporary struggle against the neo-colonial forces that attempt to exploit the entire natural resources at a fast rate simply for quenching the wants of the small minority section of the earth's population.

The Concept of Stewardship

When everything was created and God declared all creations as good, God entrusted human beings to look after or be God's steward over the entire creation. Both the sources, Yahwhistic and Priestly source illustrate that God handed down to humans the role and responsibility to look after all of God's creation. For a long period, the two terms *radhash* meaning 'dominion' and *kabash* 'to subdue' in Genesis 1, have been misinterpreted and misunderstood as God's license to human beings to take control and dominate over the other creations. Coupled with the concept image of God bestowed upon humans the text is understood to convey that humans have the right or are empowered to rule over and become master over the entire God's creation. Kochupuracal argues that these two concepts have "often been misinterpreted to justify man's [sic] greed for power and his[sic] limitless exploitation of the earth for his [sic] selfish ends."[274]

Lynn White as cited by R. J. Berry, in his paper "The Historic Roots of our Ecological Crisis" first published in *Science* in 1967 put the blame on Christianity as the root cause for ecological disaster in the entire planet. That is, this is the outcome of the Genesis mandate that legitimated human beings to have dominion over the other species. To state differently, Christianity has mistreated nature, "allowing it to be exploited without restraint."[275] White as cited by Anne M. Clifford, it is the concept of created in God's image that guarantees human beings to exploit and dominate other creation.[276] Consequently, for White as cited by Peter Harisson Christianity "bears a huge burden of guilt for environmental deterioration."[277] Commenting on the misinterpretation of the biblical view, Berry argues that the world here is recognized in "strongly utilitarian term" and all other creations came into being for the benefit of humans. Creations are inferior

---

[274] Sebastian Kochupurackal, *Eco-Mission: A Paradigm Shift in Missiology* (Bangalore: Asian Trading Corporation, 2007), 127.

[275] R. J. Berry, "Introduction: Stewardship- A Default Position," in *Environmental Stewardship: Critical Perspectives- Past and Present,* edited by R. J Berry (London: T & T Clark International, 2006), 4. See also R. L. Sarkar, *The Bible Ecology and Environment* (Delhi: ISPCK, 2000), 146-149.

[276] Anne M. Clifford, "From Ecological Lament to a Sustainable Oikos," in *God's Steward: The Role of Christian in Creation Care,* edited by Don Brandt (California: World Vision Publications, 2002), 54.

[277] Peter Harisson, "Having Dominion: Genesis and the Mastery of Nature," in *Environmental Stewardship: Critical Perspectives- Past and Present,* edited by R. J. Berry (London: T & T Clark International, 2006), 17.

to humans as only humans acquired reasoning power.[278] Hence, human beings have the power to do whatever he/she like over the entire creation.

Nevertheless, a closer look into these passages indicates that humans' role is not one of dominating or exploiting rather it conveys a covenantal relationship that God made with humans and other creations. Northcott maintains that the Genesis account reveals that humanity is bequeathed on the earth not as a possession but as a gift. The word 'dominion' is not to be understood as "ownership but trusteeship or stewardship."[279] W. M. Swartley as cited by Therukattil maintains that it is in the relationship between created in God's image and the command to have dominion that we understood the responsibility given to human as stewardship of God. The Biblical synonym for this concept is faithfulness, obedience, justice, love for God and one's neighbour.[280] Brandt argues that those words like multiply, dominion, subjugate and naming when we put them in the wider context of the Bible they seems to empower human not as "environmental autocrat" rather humans are portrayed as created being with the responsibility to care and look after the other creations.[281] The first human Adam was not given the role to dominate over other creation but the role to manage or care, which is the task of guardianship. According to Genesis 3:20, Eve was also called the mother of all living things. The word mother here is not to be understood in biological sense, rather in terms of "special relationship or protecting and caring for the non-human members of the creation."[282]

At the same time, dominion or subdue here is not to be considered as conquest, subjugation, tampering or damaging. Rather it conveys that being created in the image of God human has a royal function. The word 'royal' and 'king' in the context of Israel does not entail the exploitation of the subjects, but it connotes a huge responsibility with strict codes of conduct in accordance with the will of God. The Kings of Israel has to be the defenders of the nation and institutions, uphold justice in the land, judging and settling different matters, and the like (Psalm 72). Here, to do justice to the land has ecological significance too. As a king he has to rule over God's creation, protect them, and care for them in tune with the will of God. For the Israelites as long as the King established good relationship with God the Creator the entire land and humans prosper, but if the

---

[278] Berry, "Introduction: Stewardship-A Default Position," 5.

[279] Michael S. Northcott, "Ecology and Christian Ethics," in *God's Stewards: The Role of Christian in Creation Care,* edited by Don Brandt (California: World Vision Publications, 2002), 35.

[280] G. Therukattil, "Towards a Biblical Eco-Theology" in *Jeevardhara* XXI/126 (November 1991), 468.

[281] Don Brandt, "Introduction," in *God's Stewards: The Role of Christians in Creation Care,* edited by Don Brandt (California: World Vision Publications, 2002), 1.

[282] Paulson Pulikottil, "God, Creation and Humankind: Old Testament Themes in Ecological Perspective," in *Ecological Challenge and Christian Mission,* edited by Krickwin C. Marak and Atul Y. Aghamkar (Delhi: CMS/ISPCK, 1998), 52-53.

King wanders away from the will of God his power diminishes and even prosperity of the land is affected.[283] This is true not only for the King but also for the people of Israel. For them, the entire land belongs to God and the people are only the caretakers of the divine land (Lev. 25:23). If they follow God's commandment, God will send rains to their field and they will prosper (Deut 11:14-15, Deut 8:18, Is 28:24-26).[284] Hence the "royal authority of Human Being in creation is thus a call to responsibility to care for nature and keep its balance that is the gift of God." [285] "It is not a dominion of caprice or exploitation," observes Kochupurackal "but one of justice and benevolence patterned on God's own benevolent justice patterned on the model of ancient King."[286]

According to Genesis 2:15, humans were entrusted with the task of tilling and keeping the garden. Sider argues that the term 'dominion' does not mean to dominate but "tilling and taking care of the garden." Humans are expected not to cause any damage but to transform the earth into a better place where both human and non-human creatures could co-exist together. As he rightly put it,

> Therefore all works must have not only productive but also a protective aspect. Economic system must be shaped so that a healthy ecological system is maintained over time. All responsible human work done by the steward of God the sustainer must contain an element of cooperation with the environment.[287]

Hence, though humans are created in God's image they are not supposed to dominate over the other creation. But their role is to be the keeper of the garden. Nash maintains that the term image and dominion in Genesis 1, is not a mandate for oppression or a sanction of totalitarian rule over creation but they are entrusted to 'till' and 'keep' the garden in accordance with the will of God the Creator.[288] Hence, any act that damage and destroy the equilibrium of the eco-system merely for selfish economic profit needs to be confronted and challenged keeping in mind the well being of other creations as intended by the Creator.

---

[283] Robert R. Gotfried, *Economics, Ecology, and the Roots of Western Faith: Perspective from the Garden* (Maryland: Rowman & Littlefield Publishers, Inc. 1995), 37.

[284] William Dyrness, "Stewardship of the Earth in the Old Testament" in *Tending the Garden: Essay on the Gospel and the Earth* edited by Wesley Granberg-Michaelson (Grand Rapids, Michigan: William B. Eerdmans Publishing Company, 1987), 56.

[285] Pulikottil, God, Creation and Humankind: Old Testament Themes in Ecological Perspective, 56.

[286] Sebastian Kochupurackal, *Eco-Mission: A Paradigm Shift in Missiology* (Bangalore: Asian Trading Corporation, 2007), 127.

[287] Ronald J. Sider, "Introduction," in *Christianity and Economics in the Post-Cold War Era: The Oxford Declaration and Beyond,* edited by Herbert Schlossberg, Vinay Samuel and Ronald J. Sider, (Grand Rapids, Michigan: William B. Eerdmans Publishing Company, 1994), 14.

[288] James A. Nash, *Loving Nature: Ecological Integrity and Christian Responsibility* (Nashville: Abingdon Press, 1991), 103.

In the New Testament, the concept of stewardship is depicted in the different parables like the parable of unjust steward (Lk 16:1-13), the parable of the talents (Mt 25:14-39), and parable of the pounds (Lk 19: 12-27). These parables demonstrate that the master was not happy at all with the lazy or idle stewards. God has endowed humans with diverse talents that need to be utilized wisely and creatively. It is human responsibility to employ his/her respective talents that are God given in a proper manner for the common good and good of the future.[289] Responsible stewardship portrays the concept of respect and reverence for the orderliness of the entire eco-system which is supposed to offer a happy dwelling place for the whole creations. When Jesus used these parables to address his audience, one could notice his main concern not only about the specific work of those persons involved, but also about the economic well being of the entire community, both present and the future. Consequently, each and every one either poor or rich are accountable for their economic behavior. Commenting on Jesus' speaking in parables, Goudzwaard argues that behind Jesus' word one could capture his deep respect for the "God-given rule of *Oikonomia,* the good care which is needed for the *oikos,* the household." He further states that

> For Jesus, the word economy-Greek *oikonomia*-was primarily a divine mandate. It included the care of the land and a concern for the well being of those who live from its fruits. So for Jesus, it was an economic not just an ethical rule that workers should receive their food on time. Remarkably, in Jesus' word about human economic life there is also an eschatological perspective. The Lord of the land himself will come back to ask all his servants to render account of their style of economic behavior (Lk 16: 1-13). And that accountability required of persons but also of the *ethne,* the people or nations of this world (Mt 25:32).[290]

The above discussion portrays that humans are accountable not only about their ethical but also about economic behavior. It is well suited to the present day era of globalization where the agencies of globalization attempt all efforts to capture economic benefits of today's world at the expense of the marginalised poor sections and the eco-system as well. Hence, to have 'dominion' does not imply to dominate or to exploit the other creation for one's own profit or gain, rather it implies the idea of concern. To state differently, it indicates to watch over it, keep and preserve it from exploitation. The notion of stewardship here is not an indication of caring for one's own property but God's property. Bradley rightly affirms that this is not a matter of someone handing power to the other, but it is

---

[289] G. Theru kattil, "Towards a Biblical Eco-Theology," *Jeevardhara,* XXI/126 (November, 1991): 472.

[290] Bob Goudzwaard, "Economic Growth: Is more always better?," in *Christianity and the Culture of Economics,* edited by Donald A. Hay and Alan Greider (Cardiff: University of Wales Press, 2001), 157.

the Lord of all things, giving a solemn trust and responsibility to his creatures for the welfare and order of the rest.[291] Rowan Williams maintains that humans are expected to take the responsibility of caring for creations "with the understanding that it is a gift from God, knowing that once the transformation is effected, the creation must be offered back to God."[292]

Humans as responsible stewards must be worthy of that trust. Human beings as responsible steward are accountable to God. Commenting on Lk 16: 1-13; Mt 25:23-32, Goudzwaard maintains that, in many of these "New Testament texts, economy, responsibility and accountability are closely interrelated, they simply cannot be separated."[293] So, any attempt to extract or subjugate the other creation for merely economic advantage is considered not only a violation of that trust, but at the same time they indicate an insult to stewardship and to the divine as well. In other words, it can be considered as deviation from God's will. In the creation account of the Khasis it is clearly stated that on account of the urgent petition of the mother earth, God sent down the *Hynniew Trep* or the seven families to look after the mother earth and all its resources. Here, one could see that the task entrusted to human beings is to look after and keep the orderliness of the mother earth as the Creator God has intent it to be. It does not sanction domination or to subdue the earth and its resources, rather to look after the entire creation with love and care. As long as humans obey this commandment of God there was peace and tranquility. But the moment they turn away from God the Creator chaos has taken place in the entire earth.[294] To state differently, humans are expected to transform the earth making it a suitable dwelling place for peaceful co-existence of the entire creation of God. Humans are given the responsibility of caring and keeping the *oikos* of God. This responsibility assigned to humans does not mean that he/she can do whatever they please to the earth rather they are subjected in accordance to God's will and directions of caring for it.

Beyond Stewardship: Towards Kinship with the Earth

It may be noted that in the contemporary theological debate today, the concept of stewardship is understood as having its own problem. The first problem with the term is the absence of God in the overall affairs of the world, while leaving everything in the hands of humans. According to this term human are not only considered as superior to other creation, but God is understood as transcendence

---

[291] I. Bradley, *God is Green* (London: Darton, Longman and Todd, 1990), 18.

[292] Rowan Williams, *Sharing God's Planet: A Christian Vision for a Sustainable Future* (London: Church Publishing House, 2005), 24.

[293] Goudzwaard, "Economic Growth: Is more always better?," 157.

[294] This chaos is well described by Kynpham Sing Nongkynrih in the story of "The Seven Clans," and the Story of "The Purple Crest." For detail see Nong Kynrih, Around the Hearth: Khasi Legends, 1-15.

or sovereign operating from a distance.[295] Everything here on earth is left within the command of human. Kochupurackal argues that "God is viewed as an absentee landlord, who has put human beings in charge of the rest of creation. Having created the world, God left its day to day affairs to human."[296] Having portrayed God as the absentee landlord this model not only exclude God's presence from the natural world but also even at the realm of humanity. Palmer states that "within the framework of the model, God's action and presence in the world are largely mediated through humans."[297] This model not only bestows superior status to human, but it also separates humans from the rest of creation.[298] Besides perceiving the natural world as resources for and under control of human, this model portrays that "nature is dependent on humanity for its management."[299] As the manager over the rest of creations humans feel that they are potentially capable of doing what they want to the rest of creation. Kochupurackal sees this as danger as "it gives humans some propriety rights over the rest of creation."[300] Creation is depicted as existing for the benefit of humans not as having good in itself.

Wilfred maintains that the term stewardship has its own problem as it "would be still infected by anthropocentrism."[301] As stated above, human beings would still picture nature as nothing but an object given to humans for good management. Commenting on the anthropocentric aspect of stewardship, Palmer maintains that "stewardship would not only allow but actually encourage total use or cultivation of the natural world for human benefit."[302] Stewardship ministry towards creation depicts more concern for the benefit and welfare of human communities rather than the welfare of other creations. Hence, it would not able to save the earth from ecological crisis in the present day era of economic globalization. Nalunnakal rightly declares when he states,

> "Stewardship," can go hand in hand with the oppressive structures without necessarily challenging them. In other words, the stewardship image does still

---

[295] Ruth Page, "The Fellowship of all Creation," in *Environmental Stewardship: Critical Perspectives- Past and Present,* edited by R. J. Berry (London: T&T Clark International, 2006), 102.

[296] Kochupurackal, *Eco-Mission: A Paradigm Shift in Missiology,* 129. See also John Black, "The Dominion of Man," in *Environmental Steward: Critical Perspectives- Past and Presence,* edited by R. J. Berry (London: T&T Clark International, 2006), 95.

[297] Clare Palmer, "Stewardship: A Case Study in Environmental Ethics," in *Environmental Stewardship: Critical Perspectives- Past and Present* (London: T&T Clark International, 2006), 68.

[298] Sarkar, *The Bible Ecology and Environment,* 160.

[299] Palmer, "Stewardship: A Case Study in Environmental Ethics," 70.

[300] Kochupurackal, *Eco-Mission: A Paradigm Shift in Missiology*, 129.

[301] Felix Wilfred, "Eco-Justice...," 10.

[302] Palmer, "Stewardship: A Case Study in Environmental Ethics," 73.

> retain anthropocentric and instrumental approaches and therefore does not take us far enough.[303]

Wilfred asserts that, we have to go beyond mere stewardship which may be still tainted by the element of anthropocentrism and "move towards kinship with the earth."[304] Kinship with the earth for him is based on the interdependence of human and nature. Williams observes that human body is not made from different but the same matter with other creations. Hence, they are not to be treated separately even at the physical level, rather they are to be seen as connected to the entire creation. He further says that

> This is not a call to earth-worship. It is recognition of the unbreakable kinship of all God's creatures. It points to the underlying unity of all things and if that can be connected with, then there is a connection with the cosmic Christ because his body is the whole universe.[305]

Human beings need to be seen as part and parcel of the creation. Genesis account reveals that human body is made out of dust. It indicates that even at the physical level, human share the same matter with other creations like trees, plants and so on who depend on the soil for their existence. Ruth Page affirms that our familiar environment like stone, water, air grass, birds, etc share the same molecular substance with us. Hence, "the very stuff of which we are made and the way it has become organized as ourselves is an inherent part of the ongoing development of the physical cosmos…" [306] The dust which becomes part of our body is also the essential part of other creations like trees, plants, etc. It is therefore a new way of looking at humans as integral part of the earth community. Human beings are not only interconnected with other species but also totally dependent on the eco-system for their survival. Consequently, this come to mean that human "have a natural kinship with members of the earth community-a kinship that reaches beyond pure biological dependency."[307] Many indigenous communities observe this kinship relationship with the earth.

Kinship with the earth is part and parcel of the indigenous communities' traditional way of life like the tribal of North East India.[308] Many among the tribal people like the Khasis of North East India have this kinship relationship with the

[303] George Matthew Nalunnakal, *Green Liberation: Towards an Integral Ecotheology* (Delhi: ISPCK/NCCI, 1999), 257.

[304] Wilfred, "Eco –Justice…," 10.

[305] Rowan Williams, *Sharing God's Planet: A Christian Vision for a Sustainable Future* (London: Church Publishing House, 2005), 19.

[306] Page, "The Fellowship of all Creation," 100.

[307] The Earth Bible Team, "Guiding Eco-justice Principles," in *Reading from the Perspective of the Earth,* edited by Norman C. Habel (Sheffield: Sheffield Academic Press, 2000), 51.

[308] Cf. Vashum, "The Stars are our Relatives: Tribal/Indigenous People's Stellar Theology," 169-188.

earth. This indicates that there are some among several clans that have totemic relationship with either plants or animals. Oxford Dictionary defines totem as "a natural object or animal believed by a particular society to have spiritual meaning and adopted by it as an emblem."[309] By virtue of this totemic relationship a particular clan will not eat certain animals or vegetation but respect and revere them to a certain extend. For instance, while some families within the the Warjri clan will not eat Khasi pumpkin and Khasi beans,[310] the Wahlang Pahsyntiew clan will not eat plantain or the banana stem.[311] Such a practice enables the people to restrain themselves from destroying or exploiting certain species of animals or vegetations which in turn contributes to maintaining ecological order and harmony. Longchar maintains that totemic relationship with certain plants and vegetation not only protects certain species of nature from being exploited but also "ensures balance and harmony in society as well as environment." He further states that by virtue of totemic relationship coupled with associated to certain animals and plants "the indigenous communities revere them greatly. In that way, the natural resources were protected and preserved from being over-exploited."[312]

Kinship with the nature and environment poses strong reservation against the neoliberalism ideologies promoted by the forces of economic globalization that emphasized on wealth accumulation through over exploitation of the earth resources. According to this model any sort of exploitation or subjugation that is harmful to other species is against meaningful peaceful co-existence and harmonious relationship in the eco-system. In other words, such action led to the distortion and fracture of the interconnectedness and interdependence of all God's creation. Hence, it is against a meaningful interrelationship among God's creation which therefore needed to be discarded and demoted. Commenting on the Kinship model Edwards rightly states that,

> It challenges the model of domination and exploitation. Adopting the kinship model demands a form of conversion. It involves a new way of seeing and acting. It involves extending the love of neighbour to embrace creatures of other species. It involves extending the love of enemy to involve creatures that confront us as other and inspire fear in us. It involves loving and valuing others as God loves and values them. Ultimately, it is God-centered (Theocentric) view of an interconnected community of creatures that have their own intrinsic value.[313]

---

[309] Catherine Soanes, Alan Spooner, and Sarah Hawker, *Compact Oxford Dictionary, Thesaurus, and Wordpower Guide* (Oxford: Oxford University Press, 2001), 961.

[310] Discussion with Ayesha D. Warjri on the 17 August 2012.

[311] Banana stem is one of the local delicious foods of the Khasis. Discussion with Wanbansain Wahlang on the 17 August 2012.

[312] Longchar, "Natural Resources: Perspectives of Primeval Traditions," 35.

[313] Denis Edwards, *Ecology at the Heart of Faith* (New York, Orbis Books, 2006), 24.

The Concept of Sabbath

The traditional Christian understanding of creation is generally understood as the six days work. The seventh day or the day when God completed the work is often ignored. But the biblical concept of creation underlines that creation and Sabbath belong together. One cannot have proper understanding of creation or its true meaning without the inclusion of the Sabbath. After the creation of the world ended on the sixth day, God saw that everything was very good (Gen 1:31). The word very good consists in God's completion through rest. Here God's rest means that He/She is resting from all the work that He/She has done. In the Sabbath's rest, God becomes free from His/Her work and returns to Godself but not apart from creation. He/She is resting together with creation. God's rest and God pleasure becomes the rest and joy for all the creation too. This indicates that God does not merely create the creation but let His/Her creation to exist and co-exist with Him/Herself.[314] Commenting on the Sabbath rest Moltmann maintains that God,

> blesses his creation through his presence at rest. God no longer acted, but he was wholly there and allowed his [sic] creatures to be there. This divine Sabbath is the 'crown of creation;' humankind is not. Rather humankind along with all other creatures is 'crowned' and blessed by the Sabbath. In his rest on the Sabbath the creator God achieves his goal, and human beings who celebrate the Sabbath perceive nature as God's Sabbath and allow the world to be God's creation.[315]

The above quotation indicates that the creation account cannot be separated from the Sabbath. Without the Sabbath, creation is incomplete. The rest that God took was after the six days work when God finished all what He/She had done. Von Rad maintains that creation "was not and is not incomplete but it has been completed by God." The phrase "has blessed" and "sanctified" indicates that rest here is not meant for God alone but for the entire creation.[316] Simultaneously with God's rest, creations also need to take rest along with God. Hence, the Sabbath holds peculiar character as it is considered "holy, set apart, differentiated from all other days which have been filled with creative activities."[317] According to the Priestly narratives after the creation of the beast of the sea (Gen 1:22) and the creation of human beings (Gen 1:28) God imparts blessings to them with the command to be fruitful. But the blessing of the Sabbath is not limited to any particular creature but is extended to the entire creation. God hallows the Sabbath

---

[314] Jurgen Moltmann, *God in Creation: An Ecological Doctrine of Creation* (London: SCM Press Ltd, 1985), 279.

[315] Jurgen, Moltmann, *Creating a Just Future* (London: SCM Press, 1989), 61.

[316] Gerhard Von Rad, *Genesis* (London: SCM Press Ltd., 1972), 62.

[317] R. Davidson, *The Cambridge Bible Commentary* (Cambridge: University Press, 1973), 27.

means declaring something to be one's own property and that is inviolable. The Sabbath commandment declares to human beings to bring interruption, interval and rhythm into humans' daily chores and give special rest to the rest of creation. This implies that it is not only humans who need rest but also the whole of creation need to have rest and peace. The peace of Sabbath is peace with God and also involves the beginning of that peace with nature. Commenting on the important of Sabbath for preserving the eco-system Moltmann declares,

> According to the Bible, Sabbath rules are God's ecological strategy to protect the life which God has made. With its rest and its rhythm of time, the Sabbath is also the strategy which will take us out of ecological crisis and after one-sided progress at the expense of others show us the values of abiding equilibrium and accord with nature.[318]

The above discussion indicates the importance of Sabbath for ecological preservation. Corresponding to the weekly Sabbath is the Sabbath year (Lev. 25:1-7) celebrated every seventh year after entering the promise land. Six years they are allowed to toil their fields and in the seventh year they have to give solemn rest to the land, that is, they are commanded neither to sow their seeds nor to prune their vineyard. Hyatt argues that the main idea for "allowing the land to lie fallow every seventh year is a humanitarian one," so that the poor as well as the wild beasts could have a share in it.[319] Martin Noth maintains that the Sabbath year begins from the autumn is "a full agricultural year, from ploughing and sowing to harvest." Nevertheless, "the fallow year is to be at the disposal of the poor" or "those who have no stake in the soil" and the "wild beast."[320] Hence, everyone can share the fruits of the land, which becomes a "special benefit to slaves and other landless persons (Lev. 25:6; Ex. 23: 11).[321] Ronald E. Clement asserts that the institution of the fallow year originated from the religious aspect as the land belongs to God. Hence, every seventh year the land needs to be restored to its original state as intended by the Creator. He further states that the idea that lies in the background is the social benefit to the poor where the non-land owning members are placed in the forefront. For him, the fallow land is supposed to be accessible to both the poor and the wild animals.[322] This could help not only the poor but other creatures as well who can also share the fruits of the land.

---

318 Moltmann, *Creating a Just Future,* 66.

319 J. P. Hyatt, *The New Century Bible Commentary- Exodus* (Michigan: WM B. Eerdmans Publication Co., 1980), 247.

320 Martin Noth, *Leviticus: A Commentary* –Revised edition (London: SCM Press LTD, 1977), 186.

321 Gordon J. Wenham, *The Book of Leviticus* (Michigan: William B. Eerdmans Publishing Company, 1979), 318.

322 Ronald E. Clements, *The Cambridge Bible Commentary: Exodus* (Cambridge: University Press, 1972), 151. See also George V. Pixley, *On Exodus: A Liberation Perspective* (New York: Orbis

Moltmann maintains that the Sabbath year is the year for celebration. It is not merely the feast for humans but for the entire creation.[323]

Together with the Sabbath year is the Jubilee year (Lev. 25:8-55) which is celebrated after every seventh Sabbath year of the Lord.[324] The word Jubilee derives from the Hebrew word *Yobel* which means "ram" or "ram's horn."[325] This can be referred to the blowing of the trumpets at the beginning of the Jubilee year to proclaim "God's year of release."[326] In the Jubilee year, the year will be hallowed, and liberty is proclaimed throughout the land to all its inhabitants, property shall be returned back to the one who has sold it, slaves shall be released, they shall neither sow nor reap but eat what is yielded out of the fields (Lev. 25:10-12). Nallunnakkal argues that "the theological principle underlying the Jubilee is that the land must not be sold off permanently, for the land is Yahweh's. (Ps. 24:1)"[327] Consequently, while the Sabbatical year helps reduce the plight of the poor; in the Jubilee year an attempt will be made to give them a new start. "Everyone had the chance to make a fresh start."[328] Hence, the Jubilee year offered freedom not only for human beings, but the entire land as well as other creations who are expected to enjoy freedom and rest.

The question may be asked whether the law of the Sabbatical year was regularly observed. Wenham maintains that "as a social institution the Jubilee year remains an ideal, which was rarely, if ever, realized."[329] Whatever the case may be, both Sabbatical and Jubilee year offer deep ecological significance. Noth argues that the idea behind the Sabbatical year and the Jubilee year is that of the return of the land to its original state. In Noth's term "*restitution in integrum* or restoration to an original state."[330] If that is the case, it convey a rich ecological nuance that could help not only the poor and the animals to share the fruits of the earth but the entire land could obtained and its fertility recaptured. Hence, it is not humans alone but the whole creation will achieve freedom. Nalunnnakal argues that "it

---

Books, 1983), 183. See also, Hans Walter Wolff, *Anthropology of the Old Testament* (London, SCM Press Ltd, 1974), 137.

323 Moltmann, *God in Creation,* 289.

324 Wenham maintains that the main purpose of Jubilee is to prevent the utter ruin of the debtors. In the biblical period a person who could not repay his/her debts are forced to sell his land or even his personal freedom by becoming a slave. If such kind of practice is left unchecked it would lead to great social disparities in the Israel society with the rich section continued to exploit the weaker section. See Wenham, *The Book of Leviticus,* 317.

325 Noth, *Leviticus: A Commentary,* 184.

326 Moltmann, *God in Creation,* 289.

327 Nalunnakkal, *Green Liberation: Towards an Integral Ecotheology,* 73.

328 Wenham, *The Book of Leviticus,* 317, 319.

329 Wenham, *The Book of Leviticus,* 318.

330 Noth, *Leviticus: A Commentary,* 183.

has strong ecological connotations as the 'original rest' (as at the time of creation) should be given back to the land, undisturbed by the hand of humanity."[331]

Theology of Sabbatical year and Jubilee year convey a strong message to the agencies of globalization or the neo-colonial forces promoted by the ideologies of neoliberalism. It speaks against the paradigm of unlimited economic growth in a very short span of time. In their eagerness for quick profit they continue to exploit not only the earth resources at alarming speed but also put the entire eco-system at risk. The idea behind the Sabbatical year and Jubilee year is to grant equal opportunity to everyone to restart and rebuild their lost economic life. Hence, as stated above, everyone is given the chance to have a fresh start. This is done to remind the Israelites that the entire earth and its resources belong to God (Ps. 24:1). If the earth and its resources belong to God, no one has the right to monopolize it for one's own advantage at the expense of others. Rather the entire earth's resources need to be shared and enjoyed by all sections of the earth's community.

For the tribal communities who are practicing *Jhuming* or shifting cultivation, the concept of fallow period is not alien to them. In the earlier time, as the available land for shifting cultivation was plenty, the fallow period was practiced up to seven or eight years. But today due to the increase of population and the pressure on land, the fallow period was reduced to one or two years. Even though the shifting cultivation is dangerous to the environment, the concept of fallow period according to the tribal understanding has deep ecological significance. The main idea for keeping the land fallow is that the land could regain and recover its fertility and production. Till the time the person concerned comes back to the same land for cultivation, the land has already replenished its productive capacities. Hence, all is not lost. This is not to romanticize shifting cultivation and today shifting cultivation is practically not viable, rather an attempt is to recover the concept of fallow period making it relevance in today's context. Looking in the context of globalization where the advocates of economic globalization make all efforts to exploit the earth resources at the expense of the entire eco-system, Basaiawmoit argues that if one is concerned for the survival of the earth today, there is no better alternative but to practice ecological Sabbath. Ecological Sabbath for him is to practice the concept of fallow period. This does not mean that the entire land is to be left fallow at the same time, rather it means to practice it sporadically or on a rotational basis.[332] This is more feasible especially for the people who have big areas of cultivated land. Citing from Isaiah 61:1-2, Moltmann says that when the Messiah will come at the end-time year of Jubilee "to bring good tidings to the afflicted; to bind up the broken hearted, to proclaim liberty to the captives, and the opening of prison to those who are bound; to proclaim the year of the Lord's

[331] Nalunnakkal, *Green Liberation: Towards an Integral Ecotheology*, 74.

[332] Interview with PBM Basaiawmoit on the 9 May 2012.

favor, and the day of vengeance of our God" the messianic era will dawn and this will exemplify the image of the Sabbath. He further states that,

> Looking back to the year of Jubilee, the image tells us that the messianic era will bring the liberation of the oppressed, and God's justice and righteousness in everything. Looking back to the Sabbath year, it means that the messianic era will allow the land to be free, and everything that lives to have the nourishment it is properly due. Looking back to the Sabbath day, finally, it means that rest and peace will spread out in the presence of God.[333]

Biblical and Theological Concept of the Poor

Poor and poverty are two among the widely discussed terms in the Bible both in the Old Testament and the New Testament. Gutierrez maintains that term like *ebyon* or the 'beggar,' *dal* the 'weak or frail one,' *ani* or the 'bent over,' and *anaw* the 'humble before God' are the terms that express the downgrading living situation of the poor and the marginalised section. He further states that using the terms indigent, weak, bent over, wretched and so on is not merely to describe the living condition of the poor, but at the same time it is to express protest against the injustices done by the oppressors.[334] People becomes poor not because of their fate rather because they are denied and deprived of their rights and privileges by the powerful section in the society. In the context of the Khasi people the powerful section are the neo-colonial forces that come in the name of giant companies to exploit and extract the entire resources of the land without any limits. With the support of a tiny section of the elite in the community, neo-colonial forces make all efforts to take control of the rich resources of the land at the expense of both the local poor people and the environment. Hence, the coming of big companies to the land, instead of bringing development to the people of the area conversely make their condition more impoverished than before.

The Biblical narratives tell us that the prophets denounce every kind of abuse, every form of keeping the poor in poverty, or of creating new poor. Gutierrez maintains that the prophets speak against fraudulence commerce and exploitation (Hos. 12:8; Amos 8:5, etc.), hoarding of lands (Mic. 2:1-3; Ezek. 22:29; etc), dishonest courts (Amos 5:7; Jer.22:13-17; etc.), violence of the ruling classes (2 Kings 23:30, 35; Amos 4:1), slavery (Neh. 5:1-5; Amos 2:6; 8:6), unjust taxes (Amos 4:1; 5:11-12), unjust functionaries (Amos 5:7; Jer. 5:28), oppression by the rich (Lk. 6:24-25; 12:13-21; etc).[335] Pieris argues that the gospel message tells us that there is conflicting relationship between God and money or as he puts it between *Abba* and *Mamona.* He further states that according to the message preached by Jesus, human's "growing intimacy with the one" resulted to

[333] Moltmann, *God in Creation,* 289-290.

[334] Gustavo Gutierrez, *A Theology of Liberation.* Reprinted (New York: Orbis Books, 1988), 165.

[335] Gutierrez, *A Theology of Liberation,* 167.

"constant repudiation of the other." For it is impossible to serve two masters.[336] It is important to note that God is not against richness (Job 42:12-16), but God is against accumulation of wealth where a person is not ready to share his/her resources with the poor and the needy (Mt. 19:21). The Bible speaks against people who are rich and often busy in accumulating wealth thereby ignore their nearest neighbour especially the poor and the needy.

Gutierrez argues that this is "not simply a matter of denouncing poverty" rather it speaks about "positive and concrete measures to prevent poverty from becoming established among the People of God." There are many occasions in the Bible where God opted for helping the poor and the needy to come out of the clutch of poverty.[337] For instance, Deut. 24:19-21 and Lev. 19:9-10 tells us that during the harvest time, the owner should not gather everything from the field; rather they should leave some grain, for such is meant for the widows, the orphans and the aliens. Notably, while the Sabbath is a day of rest for everyone including the slaves and aliens, the main characteristic of the Sabbatical year is to leave the land fallow so that the poor, the widow can have some share from the fruits of the mother earth. As stated earlier, in the Jubilee year everyone gets the chance to start their life anew; slaves should be made free, land should be returned to the one who sold it and so on. This is done with the conviction that the land is Yahweh's. Hence the above discussion indicates that God has a preferential option for the poor and the vulnerable section in the society. This contrasts the practices of the neo-colonial forces who driven by neo-liberal ideologies they make all efforts to strive for unlimited profit.

Preferential Option for the Poor

The term preferential option for the poor has become a widely discussed topic especially in the context of liberation theology. The perception of the term preferential option for the poor was developed at the Conference of Latin American Bishops held at Medellin, Columbia in 1968.[338] Here, the preferential option for the poor indicates that though God loves all people, He/She often sides with the poor, reveals Him/Herself to them and identifies with them. In the context of class struggle, "God sides with the poor against every oppressor who

---

[336] Aloysius Pieris, *An Asian Theology of Liberation* (Edinburg: T & T Clark, 1988), 15.

[337] Gutierrez, *A Theology of Liberation,* 167.

[338] The Conference of Latin American Bishops was a Bishops Conference held in 1968 in Medellin, Columbia. In this conference the Bishops agreed that the church should take "a preferential option for the poor." The bishops decided to form Christian base communities in which they would teach the poor how to read by using the Bible. The goal of the bishops was to liberate the people from the institutionalized violence of poverty. They informed the people that poverty and hunger were preventable. This movement led to the development of Liberation Theology. http://en.wikipedia.org/wiki/conference_of_latin_American_Bishops (25.8.2012).

would exploit and dehumanize them."[339] Nevertheless, this does "not necessarily mean an option against the rich, although it does not deny the rejection of evil systems and of bad structures in society."[340] This implies that preferential option for the poor means to be in solidarity with the poor and the weaker sections of the society. Here, solidarity can be understood as "readiness to accept the differences, respecting them. There is no domination; everyone is free to be what he or she is."[341] To be in solidarity with the poor also involve an understanding of their social setting, their worldview, their living conditions, and their daily struggles in their attempt to fight for survival. In short, living experience and the entire context of the poor must be an important ground for theological reflection. Gerald West maintains that preferential option for the poor also "involves an epistemological paradigm shift in which the poor and the marginalised are seen as the primary dialogue partners of theology. Theology begins with the reality, experience, needs, interests, questions, and resources of the poor and the marginalised."[342]

Hence, it entails the necessity of solidarity with the poor in their struggle against power relations and discrimination by the powerful section in the society. The preferential option for the poor reminds us that the God of the Bible is one who takes sides with the poor and marginalized. It may be noted that the God who is revealed in the entire exodus event is the God of the abused, the poor and the despised. "This God" argues Field "is sensitive to the cries of the oppressed and marginalised and responds to them."[343] On the other, this God is always against the powerful and the oppressors, who not only exploit the source of livelihood of the marginalised poor, but also push them towards the margins of economic life. God's preferential option for the poor does not merely mean that God is on the side of the poor, or that God's justice will be demonstrated through the life experience of the poor. Rather it indicates that "God speaks through these oppressed and marginalised in the society."[344] They are the vehicle through which God's messages and blessings are to be realized in the society. Gutierrez asserts that God takes the side or show special care towards the poor not because they good rather because they are poor. He further states that,

---

[339] Stanley J. Grenz & Roger E. Olson, *20th Century Theology: God & the World in a Transitional Age* (Secunderabad: OM Books, 2004), 218.

[340] Josey Thamarassery, *Church: Sign and Sacrament of Unity: A Contextual Mission Theology* (Kottayam: Oriental Institute of Religious Studies, 2009), 497.

[341] Thamarassery, *Church: Sign and Sacrament of Unity: A Contextual Mission Theology,* 498.

[342] Gerald West, "The Bible and the poor: a new way of doing theology," in *The Cambridge Companion to Liberation Theology* (Reprinted), edited by Christopher Rowland (Cambridge: Cambridge University Press, 2001), 131.

[343] Field, "On (Re)centering the Margins…," 51.

[344] Thamarassery, *Church: Sign and Sacrament of Unity: A Contextual Mission Theology,* 489.

> The Beatitudes tell us more about the goodness of God than about the goodness of the poor. They reveal a *Go'el* God, defender and protector of the real-life poor, those deprived of what is necessary to live as human beings. It is this conditions that makes them the preferred people of God.[345]

The above discussion reflects that God is against all powers and structures that attempts to dehumanize and discriminate the poor and marginalised. He/She is always found to be on the side of the poor and the vulnerable sections of humanity. The God of the exodus who reveals Himself/Herself to and takes sides with the poor chooses to be incarnated in Jesus in very poor conditions and poor surroundings. The Bible says "the word became flesh and dwelt among us (John 1:14)." God chooses to be incarnated in a poor stable, born through poor parents and even brought up in a poor surrounding from Nazareth. "This poor carpenter" asserts Field "was not only a member of a defeated and colonized nation but came from Galilee, an area despised by his fellow Jews."[346] At the very beginning of his ministry Jesus preached the good news to the poor by reading the so called famous Nazareth Manifesto based on Isa. 61:1-2 which says,

> The Spirit of the Lord is upon me, because he has anointed me to preach the good news to the poor. He has sent me to proclaim release to the captives and recovering of sight to the blind, to set at liberty those who are oppressed, to proclaim the acceptable year of the Lord.(Lk. 4:18-19).

Jesus ministry is mostly found among the despised and rejected in the society. His ministry to the Samaritan woman (Jn. 4:4-30); Lazarus (Jn. 11: 1-44), healing of ten lepers (Lk. 17:11-19) to name a few, all point to the fact that Jesus spent the main part of his ministry among the poor and the rejected of the society. Field further argues "at the beginning of his ministry, Jesus abandoned the relative security of his trade and joined the landless poor, in so doing he became an outcast by choice."[347] Paul's letter to the Corinthians explain well how Jesus became poor in order to identify himself with the least in the community, so that they will experience life in all its fullness. "For you know the grace of Lord Jesus Christ, that though he was rich, yet for your sake he became poor, so that by his poverty you might become rich.(II Cor. 8:9)" His entire life and ministry is concentrated mostly with the poor, the despised, the rejected, the lepers and the least among the community. For he came that they might have life, and have it abundantly (Jn. 10:10). Abraham maintains that,

> Jesus' proclamation includes the full dimensions of a truly human life-physical and mental healing, bringing new life to the poor, a new stewardship of all resources of the earth and the gifts of the grace of God for the flowering

---

[345] Gustavo Gutierrez, *The Power of the Poor in History* (London: SCM Press Ltd., 1983), 116.

[346] Field, "On (Re)centering the Margins…," 51.

[347] Field, "On (Re)centering the Margins…," 52.

> of human life and to enable the principalities and powers to perform their true political function.[348]

Hence, the God of the Bible, the one who incarnated in Jesus of Nazareth is the God who not only takes care of the poor but also shares their experiences by identifying and becoming as one of them. This is against the practices of the neo-colonial forces in the present day context of economic globalization, where the poor and the weaker sections of the society are not only discriminated and denied of their rights and privileges, but are also pushed back to the margin and periphery of economic life.

Conclusion

The above discussion portrays the number of resources from the indigenous Khasi Tribal perspective offers valuable insights for correcting the drawbacks of the neo-colonial forces. Driven by the ideologies of neo-liberalism, neo-colonial agencies make all efforts to strive for unlimited economic growth. In the process they brought certain damages to both humans and natural environment. Hence, corrective measures from the indigenous Khasi perspective could offer other alternatives that would help do justice to both humans and the natural environment. Secondly, the perception of top-down development instead of bringing development to the people concerned, make their situation more impoverished than before. Hence, the researcher found that we have to move beyond sustainable development towards realizing the value and worth of the natural environment thereby bringing justice to the health of nature as well as humans. Thirdly, misinterpretation of certain biblical passages as giving license to exploit and abuse the earth resources has been re-read and re-interpreted. The researcher found that the Bible did not suggest or permit exploitation of the earth resources. The earth's resources is for use not misuse. The above discussion reveals that there are a number of biblical passages that emphasize on the importance of caring and protecting the entire environment as the *oikos* of God, so as to make it beautiful and secured place to live in both for humans and non human creatures.

---

[348] K. C. Abraham, *Transforming Vision: Theological-Methodological Paradigm Shift* (Thiruvalla: Christava Sahitya Samithy, 2006), 142.

Conclusion

The research work has investigated the challenges posed by globalization to the economic life of the tribal people with special reference to the Khasi people of Meghalaya. The process of globalization has penetrated and permeated in every nook and corner of the globe. There is no area or region that is free from the impact or the influence of globalization. Whether people like it or not, and agree or disagree with its ideologies, globalization is here to stay. The advent of globalization not only divided the countries of the world between the rich and the poor countries or the north and the south, but within the country it has divided the population between the rich affluent and the poor marginalised sections. In addition, it has broken the delicate balance of the entire eco-system, especially in the context of the tribals. Such a situation demands concrete and authentic response with practical suggestion that would help facilitate the tribal people in general and the Khasi people in particular in their daily struggle against the challenges of globalization that has affected their entire life situation.

The Khasi Setting

The study testifies that the traditional social, political, cultural, and religious life of the Khasis have to a certain extent contributed to the growth and development of the economic life of the people. Prior to the coming of the British colonial rule, the economy of the people was generally self sufficient. In course of time, the Khasi people developed good trade relationship with their neighbours both in the plains of Assam and Bengal. The study reveals that though the people have to import some items for their domestic needs, the amount of export are more in comparison with the imports. This point to the fact that, besides agriculture, trade and commerce is another income generating activity of the Khasi people. The advent of the British colonial rule to this part of the land had adverse affect on the tribal life in general and their economic life in particular. With the motive to exploit the economic advantage of the region the colonial master make all efforts to capture trade activities from the control of the local indigenous people particularly those items that could generated high amount of economic benefits like coal, lime stone and orange. What is left in the hands of the natives were those items that have less economic importance. In addition, to establish their complete control over the natives, the colonial ruler brought with them people from outside the region employing them in different services like office work, trade activities and the like. While this assisted them in extending the horizon of their empire, it however caused large influx of the people from outside the Khasi region to these hills. In course of time, people from outside the region also took control of the whole trade and commerce in the region, which denied significant job/employment opportunities to the local indigenous population. For the indigenous and simple tribal people like the Khasis, this has not only hindered their source of livelihood but it has obstructed the entire growth and development of their economy. Hence, by the time the colonial rulers left these hills the economy of the people was in a deplorable state. With the partition of the country into India and East Pakistan (later Bangladesh) trade activities both exports and imports that have flourished since the pre-colonial period has been severely affected. With no proper transport communication developed in the hills on one hand and no market readily available in the hills on the other, agricultural products that were in great demand in the plains of Bengal was then left to rot in the fields. This brought untold misery to the life of the local people. In due course, tribal people that were economically self sufficient prior to the advent of the British colonial rulers, now need to depend on the financial support of the central government. At the time when the tribal economy was insecure and weak, the advent of globalization worsened the economic situation of the tribal people.

Globalization: An Overview

The study reveals that globalization is not a new phenomenon. Globalization originates when people or nations begin to move out of their geographical or territorial boundaries either for domination or having trade relationship with the other in other parts of the globe. Consequently, this study examines three different phases of globalization that have influenced the world in different time and capacities. The first phase or the colonialist globalization portrays that with the motive to exploit the land and economic resources of the colonies, the colonial ruler went on to plunder and extract the mineral resources of the colonies without limits. Besides exploiting the economic resources of the colonies, the colonial rulers went further to colonize the mind of the native people, thus, preparing them for the global economic phenomenon. The second phase demonstrates the emergence of two super powers the USA and the USSR who in their attempt to capture the entire globe led to the bipolarization of the world. However, with the collapse of the Berlin wall and the disintegration of the USSR, USA became the lone super power to dominate and influence the entire globe. The third phase or the present day globalization testifies the emergence of the agencies of globalization that has erased the national or territorial borders and pushed back the role of the nation states to the back seat. In the present day globalization it is the MNCs/TNCs, not the nation states that makes the decision as what to produce, how much to produce, where to invest and so on. The present day globalization not only divides the world's countries between the rich and the poor, or the North and the South, but within the country, the populations are divided between the rich and the poor section. The worst sufferers are the poor and marginalized people of the Third World countries like India.

India and Globalization

Right after independence, India adopted a planned economy based on the USSR model with certain restrictions to protect the country's economy from outside influence. However, with the country facing severe economic crisis in the 1990s, India opened up its economy by implementing the New Economic Policy based on liberalisation, privatization and globalization or the so called LPG model. It is believed that by integrating its economy with the global economy, the country has nothing to lose but many things to gain in the process. In other words, this will not only help raise the economic position of the country but will also improve the living conditions of different sections of population including the vulnerable section of the society. Nevertheless, though the country achieves rapid economic growth rate within short span of time, it is only one sided. To state differently, in the global economic competition, it is only the fittest that could survive. In reality, it is only the rich and the powerful that are benefitted whereas the poor and the marginalised section of population are pushed back to the margin of economic life, with little hope for a better future.

The Challenges of Globalization to Tribal Economy: Khasi Perspective

In the context of the Khasi people the challenges of globalization is experienced both in the first phase or the colonialist globalization and the present day globalization. The capturing of important trade activities and the dismantling of the iron industries posed severe challenges to the economic life of the Khasi people. What were left to the native people were only those trade activities with less economic value. By the time the colonial rulers left Khasi Jaintia Hills, the economy of the people was in deplorable state. In the post independence era, the development activities implemented by the government of India in the context of the tribal people using the "top-down" model and the Five Year Plan developmental activities did not help improve the living conditions of the majority poor tribals. Moreover, the advent of the present phase of globalization, make the situation no better for the Khasi people. With the motive to achieve quick and unlimited profit within short span of time as influenced by the neoliberal ideologies, the agencies of globalization inflict severe damage not only to the sources of livelihood of the tribal people but also to the entire surrounding environment. It is such situation that impels a serious response from the theological point of view as well as the Khasi perspective.

An Indigenous Khasi Tribal Theological Response

As indicated above, such situation demands authentic response both from the theological point of view and the Khasi perspective. From the Khasi perspective, the researcher employ rediscovery of Khasi traditional ethical teachings like the concept of *Tipbriew Tipblei* and the concept of *Kamai ia ka Hok*. Both the concepts speak against the neo-liberal ideologies of quick and unlimited profit within short period at the expense of the poor and the entire natural surroundings. At the same time, the study made an attempt to re-visit the eco-spirituality of the Khasis that emphasized on the value and worth of the mother earth. Eco-spirituality of Khasi in particular and the tribal in general, portrays that the earth is like a mother which provide not only the source of livelihood but also identity and personhood to human persons. It is a home to both human and non-human creatures. Hence, if globalization is to be corrected, resources from the traditional tribal heritage need to be considered seriously. The study demonstrates that misinterpretation of certain passages like the genesis creation account that stress on the centrality of human persons at the expense of other creatures led to serious ecological crisis that has threaten the survival not only of humans but also other non-human creatures. However, the study testifies that there are many biblical passages that also stress on the importance of caring and preserving the earth and other creatures. Hence, re-reading and re-interpretation of the biblical passages need to be taken seriously. That is, re-reading and re-interpretation of certain biblical passages like the creation narratives will not only help to correct the drawback of globalization, but also to reconsider the earth as the *oikos* of God that provide secured environment and happy home not only for human persons but also for the entire creation.

Bibliography

Books

Abraham, K. C. *Liberative Solidarity: Contemporary Perspectives on Mission.* Thiruvalla: Christava Sahitya Samithi, 2001.

Abraham, K. C. *Transforming Vision: Theological-Methodological Paradigm Shifts.* Thiruvalla: Christava Sahitya Samithi, 2006.

Acharya, M. N. *The History of Medieval Assam.* Guwahati: Dulla Barua and Company, 1966.

Annie, W. S. *Globalization and Women Subsistence Labour: A Third World Theological Perspective.* Bangalore: BTESSC/SATHRI, 2009.

Anthuvan, M. Victor Louis. *The Dynamics and the Impact of Globalization- A Subaltern Perspectives.* Madurai: Amirtham Publications, 2006.

Arthur, Chris. *The Globalization and Communications: Some Religious Implications.* Geneva: WCC Publications, 1998.

Aschroft, Bill, Gareth Griffiths and Helen Tiffin. *The Empire Write Back.* 2nd ed. London: Routledge, 1989.

Balasuriya, Tissa. *Globalization and Human Solidarity.* Thiruvalla: Christava Sahitya Samithy, 2000.

Bandyopadhayay, P. K. *The North East Saga.* New Delhi: Publication Division, Ministry of Information and Broadcasting, Government of India, 1978.

Banerjee, Brojendra Nath. *Globalization: Rough and Risky Road.* New Delhi: New Age International (P) Limited, Publishers, 1998.

Bareh, H. *The History and Culture of the Khasi People.* 3rd ed. Guwahati: Spectrum Publications, 1997.

Barry, Peter. *Beginning Theory: An Introduction to Literary and Cultural Theory.* New Delhi: Viva Books, 2010.

Basu, Nirmal Kumar, *Assam in the Ahom Age, 1228-1826.* Calcutta: Sanskrit Pustak Bandar, 1970.

Bhagawati, Dhiren. *Meghalaya: Issues and Legacies of its Early Years.* Guwahati: D. V. S. Publishers, 2007.

Bhattacharji, Tanmay. *Political Economy of North East India.* Silchar: Published by the Author, 2004.

Blah, Toki. *Good Governance for Transformation and Development of Meghalaya.* Shillong: ICARE, 2007.

Bradley, I. *God is Green.* London: Darton, Longman and Todd, 1990.

Buckman, Greg. *Globalization: Tame it or Scrap it?.* Bangalore: Books for Change, 2004.

Cantlie's, Sir Keith. *Notes on Khasi Law.* Shillong: Chapala Book Stall, 2008-2009.

Cayre, F. *Manual of Patrology and History of Theology.* Paris: Desclee & Co, 1927.

Chandra, Bipan, Mirdula Mukherjee and Aditya Mukherjee, *India After Independence, 1947-2000.* New Delhi: Penguin Books, 2000.

Chandra, Kakati. *Discovery of Assam.* Guwahati: The Tribune Press, 1954.

Chattopadhyay, S. K. *Tribal Institution of Meghalaya.* Guwahati: Spectrum Publications, 1985.

Chaudhury, J. N. *Ki Khun Khasi Khara (The Khasi People).* Shillong: Published by the Author, 1996.

Chib, Sukhdev Singh. *This Beautiful India: Meghalaya.* New Delhi: Light & Life Publishers, 1980.

Chossudovsky, Michel. *The Globalization of Poverty: Impacts of IMF and the World Bank Reforms.* Penang: Third World Network, 1997.

Chowdhury, J. N. *The Khasi Canvas.* Calcutta: Srimati Jaya Chowdhury, 1978.

Chowdhury, J. N. *Ki Khun Khasi Khara (The Khasi People).* Shillong: Published by the Author, 1996.

Claar, Victor V. & Robin J. Klay. *Economic in Christian Perspective: Theory, Policy and Life Choices.* Illinois: IVP Academic, 2007.

Clement, Ronald E. *The Cambridge Bible Commentary: Exodus.* Cambridge: University Press, 1972.

Cob Jr., John B., *Sustainability: Economics Ecology & Justice.* New York: Orbis Books, 1992.

______________. *The Earthist Challenge to Economism: A Theological Critique of the World Bank.* New York: St. Martin's Press INC, 1999.

Cobb Jr., John B. and Jeanyne B. Slettom, *The Process Perspective: Frequently Asked Question about Process Theology.* St. Louis Missouri: Challice Press, 2003.

Dasgupta, Biplab. *Structural Adjustment, Global Trade and the New Political Economy of Development.* New Delhi: Vistaar Publications, 1998.

______________.*Globalization.* New Delhi: Sage Publications, 2005.

Dasgupta, Samir and Ray Kiely. *Globalization and After.* New Delhi: Sage Publications, 2006.

Davidson, R. *The Cambridge Bible Commentary.* Cambridge: University Press, 1973.

Desai, S. S. M. *Development of Indian Econoic Thought.* Bombay: Himalaya Publishing House, 1981.

Devi, Lakshmi. *Ahom Tribal Relations.* Guwahati: Assam Book Depot, 1968.

Dey, Shumboo Chunder. *Sylhet.* Calcutta: G. P. Roy & Co, 1880.

Doshi, S. L. *Modernity, Postmodernity and Neo-sociological Theories.* Jaipur: Rawat Publications, 2006.

Dube, Musa W. *Postcolonial Feminist Interpretation of the Bible.* Missouri: Chalice Press, 2001.

Dutt, Romesh. *The Economic History of India.* Vol. I. New Delhi: Publication Division, 1989.

Dutt, Romesh. *The Economic History of India.* Vol. 2. New Delhi: Publication Division, 1989.

Dutta, Promatha Nath. *Impact of the West on Khasis and Jaintias.* New Delhi: Cosmo Publications, 1982.

Edwards, Denis. *Ecology at the Heart of Faith.* New York: Orbis Books, 2006.

Epperly, Bruce G. *Process Theology: A Guide for the Perplexed.* London: T & T Clark International, 2011.

Fanon, Frantz. *The Wretched of the Earth.* Middlesex: Penguin Books, 1963.

Fernandez, Walter and Anupama Dutta. *Colonialism to Globalization: Five Centuries after Vasco da Gama.* New Delhi: Indian Social Institute, 1999.

Friedman, Thomas. *The World is Flat.* London: Penguin Books, 2006.

Frowde, Henry. *Imperial Gazetteer of India: Karachi to Kottayam.* New ed. Oxford: Clarendon Press, 1908.

Gait, Edward. *A History of Assam.* 5th ed. Guwahati: Lawyer's Book Stall, 1992.

Gandhi, Leela. *Postcolonial Theory- A Critical Introduction.* Delhi: Oxford University Press, 1999.

Gatphoh, Primrose. *Ki Umjer Ksiar.* Guwahati: Dispur Print House, 1941.

Gill, Stephen and David Law. *The Global Political Economy.* Baltimore: The John Hopkin University Press, 1989.

Gilpin, Robert. *The Challenge of Global Capitalism: The World Economy in the 21st Century.* Princeton: Princeton University Press, 2000.

Giri, Helen. *The Khasis Under the British Rule, 1824-1947.* New Delhi: Regency Publications, 1998.

Gocmen, Dogan. *The Adam Smith Problem: Human Nature and Society in the Theory of Moral Sentiments and The Wealth of the Nations.* London: Tauris Academic Studies, 2007.

Gregorious, Paulus Mar. *A Light too Bright: The Enlightenment Today.* Albany: State University of New York Press, 1992.

Grenz, Stanley J. and Roger E. Olson. *Twentieth Century Theology: God and the World in a Transitional Age.* Secunderabad: OM Books, 2004.

Griffith, Brian. *The Creation of Wealth: A Christian Case for Capitalism.* Illinois: InterVarsity Press, 1984.

Guha, Amalendu. *Medieval and Early Colonial Assam: Society, Polity and Economy.* Calcutta: K. P. Bakchi & Company, 1991.

Gunton, Colin E. *The Triune Creator.* Cambridge: William B. Eerdmans Publishing Co., 1998.

Gupta, K. R., ed. *Liberalisation and Globalization of Indian Economy.* Vol. I. New Delhi: Atlantic Publishers and Distributors, 2000.

Gurdon, P. R. T., *The Khasis.* 6th ed. Delhi: Low Price Publications, 2010.

Gurudas, Das. *Structural Change and Strategy of Development Resource-Industry Linkages in North East India.* New Delhi: Akansha Publishing House, 2005.

Gutierrez, Gustavo. *A Theology of Liberation.* Reprinted. Maryknoll: Orbis Books, 1973.

_______________. *The Power of the Poor in History.* London: SCM Press Ltd., 1983.

Hirst, Paul and Grahame Thompson. *Globalization in Question.* Cambridge: Polity Press, 1999.

Hunter, W. W. *A Statistical Account of Assam.* 2 vol. Reprinted. Guwahati: Spectrum Publications, 1998.

Hyatt, J. P. *The New Century Bible Commentary-Exodus.* Michigan: Wm B. Eerdmans Publication Co., 1980.

Jaitdkhar, Sib Charan Roy, *Ka Niam-Ki-Khasi: Ka Niam Tipbriew Tipblei.* Reprinted. Shillong: Ri Khasi Press, 1966.

Jawara, Fatoumata and Aileen Kwa. *Behind the Scene at WTO.* London. Zed Books, 2003.

Jayapalan, N. *Economic History of India: Ancient to Present Day.* 2nd edition. New Delhi: Atlantic Publishers & Distributors (P) Ltd., 2008.

Jenkins, Nigel. *Gwalia in Khasia.* Llandysul, Dyfed: Gomer Press, 1995.

Jha, Avinash. *Background to Globalization.* Reprinted. Mumbai: Centre for Education and Documentation, 2001.

Jha, Shiva Chandra. *Indian Ecomomic Thought: Mahatma Gandhi to Indira Gandhi.* New Delhi: Deep & Deep Publications, 1990.

Jyrwa, J. F. *Christianity in Khasi Culture.* Shillong: K. J. P. Assembly Press, 2011.

Kalita, Ramesh Chandra. *Assam in the Eighteenth Century.* New Delhi: Omson Publications, 1992.

Kharakor, Philomena. *Ka Kolshor Khasi kumba pawha ka Literashor Khasi (1930-1940).* Shillong: St. Mary's College, 2006.

Khor, Martin. *Rethinking Globalization: Critical Issues and Policy Choices.* London: Zed Book, 2001.

Khor, Martin. *Globalization & the Crisis of Sustainable Development.* 2nd ed. Penang: Third World Network, 2002.

Kochupurakal, Sebastian. *Eco-Mission: A Paradigm Shift in Missiology.* Bangalore: Asian Trading Corporation, 2007.

Kurien, C. T. *Global Capitalism and the Indian Economy.* New Delhi: Orient Longman Limited, 1994.

Kynta, Hamlet Bareh Ngap. *The Economy of Meghalaya.* Guwahati: Spectrum Publication, 2001.

Lamare, Shobhan. *The Jaintias: Studies in Society and Change.* New Delhi: Regency Publication, 2005.

Lamin, Henry. *Economy and Society in Meghalaya.* New Delhi: Har-Anand Publications, 1995.

Longchar, A. Wati. *The Tribal Religious Traditions in North East India.* Jorhat: Eastern Theological College, 2000.

Loomba, Ania. *Colonialism/Postcolonialism.* London: Routledge, 1998.

Lyngdoh, H. *Ka Niam Khasi.* Shillong: Ri Khasi Press, 1937.

Lyngdoh, Homiwell, *Ki Syiem Khasi bad Synteng.* 3rd ed. Shillong: Desmond P. Reade Diengdoh, 2003.

Lyngdoh, Mary Pristilla Rina. *The Festivals in the History and Culture of the Khasi.* New Delhi: Radha Publications, 2009.

Lyngdoh, Sngi, *Ki Riti Khyndew ba la buh u Longshwa Manshwa jong ka Ri Bhoi.* Shillong: Ribhoi Durbar, 1965.

Malngiang, Pascal. *Aspect, of Khasi Religion.* Shillong: Seven Hut Enterprise, 1981.

Marbaniang, Iskot. *Assam in a Nutshell.* Shillong: Chapala Book Stall, 1970.

Mathur, P. R. G. *Khasi of Meghalaya: A Study in Tribalism and Religion.* New Delhi: Spectrum Publications, 1980.

Matthew, T. *Tribal Economy of North Eastern Region.* Guwahati: Spectrum Publication, 1980.

Mawrie, Barness L. *Introduction to Khasi Ethics.* Shillong: DBCIC Publications, 2005.

______________. *The Khasis and their Natural Environment: A Study of Eco-consciousness and Eco-spirituality of the Khasis.* 2nd edition. Shillong: Vendrame Institute Publications. 2009.

Mawrie, H. Onderson. *The Essence of Khasi Religion.* Shillong: Ri Khasi Press, 1981.

______________. *Ka Theology Ka Niam Khasi.* Shillong: Ri Khasi Press, 1991.

______________. *Ka Pyrkhat U Khasi.* 5th ed. Guwahati: Silpi Printers, 1997.

McLeod. *Biginning Postcolonialism.* New Delhi: Viva Books Private Limited, 2010.

Medhi, S. B. *Transport System and Economic Development in Assam.* Guwahati: Publication Board Assam, 1978.

Mesle, C. Robert. *Process Theology: A Basic Introduction.* Missouri: Chalice Press, 1993.

Mills, A. J. M. *Reports of the Khasi and Jaintia Hills, 1853.* Shillong: North Eastern Hill University, 1985.

Moltmann. Jurgen. *God in Creation: An Ecological Doctrine of Creation.* London: SCM Press Ltd., 1985.

______________. *Creating a Just Future.* London: SCM Press, 1989.

More, William and Henry Austin Wilson, *Sellect Writings and Letters of Gregory of Nyssa.* Michigan: William B. Eerdmans Publishing Company, 1988.

Morris, John Hugh. *The Story of our Foreign Mission (Presbyterian Church of Wales).* 2nd ed. Aizawl: Synod Publication Board, 1990.

Muralivalabhan, T. V. *Dimensions of Sustainable Economic Development.* Nooranad. UNMA Publications, 2005.

Nakane, Chie, *Khasi and Garo: A Comparative Study in Matrilineal System.* Paris: Mouton and Company, 1967.

Naoroji, Dadabhai. *Poverty and Un-British Rule in India.* London, 1901.

Nash, James A. *Loving Nature: Ecological Integrity and Christian Responsibility.* Nashville: Abingdon Press, 1991.

Nataranjan, Nalini. *The Missionary among the Khasis.* Guwahati: United Publishers, 1997.

Nayak, P. and E. D. Thomas, *Human Development and Deprivation in Meghalaya.* New Delhi: Akansha Publishing House, 2007.

Nongkynrih, Kynpham Singh. *Around the Hearth: Khasi Legends.* New Delhi: Penguin Books, 2007.

Noris, Christopher. *The Truth About Post Modernism.* Oxford: Blackwell Publishers, 1993.

Noth, Martin. *Leviticus: A Commentary.* Revised Edition. London: SCM Press LTD., 1977.

Nulunnakkal, George Matthew. *Green Liberation: Towards an Integral Ecotheology.* Delhi: ISPCK/NCCI, 1991.

Oldham, Thomas. *Geological Structure of Parts of Khasi Hills.* Calcutta: F Carbery, Bengal Millitary Orphan Press, 1854.

Olson, Roger E. *The Story of Christian Theology.* Secunderabad: OM Books, 1999.

Osborn, L. *Guardian of Creation.* Leicester: Appolos, 1993.

Pamberton, B. R. *The Eastern Frontier of India.* Reprinted, New Delhi: Mittal Publications, 2000.

Patel, I. G. *Glimpse of Indian Economic Policy: An Insider's View.* Oxford: Oxford University Press, 2002.

Pde, L. H. Ka Law Lyngdoh bad ka Knia Phodsohlang. Shillong: Kaiser Mussinghoft Schuetz, 1994.

Peters, Rabecca Todd, *In Search of the Good Life: The Ethics of Globalization.* New York: Continuum International Publishing Group, 2004.

Pieris, Aloysius. *An Asian Theology of Liberation.* Edinburg: T & T Clark, 1988.

Pixley, George V. *On Exodus: A Liberation Perspective.* New York: Orbis Books, 1983.

Playne, Somerset, *Bengal and Assam, Behar and Orissa: Their History, People, Commerce and Industrial Resources.* London: The Foreign and Colonial Compiling and Publishing Company, 1917.

Premkumar, Daniel. *Bonding with Mission: Faith Activism in Local Congregations.* Chennai: Inter Church Service Association, 2008.

Prestige, G. L. *God in Patristic Thought.* London: SPCK, 1952.

Ramaswami, S. R. *In the Woods of Globalization.* Bangalore: Sahitya Sindhu Prakashana, 1995.

Ramsiej, K. D. *Ka Mariang ha u Khasi.* Shillong, Bonsen Press, 1992.

Rana, B. S. *The People of Meghalaya.* Calcutta: Punthi Pustak, 1989.

Rangritz, Hassan, *Human Resource in the Globalized World.* Delhi: Abhijeet Publications, 2004.

Ray, Ashok Kumar. *Revisiting North East India in the Era of Globalization.* New Delhi: OM Publications, 2007.

Reid, David. *Sustainable Development: An Introduction Guide.* London: Earthscan Publications Ltd, 1995.

Rieger, Joerg. *Globalization and Theology*. Nashville: Abingdon Press, 2010.

Riggs, John W. *Post Modern Christianity.* Harrisburg: Trinity Press International, 2003.

Robinson, William. *A Descriptive Account of Assam.* Calcutta: Ostel and Lepage, 1841.

Rongsen, M. *Development and Ecology.* Delhi: ISPCK, 1999.

Roy, Jeebon, *Ka Kitab ba Batai Pynshynna Shaphang U Wei U Blei.* 2nd edition. Shillong: Ri Khasi Press, 1979.

_______________. *Ka Niam jong ki Khasi.* Reprinted. Shillong: Ri Khasi Press, 2009.

Roy, Tirthankar. *The Economic History of India (1857-1947).* 2nd ed. New Delhi: Oxford University Press, 2006.

Said, Edward W. *Orientalism.* New Delhi: Penguin Books Pvt. Ltd., 2001.

Sampat, Preeti. *Economic Globalization Today: Resource Book.* Bangalore: Books for Change, 2003.

Santmire, H. Paul. *The Trivial of Nature.* Philadelphia: Fortress Press, 1985.

Sarkar, R. L. *The Bible, Ecology and Environment.* Delhi: ISPCK, 2000.

Schlossberg, Vinay Samuel, Ronals J. Sider. *Christianity and Economics in Post-Cold War Era: The Oxford Declaration and Beyond.* Grand Rapids, Michigan: William B. Eerdmans Publishing Company, 1994.

Sebastian, Thomas. *Globalization and Uneven Development: Neo-colonialism, Multinational Corporations, Space and Society.* Jaipur: Rawat Publications, 2007.

Sen, Amartya. *Development as Freedom.* New York: Anchor Books, 1999.

Sen, Soumen, *Social and State Formations in Khasi-Jaintia Hills.* Delhi: B. R. Publishing Corporation, 1985.

Shadap-Sen, Catherine. *The Origin and Early History of the Khasi-Synteng People.* Calcutta: Firma Private Limited, 1981.

Sharma, P. D. *Ecology and Environment.* Meerut: Rastogi Publications, 1995.

Shreeranjan, *Perspective on Development in Meghalaya.* Shillong: A Publication of State Institute of Rural Development (SIRD), Meghalaya, 2001.

Shulai L. Gilbert, *Ka Shillong: Naduh ka snem, 1863.* Shillong: Riwar Offset Press, 1998.

Sing, Kynpham, *Around the Hearth: Khasi Legends.* New Delhi: Penguin Books, 2007.

Smith, Adam. *The Wealth of Nations.* Vol. I, Reprinted. London: J. M. Dent & Sons LTD, 1960.

Snaitang, O. L. *Christianity and Social Change in Northeast India.* Shillong: Vendrame Institute, 1993.

Sreedharan, E. *A Text Book of Historiography.* New Delhi: Orients Blackswan Private Limited, 2009.

Stephen, M. *New Trends in Christian Theology.* New Delhi: Serial Publications, 2009.

Stiglitz, Joseph. *Globalization and Its Discontent.* New Delhi: Penguin Book India (P) Ltd., 2002.

______________. *Making Globalization Work.* London: Penguin Books, 2006.

Sugirtharajah, R. S. *The Bible and the Third World.* Cambridge: Cambridge University Press, 2001.

______________. *Asian Biblical Hermeneutics and Postcolonialism.* Sheffield: Sheffield Academic Press Ltd. 1999.

Szentes, Tamas, *The Transformation of the World Economy: New Directions and New Interests.* London: Zed Books Ltd, 1988.

Talukdar, Sharmila Das. *Khasi Cultural Resistance to Colonialism.* Guwahati: Spectrum Publications, 2004.

Tham, Soso, *Ki Sngi Barim U Hynniew Trep.* Shillong. Ri Khasi Press, 1987.

Thamarassery, Josey James. *Church Sign and Sacrament of Unity.* Kottayam: Oriental Institute of Religious Studies, 2009.

Thanzauva, K. *Transforming Theology: A Theological Basis for Social Transformation.* Bangalore: Asian Trading Corporation, 2002.

______________.*Theology of Community: Tribal Theology in the Making.* Bangalore: Asian Trading Corporation, 2004.

Thomas, Eugene D. *Poverty and Rural Development in Meghalaya (India).* New Delhi: Akansha Publishing House, 2004.

Tomlinson, B. R. *The Political Economy of the Raj (1914-1947): The Economics of Decolonization in India.* Cambridge: Cambridge Commonwealth Series, 1979.

Von Rad, Gerhard. *Genesis.* London: SCM Press Ltd., 1972.

Wenham, Gordon J. *The Book of Leviticus.* Michigan: William B. Eerdmans Publishing Company, 1979.

White, Sarah and Romy Tiongco. *Doing Theology and Development: Meeting the Challenge of Poverty.* Edinburg: St. Andrew Press, 1997.

Wilfred, Felix, *Asian Dreams and Christian Hope.* 2nd edition. Delhi: ISPCK, 2003.

Williams, Rowan. *Sharing God's Planet: A Christian Vision for a Sustainable Future.* London: Church Publishing House, 2005.

Wolff, Hans Walter. *Anthropology of the Old Testament.* London: SCM Press Ltd., 1974.

Young, Richard A. *Healing the Earth.* Nashville: Broadman and Holman Publishers, 1994.

Articles

Abraham, K. C. "A Theological Response to Ecological Crisis." In *Eco-Theology: Voices from South and North.* Edited by David G. Hallman. Geneva WCC Publications, 1994.

______________. "Globalization and Liberative Solidarity." In *Globalization and Its Impact on Human Rights.* Edited by Matthew George Chunakara. Thiruvalla: Christava Sahitya Samithy, 2000.

Arambam, Lokendra. "Globalization and Cultural Encounters: The Manipuri Perspective." In *Globalization and the Changing Scenario of Cultural Interaction (Manipur Experience).* Edited by N. Joykumar Singh. New Delhi: Akansha Publishing House, 2007.

"Liberalising the Indian Economy." In *Liberalization and Globalization of Indian Economy.* Vol. I. Edited by K. R. Gupta. New Delhi: Atlantic Publishers and Distributors, 2000.

Bagchi, Amiya K. "The Great Depression (1873-96) and the Third World: With Special Reference to India." In *India and the World Economy: 1850-1950.* Edited by G. Balachandran. Delhi: Oxford University Press, 2003.

Banerjee, Amalesh. "Reform and Inclusive Growth of North East Economy." In *Globalization and North East India.* Edited by Bimal J. Deb, Keya Sengupta and B. Datta Ray. New Delhi: Concept Publishing Company, 2008.

Berry, R. J. "Introduction: Stewardship-A Default Position." In *Environmental Stewardship: Critical Perspectives- Past and Present.* Edited by R. J. Berry. London: T & T Clark International, 2006.

Bhagawati, Jagdish. "The Design of Indian Development." In *India's Economic Reforms and Development: Essays for Mohan Singh.* Edited by Isher Judge Ahluwalia and I. M. D. Little. New Delhi: Oxford University Press, 1998.

Bhattacharjee, J. B. "The Eastern Himalayan Trade of Assam in the Colonial Period." In *Studies in the Economic History of North East India.* Edited by J. B. Bhattacharjee. New Delhi: Har-Anand Publications, 1994.

Bisht, Pushpa, "India under Globalization: Facing an Unequal World." In *Globalization: Myth and Reality.* Edited by Govind Prasad and Anil Dutta Mishra. New Delhi: Concept Publishing Company, 2004.

Biswas, Saswati. "Preservation of Tribal Culture in North East India: How Strong is the Non Tribal Threat." In *Tribal Studies in North East India.* Edited by Sarthak Sen Gupta. New Delhi: Mittal Publications, 2002.

Black, John. "The Dominion of Man." In *Environmental Steward: Critical Perspectives- Past and Present.* Edited by R. J. Berry. London: T & T Clark International, 2006.

Boff, Leonardo. "Social Ecology: Poverty and Misery." In *Eco Theology: Voices from South and North.* Edited by David G. Hallman. Geneva: WCC Publications, 1994.

Boral, L and T. Lyngdoh. "Degradation of Eco-System due to coal mines." In *Forest: A Global Perspectives.* Edited by S. K. Majumdar (Pennsylvania: Academy of Science, 1996).

Brandt, Don. "Introduction." In *God's Steward: The Role of Christians in Creation Care.* Edited by Don Brandt. California: World Vision Publications, 2002.

Brar, Bhupinder. "Theorising Transitions: Post-Coloniality, Post-Socialism and the Coming Age of Globalization." In *Interpreting Globalization: Perspectives in International Relations.* Edited by Rajen Harshe. Jaipur: Rawat Publications, 2004.

Butola, B. S. "Structural Adjustment and the Politics of Recognition and Redistribution in the North Eastern Region of India." In *Liberalization and India's North East.* Edited by Gurudas Das and R. K. Purkayastha. New Delhi: Commonwealth Publishers, 1998.

Chakravarty, Gorgy. "Economic Policy and the North East: Looking Beyond Neo-Classical Praxis." In *Globalization and North East India.* Edited by Bimal J. Deb, Keya Sengupta and B. Datta Ray. New Delhi: Concept Publishing Company, 2008.

Chaudhury, K. N. "India's International Economy in the Nineteenth Century: A Historical Survey." In *India and the World Economy (1850-1950).* Edited by G. Balachandran. New Delhi: Oxford University Press, 2003.

Chellakan, Amal Raj, *Eradicating the Poverty and Empowerment of the Poor.* Delhi: ISPCK, 2007.

Cherian, George, "Globalization-A Conspiracy of the Rich against the Poor." In *Globalization: A Challenge to the Church.* Edited by P. Jegadish Gandhi and George Cherian. Chennai: Association of Christian Institute for Social Concern in Asia, 1998.

Chunakara, Mathews George. "Globalization and its Impact on Human Rights." In *Globalization and its Impact on Human Rights.* Edited by Mathews George Chunakara. Thiruvalla: Christava Sahitya Samithy, 2000.

Churchchil, Laishram. "India's LEP and the North East: A Study on Environment Impact." In *Look East Policy & Polemics and Perspectives.* Edited by Thingnam Kishan Singh. New Delhi. Concept Publishing Company, 2009.

Clifford, Anne M. "From Ecological Lament to a Sustainable Oikos." In *God's Stewards: The Role of Christians in Creation Care.* Edited by Don Brandt. California: World Vision Publications, 2002.

Cobb Jr., John B. "The World and God." In *Process Theology.* Edited by Ewert H. Cousins. New York: Newman Press, 1971.

______________. "Christology in 'Process-Relational' Perspectives." In *Word and Spirit- A Monastic Review-8: Process Theology and the Christian Doctrine of God.* Edited by Santiago Sia. Petersham: St. Bede's Publications, 1986.

______________. "Jesus and Christ in Process Perspectives." In *Handbook of Process Theology.* Edited by Jay McDaniel and Donna Bowman. St. Louis: Chalice Press, 2006.

Das, Gurudas. "Liberalization and Internal Periphery: Understanding the Implications for India's North East." In *Liberalization and India's North East.* Edited by Gurudas Das and R. K. Purkayastha. New Delhi: Commonwealth Publishers, 1998.

David, James. "The Backlash against Globalization." In *Dimension of Globalization.* Edited by James David and John Desrochers. Bangalore: Centre for Social Action, 1998.

De, Utpal Kumar. "Human Development and the Management of Natural Resources: Some Basic Issues." In *Human Development-Experience of North East India.* Edited by Kiran Sankar Chakravarti and Guru Das. New Delhi: Akansha Public House, 2007.

Dennis, Edwards, *Earth Revealing, Earth Healing: Ecology and Christian Theology.* Minnesota: The Liturgical Press, 2001.

Devasahayam, V. "Biblical Perspective on Creation: Some Reflection Text Gen 2:4-17, Rom 8: 18-25." In *Towards an Ecological World View.* Edited by B. Benjamin. Nagpur: NCCI, 1990.

Dube, Musa W. and JeFfrey L. Staley. "Descending from an Ascending to heaven: A Postcolonial Analysis of Travel, Space and Power in John." In *John and Postcolonialism.* Edited by Musa W. Dube and Jeffrey L. Staley. London: Sheffield Academy Press, 2002.

Dutta, B. B. "Tribal Development in Khasi-Jaintia Setting." In *Tribal Demography and Development in North East India.* Edited by J. Matthew: Delhi: B. R. Publications Corporations, 1990.

Dutta P. C. and B. C. Pradhan, "New Economic Policy and Development in NER of India." In *Globalization and North East India.* Edited by Bimal J. Deb, Keya Sengupta and B. Datta Ray. New Delhi: Concept Publishing Company, 2008.

Dyrness, William. "Stewardship of the Earth in the Old Testament." In *Tending the Garden: Essay on the Gospel and the Earth.* Edited by Wesley Granberg-Michaelson. Grand Rapids, Michigan: William B. Eerdmans Publishing Company, 1987.

Evans, S. "Ka Jingpyniaid Balang." In *Ka Centenary History Ka Balang Presbyterian ha Ri-Khasi-Jaintia Naduh, 1841-1940.* Edited by D. Ropmay. Shillong: Literature Committee Ka Assembly, 1940.

Fernandes, Walter. "Globalization, Liberalization and the victims of Colonialism." In *Globalization and its Victims.* Edited by Michael Amalados. Delhi: Vidyajyoti Education & Welfare Society/ISPCK, 1999.

______________. "Tribal Identity, Customary Law and Modernisation in Northeastern India. In *Tribes of North East India: Issues and Challenges.*

Edited by Brinchi K. Medhi, R. P. Athparia and K. Jose. New Delhi: Omsons Publications, 2009.

Field, David N. "On (Re)Centering the Margins: A Euro-African Perspective on the Option of the Poor." In *Opting for the Margins: Postmodernity and Liberation in Christianity.* Edited by Joerg Rieger. Oxford: Oxford University Press, 2003.

Gajwala, Astrid Lobo. "Making a Path to the Womb: Eco-Feminism and its Implications." In *Ecological Cocerns: An Indian Christian Response.* Edited by Joseph Mattam and Jacob Kuvunkal. Bangalore: NBCLC, 1998.

Gassah, L. S. "Effects of Partiation on the Border Marketting of Jaintia Hills." In *Marketting in North East India.* Edited by J. B. Ganguly. New Delhi: Omsons Publications, 1984.

______________. "Self-Management in North East India." In *Antiquity to Modernity in Tribal India: Tribal Self Management in North East India.* Vol. II. Edited by Bhupinder Singh. New Delhi: Inter-India Publications, 1998.

Ghosh, R. N. and R. Gabbay. "Prospect of the Indian Economy: The 1990 and Beyond." In *Sustainable Development: Human Resources, Gender and Environment.* Edited by R. N. Ghosh, R. Gabbay and K. C. Roy. Delhi: Atlantic Publishers and Distributors, 1999.

Gibson, William E. "Eco-Justice New Perspective for a Time of Turning." In *For Creation's Sake: Preaching Ecology and Justice.* Edited by Dieter T. Hassel. Philadelphia: The Geneva Press, 1985.

Giri, Pabitra, "Implementations of New Economic Policy for Development of North-East India." In *Globalization and North East India.* Edited by Bimal J. Deb, Keya Sengupta and B. Data Ray. New Delhi: Concept Publishing Company, 2008.

Goudzwaard, "Economic Growth: Is More always better?." In *Christianity and the Culture of Economics.* Edited by Donald A, Hay and Alan Greider. Cardiff: University of Wales Press, 2001.

Grainger, Alan. "The Role of Special Scale and Special Interactions in Sustainable Development." In *Exploring Sustainable Development: Geographical Perspectives.* Edited by Martin Purvis and Alan Grainger. London: Earthscan Publications Limited, 2004.

Gulati, Ashok. "Indian Agriculture in an open Economy: Will it Prosper?" In *India's Economic Reforms and Development: Essays for Manmohan Singh.* Edited by Isher Judge Ahluwalia and I. M. D. Litle. New Delhi: Oxford University Press, 1998.

Gunnam, Amar. "Globalization, Culture and Development: An Economist's Perspective." In *Globalization and the Changing Scenario of Culture*

Interaction. Edited by N. Joy. Kumar Singh. Imphal: Centre for Manipur Studies, 2007.

Gupta, K. R. Liberalisation and Globalization of Indian Economy." In *Liberalization and Globalization of Indian Economy.* Vol. I. New Delhi: Atlantic Publishers and Distributors, 2000.

Gupta, Saroj. "Privatisation in India." In *Liberalisation: Its Impact on the Indian Economy.* Edited by S. P. Gupta. New Delhi: Macmillan India Limited, 1993.

Gupta, S. P. "Introduction: Recent Economic Reforms and their Impact." In *Liberalisation: Its Impact on the Indian Economy.* Edited by S. P. Gupta. Delhi: Macmillan India Limited, 1993.

Gupta, S. P. and A. K. Sarkar. "Economic Reforms and Growth." In *Liberalisation: Its Impact on the Indian Economy.* Vol. I. Edited by S. P. Gupta. Delhi: Macmillan India Limited, 1993.

Gutierrez, Gustavo. "The Situation and Task of Liberation Theology Today." In *Opting for the Margins: Postmodernity and Liberation in Christian Theology.* Edited by Joerg Rieger. Oxford: Oxford University Press, 2003.

Haokip, Peter, "Major Challenges faced by the Tribals of North East India." In *Tribes of North-East India: Issues and Challenges.* Edited by Brinchi K. Medhi, R.P. Atpharia and K. Jose. New Delhi: Omsons Publications, 2009.

Harrison, Peter. "Having Dominion: Genesis and the Mastery of Nature." In *Environmental Stewardship: Critical Perspectives- Past and Present.* Edited by R. J. Berry. London: T & T Clark International, 2006.

Hart, David Bentley. "The Miror of the Infinite: Gregory of Nyssa on *Vestigia Trinitatis.*" In *Re-thinking Gregory of Nyssa.* Edited by Sarah Coakley. Malden: Blackwell Publishing Ltd. 2002.

Hayong, S. "The Concept of Sin in Khasi Traditional Religion." In *Doing Tribal Christian Theology with Tribal Resources: Cultural Resources in North East India.* Edited by Razouselie Lasetso and Eyingbeni Humtsoe. Jorhat: ETC Programme Coordination, 2009.

Henley, Andrew, "Work and Unemployment." In *Christianity and the Culture of Economics.* Edited by Donald A. Hay and Alan Kreider. Cardiff: University of Wales Press, 2001.

Indrakumar, Konthoujam, "Mapping India's Look East Policy: Shifting Alignments." In *Look East Policy & India's North East: Polemics and Perspectives.* Edited by Thingnam Kishan Singh. New Delhi: Concept Publishing Company, 2009.

Indrakumar, Konthoujam. "Imagining the North East through Look East Policy: Towards a Contextual Understanding." In *Look East Policy & India's North*

East: Polemics and Perspectives. Edited by Thingnam Kishan Singh. New Delhi: Concept Publishing Company, 2009.

Joseph, M. P. "Forward-Towards a Theological Critique of Globalization." In *Globalization and Human Solidarity.* By Tissa Balasuryia. Thiruvalla: Christava Sahitya Samithi, 2000.

______________. "Where is your Sister/Brother?" Carbon Civilization Defiles Faith in God." In *A Christian Response to Ecological Crisis.* Edited by Thomas Samuel and Mathew Koshy Punnakadu. Thiruvalla: Christava Sahitya Samithi, 2009.

Karna, M. N. "Socio-Economic Aspect of Ethnic Identity in North–Eastern India." In *Liberalisation and India's North East.* Edited by Gurudas Das and S. K. Purkayastha. New Delhi: Commonwealth Publishers, 1998.

Keitzer, Renthy. "Tribal Theological Trend in North East India." In *Tribal Theology: A Reader.* Edited by Shimreingam Shimray. Jorhat: Tribal Study Centre, 2003.

Kendra, Vikas Adhyayan. "The Myth of Globalization." In *Dimension of Globalization.* Edited by James David and John Desrachers. Bangalore: Centre for Social Action, 1998.

Kharakor, Spiton. "Ki 'Lawblei 'Lawkyntang." In *Sengkutsnem 1989: Ninetieth Year Souvenir (1899-1989).* Shillong: Seng Khasi, 1989.

Khongphai, A. S. "Shad Suk Mynsiem (Thanksgiving Dance)." In *Khasi Heritage.* Edited by Hipshon Roy Kharshiing. Shillong: Seng Khasi, 1979.

Kipgen, M. "*Tlawngaihna* and Christianity." In *Encounter Between Gospel and Khasi Culture.* Edited by A. Wati Longchar. Jorhat: Tribal Study Centre, 1999.

La, Kwock Pui. "Liberation Theology in the Twenty-First Century." In *Opting for the Margins: Postmodernity and Liberation in Christian Theology.* Edited by Joerg Rieger. Oxford: Oxford University Press, 2003.

Legrant, Lucien. "Jesus and Jesus' Movement in the Globalized World." In *Theology of Economics in the Globalized World: Indian Approaches.* Edited by Jacob Parapally & Antony Kalliath. Bangalore: Indian Theological Association, 2010.

Longchar, A. Wati. "The Need for Doing Tribal Theology." In *An Exploration of Tribal Theology.* Edited by I. Wati Longchar. Jorhat: Tribal Study Centre, 1997.

______________."Indian Christian Theology and Tribals in India." In *Encounter Between Gospel and Tribal Culture.* Edited by A. Wati Longchar. Jorhat: Tribal Study Centre, 1999.

______________. "Interaction Between Gospel and Culture among the Nagas." In *Encounter Between Gospel and Tribal Culture.* Edited by A. Wati Longchar. Jorhat: Tribal Study Centre, 1999.

______________. "A Critic of Christian Theology of Creation." In *Doing Theology with the Tribal Resources.* Edited by A. Wati Longchar and W. Davies. Jorhat: Tribal Study Centre, 1999.

______________. "The Need for Doing Tribal Theology." In *Tribal Theology: A Reader.* Edited by Shimreingam Shimray. Jorhat: Tribal Study Centre, 2003.

______________. "Globalization and Indigenous People: Challenges for Doing Theology in Asia." In *Tribal Theology: A Reader.* Edited by Shimreingam Shimray. Jorhat: Tribal Study Centre, 2003.

______________. "The Continuity of Indigenous People in Today's World." In *Theologizing Tribal Heritage: A Critical Re-Look.* Edited by Hrangthan Chungi. Delhi: ISPCK, 2008.

Lyngdoh, Ladbasuk. "Life after Death in Khasi Religion and Ressurection in the Bible." In *Garnering Tribal Resources for doing Tribal Christian Theology.* Edited by Razouselie Lasetso. Jorhat: ETC Programme Coordination, 2008.

Mallick, Saroj. "Contradictions and Challenges of Globalization: Need for Alternatives." In *Globalization: Myth and Reality.* Edited by Govind Prasad and Anil Dutta Mishra. New Delhi: Concept Publishing Company, 2004.

Mane, Suresh. "Constitutional Dimensions of Social Justice in the Era of Globalization." In *Globalization and Social Justice: Perspective, Challenges and Praxis.* Edited by J. G. Jogdand, Prashant P. Bandsode and N. G. Meshram. Jaipur: Rawat Publications, 2008.

Martin, Chandran Paul. "India Case Study Paper on Christianity, Wealth and Poverty." In *Christianity, Wealth and Poverty.* Edited by Chandran Paul Martin. NCCI/ISPCK, 2004.

Mawlong, Cecile A. "Megalith and Social Formation in Khasi-Jaintia Hills." In *Society and Economy in North-East India.* Edited by Mignonette Momin and Cecile A. Mawlong. New Delhi: Regency Publications, 2004.

Mawrie, Barness. "Khasi Society and the Impact of Modernity: Challenges to Identity and Integrity." In *Tribes of North-East India: Issues and Challenges.* Edited by Brinchi K. Medhi, R. P. Athparia and K. Jose. New Delhi: Omsons Publications, 2009.

Mawrie, H. O. *The Khasi Millieu.* Reprinted. New Delhi: Concept Publishing Company (P) LTD., 2010.

Mazumdar, Apurbananda. "Globalization and Regional Imbalance: Prospect of North East India in a Super-colonial World Order." In *Liberalization and India's North East.* Edited by Gurudas Das and R. K. Purkayastha. New Delhi: Commonwealth Publishers, 1998.

McLane, John. "The Drain of Wealth and Indian Nationalism at the Turn of the Century." In *India and the World Economy, 1850-1950.* Edited by G. Balachandran. New Delhi; Oxford University Press, 2003.

Medury, Uma. "Changing Complexion of Public Administration in the Globalised Era: Some Emerging Issues. In *Globalization: Myth and Reality.* Edited by Govind Prasad and Anil Dutta Mishra. New Delhi: Concept Publishing Company, 2004.

Menon, Geetha, "New Colonialism and the Campaign against Foreign Debt: A Woman's Perspective." In *Globalization.* Edited by P. Jagadish Gandhi and George Cherian. Chennai: Association of Christian Institutes for Social Concern in Asia, 1998.

Meye, Robert P. "Invitation to Wonder: Towards a Theology of Nature." In *Tending the Garden: Essay on the Gospel and the Earth.* Edited by Wesley Granberg-Michaelson. Grand Rapids, Michigan: William B. Eerdmans Publishing Company, 1987.

Minz, Nirmal. "Tribal Perspective on Ecology." In *The Tribal Worldview and Ecology.* Edited by Wati, A. Longchar and Yangkahao, Vashum. Jorhat: Tribal Study Centre, 1998.

Mishra, Anil Dutta. "Globalization: Concept and Nature." In *Globalization: Myth and Reality.*Edited by Govind Prasad and Anil Dutta Mishra. New Delhi: Concept Publishing Company, 2004.

Mishra, Pramod. "Globalization poses new challenge to South-South Solidarity. In *Globalization: Myth and Reality.* Edited by Govind Prasad and Anil Dutta Mishra. New Delhi: Concept Publishing Company, 2004.

Mohamed, Naina Shaik. "Impact of Globalization: India and Canada." In *Globalization: Myth and Reality.* Edited by Govind Prasad and Anil Dutta Mishra. New Delhi: Concept Publishing Company, 2004.

Mohapatra, A. C. "Locational Pattern of Market in Pre and Early British Period in North East India (Khasi, Jaintia and Garo Hills." In *Studies in the Economic History of North East India.* Edited by J. B. Bhattacharjee. New Delhi: Har-Anand Publications, 1994.

Mulan, C. S. "Hill Tribes of Assam." In *Introducing India.* Edited by K. N. Bagchi & W. C. Griffiths. Calcutta: The Royal Asiatic Society of Bengal, 1947.

Muricken, Ajit. "Globalization-Overview." In *Dimension of Globalization.* Edited by James David and John Desrochers. Bangalore: Centre for Social Action, 1998.

Murray, Leslie A. "Politics in Process Perspective." In *Handbook of Process Theology.* Edited by Jay Mc Daniel and Donna Bowman. St, Louis: Chalice Press, 2006.

Nash, James A. *Loving Nature: Ecological Integrity and Christian Responsibility.* Nashville: Abingdon Press, 1991.

Nash, Ronald H. "Process Theology and Classical Theism." In *Process Theology.* Edited by Ronald H. Nash. Michigan: Baker Book House, 1987.

Niumai, Ajailiu. "Development and Discontent Meet in the North East: Perspective on India's Look East Policy." In *Look East Policy & India's North East: Polemics and Perspectives.* Edited by Thingam Kishan Singh. New Delhi: Concept Publishing Company, 2009.

Nongbri, T. "The Khasi Land Tenure System: Need For Conceptual Refinement." In *Land Relation in North East India.* Edited by B. B. Dutta and M. N. Karna. New Delhi: People Publishing House, 1987.

Nongbri, Tiplut. "Impact of the State Logging Ban in Meghalaya, India." In *Globalization and Indigenous People in Asia.* Edited by Dev Nathan, Govind Kelkar and Pierre Walter. New Delhi: Sage Publications, 2004.

Northcott, Michael S. "Ecology and Christian Ethics." In *God's Steward: The Role of Christian in Creation Care.* Edited by Don Brandt. California: World Vision Publications, 2002.

Oliver, Jeti A. "Recolonization, Globalization and the Role of the Church." In *Globalization: A Challenge to the Church.* Edited by Jagadish Gandhi and George Cherian. Chennai: Association of Christian Institutes for Social Concern in Asia, 1998.

Oomen, M. A. "More a Moral Crisis than a Development Dilemma: An Examination of Some Issues of Globalization." In *Globalization and SAP: Trends and Impact- An Overview.* Edited by Ajit Muricken. Mumbai: Vikas Adhyayan Kendra, 1997.

______________. "Globalization and Decolonization: The Contemporary Challenges." In *Globalization: A Challenge to the Church.* Edited by P. Jegadish Gandhi and George Cherian. Chennai: Association of Christian Institutes for Social Concern in Asia, 1998.

______________. "Globalization and Working Towards Alternative Development Paradigms." In *Globalization and its Impact on Human Rights.* Edited by Mathew George Chunakara. Thiruvalla: Christava Sahitya Samithy, 2000.

Page, Ruth. "The Fellowship of all Creation." In *Environmental Stewardship: Critical Perspectives- Past and Present.* Edited by R. J. Berry. London: T & T Clark International, 2006.

Pakem, B. "State Formation in Pre-Colonial Jaintia." In *Tribal Polities and State System in Pre-Colonial Eastern and North Eastern India.* Edited by Surajit Sinha. Calcutta: K. P. Bagchi & Company, 1987.

Palmer, Clare. "Stewardship: A Case Study in Environmental Ethics." In *Environmental Stewardship: Critical Perspectives-Past and Present.* London: T & T Clark International, 2006.

Pandey, Shridhar. "Liberalisation, Globalisation and the State in Indian Economy." In *Liberalisation and Globalisation of Indian Economy.* Vol. III. Edited by K. R. Gupta. New Delhi: Atlantic Publishers and Distributors, 1999.

Panikkar, K. N. "Globalization and Culture- 1." In *Globalization and SAP: Trends and Impact- An Overview.* Edited by Ajit Muricken. Mumbai: Vikas Adhyayan Kandra, 1997.

Patel, S. K. and R. C. Talati, "Globalisation of the Indian Economy." In *Liberalisation and Globalization of Indian Economy.* Vol. I. Edited by K. R. Gupta. New Delhi: Atlantic Publishers and Distributors, 2000.

Patmury, J. "Ecofeminism, Ecojustice and Ecospirituality." *Theology of our Times* 6 (August, 1999): 57-74.

Patten, Chris. "Governance." In *Respect for the Earth: Sustainable Development.* Edited by Chris Patten, et al. London: Profile Books Ltd, 2000.

Pohsngap, L. "Ecology and Tribal Culture." In *Ecological Challenge and Christian Mission.* Edited by Krickwin C. Marak and Atul Y. Aghamkar. Delhi: CMS/ ISPCK, 1998.

Prasad, Govind. "Globalization and Foreign Direct Investment: India and Canada." In *Globalization: Myth and Reality.* Edited by Govind Prasad and Anil Dutta Mishra. New Delhi: Concept Publishing Company, 2004.

Prasad, Khrishna Mohan. "Changing Economic Scenario and Globalization of Indian Economy." In *Liberalisation and Globalization of Indian Economy.* Vol. 3. Edited by K. R. Gupta. New Delhi: Atlantic Publishers and Distributors, 2000.

Prasad, M. K. "Ecology, Science and Sustainable Development." In *Ecological Concerns: An Indian Christian Response.* Edited by Joseph Mattam and Jacob Kuvunkal. Bangalore: NBCLC, 1998.

Prasad, Narendra. "Efficacy and Impact of a decade of Economic Reforms on the Indian Economy." In *Economic Reforms in India.* Edited by Bishwa Nath Singh, Mohan Prasad Srivastava, Narendra Prasad. New Delhi: APH Publishing Corporation, 2003.

Prasain, G. P. and E. Nixon Singh, "Globalization and FDI in North East India." In *Globalization and North East India.* Edited By Bimal J. Deb, Keya Sengupta and B, Datta Ray. New Delhi: Concept Publishing Company, 2008.

Predamanda, Hidam. "India's Look East Policy and the Political: An Interrogation into the Survey of the 'Global' in Manipur." In *Look East Policy & India's*

North East: Polemics and Perspectives. Edited by Thingnam Kishan Singh. New Delhi: Concept Publishing Company, 2009.

Pulikottil, Paulson. "God, Creation and Humankind: Old Testament Themes in Ecological Perspectives." In *Ecological Challenges and Christian Mission.* Edited by Krickwin C. Marak and Atul Y. Aghamkar. Delhi: CMS/ISPCK, 1998.

Raju, C. S. N. "New Economic Policy and GATT." In *Liberalisation and Globalization of Indian Economy.* Vol. I. Edited by K. R. Gupta. New Delhi: Atlantic Publishers and Distributors, 2000.

Ramakhrishnan, P. S. "Conserving the Sacred for Biodiversity: The Conceptual Framework." In *Conserving the Sacred: For Biodiversity Management.* Edited by P. S. Ramakhrishnan, K. G. Saxena and U. M. Chandrasekhar. New Delhi: Oxford & IBH Publishing CO. PVT. LTD., 1998.

Ramanjaneyulu, M. "Pros and Cons of Indian Economic Liberalisation." In *Liberalisation and Globalization of Indian Economy.* Vol. I. Edited by K. R. Gupta. New Delhi: Atlantic Publishers and Distributors, 2000.

Rangriz, Hassan. "Globalization: The Nature and its Dynamics." In *Globalization: Myth and Reality.* Edited by Govind Prasad and Anil Dutta Mishra. New Delhi: Concept Publishing Company, 2004.

Rao, J. V. Raghavendra. "Globalization, Dalits and Social Justice." In *Globalization and Social Justice.* Edited by P. G. Jogdand, Prashant P. Bansode and N. G. Meshram. Jaipur: Rawat Publications, 2008.

Rao, S. N. "Megalith Practice among Khasi and Naga of North East India." In *Archeology of North East India.* Edited by G. P. Singh & Sen Gupta. Delhi: Vikas Publishing House Pvt. Ltd, 1991.

Rao, V. Venkata. "The Khasi Political System- The Syiemship." In *Tribal Institution of* Meghalaya. Edited by S. K. Chattopadhya. Guwahati: Spectrum Publications, 1985.

Rasmussen, Larrry L. "Creation, Church and Christian Responsibility." In *Tending the Garden: Essay on the Gospel and the Earth.* Edited by Wesley Granberg Michaelson. Grand Rapids: William B. Eerdmans Publishing Company, 1987.

Rasmussen, Larry L. "Theology of Life and Ecumenical Ethics." In *Eco Theology: Voices from South and North.* Edited by David G. Hallman. Geneva: WCC Publications, 1994.

Ray, B. Datta, "North East India in the Context of New Economic Policy." In *Globalization and North East India.* Edited by Bimal J. Deb, Keya Sengupta and B. Datta Ray. New Delhi: Concept Publishing Company, 2008.

Razu, I. John Mohan. "Towards an Understanding of the Phenomenon of Globalization: An Attempt." In *Globalization.* Edited by Rose Mary Vishwanath. Bangalore: Verba Network Service, 1998.

______________. "Globalization, TNCs and the Exploitation of the Poor." In *Globalization: A Challenge to the Church.* Edited by P. Jegadish Gandhi and George Cheryian. Chennai: Association of Christian Institute for Social Concern in Asia, 1998.

Robra, Martin, Deenabandhu Manchala and Sarah Anderson-Rajarigam. "Affirming Life for the Disregard Many." In *Earth Habitat: Eco- Injustice and the Church's Response.* Edited by Dieter T. Hessel and Larry L. Rasmussen. Augsberg: Fortress Press, 2001.

Rockfeller, Steven C. "Global Interdependence, The Earth Charter, and Christian Faith." In *Earth Habitat: Eco-Injustice and the Church's Response.* Edited by Dieter T. Hessel and Larry L. Rasmussen. Augsburg: Fortress Press, 2001.

Roy, David. "Land Tenure in the States." In *Notes on Khasi Law.* Edited by Sir Keith, Cantlie's. Shillong: Chapala Publishing House, 2008-2009.

Rymbai, R. T. "Evolution of Modern Khasi Society." In *Khasi Heritage.* Edited by Hipshon Roy, Kharshiing. Shillong: Seng Khasi, 1979.

______________. "Some Aspect of the Religion of the Khasi-Pnars." In *Khasi Heritage.* Edited by Hipshon Roy Kharshiing. Shillong: Seng Khasi, 1979.

______________. "The Festivals of the Khasi and their influence on his Life." In *Khasi Heritage.* Edited by Hipshon Roy Kharshiing. Shillong: Seng Khasi, 1979.

______________. "Behdiengkhlam." In *Khasi Heritage.* Edited by Hipshon Roy Kharshiing. Shillong: Seng Khasi, 1979.

______________. "U Hynniew Trep bad la ka Niam." In *Seng Khasi Souvenir.* Shillong: Seng Khasi, 1986.

______________. "Christian Mission and the Indigenous Religion of the Khasi-Pnar." In *Religion in North East India.* Edited by Soumen Sen. New Delhi: Uppal Publishing House, 1993.

______________. "The Traditional Ecological Concept of the Khasi-Pnars." In *Tribal Worldview and Ecology.* Edited by A. Wati Longchar and Yangkahao Vashum. Jorhat: Tribal Study Centre, 1998.

Sankar, Ulaganathan. "Introduction." *Environmental Economics.* Edited by Ulaganathan Sankar. New Delhi: Oxford University Press, 2001.

Sarangi, Prakash. "Role of the State in the Era of Globalization." In *Interpreting Globalization-Perspectives in International Relations.* Edited by Rajen Harshe. New Delhi: Rawat Publications, 2004.

Sawian, Sumar Sing. "The Evolution of the Hynniew Trep Polity." In *Khanasamari-U Khun U Hajar ka Ri u Hynniew Trep*. Edited by Sumar Sing Sawian. Shillong: Apphira Publications, 1998.

Sen, Sunanda. "Tributes and Transfers from Colonial India." In *India and the World Economy, 1850-1950*. Edited by B. Balachandran. New Delhi: Oxford University Press, 2003.

Shaik, A. A. "Globalization: Its Clashes, Contents and Discontents." In *Globalization: Myth and Reality*. Edited by Govind Prasad and Anil Dutta Mishra. New Delhi: Concept Publishing Company, 2004.

Sharma, Jainarain. "Cosumers in the Globalized World." In *Globalization: Myth and Reality*. Edited by Govind Prasad and Anil Dutta Mishra. New Delhi: Concept Publishing Company, 2004.

Sharma, Meenalshi and Roona, " Globalization and its Implications for Indian agriculture." In *Impact of Globalization and Development*. Edited by Meenu Agarwal. New Delhi: Deep & Deep Publications (P) LTD, 2008.

Shastri, Siddharth, "Globalising the Indian Economy: A Disastrous Move." In *Liberalisation and Globalization of Indian Economy*. Vol. I. Edited by K. R. Gupta. New Delhi: Atlantic Publishers and Distributors, 2000.

Shimray, Shimreingam. "Globalization Process and Tribal People." In *Tribal Women and Globalization*. Edited by Narola Imchen. Jorhat: Women Study Center, 2008.

Shiva, Vandana. *Globalization's New Wars: Seed, Water and Life Forms*. New Delhi: Women Unlimited, 2005.

Shrivastava, Mohan P., et al. "Relevance and Incidence of Globalization in Indian Economy." In *Liberalisation and Globalisation of Indian Economy*. Vol. III. Edited by K. R. Gupta. New Delhi: Atlantic Publishers and Distributors, 1999.

Shrivastava, Mohan Prasad. "A Decade of Globalization, Liberalisation and Economic Reforms in India: An Assessment" In *Economic Reforms in India*. Edited by Bishwanath Singh, Mohan Prasad Srivastava and Narendra Prasad. New Delhi: APH Publishing Corporation, 2003.

Shuurman, Frans J. "Globalization and Developmental Studies: Introducing the Challenged." In *Globalization and Development Studies*. Edited by Frans J. Shuurman. New Delhi: Vistaar Publications, 2001.

Sider, Ronald J. "Introduction." In *Christianity and Economics in the Post-Cold War Era: The Oxford Declaration and Beyond*. Edited by Herbert Schlossberg, Vinay Samuel and Ronald J. Sider. Grand Rapids, Michigan: William B. Eerdmans Publishing Company, 1994.

Sing, Kynpham. "Khasi and Jaintia Religion." In *Khasi Heritage*. Edited by Hipshon Roy Kharshiing. Shillong: Seng Khasi, 1979.

______________. Sing, Kynpham, "Khasi Hills and Jaintia Hills up to 1874." In *Tribal Heritage.* Edited by Hipshon Roy Kharshiing. Shillong: Seng Khasi, 1979.

______________. "Syiems and Durbars in Khasi Polity." In *Tribal Institution of Meghalaya.* Edited by S. K. Chattopadhyay. Guwahati: Spectrum Publications, 1985.

Sing, Maham. "Nongkrem Festival." In *Khasi Heritage.* Edited by Hipshon Roy Kharshiing. Shillong: Seng Khasi, 1979.

Singh, Arun Kumar. "Globalization, Sovereignty and Human Rights." In *Globalization: Myth and Reality.* Edited by Govind Prasad and Anil Dutta Mishra. New Delhi: Concept Publishing Company, 2004.

Singh, Gajendra, "Globalization and its Impact on Indian Agriculture." In Impact of Globalization on Development. Edited by Meenu Agarval. New Delhi: Deep and Deep Publications (P) LTD, 2008.

Singh, Thingnam Kishan. "India's Look East Policy: Origin and Conceptualization." In *Look East Policy & India's North East: Polemics and Perspectives.* Edited by Thingnam Kishan Singh. New Delhi: Concept Publishing Company, 2009.

Sinha, Manoj. "Globalization and Consumerism: A Study of its Impact." In *Globalization: Myth and Reality.* Edited by Govind Prasad and Anil Dutta Mishra. New Delhi: Concept Publishing Company, 2004.

Srikanth, H. "Liberalization and Development of India's North East: Learning from Experience." In *Liberalization and India's North East.* Edited by Gurudas Das and R. K. Purkayastha. New Delhi: Commonwealth Publishers, 1998.

Srivastava, Madhury. "Globalisation of Indian Economy: Direction and Challenges." In *Liberalisation and Globalization of Indian Economy.* Vol. I. Edited by K. R. Gupta. New Delhi: Atlantic Publishers and Distributors, 2000.

Suderbaum, Peter. *Understanding Sustainable Economics: Towards Pluralism in Economics.* London: Earthscan, 2008.

Sugirtharajah, R. S. "A Postcolonial Exploration of collusion and Construction in Biblical Interpretation." In *The Postcolonial Bible.* Edited by S. R. S. Sugirtharajah. Sheffield: Sheffield Academy Press, 1998.

Syiemlieh, David R. "Trade and Markets in Khasi Jaintia Hills: Changed Conditions in the 19th and 20th Centuries." In *Society and Economy in North East India.* Vol. III. Edited by David R. *Syiemlieh* and Manorama Sharma. New Delhi: Regency Publications, 2008.

_________________."Khasi Iron Culture and Iron Trade in the Late Eighteenth and Early Nineteenth Century." In *Studies in the Economic History of*

North East India. Edited by J. B. Bhattacharjee. New Delhi: Har-Anand Publications, 1994.

________________."Technology and Socio-Economic Linkages of the Khasi-Jaintias in Precolonial Times." In *Society and Economy in North-East India.* Vol. I . Edited by Mignonette Momin and Cecile A. Mawlong. New Delhi: Regency Publications, 2004.

Team, VAK. "The New Economic Path-Trends and Impact." In *Globalization and SAP: Trends and Impact- An Overview.* Edited by Ajit Muricken. Mumbai: Vikas Adhyayan Kendra, 1997.

The Earth Bible Team. "Guiding Eco-Justice Principles." In *Reading from the Perspective of the Earth.* Edited by Norman C. Habel. Sheffield: Sheffield Economic Press, 2000.

Thimmaiah, G. "Impact of Trade Liberalization on Indian Agriculture." In *Economic Reforms in India.* Edited by Bishwa Nath Singh, Mohan Prasad Srivastha and Narendra Prasad. New Delhi: APH Publishing Corporation, 2003.

Thonbiparambil, Joseph. "The Challenge of the Old Testament Prophets to Economic Structures. In *Theology of Economics in the Globalised World: Indian Approaches.* Edited by Jacob Parappally & Antony Kalliath. Bangalore: Indian Theological Association, 2010.

Tiwari, B. K., S. K. Barik and R. S. Tripathi, "Sacred Groves of Meghalaya." In *Conserving the Sacred: For Biodiversity Management.* Edited by P. S. Ramakrishnan, K. G. Saxena and U. M. Chandrasekhar. New Delhi: Oxford & IBH Publishing CO. Pvt. Ltd., 1998.

Tomlinson, B. R. "Britain and the Indian Currency Crisis, 1930-2." In *India and the World Economy, 1850-1950.* Edited by G. Balachandran. New Delhi: Oxford University Press, 2003.

Tomlinson, John. "Vicious and Benign Universalism." In *Globalization and Development Studies.* Edited by Frans J. Shuurman. New Delhi: Vistaar Publications, 2001.

Upadhyay, Vandana. "Globalization and Development in North East India." In *Globalization and Development Dilemma.* Edited by M. C. Behera. New Delhi: Mittal Publications, 2004.

Vanhoozer, Kevin. "Human Beings, Individual and Social." In *The Cambridge Companion to Christian Doctrine.* Cambridge: Cambridge University Press, 1977.

Varadarajan, Dhulasi Birundha. "Impact of New Economic Policy on Foreign Trade." In *Liberalisation and Globalization of Indian Economy (Vol. I).* Edited by K. R. Gupta. New Delhi: Atlantic Publishers and Distributors (P) Ltd., 2000.

Vashum, Yangkahao. "A Thankhul Myth of Creation: Implication of a Holistic View of Human Right." In *Tribal Worldview and Ecology.* Edited by A. Wati Longchar and Yangkahao Vashum. Jorhat: Tribal Study Centre, 1998.

________________. "The Stars are our Relatives: Tribal/ Indigenous People's Stellar Theology." In *Doing Tribal Christian Theology with Tribal Resources: Cultural Resources from North East India.* Edited by Razouselir Lasetso and Eyingbeni Humtsoe. Jorhat: ETC Programme Coordinator, 2009.

Wali, R. L. "New World Disorder and India's Driven Reforms." In *Liberalization and India's North East.* Edited by Gurudas Das and R. K. Purkayastha. New Delhi: Commonwealth Publishers, 1998.

War, Junita. "The Khasi Concept of Nature." In *The Tribal Worldview and Ecology.* Edited by A. Wati Longchar and Yangkahao Vashum. Jorhat: The Tribal Study Centre, 1998.

West, Gerald. "The Bible and the Poor: A New Way of Doing Theology." In *The Cambridge Companion to Liberation Theology.* Cambridge: University Press, 2001.

Articles in Journals

Abraham, K. C. "Theological Response to Ecological Crisis." *Bangalore Theological Forum* XXV /1 (March, 1993): 3-14.

Arun, Joe. "Taming the Global Demagogue I." *Vidyajyoti Journal of Theological Reflection* 66/6 (June, 2002): 419-435.

________________. "Taming the Global DemagogueII." *Vidyajyoti Journal of Theological Reflection.*" 66/7 (July, 2002): 526-535.

Bose, Ashish. "Globalization, Migration and Urbanization." *Religion and Society* XLI/2 (June, 1994): 30-41.

Christie, P. Maria Joseph. "Conflict of Values the Globalized Era." *SNC Journal of Intercultural Philosophy,* 10 (August, 2006): 2-15.

Downs, F. S. "Christianity as a Tribal Response to Change in North East India." *Missiology* VIII/4 (October, 1980): 407-416.

Fischer, Thomas. "Memoirs of Sylhet, Kachar and the Adjacent Districts." *Asiatic Journal* IX (1840): 830-838.

Fonseca, Joseph. "The Globalization of Business- an Ethical Enquiry: With Special Reference to India." *Jeevardhara* XXVI/156 (November, 1956): 411-434.

Gait, E. A. "Some Notes in Jaintia History." *Journal of Asiatic Society of Bengal* LXIV (1895): 242-248.

Ghosh, Partha S. "Challenges of Governance and Globalization: A Case Study of India's North East." *Man and Society: A Journal of North East Studies* 2/1 (Spring, 2005): 21-55.

Gurdon, P. R. T. "Notes on the Khasi, Synteng and allied Tribes, inhabiting the Khasi and Jaintia Hills District in Assam." *Journal of Asiatic Society of Bengal* LXXIII/4 (1904): 56-69.

Hayong, S. "The Khasi Concept of Ecology." *Indian Theological Journal* 2/1 (January-June, 2008): 86-99.

Hutton, J. H. "Some Meghalitic Works in Jaintia Hills." *Journal of the Asiatic Society of Bengal.* New Series. 22/6 (1926): 333-345.

Jeyaraj, Xavier. "An SEZ with a Difference." *Social Action* 58/3 (July-September, 2008): 272-282.

Joseph, M. P. "Denying Life: Theological Meaning of Globalization." *National Council of Churches Review.* CXVI/7 (August, 1996): 453-468.

Katiyar, Impact of Coal Mining in Jaintia Hills. *Eastern Panorama* (December, 1997).

Koshy, Ninan. "Issues and Challenges facing the Indian Churches in the Twenty-First Century." *National Council of Churches Review* CXX/7 (August, 2002): 665-676.

Kumar, Arun. "Socio-economic Aspects of SEZs." *Social Action* 58/3 (July-September, 2008): 235-245.

Laitphlang, W. R. "Ka Niam ha u Khasi." *Sneng Khasi* 5/19 (December, 1981): 4-10.

Lish, A. B. "A Brief Account of the Khasees." *Calcutta Christian Observer* VII/70 (March, 1838): 129-143.

Longchar, Wati. "Natural Resources: Perspectives of Primeval Traditions." *Jeevardhara* XL/235 (January, 2010): 26-36.

________________. "Indigenous Peoples and Christian Theology." *Indian Theological Journal* 2/1 (January-June, 2008): 17-33.

Matthew, Prasad. "Free India Today: In the Context of Globalization." *National Council of Churches Review* CXVIII/8 (September, 1998): 579-585.

Nath, Brojendra. "Globalization of Agriculture." *Religion and Society* LXI/2 (June, 1994), 46-61.

Nayak, Arun Kumar. "SEZs and Displacement." *Social Action* 58/3 (July-September, 2008): 254-263.

Nirmal, A. P. "Ecology, Ecumenics and Economics in Relation: A New Theological Paradigm." *National Council of Churches Review* CXI/3 (March, 1991): 879-890.

Nongbri, B. L. "Serampore Mission in North East India with Special Reference to Khasi Hills (1813-1835): A Historical Survey." *Indian Theological Journal* 2/2 (July-December, 2008): 38-48.

Nongkhlaw, Dondor Giri. "That elusive Niamkur (Clan Religion) of the Hynniew Trep Geographical Landscape." *Indian Theological Journal* 1/1 (January-June, 2007), 54-74.

Oldham, Thomas. "The Geological Structure of Part of Khasi Hills, with Observation on the Meteorology and Ethnology in that District." *The Culcutta Review* XXVII (July-December, 1856): 87-90.

Oomen, T. K. "Globalization and Structural Change: Historicity and Implications." In *Religion and Society* XLI/2 (June, 1994): 16-22.

Patrick, Gnana. "Empovering Modernity and Ambivalent Globalization: A Perspective of the Indian 'social' Minorities." *Jeevardhara* XXXIV/199 (January, 2004): 32-53.

Pinto, Ambrose, "Vasco da Gama: Culture, Colonisation and Globalization." *Social Action* 49/3 (July-September, 2000): iii-v.

Raj, J. Felix and Samrat Roy, "SEZs: Broken Promise in West Bengal." *Social Action* 58/3 (July-September, 2008): 283-290.

Ralte, R. D. Mawia. "An enquiry into the Divine, Human and Nature Relationship in the Northeast Indian Primal Religious Traditions and its contemporary Relevance." *Sathri Journal: A Journal of Contextual Theology* VI/I (April, 2012): 71-114.

Rao, V. Khrishna. "Globalization Unleashes English Tsunami." *Indian Currents.* (11-17, December, 2006): 34-37.

Rayan, Samuel. "Theological Perspective on the Environmental Crisis." *Religion and Society* XXXVII/2 (June, 1990): 18-34.

_______________. "Ecology and Faith: The Mystery of the Earth" *National Council of Churches Review.* CXI (October, 1991): 1281-1295

Razu, I. John Mohan. "The Symbiosis between Poverty and Globalization: A Need for a Critique from Political Ethics." *National Council of Churches Review* CXX/10 (November, 2000): 875-890.

Robra, Martin. "People's Struggle for life are a source of inspiration for an enriching spirituality." In *National Council of Churches Review* CXXII/1 (January-February, 2002): 3-8.

Samuel, Simon, "A Postcolonial Historiography: Towards Postcolonial Approach to Reading the Discourse of Colonial Subject Community." *Doon Theological Journal* 1/1 (2004): 5-19.

Scott, David C. "Some Reflection on a Theological Response to Ecological Crisis." *Bangalore Theological Forum.* XXV/ 1 (March, 1993): 15-24.

Shobha SV. "Ostracised for Demanding Information." *Open* (24 October, 2011): 26-28.

Singh, Kynpham. "Seng Khasi." *Sneng Khasi* 3/10 (November, 1980): 4-6.

_______________. Ka Shad Suk Mynsiem (The Thanksgiving Dance). *Sneng Khasi* 3/11 (April, 1981): 2-4.

Srikanth, H. "British Colonialism and the Hill Tribes of Composite Assam." *Man and Society: A Journal of North East Studies 6.* (Spring, 2006): 90-102.

Syiemlieh, David R. "Traditional Institutions of Governance in the Hills of North East India: The Khasi Experience." *Man and Society: A Journal of North East Studies* III (Spring, 2006): 117-137.

Sugirtharajah, R. S. "Postcolonialism and Indian Christian Theology." *Studies in World Christianity* 5/2 (1999): 229-240.

Therukattil, G. "Towards a Biblical Eco-Theology." In *Jeevardhara* XXI/126 (November, 1991): 465-483.

Tirimana, Vimal. "Moral Theological Implications of Globalization from a Third World Perspective." *Vidyajyoti Journal of Theological Reflection* 65/4 (April, 2001): 288-289.

Walters, H. "Journey Across the Pandua Hills near Sylhet in Bengal." *Asiatic Research* 17/333 (1832): 500-506.

Watson, Thomas C. "Chirrapunji and a detail of some of the Favourable Circumstances which render it an Advantageous Site for the Erection of an Iron and Steel Manufactory on an Extensive Scale." *Journal of the Asiatic society of Bengal* 3/26 (1834): 25-30.

Wilfred, Felix. "Eco-Justice: Expanding the Horizons for a Common Future." *Jeevardhara* XL/235 (January, 2010): 5-17.

Yule, Henry. "Notes on the Khasi Hills and People." *Journal of Asiatic Society of Bengal* XIII/152 (1844): 614-627.

Yule, Lt. "Notes on the Iron of Khasia Hills." *Journal of Asiatic Society of Bengal* XI (II)/129 (1842): 833-856.

Reports

Allen, B. C. *The Census of India, 1901.* Shillong: Assam Secretariat Printing Office, 1902.

Allen, B. C. *Gazetteer of the Khasi & Jaintia Hills Garo Hills Lushai Hills.* Delhi: Gyan Publications, 1905.

Allen, B. C. *Assam District Gazetteer: The Khasi and Jaintia Hills, the Garo Hills and the Lushai Hills.* Vol. X. Allahabad: Pioneer Press, 1906.

Allen, B. C. *Gazetteer of the Khasi & Jaintia Hills, Garo Hills, Lushai Hills,* 2nd ed. Delhi: Giant Publications, 1980.

Allen, W. J. *Report of the Administration of the Cosseah and Jynteah Hill Territory.* Calcutta: John Gray "Bengal Hurkary" Press, 1858.

An Account of the Province of Assam and its Administration. Shillong: Assam Secretariat Printing Office, 1903.

Board of Revenue (Part II) Proceedings on Deputation, Cherapunjee: 25th October, 1858.

Census of India, 1931. Vol. III.

Directorate of Economics and Statistics, *Statistical Hand Book Meghalaya, 2008-2009.* Shillong: Government of Meghalaya, 2009.

Firminger, W. K. *Sylhet District Gazetteer.* III/172. Letter of John Willes, Collector of Sylhet to Earl Cornwallis, 15 September, 1789.

Gait, E. A. *Census of India, 1891.* Shillong: Assam Secretariat Printing Office, 1892.

"Keeping and Healing the Creation." Committee on Social Witness Policy, PCUSA.

Maran, K. W. P. *The Census of India, 1941.* Shimla: Government of India Press, 1942.

Meghalaya District Gazetteers Khasi Hills District Shillong: Government of Meghalaya, Art & Culture Department, 1991.

Pamberton, R. Boileau. *Report of the Eastern Frontier of British India.* Calcutta: Baptist Mission Press, 1835.

Rawat, Vidya Bhushan, Namidi Bharath Bhushan and Sujata Surepally. "The Impact of Special Economic Zones in India: A Case Study of Polepally SEZ." New Delhi: Social Development Foundation, August, 2011.

Report of the Administration of the Province of Assam for the Year, 1901-1902. Shillong: Assam Secretariat Printing Office, 1902.

Report of the Land Reforms Commission on Khasi Hills, 1974.

Simon, I. M. *Meghalaya District Gazetteer: Khasi Hills District.* Shillong: Art and Culture Department, Meghalaya, 1991.

Statistical Hand Book of Meghalaya, 2007. Government of Meghalaya, Directorate of Economic and Statistics.

Suchiang, F. S. *Meghalaya Eco-Resource Development Project (A Report),* 1994.

The Agriculture Ledger. Vol. 14. Calcutta: Office of the Superintendent Government Printing, India, 1898.

The Census of Assam, 1881. Calcutta: Office of Superintendent Printing, 1883.

Vaghaiwalla, B.B. *Census of India, 1951.* Bombay: Municipal Printing Press, 1954.

Dictionaries and Encyclopedias

Habgood, J. "Creation." In *A New Dictionary of Christian Theology.* Edited by A. Richardson and J. Bowden. London: Scm Press Ltd., 1983.

Reade, Allen Walker. *The New International Webster Comprehensive Dictionary of the English Language.* Florida: Trident Press International, 1996.

Roth, John K. *International Encyclopedia of Ethics.* New Delhi: S. Chand & Company Ltd, 1996.

Singh, Nissor. *English Khasi Dictionary.* Reprinted. New Delhi: Mittal Publications, 2010.

Soanes, Catherine and Spooner, Alan. *Compact Oxford Dictionary Thesaurus & Word Power Guide.* New Delhi: Oxford University Press, 2003.

Newspapers

Mawphor, 10 May 2002.

Mawphor, 27 March 2007.

Mawphor, 14 July 2007.

Mawphor, 14 May 2008.

Mawphor, 6 October 2009.

Mawphor, 1 December 2009.

Mawphor, 22 December 2009.

Mawphor, 20 January 2010.

Mawphor, 21 January 2010.

Mawphor, 6 February 2010.

Mawphor, 12 April 2010.

Mawphor, 4 June 2010.

Mawphor, 8 May 2011.

Mawphor, 19 May 2011.

The Hindu, (Kochi) 5 August 2009.

The Hindu, (Kochi) 22 January 2011.

The Meghalaya Guardian, 6 June 1996.

The Meghalaya Guardian, 27 June 1996.

The Shillong Times, 6 June 1981.

The Shillong Times, 6 June 1996.

The Shillong Times, 10 May 2002.

The Shillong Times, 12 June 2004.

The Shillong Times, 23 August 2004.

The Shillong Times, 26 May 2006.

The Shillong Times, 17 August 2006.

The Shillong Times, 4 June 2007.

The Shillong Times, 28 June, 2007.

The Shillong Times, 4 July 2007.

The Shillong Times, 26 July 2012.

The Shillong Times, 20 August 2007.

The Shillong Times, 26 October 2007.
The Shillong Times, 31 October 2007.
The Shillong Times, 8 January 2008.
The Shillong Times, 16 January 2008.
The Shillong Times, 31 January 2008.
The Shillong Times, 21 April 2008.
The Shillong Times, 3 May 2008.
The Shillong Times, 9 May 2008.
The Shillong Times, 5 June 2008.
The Shillong Times, 21 August 2008.
The Shillong Times, 20 September 2008.
The Shillong Times, 30 September 2008.
The Shillong Times, 22 October 2008.
The Shillong Times, 8 November 2008.
The Shillong Times, 8 March 2009.
The Shillong Times, 6 April 2009.
The Shillong Times, 13 May 2010.
The Shillong Times, 15 May 2010.
The Shillong Times, 17 June 2010.
The Shillong Times, 5 November 2010.
The Shillong Times, 15 November 2010.
The Shillong Times, 29 April 2011.
The Shillong Times, 18 May 2011.
The Shillong Times, 20 May 2011.
The Shillong Times, 28 May 2011.
The Shillong Times, 5 April 2012.
The Telegraph, (Guwahati) 22 December 2009.
U Nongphira, 6 Naiwieng 1914.
U Nongsain Hima, 15 December 2008.
U Nongsain Hima, 28 October 2009.
U Nongsain Hima, 18 January 2010.

Webliography

Amedeo, Kimberly. India's Economy. http://useconomy.about.com/od/worldeconomy/p/india_economy.htm (4 Nov 2011).

Balakhrishnan, Chandrasekaran. "Impact of Globalization on Developing Countries and India." http://economics.about.com/od/globalizationtrade/l/aaglobalization.htm (4 Nov 2011).

Chand, Ramesh. "Effects of Trade Liberalization on Agriculture in India: Commodity Aspects." www.uncapsa.org/publication/wp45.pdf (5 Dec 2011).

Chekutty, N. P. "The whole World's Bhujia." www.indiatogether.org/2005jul/eco-bikaner.htm#continue (15 Nov 2011).

Cobb, Jr John B. "Marx and Whitehead." http://www.religion-online.org/showarticle.asp?title=3359 (8 July 2009).

______________. A Theology of Enjoyment for a Post Capitalist Life. http://www.religion-online.org/showarticle.asp?title=3544 (8 July 2009).

Collyer, Tran M. "Theorising Privatisation: Policy, Network Analysis and Class." In *Electric Journal in Sociology, 2003.* See www.sociology.org/content/vol7.3/01_collyer.html (31 Oct 2011).

Cummings, Charles. "Exploring Eco-Spirituality." http://www.spiritualitytoday.org/spir2day/894113cummings.html (8 Feb 2011).

Dohrmann, Jona Aravind. "Special Economic Zones in India- An Introduction." http://www.asienkunde.de/articles/a106_asien_aktuell_dohrmann.pdf (29 Nov 2011).

Economic and Social Development Department, "The State of Food and Agriculture 1995." www.fao.org/docrep/v6800e/v6800EOD.htm (5 Dec 2011).

Einhorn, Jessica, "Millions of Indians Awaits benefits of Globalization." www.yale.edu/content/millions-indians-awaits-benefits-globalization (3 Nov 2011).

Emde Matthew, "An Analysis of the effects of the MNCs on India since Liberation." www.arts.usask.ca/economics/skjournal/sej-2nd/sej2-emde.pdf (15 Nov 2011).

Fernando, Vincent. "Faber: India's Middle Class will soon be larger than Americas." www.articles.businessinsider.com/2010-02-15/markets/30074431_1_rupees-population-vehicle-sales (15 Nov 2011).

Follath, Eric. "The Paradox of Mumbai: Slums, Stocks, Stars and the New India." www.spiegel.de/international/spiegel/0,1518,469031,00.html (29 Nov 2011).

"Globalization Impact on Indian Agricultural Sector." http://wiki.answers.com/Q/Globalization_impact_on_Indian_agriculture (7 Dec 2011).

Haub, Carl and O. P. Sharma, "What is Poverty, Really? The case of India." www.prb.org/Articles/2010/indiapoverty.aspx (21 Nov 2011).

"How Poverty is calculated in India." http://business.rediff.com/slide-show.2010/apr/21/slide-show-1-bcrisis-how-poverty-is-calculated-in-india.htm (21 Nov 2011).

http://encyclopedia2.thefreedictionery.com/modernization (8 Feb 2011).

http://en.wikipedia.org/wiki/conferenceoflatinAmericanBishops (25 Aug 2012).

http://en.wikipedia.org/wiki/swadeshi-Movement (3 Oct 2011).

http://caravan.squat.net/ICC-en/Krrs-en/ghandhi-econ-en.htm (3 Oct 2011).

http://www.indohistory.com (6 Oct 2011).

http://www.zimbio.com/Mukesh+Ambani/articles/uPPuHlivy7w/Top+50+Richest+person+India+list+Forbes+World (28 Nov 2011).

http://timesofindia.indiatimes.com/business/india-business/Indias-external-debt-rise (5 Oct 2012).

"Impact of Globalization on Indian Agriculture." http://www.ssmrae.com/admin/images/168d52131d54abe17f22e88f58d21327.pdf (5 Nov 2011).

Jona, Aravind Dohrmann, "Special Economic Zones in India- An Introduction," http://www.asienkunde.de/articles/a106_asien_aktuell_dohrmann.pdf (15 Nov 2011).

Kalirajan, Kallipa. "Liberalisation Strategies and Poverty Reduction in India. www.eastasiaforum.org/2010/09/06/liberalisation-strategies-and-poverty-reduction-in-india (28 Oct 2011).

Kasturi, Kannan. "SEZs: Engine derailed?" www.indiatogether.org/2009/jan/eco-Sezbust.htm (29 Nov 2011).

Kumar, Arun. "Half of India's Population lives below Poverty line," www.wsws.org/articles/2010/aug2010/india-aoz.shtml (21 Nov 2011).

Malhotra, Jyoti. Globalization and the Indian Economy. www.indiastudychannel.com/resources/74993-globalization-indian-economy.aspx (5 Nov 2011).

Ministry of Commerce and Industry. "Special Economic Zones in India." http://www.sezindia.nic.in/about-introduction.asp (29 Nov 2011).

Nagaraj, R. "Growth Rate of India's GDP, 1950-51 to 1987-88; Examination of Alternative Hypothesis." *Economic and Political Weekly* 25/26 (June 30, 1990). www.jstor.org/pss4396440 (7 Oct 2011).

"Numbers of MNCs in India." www.numberof.net/numberofmncsinindia/ (14 Nov 2011).

Pal, Amitabh. "Indian Farmers Bear the Brunt of Globalization." www.progressive.org/mag_apb091906 (8 Dec 2011).

"Perspective on Trans-National Companies."www.grips.ac.jp/csids/perspectives/perspective03.pdf (15 Nov 2011).

"Poverty in India." http://en.wikipedia.org/wiki/Wiki/Poverty_in_India (20 Nov 2011).

"Poverty In India," http://wikipedia.org/wiki/poverty_in_India (5 Oct 2012).

Prabhudesai, Arun. "How India's Rich spend & invest their money." http://trak.in/Tags/Business/category/indi-business-news-everything-you-want-to-know-about-india/what-are-indian-people-how-do-they-live-what-i (27 Nov 2011).

Prasad, Mahesh. "India: TNCs musling into Cottage Industry Sectors." www.twnside.org.sg/title/tnc-ch.htm (25 Nov 2011).

"Press Note on Poverty Estimates." http://planningcommission.nic.in/reports/genrep/Press_pov_27jan11.pdf (28 Nov 2011).

Pujari, Y. D. "Socio-Economic Impact of Globalization on Indian Agriculture." *Golden Research Thought* 1/IV (October, 2011). http://aygrt.net/oct/2011/Economic%20_GLOBALIZATION_ON_INDIAN_AGRICULTURE>aspx (3 Dec 2011).

Rao, R. Sunitha. "Every 3rd B'lorean lives in sub-human slum." *The Times of India* http://articles.timesofindia.indiatimes.com/2011-03-17/bangalore/29137890_1_slum-population-slum-dwellers-urban-poverty (29 Nov 2011).

Shiva, Vandana. "The Green Revolution in Punjab." http://livingheritage.org/green-revolution.htm (1 Dec 2011).

"Slums." www.macalester.edu/courses/geog61/espencer/slums.html (29 Nov 2011).

"Sngewkhia Ka KSU ba thombor ka Amrit Cement ia ki Jaka Rep." *Mawphor* 14 November 2011. http://mawphor.com (14 Nov 2012).

The Benefit of Job Outsourcing to O21. www.outsourcing2india.com/why_india/articles/job-outsourcing-to-india.asp (7 Nov 2011).

"The end of India Green Revolution?" http://news.bbc.co.uk/2/hi/south_asia/4994590.stm (1 Dec 2011).

"The Impact of New Economic Policy on Agricultural Sector." www.shodhganga.inflibnet.ac.in/bitstream/10603/604/11/11_chapter5.pdf (3 Dec 2011).

"Unrestricted Globalization: Boon or Hazard?" in *South Asian Voice.* http://india_resource.tripod.com/globalization.html (5 Nov 2011).

www.mapsofindia.com/personalities/nehru/economic-policies:html (4 Oct 2011).

www.istr.org/conferences/bankok/WPVolume/Kumar.Mauday.pdf (4 Oct 2011).

www.en.wikipedia.org/wiki/Bikaneri_Bhujia (15 Oct 2011).

Interview

Basaiawmoit, P. B. M., Interview 9 May 2012.

Blah, Toki, Retired IAS, Interview 12 May 2011.

Focus Group Nonglait, Interview with Mr. B. Lyngdoh- Headman, T.bn T. L. Rapmai and Mr. T. Shabong 11 May 2012.

Gassah, L. S., Interview 3 May 2012.

Gympad, Brian, Interview 17 May 2002.

Gympad, Presbyter, Interview 21 May 2012.

Hayong, Minsah P., Interview 17 July 2012.

Hayong, Wansalan, Interview 18 May 2012.

Jungai, W., Interview 17 July 2010.
Kharlukhi, Bajubon, Interview 2 May 2012.
Khonglah, Rangbahduh, 17 May 2012.
Khonglah, T. D., Interview 2 May 2012.
Lawrinniang, Pynskhem, Interview 28 June 2012.
Lyngdoh, Ladbasuk, Interview 30 June 2012.
Marsing, Emoral, Interview 25 May 2012.
Mukhim, Patricia, Interview 16 May 2012.
Muktieh, Eltis, Interview 24 May 2012.
Nongtrai Focus Group, Interview 11 May 2012.
Rynjah, Sweetymon, Interview 30 April 2012.
Sawian, Sumar Sing, Interview 2 May 2012.
Wahlang, Wanbansain, Interview on 17 August 2012.
Warjri, Ayesha D., Interview on 17 August 2012.